D0778701

The African
Diaspora

EDITED BY

Martin L. Kilson

Robert I. Rotberg

The African
Diaspora

Interpretive

Essays

HARVARD UNIVERSITY PRESS

Cambridge, Massachusetts, and London, England 1976

Library of Congress Cataloging in Publication Data

Main entry under title:

The African diaspora.

   Includes index.
   1. Blacks—Addresses, essays, lectures. 2. Slave-
trade—Addresses, essays, lectures. I. Kilson, Martin.
II. Rotberg, Robert I.
GN645.A36   909'.04'96   75-30643
ISBN 0-674-00779-4

In memory of
Henry Blasius Masauko Chipembere,
loyal son and patriot of Malawi
and member of the new diaspora

Preface

The dispersion of Africans is a phenomenon of the modern world. Although Africans have always been in motion, their enforced exodus greatly increased their numbers abroad and permanently established communities of overseas Africans. George Shepperson's introduction makes this point at greater length. The first two essays, by Frank Snowden and Bernard Lewis, discuss the role and image of blacks in the ancient and Islamic worlds. The next four chapters, by Christopher Fyfe, Joseph Miller, W. Robert Higgins, and Leslie Rout, examine aspects of the slave trade—that cataclysm which drastically altered the horizons of individuals and nationalities and gave to the earlier numerically insignificant diaspora a significant dimension. The next three chapters in this collection, by Paul Edwards and James Walvin, James W. St. G. Walker, and Brian Weinstein, look at the experience of slaves and ex-slaves in Britain, Nova Scotia, and the French West Indies. Three subsequent chapters, by George Simpson, Raymond Smith, and Robert I. Rotberg, discuss the religion of the diaspora in its Caribbean setting. Adele Simmons and I. K. Sundiata look at two particular aspects of creole (part ex-slave) adaptation to different surroundings, the one an African island, the other an Indian Ocean island. The last two chapters in this book, by Marion Kilson and Martin Kilson, analyze the growth of black sociocultural and political adaptation in the new world of the United States.

This is not a study of every aspect of the African diaspora. As originally conceived, it was. The editors had hoped to publish chapters on virtually all important dimensions of the diaspora. Chapters were commissioned on the experience of Africans in China, in India, in the city-states along the Persian Gulf, in France, in North Africa, in Peru, in Venezuela, in Cuba, and so on. The editors wanted essays on the views of the inhabitants of Biblical Israel toward blacks, on internal African migration, on the economic consequences of the slave trade, on black culture in the New World, on the musical development of ex-Africans overseas; on the trans-Saharan as well as the trans-Atlantic slave trades; and so on.

The editorial design was overarching and ambitious. It was stimulated by long-term professional and personal involvements in various consequences of the diaspora—in the American as well as the modern African experience with the acculturation and socialization which are the contemporary artifacts of a portion of that diasporic experience. There was a precipitating stimulation, too. Along with Shepperson, the editors had both long known of the need for a multi-volume appreciation of the entire diaspora which would, it was hoped, stimulate further research and book-length examinations of the particular questions addressed in a series of essays in a more general publication. In a famous talk at Harvard University Shepperson spoke to this same scholarly and cultural need. The Harvard University Press, especially Ann Orlov, then editor for the behavioral sciences, was quick to appreciate the importance of the idea.

She persisted in encouraging the editors when their energies flagged and managed to steer this volume—the distillation of an original, larger conception—through the vicissitudes of many crises of different orders of magnitude. The resulting volume is a tribute to her foresight and acumen.

We are grateful for the patience of the contributors and the unheralded understanding of those writers whose chapters, for one reason or another, could not be incorporated into this volume: we regret the absence from this book of those many chapters. There is room for further collections and long, specialized books on an array of fascinating topics which are either mentioned too briefly in what follows or, alas, ignored completely.

Our wives and children have endured this as well as our other enterprises. Evalyn Seidman coped with many of the necessary administrative chores. Gail Stewart was an exemplary and assiduous copyeditor. Kay Bruner prepared the index. As to the gallon of blueberries which fueled the cells which finally made an idea into a workable proposal, its provenance goes unrecorded.

R.I.R. and M.L.K.

Contents

CONTENTS

Maps

Tables

The African
Diaspora

George Shepperson

Introduction

Thou . . . shalt be removed into all the kingdoms of the earth
(Deuteronomy, 28:25).

Ethiopia shall soon stretch out her hands unto God
(Psalms, 68:31).

I am black, but comely . . .
(The Song of Solomon, 1:5).

The history of the world is the history of the great migrations. One does
not have to be a diffusionist or a Biblical fundamentalist to appreciate the
truth in this assertion. If one is a student of the history of the Western
Hemisphere, particularly of the United States of America, it is self-
evident. The historian who looks eastward, confronting the vast movements of men and women across Asia, will take it for granted.

Too often, however, the study of the great human migrations has
become—and becomes—the study of ruling races. Their subject peoples
have tended to be neglected, to be taken for granted and thus overlooked. "For ye have the poor with you always," or, from the point of
view of Oswald Spengler, "All higher economic life develops itself on
and over a peasantry. Peasantry, *per se*, does not presuppose any basis
but itself. It is, so to say, race-in-itself, plantlike and historyless."[1]

To this tendency to neglect the subject peoples in the study of the
great migrations, there is, of course, one major exception: the Jews and
their dispersal, from the times of the Babylonian captivity onward. The

---

1. Oswald Spengler, *The Decline of the West* (New York, 1939), 474.

GEORGE SHEPPERSON

application of the Greek word for dispersion, *diaspora*, to this process of Jewish migration from their homeland into all parts of the world not only created a term which could be applied to any other substantial and significant group of migrants, but also provided a concept which could be used to interpret the experiences (often very bitter experiences) of other peoples who had been driven out of their native countries by forces similar to those which had dispersed the Jews: in particular, slavery and imperialism.

It was perhaps inevitable that "diaspora" should come to be used of another great human migration which had been the result, too often, of slavery and imperialism but which, unlike the Jewish dispersion, did not become until recently the matter for intense study. When the expression "the African diaspora" was first used it is difficult to say: probably the 1960s could be claimed as its gestation period.[2] However, the parallels and links between the Jewish and black African experiences of uprooting from their homelands had been noticed at least from the early nineteenth century.

In 1802 the British writer William Mavor included in his *Universal History* a volume entitled *The History of the Dispersion of the Jews; of Modern Egypt; and of other African Nations*. By the middle of the nineteenth century, the fascination of the parallels between the black African and the Jewish experiences had spread to African writers. James Africanus Beale Horton, the Sierra Leonean doctor whose Ibo father was a liberated slave, examined some of these parallels in his *West African Countries and Peoples* of 1868.[3] But it was left to the greatest black savant of the nineteenth century, Dr. Edward W. Blyden, to take these parallels further; in an address which he delivered in America in 1880 on Africa's service to the world, he gave a succinct description of the African diaspora, without actually using this expression, and compared it to the dispersion of the Jews:

---

2. The expression was certainly established by the time that the International Congress of African Historians was held in Dar es Salaam in 1965. See Joseph E. Harris, "Introduction to the African Diaspora," and George Shepperson, "The African Abroad or the African Diaspora," in T. O. Ranger (ed.), *Emerging Themes in African History* (Nairobi, 1968), 147-151, 152-176.

3. James Africanus Horton, *West African Countries and Peoples* (1868; reprint, Edinburgh, 1969), 167-171.

The Negro is, at this moment, the opposite of the Anglo-Saxon. These everywhere serve the world; these everywhere govern the world. The empire of the one is more widespread than that of any other nation; the service of the other is more widespread than that of any other people. The Negro is found in all parts of the world. He has gone across Arabia, Persia, and India to China. He has crossed the Atlantic to the Western Hemisphere, and here he has laboured in the new and in the old settlements of America; in the Eastern, Western, Northern and Southern States; in Mexico, Venezuela, the West Indies and Brazil. He is everywhere a familar object, and he is, everywhere out of Africa, the servant of others. . . . Africa is distinguished as having *served* and *suffered*. In this, her lot is not unlike that of God's ancient people, the Hebrews, who were known among the Egyptians as the servants of all; and among the Romans, in later times, they were numbered by Cicero with the 'nations born to servitude', and were protected, in the midst of a haughty population, only 'by the contempt which they inspired'.[4]

Considering Blyden's knowledge of Hebrew, his interest in Jewish history, and his sympathy with Zionist aspirations,[5] it is surprising that he did not employ the expression "the African diaspora."

If, however, Blyden had popularized the expression "African diaspora" in the nineteenth century and it had gained support amongst early African nationalist intellectuals, it could have acquired political overtones which would have rendered it useless for scholars today who find it convenient to employ in their studies of the too long neglected subject of the African abroad. Without political overtones, it serves as a satisfactory although sometimes fluctuating focus for the various aspects of the African outside of Africa which are examined by the writers in this volume.

It should be noted, however, that the serious study of the many and highly complex aspects of the African diaspora—not only in its *locus classicus*, the European slave trade to the Americas and the Caribbean, but also well before this period and well after it—is in its infancy. The

---

4. Edward W. Blyden, *Christianity, Islam and the Negro Race* (1887; reprint, Edinburgh, 1967), 120.

5. See, e.g., Edward W. Blyden, *The Jewish Question* (Liverpool, 1898), extracts reprinted in Hollis R. Lynch (ed.), *Black Spokesman: Selected Published Writings of Edward Wilmot Blyden* (London, 1971), 209-214.

GEORGE SHEPPERSON

reader of this volume must not expect it to cover all the aspects of the rough diamond of the diaspora from Africa.

Indeed, Blyden himself, in the address which has been quoted above, drew attention to one interesting aspect of the African diaspora which is not made the subject of a special article in this volume, although its ramifications into the ancient and Arab world are suggested: what Harris has called "the African presence in Asia."[6] As Blyden put it,

> The countless caravans and dhow-loads of Negroes who have been imported into Asia have not produced, so far as we know, any great historical results; but the slaves exported to America have profoundly influenced civilization.[7]

Whether Blyden was correct in dismissing the historical importance of blacks in the East (especially in India) so rapidly, remains to be seen in the light of future research—and it is to be hoped that one result of this volume will be to encourage Asian scholars to enter the study of the African diaspora. What this volume does offer, however, is material by which the reader, in the light of his knowledge of world history, can judge the validity of Blyden's assertion on the role of American slavery.

On the other hand, Blyden, in his succinct summary of the African diaspora which was quoted above, omitted one feature of this process to which this volume draws some attention: blacks in Europe. The articles here on blacks and the world of Greece and Rome, on Arab culture (which, it should not be forgotten, ramified into the Iberian Peninsula) and the African diaspora, and on Africans in sixteenth-to-eighteenth century Britain[8] indicate a subject on which serious scholarly work is

---

6. Joseph E. Harris, *The African Presence in Asia: Consequences of the East African Slave Trade* (Evanston, 1971). See also D. R. Banaji, *Bombay and the Siddis* (Bombay, 1932); idem, *Slavery in British India* (Bombay, 1933); R. V. Ramdas, "Relations between the Marathas and the Siddis of Janira," unpub. Ph.D. thesis (University of Bombay, 1965). I am indebted for this last reference to Vasant Rao, who supervised the dissertation and is engaged in research on Africans in India. See also G. S. P. Freeman-Grenville, "The Sidi and the Swahili," *Bulletin of the British Association of Orientalists*, VI (1971), 3-18.

7. Blyden, *Christianity, Islam and the Negro Race*, 119.

8. To the British documentation here, a recent dissertation is worth adding: Ruth M. Cowhig, " 'Haply for I am Black': A Study of Othello's Race, of Changing Racial Attitudes, and of the Implications of Such Changes for the Production and Interpretation of the Play," unpub. Ph.D. thesis (University of Manchester, 1974).

only just beginning. Just as the emphasis on the African diaspora in the New World has served largely to veil from the sight of scholars the significance of the African presence in Asia, it has, in the main, concealed the presence of Africans and people of African descent in European countries. There are, to be sure, a few indications in that pioneering study of the African diaspora, Sir Harry Johnston's *The Negro in the New World* (London, 1910)—a volume which deserves to be read in conjunction with this present work to show how much progress has been made in the study of the African diaspora—that serious students of the subject have never entirely neglected the African in Europe. Yet, at the present state of scholarly reckoning, his presence in that continent seems peripheral in the extreme.

But is this really so? Anyone who has seen the four large stone statues of Negroes who seem to be holding up the main door—almost the whole façade—of the Church of S. Maria Gloriosa dei Frari in Venice could be forgiven for thinking that the presence of blacks in this maritime republic was much greater than is commonly supposed. Indeed, black men are to be encountered in countless corners of European history—and if the orthodox historian of Europe has failed to see them, perhaps it is because the black in European history, like his counterpart in American history, is also an "Invisible Man." Too often, however, when blacks are noticed in European history, they appear as striking but isolated individuals, once seen and soon forgotten, such as the black Dalmatian stonemason who helped to build the bridge across the river Drina in sixteenth-century Bosnia. According to Andrić, the assistant to the master mason "was a Negro, a real Negro, a young and merry man whom the whole town and all the workmen soon nicknamed 'the Arab.' "[9] When the study of the African diaspora in Europe is taken more seriously than it is at the moment, the significance of such fascinating African characters as Andrić's black stonemason of the sixteenth century may be more apparent.

It could hardly be expected that, in a series of essays such as those in the present collection, the individual African or person of African descent overseas would be emphasized. In this collection, although occasionally attention is drawn to important individuals in various

9. Ivo Andrić, *Na Drini Cuprija* (Belgrade, 1945), ch. 3: English trans., *The Bridge on the Drina* (New York, 1967), 27.

GEORGE SHEPPERSON

aspects of the African diaspora, the emphasis is upon the anonymous black masses or upon substantial groups. This follows naturally from a concentration by most of the writers on the slave trade, particularly the commerce in Africans in the New World.

Yet the African diaspora was—and indeed still is—more than the transmission across the Atlantic, over the Sahara Desert, through the Mediterranean, or over the Indian Ocean of masses of anonymous blacks. Of course, as with so much of human history, enormous numbers of once living, identifiable individuals have been swallowed up into the anonymity of the past—and probably there has been no greater agent of anonymity than the dehumanizing trade in slaves across the Atlantic from Africa. But records of individuals, often tantalizing in the extreme, survive at all stages in time and space of the African diaspora. Their existence and their fascination ought not to be forgotten.

In the days of the great European migrations to the Americas, especially in the nineteenth century, black men, in spite of their often lowly social status and the smallness of their finances, moved as individuals into many parts of the world with an apparent facility which may surprise the modern reader whose only image of men of African descent at that time is in the immobilizing shackles of slavery. In the heyday of American slavery, in 1854, there was a black man from America standing with the 500 rebels who stockaded themselves on Bakery Hill, Ballarat, Australia, against the autocracy of the government of Victoria and the goldfields police: "John Joseph, a native of New York, under a dark skin possessed a warm, good, honest, kind, cheerful heart," as the idiosyncratic and sentimental historian of this democratic episode in Antipodean history described him.[10] What forces in the African diaspora took his ancestors to the New World in the first place, and then thrust him amongst the Australian Eureka Stockaders in the mid-nineteenth century, with the result that one report of the trials of the militant gold-diggers early in 1855 was headed "Nigger-Rebel State Trial"? A few lines about him may be all that has survived—and yet, considering all the complexities of the African diaspora, with its multitudinous byways where evidence may lie hidden, who can be sure?

10. Carboni Raffaello, *The Eureka Stockade* (orig. pub. Melbourne, 1855; citation from edition of Melbourne, 1947), 135.

A similar example is the unknown Afro-American who is commended at the start of the tenth chapter of the second part of Mahatma Gandhi's autobiography.[11] On his first visit to the heart of Afrikanerdom, Pretoria, in 1893, Gandhi, a young barrister who had only been a few months in South Africa, was left on the station platform at night with no one to meet him or to tell him where he could stay in this strange, color-conscious city. And then "an American Negro who was standing nearby" and who saw his plight went up to him and directed him to a hotel where he could get a night's rest without too much attention being paid to his brown skin by the white guests in the establishment. How, one may ask, did a black American come to be residing in this very white-conscious South African city in the years just before the Boer War? Was he, like John Joseph in Australia, attracted to the country by the opportunities offered in the mines? Whatever the reason, at the moment he too remains a puzzle wrapped up in a few lines.

Equally puzzling are some men of American descent who have written about themselves and their exploits in strange corners of the African diaspora. An obvious example is the Afro-American Captain Harry F. Dean, who claimed descent from the pioneer black sea captain, Paul Cuffee, and who made his mark on race relations in South Africa, Liberia, and the United States. Dean produced his autobiography in 1929, a fascinating volume in the development of the African diaspora around the world; but how much of it is fact and how much fiction remains to be established.[12] Similarly, there is the even more fascinating autobiography by Bata Kindai Amgoza Ibn LoBagola which appeared the following year.[13] LoBagola claimed to be a black Jew from Dahomey whom accident and adventure took to Scotland, England, Africa, and America, and into the British army in Palestine and Egypt during World War I. Again, the problem of fact and fiction in his work puzzles the historian. And yet, as research into the bewildering ramifications of the African diaspora goes forward, fact often comes to predominate in these accounts of adventurers of African descent around the world. This has

---

11. Mohandas K. Gandhi, *An Autobiography: The Story of My Experiments with Truth* (Boston, 1962), 118-119.

12. Harry Dean and Sterling North, *The Pedro Gerino* (Boston, 1929).

13. Bata Kindai Amgoza Ibn LoBagola, *An African Savage's Own Story* (London, 1930).

GEORGE SHEPPERSON

become clear from studies which have been made recently of the career of Dusé Mohamed Ali, that remarkable Sudanese-Egyptian who, in the late nineteenth and early twentieth centuries, influenced African and Afro-American movements in North and West Africa, the United States, and Great Britain.[14] When these studies began, Dusé Mohamed Ali's claims seemed exaggerated and the tales told about him a tissue of fiction covering only a little fact. Yet recent research indicates that most of the reports of his adventures are not exaggerated.

The studies in this volume, chosen from a range of differing research interests, can hardly do more than suggest such ramifications; the percipient reader, however, should find here a chart which, although it will not carry him safely through all the currents of the African diaspora, should help him across the major seas of the subject and, if he provides a compass from his own determination and ingenuity, may eventually direct him into many undiscovered fields of the African abroad. The use of the maritime metaphor here is intended to be functional rather than fanciful, and to draw attention to the role of the sea as much as the land in the African *völkerwanderung*. Again, the image of the slave ship, crammed to capacity with unwilling Africans, is pertinent here. It is an image which, while it illustrates the maritime side of the African diaspora, distorts it by laying emphasis on the involuntary side of African migrations. There is a new world to be discovered in the voluntary aspects of movement around the world by people of African descent.

People of African descent abroad played a major role in the emergence of the idea of African unity, political and cultural, which has come to be known as pan-Africanism and which, in its ideological and organizational complications, is almost as ramified as the African diaspora itself. Indeed, it is no exaggeration to call pan-Africanism the latter-day ideology of the African diaspora.

Like all ideologies, it has been and is subject to change and conflict. One can imagine some of the studies in this book being both commended and criticized by exponents of its various groupings. It is, therefore,

14. Shepperson, "African Abroad," 171-172; and, especially, Ian Duffield's monumental "Dusé Mohamed Ali and the Development of Pan-Africanism, 1866-1945," unpub. Ph.D. thesis (University of Edinburgh, 1971).

fortunate that this book contains no chapter on pan-Africanism,[15] although, from another angle, this reveals one of its limitations: its lack of attention to the history of ideas in the African diaspora.[16]

But one must not ask too much of a pioneering study. This is, I believe, the first book, academic or otherwise, to contain the words "African diaspora" in its title. The reader who knows nothing about Africans and people of African descent in the story of the great human migrations should discover here a convenient guide to many of the major aspects of the African diaspora. The scholar and student whose eyes have already been opened to the importance and fascination of this subject should find this a challenging book—as much, perhaps, by what it does not say as by what it does. Africa, the once "unknown continent," receives in these pages further illumination; it is becoming virtually impossible for the serious reader to deny it a place in universal history,[17] as Hegel did in his famous lectures on the philosophy of history at Berlin in the early nineteenth century.

Perhaps, too, this book or individual essays in it will serve to persuade many historians of Africa, who have hitherto been reluctant to accept the proposition, that the study of the African diaspora is an integral part of the history of Africa, and that to limit the historiography of Africa to its continental boundaries is to distort its true features.

But very much remains to be done before even the main elements, not to speak of the multitude of fascinating minutiae in the African diaspora, can be adequately revealed. The refinement of techniques of his-

15. A useful scholarly guide to the ramifications of pan-Africanism is Imanuel Geiss, *Panafrikanismus* (Frankfurt, 1968), trans. into English as *The Pan-African Movement* (London, 1974).

16. In addition to *ibid.*, other useful volumes for the history of ideas in the African diaspora are Robert W. July, *The Origins of Modern African Thought* (London, 1968); Adelaide Cromwell Hill and Martin Kilson (eds.), *Apropos of Africa: Sentiments of Negro American Leaders on Africa from the 1800s to the 1950s* (London, 1969); E. A. Ayandele, *Holy Johnson, Pioneer of African Nationalism, 1836-1917* (London, 1970); Jacques Louis Hymans, *Léopold Sédar Senghor: An Intellectual Biography* (Edinburgh, 1971); Philip D. Curtin (ed.), *Africa and the West: Intellectual Responses to European Culture* (Madison, 1972); J. Ayodele Langley, *Pan-Africanism and Nationalism in West Africa 1900-45* (Oxford, 1973); Ras Makonnen (recorded and edited by Kenneth King), *Pan-Africanism from Within* (London, 1973).

17. Georg Wilhelm Friedrich Hegel, *The Philosophy of History* (New York, 1956), 99. The lectures were given in 1830-1831.

torical research makes it possible to do much in this field which past scholars have been prevented from tackling. And yet I believe that the major task before students of the African diaspora is the retrieval of records, collective and individual, which are scattered around the world in many languages. The time to do so is short, and I hope that this book will stimulate the search. In the Swahili words from a marching song of East and Central African soldiers, with whom I had the privilege of serving over thirty years ago in the eastward-moving African diaspora, and who first revealed to me its existence, "Tufunge safari, tufunge upesi." Let's get on with the journey, let's get on with it *quickly*.

1
Frank M. Snowden, Jr.

Ethiopians and the Graeco-Roman World

Ethiopians—the name which the Greeks and Romans applied to a number of dark- and black-skinned African peoples—are mentioned frequently in classical literature. Negroes interested Greek and Roman artists in every major period of classical art. Who were these blacks? What did they look like? Whence and when did they come to Greece and Italy? What did they do and how did they fare in alien lands? The answers to these and similar questions constitute the first recorded experience in European records of blacks in a predominantly white society. The purpose of this essay is to present certain aspects of the black man's presence in the classical world hitherto inadequately treated.[1]

One of the most serious shortcomings in traditional approaches to blacks in classical antiquity has been the scant consideration given to the experience of these peoples in Africa and its pertinence to the classical evidence. Another weakness has been a failure to appreciate the full import of the combined documentary and archaeological evidence: often scholars have not related the "Ethiopians" of texts and inscriptions to the Negroes of the graphic and plastic arts and crafts. Moreover, the importance of the frequent portrayal of the Negro in ancient art has been underestimated in evaluations of the black population. And finally, in complex questions of racial attitudes it is important to let the ancients speak for themselves and not to attribute to antiquity nonexistent

---

1. For a more detailed treatment of the subject of this study, see Frank Snowden, *Blacks in Antiquity: Ethiopians in the Greco-Roman Experience* (Cambridge, Mass., 1970).

FRANK M. SNOWDEN, JR.

modern concepts. Such an approach, however, has not usually been adopted in assessing the classical image of the Negro.

The Egyptians were among the first of several predominantly white peoples who had extended contacts with blacks living in the lands south of Egypt. The word Kush, which the Egyptians used initially in a restricted geographical sense, acquired in time an enlarged significance and embraced lands farther south. The Greeks, and later the Romans, followed a similar practice in applying a single general term, Ethiopia, to the same region. (Today Kush, Ethiopia, and Nubia are frequently used interchangeably.)² The Greek word Ethiopia, however, although having a geographical meaning like Kush, emphasized the color of the inhabitants since it meant the land of "burnt-faced men." The term Ethiopians embraced a variety of brown, dark, and black peoples, including the so-called true or pure Negro, a type with less pronounced Negroid characteristics, sometimes called Nilotic, and various mixed black-white types. Thus, to the Greeks and Romans, the inhabitants of certain areas of both East and West Africa, whether classified today as Hamites, Nubians, or Negroes, were *all* Ethiopians, or persons with burnt faces.

Opinions differ as to the nature of the black element in the population of Kush at various periods in its history. Murdock, for example, holds that Nubians are Negroid in origin but reveal a strong Caucasoid admixture.³ According to Trigger, the population of Nubia has intermarried with individuals or groups of many different types from outside and should be described as Nubians and not as a mixture of any one type with another.⁴ Shinnie sees no reason to believe that the ancient populations of Nubia were different from the present-day inhabitants, i.e., "predominantly brown-skinned people of aquiline features having in varying degrees an admixture of Negro."⁵ Adams maintains that the evidence

---

2. In this essay I have in general employed the terms Kushite and Nubian for the preclassical periods and Ethiopian for the Greek and Roman period. Negro or Negroid is used when an art object warrants such a classification according to the criteria of physical anthropologists or when justified on the basis of the physical characteristics mentioned in classical sources. The modern term "black" is sometimes used, especially as a substitute for "Ethiopian," since that word emphasized color. For Graeco-Roman usage of "Ethiopian" and acquaintance with the Negroid type, see Snowden, *Blacks*, 1-99.

3. George Peter Murdock, *Africa: Its People and Their Culture History* (New York, 1959), 161.

4. B. G. Trigger, *History and Settlement in Lower Nubia* (New Haven, 1965), 17.

5. P. L. Shinnie, *Meroe: A Civilization of the Sudan* (New York, 1967), 155.

requires adopting "as a working hypothesis the idea that the Nubian population has remained basically the same since Neolithic times— neither markedly Negroid nor markedly 'Egyptian,' but a stable blend of the two strains," and adds, "The stock has certainly been augmented by immigration at many times, but probably never to the extent of upsetting the existing balance, either biological or social."[6] Hence, although views differ as to the precise nature of the Negroid element, such a component, varying from period to period and from region to region, must be kept in mind whenever the words Kushite, Nubian, and Ethiopian are used.

Ethiopians in Africa

The experience of blacks in Graeco-Roman Egypt and in other parts of the classical world cannot be fully understood without a consideration of the history of Kush, especially during the Meroitic period, i.e., from the sixth century B.C. to the end of the third or middle of the fourth century A.D. A very large part, perhaps the majority, of Ethiopians came to Greece and Italy either directly from Nubia via Egypt or indirectly from Nubia after a period of residence in Egypt. The Ethiopians who lived to the south of Egypt are mentioned more frequently in classical texts than those who resided in North Africa. Reports of blacks in Egypt and of black kingdoms to the south of Egypt reached the Greeks at a very early date. These first reports, often meaningful if examined in the light of relevant Kushite documents, were important factors in molding the Greek image of blacks, an image which never changed fundamentally and later influenced greatly the Roman attitude toward Ethiopians.

Shadows of the Napatan kingdom of Kush are reflected in Herod-otus. The Meroitic kingdom of Kush, whose beginning is associated with the removal of the Kushite capital in the early part of the sixth century B.C. from Napata, near the Fourth Cataract, further south to Meroe, was much better known to the Greeks and, later, to the Romans. In fact, as early as the fifth century B.C. Herodotus described Meroe, situated between the Fifth and Sixth Cataracts, as a great city, the capital of the other Ethiopians.[7] In the course of time the Ethiopian peoples and civili-

---

6. W. Y. Adams, "Continuity and Change in Nubian Cultural History," *Sudan Notes and Records*, XLVIII (1967), 18.
   7. Herodotus 2.29.

FRANK M. SNOWDEN, JR.

zation of the Meroitic era evoked the attention of a number of classical writers and attracted a number of Greek and Roman visitors. Two of the earliest of these, if our records are accurate, were the well-traveled Democritus[8] and Simonides the Younger, the latter reportedly having spent five years in Meroe in preparation for writing a book,[9] perhaps entitled *Aethiopica* like several other lost works on the region. It is appropriate, therefore, to call attention to a few pertinent highlights of Kushite history and, especially, of Meroitic civilization.

The military experience of the southern neighbors of Egypt, particularly as mercenaries, has rarely been given its due weight in accounting for the presence of the Ethiopian in the classical world or in explanations of Negro soldiers in Greek and Roman art. As early as the Seventeenth Dynasty (c. 1650-1567 B.C.) the Kushites were powerful enough to be an important force in the politics of the times. About 1600 B.C. a Kushite ruler was sent an invitation from the Hyksos king, Apophis, to join his expedition against the Egyptian Pharoah Kamose.[10] The Kushite reply to this overture, which promised to divide Egypt between them, is not known, but the incident is a significant commentary on the high regard in which Kushite soldiers were held. Another illustration of respect for Kushite military skill is apparent in the Egyptian policy of employing Nubian auxiliaries. Mercenaries from various parts of the south have been considered one of the most important factors responsible for revolutionizing Egypt's military effectiveness and assuring her success during the expansion of the empire.[11] "Men of Nubian race," Hayes points out, "have continued to serve in the Egyptian army and police force until the present day, and we may be sure that throughout the Dynastic Period many Nubian tribesmen, particularly the warlike Medjay, resided with their families within the boundaries of Egypt itself."[12]

Relations between Egypt and Kush were shrouded in obscurity from the eleventh to the middle of the eighth century B.C. About 750 B.C.,

---

8. Diogenes Laertius 9.35.

9. Pliny *Naturalis historia* 6.35.183.

10. George Steindorff and Keith C. Seele, *When Egypt Ruled the East*, 2d ed. rev. (Chicago, 1957), 31.

11. *Ibid.*, 28.

12. William C. Hayes, ch. II in I. E. S. Edwards, C. J. Gadd, N. G. L. Hammond, and E. Sollberger (eds.), *The Cambridge Ancient History*, 3d ed. (Cambridge, 1973), II, pt. 1, 76.

however, a new day began for Kush, a region which had interested the Egyptians since the Old Kingdom. Under the leadership of Kashta the independent Napatan kingdom of Kush took advantage of Egyptian weaknesses, invaded, and conquered Egypt. Kashta's son, Piankhi, completed the conquest of Egypt about 730 B.C., and, according to the detailed record of his campaign preserved on a stele erected near Napata, respected the temples and gods of the Egyptians, was scrupulously attentive to religious ritual, and was moderate with his enemies.[13] Piankhi and his successors constituted the Twenty-fifth Dynasty, known as the Ethiopian, which for about sixty years ruled Egypt and occupied an area from deep in the south to the shores of the Mediterranean.[14] This was, as Hallett has pointed out, "the first and indeed the only time in history, a state based on the interior of Africa played an active part in the politics of the Mediterranean."[15] In 663 B.C. the Ethiopians were defeated by the Assyrians, expelled from Egypt, and forced to withdraw to Napata.

The history of the Meroitic kingdom of Kush from the middle of the sixth century B.C. to the early fourth century A.D. has a particular relevance for the Graeco-Roman image of Ethiopians, since it was the Ethiopia of this period which the Greeks and Romans knew best. Meroitic civilization has been regarded as a creative synthesis of native and foreign cultures, influenced to a great extent in its early stages by Egypt and later by other foreign elements, especially Hellenistic. Though heavily indebted to the Egyptians throughout their history in language, religion, and art, the Meroites gradually developed their own distinctive writing, worshiped their own gods, and created a style of their own in architecture, statuary, reliefs, and ceramics.[16] Their pottery has been described

---

13. James Henry Breasted, *Ancient Records of Egypt*, rev. ed. (New York, 1962), IV, 406-444.

14. For a discussion of the question of a Negro element in the Twenty-fifth Ethiopian Dynasty, see D. M. Dixon, "The Origin of the Kingdom of Kush (Napata-Meroë)," *Journal of Egyptian Archaeology*, L (1964), 130-132.

15. Robin Hallett, *Africa to 1875: A Modern History* (Ann Arbor, 1970), 82. For a recent evaluation of early Egyptian contact with southerners, see David O'Connor, "Ancient Egypt and Black Africa—Early Contacts," *Expedition: The Magazine of Archaeology/Anthropology*, XIV (1971), 2-9.

16. My summary of Meroitic culture is based especially on the following: Fritz Hintze and Ursula Hintze, *Civilizations of the Old Sudan: Kerma. Kush. Christian Nubia* (Amsterdam, 1968); B. G. Haycock, "Landmarks in Cushite History," *Journal of Egyptian Archaeology*, LVIII (1972), 225-244; Shinnie, *Meroe*.

FRANK M. SNOWDEN, JR.

The Ethiopian military presence continued to be felt in the Ptolemaic world. Although the second Ptolemy (Philadelphus, 283-246 B.C.), according to Theocritus, conquered a portion of the country of the black Ethiopians,[27] the central Meroitic power suffered no permanent effect. The fifth Ptolemy (Epiphanes, 205-180 B.C.) was confronted with a lengthy Theban rebellion in which Nubian officers or chiefs participated.[28] A regent warned an unidentified youthful Ptolemy, perhaps Epiphanes, of the undesirability of launching an expedition against the Ethiopians and of the need for vigilance in dealing with them because of their well-known courage and skill in warfare.[29] Arrian informs us that Indian and Ethiopian armies employed war elephants before the Macedonians and Carthaginians used them for military purposes.[30] Noting the importance of elephants in the life of Ethiopians at Meroe, some specialists maintain that African elephants used in Ptolemaic and Roman times were trained by Meroites and that Ethiopians were among the mahouts whom the Ptolemies employed.[31] Bronze coins depicting a Negro on the obverse and an elephant on the reverse have been regarded as evidence that Negro mahouts rode Carthaginian elephants in the First or Second Punic Wars.[32]

At various times during their occupation of Egypt until late in the sixth century A.D. the Romans found southern opposition a threat to their presence in Ethiopia as the Egyptians and Ptolemies had before them. In the last quarter of the first century B.C. Ethiopian troops, many of whom were certainly Negroes, crossed the Roman frontiers, captured several towns, enslaved the inhabitants, and seized statues of Augustus erected there. The countermeasures of the prefect of Egypt, C. Petronius,

---

27. Theocritus 17.87.

28. P. J. Pestman, "Harmachis et Anchmachis, deux rois indigènes du temps des Ptolémées," *Chronique d'Egypte*, XL (1965), 168-169; Haycock, "Landmarks," 234.

29. Agatharchides *De Mari Erythraeo* 16 in *Geographi Graeci Minores* (Paris, 1882), I, 118; P. M. Fraser, *Ptolemaic Alexandria* (Oxford, 1972), I, 541-542, and II, 775-777.

30. Arrian *Tactica* 2.2 and 19.6.

31. Shinnie, *Meroe*, 101; Hintze and Hintze, *Civilizations of the Old Sudan*, 23, 25; Haycock, "Landmarks," 230, 237.

32. See Snowden, *Blacks*, 130-131, and literature there cited; F. Panvini Rosati, "La monetazione annibalica," in *Studi Annibalici, Atti del Convegno svoltosi a Cortona, Tuoro sul Trasimeno, Perugia, Ottobre 1961*, n.s. V (1961-1964) (Cortona, 1964), 178-180; Jehan Desanges, "Les Chasseurs d'éléphants d'Abou-Simbel," *Actes du Quatre-vingt-douzième Congrès des Sociétés Savantes* (Paris, 1970), 36, n. 28.

were not minor skirmishes as the ancient sources imply,[33] and as some scholars have maintained. Although Augustus considered his Ethiopian campaign of sufficient importance to mention it in his *Monumentum Ancyranum*,[34] he granted the Ethiopian queen's ambassadors everything they pleaded for, according to Strabo, including the remission of tribute which the emperor had imposed.[35] "The sources throughout smack of apologia," Jameson concludes, and adds, "Augustus was aiming at territorial expansion and failed."[36] The Blemmyes, a difficult-to-locate nomad Ethiopian people, mentioned as early as Theocritus,[37] threatened the Roman presence in Africa intermittently from the middle of the third century A.D. until late in the sixth century. The emperor Diocletian (284-305 A.D.), in an attempt to keep peace, decided to make an annual grant of money (which continued to be paid for 200 years) to the Blemmyes, with the stipulation that they were no longer to plunder Roman territory.[38] An Ethiopian was among the auxiliaries of Septimius Severus in distant Britain [39] and perhaps part of the *numerus Maurorum* billeted at Burgh-by-Sands.[40] At least one of the soldiers on the Arch of the African-born Septimius Severus in the Roman Forum seems to be Negroid.[41] It has been argued that Constantine in the siege of Verona and at the battle of Milvian Bridge employed Ethiopian archers and that Ethiopians fought in the great imperial armies on all fronts.[42]

Certain classical references to Ethiopian warriors and representations of Negroes in art, we have seen, become more comprehensible when interpreted in the light of Meroitic history. Similarly, many other

---

33. Strabo 17.1.53-1.54.

34. *Monumentum Ancyranum* 5.26.22.

35. Strabo 17.1.

36. Shelagh Jameson, "Chronology of the Campaign of Aelius Gallus and C. Petronius," *The Journal of Roman Studies*, LVIII (1968), 82.

37. Theocritus 7.114.

38. Procopius *De bello Persico* 1.19.29-35.

39. Scriptores Historiae Augustae *Septimius Severus* 22.4-5.

40. R. G. Collingwood and R. P. Wright, *The Roman Inscriptions of Britain* (Oxford, 1965), I, 626, no. 2042; Anthony Birley, *Septimius Severus: The African Emperor* (London, 1971), 265-266.

41. See Richard Brilliant, *The Arch of Septimius Severus in the Roman Forum* (Rome, 1967), 247 and pls. 78c, d.

42. H. P. L'Orange, "Una strana testimonianza finora inosservata nei rilievi dell'Arco di Costantino: Guerrieri etiopici nelle armate imperiali romane," *Roma: Rivista di studi e di vita romana*, XIV (1936), 21.

FRANK M. SNOWDEN, JR.

allusions to Ethiopians have puzzled scholars and caused them to under-
estimate their significance—pointing to a need for a closer examination
of classical texts and monuments in the light of pertinent African materials.

Doubt, for example, has been expressed as to whether Homer had
heard of African blacks. It is very likely that, in view of evidence of acquaintance with blacks outside Africa as early as the Early Minoan period, reports of African blacks had reached the Greek world by the time
of the Homeric poems. Connor is correct in pointing out that the first
Greek allusions to blacks appear at approximately a time of military and
diplomatic activity among the Ethiopians of Kush, who had conquered
Egypt about 730 B.C. and had not only left a record of their military
prowess but also apparently won a reputation for their piety. Connor has
suggested as reasonable the hypothesis that "Homer's allusion to 'blameless Ethiopians,' his picture of Ethiopia as a land particularly pleasing to
the gods, his selection of a black-skinned and woolly-haired herald for
Odysseus, Eurybates, are part of the respectful consciousness of black
power on the edge of the Greek world."[43] The popularity of Negro warriors in the art of the sixth and early fifth centuries B.C., another important factor in molding the Greek image of the Negro, may have owed its
origin to a similar consciousness of a military tradition among African
blacks. Greek settlements in Naucratis and residence elsewhere in Egypt
in the sixth century B.C. provided artists with first-hand contacts with
Negroes. These contacts not only presented the artists with a challenge to
represent the black man's features but also undoubtedly brought to their
attention stories about his military past. In such a way early vase-painters
were influenced to give prominence to Negro soldiers in the Memnon
cycle and to paint episodes such as a shield-bearing Negro between two
Amazons, a woolly-haired Negro armed with lance and shield, advancing on the run, and a helmeted Negro bending intently forward as he
raises his shield.[44]

---

43. W. Robert Connor, review of Snowden, *Blacks*, in *Good Reading: Review of
Books Recommended by the Princeton Faculty*, XXI (May 1970), 4.
44. For Negro military companions of Memnon, see black-figured neck-amphora,
c. 530 B.C. , in New York, Metropolitan Museum of Art, 98.8.13 and similar vase in
London, British Museum, B209; for a shield-bearing Negro between two Amazons,
mid-sixth century B.C. black-figured amphora in Brussels, Musées Royaux du Cin-

The "blameless Ethiopians" of the *Iliad* and the *Odyssey* may have derived from reports of Ethiopian piety resembling the account on Piankhi's stele and similar documents no longer extant. Herodotus' more detailed account of Sabacos provides a fifth-century version of the Twenty-fifth Dynasty's generosity and piety. Sabacos, when king of Egypt, according to Herodotus, never put wrongdoers to death and was deeply concerned lest he commit sacrilege.[45] Since such reports continued to be circulated in the fifth century, there is no reason to consider the Negroes depicted on a late fourth-century gold phiale as "almost caricatures" and to maintain that they reveal "little of the Homeric spirit," which represented Ethiopians as friends of the gods.[46] Such an interpretation overlooks the fact that the creator of the phiale—working in the tradition of Homer's "blameless" Ethiopians, amplified by Herodotus' more recent account of the just Sabacos—considered it appropriate to include three concentric circles, with twenty-four Negro heads in each, as a major motif in a design also reminiscent of Hesiod's "just" city.[47]

The all-too-frequent penchant of some scholars for "explaining away" Ethiopians who do not fit a preconceived stereotype of barbarians or slaves perhaps would not have developed if adequate attention had been given to the history of Meroe. That all Ethiopians were not considered as savages or slaves by the Greeks and Romans is, of course, amply attested by classical art and literature, which, more frequently than has been realized, reflects an actual acquaintance with aspects of Meroitic civilization. Although the Greeks had knowledge of primitive Ethiopians living beyond Napata and Meroe, whose practices presented a striking contrast to their own customs, they also spoke highly of the Ethiopians who inhabited Meroe and the land adjoining Egypt. Accounts of some Ethiopians who resembled wild beasts in their way of living, of others who went about entirely naked, or of a few who did not believe in the existence of any gods at all did not blind the Greeks and Romans to those

quantenaire, A13; for a woolly-haired Negro on interior of red-figured kylix, c.520-500 B.C. , in Paris, Louvre, G93; and for a heavily armed Negro on lekythos in Six's style, Naples, Museo Nazionale, 86339.

45. Herodotus 2.137, 139.

46. Dietrich von Bothmer, "A Gold Libation Bowl," *Bulletin of the Metropolitan Museum of Art*, XXI (1962), 161.

47. Hesiod *Opera et dies* 232-233.

FRANK M. SNOWDEN, JR.

highly developed Ethiopians whose reputation for wisdom was great and whose religious practices made them the favorites of the gods.[48]

Lucian notes the preeminence of the Ethiopians in wisdom and informs us that they gave the doctrine of astrology to men[49]—an interesting reference in view of second-century B.C. evidence from Meroe of astronomical equipment and of graffiti representing actual sketches of instruments and astronomical calculations.[50] It is tempting to surmise that visitors to Meroe, impressed at seeing such instruments, circulated reports that Ethiopians invented astrology. Undoubtedly other visitors, fascinated by impressive temples and religious ceremonies "at the ends of the earth," returned with accounts which influenced historians in the views detailed by Diodorus, that many Egyptian institutions were derivatives of Ethiopian civilization. It is not unlikely that such historians, as they reflected upon similarities in certain Egyptian and Ethiopian practices, recalled Homer's "blameless Ethiopians,"[51] "the farthermost of men,"[52] and concluded that the distant southerners were the first of men and, hence, dearest to the gods. One version of such a view is preserved in Diodorus, who writes that the Ethiopians "were the first to be taught to honour the gods and to hold sacrifices and festivals and the other rites by which men honour the deity; and it is generally held that the sacrifices practiced among the Ethiopians are those which are most pleasing to heaven."[53]

The Black Population in the Graeco-Roman World

Quantitative precision is impossible, but the black population in the Graeco-Roman world was certainly larger than has been generally realized, especially in the Roman world. Several scholars, though impressed by the archaeological evidence, have underestimated the significance of the many blacks depicted in classical art.

---

48. See, e.g., the account of Ethiopians as given by Diodorus 3.2-3.35.
49. Lucian *De astrologia* 3.
50. J. Garstang, "Fifth Interim Report on the Excavations at Meroë in Ethiopia," *Annals of Archaeology and Anthropology* (Liverpool), VII (1944), 4-6.
51. Homer *Iliad* 1.423-424.
52. Homer *Odyssey* 1.22-24.
53. Diodorus 3.3.1 (trans. C. H. Oldfather in the Loeb edition).

Smith, for example, believes "that in the Greco-Roman world Negroes were not extremely rare, but were sufficiently uncommon to interest both artists and the public as exotic types."[54] "The abundance of archaeological material is . . . quite remarkable," according to Costelloe, "though probably more indicative of an ancient curiosity in foreign types than of any great number of blacks in the Greco-Roman world."[55] The enigma which some have seen in the frequent representations of Negroes is stated in another fashion by Kiang: " . . . it appears to me that in classical art there were more representations of Blacks as slaves than in a sense were justified by the proportion of black slaves, even in Egypt."[56] The Negroes, Kiang believes, are the result of a selective process which "abstracts from real life those limited images which once formulated, and launched into the public consciousness, have a disturbing tendency to persist . . . whose success as decorative motives were insured by their very exoticism."[57]

Interpretations such as these, however, do not adequately answer several questions: Why were there so many representations of Negroes? Why does the Negro appear over such a long span of time? Why is the archaeological evidence so often corroborated by written sources and vice versa? And at what point would "curiosity" or "exoticism" be expected to cease? Nor can the importance of the artistic evidence be minimized by arguing, as some have, that the Negroes of classical artists are usually "types" and that their Negroid features are the result of artistic conventions. Some, of course, are "types," but one of the astonishing facts about classical representations of Negroes is their freshness and great variety of physical types, "pure," Nilotic, and mulatto. All Negroes may look alike to some whites, but Greek and Roman artists did not see Negroes in such a manner.[58] Even Roman craftsmen, working in Hellen-

---

54. Morton Smith, review of Snowden, *Blacks,* in *American Historical Review,* LXXVI (1971), 140.

55. M. Joseph Costelloe, review of Snowden, *Blacks,* in *Review for Religious,* XIX (1970), 588.

56. Dawson Kiang, "The Brooklyn Museum's New Head of a Black," *Archaeology,* XXV (1972), 6.

57. *Ibid.*

58. On the classical representations of Negroes as an important source for a quite accurate and minutely characterized picture of the most diversified variants of dark-skinned Africans, see L. Castiglione, review of Snowden, *Blacks,* in *Acta Archaeolog-*

FRANK M. SNOWDEN, JR.

istic traditions, often portrayed the individual characteristics of Negroes whom they had seen.

The total output of classical artists was obviously much larger than that which has survived. All the more significant, therefore, is the large number of Negroes in every major period. The number, great as it is, represents only a very small proportion of the works depicting Negroes, in a variety of media and designed for many different purposes, which must have come from the workshops of artists. If one considers the occasions when it is possible to relate a particular Negro or group of blacks to a specific fact or event, it becomes clear that the historical value of classical art has been greatly underestimated. Further, the artistic evidence, much more than literature, produces valuable information concerning the physical characteristics of Negroes in antiquity, an important function in view of the paucity of pertinent anthropological studies. The findings of anthropology, however, though few, do tend to confirm the black man's presence at various times. Angel's study of skeletal samples from Greece, for example, has noted Negroid traits in samples from the classical, Hellenistic, and Roman periods, including four clearly Negroid types among ninety-five skeletons from one area of early Christian Corinth.[59] In addition, anthropological investigations pointing to Negroes in the Maghrib in antiquity are a useful supplement to the notices concerning North Afcan Ethiopians mentioned in classical texts.

References to Ethiopians in classical, especially Roman, literature are by no means few. Yet some scholars suggest that had the black population been significant, allusions would have been more frequent. Such a conclusion does not take into consideration the fact that, since there was no complex color problem or intense color prejudice (a subject to which I shall return), specific references to blacks were made on fewer occasions than today. It is largely, for example, because of the discovery of a marble head of a Negro on an estate of Herodes Atticus that it has been con-

---

ica *Academiae Scientiarum Hungaricae*, XXIV (1972), 440. Engelbert Mveng, *Les Sources grecques de l'histoire négro-africaine* (Paris, 1972), 70, describes the Negroes of the Greek and Roman artists as "un vaste tableau des principaux types négro-africains connus de nos jours" and as representing "authentiquement le monde négro-africain, dans son unité et dans sa diversité."

59. J. Lawrence Angel, review of Snowden, *Blacks*, in *American Anthropologist*, LXXIV (1972), 159.

cluded that Memnon, a favorite pupil and foster son of the influential member of the international aristocracy of the second century A.D., was a Negro.[60] Accounts of the life of Herodes Atticus, however, do not identify Memnon as an Ethiopian. In many later more color-conscious societies a black in a comparable relationship would receive extended comment. That blacks were constantly being assimilated in the predominantly white societies of antiquity is attested by both written and archaeological evidence. Race mixture of blacks and whites, though a subject of frequent comment in many postclassical societies, was mentioned only incidentally by classical authors, and therefore it is usually difficult to identify mixed black-white types in literature. Unless further excavations yield other relevant art objects, we perhaps shall never know how many more blacks were as devoted to learning as Memnon, or how many more North Africans achieved the financial success of the obviously Negroid Julius Serenus, the well-to-do resident of Thaenae in southern Tunisia, whose happy life with his white wife Julia Numitoria is known only through a mosaic.[61] It should not be concluded, therefore, that blacks were rare or even a small part of Graeco-Roman communities, merely because the ancients did not always apply an ethnic tag to Ethiopians.

The role of blacks in various military operations from Minoan to Roman times must have accounted for a substantial, if not the largest, segment of blacks. When one considers the scale of Xerxes' expedition into Greece, Ptolemaic activity in Ethiopia, the scope of the Carthaginian wars, Roman involvement south of Egypt, and Rome's long occupation of North Africa, it is reasonable to conclude that this representation of blacks in the Roman world has been underestimated. Although specific numbers of Ethiopians are mentioned only infrequently in accounts of military campaigns, the numerous military actions over the centuries nevertheless suggest thousands rather than hundreds. Of the black warriors who survived in battle, some were captured and enslaved. Other survivors returned to their homelands, and still others, perhaps attracted by

---

60. Philostratus *Vita Apollonii* 3.11 and *Vitae Sophistarum* 2.558; Paul Graindor, "Tête de nègre du Musée de Berlin," *Bulletin de correspondance hellénique*, XXXIX (1915), 402-412; idem, *Un Milliardaire antique: Hérode Atticus et sa famille* (Cairo, 1930), 114-116.

61. Mohamed Yacoub, *Guide du Musée de Sfax* (Tunis, 1966), 44, and pl. XIV, figs. 2, 3.

FRANK M. SNOWDEN, JR.

what they had seen in the countries where they had fought, came back later, either in a spirit of adventure or in pursuit of economic gain. Some returned perhaps to join women whose affection they had won. That a mulatto element began to appear in the Greek population about the middle of the fifth century B.C. is suggested by Greek art. Prior to that time only blacks with pronounced Negroid features had been depicted. The mulatto features of children born of Greek women by Xerxes' black soldiers had apparently caught the eye of vase-painters, who in the latter part of the fifth century for the first time depicted mulattoes, often youthful figures.[62] Crossings between Greek women and Ethiopians are attested also by Aristotle in the next century in his comments on the transmission of physical characteristics in the family of a woman from Elis and an Ethiopian.[63]

Blacks, in the opinion of Fraser, were as familiar a part of the Alexandrian scene in antiquity as they are today.[64] Fraser suggests that the economic factors which in modern times have attracted Sudanese to Cairo and Alexandria may have also been responsible for northward migrations of Negroes in antiquity. That there were numerous Negroes in Egypt, and especially Alexandria, is attested by the striking evidence of terracottas. The many Negro dancers, musicians, actors, and slaves whom Hellenistic craftsmen produced in terracotta and bronze were not studies of museum pieces but were inspired by peoples whom the artists had seen in Egypt, in town and in country.

In most instances, Fraser believes Alexandrian Negroes were the "house-boys" of the age or slaves acquired during Ptolemaic activity in Ethiopia. There were certainly black slaves, but Fraser, like others, has minimized the mobility of many Ethiopians in antiquity. The resources of Ethiopia and the condition of the Meroitic kingdom of Kush at that time would have both permitted and encouraged a number of Ethiopians

---

62. See, e.g., the mixed black-white types on the following: red-figured stamnos (c. 460 B.C.) in Bologna, Museo Civico Archeologico, 174; red-figured pelike (c. 460 B.C.) in Boston, Museum of Fine Arts, 63.2663 (note upturned nose and thick lips of Cepheus as contrasted with the leptorrhine nose and thin lips of his daughter); and red-figured kylix (c. 450 B.C.) in West Berlin, Staatliche Museen, Antikenabteilung, F2534.

63. Aristotle De generatione animalium 1.18.722a; Historia animalium 7.6.586a.

64. Fraser, Alexandria, I, 74. Cf. Trigger, Lower Nubia, 16, 19.

to migrate to Egypt and elsewhere in the Graeco-Roman world. The advantages of centers like Rome and Campania must have been as attractive to enterprising blacks as they were to Jews, Greeks, Syrians, and Egyptians. Worthy of note in this connection is the substantial evidence for the presence of Negroes in Campania—not unexpected, however, since Puteoli docked a steady flow of ships from Alexandria.

Ethiopians of various social classes, like others of non-Greek and non-Roman origin, voluntarily went to Greece and Italy for a variety of reasons. Amasis, the sixth-century B.C. painter-potter in Athens, Boardman has argued, was perhaps a dusky-skinned metic, born in Egypt.[65] It is not unreasonable to suggest that some other unknown craftsmen of the Greek and Roman world were blacks who, coming from Meroe, steeped in a rich artistic tradition, saw the advantages of working as goldsmiths and especially as potters and vase-painters. Some Ethiopians went abroad to study. The Ethiopian king Ergamenes (c. 268-220 B.C.), a contemporary of Ptolemy II, according to Diodorus, had a Greek education,[66] and other Ethiopian rulers, aristocrats, and well-to-do Meroites acquainted with the advantages of a Greek education doubtlessly sent their children to Alexandria and other foreign centers. A Hellenistic bronze of a boyish Negro orator has been interpreted as an aristocratic lad from Upper Egypt or beyond, sent to study among the philosophers and teachers of rhetoric in Alexandria.[67] Included among the distinguished disciples of Epicurus were two Ptolemaei of Alexandria, the one black and the other white.[68]

Ethiopian diplomats were not uncommon, since Ethiopian relations with the Ptolemies and Romans involved diplomatic exchanges. Diodorus interviewed Ethiopian ambassadors resident in Egypt.[69] Some Ethiopian diplomats remained in their foreign posts or returned after completion of their missions. Among ambassadors accredited to Constantine

---

65. John Boardman, "The Amasis Painter," *Journal of Hellenic Studies*, LXXVIII (1958), 1-3; *idem, The Greeks Overseas* (Harmondsworth, 1964), 169.

66. Diodorus 3.6.3.

67. Cornelius C. Vermeule, "Greek, Etruscan and Roman Bronzes Acquired by the Museum of Fine Arts, Boston," *Classical Journal*, LV (1960), 198.

68. Diogenes Laertius 10.25. I am indebted to Werner A. Krenkel of the University of Rostock for this reference.

69. Diodorus 3.11.3.

FRANK M. SNOWDEN, JR.

were Blemmyes and Ethiopians, some of whom had no desire to return to their homelands but preferred to remain in Italy.[70] A life-size bust of the Flavian period has been thought to be that of a Negro who came to Rome as an ambassador or a hostage and during his stay had his portrait made.[71] Such an interpretation may be correct, but he may have been, on the other hand, one of a number of well-to-do Ethiopians from the Meroitic kingdom of Kush who had voluntarily settled abroad to seek their fortunes, and had achieved distinction. Although the slightly under life-size head of dark gray marble in the Brooklyn Museum may have been, as has been suggested, that of a soldier or official in the administration of a Greek ruler or perhaps a member of the household of a prominent Greek,[72] independent Meroe should not be overlooked as the origin of this Negro as well as that of several other nameless marble heads and busts of Negroes from the early centuries of the Empire.

Graeco-Roman Attitudes toward Blacks

The first blacks in the Mediterranean world outside Africa are known to us primarily through art. These blacks were neither slaves nor savages but mercenaries in Crete, a participant in a procession at Pylos,[73] and a local dignitary or distinguished visitor to Thera.[74] The first Ethiopians in European literature are Homer's "blameless Ethiopians." Warmington emphasizes the importance of the initial Homeric image of Ethiopians:

> It cannot be said what dim memory of the Bronze Age lies behind Homer's few but much discussed lines about the "blameless Ethiopians" who were visited by the immortal gods, and some Homeric scholars would deny them any historical significance. Their real importance, given the place of the the Homeric epics in the Greek con-

---

70. Eusebius De vita Constantini 4.7.

71. Wolfgang Helbig (trans. J. F. and F. Muirhead), Guide to the Public Collections of Classical Antiquities in Rome (Leipzig, 1896), II, 86, no. 847.

72. Bernard V. Bothmer, "A Young Nubian Immortalized: Brooklyn's New Acquisition, Apollo, XCII (February 1971), 126-127; Kiang, "New Head of a Black," 4-7.

73. See above, nn. 20 and 21.

74. Sp. Marinatos, "An African in Thera (?)," Athens Annals of Archaeology, II, fasc. 3 (1969), 374-375 and color pl. 1; idem, A Brief Guide to the Temporary Exhibition of the Antiquities of Thera (Athens, 1971), 22-23.

sciousness, lies in the fact that they were there at all; it was inevitable that in later Greek times, geographers and philosophers would discover what would explain and amplify the Homeric references, and in particular the religious practices which would account for the favor of the gods. The fact that these as recorded are in no way remarkable, and that some Ethiopians lived in a state of savagery, made no difference to the generally favorable judgment.[75]

Whatever the origin and full significance of Homer's "blameless Ethiopians" and whatever their precise physical characteristics, Ethiopian-Olympian consortia and pious and just Ethiopians continued to be mentioned throughout the history of classical literature long after African Negroes were a reality in the ancient world. To the Augustan world Diodorus presented an image of just Ethiopians who, because of their piety, had been protected from invaders by the gods. "Although many and powerful rulers have made war upon them," Diodorus wrote, "not one of these has succeeded in his undertaking."[76] Seneca admired the freedom-loving Ethiopians who rejected slavery and replied to Persian spies "with the independent words which kings call insults."[77] As late as the third century A.D. Heliodorus described the Ethiopian king Hydaspes' attitude toward the vanquished in language reminiscent of Anchises' famous statement on the destiny of Rome.[78]

The favorable view of Ethiopians was also amplified in early descriptions, environmental explanations of racial differences, ideas of the unity of mankind, and the exegesis of early Christian writers. And there was nothing in the experience of blacks as slaves, freedmen, or freemen which did not confirm formal and informal expressions of these views.

Xenophanes, the first author in European literature to apply to Ethiopians a physical characteristic other than color, contrasted, in an unbiased description of physical types, black-skinned, platyrrhine Ethiopians and blue-eyed, red-haired Thracians.[79] Herodotus described Ethi-

---

75. B. M. Warmington, review of Snowden, *Blacks*, in *African Historical Studies*, IV (1971), 385.

76. Diodorus 3.2.4.

77. Seneca *De ira* 3.20.2.

78. Heliodorus 9.21, where Hydaspes says: "A noble thing it is to surpass an enemy in battle when he is standing but in generosity when he has fallen."

79. Xenophanes, *Fragment* 16, in Hermann Diels, *Die Fragmente der Vorsokratiker* (Berlin, 1961).

FRANK M. SNOWDEN, JR.

opians as the tallest and most handsome men on earth.[80] Classical anthropology accounted for the characteristics of the Ethiopians by an environment theory in the same way it explained the physical traits of the Scythians, Thracians, or any other people. The Greeks recognized Greeks and non-Greeks, frequent examples of the latter being Scythians and Ethiopians—a practice which the Romans continued as illustrations of racial extremes differing from themselves. The ancients attached no special stigma to color, regarding black skin or yellow hair mere geographical accidents, and developed no special racial theory about the inferiority of darker peoples or the superiority of whites. It makes no difference, declared Menander, whether one is as racially different from a Greek as an Ethiopian or Scythian; it is merit, not race, that counts.[81] In this statement Menander was attacking a traditional Greek distinction based on birth, not rejecting some special concept concerning the inferiority of the Ethiopian qua Ethiopian. When the early Christians proclaimed that it was the whiteness of the spirit, not the skin that mattered, that it made no difference whether a man was born among the Hebrews, Greeks, Ethiopians, Scythians, or Taurians, they were echoing Menander and adapting a formula which left no doubt as to its meaning and comprehensiveness.

Allusions in classical literature to the Ethiopian's blackness continued the unbiased approach of Xenophanes and the early environmentalists. It was to be expected that a predominantly white society should note the Negro's blackness and that the distinguishing mark of an Ethiopian continued to be the color of his skin. Though Xenophanes had mentioned the color of the skin, together with playtrrhiny, as the Ethiopian's distinctive characteristics, he had not included skin color in his description of the Thracians—the northerners in his contrast—but only their blue eyes and red hair. In other words, it was the Ethiopian's blackness and the color of the Thracian's eyes and hair that were unusual and distinctive from the Greek point of view. Thus blackness and Ethiopians were closely associated, and prominence was given to the Ethiopian's color in Greek, Roman, and early Christian imagery.[82]

---

80. Herodotus 3.20.
81. Menander, *Fragment* 612, in Alfred Koerte, *Menandri Quae Supersunt*, 2d ed., rev. and enlarged (Leipzig, 1959) [= *Frg.* 533 in Theodore Kock, *Comicorum Atticorum Fragmenta* (Leipzig, 1888), 157].
82. Ibn Khaldun's later observation throws some light on the Graeco-Roman practice: "The inhabitants of the north are not called by their color, because the peo-

A third-century A.D. epitaph found in Egypt includes an interesting example of this imagery. The epitaph, in which a master memorializes his Negro slave, reads in part: "Among the living I was very black, darkened by the rays of the sun, but my soul, ever blooming with white blossoms, won my prudent master's good will."[83] Commenting on Westermann's opinion that the sentiment expressed was a "remarkable example of the lack of race feeling based on distinctions of color," Davis compares the epitaph with two lines in William Blake's "The Little Black Boy": "My mother bore me in the southern wild, / And I am black, but O! my soul is white," and then remarks: "without doubting the general truth of Westermann's argument, we may still observe . . . that the dominant thought in both cases is that a Negro's soul may be white, in spite of his color, and that white is somehow better."[84] There is nothing, however, in the long history of the imagery to prove Davis's assumption. The Negro's blackness was merely *different* from the white man's whiteness. Such was the basic significance of the color of the skin in Graeco-Roman thought— whether mentioned in anthropological theories, in philosophical reflections, or in spiritual imagery. The traditional black-white, often deeply spiritual, symbolism had its roots firmly embedded in a Weltanschauung in which color was not emotionally charged as in some postclassical societies.

Father Moses, a black father of the Desert of Scetis, applied to himself the well-known Christian symbolism of spiritual blackness and whiteness. Even if the account is apocryphal, it illustrates the nature of the Graeco-Roman spirit. In response to the bishop's observation that he had upon consecration become all white because he was clad in white vestments, Moses replied, "Outwardly, holy Father, would that I were inwardly too!"[85] The sentiment is not unlike that which the master has left in memory of his Negro slave in the Egyptian epitaph.

---

ple who established the conventional meanings of words were themselves white. Thus, whiteness was something usual and common (to them), and they did not see anything sufficiently remarkable in it to cause them to use it as a specific term. Therefore, the inhabitants of the north, the Turks, the Slavs . . . [and others] are found to be separate nations and numerous races called by a variety of names" (Ibn Khaldun [trans. Franz Rosenthal], *The Muqaddimah: An Introduction to History* [New York, 1958], I, 172).

83. Werner Peek, *Griechische Vers-Inschriften* (Berlin, 1955), no. 1167.

84. David Brion Davis, *The Problems of Slavery in Western Culture* (Ithaca, 1966), 49-50.

85. *Apophthegmata Patrum, De abbate Mose* 4 in J. P. Migne (ed.), *Patrologiae Cursus Completus*, Series Graeca (Paris, 1864), LXV, col. 284.

FRANK M. SNOWDEN, JR.

There are only a few passages in the entire corpus of classical or early Christian literature which are sometimes cited as suggesting color prejudice. None of these passages, however, appears earlier than the literature of the Empire, long after the highly favorable image of Ethiopians had been firmly established and the unbiased environmental explanations of races and customs had taken root. Several authors of the early Empire associated the presence of an Ethiopian with omens portending disaster. The association of the color black with death and the underworld (the god of the nether regions was himself described as "niger Jupiter" and "niger Dis")[86] had nothing to do with the color of the skin, and the origin antedated an intimate acquaintance with blacks. It is not surprising, therefore, that as knowledge of blacks increased, the color of the Ethiopian's and the Egyptian's skin came to be associated in the minds of some with death and the lower world. It was reported, for example, that at the time of Caligula's death, a nocturnal performance was in rehearsal in which scenes from the lower world were enacted by Egyptians and Ethiopians.[87] If an occasion called for a dramatization of underworld scenes, why not add a bit of realism and cast darker peoples in such episodes, since the ancient world, unlike some postclassical societies, did not discriminate against black actors? Shortly before his death in Britain, Septimius Severus was said to have seen an Ethiopian and to have been dismayed because the color of the Ethiopian and the cypress bough which he carried were ill-omened.[88] It was a natural development for a biographer in compiling exhaustive collections of prodigies— dreams, falling statues, black victims provided for a sacrifice—to note the presence of black Ethiopians who happened to be in the vicinity of an emperor on the eve of his departure to the black underworld and the "black" Jupiter.

The tradition of underworld blackness seems also to have influenced

---

86. E.g., Seneca *Hercules Oetaeus* 1705; Statius *Thebais* 2.49, 4.291; Ovid *Metamorphoses* 4.438.

87. Suetonius *Caligula* 57.4.

88. Scriptores Historiae Augustae *Septimius Severus* 22.4-5. For two other examples of this belief, see a report of an Ethiopian who met the troops of Brutus before the battle of Philippi (Appian *Bella civilia* 4.17.134; Florus 2.17.7.7-8; Plutarch *Brutus* 48), and a reference to the ill-omened assistance which Priam received from Memnon and his black troops: Alexander Riese (ed.), *Anthologia Latina* (Leipzig, 1894), 157-158, no. 189.

some early Christian writers who depicted the devil at times as black, Ethiopian, or Egyptian.[89] The devil, for example, is described as "the black one" in the so-called *Epistle of Barnabas*,[90] and as a black boy, one of the visitors to St. Anthony.[91] A demon "in appearance like an Ethiopian altogether black and filthy" appeared in the dream of Marcellus in the *Acts of Peter*.[92] Such descriptions of the devil no doubt hark back to the pagan practice of describing Dis as *niger* and Charon as *horrendus*.[93] If the lord of the pagan underworld were "black," why was it not appropriate to depict a prominent figure of Christian hell in a similar manner?

What was the effect of a belief in black as a portent of evil on Graeco-Roman views of blacks and of the depiction of black devils and demons on early Christian attitudes toward Ethiopians? With respect to the classical view, there is nothing to suggest that the existence of the superstition resulted in fear or hostility or detracted from the generally favorable image otherwise amply documented. Nor did the daily lives of blacks seem in any way to be adversely affected by the superstition. Whether slaves or freedmen, auxiliaries in the Roman army, or freemen, Ethiopians enjoyed the same opportunities and received the same treatment as others of foreign origin. A former slave from Carthage, the dark- or black-skinned Terence, received recognition in the literary circles of the day. Popular black athletes won the plaudits of the crowds in the amphitheater and were eulogized by poets. Glycon, a tall, dark actor

89. Franz Jos. Dölger, *Die Sonne der Gerechtigkeit und der Schwarze; Eine religionsgeschichtliche Studie zum Taufgelöbnis*, Liturgiegeschichtliche Forschungen II (Münster, 1918) contains the major references in classical and early Christian literature to black devils and demons, 49-57; to black and evil, 57-64; to the devil and black Zeus, 64-75.

90. *Epistula Barnabae* 4.10 in Franz Xaver Funk, *Patres Apostolici* (Tubingen, 1901), I, 48.

91. Athanasius *Vita S. Antonii* 6 in *Patrologiae Cursus Completus*, Series Graeca (Paris, 1887), XXVI, col. 849A.

92. *Actus Petri cum Simone* 22 in Richard A. Lipsius and Max Bonnet, *Acta Apostolorum Apocrypha* (Leipzig, 1891), I, 70.

93. Charon is described as "portitor . . . horrendus . . . terribili squalore" (The grim ferryman and customs-officer, terrible in his squalor) in Vergil *Aeneid* 6.298-299. A poem in the *Anthologia Latina*, 155, no. 183, says of a pitch-black slave: "If the voice issuing from his lips did not make him sound human, the grim ghost would be frightening upon sight. Hadrumetum (Sousse in southern Tunisia), may ill-omened Tartarus carry off your monster for itself! The abode of Dis should have him as a guardian." The author of this poem is reflecting conventional language applied to the blackness of death and the underworld.

FRANK M. SNOWDEN, JR.

with a hanging lower lip, attained great popularity in the time of Nero.[94] Julius Serenus was a prosperous resident of southern Tunisia, his villa and golden goblets pointing to a considerable fortune, if not equal to Trimalchio's.[95] The skillful diplomacy of the Ethiopian queen's ambassadors gained the respect of Augustus, who granted them a very favorable peace. There was no repugnance to the intermarriage of black and white. Sextus Empiricus may have described accurately the preferences of the majority when he wrote that whites prefer the whitest and blacks, the blackest,[96] but it is noteworthy that many Greek and Roman men felt otherwise and had no reluctance in saying so. Many blacks were assimilated into the predominantly white society.[97]

There is substantial evidence that "black devils or demons" had no negative effect on early Christian attitudes toward blacks. Christianity reinforced a bond that had united black and white in the common worship of Isis,[98] which itself followed the tradition of Homer's gods who knew no color line. No stereotyped concept of the Ethiopian as wicked or unworthy of conversion ever arose. On the contrary, early Christian writers, whether employing the imagery of blackness and whiteness or interpreting lines from the Scriptures, gave dramatic expression to a credo that considered all men, regardless of the color of the skin, as potential Christians. This credo was translated into practice from the very beginning. By the baptism of the Ethiopian eunuch, reported as the first of the Gentiles to receive the mysteries of the divine word from Philip, it was proclaimed that considerations of race were to be of no significance in determining membership in the Church.[99] The early history of the Church attests that a predominantly white religion was as zealous about the spiritual welfare of the blackest Ethiopian from the south as that of the fairest Scythian from the north. But blacks were not to be only humble converts. The lives of two men, one perhaps and the

94. *Scholia ad Persium* 5.9 in Otto Iahn, *Auli Persii Flacci Satirarum Liber cum Scholiis Antiquis* (Leipzig, 1843).

95. See above, n. 61.

96. Sextus Empiricus *Adversus mathematicos* xi.43.

97. On Greek and Roman attitudes toward racial mixture between blacks and whites, see Snowden, *Blacks*, 178-179, 192-195.

98. Cf. R. E. Witt, *Isis in the Graeco-Roman World* (London, 1971), 22-24, 268.

99. Snowden, *Blacks*, 206-207. See *idem*, 196-218, for Ethiopians and early Christianity.

other certainly black, illustrate another aspect of the spirit of early Christianity. Many pilgrims from Africa, Asia, and Europe flocked to the Egyptian shrine of St. Menas (c. third-fourth century A.D.), sometimes represented as a Negro on pottery flasks which the visitors used as vessels to hold holy oil from the saint's shrine or water from a sacred spring near his tomb. The life of Moses, the black father mentioned above who died at the end of the fourth or in the early years of the fifth century A.D., was a source of inspiration to many. Known especially for his courage and humility, Moses was everything to all, an excellent teacher, and a model of the monastic life. Moses, whose body was black, had a soul more radiantly bright than the splendor of the sun, and by his life showed the incorrectness of the proverb that it is impossible to wash an Ethiopian white.[100]

Just as there are scholars who imply that if the ancients had been free from color prejudice they would not have mentioned color at all, there are those who argue that Greek artists, if unbiased, would not have depicted a Negro in comic or satirical scenes. Whites of many races received such treatment in classical art; why should Negroes have been excluded? If Negroes had been depicted only as caricatures or grotesques, or if representations of this kind were the rule, there might be some justification for seeing evidence of bias. But there was in art no *stereotyped* concept of the Negro as ugly or comic. On the contrary, the varied—and often sympathetic—treatment which the Negro received over many centuries in a wide variety of media and art forms suggests strongly not only that classical artists turned to the Negro as a subject for the same reasons that motivated the selection of individuals of various other races, but also that they were often motivated in their choice of the Negro by aesthetic considerations.

How widespread were views that color was of no importance in judging the worth of a man? How representative were the unbiased sentiments of classical or Christian writers? Even modern sociologists and historians who have developed elaborate techniques for gauging racial attitudes are confronted with difficulties in determining the attitudes of whites toward blacks. Hence, precise answers to the above questions

---

100. *Vita S. Moysis Aethiopis* in V. V. Latyšev, *Menologii Anonymi Byzantini Saeculi X Quae Supersunt* (St. Petersburg, 1912), fasc. 2, 330-334.

FRANK M. SNOWDEN, JR.

may never be known. Although it is true that the attitudes toward Ethiopians expressed in ancient literature may in large part represent the views of the educated upper classes, there is little evidence, as Warmington has pointed out, that the feelings of the majority were different.[101] On the contrary, there is much in the *total* picture which, as we have seen, suggests that the views preserved in our texts were representative of the attitude of the majority. In the ancient world the color of the Ethiopian's skin often went unnoticed on occasions when today it would be subject to comment. When Ethiopians were mentioned, their blackness did not convey the meaning or evoke the hostilities which have developed in color-conscious societies. Though there were black slaves in antiquity, they were not the only nor even the largest part of enslaved peoples. Further, the association of "black" and "slave" never acquired the meanings which accompanied the combination of these two words in several postclassical societies. No stereotyped conception of blacks ever flourished in either art or literature, and color per se was never a barrier. Although there are those who minimize its significance, the evidence leads me to agree with those who believe that the unprejudiced attitude of the Greeks and Romans toward blacks was one of the great achievements of the ancient world.

101. Warmington, review of Snowden, *Blacks*, 386.

2 Bernard Lewis

The African Diaspora
and the Civilization of Islam

There are reports of black African slaves in the Arabian peninsula in pre-Islamic times. This is not in itself surprising. Black slaves, though comparatively rare, were known in the ancient world, where they formed part of the vast mixed slave population. The import of black slaves to Egypt dates back to Pharaonic times, when some of them were depicted on friezes. In the Hellenistic and Roman periods, slaves, with other commodities, were exported from Nubia and from further south to the Mediterranean lands, both by the inland route down the Nile and by sea from the ports of the Horn of Africa to Clysma, the Egyptian port in the Gulf of Suez. According to a Greek author writing in the second half of the first century A.D., South Arabians were well established on the East African coast and played an important part as middlemen in the trade with the Graeco-Roman world.[1] Arabia was not actually part of that world, but had many connections with it and was in many respects influenced by its practices and affected by its politics.

References to black people in pre-Islamic Arabia have usually been taken to mean Abyssinians—commonly called Habash, the Arabic name from which our word Abyssinian is derived.[2] Habash was probably used

1. See L.A. Thompson, "Eastern Africa and the Graeco-Roman World," in L.A. Thompson and John Ferguson, *Africa in Classical Antiquity* (Ibadan, 1969), 32.

2. I have used the name Abyssinia in preference to Ethiopia, although the latter is now the correct official name of the country, and the name Abyssinia is falling into disuse. In antiquity, the Greek word *Aithiopes*, "burnt faces," was used loosely and generally of dark-skinned peoples, both African and Asian, and therefore lacks precision. On the Abyssinians in Arabia see N. V. Pigulewskaja, *Byzanz auf den Wegen nach, Indian* (Berlin-Amsterdam 1969), 211-271; Sidney Smith, "Events in Arabia in

BERNARD LEWIS

for the peoples of the Horn of Africa and their immediate neighbors. Apart from a few questionable references to Nubians, no other specific ethnic term relating to an African people is used in the most ancient Arabic sources; such terms do not appear until after the great waves of Islamic conquests had carried the Arabs out of Arabia and made them masters of a vast empire in southwest Asia and northern Africa.

Abyssinians were active in Arabia in the sixth century as allies of the Byzantines in the great struggle for power and influence between the Christian Roman Empire on the one hand and the Persian Empire on the other. An Abyssinian expedition seems to have crossed the Red Sea in about 512 A.D. to help the Christians in southern Arabia. After fighting a victorious campaign they returned home, leaving garrisons behind them. These were, however, overwhelmed in a local reaction. The Abyssinians returned in about 525 A.D., to restore their authority and protect the Christians. Having done this, they once again withdrew, leaving the country in the hands of a local puppet ruler. Later, he was overthrown by a group of Abyssinian deserters who had remained in the country. Their leader, who now became king, was Abraha, a former slave of a Byzantine merchant in the Abyssinian port of Adulis. The Abyssinians tried unsuccessfully to remove him and then agreed to grant him some form of recognition. He probably led the Abyssinian force which advanced northward from the Yemen and attacked Mecca, at that time a Yemenite trading post on the caravan route to Syria.[3] The attempt, which was probably part of a campaign against the Persians, failed, and in about 570 the Persians sent a naval expedition which brought the Yemen under their control.

Some Abyssinians remained in Arabia, mostly as slaves—that is to say as captives—or as mercenaries. These at times played a role of some importance, which is attested by the Arabic sources and also by ancient Ethiopic loanwords in classical Arabic. The early poets also make frequent references to Abyssinians serving the Arab tribesmen as shepherds and herdsmen.

---

the Sixth Century A.D.," *Bulletin of the School of Oriental and African Studies*, XVI (1954), 425-468; *Encyclopaedia of Islam*, 2nd ed., s.v. "Abraha" (by A. F. L. Beeston); Thompson, "Eastern Africa."

3. The expedition is referred to in the Qur'ān, ch. cv.

Apart from some inscriptions there is no contemporary internal historical evidence on Arabia on the eve of the birth of the Prophet Muhammad. There is, however, a great deal of poetry and narrative, committed to writing in later (that is, Islamic) times. Although very detailed and informative, it needs careful critical scrutiny in that it often tends to project back into the pre-Islamic Arabian past the situations and attitudes of the very different later age in which the texts were compiled and written. This consideration applies particularly to the poems and traditions relating to blacks, whose situation changed radically after the great Arab conquests, as did also the attitude of the Arabs towards them.

The normal fate of captives of those times was enslavement, and Abyssinians appear together with Persians, Greeks, and others among the foreign slave population of sixth-century Arabia. The proportion of black slaves is unknown, but from lists of the slaves and freedmen of the Prophet, and of some of his companions, it would seem that they formed a minority. Slave women were normally and lawfully used as concubines, and it was not unusual for a man to have a free, noble Arab as father and a slave concubine as mother. In such a case, according to ancient Arabian custom, he was a slave unless he was recognized and liberated by his father.

Arab poetry and legend have preserved the names of several famous figures in ancient Arabia who are said to have been born to Abyssinian mothers and who in consequence were of dark complexion. The most famous of these was the great poet and warrior 'Antara, whose father was of the Arab tribe of 'Abs and whose mother was an Abyssinian slave woman called Zabība. A verse ascribed to him runs:

> I am a man, of whom one half ranks with the best of 'Abs.
> The other half I defend with my sword.

This may mean no more than that his mother was a slave, without reference to race or color. There are, however, other verses ascribed to him, indicating that his African blood and dark skin marked him as socially inferior and exposed him to insult and abuse. For example:

> Indeed, I am black, and musk is my colour
>   and there is no cure for the blackness of my skin.

BERNARD LEWIS

And again:

> Enemies revile me for the blackness of my skin
>> but the whiteness of my character effaces the blackness.[4]

In another poem, he is even quoted as insulting his own mother:

> I am the son of a black-browed woman
>> like the hyena that thrives on an abandoned camping ground
> Her leg is like the leg of an ostrich, and her
>> hair like peppercorns
> Her front teeth gleam behind her veil like lightning
>> in curtained darkness.[5]

Similar complaints are ascribed to other figures of the pre-Islamic and early Islamic period, including, for example, a tribal chief called Khufāf ibn Nadba, a contemporary of the Prophet. The son of an Arab father and a black slave mother, Khufāf was an important man in his tribe. A verse ascribed to him remarks that his tribe had made him chief "despite this dark pedigree."[6]

These stories and verses almost certainly belong to a later period and reflect a situation which did not yet exist at that time. This is indicated by the very fact that such men as 'Antara, Khufāf, and others could rise to the social eminence they attained, something which would have been very difficult a century later. In pre-Islamic and early Islamic Arabia there would have been no reason whatever for Arabs to regard Abyssinians as inferior, or to regard Abyssinian ancestry as a mark of base origin. On the contrary, there is a good deal of evidence that Abyssinians were regarded with respect as a people on a level of civilization substantially higher than that of the Arabs themselves. A slave as such was of course inferior—but the black slave was no worse than the white. In this respect pagan Arabia seems to have shared the general attitude of the ancient world, which attached no stigma to blackness and imposed no restrictions on black freemen.[7]

---

4. 'Antara, *Dīwān* (Cairo, A.H. 1329 [A.D. 1911]), 167, 17, 73.

5. *Ibid.*, 196.

6. Ibn Qutayba (ed. M. J. de Goeje), *Kitāb al-Shi 'r wa' l-Shu 'arā'* (Leiden, 1904), 196. See also Bernard Lewis, *Race and Color in Islam* (New York, 1971), 26.

7. See Frank M. Snowden, *Blacks in Antiquity: Ethiopians in the Greco-Roman Experience* (Cambridge, Mass., 1970).

There were many contacts between Arabs and Abyssinians, both in Arabia and in Africa, and during the career of the Prophet several of his Meccan companions were able, for a while, to find refuge in Abyssinia from the persecution of their pagan compatriots. Many prominent figures of the earliest Islamic period had Abyssinian women among their ancestresses, including no less a person than the caliph Omar himself, whose father, al-Khattāb, had an Abyssinian mother. Another was 'Amr ibn al-'Ās, the conqueror of Palestine and Egypt and one of the architects of the Arab Empire. There were several others of Abyssinian or partly Abyssinian origin among the companions of the Prophet.[8] One of the most famous was Bilāl ibn Rabāh. Born a slave in Mecca, he was an early and devoted convert to Islam, and was acquired and manumitted by Abū Bakr, the Prophet's father-in-law and eventual successor as first caliph. Bilāl became the personal attendant of the Prophet, whom he accompanied on all his expeditions. He is remembered chiefly as the first muezzin, when the call to prayer was instituted shortly after the Prophet's arrival in Medina. Another companion was Abū Bakra, literally "the father of the pulley," an Abyssinian slave in Tā'if. He acquired this nickname by letting himself down with a pulley during the Muslim siege of Tā'if, and joining the Muslims. He was accepted and manumitted by the Prophet, and later settled in Basra, where he died in about 672 A.D.

During the lifetime of the Prophet, color—as distinct from social status—was not an issue. The Qur'ān—the most reliable source of information of the lifetime of the Prophet—contains only two passages which have any bearing at all on this problem. The first of these (xxx, 22) reads: "Among God's signs are the creation of the heavens and of the earth and the diversity of your languages and of your colors. In this indeed are signs for those who know." This is part of a larger section setting forth the signs and wonders of God. The diversity of languages and colors among mankind is adduced as another example of God's universal power—no more than that. The second passage (xlix, 13) is rather more specific: "O people! We have created you from a male and a female and we have made you into confederacies and tribes so that you may come to know one another. The noblest among you in the eyes of God is the most pious,

---

8. These are listed by Muhammad ibn Habib (ed. Ilse Lichtenstädter), *Kitāb al-Muhabbar* (Haydarabad, 1361/1942), 306-309.

BERNARD LEWIS

for God is omniscient and well informed." The Qur'ān, in short, expresses no prejudice in matters of race or color.[9] Even more significantly, it does not even reveal any awareness of such prejudice. The two passages quoted show a consciousness of difference and the second of them insists that piety is more important than birth. The point made, however, is social rather than ethnic, and is directed against aristocratic rather than racial arrogance. The Qur'ān makes no specific references to blacks, to Africa, or to Abyssinia. It does, however, recognize and regulate the institution of slavery. This was to be of great consequence in the dealings between Arabs and Africans in the centuries following the death of the Prophet.

Under the early caliphs, in the age when the Islamic Empire was created by conquest and Islamic civilization grew by the efforts of men of many races, three major changes took place which transformed the relationship between the Arab and the African.

The first development was the conquest itself—the establishment by the Muslim Arabs of a vast empire with the normal distinctions and barriers between the conquerors and the conquered. In time many of the conquered were converted to Islam, but their conversion did not admit them to full equality with the Arabs. Even children of an Arab father and a non-Arab mother—the reverse was inconceivable—were regarded as socially inferior to those of pure Arab parentage on both sides. Their grievances form one of the main themes of the early Islamic period, and their attempts to remedy those grievances one of the main issues of social and religious struggle. Among the socially inferior non-Arab or half-Arab Muslims, color as such was not at first a factor. What marked them as inferior was the negative fact of their not being Arabs, not the positive fact of their belonging to any other particular group. Those, however, of black or partly black parentage were at a disadvantage, as compared with others, in one important respect—their visibility. The son of an Arab

---

9. In a well-known passage (iii, 102), the Qur'ān refers to "the day when some faces will become white and some faces will become black. As for those whose faces have become black—will you disbelieve after having believed? Then taste the punishment for the unbelief which you have been showing. But as for those whose faces have become white—in the mercy of Allah will they be, therein to abide." It is clear that white and black in this verse have no racial meaning, but are used in the idiomatic sense, shared by Arabic with many other languages, by which white connotes light, bliss, and goodness, while black is associated with darkness, affliction, and evil.

father and a Persian or Syrian or Greek or Egyptian mother might pass unnoticed; the son of an Arab father and a black mother could not.

This visibility acquired increasing importance as the result of a second factor of change—the wider range of experience which conquest brought to the Arabs. Before Islam, their acquaintance with Africans was substantially limited to the Abyssinians, a people whom they rightly respected as the possessors of a revealed religion and a high level of culture. After the conquest, however, the world view of the Arabs was modified by experience. As they advanced into Asia and Africa and invaded parts of Europe, they encountered fairer-skinned peoples in Persia and the Mediterranean lands who were of higher civilization; they also encountered darker-skinned peoples in Africa who were at a more primitive level of development. In the experience of the advancing Arab conquerors and explorers, the white- or brown-skinned were advanced and civilized people like the Greeks, the Persians, the Syrians, the Egyptians, and the North Africans; the dark-skinned were the primitive and backward peoples of eastern and sub-Saharan Africa. Already during the first century of Islam—this time on sounder historical evidence—there are indications of a growing prejudice against those of darker skin and of Negro parentage.

The fact of conquest created a new relationship; the range of conquest evoked new attitudes. The final determining factor was the third major development of the early Islamic centuries—slavery and the slave trade. The Muslim Arabs did not initiate the black slave trade, which dated back to Pharaonic times. They did, however, give it an importance and extension unknown to either classical or preclassical antiquity. During the medieval Islamic period there was a massive development in the import of black slaves to the North African and Middle Eastern countries by a number of routes and for a variety of purposes. This vast expansion of black slavery inevitably influenced the attitude of Arabs toward blacks, whom they normally encountered only in the role of slaves. In the Muslim world, slavery was never an exclusively black phenomenon. At all times there were white slaves imported from northern countries, as well as black slaves imported from Africa. The latter, however, gradually became more numerous, the former fewer. Moreover, there was an increasing tendency to reserve black slaves for the more menial and humble tasks. This process is illustrated by the semantic development of the Ara-

BERNARD LEWIS

bic word 'abd. Originally meaning "slave," and in early texts used indifferently of both black and white slaves, it was then specialized to mean "black slave" in contrast to slaves of other colors, and finally came to mean simply "black man" of whatever status.

This changing attitude affected even freemen of African ancestry— even descendants of the companions of the Prophet. Thus, 'Ubaydallah, the son of Abū Bakra, was appointed governor of Sistan in 671 and again in 697. Already by that time blackness had become a reproach, and a poet, in a satire against him, said:

> The blacks do not earn their pay
>> by good deeds, and are not of good repute
> The children of a stinking Nubian black—
>> God put no light in their complexions!

Even the caliph, who had appointed him, remarked: "The black man is lord of the people of the East."[10] The descendants of Abū Bakra had acquired a prominent social position in Basra, and had forged themselves an Arab pedigree. This was rejected by the caliph al-Mahdī (reigned 775- 785 A.D.), who compelled them to revert to the status of freedmen of the Prophet.

Black slaves were imported into the Islamic world by several routes. The first group to be imported were the Nubians and their immediate neighbors, who came down the Nile to Egypt. The black peoples of East Africa were taken by sea to Arabia, Iraq, and further east, while those of West Africa were transported by overland routes to the western and eastern Maghrib. The generic Arabic term for these peoples was Sūdān, a word meaning simply "blacks" and applied to the whole area of black Africa south of the Sahara, from the Atlantic to the Red Sea. It was not applied to the Egyptians, Berbers, or other people north of the Sahara and only rarely to the Abyssinians. The term Ifrīqiya, the Arabic adaptation of the Latin name Africa, was applied in classical Arabic usage only to the Maghrib, usually just to the area of Tunisia and eastern Algeria. It was never used of the blacks, nor of their countries of origin.

---

10. Al-Balādhurī (ed. Muhammad Hamidullah), *Ansab al-ashrāf* (Cairo, 1959), I, 505.

We have no precise information as to the numbers of slaves imported, but the indications are that they were considerable. They were required for a number of purposes. Sometimes they were employed for rough labor of one sort or another. Thus, in Upper Egypt, black slaves were used to work the mines. We hear of others in the salt mines and in the copper mines of the Sahara, where both male and female black slaves were employed. The most famous were the East African slave gangs known by their ethnic name as Zanj, who worked in southern Iraq on the salt flats of Basra. They are said to have numbered some tens of thousands and to have lived and worked in conditions of extreme misery. They rose in rebellion several times. The first recorded outbreak was in 689, a mere half-century after the Arab conquest of Iraq;[11] the most important Zanj rebellion lasted for fifteen years, from 868 to 883 A.D., and for a while constituted a serious military threat to the caliphate. In Egypt, too, black slaves were used on sugar plantations and irrigation work. As late as the nineteenth century we hear of Egyptian farmers, newly enriched by the opportunities offered to them as the result of the American Civil War and the new markets for their cotton which this created, spending some of their profits on the purchase of black slaves to help them in the cultivation of their lands.

Sometimes black slaves were required for military purposes. After the slave rebellion in southern Iraq, when the blacks showed remarkable military prowess, they were recruited in large numbers into the army of the caliphs in Baghdad. Several Muslim rulers in medieval Egypt relied very heavily on black slaves, probably Nubians. One of them is said to have had an army of 45,000 blacks and 24,000 whites. Black and white slave troops were normally separately organized and accommodated, and from time to time we hear of outbreaks of violence between them. In 930 A.D. the black infantry in Baghdad were attacked and massacred by the white cavalry with the help of local troops and the civil population, and their quarters were burnt.

---

11. On the risings of the Zanj slaves in Iraq in 689-690 and 694-695, see Al-Balādhurī, Ansāb al-ashrāf, xi, ed. Wilhelm Ahlwardt as Anonyme arabische Chronik (Leipzig, 1883), 303-307, followed by Ibn al-Athır, iv, 314-315; Ibn Khaldūn, 'Ibar, iii, 98. See also Charles Pellat, Le milieu basrien et la formation de Gahiz (Paris, 1953), 41-42.

BERNARD LEWIS

Black troops in Egypt were several times attacked by their white colleagues. Most notable of such occasions was the great battle in 1169 when Saladin, then vizier of Egypt, discovered a plot by the chief black eunuch to unseat him, allegedly in collusion with the Crusaders in Palestine. The black eunuchs in the palace were dismissed. The black troops in Cairo, moved, according to a medieval Arabic chronicler, by "racial solidarity," prepared for battle. In two hot days in August an estimated 50,000 black troops fought against Saladin's army in the space between the two palaces, the caliph's and the vizier's. The chroniclers give two reasons for the defeat of the blacks. One was their betrayal and abandonment by the caliph, in whose cause they believed they were fighting against a usurping vizier. The other reason was Saladin's stratagem in sending a detachment of troops to the blacks' quarters with orders "to burn them down on their possessions and their children." Hearing of this, the black troops tried to disengage from the fighting and save their families, but were caught in the streets and annihilated. This event is known in the Arabic chronicles as "the battle of the blacks" or, sometimes, "the battle of the slaves." A late medieval Egyptian historian, describing this encounter, remarks of the blacks: "If they had a grievance against a vizier, they killed him, and they caused much damage by stretching out their hands against people's property and families. When their outrages were many and their misdeeds increased, God destroyed them for their sins."[12] After this, black troops were rare in the east though they still played a role of some importance in the armies of the Muslim west.

The main function of slavery in medieval Islam, however, was not economic, as in the Graeco-Roman world and in the Americas, nor, for black slaves, was it military—except to some extent in Egypt and North Africa. White slaves did play a role of major importance in the armies of Islam. The main purpose of black slaves was domestic, and they were used principally as household and office servants and menials. A certain proportion of males were castrated before being brought into Islamic territory, since eunuchs were required in considerable numbers, not only for guarding homes but also in mosques.

One other role is mentioned by the sources, more frequently in the

---

12. Al-Maqrīzī, *Al-Khitat* (Bulaq, A.H. 1270 [A.D. 1853/54]), II, 19.

earlier than in the later period: that is, entertainment. Black slaves were used as dancers and more especially as singers, and some of these seem to have won great fame and also to have earned considerable wealth for their owners, and even occasionally, for themselves.

In the attitude of Arab Islamic society to the blacks who lived in their midst there was an inherent and continuing contradiction between Islamic doctrine on the one hand and social reality on the other. The Islamic religious tradition is overwhelmingly hostile to racial discrimination. A phrase commonly ascribed to the Prophet runs: "I was sent to the red and the black," an expression which is usually taken to embrace the whole of mankind. Numerous traditions deplore racial prejudice and insist that piety and good works, not pedigree or race, are what determine merit. In only one respect does the Islamic law admit the principle of inequality, and that is in the law relating to marriage. According to some, though not all, of the legal schools of Islam, a man should be the social equal of the woman that he marries, so that her family does not suffer dishonor by the match. The jurists give various definitions of social equality, in all of which ancestry and origin are elements of importance. The non-Arab is not equal to the Arab, the slave is not equal to the freeman; even the descendant of a slave or a convert is not equal to a descendant of freeborn Muslims, to three generations. For Arab men to take black women to their beds was considered acceptable—indeed, Arab poets show a prurient interest in what they regarded as the high sexuality of black women. On the other hand, for an Arab woman to become the wife of a black was regarded as a mésalliance and could, according to some jurists, be grounds for divorce or dissolution of marriage.

With this important exception, Islamic religious tradition insists on the equality of all men and all races in Islam before God. The argument is forcibly made by a famous writer, Ibn Hazm (994-1064) who said: "God has decreed that the most devout is the noblest, even if he be a negress's bastard, and that the sinner and unbeliever is at the lowest level, even if he be the son of prophets."[13]

---

13. Ibn Hazm (ed. E. Lévi-Provençal), *Jamharat ansāb al- 'Arab* (Cairo, 1948), I. See also Lewis, *Race and Color*, 21.

BERNARD LEWIS

ened form 'Antar, his name appears as the hero of a famous Arab romance of chivalry, covering the wars against Persia, Byzantium, the Crusaders, and many other enemies. On one campaign, against the blacks, the hero penetrates further and further into Africa until he reaches the empire of Abyssinia and discovers, in true fairy-tale style, that his mother, the slave girl Zabība, was the granddaughter of the emperor.

All this is clearly fiction, but even the early historical accounts of 'Antara are questionable, and only a very small part of the poetry extant in his name can be ascribed to him with any certainty. The greater part, and especially the verses in which he complains of the insult and abuse which he suffered because of his blackness, is of later composition and is probably the work of later poets of African origin. Some of these verses do indeed recur in collections ascribed to later poets of African or part African birth. And it is not uncommon to find the same verses ascribed to more than one of these poets.

One of the earliest was Suhaym (died 660). He was of Abyssinian origin, and was brought to Medina as a slave while very young. His name, presumably a nickname, might be translated as "little blackie." In one poem he laments:

> If my colour were pink women would love me
> but the Lord has marred me with blackness.

In another he gives expression to a sentiment which recurred many centuries later in a famous poem of William Blake.

> Though I am a slave my soul is nobly free
> though I am black of colour my character is white.

In the same mood Suhaym remarks in another poem:

> My blackness does not harm my habit, for I am like musk;
> who tastes it does not forget.
> I am covered with a black garment,
> but under it is a lustrous garment with white tails.[17]

---

17. On Suhaym, see Lewis, *Race and Color*, 11-12, where further references are given.

The same verses are also attributed to another black poet, Nusayb (died between 726 and 731 A.D.), probably the most gifted of the group. He too was born black and a slave, at Waddān, a small oasis between Mecca and Medina. After spending his childhood and youth in Arabia, he gained the favor of 'Abd al-'Azīz b. Marwān, the caliph's brother and governor of Egypt. The prince bought and manumitted him, and thereafter kept him as his freedman and protégé in Egypt. Nusayb went on frequent visits to Damascus, where he gained the favor of successive caliphs.

Nusayb's poetry reveals an acute consciousness of his birth and color. Because of them he endured many insults, which he bore with dignity and fortitude. On one occasion he was mocked because of his color by the great Arab poet and satirist Kuthayyir. Nusayb was invited by his friends to reply in kind but refused with dignity. God, he said, had given him the gift of poetry to use for good; he would not misuse it for satire and insult. For another thing, "all he has done is call me black—and in that he speaks truth." Nusayb felt his color to be an affliction.

> If I am jet black, musk too is very dark—
> and there is no medicine for this blackness of my skin.[18]

At the same time, he felt that he could rise above his dark color and humble origin.

> Blackness does not diminish me, as long as I
>   have this tongue and this stout heart.
> Some are raised up by means of their lineage;
>   the verses of my poems are my lineage!
> How much better a keen-minded, clear-spoken black
>   than a mute white![19]

The last of these early black poets writing in Arabic was Abu Dulāma, again a nickname, meaning "father of blackness." He died in about 776 A.D. A black slave by origin, he became the court poet and jester of the first caliph of the 'Abbasid Dynasty which came to power in about

---

18. Cf. the verse ascribed to 'Antara, cited above, 39-40.
19. On Nusayb, see Lewis, *Race and Color*, 12-14, where further references are given.

BERNARD LEWIS

750 A.D. In Abu Dulāma's poetry the acceptance of inferiority is unmis-
takable. To amuse his royal master, Abu Dulāma makes fun of his own
appearance, of his mother, and of his family.

The Arab anthologists and literary historians tell us something about
the lives of these men and others, and show some of the difficulties from
which they suffered. In an autobiographical fragment which has been
preserved Nusayb tells how, before he went on his first trip to Egypt, he
consulted his sister, who was a wise woman. She reminded him that he
was black and ridiculous in men's eyes. He then recited some of his verses
to her and she was persuaded that their quality gave him some prospect
of success. Another characteristic anecdote relates to the black poet
Da'ud ibn Salm, who died in about 750 A.D. He was known as Da'ud the
Black, and according to the Arabic chroniclers was famous for his ugli-
ness. On one occasion he was arrested together with an Arab called Zayd
ibn Ja'far and brought to trial before a judge in Mecca on a charge of
flaunting luxurious clothes, an offense against Islamic law. The Arab and
the black received different treatment from the judge. The Arab, says the
chronicler, was released; the black was flogged. "The judge said: 'I can
stand this from Ibn Ja'far, but why should I stand it from you? Because of
your base origin, or your ugly face? Flog him, boy!'—and he flogged
him."[20]

Despite this and similar disabilities, gifted blacks were able to make
their way as poets and entertainers. One of the most famous of all was
the singer Sa'īd ibn Misjah, who died between 705 and 715 A.D., and was
considered the greatest Muslim musician of his century. An anecdote preserved by an early writer illustrates vividly both the nature and the limits
of discrimination against blacks. One night Ibn Misjah, we are told, was
seeking a lodging in Damascus, where he had just arrived, and got himself accepted by one of a group of young men, the others of whom were
reluctant. The party went to the house of a singing girl, and when food
was brought Ibn Misjah withdrew, saying, "I am a black man. Some of
you may find me offensive. I shall therefore sit and eat apart." The party,
says the chronicler, were embarrassed but nevertheless arranged for him
to take his food, and later his wine, separately. Then slave girls appeared
and sang, and Ibn Misjah complimented them. Both the singers and their

20. Lewis, *Race and Color*, 14.

owners were affronted by what they regarded as the impudence of "this black man" toward the girls. The young man who had first accepted him offered to leave with him and take him to his own house, but the others thought this was too much. They were permitted to stay but were warned to behave better. Later, however, his identity was revealed, and when it was realized that this black man was the famous singer, all present competed in seeking the honor of his company.[21]

Abu Dulāma seems to have been the last known black poet of any consequence. Thereafter a few very minor figures are mentioned as being of black or partly black ancestry, but with one exception little is known of them or of their work. The one exception is Dhu'l-Nūn al-Misrī, born in Upper Egypt in about 796 A.D. He is known as al-Misrī the Egyptian because of his Egyptian birth, but his parents were Nubian and his father is said to have been a freed slave. Dhu'l-Nun traveled and studied extensively and at one time was arrested and imprisoned in Baghdad but was released by the order of the caliph. He returned to Egypt where he died in 861 A.D. He is known as "the head of the Sūfīs" and is regarded as a founder of the Sūfī doctrine of Islamic mysticism. Some books on magic and alchemy are attributed to him but are probably not authentic. A number of his prayers and some of his poems are preserved by other writers and it is on these and on his disciples that we must rely, in the main, for knowledge of his mystical doctrines. He is said to have been the first to formulate the characteristic Sūfī doctrine of the ecstatic states, the stations on the mystic way towards gnosis, the true knowledge of God. Interestingly, he is credited with having named music as a means to this end. "Music is a divine influence which stirs the heart to seek God: those who listen to it spiritually attain to God, and those who listen to it sensually fall into unbelief."[22] Like other Sūfīs, he preached the merits of penitence, renunciation, self-discipline, and sincerity, and saw in affliction and solitude aids toward spiritual progress. He was among the first to use the language of passionate love in his religious poems, thus helping to establish what became a major feature of the Sūfī tradition.

The role of blacks in the political and public life of medieval Islam was minimal. White slaves of Turkish, Caucasian, or Slav origin could,

21. *Ibid.*, 14-15.
22. Cited in R. A. Nicholson, *The Mystics of Islam* (London, 1914), 65.

BERNARD LEWIS

and frequently did, become generals, provincial governors, sovereigns, and even founders of dynasties. With black slaves in the central Islamic lands this hardly ever happened. One reason of course is that a fair proportion of them were eunuchs. But even for those who were allowed to retain their manhood, opportunities for advancement, inside or outside the condition of servitude, were limited. It was indeed only as eunuchs that, through the positions of influence which they were thus able to acquire in the palaces of Islam, blacks were sometimes able to play political roles of some importance. From late medieval times onward white eunuchs became fewer and fewer and the numbers and influence of the black eunuchs increased correspondingly. Their chief at the Ottoman court was known as the Kizlar Agasi, "the *aga* of the girls," and he was one of the most powerful figures at the Ottoman court. The gelder's knife and the corps of eunuchs were virtually the only route by which a black could attain high office.

One outstanding figure among these was the Nubian eunuch known by the slave name Abu'l-Misk Kāfūr, "musky camphor," who in the tenth century, during an interregnum, became the regent of Egypt. He was a capable and effective ruler and Egypt enjoyed peace and prosperity during his time of office. For a while he was the patron of the great Arab poet al-Mutanabbī, who served him as eulogist. Later al-Mutanabbī quarreled with Kāfūr and went to serve one of his enemies in Syria. He then subjected his former master to satirical abuse and found in Kāfūr's slave origin and black skin rich material for his satirical talents.[23]

An interesting phenomenon of medieval Islam was the emergence of a literature defending the blacks against their detractors. The earliest example to have survived is "The Boast of the Blacks against the Whites" by the great Arab essayist Jāhiz (died 868 A.D.), himself said to have been of partly African descent. The text is of great interest—first, in showing that such a defense was felt to be needed; second, in describing some of the prejudices and accusations that were current; and third—and perhaps most important—in indicating that the belief in the inferiority of the

---

23. For examples see Lewis, *Race and Color,* 78-80. For an Arabic biography of Kāfūr, see Bernard Lewis, *Islam from the Prophet Muhammad to the Capture of Constantinople* (New York, 1974), I, 43-46. Vol. II of the same work includes translations of a number of texts on Africa and Africans (see index, s.vv. Africa, blacks, Nubians, Zanj, etc.).

blacks had arisen *after* the advent of Islam, though not of course as part of it. It is to be feared that Jāhiz's purpose was at least partly satirical, since in other writings he himself reflects some of the prejudices which he purports to refute in this tract.

Later writers of such defenses were more serious in their purpose, and were usually chiefly concerned with the Abyssinians. There are a few such books; they have survived in only a few copies and none of them has as yet been printed. One of the earliest, written by Jamāl al-Dīn Abu'l-Faraj ibn al-Jawzī (died 1208 A.D.), is entitled *The Lightening of the Darkness on the Merits of the Blacks and the Abyssinians.* In this the author attempts to defend both groups against the various accusations made against them. A second work, based in part on the previous one and written by the famous Egyptian polyhistor Jalāl al-Dīn al-Suyutī (died 1505 A.D.), is *The Raising of the Status of the Abyssinians.* Another, by a sixteenth-century author, is entitled *The Treasure of Kindling on the Sons of Concubines* and yet another *The Colored Brocade on the Good Qualities of the Abyssinians.* A similar work in Turkish was written by an Abyssinian protégé of the chief black eunuch, who was brought to Istanbul, studied there, and rose to high rank as a judge in the Ottoman service. There were also other, earlier works of the same type but these have not survived.

The books that have come down to us follow the same main pattern. They discuss the origins of the blacks and deal with the reasons for their blackness, rejecting hostile myths concerning this. They set forth the good qualities of blacks and also draw attention to blackness as a good quality in certain plants, stones, and animals. They insist that whites cannot claim superior merit because of their whiteness but must earn it by piety and good deeds. Most of them then discuss Abyssinians among the slaves and freedmen of the Prophet and his companions, the asylum given in Abyssinia to some of the Prophet's companions who fled from Arabia, the words of Ethiopic origin in the Qur'ān and more generally in Arabic, utterances of the Prophet concerning Abyssinians, and the like. There are also collections of anecdotes illustrating good and pious deeds by blacks, though here the usual line is that simple piety is better than sophisticated wickedness, with the black used as the example of simplicity as much as of piety.

All in all, the cultural role of blacks in medieval Arab Islam was

BERNARD LEWIS

small and, as compared with the role of the Arabs, Persians, and Turks, of minor significance. It was primarily as slaves that they were imported to the Islamic lands, and it was as slaves of various kinds that they rendered their service to Islam. With minor changes, this remained the case until the nineteenth century, when legal slavery was abolished in most of the countries of the Middle East and North Africa under the pressure of the European powers. Effective abolition of slavery was slow and of its social consequences even slower, and even today black slavery still lingers on in parts of the Arabian peninsula.

3 Christopher Fyfe

The Dynamics of African Dispersal: The Transatlantic Slave Trade

The historiography of the Atlantic slave trade can be roughly period-ized.[1] After it ended in the 1860s it passed through an eighty-year phase of neglect. White scholars tended to avert their attention from this dis-creditable episode of the recent past. When mentioned, it was usually less as an activity in itself than as an aspect of the history of the European maritime empires or of the United States. British imperial historians of the early twentieth century fitted the slave trade into a complacent pic-ture of expanding British humanitarianism—its horrors eclipsed by the glories of its abolition—on which they could congratulate themselves and the national genius.

Similarly, white American historians could congratulate themselves that the shame of the slave trade had been washed away by the blood shed during the American Civil War. They could also take comfort in feeling that, however deplorable in itself, it had at least served the beneficent purpose of bringing their black countrymen across the Atlantic, thus raising them from African savagery to a place in a nobler American civi-lization.

Black historians obviously could not disregard the process that had forced their ancestors into American slavery. But no major study of the slave trade appeared. W. E. B. DuBois's famous *The Suppression of the Atlantic Slave Trade to the United States of America, 1638-1870*, pub-

---

1. Christopher Fyfe, "A Historiographical Survey," in "The Transatlantic Slave Trade from West Africa" (Edinburgh, 1965), 1-13, mimeo.

CHRISTOPHER FYFE

lished in 1896, was primarily a contribution to the history of mainland America. The economic aspects of the slave trade, its contribution to the building up of Euro-American capitalism, or the economic motives that might have inspired its opponents remained largely unexamined.

Two Afro-Trinidadian historians, C. L. R. James and Eric Williams, at last raised these economic issues—"the role of Negro slavery and the slave trade in providing the capital which financed the Industrial Revolution in England, and of mature industrial capitalism in destroying the slave system."[2] Williams demonstrated that the slave trade was suppressed for economic as well as humanitarian reasons. His arguments were greeted with anger and derision by many white historians. But in a period of growing black political awareness they had to be taken seriously, particularly by those historians of the 1950s who were moving toward a new Afro-centered historiography.

The slave trade could in any case no longer be ignored in the era of African decolonization, when it inevitably emerged as a major theme in the history of European exploitation of Africa. "The slave trade," cried Léopold Sédar Senghor, poet and first president of the Republic of the Senegal, "ravaged black Africa like a bush fire, wiping out images and values in one vast carnage."[3]

In the United States, Elkins identified the slave ship experience with the German concentration camp experience. Though the details of his work have been much criticized, he destroyed forever the complacent old attempts to justify the slave trade as a bad means to a good end.[4]

The Atlantic slave trade has therefore now been unequivocally revealed in all its atrocity as a prolonged exploitative device by which millions of Africans were brutalized and dehumanized in order to bring wealth to those who organized it. Most contemporary historians now no longer feel the need to denounce (any more than they would justify) its horrors. They can take them for granted, and concentrate on examining how it worked—how it affected its victims and beneficiaries, how it af-

2. Eric E. Williams, *Capitalism and Slavery* (Chapel Hill, 1944), v; C. L. R. James, *The Black Jacobins* (London, 1938), 37-39.

3. Lecture given at the University of Oxford, October 26, 1961, quoted in *West Africa*, November 4, 1961, 1211.

4. Stanley M. Elkins, *Slavery* (Chicago, 1959); Ann J. Lane, *The Debate over Slavery: Stanley Elkins and his Critics* (Urbana, 1971).

fected the economies and societies of Africa, America, and Europe, and similar lines of enquiry. A wide field is open. Nevertheless this self-consciously dispassionate approach risks provoking, particularly among those who still feel themselves to be the vicarious victims of the slave trade, the same kind of angry critical reaction that was once provoked by the complacency of earlier historians.

It is impossible to generalize more than very superficially about the organization of the Atlantic slave trade.[5] Europeans shipped Africans regularly over the Atlantic as slaves, to Europe or to America, for a period of over four hundred years, from places dispersed over the vast African continent. Inevitably generalizations that are valid for one era and area are invalid for another. It must therefore be seen in the changing context of time and place, not as an unvarying activity conducted by unchanging methods.

The trade was started by the Portuguese. After capturing the Moroccan port of Ceuta in 1415, they began venturing down the West African coast, primarily in search of gold. At first most of the slaves they took were kidnapped. But by the middle of the fifteenth century the Portuguese government realized that West Africa was a valuable source of labor, and that a steady labor supply could not be permanently maintained by violent means. Instructions were therefore given that slaves must henceforth be purchased, not captured. From then on, with occasional exceptions, Europeans obtained slaves in Africa by a willing exchange of commodities with African vendors—human beings exchanged for consumer goods.

In succeeding decades Portuguese and then Spanish traders bought slaves regularly to work in Europe and on the offshore African islands. In 1518 the first cargo of slaves was shipped directly from Africa across the Atlantic. For another century and more the trade, still largely Portuguese and Spanish, grew at a steady rate as the demand for plantation labor in

---

5. The best general account of the Atlantic slave trade is still Basil Davidson, *Black Mother* (London, 1961); there are good short surveys by Philip D. Curtin, "The Atlantic Slave Trade, 1600-1800," in J. F. Ade Ajayi and Michael Crowder (eds.), *A History of West Africa* (London, 1971), I, 240-268, and by John D. Hargreaves, "Relations with Africa," in Albert Goodwin (ed.), *The New Cambridge Modern History* (Cambridge, 1965), VIII, 236-251.

CHRISTOPHER FYFE

the American colonies increased.[6] In the early seventeenth century the governments of northern Europe, particularly England, France and the Netherlands, whose traders were already participating in a small way, began seizing land on a large scale in America and the Caribbean for slave-labor plantation colonies. Traders from northern Europe soon dominated the slave trade. From the middle of the seventeenth century the export of slaves increased terrifyingly as Africa and America were drawn into the developing system of European capitalism—Africa as a market for European manufactures and as a slave supply, America as a market and as a source of slave-grown produce.

The African catchment areas from which slaves were drawn also varied over the centuries. Often they were affected by the wars fought between African rulers, which provided prisoners to sell to the white traders. It has, for instance, been noted that during the sixteenth century, a period of prolonged internal warfare among the Wolof of the Senegambia, a high proportion of the slaves imported into America were Wolof. Later, in more peaceful times, few seem to have been imported. Similarly, in the early nineteenth century, at the time of the Yoruba civil wars and the Fulani *jihads* (Muslim "holy wars"), the proportion of Hausa and Yoruba rose greatly.[7]

Slaves were also exported from East Africa, from Moçambique, and from the island of Madagascar. Shipments from East Africa increased greatly in the late eighteenth century, the catchment areas extending inland into the country now occupied by the modern state of Malawi. Though Europeans have tried to justify the East African slave trade as the mere continuation of an existing trade, centuries old, there is insufficient evidence to justify the assumption of a large-scale export of slaves from the coastal East African cities south of Mogadishu in the pre-European period.

It is also worth recalling that the Dutch East India Company imported Malay slaves into South Africa during the seventeenth and eighteenth centuries. This refutes the theory that Africa was in some way the

6. Most of the quantitative statements in this section are derived from Philip D. Curtin, *The Atlantic Slave Trade* (Madison, 1969). But some of them, notably that slave exports began to decline in the 1790s, will need revision when Seymour Drescher publishes his research.

7. Curtin, *Atlantic Slave Trade*, 102, 260.

natural slave supply of the world, and that Africans were particularly suited by nature to be slaves. The white slave-owners in Cape Town, like those across the Atlantic, knew that it is always easier to control and exploit nonindigenous slaves who have been imported from overseas— whether they are African, Asian, or European—because they cannot run away to their homes.

From the 1790s the number of slaves exported from Africa across the Atlantic began to decline. Historians are therefore wrong in assuming (as some have) that the decline was caused by the successive legal enactments passed against the slave trade during the early years of the nineteenth century—by the Danish government in 1804, by the British government in 1807, by the United States government in 1808. Plainly the slave trade was already becoming a less attractive field for investment. Free-trade economists preached, and businessmen came to understand, that in an increasingly industrialized capitalist economy it was cheaper to hire labor than to buy and maintain it. Those seeking to abolish the slave trade for humanitarian reasons could therefore join with those who disliked it for the economic reason that it was an anachronism no longer suited to a free trade world.

But, despite an overall decline, in some places the slave trade actually increased during the nineteenth century. In the 1820s and 1830s slaves were shipped on a large scale, chiefly from Africa south of the equator, to Brazil and Cuba, where the plantation economy was being intensively developed and slaves were in great demand. Not until the mid-1860s did this by now outmoded and almost universally denounced means of supplying labor come gradually to a belated end. It is possible (though not clearly proved) that occasional shipments may even have continued into the 1870s.[8]

Though the Atlantic slave trade ended, the economic system that it had maintained continued within Africa. Manufactured goods were still imported on a large scale in return for produce. The produce was now vegetable, not human. But it was often produced by slave labor—for the "legitimate commerce" with which Europeans replaced the Atlantic slave trade, and sustained the African market for European imports, created a new demand for slaves within Africa, to grow and harvest exports for

8. Hugh Thomas, *Cuba, or the Pursuit of Freedom* (London, 1971), 235n.

CHRISTOPHER FYFE

Europe.[9] During the colonial era slavery was gradually suppressed. Yet still in the colonial era, indeed into the post-colonial era, the African economy remained as firmly tied to an economic system devised to make profits for non-Africans as it had been in the days of the Atlantic slave trade.

The new "dispassionate" historiography of the slave trade has begun to evaluate systematically the number of slaves shipped across the Atlantic. Curtin (drawing on the pioneer work of Noel Deerr) has shown that the customary estimates, varying from 15 to 20 million, were based on guesswork and must be discarded.[10]

To reach this conclusion he has put together the available published evidence, much of it fragmentary and inferential. Extensive shipping and port records have survived, but only for some periods and places. They are inadequate, or totally lacking, for others. He has also used slave population censuses, contemporary estimates (which are often prejudiced), and inferences from the volume of goods exported into Africa in exchange for slaves. He concludes that it is impossible to make any precise overall estimate. There is not enough evidence. Nevertheless he feels that the guesswork estimates of the past were grossly exaggerated, and that the traditional 15 to 20 million should be scaled down to something nearer 10 million.

Curtin has, however, emphasized that his revised figure in no way reduces or excuses the horrors of the slave trade. "Whether the figure is 8 million, 10 million, or 15 million, this largest dimension of the Atlantic slave trade is simply too all-embracing for comparison. As a measure of human misery, 2 million slaves brought to the Americas is already such a terrifying thought that no multiplier could make it seem any worse."[11]

Some historians are skeptical of his figures, and consider that the margin of error allowed for—plus or minus 20 percent—is unwarrantably large for generalization. But the revision of his figures downwards is

9. A. G. Hopkins, "The Lagos Strike of 1897," *Past and Present*, 35 (1966), 138-139; John D. Hargreaves, *Prelude to the Partition of West Africa* (London, 1963), 22.

10. Curtin, *Atlantic Slave Trade*, 3-13.

11. *Ibid.*, 87.

no surprise to those who have puzzled over the demographic aspects of the slave trade. In coastal West Africa there is no sign that the population decreased as a result of it. Indeed the Niger Delta and its hinterland, one of the largest slave export centers, remained densely populated despite the constant drain of human beings across the Atlantic. Elsewhere, too, the supply kept up. As John Matthews, an English slave trader, commented with surprise in 1788, "one would be led to imagine the country would, in time, be depopulated; instead of which no diminution of their numbers is perceived."[12]

This maintenance of demographic continuity in coastal West Africa has been confirmed by linguistic evidence assembled by Hair.[13] Using linguistic samples recorded by early European travelers, he has shown that the language map of coastal West Africa has scarcely changed over a period of 400 to 500 years. With a few exceptions, he has found that present-day speech groupings are virtually identical with those recorded in the fifteenth and sixteenth centuries. There is no sign of any coastal population having been exterminated by the slave trade. Senghor's emotional rhetoric is not confirmed here demographically.

As the coastal peoples were slave suppliers who often obtained their victims from inland, one should perhaps look for depopulation in the West African interior. Here early linguistic evidence of the type Hair used is lacking, as the coastal peoples would not permit Europeans to travel inland, and the languages of the interior remained almost unknown to them. There are grassland areas of northern Ghana and Upper Volta which appear to be depopulated. But the depopulation may be from other causes. It cannot be proved to be the result of the slave trade, which, it has been suggested, "may be likened to the collection of honey—never in excess of the natural rate of replacement."[14]

Possibly the introduction of prolific American food plants, maize

12. John Matthews, *A Voyage to the River Sierra Leone* (London, 1788), 145.

13. P. E. H. Hair, "Ethnolinguistic Continuity on the Guinea Coast," *Journal of African History*, VIII (1967), 247-268; *idem*, "An Ethnolinguistic Inventory of the Upper Guinea Coast before 1700," *African Language Review*, VI (1967), 32-70.

14. Quoted from Ivor Wilks in John M. Hunter, "River Blindness in Nangodi, Northern Ghana: A Hypothesis of Cyclical Advance and Retreat," *The Geographical Review*, LVI (1966), 410. See also Michael Mason, "Population Density and Slave Raiding," *Journal of African History*, X (1969), 551-564.

CHRISTOPHER FYFE

and cassava, may have provided an increased food supply to rear a larger population and offset the losses drained away by the slave trade. Nor does population loss always reduce a population. During the second half of the nineteenth century nearly 5 million people emigrated from Europe, yet the overall population rose astonishingly. Demographic estimates vary greatly (allowing for inadequate data and for lack of an agreed definition of what constitutes Europe), but at the very least it seems to have risen by some 88 million.

Historians are also trying to evaluate the profitability of the slave trade.[15] Here too many estimates can be shown to have been based on guesswork—indeed, profits can never be accurately calculated when the number of slaves transshipped remains unknown. Research into individual cases shows that profitability varied over time and place. Sometimes slave trading brought enormous profits, sometimes a loss.

But working out the statistics of individual profit and loss tells us little. Profitability should not be calculated in terms of slaving voyages or even series of voyages, or of the fluctuating profits of those who operated them. "Profits of the slave-carrying trade alone cannot be dissociated from the profits of the trade as a whole."[16] The slave trade must be seen as part of a vast system which spread wealth right through the economies of the organizing countries and their dependencies—a system that helped to build up Liverpool and Nantes into great cities, and stimulated the investment that fed developing European and American capitalism, breeding profits to invest in manufacturing, banking, shipping, insurance, wholesale and retail trading, real estate ownership, planting and processing, and giving employment to an army of factory workers, dock workers, ships' crews, construction workers, traders, shopkeepers, plantation owners, lawyers, clerks, and a variety of officials, from the governors of extensive plantation colonies down to the humblest customs employees.

Yet even if it could be proved that the Atlantic slave trade was un-

15. For example, Roger Anstey, *The Atlantic Slave Trade and British Abolition, 1760-1810* (London, 1975), 38-57.

16. F. E. Hyde, B. P. Parkinson, and Sheila Marriner, "The Nature and Profitability of the Liverpool Slave Trade," *Economic History Review*, V (1953), 372.

profitable, and that it involved its organizers only in losses, that would still be no argument in its favor. Indeed it would be yet another argument against it. For it would destroy even the self-interested defense which has sought to justify it on the grounds of efficiency and economic development, and would reveal it as an inefficient system of mass torture, wantonly indulged in, not even for profit, but as a brutal end in itself.

Unquestionably its organizers hoped for profit. In the initial stages most of the European governments concerned tried to enforce official monopolies, directly or through chartered companies, to get the profits for themselves or their agents. But in the long run their efforts were unsuccessful. Private traders could not be excluded from such a widespread international trade. In any case, at that period the overheads of the directing agencies were too high, and the problems of enforcement too complex, for the slave trade to be permanently maintained on a monopolistic basis.[17]

After the middle of the fifteenth century, when regular kidnapping ceased, the organization tended to follow a general pattern along most of the African coastline. European traders, singly or in groups, would establish themselves under the protection of African rulers, who welcomed them for the sake of the imported manufactured goods they offered in return for slaves or other produce. The imported commodities were chiefly luxuries—textiles, hardware, tobacco, liquor—of a kind that seemed more attractive than those produced locally. They also included firearms. Slaves were exchanged for guns, to fight wars to capture slaves to exchange for more guns.

Nevertheless, the importance of firearms as a trading commodity must not be overestimated. Until the later seventeenth century few were imported, and though after that period they were sold indiscriminately on a large scale, the inefficient guns used in the African trade before the nineteenth century were not in themselves always decisive in warfare. They supplemented rather than replaced existing weaponry.[18]

---

17. For examples, J. W. Blake, *Europeans in West Africa, 1450-1560* (London, 1942), I; K. G. Davies, *The Royal African Company* (London, 1957); Johannes Postma, "The Dimension of the Dutch Slave Trade from Western Africa," *Journal of African History*, XIII (1972), 237-248.

18. See the series of articles on this subject in *Journal of African History*, XII (1971), 173-254.

CHRISTOPHER FYFE

Exchange of goods between Europeans and Africans necessitated a conventional exchange medium. In Europe metal currencies were in use. Commodities were given currency prices and were sold to give a profit to the vendor. But in West Africa goods were usually exchanged directly, one against another, by recognized systems of equivalence (so much of one commodity against so much of another), without profit-and-loss accounting. In some places an exchange medium was used—cowries (small seashells imported from the Indian Ocean islands) or metal tokens —but they were of no use to Europeans, any more than European coins were of any use to Africans.[19]

Compromise between the two currency systems was impossible. The European traders were therefore forced to adjust theirs to the African concept of the exchange of equivalent commodities, or notional commodities. Notional standards of account became recognized. A "bar" (originally a bar of iron) in some parts of West Africa, or an "ounce" (originally an ounce of gold) or a "stick" (originally a cylinder of salt) in other parts, came to represent a conventional unit of value.[20] Each commodity used in the trade would have its value in "bars" or "ounces" or "sticks." Slaves worth 100 bars would be exchanged for imported goods worth 100 bars—the imports made up perhaps of 50 bars of tobacco, 25 of cloth, 15 of rum, 10 of gunpowder. The bar value of each commodity fluctuated with supply and demand on the coast. If imported tobacco were plentiful, the African trader would insist on taking most, or perhaps all, of his 100 bars in some other scarcer commodity. The European meanwhile would try and combine his bars in such a way that the goods he could make most profit on (in terms of his own profit-and-loss accounting) outweighed the rest.

This sophisticated exchange system enabled an intelligent trader, African or European, to outwit a more stupid trading partner. Each partner also sought to gain advantage over the other in the arrangement of

19. For trade and currency systems in West Africa see Karl Polyani, *Dahomey and the Slave Trade* (Seattle, 1966). For cowries see Marion Johnson, "The Cowrie Currency of West Africa," *Journal of African History*, XI (1970), 17-49, 331-353.

20. For "ounces" see Polyani, *Dahomey*; Marion Johnson, "The Ounce in the Eighteenth Century West African Trade," *Journal of African History*, VII (1966), 187-214. For "sticks" see Svend E. Holsoe, "The Manding in Western Liberia," unpub. paper read at Conference on Manding Studies, London, 1972, 6.

commodities. The European would try to give short weight or poor quality undetected. The African would palm off sick slaves as healthy, or insist on selling a group of slaves in one lot so that the purchaser had to take some old and infirm people to get the young and healthy. But even if the African trader got the best of a specific bargain, overall the ultimate advantage remained with the European, who received wealth-producing slaves in return for expendable consumer goods.

The large-scale import of European manufactures damaged local manufacturing. Weaving still continued, for the imported textiles were often of inferior quality to those woven in Africa, but African weavers had to face competition from the great variety of imported cloth which flooded the market. During the 1780s textile imports into West Africa from Great Britain alone averaged about £250,000 in value every year. Metal workers and potters had little incentive to improve their own simple domestic products when better-made imported hardware was so easily obtainable.

But sculptors and jewelers went on practicing their skills, sometimes using imported silver or bronze. Occasionally an African government intervened to protect a local product. For a while some eighteenth-century coastal rulers refused to allow the import of European salt in order to protect their own seaside salt-making industry. But this was exceptional. Normally imports were allowed to compete freely with indigenous products, and inevitably tended to supplant them. African ingenuity and skill turned from manufacturing to trading, and the African market became increasingly dependent on imported goods.

Coastal African rulers welcomed the white traders for the sake of the economic advantages they provided, and extracted all they could from them. Every trader had to come under the protection of an African "landlord," to whom he paid regular recognized dues.[21] These included rent for his trading post, which remained the landlord's property. Land was not alienated. Hence it is inaccurate to refer to the European trading settlements in West Africa as "colonies." They remained under the sovereignty of African rulers, who received rent for them from the Euro-

---

21. Vernon R. Dorjahn and Christopher Fyfe, "Landlord and Stranger," *Journal of African History*, III (1962), 391-397.

pean occupiers—even for the large stone-built castles still standing along the coast of Ghana, whose white inhabitants had to make regular payments for them to an African landlord.

These castles, modeled on those of medieval Europe, were fortified primarily against attack from other Europeans, rather than from their African neighbors with whom (apart from inevitable disputes and occasional wars) they tended to stay on good terms. Each depended on the other. The Europeans depended on their landlords to bring them slaves. Without their landlords' agency they could get none. The landlords depended on them for imported manufactures. If they quarreled, trade ceased. So, as each relied on the other for the commodities they needed, neither could afford any very protracted dispute.

The African landlord protected his "strangers" and provided them with trading opportunities. He would not let them go inland to trade directly with suppliers in the interior, for fear of losing his own privileged monopoly position as landlord. He or his subjects acted as middlemen in the trade. They alone were permitted to trade directly with Europeans—a constant source of grievance among the inland peoples, who resented having to pay commissions to coastal middlemen.

The landlord also assumed responsibility for debts owing to his strangers. This meant that trade could be conducted on credit. The European trader would advance goods to trading agents (his landlord's subordinates), who would take them inland and return eventually with slaves or other produce. If the agent defaulted, the landlord paid the debt, and reimbursed himself by selling the defaulter's family or neighbors.

The Europeans were therefore closely tied to their landlords and their landlords' people. Far from subjecting their African customers to European norms, they had themselves to conform to African norms. Most Europeans married African wives. Even if they had white wives at home, the marriages that they contracted in Africa were valid by the laws of the polygamous society they were living in. In this way their business ties with their suppliers might be reinforced by ties not only of friendship but of kinship.[22]

---

22. For an example see Margaret Priestley, *West African Trade and Coast Society* (London, 1969).

Thus white buyer and black vendor were bound together in a close, regulated "moral community" (one should in this case more properly say "immoral community") of trade, based on mutual trust and economic advantage.[23] Though only Africans were sold, race was no barrier between exploiters and exploited. Each, black and white, shared the advantages of the trade at the expense of their black victims—prisoners of war, debtors, real or imputed criminals or witches, and those who offended their superiors. All these were liable to be sold, under a social system which disguised a process of dehumanization, the reduction of a human being to a piece of merchandise, under forms of custom and legality. From this dehumanization both buyers and sellers derived benefits. As the Guyanese historian Rodney has put it, "the ruling classes joined hands with the Europeans in exploiting the African masses—a not unfamiliar situation on the African continent today."[24]

This collaborative relationship of white traders and black rulers maintained the slave trade along most of the West African coast. But south of the equator the Portuguese established a settlement of a different kind, based on violence rather than collaboration. They conquered the coastal Mbundu kingdom, and annexed it as the colony of Angola. Portuguese sovereignty was asserted and maintained. No rent was paid.

The city of Luanda was built as a center for the export of slaves across the Atlantic to Brazil. Here a substantial white population settled and lived off the slave trade—the only form of wealth Angola provided for them. The colony's officials were not paid salaries, and had therefore to earn their living by trading in slaves and extortionately oppressing the African population.

Here, as elsewhere, Africans were used as agents and were sent into the interior to obtain slaves. But as under Portuguese sovereignty there were no powerful coastal landlords to keep European traders from going inland, Europeans played a much larger direct part in the trade, going out themselves as agents for Luanda merchants, and provoking wars in order to get the prisoners. Hence the Angolan slave trade was different

---

23. For the concept of a moral community of trade see Abner Cohen, "The Politics of the Kola Trade," *Africa*, XXXVI (1966), 25; Abner Cohen, *Custom and Politics in Urban Africa* (London, 1969), 36-37, 90-91, 96.

24. Walter Rodney, "African Slavery and Other Forms of Social Oppression on the Upper Guinea Coast," *Journal of African History*, VII (1966), 434.

from the slave trade further north. The Portuguese were in Angola as masters and colonizers, determined to extract from their colony as many slaves as possible without respect for African rights. "From the point of view of the African subject," wrote the Belgian historian Vansina, "Angola was sheer terror."[25]

In the neighboring Kongo kingdom the Portuguese were at first friendly. Christian missionaries converted members of the royal family, one of whom succeeded to the throne in 1505, with Portuguese help, as King Affonso I. In the Kongo kingdom, as in other African states, disputes over royal succession were built into the constitution to prevent the emergence of a despotic royal family. The Portuguese exploited this constitutional mechanism, deliberately using succession disputes as a pretext to stir up constant civil war in order to acquire the prisoners. Eventually, after 1678, the kingdom virtually disintegrated. The king became a nominal overlord over his warring nobility, whose struggles provided a steady supply of slaves for the Portuguese.

Here, then, in Angola and in Kongo, Senghor's emotional rhetoric is confirmed by dispassionate historiography—another reminder that the methods used to organize the Atlantic slave trade are not easily subject to generalization but varied from place to place.

A related subject for historians to examine is how the European organization of the slave trade affected African political and social systems. The Portuguese destroyed the Mbundu and Kongo kingdoms. But elsewhere kings (using the word "king" to mean a sovereign ruler, irrespective of the size of his territory) tended to use Europeans to their advantage, finding in the slave trade a means to strengthen their own authority. Enriched by rents, by presents, which often became regularized as taxes, by customs duties, and by other exactions deriving from a trade which they controlled, they could build up their own power, sometimes using their European customers as allies in war. Those with imperial ambitions found that war was profitable as well as glorious, since they could sell their captives. Even the legal systems now worked to their advantage, as convicted criminals could be sold.

Hence the slave trade gave them increased opportunities for

---

25. Jan Vansina, *Kingdoms of the Savanna* (Madison, 1966), 147.

extending their territory and for exploiting their own people—opportunities most of them were only too ready to take.[26] As salable objects, the dehumanized victims lost their status as human beings and became commodities. Here again Senghor's evaluation is confirmed. But his "bush fire," kindled originally by Europeans, was fed by their African partners.

Daaku has called attention to "the correlation between the growth of empires and the European trade" in seventeenth-century Ghana.[27] Fage has ventured the more extensive generalization that the slave trade in West (as distinct from East and Central) Africa was the agent of centralizing state formation. This process he has presented not merely as "purposive and perhaps more or less inevitable" but even as "part of a sustained process of economic and social development," thus giving the slave trade a positive role in an integrative model.[28]

But here dispassionate historiography has drifted back into complacency. For, as Wrigley has sharply pointed out, Fage's teleological interpretation is a revival in a new dress of the old Eurocentric determinism, which justified the slave trade and colonial rule as necessary, perhaps even desirable, evolutionary stages in the progressive development of Africa.[29]

Whether or not the slave trade involved West Africa in an evolutionary process, it certainly brought no radical change in the structure of society. The balance of power between rival kings, or between kings and their subjects, might alter.[30] But the existing social system remained as it was, manipulated by its rulers to bring them more benefits and to increase their own authority at their people's expense.

Sometimes kings engaged directly in trade themselves. Elsewhere, as in Ashanti, they left the actual trading to their subjects, some of whom

26. Walter Rodney, *A History of the Upper Guinea Coast* (Oxford, 1970), 252-254.

27. Kwame Daaku, *Trade and Politics on the Gold Coast, 1600-1720* (Oxford, 1970), 29.

28. John D. Fage, "Slavery and the Slave Trade in the Context of West African History," *Journal of African History,* X (1969), 393-404.

29. Christopher Wrigley, "Historicism in Africa," *African Affairs,* LXX (1971), 113-124.

30. For Senegambian examples see Martin A. Klein, "Social and Economic Factors in the Muslim Revolution in the Senegambia," *Journal of African History,* XIII (1972), 419-441.

CHRISTOPHER FYFE

gained wealth and power.[31] A new trading group grew up, whom Daaku has called "a new class."[32] Whether such a label is acceptable must depend on the definition of the term "class." African traders did undoubtedly gain wealth and power of a new kind. But they were very different from the "new class," the bourgeoisie, that was emerging in capitalist Europe. They did not create wealth for themselves.

Instead of generating wealth, they remained dependent on the wealth generated abroad by foreigners. They invested their profits in foreign-made consumer goods, or else in slaves who were to be used either in acquiring more consumer goods or in nonproductive prestige activities.[33] For, as Davidson has put it, the slave trade "contained and could contain no single developmental feature capable of advancing methods of production as distinct from methods of trade. It could lead in Africa to no improved technologies, no enlarged productive systems, no creative change in productive relationships."[34]

The new power African traders gained was political, not economic. They might try, sometimes successfully, to become kings themselves. But their aim was to take over an existing system, not to introduce any new system. Even those who were the children of European fathers integrated into the sociopolitical world of their African mothers.

In the inland states of the middle Niger and the upper Senegal specialized trading groups were already established, centuries before the period of the Atlantic slave trade. These *jula* (or *dyula*), whose shared Muslim faith held them together as a distinct trading community, operated the long-distance trade throughout West Africa, and have been described as representing a type of "commercial capitalism."[35] When the Atlantic slave trade started, they extended their networks to the coast to trade with Europeans, particularly in the Senegambia country, and sold

31. Kwame Daaku, "Aspects of Precolonial Akan Economy," *African Historical Studies*, V (1972), 241.

32. Daaku, *Gold Coast*, 96.

33. A. J. H. Latham, "Currency, Credit and Capitalism on the Cross River in the Pre-Colonial Era," *Journal of African History*, XII (1971), 599-605.

34. Basil Davidson, *In the Eye of the Storm: Angola's People* (London, 1972), 95.

35. Yves Person, "The Dyula and the Manding World," unpub. paper read at Conference on Manding Studies, London, 1972, 6.

them slaves. But they did not develop and diversify like capitalists in Europe. They merely added new commodities to their stock.

Even where, in the Niger Delta, a trading society grew up in which power tended to go (untypically in West Africa) to those with achieved rather than ascribed status, it was rooted in seafaring, fishing communities where authority was already being given to achievement before the arrival of Europeans.[36] As elsewhere, the old authority pattern remained, though adjusted to a new situation.

The reciprocity system, deeply rooted in West African society, which obliged those with wealth to share it with their dependents and neighbors, also worked against the accumulation of capital. Kings might collect large revenues from the Europeans, but they had to redistribute their wealth to their subjects. They could not accumulate it indefinitely. As Daaku has put it, "the king's wealth and indirectly that of the state was potential rather than real."[37] Indeed, similar restrictions hindered capital accumulation in precapitalist Europe. There, however, they were swept aside. In Africa they remained.

There is no reason for supposing that African societies were in some way more static and resistant to innovation than those of Europe.[38] In Africa too, given other conditions, we must assume that they would have been destroyed and supplanted by new forms of social organization. But the opportunities and incentives lay in Europe and America with the already established entrepreneurs of Britain, France, the Netherlands, Spain, Portugal, and their dependencies. They had been the pioneers in the development of capitalism. Now they were in a position to maintain their entrenched monopoly of wealth creation, and to harness increasingly the productive capacity of the rest of the world to make profits for themselves.

36. E. J. Alagoa, "The Development of Institutions in the States of the Eastern Niger Delta," *Journal of African History*, XII (1967), 269-278; Robin Horton, "From Fishing Village to City-State," in Mary Douglas and Phyllis Kaberry (eds.), *Man in Africa* (London, 1969), 37-58.

37. Daaku, "Precolonial Akan Economy," 245.

38. A. G. Hopkins's distinguished *An Economic History of West Africa* (London, 1973), which appeared after my contribution to this volume was completed, confirms this judgment, and analyzes in brilliant and original detail many of the issues I have raised.

CHRISTOPHER FYFE

African political systems therefore were resilient enough to adapt to the Atlantic slave trade. Kings could gain more power. Clever traders could make themselves kings. But the economic systems, though they forced the Europeans to adopt unfamiliar methods, were ultimately overwhelmed by outside forces. The "dynamics of African dispersal" did not lead to the emergence of any new type of autonomous socioeconomic organization within Africa. The economy became, and to this day remains, an adjunct to that of Europe and America.

4

Joseph C. Miller

The Slave Trade
in Congo and Angola

Approximately 40 percent of the 10 million or so African slaves landed in the New World between 1500 and 1870 began the dreaded Middle Passage at the ports of the Congo and Angola coast, roughly the Atlantic shores of Africa south from Cape Lopez (1° S) to the vicinity of Cabo Frio (18° S).[1] The mainland trading networks which channeled slaves toward these ports form the primary focus of this chapter, although aspects of the trade on the high seas which affected inland trading operations also receive some attention. The chapter seeks to identify the economic and political tensions which drove uncounted lineage headmen and petty political officials on the African side, as well as kings in several large and well-known states, to furnish their kinsmen, dependents, and subjects to a variety of European and African traders, who then conducted chains of these unfortunate captives down the maze of trails leading west to embarkation points spaced all along the coast.

The horrors which attended the forced movement of people through this system receive little emphasis except as they illustrate the relatively impersonal demographic, ideological, financial, and technological conditions which encouraged the trade's well-known cruelties, painfully

I am deeply indebted to Susan Herlin Broadhead, Philip D. Curtin, Robert Garfield, Harold B. Johnson, Jr., and Phyllis M. Martin for their careful reading and criticism of an earlier draft of this chapter. I have incorporated a number of their suggestions but claim full responsibility for such errors of fact and interpretation as may remain.

1. Gross estimates based on Philip D. Curtin, *The African Slave Trade: A Census* (Madison, 1969). The tentative phrasing of the statement derives from the extreme difficulty of reaching precise estimates of the numbers of slaves embarked from Congo and Angola—as the following pages amply demonstrate.

JOSEPH C. MILLER

evident to twentieth-century observers but apparently less obvious to those responsible for them. The gross export figures cited at the outset, while useful for relating the volume of the Congo-Angola slave trade to the overall movement of Africans to the Americas, have no meaning either in human terms or in perceiving the operational complexity and diversity of the trade, and so I have chosen not to play the "numbers game" at any length. I instead try to present the dimensions of the trade which influenced its participants without losing sight of major structural changes over the four centuries of its history.

Western Central Africa, c. Sixteenth Century

The economic bases of the regions behind the Congo-Angola coast ranged from shifting cultivation in the more northerly forest-savanna mosaic, where plentiful rains made agriculture viable, through near-total dependence on cattle in the south as moisture supplies became less dependable toward the dry hills above the lower Kunene River. Nearly all the inhabitants of these regions organized themselves in terms of lineages, a social system which typically engendered a particularistic worldview in which everyone held loyalty to his descent group as the prime social value; few felt much responsibility for persons not considered relatives. The absence of concern for persons defined as outsiders essentially eliminated moral restraints on the disposition of strangers as slaves. Another element in the dominant lineage ethic, an emphasis on the subordination of individual interests to those of the collectivity (usually the lineage), encouraged kinsmen to expel even relatives who seemed to threaten harmony within the descent group. Together, these attitudes encouraged the lineages of the Congo-Angola region to dispose of many more than the 10,000 persons sold each year for over four centuries to alien slave traders.

Several established techniques of transferring undesirables from one descent group to another (where they assumed a variety of semi-lineageless dependent statuses customarily categorized in the anthropological literature as varieties of "pawnship" and "slavery" but in fact only roughly analogous to the corresponding European institutions)[2] gave

2. I draw here on Mary Douglas, "Matriliny and Pawnship in Central Africa," *Africa*, XXXIV (1964), 301-313; Joseph C. Miller, "Imbangala Lineage Slavery," Wyatt MacGaffey, "Economic and Social Dimensions of Kongo Slavery," both in Igor Kopy-

effect to the willingness to sell one another. These essentially social and political devices touched more purely economic systems at several points. Traders active in wide-ranging commercial networks dealt in such commodities as iron and salt, copper, cloths woven from the fibers of the raphia palm, dyewoods, and other prestige goods, and few descent groups could have lacked entrepreneurs skilled in turning contacts with outsiders to their own profit.[3] Given the coincidental transfers of kinsmen and affiliated dependents, numerous precedents must have justified the conversion of unwanted persons into goods circulating in the prestige spheres of the commercial system. Although the sixteenth-century economic networks probably overlapped only intermittently with the systems of transferring individuals from one descent group to another, these tenuous links clearly held the potential for more intensive contact if wealthy strangers should introduce large quantities of new and desirable prestige goods into the system.

The transfer of former lineage mates to dependent positions in other groups tended to occur more frequently in areas subject to several larger and more centralized political institutions, usually headed by kings, in the Congo-Angola region. These kings' authority depended in no small part on their ability to hire or force people away from their primary loyalty to kin and to incorporate these slave-like lineageless dependents as royal retainers residing at the court; there they became personal servants, craftsmen, mercenaries, and other sorts of agents of the king. From the point of view of the lineages, the position of the king remained outside the otherwise comprehensive structure of descent groups and resembled the similarly lineageless dependents who congregated at the royal capitals and were seen as natural complements to their rulers. Most sixteenth-century inhabitants of the hills and plateaux behind the Congo-Angola coast, even in the larger kingdoms, could still expect to spend

toff and Suzanne Meiers (eds.), *Slavery in Africa: Historical and Anthropological Perspectives*, forthcoming. I am, of course, aware of the speculative element necessarily present in an attempt to describe the undocumented social structures of the fifteenth and sixteenth centuries but feel that the present general description does not exceed limits permissible by anthropological theory. My approach may be compared to that of Robin Horton, "Stateless Societies in the History of West Africa," in J. F. A. Ajayi and Michael Crowder (eds.), *A History of West Africa* (New York, 1971), I, 78-119.

3. On early trade, see David Birmingham, "Early African Trade in Angola and its Hinterland," in Richard Gray and David Birmingham (eds.), *Pre-Colonial African Trade* (London, 1970), 163-174; Joseph C. Miller, "Requiem for the 'Jaga,' " *Cahiers d'études africaines*, XIII (1973), 136-141.

JOSEPH C. MILLER

their entire lives within the protective embrace of their own lineages, but the circulation of semi-lineageless dependents accelerated under the domination of strong kings who extracted their numerous retainers from the descent groups almost at will. Outsiders interested in exchanging prestige goods for slaves thus found greater commercial potential in the kingdoms than in the less centralized areas, and within the kingdoms they found the central rulers their most valued trading partners, since the kings alone possessed institutionalized methods of acquiring and disposing of such persons.

The largest states—presumably with the greatest numbers of lineageless dependents—had emerged among the lineages living behind the northern parts of the Congo-Angola coast. The best-known of these kingdoms, that of the so-called Kongo peoples who lived south from the great bend of the Ogowe to the banks of the Dande and roughly as far east as the lower Kwango River, had its center south of the Zaïre (Congo) River at the court of rulers who called themselves *mani* Kongo.[4] North of the main Kongo state, a number of smaller principalities (of which Loango, Kakongo, and Ngoyo later became prominent) dotted the coastline from the mouth of the Zaïre River all the way to Cape Lopez.[5] Just to the east of the Kongo lived a variety of smaller groups with one significant state—that of the kings who later became famous under the title of the "great Makoko" of the Tio (Teke) of the Mbé Plateau north and east

---

4. For Kongo, see Georges Balandier (trans. Helen Weaver), *Daily Life in the Kingdom of the Congo* (New York, 1969), esp. 27-41; Jan Vansina, *Kingdoms of the Savanna* (Madison, 1966), 38-45. I introduce such ethnolinguistic labels as Kongo, etc., only to facilitate description, since they had no meaning in the sixteenth century and even now represent little more than the abstractions of modern linguists and ethnographers. I have avoided the even less meaningful designation of all Africans in the Congo-Angola region as "Bantu" found in most Portuguese language sources; the term derives, of course, from the class of central, eastern, and southern African languages of which those spoken in the area under consideration form a small part.

5. None of the authorities who have described the early history of the coast north of the Congo have distinguished fifteenth- and sixteenth-century social and political structures from the obviously altered (and stronger) states of the seventeenth century and after. The most extensive treatment is in Phyllis M. Martin, *The External Trade of the Loango Coast, 1576-1870* (Oxford, 1972), 1-32. The prevalence of fishing and the nearness of the later states to the coast suggest that the earlier situation may have resembled that described for the Niger Delta by E. J. Alagoa, "The Development of Institutions in the States of the Eastern Niger Delta," *Journal of African History*, XII (1971), 169-178.

of Malebo (Stanley) Pool.[6] Two other states controlled most of the Mbundu lineages on the highlands above the middle Kwanza River; in the southern highlands lay a kingdom known as Libolo, while north of the river another state under kings bearing the title of *ngola a kiluanje* grew dramatically during the sixteenth century.[7] The population shaded gradually from Mbundu in the mountainous area just south of the Kwanza to Ovimbundu groups on the drier and higher (6,000 to 7,000 feet) Benguela Plateau. The Ovimbundu seem to have been ruled by very early kings but by the sixteenth century were entering a period of relative decentralization and political disorder.[8]

The people living east of the Mbundu and south of the Ovimbundu in the sixteenth century have as yet yielded little of their past to historians. Lineages of speakers of the Cokwe/Lwena languages occupied the high plains beyond the Kwango as far as the Kasai and upper Zambezi but had achieved little significant political centralization by that time.[9] The inhabitants of the desert coasts south of the bay later known as Benguela (or Baia das Vacas, the Bay of Cows) were sparsely scattered bands of hunters and gatherers with no states, but the cattle-keeping Nyanyeka, Humbe, Ambo, and Herero seem to have begun to organize themselves into powerful kingdoms about that time.[10] The slave trade only belatedly entered the trans-Kwango region but remained concentrated among the politically more centralized farmers to the north and west and among the Humbe cattle-keepers of the far southern plateaux, the ethnic and economic boundaries of the Congo-Angola region adopted for present purposes.

Beginnings: The Kongo-São Tomé Axis, 1500-1570

The initial phases of the Congo-Angola slave trade were entirely intra-African, as European traders based on the equatorial island of São Tomé

6. See Jan Vansina, *The Tio Kingdom of the Middle Congo 1880-1892* (London, 1973).

7. See Joseph C. Miller, *Kings and Kinsmen: Early Mbundu States in Angola* (Oxford, 1975), 73-106.

8. On the Ovimbundu, see Gladwyn M. Childs, *Umbundu Kinship and Character* (London, 1949) for the best introduction. Miller, *Kings and Kinsmen* contains some modifications.

9. Miller, *Kings and Kinsmen.*

10. Carlos Estermann, *Etnografia do Sudoeste de Angola* (Lisboa, 1960-1961), 3 v., remains the major source for this area.

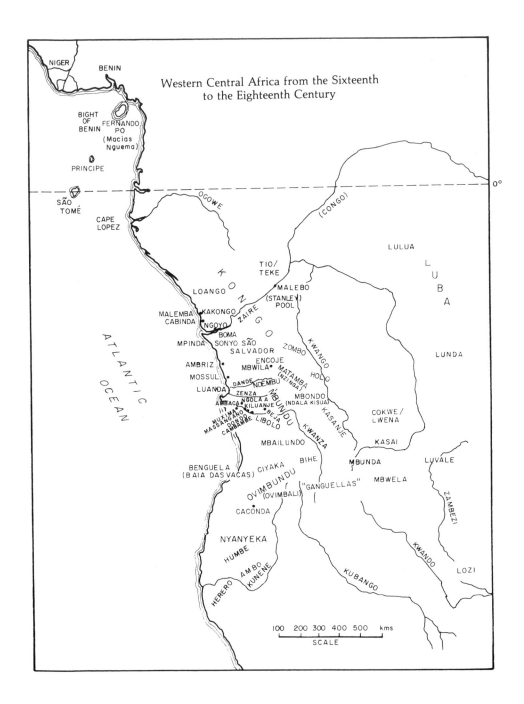

Western Central Africa from the Sixteenth
to the Eighteenth Century

port at Mpinda (on the south bank of the Zaïre near the ocean) each year.[18]

Since the Kongo kings could not meet this demand from their own resources, European traders in search of slaves began to bypass the royal marketplace at São Salvador. With the encouragement of provincial lords eager both to obtain direct access to the sources of new wealth and to diminish the power of their royal overlords, the once-centralized trade spread throughout Kongo. As local chiefs prospered from the trade and grew correspondingly powerful and restive, the kingdom began by the 1560s to exhibit signs of impending dissolution. The relatively peaceful former methods of transferring dependents gave way to outright slave raiding and, by the mid-seventeenth century, the changes induced by an expanding slave trade culminated in an entirely new Kongo social and political structure. A new class of wealthy traders "owned" the majority of the population as lineageless dependents torn from their native descent groups and reincorporated into new villages under the domination of rich merchant chiefs.[19]

São Toméan merchants also actively contributed to the downfall of the Kongo kings as they sought the most profitable means of acquiring slaves. Island interests had obtained Portuguese royal recognition of a monopoly over the officially authorized slave exports through São Salvador and Mpinda as early as 1500 but had taxed slaves only upon their entry into Portuguese territory in São Tomé, thus leaving the collection of export duties on the mainland to the sovereign *mani* Kongo. The Kongo kings lost this important source of revenue sometime in the 1540s when European tax farmers acquired a Portuguese contract allowing them to collect taxes paid at Mpinda.[20] The Europeans also tampered

18. Estimates in letter from Manuel Pacheco to D. João III, 3/28/1536, Arquivo Nacional da Torre do Tombo, Lisbon (hereafter ANTT), Gav. 20-5-24; António Brásio, *Monumenta Missionária Africana—Africa Occidental* (Lisboa, 1952-1965), II, 57-60. Data for 1548 are calculated from an Inquirição sobre o comércio de S. Tomé com Angola ordenada por D. João III, 11/12/1548, ANTT, Corpo Chronológico, I-80-105; Brásio, *Monumenta*, II, 197-206.
19. Miller, "Requiem for the 'Jaga,' " 145-147 and *passim*; Vansina, *Kingdoms*, 138-142, 152-154.
20. Garfield, "History of São Tomé," 19-20; Alfredo de Albuquerque Felner, *Angola: Apontamentos sobre a occupação e início do estabelecimento dos Portugueses no Congo, Angola, e Benguela* (Coimbra, 1933), 70-71.

JOSEPH C. MILLER

with another crucial component in the *mani* Kongo's economic position—a royal monopoly over a specialized currency based on a small marine shell (called an *nzimbu*) obtained from bays near Luanda Island just south of the Dande. The São Toméans imported similar shells from Benin, Cabo Verde, and Brazil and ultimately undercut the *mani* Kongo's monopoly by exchanging the counterfeit shells for slaves obtained from sources outside the capital and by inflating the royal currency.[21]

São Tomean merchants and planters had thus established the Congo-Angola slave trade on a basis which largely excluded metropolitan Portuguese merchants and shippers from direct participation. With the equatorial island as the hub of this commercial network, trade in slaves, shells, and other commodities linked Kongo to parts of Guinea, to the Americas, and to other portions of adjacent African coasts. Imports to Kongo, other than the counterfeit shell currencies, are hardly known, but one significant trade tie to other parts of the Congo-Angola region involved cattle, brought from the Ovimbundu regions south of the Kwanza.[22] The relatively autonomous São Tomean trade encouraged merchants from the island to violate Portuguese royal injunctions forbidding mainland trade outside the port at Mpinda, and they began to spread north and south along the coast in response to slaving opportunities. This geographical expansion led directly to the succeeding phase of the Congo-Angola slave trade.

Relocation in Angola, 1570-1650

At the same time that the increasing volume of the slave trade forced São Tomé's merchants into remote corners of sixteenth-century Kongo, the search for more slaves drove others south toward the mouth of the Kwanza, where they settled near the *mani* Kongo's *nzimbu* fisheries at Luanda Bay and created a second, different commercial system. Although the earliest trading ventures in this direction originally sustained the Kongo slave trade by providing cattle and *nzimbu*, later ones ended by sup-

---

21. W. G. L. Randles, *L'ancien royaume du Congo* (Paris, 1968), 137.
22. *Ibid,* 5. The trade in cattle probably accounted for the original name of the area which later became the port of Benguela—the Baia das Vacas or Bay of Cows.

planting it, since they brought traders into contact with new sources of slaves, particularly at the court of the *ngola a kiluanje* of the Mbundu. São Toméan traders began to penetrate the highlands between the Bengo and Kwanza rivers and to relocate their operations at Luanda Bay, and, by the last third of the century, they had largely replaced the old Kongo trade through Mpinda with a new Angola-São Tomé trading axis. The first half of the seventeenth century saw the emergence of two other new patterns characteristic of the mature Congo-Angola trade: slaves were transported directly from Angola to Brazil, thus ending the old barracoon function of São Tomé, and European governments (at first a Spanish bureaucracy in temporary control of Portuguese overseas possessions during the "double monarchy" from 1580 to 1640) attempted to extend their direct control to a southern Atlantic trade which had contributed little to Lisbon's commercial interests or to the royal treasury. By the mid-seventeenth century, a government-dominated trading system based at Luanda had emerged from the carnage of the "Angolan Wars" that stained the transition to the mature eighteenth-century trade.

The initial phases of the Angolan trade repeated the history of slave trading in Kongo. São Tomé's traders bought semidependent "slaves"—criminals and other outcasts from the Mbundu lineages—from the most powerful political authorities of the Luanda hinterland, mainly at the capitals of the *ngola a kiluanje* located a hundred or more miles inland between the Kwanza and Bengo rivers. They offered significant competition to Kongo traders by the 1540s and were conducting a thriving trade by the 1560s and 1570s, when, it was believed, some 10,000 slaves passed through their barracoons each year.[23] Parallels to the old Kongo trade included an absence of interference from royal officials (then largely concentrated at São Salvador), relatively few direct European imports, and initially increased power in the hands of their major African partners.

Metropolitan government nominees arrived to tax this commerce

---

23. Based on the allegations of resentful competitors at Mpinda (see Inquirição cited in n. 18) and the presence of a number of Kimbundu-speaking "Angolares" (slaves escaped from a vessel shipwrecked in 1544) in São Tomé (see Garfield, "History of São Tomé," 56-58). For the estimate from the 1570s, see letter from Padre Garcia Simões to the Provincial, 10/20/1575, Biblioteca Nacional de Lisboa (hereafter BNL), Coleção Alcobacense, ms. 308, fls. 215-220v; Brásio, *Monumenta*, III, 129-142.

JOSEPH C. MILLER

after 1575, but the São Toméan traders waited with the Mbundu and southern Kongo political authorities near Luanda to defend their free trade from royal interference. A Portuguese nobleman named Paulo Dias de Novaes arrived in 1575 to tax the main economic resources in the region: the *nzimbu* fisheries in Luanda Bay, a number of important salt sources, edible fish taken in adjacent waters, and—most significantly— slaves.[24] Dias de Novaes and his successors made little headway against the prevailing economic winds before 1611 or 1612. In 1579, the São Toméan traders, whose activities had been declared illegal through Lisbon's intervention, attacked merchants loyal to Dias de Novaes in conjunction with the *ngola a kiluanje*. Throughout those early decades, the official Portuguese forces, burdened by expensive provisions in the charter of donation, found themselves unable to compete with the entrenched traders and their African partners.[25] Economic weakness forced them to seize by warfare what they could not gain in any other way, and the resulting battles against the armies of the *ngola a kiluanje* began the "Angolan Wars" in which royal forces eventually carved out the colony (*"reino* and *conquista"*) of Portuguese Angola.[26]

Up to 1610, official Portuguese troops in Angola clung to a few tenuously held positions near Luanda Bay and along the lower Kwanza (fortifications on the river bank at Massangano, Muxima, and Cambambe), forfeiting the Bengo River valley to the illegal traders who continued to embark some 3,000 slaves per year through the 1580s.[27] If estimates that an approximately equal number of slaves passed through the Luanda factory of the royal contractors around 1600 were accurate—and they can

24. The Carta de Doação a Paulo Dias, 9/17/1571, is in the ANTT, Chancelaria de D. Sebastião (Doações), liv. 26, fls. 295-299; Brásio, *Monumenta*, III, 36-51. David Birmingham, *Trade and Conflict in Angola* (Oxford, 1966), 46-47, has a convenient English summary of the provisions of this document.

25. Auto of Pero da Fonseca, 4/18/1579, British Museum, Add. Ms. 20,786, fls. 145-145v; Brásio, *Monumenta*, IV, 308-309. Also the "História da residencia dos padres da companhia de Jesus em Angola e cousas tocantes ao Reino, e conquista," 5/1/1594, Arquivo Romano da Companhia de Jesus, lus. 72, fls. 230-231v, also lus. 106, fls. 25-27, 58-64; Brásio, *Monumenta*, IV, 546-581.

26. The best English summary of the Portuguese conquest is that of Birmingham in *Trade and Conflict*, 49-63, 78-132.

27. Based on an estimate of Domingos de Abreu e Brito, "Rellação breve das cousas que se contem neste tratado dangolla e do Brazil," published as *Um Inquérito à vida administrativa de Angola e do Brasil* (Alfredo de Albuquerque Felner, ed.) (Coimbra, 1931), 30-31.

be accepted as only the roughest of guesses—the first thirty years of official governmental warfare in Angola had diminished the total number of slaves exported[28] but had divided them almost evenly between official channels down the Kwanza to Luanda and unofficial exports down the Bengo to São Tomé.

The crown's interventionist economic policies enjoyed greater success north of the mouth of the Zaïre River, where Portuguese traders began for the first time to trade in the bays of the Loango coast.[29] The people of the Loango coast, who had had little regular contact with Europeans before 1576, emerged after that date as important suppliers of palm or raphia cloth, red dyewoods, the tail hairs from elephants (potent magical charms), and copper, all commodities which the Mbundu regarded as vital components in any commercial transaction. Lisbon consigned control of the crucial trade in raphia cloth, which circulated as a currency within the European slave-trading community in Angola, to royal contractors who maintained a factory in Loango for that purpose. Imports to Loango, which seem to have included much higher proportions of European manufactured wares—textiles, beads, rugs, mirrors, etc.—than the regions farther south, also indicated the greater extent of metropolitan control over this phase of the trade. The important role played by Loango exports in the slave trade at Luanda thus indirectly supported the imposition of government authority in the south.

Portuguese royal officials definitively established their control over the Luandan trade on the wings of a dramatic increase in the numbers of slaves sent from the Congo-Angola coast during the decade after 1610. Expanded sugar planting in Brazil and an unexplained shift in the slave trade from other parts of Africa toward Angola coincided with the beginnings of close cooperation between Portuguese governors at Luanda and mobile bands of highly effective African warriors (known as Imbangala) from the Ovimbundu region south of the Kwanza. Together they fought

---

28. From the 10,000 estimated in 1575 to slightly more than 6,000 per year in later decades. The Luandan contractors issued 15,768 permits to private traders wishing to embark slaves in Angola between 1603 and 1607, an annual average of about 3,150. See List of Slave Export Taxes from Angola, 12/9/1608, Arquivo Geral de Simancas, Secretarias Provinciales (Portugal), liv. 1499, fl. 46; Brásio, *Monumenta*, V, 487-488.

29. The remainder of this paragraph is based on portions of Martin's summary of late sixteenth-century Loango trade, *External Trade*, 33-52.

JOSEPH C. MILLER

the major opponents of official expansion and hunted slaves for the official traders.[30] The devastating military effectiveness of the Imbangala gave the initiative to the Portuguese and opened a decade (roughly 1612 to 1622) of rampant warfare in which they defeated the *ngola a kiluanje* and all nearby Kongo and Mbundu political authorities. These wars boosted the annual totals of slaves embarked through official channels from the approximately 3,000 of preceding years to a much higher (but unknown) figure.[31]

Royal officials exploited their new administrative/military control over the area between the Bengo and Kwanza rivers (as far east as fortified posts at Ambaca and Cambambe) to bring the existing trade under their own control and to extend it into new areas during the 1620s and 1630s. Within the conquered region, they appointed military officials (with the patents of *capitães mores*, or captains-major), similar in function to the contemporaneous civilian holders of *repartimientos* in New Spain, who collected tribute in slaves from local Mbundu lineage and political authorities. Outside the boundaries of direct government control, governors fostered the establishment of a ring of nominally independent African kingdoms, headed by alien Imbangala kings whose power over the local Mbundu lineages depended on sales of slaves to Portuguese merchants.[32] East of Ambaca and Cambambe, the governors imposed a new line of puppet kings in the old *ngola a kiluanje* title and

30. On the overall currents of the South Atlantic system, see Curtin, *Atlantic Slave Trade,* 108-116 and tables 33 (p. 116) and 34 (p. 119). The causes of the shift to Angola were not clear to Curtin, but they obviously lay outside events on the Angolan mainland since they were well underway before the post-1611 surge in official exports connected with the Portuguese-Imbangala alliance. On the Imbangala, see Joseph C. Miller, *Kings and Kinsmen,* 176-201.

31. The documents give no indication of the absolute volume of slave exports at this period, but figures from the Spanish *asientistas* (slave contractors) show that their share of slaves from Angola jumped ten- to twenty-fold between the 1606-1615 decennium and the period from 1616 to 1625. Official exports were estimated at approximately 10,000 per year as early as 1612, and slaves taxed during the early 1620s have been calculated at some 13,000 per year. See letter from André Velho da Fonseca to el-Rei, 2/28/1612, in Brásio, *Monumenta,* VI, 64-70; also calculation in Birmingham, *Trade and Conflict,* 80, n. 2.

32. Principally in the northeast along the middle Lukala, where two friendly Imbangala kings, Kabuku ka Ndonga and Kalandula, defended Portuguese territory from the hostile *ndembu* title-holders in southern Kongo and also provided slaves at the market of Lukamba near Ambaca.

sent official slave traders to government-regulated marketplaces, or *feiras*, located in their lands.[33] The nucleus of a second trading system based at Luanda also appeared at this time, as private Portuguese merchants began to send out far-ranging half-caste and African traders, known as *pombeiros*,[34] who developed their own commercial networks extending into southern Kongo, east toward the Kwango, and south across the Kwanza. The most important of these routes probed east from Ambaca through the Mbondo kingdom of the *ndala kisua* to the Kwango River valley, where another band of Imbangala, settled in a nascent state known as Kasanje, had already become important suppliers of slaves.[35] The other direction of the *pombeiro* advance during this period ran through *feiras* held near Cambambe toward the old Libolo areas south of the middle Kwanza.

No sooner had the Angolan wars of 1612-1622 expanded the Luanda slave trade from the court of the *ngola a kiluanje* to the entire Kwanza basin than a still wider dispersion along the coasts and in the interior duplicated another aspect of the history of the Kongo slave trade. Unrestrained exploitation of the conquered territories near Luanda quickly depleted their population through tribute collected in slaves and the flight of the remaining Mbundu. The local Portuguese military elite and the Luandan merchants sought additional sources of slaves beyond the Kwanza in an extension of the southward dispersal of São Toméan traders a century earlier. A former governor (Manuel Cerveira Pereira) attempted to contact Imbangala in those regions during 1617 and, despite initial failures, a few slaves began to reach Luanda from the southern coasts, along with cattle, dried and salted beef, copper, salt, and other products which had long been sought there.[36] The most enduring result

33. Letter from Governor Fernão de Sousa to el-Rei Angola Ari, 3/27/1627, Biblioteca da Ajuda, Lisbon (hereafter BAL), 51-VIII-30, fls. 142-142v; Brásio, *Monumenta*, VII, 506-507.

34. On the origins and history of the term, see Bal, "Portugais pombeiro." The *pombeiro* is one of the folk heroes of Portuguese Angola, idealized as an intrepid pathbreaker in the wilderness and in this respect not unlike the French Canadian *coureurs de bois*, the Argentine *gaucho*, the American cowboy, or the Brazilian *bandeirante*.

35. Letter from Fernão de Sousa to Capitão F. de Castro, 4/8/1628, BAL 51-VII-31, fl. 171v; Brásio, *Monumenta*, VII, 549-550.

36. Zegers Report, 1643, Archief van de Eerste West Indische Compagnie, 46; Louis Jadin, "Rivalités luso-néerlandaises au Sohio, Congo, 1600-1675," *Bulletin de*

JOSEPH C. MILLER

of these expeditions was the creation of a small trading post at the Baia das Vacas, henceforth renamed Benguela (Nova).

Meanwhile, between the Bengo and the Kwanza, royal governors and *capitães mores* had become totally dependent on exploitation of the conquered regions but lacked sufficient military strength to conduct relatively difficult and costly armed raids in the lands outside the sphere of their direct authority.[37] Most expansion in the Luandan hinterland during the 1630s and 1640s therefore benefited a different group of traders, heirs of the sixteenth-century São Toméans and their African partners who operated in defiance of government efforts to route all slaves through Luanda. Non-Portuguese shippers, mainly Dutch, who became increasingly frequent visitors to the coasts north of Luanda during this period,[38] drew slaves from the northern Kwango valley, in particular from the new and powerful kingdom of Matamba under the control of the famous queen Nzinga, down the Bengo and Dande rivers through the lands of the southern Kongo chiefs known as *ndembu*.

The 1640s saw this northern branch of the Angolan slave trade, which had grown steadily throughout the previous decade, temporarily replace Portuguese governmental commerce. An invading Dutch force captured São Tomé and expelled the Portuguese from Luanda in 1641-1642 in a final victorious codicil to their thirty-year global war against Spain and—by extension—Portugal. For most of the next seven years, through recurrent Dutch-Portuguese skirmishes and related conflicts among their respective African allies as well as through more normal

l'Institut Historique Belge de Rome, XXXVII (1966), 228. I am indebted to Phyllis Martin for this reference.

37. Wars occurred with expensive regularity during this period, but they were essentially devoted to the protection of private *pombeiros* who encountered trouble beyond the range of full Portuguese control.

38. See Johannes Postma, "The Dutch Participation in the African Slave Trade: Slaving on the Guinea Coast, 1670-1795," unpub. Ph.D. thesis (Michigan State University, 1970), 14, for the Dutch. The structure of the trade route in the interior may be inferred from the active shipping on the coast, from Luandan merchants' complaints that *pombeiros* had begun to trade goods taken on credit (with unidentified partners), and from the efforts made by Portuguese governors to defeat the main *ndembu* (southern Kongo) kingdom of Mbwila during the 1630s. See António de Oliveira Cadornega (José Matias Delgado, ed.) *História Geral das Guerras Angolanas* (Lisboa, 1940-1942, but written during the 1680's), I, 178-180. See also Gonçalo de Souza, 7/6/1633, Arquivo Histórico Ultramarino, Lisbon (hereafter AHU), Angola, cx. 1; Brásio, *Monumenta*, VIII, 241.

commercial channels, the Dutch acquired as many as 12,000 to 13,000 slaves each year from Nzinga and her allied *ndembu* neighbors,[39] while the Portuguese, who had taken refuge at Massangano, continued to buy slaves south of the Kwanza but exported a relatively insignificant number of them.[40] The brief prosperity of the northern *ndembu*-Matamba trade route ended with Dutch abandonment of Luanda in 1648 and the simultaneous Dutch retreat from the Portuguese Brazilian colonies they had seized during the 1630s. The restoration of Portuguese control on both sides of the Atlantic set the stage for a resurgence of government-authorized slave trading from Luanda after 1650.

The original Portuguese occupation of Luanda in the 1570s had brought Loango peripherally into the Congo-Angola slave trade; now, Dutch involvement during the 1630s began the slave trade directly from the coasts north of the Zaïre River. The primary contribution of the Loango coast remained dyewoods, palm cloth, and elephant-tail bristles traded for slaves in Angola during the 1640s, but the expulsion of the Dutch from Luanda sent them back to the north where they developed the commercial contacts of earlier years to buy much larger numbers of slaves in subsequent decades.[41] The growth of the Loango slave trade completed the development of the four principal seventeenth-century trading networks which fed slaves from the interior to the Congo-Angola coast. Two others in Angola (the official "Mbundu" trade at Luanda and the unofficial "Jinga" trade from Matamba) were by far the most significant in terms of quantity, while the remaining trade came from a desultory Kongo commerce which preserved the faded memory of the thriving sixteenth-century commerce at Mpinda.

---

39. Report of Pieter Mortamer, 1643, Archief van de Eerste West Indische Compagnie, 46; S. P. Honoré-Naber, "Nota van Pieter Mortamer over het gewest Angola, 1632," *Bijdragen en Medeldeelingen van het Historisch Genootschap gevestigd te Utrecht,* LIV (1933), 1-42. Confirmation from the Portuguese side in letter from Francisco de Sotomaior to el-Rei D. João IV, 12/4/1645, AHU, Angola, cx. 3; Brásio, *Monumenta,* IX, 398-411; also *Arquivos de Angola,* ser. 2, I, 3-6 (1943-1944), 169-179. Other Dutch sources disagree as to the significance of the Bengo route to Matamba. See Jadin, "Rivalités luso-néerlandaises," 238-239.

40. The volume of exports is not known but it could not have approached the Dutch totals, if for no other reason than Dutch control of the most important slave-importing regions of Brazil and the separation of the Spanish and Portuguese crowns in 1640; these events deprived the Portuguese merchants of free access to Spanish territories around the Caribbean. See Curtin, *Atlantic Slave Trade,* 117.

41. Martin, *External Trade,* 53-59; figures from the Mortamer report (n. 39).

JOSEPH C. MILLER

The Congo-Angola slave trade of 1650 bore little resemblance to its late sixteenth-century antecendents. The once-dominant exports from the mouth of the Congo had slipped into insignificance while the formerly small trade from Luanda had taken a nearly commanding position relative to its rivals. The São Toméan merchants, who had controlled both the Kongo and Angola commerce up to 1575, had been eclipsed by two other groups of traders—governors with their network of *capitães mores* in the subjugated regions, and private merchants in Luanda who sent *pombeiros* to *feiras* as distant as the banks of the Kwango and the highlands south of the Kwanza. Both these arms of the offical Luanda trade had profited from the "Angolan Wars" of conquest and the assistance of the Imbangala, but success had sown the seeds of future dissension in their ranks, since the community of private merchants, based mainly in Luanda but with a small southern outpost at Benguela, would later try to limit slave trading by the governors. A new generation of Imbangala kingdoms, as well as a few Portuguese puppet states, had succeeded the *ngola a kiluanje* in an Mbundu political revolution no less profound than the decentralization which had taken place in Kongo. Brazil had replaced São Tomé, in the throes of economic and social collapse since 1575, as the official traders' most important destination, and the Dutch had assumed the São Toméans' role as principal threats to government monopoly by conducting both a supplementary trade from Loango and an unauthorized trade in slaves from Matamba. The efforts of non-Portuguese traders to subvert Lisbon's exclusive claims to slave exports from the Congo-Angola coast furnished the key theme during the next phase— the diversion of captive labor from the Luanda hinterland to ports along the northern coasts.

The Mature Angolan Slave Trade, 1650-c.1810

The later Angolan slave trade grew from the seeds planted before 1650 and bore its sad fruit in the form of well over a million Africans shipped to all parts of the New World during the eighteenth century. Restoration of Portuguese political authority at Luanda ushered in a brief period in which governors and merchants there dominated commerce on the entire coast south of the Congo. But private commercial interests gradually eliminated the competing slave trade run by governors and *capitães mores.* Succeeding years, however, denied these merchants the profits expected from their victory, since African traders from the Loango region and competing Portuguese merchants at Benguela gradually cut into the trade from the Luandan hinterland. Dutch, English, and French interests along the Loango coast extended their activity down the Kongo coast to the very environs of Luanda. The total number of slaves exported grew haltingly, and, in the interior, the center of slave raiding and trading moved east of the Kwango for the first time. By the end of the eighteenth century, merchants in Luanda enviously eyed the prosperity of traders in Loango and Benguela and wondered why similar good fortune seemed continually to elude them.

Luandan governors and merchants came closest to realizing their intended monopoly over the Congo-Angola slave trade in the ten years after 1650. Salvador Correia de Sá e Benevides, first governor of the restored Portuguese colony (1648-1652), reestablished government-regulated trade with the African states along the Kwango (Kasanje in particular, but also Mbondo and the Holo state just north of Kasanje); and Matamba, keystone in the old illegal trade of the 1630s and 1640s, returned to Luanda's economic orbit under the terms of a 1655 treaty in which (among other provisions) Nzinga granted Portuguese traders full access to the slave resources of her state.[42] Finally, a military expedition defeated the *ndembu* Mbwila, Nzinga's western partner in the trade with the Dutch, and secured temporary Portuguese control over the seaward end of the routes down the Bengo and Dande.[43] The Luanda authorities felt as though control over the outlying coasts was also within their reach, since Loango, Kongo, and Benguela all once again lay open to Portuguese merchants.

Within the lands under direct administration, Portuguese self-confidence and power manifested themselves in a half-century of severe governmental abuse of African populations within their reach. Governors and *capitães mores* extorted heavy slave tributes from the *sobas* (government-recognized chiefs) in Angola and frequently raided more remote

---

42. The treaty exists in the form of a copy: Certidão de Bento Baptista de Parida, 2/15/1657, AHU, Angola, cx. 5 (also a second copy of 4/4/1657). Published in *Arquivos de Angola*, ser. 1, II, 7 (1936), 9-14.
43. Cadornega, *História Geral*, II, 53-62.

populations to acquire slaves in violation of explicit royal condemnations of such "unjust" wars.[44] Salvador Correia de Sá's successors complained that they received insufficient salaries to cover their expenses and habitually supplemented their incomes with profits gained from selling captives taken in wide-ranging raids through the interior. By 1658, many Mbundu had fled the region under Portuguese control and many others had died of famine and disease.[45] One notorious foray of the 1650s netted 2,000 prisoners from the *ndembu* regions, all sold to the profit of the governor and his cronies, his military commander, and other members of the army.[46]

When the late seventeenth-century trade south of the Congo operated according to the plans of its directors, perhaps 10,000 to 12,000 slaves, chained in gangs called *libambos*, trudged each year from distant markets on the south side of the Kwanza and from all along the Kwango through the large *feira* in Kasanje to Portuguese ships waiting in Luanda. This volume approached the totals of the previous peak decades of the 1620s and 1640s but, unlike earlier eras, rested almost entirely in the hands of officially-recognized parties, public and private. Upon the slaves' arrival in Luanda, a few were sold to residents of the city or to planters from surrounding agricultural areas. Most, however, were loaded on ships leaving for Brazil, while a substantial minority were taken to the Spanish Caribbean and to Mexico.[47] Representatives of slave contractors authorized by the Portuguese kings collected a tax of 3$000 (*milreis*, the metropolitan Portuguese currency) per adult male slave or equivalent sent through the port.[48] Buyers valued the adult male slave, or *peça*, at the equivalent of 22$000 in Luanda but paid lower prices for

44. "Unjust" according to European civil and canon law.

45. Relatório of Bartholemeu Paes Bulhão, 5/16/1664, AHU, Angola, cx. 6.

46. Undated letter from Padre Serafim de Cortona (arrived back in Lisbon by December 1658), cited in Birmingham, *Trade and Conflict*, 118-119.

47. Curtin, *Atlantic Slave Trade*, fig. 7 (p. 111), tables 32 (p. 113) and 34 (p. 119), and supporting text.

48. "Relatório do governador descriminando os rendimentos . . . ," *Arquivos de Angola*, ser. 1, II, 15 (1936), 653-666. The *real* or "crown" was the basic Portuguese monetary unit and values were written with the dollar sign ($) after the thousands of reis (i.e., *milreis*). An idealized adult male slave of approximately fifteen to twenty-five years of age, called a *peça* or *peça da India*, was the standard against which actual slaves were evaluated. Age, physical strength, appearance, health, and sex raised or lowered the value of people actually traded. See Rout, below, 134 n.

women or for older or younger males.[49] Although buyers and sellers reckoned these prices in terms of Portuguese metal currencies, they made the actual transactions in Loango palm cloths, salt, and other commodities which had circulated in Luanda since the beginning of the century.[50]

Governmental slave raiding diminished at the end of the century and trade at Luanda flowed increasingly through the hands of private merchants; the transition to private commerce finally received official sanction in a 1721 law which forbade governors and their *capitães mores* from further dealings in slaves.[51] But Luanda's private merchants secured their monopoly too late, since kings in Matamba and Kasanje by that time had combined with African traders from the Loango coast to divert slaves from the Luandan hinterland along a complex web of northern trade routes terminating at the ports of the Loango coast. Many slaves from the middle Kwango thus ended their long march to the sea in the holds of ships belonging to French, Dutch, and English interests rather than in Portuguese bottoms anchored in Luanda Bay. The Dutch West India Company alone traded 3,000 slaves per year through the major port at Loango by 1670.[52] Vili (also known as Mubire) traders from Loango spread south of the Zaïre River, settling small trading communities, and passed quantities of European manufactures (in particular, guns and powder, much to the displeasure of Luanda's governors, who vainly tried

---

49. Some standard equivalencies of the time (of unknown representativeness, however) included 18$000 for an older male of twenty-five to thirty-five years and 14$000 for an elderly man. Women and youths eight to fifteen years old (*molecões* and *molecanas*) brought 17$000 to 19$000 and children under eight years (*moleques*) 12$000 to 16$000 (Annex to letter from Governor Souza Chichorro to el-Rei, 3/12/1657, AHU, Angola, cx. 4).
50. See Martin, *External Trade*, 37-39, for the palm-cloth currency. The artificiality of valuation in terms of nonexistent metropolitan currencies is evident from the fact that merchants valued the same cloth at 20 reis at Loango when they purchased it and at 50 reis in Luanda when they sold it (Brásio, *Monumenta*, IX, 376, n. 10). By this sort of calculation, a merchant was able to convert goods from Brazil and Portugal valued at less than 9$000 in Loango into a slave worth 22$000 in Luanda; the paper profit in reis between actual cost in Europe or Brazil and the artificial Loango values is not known. The difference between 9$000 and 22$000, less expenses for transporting the palm cloths and buying the slave, represented profits obtained simply by revaluing the cloths.
51. In return, the merchants agreed to pay a new export duty of 1$200 per adult male slave in support of future governors' salaries (Birmingham, *Trade and Conflict*, 134-137; also "Relatório" cited in n. 48).
52. Martin, *External Trade*, 68.

to exclude firearms from the unstable politics of the Kwango kingdoms) in return for slaves.[53] Matamba became the major inland terminus for this trade, thus resuming its historic role as the principal antagonist of the traders based in Luanda.[54]

As non-Portuguese ship captains flocked to the northern coasts in search of slaves made available through Vili diversion of captives from the middle Kwango, relatively strong merchant states coalesced around the main ports at Loango (the Vili state proper), Malemba (Kakongo), and Cabinda (Ngoyo). Competing groups of African traders, Solongo from the old Kongo riverine province of Sonyo, by then almost independent of the decrepit *mani* Kongo at São Salvador, bought other slaves in the lands behind Luanda and sold them in ports located on the south bank of the Zaïre.[55] These states, once they had become established as slave exporters, turned to the development of other slave sources nearer to home than the remote kingdoms of Matamba and Kasanje. The Tio region resumed the role of provider which it had lost with the decline of the sixteenth-century trade from Malebo Pool through São Salvador to Mpinda. Intense competition among the many Europeans calling at these ports, primarily Dutch at the end of the seventeenth century but increasingly French and English (despite intermittent and unsuccessful Portuguese efforts to exlude European rivals from an area they quixotically regarded as their own), allowed the merchant princes of Loango, Kakongo, and Ngoyo to set prices and terms of trade highly advantageous to themselves.[56] Contemporary estimates of the volume of this trade showed wide discrepancies but it probably hovered between 4,000

---

53. The Vili were reported as far south as Luanda by the 1640s but became a major factor in the Kwango trade only somewhat later, probably about the time Nzinga's successors expelled the Portuguese from Matamba in the 1670s. See Martin, *External Trade*, 70; also Consulta do Conselho Ultramarino, 9/11/1683, AHU, Angola, cx. 10, published in Ralph Delgado, *História de Angola* (Lobito, 1948-1952), IV, 70-74. Also letter from Governor António de Albuquerque Coelho de Carvalho, 4/26/1722, AHU, Angola, cx. 16, which detailed the presence of English trading with Vili near the mouth of the Dande.

54. Birmingham, *Trade and Conflict*, 124-125, 128-132.

55. Letter from Governor Souza Coutinho to Martinho de Mello e Castro, 12/30/1770, AHU, Angola, cx. 32, doc. no. 131.

56. Based on descriptions in Martin, *External Trade*, 73-92, 117-135. Martin emphasizes the difficulty of distinguishing eighteenth-century trade patterns in the interior from better reported routes of the late nineteenth century.

and 6,000 annually throughout most of the eighteenth century before surging to a peak of perhaps 15,000 slaves each year during the 1780s.[57]

Some of the slaves diverted from the middle Kwango began to reach the ocean at Kongo ports closer to Luanda as the northern Vili and Solongo became more involved with the Tio and other slave sources nearer to the Loango coast. Ambriz (Mbrije) and Mossul, among several other sites, became important outlets toward the end of the eighteenth century as newly independent Vili traders living in the Dande River valley purchased slaves at a major trading junction near the lands of the *ndembu* Mbwila[58] and sold them to the captains of coasting sloops sent down from the large transoceanic ports on the northern coasts.[59] Luanda merchants and officials tried unsuccessfully to interrupt this trade, clearly an alternative outlet for their own contacts in Kasanje and elsewhere, by establishing a fortified post and market (Encoje, or Nkoje, 1759) near Mbwila, but failed to stanch the northward flow of slaves. By the end of the century, the Luanda Portuguese complained ever more bitterly about *pombeiros* who obtained trade goods on credit from merchants in the capital but sold the slaves obtained to Vili and other participants in the northern trading system.[60] The southern Vili and Solongo had thus resurrected in slightly modified form the old illegal trade founded by São Toméan merchants in the sixteenth century and revived by Matamba and the Dutch during the 1630s and 1640s.

Luanda also suffered from the competition of Portuguese merchants

---

57. Martin, *External Trade*, 86-87, gives several estimates in the range of 13,000 to 15,000. Cf. Curtin, *Atlantic Slave Trade*, table 63 (p. 211).

58. Official Portuguese estimates placed the total of slaves passing through Mbwila at 5,000 per year in the early 1770s. This figure was greater than estimated exports for the entire Loango coast at the time and may indicate the importance of the middle Kwango slave sources for the northern ports even after allowing for official "pointing with alarm" (Relação of Governor Souza Coutinho, 11/27/1772, AHU, Angola, cx. 36).

59. Susan Herlin Broadhead, "Trade and Politics on the Congo Coast, 1770-1870," unpub. Ph.D. thesis (Boston University, 1971), 52, 91-92, cited with the permission of the author. Also Elias Alexandre da Silva Corrêa, *História de Angola* (Lisboa, 1937, but written in the 1790s), II, 68.

60. The Arquivo Histórico de Angola (hereafter AHA) contains a *códice* (G[6]-2-66) in which were registered the minutes of meetings held by Luandan merchants and resulting government regulations intended to restrict this practice; some of these documents have been published in *Arquivos de Angola*. Also see Silva Corrêa, *História*, esp. I, 35-57, for the complaints of merchants during this period.

JOSEPH C. MILLER

in Benguela who duplicated the feats of the Vili in the north, simultaneously diverting slaves from the Benguela (or Ovimbundu) highlands whose predecessors had once gone to Luanda and developing new slave sources in the east.[61] Unlike the Luandan trade, which was based on expensive territorial conquest, fortified interior posts, and regulated *feiras*,[62] the Benguelan trade employed only ambulant *pombeiros* and informal Portuguese settlement in parts of the highlands.[63] The early Benguelan trade had relied on slave sources among the Humbe regions just west of the headwaters of the Kunene, contracted through a *pombeiro* community resident at Caconda. Other traders penetrated the northern plateaux of Bihe and Mbailundo during the 1720s and, by the 1760s, their successors were able to travel as far east as the upper Kwanza with some security.[64] Most slaves purchased in the eastern hinterland up to that time had come from the basin of the upper Kwanza known as the "Ganguellas." The main trade routes at the end of the century, however, had stretched eastward to the upper Zambezi kingdoms of the Luvale and drew slaves from Mbunda, Mbwela, and even the Lozi in the far southeast.[65] Such Luanda *feiras* as those on the Kwanza River at Dondo and

61. The first slave ships to sail directly to Benguela did so in order to avoid the duties payable at Luanda (Carta dos officiaes do senado da camara de São Paulo de Assumpçao de Luanda para Concelho Ultramarino, 4/17/1728, AHU, Angola, cx. 17). The Luanda merchants added that *pombeiros* had been selling slaves purchased with their capital to traders based in Benguela.

62. The major *feiras* of the time, some operated only intermittently, were those in Mbwila (Encoje), Kasanje (Cassange), Holo, and Mbondo. Other regulated marketplaces (Ambaca, Beja near Pungo Andongo, Dongo, Haco, Libolo, Calandula, and Kiteshi at the end of the eighteenth century) existed near the fortified government posts in Angola ("Angola no fim do seculo XVIII," *Boletim da Sociedade de Geographia de Lisboa,* VI [1886], 288-289). See the partial summary in Jean-Luc Vellut, "Notes sur le Lunda et la frontière luso-africaine (1700-1900)," *Etudes d'histoire africaine,* III (1972), 124.

63. Letter from Governor D. Miguel Antonio de Mello to D. Rodrigo de Sousa Coutinho, 1/3/1801, AHU, Angola, cx. 52, emphasized the contrast between the two colonies and the differences in their relative prosperity.

64. "Copia de uma rellação que deu João Pilarte da S.ª hoje falecido ao Cap.ᵐ more José Vieira de Araujo da viagē q' fez ao Cabo Negro por terra no anno de 1770 em comp.ª de José dos Santos hoje cap.ᵐ mor de Caconda," published in Alfredo de Albuquerque Felner, *Angola: Apontamentos sobre a colonização dos planaltos e litoral do sul de Angola* (Lisboa, 1940), I, 182-185. The expansion of this trade is confirmed by rises in exports from Benguela at corresponding periods. See statistics in Herbert S. Klein, "The Portuguese Slave Trade from Angola in the Eighteenth Century," *The Journal of Economic History,* XXXII (1972), 896.

65. Letter from Governor D. Fernando António de Noronha to Visconde de Anadia, 4/20/1803, in Felner, *Angola: Colonização dos planaltos,* II, 16-26.

Beja, which would once have swarmed with Ovimbundu slaves, were largely deserted by 1800.[66] Luandan merchants thus had good reason to complain of the prosperity of their compatriots in Benguela at least as much as they resented the intrusion of foreign competitors in Loango.

One important reason why Luandan merchants failed to compete successfully with the growing commercial centers both south and north of the city lay in the strength and autonomy of their main trading partners in the hinterland, the kingdoms of Matamba and Kasanje. These states blocked access to the main eighteenth-century slave producing regions—the wide savannas beyond the Kwango, and notably the powerful *mwata yamvo*, rulers of the Lunda empire in Katanga. In addition, marauders from Matamba frequently disrupted trade on the trails east of Ambaca.[67] Kasanje kings, often with the cooperation of satellite states in Holo, Mbondo, and among the Minungo, prevented Portuguese merchants from so much as viewing the Kwango River, symbol of the separation of European traders from the slave sources in the east.[68] These kings' political and military strength allowed them to trade at will with Vili from Loango.

Nowhere was the ancient complementarity between African kings and the lineageless dependents of their kingdoms clearer than in Kasanje, where control over the circulation of these "slaves" and "pawns" and a monopoly over their sale to Europeans supported the Kasanje rulers' ability to dominate the lineages of their state.[69] Royal wealth and political power peaked sometime in the middle third of the eighteenth century[70] but declined thereafter as the kings lost their monopoly over the

66. José Joaquim Lopes de Lima, *Ensaios sobre a Statistica das possessões portu-guezas* (Lisboa, 1846), III, *Angola e Benguela*, 18. Also letter from D. Miguel Antonio de Mello to D. Rodrigo de Souza Coutinho, 9/19/1799, AHA codice A-2-2, letter no. 9; published in *Arquivos de Angola*, ser. 1, I, (1933), n.p.

67. A repeated complaint mentioned in numerous documents scattered through the Oficios para Angola codices of the AHA.

68. Manoel Correia Leitão, "Viagem que eu, sargento-mór dos moradores do distrito do Dande, fiz ás remotas partes de Cassange e Olos, no ano de 1755 até o seguinte de 1756," published by Gastão Sousa Dias (ed.), "Uma viagem a Cassange nos meados do seculo XVIII," *Boletim da Sociedade de Geografia de Lisboa*, LVI (1938), 3-30.

69. I have outlined this argument in "Slaves, Slavers, and Social Change in Nine-teenth Century Kasanje," in Franz-Wilhelm Heimer (ed.), *Social Change in Angola* (Munich, 1973), 9-29.

70. For the chronological calculations, see Joseph C. Miller, "Kasanje King Lists—Miscalculating African History?", forthcoming.

JOSEPH C. MILLER

slave trade in a repetition of the sixteenth-century pattern of trade and politics in Kongo. The late-century surge in the northern trade drew slaves from the Kwango kingdoms and forced slave buyers in Kasanje to make purchases outside the kings' central market. The decentralization of trade in Kasanje meant the sale of guns and other imports to regional powers and led to a decline in royal authority. Like the events in the Kongo, decentralization worked against the Europeans most closely connected with the failing central authority. In this case, governors and merchants in Luanda lost out since they had staked their fortunes on the Kasanje kings' *feira*. Ironically, the decline of rulers who had once irked Luandan interests because of their imposition of high prices and vexing conditions at the height of their power did not admit Luandan traders to the long-sought trans-Kwango interior but merely opened the richest interior markets to a variety of other renegades—recalcitrant *pombeiros*, Vili, traders from Matamba, provincial title-holders in Kasanje, and competing Portuguese from Benguela.

The table arrays the statistics available on slave exports from all parts of the Congo-Angola coast to illustrate the dispersal of trade from relative concentration at Luanda in the 1650s to roughly equal shares for the central, northern, and southern regions by 1800.[71] Both Benguela and Loango drew in part on the same middle Kwango and northern Ovimbundu regions which Luandan merchants claimed as their own, but traders from the northern and southern regions had also penetrated portions of the interior never reached by Luandan merchants and maintained fully independent slave trading networks. In the case of Loango, these were mostly areas which had first known the slave trade in its São Tomé-Kongo phase, but in the case of Benguela, traders moved into entirely untouched areas far to the east along the headwaters of the Kasai and Zambezi rivers. The tendency of the Congo-Angola trade to expand and decentralize, first manifested in sixteenth-century Kongo, continued to shape its historical development until well into the nineteenth century.

---

71. In addition to the portions of the coast discussed, total exports included a number of slaves who left Angola illegally at several points near Luanda and Benguela, in addition to the better-known foreign shipping at Loango. See Instruçoens para o Capitão more de Ambaca Jozé Filippe Turém (from Governor Almeida e Vasconcelos), 10/20/1790, AHA, *códice* C-15-2, fls. 20-21, for a report of French slavers loading at ports south of the Kwanza (Novo Redondo, Benguela Velha, etc.).

TABLE 4.1 Summary of Various Estimates of Slave Trade Statistics from Congo and Angola (rough annual averages)

Decade	Loango	Kongo	Luanda		Benguela	
			legal	illegal	legal	illegal
1500		(several thousand)				
1510		4,000				
1520						
1530		4,000-5,000		(becoming significant)		
1540		5,000-6,000		(important)		
1550						
1560						
1570				10,000		
1580			3,000	3,000		
1590						
1600			3,150			
1610			10,000			
1620			13,000			
1630	c. 300			(growing)		
1640			(small)	12,000-13,000		
1650			10,000-12,000			
1660						
1670	3,000		8,000-10,000			
1680	8,000					
1690						
1700						
1710			3,500-7,000			
1720		3,200	6,700-7,300		(low)	
1730		5,200	8,300-9,200		1,000-2,000	
1740		6,000	9,700-10,000		1,000-2,000	
1750		4,500	9,900		2,300-2,400	

(continued)

JOSEPH C. MILLER

TABLE 4.1 *(continued)*

Decade	Loango Kongo	Luanda legal	Luanda illegal	Benguela legal	Benguela illegal
1760	5,300	8,200-8,400		4,900-5,400	
1770	4,300	7,600		5,100-5,600	
1780	13,000-15,000	9,500		6,400	
1790	12,000	9,300		7,500	
1800	10,000	11,300		5,500	
1810	c. 7,700	13,600		4,100	
1820	9,800	13,000		3,900	

Source: See accompanying notes. In addition, see Curtin, *Atlantic Slave Trade,* tables 63 (p. 211), 69 (p. 240), and 75 (p. 261), and Joseph C. Miller, "Legal Portuguese Slaving from Angola: Some Preliminary Indications of Volume and Direction," *Revue française d'histoire d'outre-mer,* XLII (1975), 135-176.

Aspects of the Maritime Portion of the Trade, c. Eighteenth Century

The organization of the Middle Passage of the Congo-Angola slave trade, including many of its infamous cruelties, derived from the high risks experienced by traders who braved the unpredictable conditions of commerce in African seas and from the extreme decentralization of financial interests and a consequent lack of responsibility for slaves' welfare. Slave traders devised two contrasting strategies to counter the vagaries of slave supplies on the African side, hazards of disease and shipwreck on the high seas, as well as danger from European wars which repeatedly spilled over into southern Atlantic waters, and sharply fluctuating slave prices in the Americas. Some organized large and relatively stable trading companies which, they hoped, could ride out short-term losses, but most—a heterogeneous swarm of individual merchants and small ad hoc partnerships (termed "interlopers" by the English)—opted for flexibility and darted into the slave trade as they heard of short-term profits to be made there relative to other commercial opportunities of the times—and then quickly moved out again. In the end, the small operators proved the superior value of their response, and with their triumph came some of the worst abuses of an inherently inhuman business.

All the major European nations trading on the Congo-Angola coast tried at one time or another to seize control of the trade through the organization of vertically integrated trading companies, but none outlasted the hordes of independent smaller firms who ultimately carried the bulk of the slaves transported to the Americas. The Dutch West India Company and the British Royal African Company compiled somewhat more successful records than their competitors, largely in the earlier, more manageable phases of the Loangan trade, but ephemeral French companies appeared there from time to time in the eighteenth century.[72] Two Portuguese chartered companies transported slaves from Angola to northeastern Brazil (a route on which few free traders had been active) from the 1760s to the 1780s but, in general, the interlopers' superior flexibility and lower overheads gave them a telling advantage in a wildly gyrating commerce where large companies tended to compete by building immobile and expensive forts and factories.[73]

The intricacies and fluctuations of African demand for imported wares defied large-scale management by the chartered companies and further favored the small local merchant who knew intimately the wants of his few customers. Africans would sell slaves only for *banzos* (or, in English, bundles), varying assortments of trade goods equivalent to the standard adult male slave (the *peça*—a "piece" in English and, for the French, a *pièce de l'Inde*). African buyers discriminated knowledgeably among the trade staples available from merchants of different European nations—mainly, for the Portuguese, metropolitan wines, Indian and European textiles, and coarse spirits (called *gerebita*) distilled from Brazilian sugar; in the case of the British and French, generally superior man-

---

72. On the second Dutch West India Company, see Postma, "Dutch Participation," *passim*; on the Dutch at Loango, Martin, *External Trade*, esp. 73-75. See K. G. Davies, *The Royal African Company* (New York, 1970), as modified and expanded by Martin, *External Trade*, 78-80, for the Royal African Company. Martin, *External Trade*, 78-80, also discusses the involvement of French companies, especially the Compagnie des Indes Occidentales.

73. For the Portuguese companies, see Klein, "Portuguese Slave Trade," 901 (table 5), 911-914, based on António Carreira, *As Companhias pombalinas de navegação e tráfico de escravos entre a costa africana e o nordeste brasileiro* (Porto, 1968). The role of the European trading companies on the northern coasts was roughly analogous to the trade-regulating functions of the Portuguese conquest of Angola; both maintained fortified positions and tried to regulate marketplaces, and both suffered from similar disadvantages relative to the more flexible private traders.

ufactures (including European imitations of favored Indian textiles), guns, and powder—and demanded *banzos* containing items obtainable only from several different nations. Successful Vili and Solongo traders therefore cultivated contacts with a variety of European sellers and performed the vital economic brokerage function of making up the diverse assortments acceptable to the sellers of slaves in the interior.[74] The Portuguese *pombeiros'* need to offer English guns together with French fabrics, in addition to the wines and *gerebita* of their Luandan sponsors, thus explains their tendency to become involved in the illegal trade in foreign imports from the north. The ability of African sellers of slaves to set the terms of trade frustrated all European attempts at monopoly and contributed to the value of flexibility in the operations of smaller-scale traders.

Accounting techniques which would barely qualify even as "fast and loose" by modern standards make it virtually impossible to determine prices and profits on the basis of presently limited data. Most traders kept their accounts in terms of metropolitan currencies but conducted all transactions in nonmonetary commodities evaluated according to local equivalencies based on the *peça* and the *banzo*. They liberally inflated the money value of the *banzo* according to the location of the goods included in it; thus goods priced at 26$800 in Lisbon in the middle of the eighteenth century, once assorted into *banzos* in Angola, acquired a (conventional) value of 40$000 in Luanda and were said to be worth 80$000 in the far interior.[75] To cite an example of the potentially misleading results of such practices, Luandan merchants used the paper losses derived from this sort of bookkeeping to show consistent deficits from slave dealing and to justify their petitions for relief from royal taxes and

---

74. Compiled from Martin, *External Trade*, 93-116, and various documents in the AHU and AHA.

75. Carta Regia, 1/14/1761 ("que regula como se deve fazer o Comercio do Sertão"), AHA, *códice* G(6)-2-66, fls. 13-23. See also the document cited by Klein, "Portuguese Slave Trade," 907n (AHU, Angola, cx. 21). To compound the confusion, the money values referred to quantities measured in terms of highly various local standards. A favorite device of traders in the hinterland was to establish a smaller "string" of beads or "yard" of cloth in interior marketplaces than that used in Luanda; they then pocketed the difference between the weights and measures used by their creditors and the elastic standards of the interior. Among the numerous documents attesting to such practices, see Bando sobre a Regulação das medidas que forão para os prezidios, e feiras, 4/9/1766, AHA, *códice* G(6)-2-66, fls. 93-96.

regulation. In fact, their losses existed only in terms of the inflated reis-values assigned to goods at the point of sale in the far interior and disguised much more consistent profits from the sale of overpriced imports.[76]

All along the coast a chain of credit, finally stretching back to Europe in many cases, facilitated the provision of slaves on the African side but introduced a sometimes disastrous rigidity for creditors on the European side. Investors in Europe retained direct ownership of the goods traded by the vertically integrated trading companies, of course, but the small traders, who shifted into and out of the slave trade, also acquired their trade goods on credit from investors in Europe or the Americas. The willingness of investors to entrust goods to these small operators made possible the agility which enabled them to survive. Even the community of merchants resident in Luanda operated largely on capital borrowed from Brazilian and Portuguese sources, and the rare Angolan trader who financed his own trade apparently achieved not only outstanding commercial success but occasionally merited knighthood in the Order of Christ.[77] Only six or eight (of the dozens of merchants active in Luanda) had acquired significant capital resources of their own by the end of the eighteenth century.[78] Most coastal traders extended the credit they received from overseas sponsors on to their trading partners on the African side—*pombeiros*, Vili, Solongo, and others—and these middlemen in turn supported the kings and lineage headmen, the ultimate sources of slaves in the interior. The chain of credit obviously lengthened through the years as the slave trade expanded into new slave-producing areas more remote from the sea.

The African kings and lineage headmen were the only participants in the trade not locked into the rigid chain of indebtedness, and they used their relative freedom to influence prices and manipulate the terms of trade to their own advantage. Their collective power to bring down the entire pyramid of credit by withholding payment in slaves for goods

---

76. Miguel Antonio de Mello, "Angola no começo do século (1802)," *Boletim da Sociedade de Geografia de Lisboa*, V (1885), 558-559. For examples of the shipping costs, taxes, and other charges borne by slave traders in Luanda, see Klein, "Portuguese Slave Trade," 908.

77. Klein, "Portuguese Slave Trade," 906-907.

78. De Mello, "Angola no começo do século," 551-552.

JOSEPH C. MILLER

received on trust put the Luandan traders, in particular, under constant pressure. These merchants were usually heavily in debt to Brazilian and metropolitan interests and could not afford to lose their only working capital if sellers in the interior refused to cover their debts, and so they repeatedly bowed to the demands of kings in Kasanje and elsewhere despite the contrary pleas of governors and others without a similar financial stake in the negotiations.[79]

A diversity of competing financial interests combined to underwrite most slaving voyages, especially in Angola, and the resulting lack of overall financial responsibility allowed sharp operators to thwart the attempts of both governments and the owners of the slaves to ameliorate shipboard conditions during the Middle Passage. Rarely enforced "leis das arqueações" required Portuguese captains to furnish minimal amenities and specified the maximum number of slaves who could be crammed into given amounts of space under Portuguese law, for example,[80] but the captains responsible for constant overcrowding seldom owned more than a few of the slaves they carried and were rarely called to account for careless treatment of slaves belonging to others.[81] Since individual captains entered and departed from the slave trade with agility and rapidity,[82] many undoubtedly calculated that their best hopes for a profitable voyage lay in overloading their ships as much as possible, skimping on expensive provisions and sanitary precautions, accepting the resultant slave mortality as a cost of doing business (but with concomitant savings from reduced expenses for food and other consumables), and then moving on to other fields of commerce if too many of their charges died

---

79. See AHA, *códice* G(6)-2-66, for repeated examples.

80. The original "leis das arqueações" (3/18/1684, published in *Arquivos de Angola,* ser. I, II, 10 [1936], 313-320) restricted ships to no more than five slaves per *tonelada,* approximately the equivalent of a space 2' by 4' by 5' for each slave. Despite the flagrant disregard of the law's provisions, the notorious overcrowding of the seventeenth century (600-700 slaves aboard the small ships of that era) may have diminished. Mid-eighteenth-century cargoes from Luanda averaged 400 slaves or less, while those of the early nineteenth century were nearly 500 (Herbert S. Klein, "Portuguese Slave Trade," 898-903, and "The Trade in African Slaves to Rio de Janeiro, 1795-1811," *Journal of African History,* X [1969], 538. Seventeenth-century estimates from n. 13 and Postma, "Dutch Participation," 15).

81. For details and abuses, see Manuel dos Anjos da Silva Rebelo, *Relações entre Angola e Brasil, 1808-1830* (Lisboa, 1970), 71-73.

82. Klein's data in "Trade in African Slaves," supported by unpublished figures I have obtained in the AHA, clearly lead to this conclusion.

en route.[83] Even the largest investors in transporting slaves never sent more than eight or ten individuals aboard a single vessel, in part as a precaution against frequent and disastrous outbreaks of smallpox but also to spread the risks of entrusting their entire fortunes (in the form of slaves owned) to the care of a single unscrupulous captain.[84]

Far too little is yet known about the slaves themselves, those who suffered most from these abuses. It is clear that slaves experienced significantly higher mortality during the Middle Passage than equivalent stable populations would have suffered; moderately higher deaths occurred among slaves embarked during the unhealthy period of the late summer African rains, and mortality increased sharply with the length of the voyage.[85] Given the sharp practices and cost-cutting techniques of most shippers, it is perhaps most remarkable that, overall, 80 to 90 percent of the slaves taken aboard managed to reach the Americas alive. The correlation between shorter voyages and higher survival rates, combined with the pattern of prevailing winds in the south Atlantic, appears to have encouraged traders to take most Congo-Angola slaves to their own countrymen's colonies nearest the point of embarkation. The Portuguese in Luanda and Benguela concentrated on the easy-to-reach ports of southern Brazil, in particular Rio de Janeiro, with some emphasis given to the Spanish colonies of the Rio de la Plata.[86] Although no clear pattern is vis-

---

83. Ship captains apparently received a stipulated flat sum to cover their expenses in delivering a slave to his/her destination in the Americas, paid upon embarkation in Angola. This system placed a premium on shaving costs during the ocean crossing when captains and slaves were far beyond the reach of the slaves' owners.

84. Klein, "Portuguese Slave Trade," 906-907; Silva Rebelo, Relações entre Angola e Brasil, 77-78.

85. On slave mortality in general, see Philip D. Curtin, "Epidemiology and the Slave Trade," Political Science Quarterly, LXXXIII (1968), 190-216; idem, "A Postscript on Mortality," Atlantic Slave Trade, 275-286. For the Congo-Angola trade, Klein, "Trade in African Slaves," estimated an overall 95 deaths per 1,000 slaves embarked to Rio, 1795-1811. Herbert S. Klein and Stanley Engerman, "Shipping Patterns and Mortality in the African Slave Trade to Rio de Janeiro, 1825-1830," Cahiers d'études africaines (forthcoming) found 62 deaths per thousand per voyage for Luanda/Benguela and 33/1000/voyage from northern ports. Miller, "Legal Portuguese Slaving," provides more detailed breakdowns for the period 1795-1830 with hypotheses to explain the nature and causes of variation in mortality rates. The aggregate estimates of mortality for 1795-1830 (based on Rio imports) were Luanda, 89/1000/voyage; Benguela, 70/1000/voyage; and northern ports, 41/1000/voyage. Overall mortality was 69/1000/voyage.

86. Estimated from figures in Mauricio Goulart, Escravidão Africana no Brasil (São Paulo, 1950), 203-209; Klein, "Trade in African Slaves," 545, and "Portuguese

JOSEPH C. MILLER

ible for the British, the French, who had a narrower range of choice, sent 95 percent of the slaves carried by Nantes traders in the latter half of the eighteenth century to the main French sugar island of Saint-Domingue.[87] The less prominent European slave traders, mainly Dutch at Loango during the later decades of the seventeenth century,[88] may also be presumed to have sent most of their captives to their own respective colonies in the New World.[89]

Ending of the Transatlantic Slave Trade, c. 1810-1870

Diplomatic constraints emanating from reform and revolution in Europe replaced economic factors as the primary determinants of the maritime portion of the Congo-Angola slave trade after 1810, altering its volume and direction, the identity of its participants, and the methods by which it was conducted. Before that time, the economics of mines and agriculture in the New World, African demands for imported wares, high risks for traders and investors, governmental taxes, and the costs of administering factories and colonies had decided the broad patterns of the trade. After that date, a succession of treaties between England, Portugal, and—after her independence in 1822—Brazil forced slave traders away from Guinea and into the southern Atlantic, where they flew the colors of Portuguese and Brazilian merchantmen and, according to terms

Slave Trade," 901; Curtin, *Atlantic Slave Trade*, 206-207. For the Rio de la Plata region, see Klein, "Trade in African Slaves," 545n, citing Elena F. S. de Struder, *La trata de negros en el Rio de la Plata durante el siglo xviii* (Buenos Aires, 1958), 323-324.

87. Curtin, *Atlantic Slave Trade*, tables 52 (p. 183) and 60 (p. 200). These tables combine to show a slight Saint-Domingue preference for Congo-Angola slaves after the middle of the eighteenth century when French slavers became active on the Loango coast.

88. Martin states that all available records on Dutch voyages from the Kongo-Loango regions show ships sailing for Surinam and Curaçao, entrepôts from which slaves were then forwarded to other Caribbean islands. See Martin, *External Trade*, 67.

89. According to Curtin's estimates, *Atlantic Slave Trade*, table 63 (p. 211), the Portuguese carried approximately 63 percent of the slaves embarked in "Central and Southeast Africa" (a term including Moçambique as well as the Congo-Angola coast) between 1701 and 1810. The British transported about 21 percent and the French the remaining 16 percent. Statistics including the late seventeenth century would add a figure for the Dutch and decrease the totals for the French (in particular) and the British.

worked out in the Anglo-Portuguese agreements, continued to transport slaves free of harassment by British naval patrols. Not until 1839, when Britain unilaterally asserted her power to search and seize all vessels discovered on the high seas with slaves (or, later, slave-trading equipment and fittings) on board, was effective pressure applied to end the trade. Further Portuguese and Brazilian concessions culminated in the formal abolition of slave imports to Brazil in 1851 and an effective stoppage of the major portion of the nineteenth century trade.[90] Cuba, the only major American importing region after mid-century, had received an increasing proportion of slaves from the Congo-Angola coast during preceding decades and took most of those embarked from 1851 until international diplomatic pressures reduced that trade after 1868.

The ubiquitous British cruisers made "mobility, speed, and secrecy . . . the keynote[s] of the mid-nineteenth century trade organization,"[91] and successful slavers of this era relied on furtive contacts with African trading partners at secluded inlets and developed techniques of loading slaves quickly to minimize the risks of detection. The ports at Loango, Malemba, and Cabinda, dominant in the eighteenth century, began to share their prosperity with a number of other, smaller points dispersed along the Kongo coast—Ambriz, Mossul, and others—which consisted of conspicuous warehouses near the shore filled with such "legitimate" commodities as ivory, wax, gum copal, and skins with slaves hidden, meanwhile, in barracoons concealed in nearby forests. Ships waited for a safe moment to enter the port, load the slaves, and then dash into the open ocean.[92]

The major African beneficiaries of the new emphasis on secrecy were the traders of the lower Zaïre, who assumed a new importance because of the river's many hidden creeks, admirably suited to trading unmolested by inquiring cruisers, and its nearness to both the old Vili routes from the middle Kwango and to slave sources near Malebo Pool. Zombo traders from eastern Kongo, active since the 1760s, became

---

90. The most comprehensive work on the progress of abolition south of the equator is Leslie Bethell, *The Abolition of the Brazilian Slave Trade* (Cambridge, 1970).

91. Martin, *External Trade*, 145.

92. Summarized from Martin, *External Trade*, 139-146, and Broadhead, "Trade and Politics," 158.

important caravan operators from Malebo Pool and Yaka territories east of the Kwango to all ports south of the Zaïre. The Solongo of Sonyo, who had permitted little direct trading at their river ports in the eighteenth century, began to sell large numbers of slaves as the nineteenth century progressed. Finally, Ngoyo kings on the north bank of the Zaïre shifted their primary outlet from Cabinda on the Atlantic side to Punta da Lenha and Boma on the river.[93] Heavily taxed slave exports from Luanda dropped precipitously after Brazilian independence, except for a small coastal commerce to the ports along the Kongo coast (defined as tax-exempt "internal trade" under Angolan law) where slaves were transferred to other vessels bound for the Americas without paying duties required at the capital town.[94] Luandan merchants thus ended their slaving days as minor tributaries of the northern factories they had fought so long and unsuccessfully to suppress. As far as can be determined from available (but imprecise) data, Benguelan traders may have increased their share of slaves exported from Angola during this period.[95]

Two groups of mixed Portuguese-African origins became the dominant forces on the trade routes east of Luanda and Benguela in the nineteenth century. The northern of the pair, known as Ambakista and based on plantation and commercial interests near the Portuguese town of Ambaca, spoke a Kimbundu lingua franca ("Ambaquista") and practiced local trading magic but were more or less Portuguese in dress, religion, and manners. The other group emerged among the Ciyaka near the Portuguese post at Caconda in the southern Ovimbundu highlands; they had fewer superficial European characteristics but became known as "Europeans," or Ovimbali, among the peoples east of the upper Kwanza. Both, like the Vili and Solongo established nearer Luanda, settled in small trading communities scattered through the high plains of the east and organized caravans to conduct slaves and trade staples back to their

---

93. Broadhead, "Trade and Politics," 43, 49, 51, 67, 134, 173.

94. Silva Rebelo, *Relações entre Angola e Brasil*, 293-296. This trade had an aura of legality from the perspective of sensitive governors in Luanda since it was "intra-Angolan" and hence not subject to inspection by British naval patrols.

95. Curtin, *Atlantic Slave Trade*, table 75 (p. 261). The uncertainty derives from the meaning of the "Angola—unspecified" category in the table, which could include slaves from almost anywhere south of the equator. But see George Tams, *Visit to the Portuguese Possessions in Southwestern Africa* (London, 1845; reprint, New York, 1969), I, 97, who reported 20,000 slaves exported there in 1838.

homelands and on to the coast. The Ambakista brought slaves from points as distant as the Lunda empire in Katanga and the Ovimbali had spread east to Loziland as early as 1835.[96] Both, dually armed with European firearms and local charms, contributed to the familiar evolution from centralized royal slaving to decentralized trading as they exhausted the kings' resources of dependent persons wherever they went and moved out to trade with provincial authorities.

Greater numbers of slaves than ever before left the Congo-Angola coast during most of the period of the "suppression of the slave trade" in response to demand from Brazil and the Spanish colonies, formerly supplied by the entire African coast but increasingly restricted to slave sources in the south Atlantic in the nineteenth century. The vast majority of these (68 percent of all slaves, probably over 90 percent of those from the Congo-Angola coast) went to Brazil in the holds of United States, Brazilian, and Portuguese ships up to 1851.[97] After that date, Spanish slavers became the almost exclusive agents of the transatlantic trade as they bought labor for Cuba's burgeoning sugar plantations in the ports of the Zaïre River.[98] Total annual exports probably exceeded 30,000 slaves in peak years before 1850, dropping to around 10,000 per annum in the 1860s and to much lower levels after that.

Aftermath and Conclusions

Although the transatlantic portion of the Congo-Angola slave trade drew to a close between 1850 and 1870, neither British cruisers nor international diplomacy affected a thriving internal slave trade which con-

96. Vellut, "Notes sur le Lunda," 94-99, on the Ambakista. On the Ovimbali (also known as Mambari), see Alfred Hauenstein, "Les voyages en caravane des Tjiaka," *Anthropos*, LIX (1964), 928-930; on their arrival in Loziland, see Eric Flint, "Trade and Politics in Barotseland during the Kololo Period," *Journal of African History*, XI (1970), 71-72.

97. Curtin, *Atlantic Slave Trade*, tables 67 (p. 234) and 69 (p. 240). Nearly 70 percent of the slaves identified by the British Foreign Office between 1817 and 1843 came from the Congo-Angola area; the sample, however, is of undetermined representativeness.

98. See Broadhead, "Trade and Politics," 173, and Martin, *External Trade*, 139-144, on Spanish slavers in the Zaïre River. Both authors also detail an ill-fated scheme entrusted to the Régis trading firm of Marseilles in which a number of "free emigrants" from the lower Zaïre were to be enlisted for service in Martinique and Guadeloupe.

JOSEPH C. MILLER

tinued to move uncounted numbers of people from one part of western central Africa to another until the 1920s. The so-called "legitimate trade" of the nineteenth century stimulated various forms of labor recruitment in the African economies which responded to European demand for palm oil, peanuts, ivory, wild rubber, wax, and all the other respectable commodities welcomed by humanitarians across the seas.[99] The tactics used to recruit the required labor were, if anything, harsher than methods long used by African kings and entrepreneurs to supply captives to European slave dealers. Ambakista and Ovimbali caravans merely shifted to the transport of legitimate commodities and continued to buy slaves who walked to the coasts very much as had their predecessors, but now with heavy burdens on their backs instead of chains around their necks. Ovimbundu and Imbangala caravans grew to enormous size, sometimes comprising 2,000 and more armed bearers, and became the dominant military forces in the Lunda empire and other areas where local political authorities declined under the pressures of the economic changes of the time. The Cokwe, in the trans-Kwango hinterland, were the prime beneficiaries of rising demands for ivory and wax and, after 1870, rubber. They acquired thousands of semi-lineageless dependents who boiled wax, tapped wild-rubber vines, and grew food to sustain their new commercial prosperity.[100] The Ovimbundu and Imbangala caravans similarly harmonized internal slaving and "legitimate" exports by selling slaves to Lulua and Luba for the rubber and ivory in heavy demand at the coast.

Portuguese planters in Angola and São Tomé continued to buy African laborers long after the Luandan merchants had ceased to send slaves to the Americas. They engaged these workers under a variety of legal euphemisms (libertos, slaves nominally "freed" by law in 1857; serviçaes, persons bought or recruited after the abolition of slavery; and other unnamed variations on the theme of essentially forced labor). The introduction of cocoa revived São Tomé's agriculture in the 1870s and, after the 1876 abolition of indentured slavery on the island allowed former slaves to flee plantations for the surrounding hills, planters

---

99. Martin A. Klein, "Slavery, the Slave Trade, and Legitimate Commerce in Late Nineteenth Century Africa," Etudes d'histoire africaine, II (1971), 5-28.

100. Joseph C. Miller, "Cokwe Trade and Conquest in the Nineteenth Century," in Gray and Birmingham (eds.), Pre-Colonial African Trade, 175-201.

imported Africans from Angola (under the title of *serviçaes*) in quantities of up to 5,000 per year.[101] The export of human labor from Angola thus ended very much as it had begun 400 years before, with São Tomé's plantations receiving some 2,000 to 4,000 unwilling workers from the mainland each year. Only the nomenclature, crops, and technology had changed.

Labor recruiting tactics in mainland Angola involved varying degrees of coercion, and thus perpetuated aspects of the nineteenth-century importation of *serviçaes* at least up to the 1960-1961 outbreak of violence in some of the areas most afflicted by these practices.[102] The Africans taken from their homes to build roads, tend coffee bushes, and harvest cotton could not have perceived many differences between the "slave trade" which preceded the middle of the nineteenth century and the continued—and, in such areas as the lower Congo during the construction of the Léopoldville and Brazzaville railways—even intensified impressment of labor after that time. It all ended as imperceptibly as it had begun, except that in the meantime at least 4 million persons had been delivered alive in the Americas, and inestimable numbers of others had been moved far from their kinsmen to other parts of Africa or had died as unrecorded casualties of the slave trade in Congo and Angola.

---

101. This "modern slavery" ended only after World War I (quote from the title of Henry Nevinson's exposé of the São Tomé *serviçal* trade, *A Modern Slavery*, published in London, 1906). See James Duffy, *A Question of Slavery* (Oxford, 1967), esp. 96-98, 168-229.

102. On later labor policies in Angola, see James Duffy, *Portuguese Africa* (Cambridge, Mass., 1959), 289-328; Douglas Wheeler and René Pélissier, *Angola* (London, 1971), 136-144, 173-192.

5

W. Robert Higgins

Charleston: Terminus and Entrepôt of the Colonial Slave Trade

Throughout the colonial period, Charleston was the preeminent port and entrepôt of the slave trade to British North America. Sea captains, British merchants, and colonial factors all recognized the major role of this single southern city within the commerce in black labor from Africa. An understanding of the significance of Charleston as the greatest North American slave market continued in the nineteenth century through the writings of eminent historians, both black and white. W. E. B. DuBois, in his doctoral dissertation at Harvard University, clearly defined the impact of the colonial port and capital of South Carolina upon the slave trade.[1] Writing simultaneously with DuBois was the former Confederate general, Dr. Edward McCrady of Charleston. In his two-volume history of colonial South Carolina during the proprietary and royal governments[2] and in a paper read before the American Historical Association in 1895,[3] McCrady claimed for Carolina the distinction of the largest mainland slave terminus. Neither of these men, however, dealt solely with the black trade, and neither buttressed his position with definitive research on the role of South Carolina in the commerce in slaves.

A shorter version of this paper was presented at the African Studies Association meeting in Denver, 1971.

1. William E. B. DuBois, *The Suppression of the African Slave-trade to the United States of America, 1638-1870* (New York, 1896), 9-11.

2. Edward McCrady, *The History of South Carolina under the Proprietary Government, 1670-1719* (New York, 1897); idem, *The History of South Carolina under the Royal Government, 1719-1776* (New York, 1899).

3. Edward McCrady, "Slavery in the Province of South Carolina, 1670-1770," *Annual Report of the American Historical Association for the Year 1895* (Washington, 1896), 631-673.

Forty years after DuBois and McCrady wrote, Donnan succinctly characterized the Charleston Negro trade in the preface to the fourth and final volume of her monumental collection of documents relating to the commerce in African slaves:

> Throughout the eighteenth century Charleston was by far the most important of the continental [slave] markets and it is there that one can best study the nature of the traffic and its economic effects.[4]

Despite the otherwise extensive presentation of materials, Donnan failed to utilize government documents available in both South Carolina and Great Britain. Thus, up to that point, even though the role of Charleston as the major slave port of North America had been known for over 200 years, no one had analyzed the available data to define the parameters of the commerce to colonial South Carolina and, in turn, to delineate the entire black trade to what presently comprises the United States.

In 1969 Curtin searched much of the published material on importations of blacks to all of the Americas. From this work he severely reduced the estimate of the number of Africans who entered the New World. Curtin, however, did not use the primary materials relating to colonial South Carolina nor recent writings analyzing importations and transshipments through the terminus and entrepôt of Charleston.[5]

The records of the slave trade to provincial Carolina are significant not only because of the great volume of Negroes who passed into plantation service through Charleston, but also because these documents are the only major body of English North American data on the origins of slaves along the west coast of Africa. Even cursory study of the records shows many of the long-held ideas of the slave trade to the Americas to be untenable. For example, no Negro offloaded in Carolina came from eastern or southern Africa. Although the idea of "seasoning" slaves in the West Indies persists, records indicate that the number of black workers imported into Charleston from any location except Africa amounted to less than 16 percent of the total volume.

4. Elizabeth Donnan (ed.), *Documents Illustrative of the History of the Slave Trade to America* (Washington, 1935), IV, Preface.

5. Philip D. Curtin, *The Atlantic Slave Trade: A Census* (Madison, 1969), chs. 1, 3, 5, 7.

W. ROBERT HIGGINS

During the colonial period, five cities—Boston, Newport, New York, Philadelphia, and Charleston—developed in English North America.[6] The dealings of Boston in the African trade were negligible. In spite of the calumny heaped upon Newport for its share in the importation of slaves, recent studies have shown that the black trade of the greatest merchants of Rhode Island was similarly small.[7] Although the settlement patterns of New York were more similar to those of the plantation colonies and more black slaves were employed in the area, the trade in Africans through the port of New York was of no great significance.[8] Philadelphia was the largest city in North America and the second largest city in the British empire during the eighteenth century. The capital of Pennsylvania was also the greatest merchant port of the English mainland colonies. In spite of the volume of its overall trade, however, the slave commerce of Philadelphia was limited not only in volume but in geographical extent. Most of the slaves who entered the port were American Negroes shipped from another British location.[9]

Although there was no city in the colony, Virginia was the oldest of the British possessions in North America and the area where English enslavement of the Negro began. Nevertheless, the demand for new black laborers in the Chesapeake region was never substantial. After rising in the seventeenth century, the trade in Negro slaves peaked in the third decade of the eighteenth century and then declined throughout the remainder of the colonial period.[10]

Only one large and dynamic colonial slave port developed in the

---

6. Carl Bridenbaugh in his two volumes, *Cities in the Wilderness: The First Century of Urban Life in America, 1625-1742* (New York, 1964) and *Cities in Revolt: Urban Life in America, 1743-1776* (New York, 1965), studied the five ports of colonial America.

7. Virginia Bever Platt, "And Don't Forget the Guinea Voyage: The Slave Trade of Aaron Lopez of Newport," unpub. paper read at African Studies Association meeting, Denver, 1971, 21 (unnumbered).

8. James G. Lydon, "The Slave Trade of Colonial New York," unpub. paper read at Missouri Valley Historical Conference, Omaha, 1972, table I.

9. Darold D. Wax, "Negro Imports into Pennsylvania, 1720-1807," *Pennsylvania History*, XXXII (1965), 261-287.

10. John Hemphill, "Virginia and the British Atlantic Slave Trade, 1660-1775: A Demographic Survey," unpub. paper read at Rocky Mountain Social Science Conference, Salt Lake City, 1972; Gerald W. Mullin, *Flight and Rebellion: Slave Resistance in Eighteenth-century Virginia* (New York, 1972).

area which today comprises the Atlantic coast of the United States. This terminus of the African trade in labor was Charleston, the capital of South Carolina and the only metropolis south of Philadelphia.

Carolina was one of the last English colonies to be established during the seventeenth century. By the time that the British settlers founded Charleston in 1670, Virginia was nearly three-quarters of a century old, and Maryland was only slightly younger. By the last quarter of the seventeenth century, the economies of the older provinces were firmly based upon the production of tobacco and each area was thriving.

Conditions in the southern province were quite different. The early Carolinians did not have a specific agricultural export until twenty years after settlement, when rice was successfully cultivated on a large scale. Another problem encountered by the colonists was the marshy lowlands of the South Carolina coastline, which were conducive to both malaria and yellow fever. Such conditions did not encourage economic productivity or extensive immigration by free whites, and therefore the European settlers within the province were always few in number.

In spite of its initial handicaps—a delay in settlement, an unhealthy climate, a limited European population, and governmental instability—South Carolina during the eighteenth century developed into one of the most flourishing colonies within the British empire. Two factors were responsible: the successful production of rice and indigo, and the widespread utilization of black slaves. Africans arrived in South Carolina at the same time as the Europeans,[11] and continued to enter the colony virtually every year from 1670 until the American Revolution temporarily ended the transatlantic slave trade. The first blacks came from the British sugar islands to the south. Barbadians constituted one-third of the passengers aboard the first three ships bringing settlers to Carolina, and these people brought with them their black chattels. Slave owners of colonial South Carolina continued to draw a portion of their labor needs from the tropical islands, but within two years of colonization the planters of the new province received their first shipment of slaves directly

---

11. South Carolina was the only British settlement where both peoples arrived at the same time. In every other case, the free people came first and then brought slaves to perform the heavy tasks. See W. Robert Higgins, *The Slave Trade of Colonial South Carolina* (Columbia, S.C., forthcoming), ch. 1.

from Africa.[12] Between that date, 1672, and 1775, nearly 90,000 black slaves entered Charleston or one of the lesser ports of South Carolina. During little more than a century, the merchants of Charleston imported and sold over one-fourth of the total number of Negroes brought to North America from 1619, when slaves first entered Virginia, until the constitutional prohibition to the trade halted legal importations at the end of 1807. One of every four Negro ancestors of the current black population of the United States, therefore, passed through the colonial port of Charleston.

Although the Carolinians received slaves from the sugar islands of the British and other European nations and also obtained a small number of Negroes from the neighboring continental colonies, the vast majority of black laborers imported through Charleston and the lesser ports of Georgetown and Beaufort came to South Carolina directly from Africa. All of the slaves received from the southern continent were shipped from the west coast within the range of the Senegal River in the north to Angola in the south. Blacks from the east coast of Africa did enter North America during the eighteenth century, but Virginia was the only southern province to receive any.[13]

The planters of Carolina had decided preferences in the type of slave they desired: age, size, origin, and sex were all determining factors in the selection of a new worker and in the price which Carolinians were willing to pay. Age was a common determinant within all of the English colonies, no matter what the geographical location of the province, nor what crop was produced on the land. The desire for young adults was sensible because of the planter's need to recoup the original investment in labor and to profit from the work of the Negro. Within Charleston, the preferred ages ranged between sixteen and twenty-five for males, and from fourteen to twenty-one for females.

---

12. Donnan, *Documents*, II, 48.

13. Virginia Bever Platt, "The East India Company and the Madagascar Slave Trade," *William and Mary Quarterly*, XXVI (1969), 548-577, records the trade from the east coast of Africa. There are no records of East African entries into South Carolina in either the South Carolina Treasury, General Duty Books A, B, and C (1735-1775), South Carolina Department of Archives and History; or CO5/509-511: Royal Naval Officer, Charleston, S.C., South Carolina Shipping Returns, Dec. 1721-Dec. 1735, March 1736-Jan. 1764, Jan. 1764-Sept. 1767, Public Record Office. Hereafter cited as "Naval Officer Shipping Returns" and "Duty Books."

Older slaves not only had a shorter period of productivity but were an expense to the owner when they were no longer able to work in the fields. Infants and black children posed a similar problem for the rice and indigo planters of South Carolina. They were not capable of mature physical labor for many years, and yet later, after they had passed prime working age, they would be a drain upon the profits of the plantation. Although the percentage of total return for black children was higher than the profits for older adults, it was much less than the yield from the labors of a young man or woman entering into maturity. These prime workers could be put directly into the fields; when acquired during the spring, they would return a profit to their owner during the year of purchase.[14]

The people of South Carolina were particular about the size of the slaves whom they purchased and employed. Tall Negroes were most sought after, and in many cases a prospective purchaser would avoid buying new labor if all the slaves in a cargo were small in size. For example, in 1756 Commodore Thomas Frankland sent to Charleston a number of slaves who had been captured from the French. They were clearly not what the colonists wanted. "They were much too small a People for the business of this Country and on this Account many [purchasers] went away [from the auction] empty handed that would otherwise have purchas'd."[15] The complement was also true. Henry Laurens, one of the greatest slave merchants in colonial Charleston, wrote to a correspondent: "A tall able People tempt many of our folks to buy when they are in no real want of them."[16]

Although the planters of Carolina had no direct knowledge of the west coast of Africa, they had decided opinions concerning the best slaving locations between Senegal and Angola. The two areas which were considered to be the most desirable points of origin for industrious, docile workers were the Gambian and Gold coasts. If the slave market

14. Report of Governor James Glen to the Board of Trade, in "Records in the British Public Record Office Relating to South Carolina," transcripts prepared by Noel Sainsbury, South Carolina Department of Archives and History, XXIII, 345-349.

15. Henry Laurens (Philip M. Hamer and George C. Rogers, Jr., eds.), *The Papers of Henry Laurens* (Columbia, S.C., 1970), II, 83.

16. Elizabeth Donnan, "The Slave Trade into South Carolina Before the Revolution," *American Historical Review*, XXXIII (1928), 818.

of Charleston could not provide Negroes from either of these two desired locations, then the planter would demand black workers from Angola. If Gambian and Gold Coast Negroes were available at the same time that a cargo of tall Angolans was ready for sale, blacks from the southern extremity of the slaving coast would be considered as suitable, because of their height, as the most preferred Negroes.[17]

Slaves from Calabar were acquired by the Carolina planters and employed successfully in the rice and indigo fields, but they were the least desired of all of the West African peoples. In the first decade of the eighteenth century, Calabar slaves were described as "those poor wretches . . . a strange sort of brutish creatures, very weak and slothful; but cruel and bloody in their temper, always quarreling, biting and fighting, and some of the times choaking and murdering one another, without any mercy. . . . "[18] Fifty years later, in the middle decade of the century, Laurens wrote to Peter Furnell, his associate in Jamaica: " . . . Callabar . . . Slaves are quite out of repute from numbers in every Cargo that have been sold with us destroying themselves."[19]

Negroes from other areas along the slaving coast of Africa were sold in Charleston with varying degrees of success, depending on the total number of Negroes available, the returns brought by Carolina produce, and the time of year. Charleston merchants attempted to educate the planters to the desirability of certain cargoes of slaves, but met with little success.[20] The geographical preferences and dislikes of the slaveholders remained constant throughout the century of the colonial black trade.

The settlers of Carolina had another concern: besides wanting to know where in Africa the blacks were acquired, they wanted to learn the specific path of shipment from the southern continent to North America. Were the Negroes directly from Africa, or had they passed through another American colony before arriving in Charleston? Blacks who came directly from Africa were preferred by the planters for a very simple reason. They had not been contaminated through association with other Europeans or other slaves; thus, it was thought that they tended to be far

---

17. Laurens, *Papers*, I, 258.
18. Donnan, *Documents*, II, 15.
19. Laurens, *Papers*, I, 331.
20. See, e.g., the advertisements of George Austin and Henry Laurens in the *South Carolina Gazette*, August 11, 1758, and June 30, 1759.

better workers. Negroes shipped from another of the American provinces, and especially from the sugar islands, were supposed to be much less docile, were prone to run away, and would physically oppose discipline. Therefore a colonial purchaser in Charleston would buy a new slave directly from one of the less desirable locations on the west coast of Africa in preference to buying a Gambian or Gold Coast Negro from another colony.[21]

The planters of Carolina were not alone in preferring new Negroes from Africa, their views being reflected in the actions of the provincial government. Although all slaves were taxed by the colonial assembly upon their arrival in Charleston, the rates of the impost were nominal. Prohibitive duties, however, were imposed upon slaves from the Americas. Throughout most of the colonial period, a black worker from another English settlement was taxed at five or six times the rate for African slaves. Negroes brought from one of the Spanish colonies faced an impost of over £20, fifteen times the rate charged for new slaves. Such taxes restricted the importations from American locations and, by limiting the number of unmanageable workers, reduced the danger of insurrection in Carolina.[22]

The vast majority of the African slaves brought to the Americas were imported to provide physical labor in agriculture. Males were stronger, and thus yielded more labor per capita than did the females. Although males were preferred because of their greater productivity, the Carolina settlers did not exclude female purchases to the extent to which the planters in the English sugar islands did. The sex ratio of Negroes brought to Charleston was therefore far closer to an even balance than the proportions found in the West Indies and Jamaica.[23]

The first record of a shipment of Negroes arriving in Carolina fol-

---

21. For this aversion of the Carolina planters, see the letters of Henry Laurens and the correspondence of Robert Pringle, *passim*: The Papers of Henry Laurens, South Carolina Historical Society; The Robert Pringle Letter Copy Book, South Carolina Historical Society.

22. See W. Robert Higgins, "The South Carolina Negro Duty Law, 1703-1775," unpub. M.A. thesis (University of South Carolina, 1967), for the role of governmental legislation upon the importation of Negroes to colonial Carolina. The £20 figure is for English sterling coin, not colonial currency.

23. Peter A. McClelland of Harvard University, in correspondence with the author, has confirmed a ratio of less than three men to two women in the trade of Carolina.

W. ROBERT HIGGINS

lowed settlement by only two years. In 1672, a Bermudan vessel brought a cargo of 125 Calabar slaves from the Niger River to Virginia, Bermuda, and Charleston. A second venture was made several years later, but at this time the black workers were sold in the northern portion of Carolina and Virginia.[24] The next known shipment from the Niger River arrived in 1719, and the last occurred only two years before the American Revolution. During this broad expanse of time, only about 1,380 slaves of all ages were imported in seven vessels from that region.[25] A comparison of Charleston's commerce from the Niger with that from other locations on the west coast of Africa reemphasizes the dislike of the Carolina planters for the Calabars.[26]

Although the first cargo of black workers to enter Carolina from the Gambia did not arrive until 1731, Negroes from that area of the slaving coast constituted the largest group of specifically enumerated blacks brought to Charleston. Trade between the Gambia and South Carolina was slight during the third decade of the eighteenth century and nonexistent throughout the 1740s. Regular trade began in 1750, however, and, with the exception of periods of prohibition, continued until the American Revolution.[27] A total of seventy cargoes from the Gambia carrying nearly 8,000 black laborers was received in Charleston during the colonial period. The preference shown by the Carolinians for Gambian slaves was thus firmly reflected by the volume and the frequency of trade in these workers.[28]

The area which supplied the second largest number of Negroes to colonial South Carolina was Angola. This southern extremity of English slaving was the point of embarkation for fifty-seven consignments received in Charleston between 1731 and 1775. Trade between the two areas was less regular than that between the Gambia and Charleston, but

24. Donnan, *Documents*, II, 48.

25. Naval Officer Shipping Returns, Duty Books. The author has prepared lists of the points of origin based upon these two voluminous sources.

26. ". . . Callabar Slaves wont go down when others can be had in plenty," Henry Laurens to DeVonsheir, Reeve, & Lloyd, May 22, 1755, in Laurens, *Papers*, I, 252.

27. Three times during the colonial period, in 1719-1722, 1741-1744, and 1766-1768, the South Carolina commons house barred the importation of slaves through the imposition of very high taxes. In 1770 the trade was interrupted by the Non-Importation Agreement.

28. Duty Books A, B, C, *passim*.

the number of Negroes in each of the consignments was significantly larger from Angola than from the northern point. Although few cargoes of black workers arriving in Carolina from Africa consisted of more than 200 slaves, many of the consignments from Angola exceeded 300, and one shipment approached 500. In 1760, during the French and Indian War, the partnership of Benjamin Smith and Joseph Nutt imported 460 children and adult slaves from Angola.[29]

The slaves brought to South Carolina from Sierra Leone followed the Gambia and Angola in total numbers. Cargoes of black workers shipped to Charleston from that area were designated as originating in Sierra Leone or in the two specific locations of Bance Island and Cape Mount Castle. In 1746 a small cargo of fifty-six adults and children from Cape Mount Castle was received by the minor slave merchant firm of Woodrop and Cathcart. Six years later a second and larger consignment of eighty-nine blacks from Cape Mount was imported to Charleston by the brothers John and James Deas. Like Woodrop and Cathcart, the Deas brothers were peripherally engaged in the slave trade rather than being a major firm providing Negroes to the settlers.[30]

The other specific location within Sierra Leone from which blacks were sent to South Carolina was Bance Island, in the mouth of the Sierra Leone River. Although the island had been used as a collection point for slaves throughout most of the period of English involvement in the trade, no black laborers were brought to Charleston from the island until the slaving station was operated by Richard Oswald of London. Oswald employed Laurens, his former business correspondent, to place the cargoes sent to Carolina between 1769 and 1774. Laurens had retired from active trade in slaves by this date, but remained a paid advisor to English slave merchants.

Through the auspices of Laurens, the six cargoes from Bance Island were sold in Charleston; two auctions were held by the cousins Thomas

---

29. Information from Naval Officer Shipping Returns and Duty Books, collated by the author.
30. See the relative position of the Deas brothers and Woodrop and Cathcart in the lists included in W. Robert Higgins, "South Carolina Merchants and Factors Dealing in the External Negro Trade, 1735-1775," *South Carolina Historical Magazine*, LXV (1964), 205-217.

Loughton Smith and Roger Smith, and the other four consignments were received and marketed by John Lewis Gervais. Laurens had long favored the Smiths with his business. Included among the magnates of Charleston, they were the scions of one of the great merchant families of Carolina. Fathers, uncles, and cousins had all been deeply involved in the importation of Negroes.[31] The two cargoes from Bance Island were only a small portion of their very extensive trade. John Lewis Gervais was a protégé and associate of Laurens; together they had speculated in western lands and planted indigo. Unlike the Smiths, Gervais was not a great slave merchant. Between 1772, when he began importing slaves, and 1774 he received only seven cargoes of black workers, four of which came from Bance Island. Of the nearly 800 slaves consigned to Charleston by Oswald from Bance Island, 524 were sold by Gervais.[32]

In addition to the shipments from Cape Mount Castle and Bance Island, the Carolinians received nine other cargoes of Negroes from the lands situated around the Sierra Leone River. These shipments, however, were designated by the more general listing of Sierra Leone. None arrived before the first year of the French and Indian War. After 1754, the cargoes arrived irregularly until the American Revolution. The age ranges in the shipments from the general area varied widely, and in this respect the cargoes differed from those originating on Bance Island. Most of Oswald's Negroes were prime hands, carefully selected on the west coast of Africa to bring the maximum prices in the Americas.[33]

Although the English did not acquire control over Senegal until the Seven Years' War, this northern area of the slave coast of West Africa supplied a large number of the Negroes in designated cargoes. Between 1759, when the British first entered Senegal, and the beginning of the War for Independence, more than 1,500 blacks of all ages were sent to Carolina. Within this period, the trade between the two areas assumed ever increasing dimensions. Had the trend not been terminated by the

31. George C. Rogers, Jr., *Evolution of a Federalist, William Loughton Smith of Charleston (1758-1812)* (Columbia, S.C., 1962), ch. 1 and genealogies.

32. Duty Book C, entries for the "Negro Duty."

33. Duty Book C, and statistics from W. Robert Higgins, "The Geographical Origins of Negroes in Colonial South Carolina," *South Atlantic Quarterly*, LXX (1971), 40-45.

American Revolution, Senegal would have become one of the major points of shipment of labor for the Carolina market.

In view of the high evaluation given black workers from the Gold Coast, the Carolina market received surprisingly few Negroes from the most preferred slaving area of West Africa. Only three consignments imported at the end of the colonial period came from locations along the Gold Coast. In 1772 and again in 1773, a single cargo of Negroes arrived in Charleston from Anamaboe. Both of the consignments were directed to Miles Brewton, the greatest of the South Carolina colonial slave merchants. The shipment in 1772 was unusually large and consisted of 345 black workers; the consignment of 1773 was smaller and differed in composition. While the vast majority of the 1772 cargo had been composed of black adults, approximately 40 percent of the shipment of 1773 was children. The latter consignment, therefore, was far less profitable than the former.[34]

The second location within the Gold Coast from which slaves were sent to Carolina was Cape Coast Castle. In 1772 a small parcel of workers arrived from Cape Castle, consigned to the brothers David and John Deas. As was the case with the first cargo of Negroes received by Brewton from Anamaboe, nearly all of the blacks shipped to the Deas brothers were fully grown. The ratio of adults to children shipped from Anamaboe and Cape Coast Castle indicates unusual care in acquiring slaves on the Gold Coast.[35]

Only one other specifically designated area on the west coast of Africa supplied blacks to South Carolina during the colonial period. In 1759, during the French and Indian War, the partners Thomas Middleton and Samuel Brailsford received a large number of Negroes from Whydah. Although the two men were deeply involved in the slave trade both alone and together, they never again sold a consignment of blacks from Whydah.[36]

Through the first third of the eighteenth century, many of the general listings for cargoes of black workers bore the name "Guinea." Al-

---

34. Higgins, *Slave Trade*, ch. 6.
35. Duty Book C, folio listings for Deas and Brewton.
36. The extent of the trade of Thomas Middleton and Samuel Brailsford is examined in Higgins, *Slave Trade*.

W. ROBERT HIGGINS

though this was a more limiting designation than "Africa," it still did not identify the exact origins of the consignments of Negroes. Between 1717, when the term was first used in the records of the Royal Naval Officer, Charleston, and 1733, when it was last recorded, twenty-one shipments of slaves were listed as having been sent from Guinea. During this seventeen-year period, over 2,500 blacks arrived in South Carolina designated as having been loaded within the broad area of West Africa known as Guinea.[37]

From the date of the first records of the colonial slave trade to South Carolina until the ending of the transatlantic commerce by the American Revolution, more than half of the cargoes of Negroes brought to Charleston from Africa bore no designation other than that of the continent as a whole. A total of 240 consignments carried this most general of all listings. For many of the black workers, no other designation would have been possible. Although the orders to a slaving captain specified the area along the west coast of Africa where he was to seek a cargo, he was also instructed to try to complete the loading if the fort or factory at that location did not have enough slaves. In order to fill the cargo, the master had to move up or down the coast to obtain the remainder of his consignment. Such wide range of movement was the rule rather than the exception, especially in the early years of the century. For a cargo consisting of black workers from two or more locations in West Africa, then, any designation more specific than the continent itself would have been difficult to make.[38]

Another reason for recording Africa rather than a specific point of origin along the west coast was that most planters of Carolina did not have strong preferences except an affinity for Gold Coast and Gambian blacks and a dislike of those from Calabar. Thus, for Negroes from locations other than these there was no real need for specification. Exact designation of the place of loading would neither increase their prices on the Charleston market nor decrease the demand for their services. In fact, generality and vagueness may even have been preferable.

There were other reasons for the failure to record a definite place of

37. Higgins, "Negro Duty Law," Appendix C, listings for Guinea.
38. Donnan, *Documents*, II, *The Eighteenth Century*, provides transcripts of many masters' logs as they moved along the west coast seeking a cargo.

origin for some of the cargoes of Negroes brought to colonial Charleston. The shipping returns and treasury ledgers were kept by clerks, most of whom were themselves recent arrivals within the province and unfamiliar with the slaving posts in Africa or with the men who dealt in the black trade. Rather than struggle with the unusual spelling of exotic place names such as Anamaboe or Whydah, it was far easier to write "Africa."[39] Also, the provincial and imperial governments required no designation more accurate than that of the continent of Africa. Regulation and taxation were based on the entire area of the southern continent, and not upon geographical locations within Africa.[40]

Three areas along the slaving coast of West Africa were not recorded as the origins of Negroes brought to South Carolina between 1672 and 1775. The Grain Coast, the Ivory Coast, and Majumba were never listed in the records of the Royal Naval Officer, Charleston, or in the duty books of the colonial treasurer. Although it is possible that some of the black cargoes bearing the general designation of Africa originated in one of these locations, it is unlikely. Surely somewhere among the hundreds of listings of consignments of Negroes these designations would have appeared had blacks been so received.

The slaves who arrived in South Carolina from one of the islands to the south of North America arrived under very different circumstances from those from Africa. While the trade from the southern continent represented over 85 percent of the traffic in black workers, the commerce from the Indies amounted to less than 15 percent. In spite of this, the number of separate parcels of workers arriving from the sugar islands exceeded the 410 consignments from Africa. Slaving ships from Africa were devoted to the single purpose of transporting black workers, but Negroes shipped to Charleston from one of the American island colonies arrived in small numbers. In virtually every case, the slaves constituted only a portion of a general cargo destined for South Carolina.[41]

39. "Africa" appears in three different spellings through the Duty Books. Although Henry Laurens was one of the major commercial and political figures of colonial South Carolina, his French Huguenot name was misspelled with regularity. One listing for him (29 Sept. 1765-25 March 1766) was even spelled Lawrence. Another slave merchant, Isaac DaCosta, suffered from similar inaccuracies.

40. See Higgins, "Negro Duty Law," 49-50, 52-53.

41. Two examples of such general cargo including slaves are found in "Naval Officer Shipping Returns:" June 9, 1739, the Schooner *Union*, John Chatfield master, from Providence. Cargo: 85 Negroes, 20 dozen Pineapples, 350 feet Madeira Plank, 9

W. ROBERT HIGGINS

The commerce in slaves from the southern islands varied from the African trade in one other significant respect: the type of merchant who received and sold the black workers in Charleston. The great magnates of the black commerce controlled the importations from Africa. Although they dealt in the American Negroes, such transactions were simply a convenience for the major merchants. In many cases, consignments of blacks were brought from the south by the magnates only to balance their trade with agents and factors in the tropical colonies. For this purpose, slaves were simply an alternative to money. Black workers were also used to complete partial cargoes sent from the sugar islands to Charleston.

Eighteen individuals and firms dominated the importation of slaves from Africa. Together, they sold over 60 percent of the blacks brought to South Carolina during the colonial period. The other 400 individuals who acquired slaves from outside Carolina supplied the remaining 40 percent; many of their workers were obtained from the neighboring American settlements rather than from the African source.[42]

Only four of the British islands made significant contributions to the labor supply of colonial South Carolina. The first blacks who came to the Ashley River were from Barbados. Throughout the following century, this sugar colony continued to dominate the intercolonial slave trade to Charleston. Following it in volume and in frequency of commerce were Antigua and Jamaica. As the seat of the legal and illegal trade between the English slavers and the Spanish colonists, Jamaica also attracted large numbers of Negroes. A portion of the blacks sent to Jamaica was later redirected to Carolina. Trade in Negroes from St. Christopher's existed at the time of the first records, and a small volume continued throughout the colonial period.

The other English island possessions, and those of the continental nations, furnished a few laborers for the fields and forests of South Carolina. The British North American colonies served the same function. With the exception of the Maritimes and New Jersey, all of the English mainland settlements at one time or another sent blacks to Carolina.

Casks Sugar, 30,000 Limes, 15 Yams. August 20, 1765, the Ship *Weatherill*, David Martin master, from St. Kitts. Cargo: 13 Negroes, 4 Barrels Sugar, 46 Hogsheads Rum, 2 Hogsheads Molasses.

42. Higgins, *Slave Trade*, ch. 6.

However, the importations from these areas were insignificant in comparison with the trade of the African coast.

The demand for slaves in South Carolina remained sizable throughout the colonial period. During only two years, 1773 and 1774, was the supply of black workers greater than could be immediately absorbed by the planters of the colony. In spite of the stable demand for additional workers, the Charleston merchants conducted a significant transshipment of Negroes through South Carolina to the neighboring English, Spanish, and French provinces. During the period from 1717 until 1775, more than 7,000 black workers passed through the entrepôt of Charleston to fill the labor needs of the adjoining colonies. The Negroes who were transshipped through the major port of South Carolina thus amounted to over 8 percent of the total importations throughout the entire colonial period.[43]

The settlement receiving the greatest number of blacks from Charleston was Georgia, the southernmost of the English mainland colonies. Approximately one-half of the 7,000 workers transshipped from Carolina went either to Savannah or to Sunbury. Georgia was not only the last of the British mainland colonies, but the only province which specifically barred the employment of Negroes, either free or slave. This prohibition was not removed until 1749, after the colony ceased to be a trusteeship and became a royal province. Despite the legal bar to the importation of slaves, a cargo of Negroes was sent from Charleston to Georgia within six years of the settlement of Savannah in 1733. The periods of heaviest trade between Carolina and the ports of Georgia were the years 1773 and 1774, when the greatest importations of Negroes occurred in Carolina. During those two years, the number of slaves sent to the colony across the Savannah River constituted a major portion of the total volume of workers brought to Charleston from all locations. For two years the transshipments to the colony of Georgia amounted to almost 15 percent of the total importations through Charleston during the same period.

The great transshipment of Negroes to Georgia was simply one as-

---

43. On a larger scale, the locations to which black workers were sent from Charleston extended from London to Campeche (Yucatan Peninsula) and from Rhode Island to Madeira and Portugal (*Higgins, Slave Trade,* ch. 4).

W. ROBERT HIGGINS

pect of the general trade pattern of the southern colony. At no time during the colonial period did the ports of Georgia develop a transatlantic market. Rather than establish their own commercial arrangements, the merchants of Savannah and Sunbury depended upon the wide business connections of the Charleston merchants to supply the needed imports of labor and manufactures and to ship and sell the produce of Georgia.[44]

The sister province of North Carolina absorbed the second largest number of slaves who passed through the entrepôt of South Carolina. The northern area of the original grant to the Lords Proprietors of Carolina remained isolated from the Atlantic world because of its inaccessible coastline as well as the lack of a major item of imperial trade. Instead of cultivating their own staple, the settlers of North Carolina competed with Virginia and Maryland in the production of tobacco, and followed the colonists of South Carolina in the planting of rice and indigo. Because of the monopoly given to the Chesapeake provinces, North Carolina tobacco was marketed only under the sufferance of the northern colonists. The northern location and the colder climate of the settlement rendered the production of tropical rice and indigo a marginal occupation. Such economic conditions created little desire and use for black slaves in North Carolina, so that virtually all of the limited labor needs of the northern colony were met with Negroes transshipped through Charleston.[45]

Limited numbers of Negroes were sent from South Carolina to the other English colonies along the eastern seaboard of North America, to the Spanish settlements in Florida, to the French colonists in Mobile and New Orleans, and to the West Indian and Caribbean plantations of all of the European nations. In many cases the use of Charleston as an entrepôt of the Atlantic slave trade did not conform to the pattern of black workers being shipped from the tropical colonies to the temperate prov-

---

44. Laurens, *Papers*, I, 309. In 1766 Governor James Wright of Georgia reported to the Board of Trade that his province had no direct commerce with the rest of the world. Instead, all trade outside the provincial coasting vessels passed through Charleston when entering or leaving Georgia. Bridenbaugh, *Cities in Revolt*, 262.

45. The trade in Negroes to North Carolina was small. In 1755 Governor Dobbs of North Carolina reported to the Board of Trade that the average number of Negroes entering the colony annually during the last seven years had been only seventeen. Donnan, *Documents*, IV, 237.

inces of the Americas. The two-way trade in new Negroes was obviously profitable, however, for it continued throughout the colonial period.

Although South Carolina was founded long after most of the English colonies of the Americas, within slightly more than a century the port of Charleston received approximately 90,000 slaves from Africa. This great importation of black workers was determined by the labor needs of the European settlers who produced agricultural staples for sale on the imperial and international markets. The cultivation and processing of rice and indigo required less brute strength than the production of sugar, but more physical labor than the tending of tobacco. For this reason, planters of Carolina demanded big strong Negroes, but they had no need to exclude women as did the West Indian slave owners.

The desire for a large and robust Negro who was also a willing worker controlled, to some extent, the choice of origins of slaves imported for sale in Charleston. The Negroes of the Gambia, the Gold Coast, and Angola, because of their preferred characteristics, were sought by the planters of Carolina and yielded higher prices on the colonial market. The settlers of South Carolina also determined, in large measure, the route traveled by slaves on their way to service in the fields and forests of the province. As we have seen, a strong dislike of blacks who had been enslaved in other settlements of the Americas limited the slave trade with the West Indies and Jamaica. Thus the needs and preferences of the South Carolina planters dictated which areas along the west coast of Africa would supply black labor, and forced direct shipment.

The merchants of the capital and port established intricate business connections and developed great financial acumen in order to meet the needs of the Carolina settlers. In time the Charleston slave merchants expanded their fields of activity and met the labor demands not only of South Carolina but of the entire southeastern area of the present United States. Charleston thus became the largest terminus of the Atlantic slave trade to English North America, and the major entrepôt for Negroes brought from Africa to work in other colonies.

6

Leslie B. Rout, Jr.

The African
in Colonial Brazil

The Transatlantic Slave Trade To Brazil

The origin of the slave trade to Brazil is rooted in the establishment of sub-Saharan Africans as useful and comparatively inexpensive labor agents by the Portuguese. They had become acquainted with the black man during the period of Moorish rule (711 A.D.-1249 A.D.) in what is today Portugal, and as early as 1258 Barbary Coast slave dealers had begun peddling black bondsmen at the semiannual fairs held in Guimar-.ães.[1] A small-scale traffic in these dusky-skinned properties would continue at least until the fifteenth century, but since the Moors monopolized the trans-Saharan trade routes and charged high prices, this trade would never develop to its full potential.[2] Then in 1443 Antão Gonçalves, whom Prince Henry the Navigator had dispatched as part of his general program of southern exploration, returned to Portugal with possibly the first cargo of blacks directly obtained by Europeans on the coast of West Africa.[3] In order to facilitate this traffic (and also that in gold dust and spices), Portuguese traders moved to create trading stations at Arguin (1445), on the African coast between Cape Verde and Sierra Leone (1446-1458), at São Jorge da Mina (1482) and on the islands of São Tomé and

---

1. Anthony Luttrell, "Slavery and Slaving in the Portuguese Atlantic (to about 1500)," in Centre of African Studies, University of Edinburgh, *The Transatlantic Slave Trade from West Africa* (Edinburgh, 1965), 64.

2. *Ibid.*, 64-65; Charles Verlinden, *Les origines de la civilisation Atlantique* (Paris, 1966), 16, 175-176.

3. Still the best history of the 1441-1442 adventures of Antão Gonçalves is Gomes Eannes de Zurara, *Chronique de Guinée* (Dakar, 1960), 78-94.

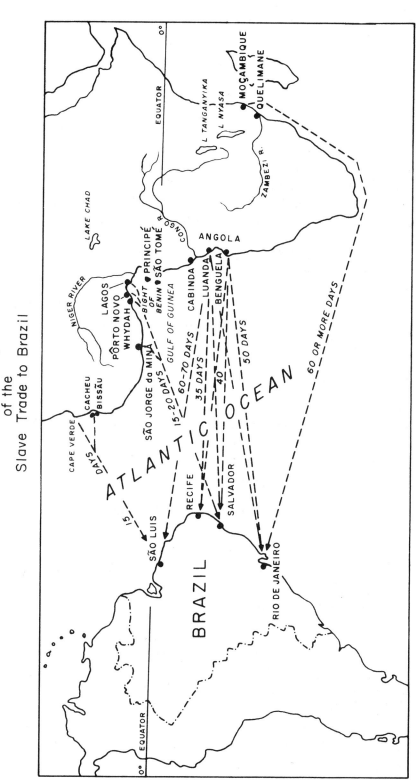

Slave Ports and Major Routes
of the
Slave Trade to Brazil

After 1700, the leading Brazilian ports per volume of slaves landed were
(1) Rio de Janeiro (2) Salvador (3) Recife (4) São Luis

LESLIE B. ROUT, JR.

Principé (1493-1495). These bases, plus those subsequently established at
the mouth of the Congo River, in Angola, Moçambique, and in the Gulf
of Guinea, would furnish virtually every African landed in Brazil.

Exactly when the first black slaves arrived in Portuguese America is
unknown, but the earliest recorded shipment from Africa to Brazil was
made in 1538 by Lopes Bixorda, a slave dealer in the *capitanía* of Bahia.[4]
The following year Duarte Coelho, grantee of the *capitanía* of Pernambuco, petitioned the crown for a license to import "merchandise" (i.e.,
slaves)[5] and in 1545 Pedro de Goes submitted a similar request. Finally,
in response to a petition by Bahian plantation owners who complained of
"the great lack of labor which is increasingly felt in the sugar mills and
the cane fields," in March 1549 João IV authorized each planter to import
up to 120 slaves.[6] The massive importation of Africans began from that
date, and the flood continued for three hundred years.

Standards and Prices

For the purposes of this study, we will commence the story of the
African's journey to Brazil with his arrival at a slave depot in Angola,
Moçambique, or Cape Verde. There he was usually baptized, branded to
show that the proper taxes had been paid on him, and then ambiguously
classified as a *peça da India*. The ideal *peça* was a male in good health,
somewhere between the ages of fifteen and thirty-five, standing "siete
quartas da altura" (5 feet, 6 or 7 inches tall).[7] Actual conformity to this

---

4. A *capitanía* was the largest political and administrative unit in colonial Brazil.
It was ruled by a governor (called a *capitão-geral*). Before 1822 fifteen *capitanías* had
been established. Many of the states of contemporary Brazil were *capitanías* during
the colonial era.

5. "Merchandise" is precisely the way Coelho referred to the African slave. See
Renato Mendonça, *A influência africana do português no Brasil* (São Paulo, 1935, 2d
ed.), 53.

6. Pierre Verger, *Bahia and the West Coast Trade: 1549-1851* (Ibadan, 1964), 1.

7. Historians differ as to the exact length of a *quarta*. Edmundo Correia Lopes, *A
escravatura* (Lisbon, 1944), 13, and Maurício Goulart, *Escravidão africana no Brasil:
Das origens a extinção do tráfico* (São Paulo, 1950, 2d ed.), 102, established 7 *quartas*
as 1.75 meters, but Affonso de Escragnolle Taunay, "Subsídios para a história do tráfico africano no Brasil colonial," *Revista do instituto de historia e geografía* (hereafter
RIHG), Anais, III Congresso de história nacional (Rio de Janeiro, 1941), III, 593-594,
insists that no one really knows how tall a prime *peça da India* was supposed to stand.
See also Miller, above, 94 n.

standard was rare, and so slave shippers had to fashion more adaptable criteria in offering captives to prospective customers. Two males between the ages of thirty-five and forty-five came to equal one *peça*, while three youths, eight to perhaps fifteen years old, were the equivalent of two *peças*. Any number of elderly, sick, or deformed slaves might also equal one *peça*. Since the female slaves could not perform the heavy mine and field labor desired, they generally sold in Africa for less than males.[8]

After he arrived in Brazil, the newly landed slave was called a *boçal*, a term which implied that he spoke no Portuguese. A captive who either understood Portuguese or displayed a familiarity with Lusitanian customs might be labeled a *ladino*, and as such was a more valuable sales item. Slaves were also categorized according to their supposed place of origin. Those blacks allegedly emanating from Angola, the mouth of the Congo River, or Moçambique were referred to as Bantu; these were the slaves most commonly found in Brazil. More highly regarded were those shipped from the Cape Verde-Portuguese Guinea region, while the *crème de la crème* were healthy captives from Gulf of Guinea ports, commonly referred to as Minas.[9]

Throughout the seventeenth century, the price of slaves rose steadily. In 1611, for example, slaves from Angola sold in Recife for 21$000[10] a *peça*, but in the same year and the same place, a *peça* from Cape Verde sold for 40$000. After 1650, Angolans sold at an average of 80$000, while Gulf of Guinea-Cape Verde blacks cost slightly more than 100$000 a *peça*. With the discovery of gold in Minas Gerais about 1695,

8. There is also serious disagreement in regard to the age span of a prime *peça*. Taunay, "Subsídios," 589, states "no more than 20 years," Goulart, *Escravidão*, 102, says 30-35 years, and C. R. Boxer, *The Dutch in Brazil: 1624-1654* (Oxford, 1957), 231, says that in Angola the age was 15-25 years. The figure in the text above is therefore a composite.

9. In Rio de Janeiro (or Minas Gerais) a Mina was any slave from territories north of the equator. In Bahia, and to some extent Pernambuco, the term originally referred only to the Ashanti people, or slaves embarked from São Jorge da Mina. Blacks from stations on the coast of Dahomey were termed Gegês. Yoruba tribesmen shipped from Pôrto Novo or Lagos were referred to as Nagôs. Muslim tribesmen from northern Nigeria, western Sudan, or the Lake Chad region were called Hausás. It should also be noted that in Bahia any and all Muslim blacks (Hausás or not) were generically termed Malês. An excellent discussion of the Brazilian practices in classifying slaves is to be found in Arthur Ramos, *Introdução à antropologia brasileira* (Rio de Janeiro, 1943), I, 324-330, 353-354, 361-362, 389, 402, 414, 423.

10. The Portuguese monetary units were established as follows: 1,000 reis = 1 milreis (1$000); 1,000 milreis = 1 conto (1:000$000).

LESLIE B. ROUT, JR.

slave prices spiraled sharply higher; responding to colonial complaint, the Portuguese government placed a ceiling of 160$000 per *peça* on newly landed slaves. This effort at price stabilization was a futile gesture, for by 1718, *peças* identified as Minas were selling in Rio de Janeiro for 300-360$000.[11]

The decline of the gold mining industry after 1770, plus the preference in European markets for West Indian sugar, were crippling blows to the Brazilian economy. The price of slaves in Pernambuco fell to 100-120$000 in 1787, but a boom in cotton production and a temporary recovery for Brazilian sugar resulted in partial stabilization around 1800. By 1810 the general price for good quality *peças* was again climbing upward to 300$000.[12]

The Legal Trade in Slaves

The right to procure slaves on the African coast and sell them in Portugal had, since 1469, been an exclusive privilege (*assento*) sold by the crown to favored national groups or persons. In 1587, for example, Pedro de Sevelha and Antonio Lomego purchased the franchise over slave sales in Moçambique. But these dealers did not arrange for the shipment of "black cargoes" to Brazil. Lisbon preferred to regulate that phase of the trade by selling licenses to individual shippers at 22-80,000 cruzados annually.[13] Not only individuals but groups such as the city council of Rio de Janeiro attempted to buy these slaves.

---

11. For these prices see Edison Carneiro, *Antología do negro brasileiro* (Pôrto Alegre, 1950), 99; *idem, Ladinos e Crioulos: Estudos sôbre o negro no Brasil* (Rio de Janeiro, 1964), 58-59; Correia Lopes, *A escravatura*, 62. Prices varied greatly from region to region. Pedro Calmon, *História social do Brasil* (São Paulo, 1937, 2d ed.), I, 174, records that in 1692 a Mina sold in Bahia for as low as 60$000, but during the same year the asking price for a prime *peça* in Maranhão was almost 160$000.

12. See Correia Lopes, *A escravatura*, 137-139, for the 1780s prices, Carneiro, *Antología*, 100, for the 1810 figure. Evidence of rising slave prices in the 1780-1800 era can be found in Dave Denslow, Jr., "Economic Considerations in the Treatment of Slaves in Brazil and Cuba," unpub. paper read at conference on An International Comparison of Systems of Slavery, University of Rochester, 1972. This paper was not included in Stanley L. Engerman and Eugene D. Genovese (eds.), *Race and Slavery in the Western Hemisphere: Quantitative Studies* (Princeton, 1975).

13. One cruzado equals 325 reis. By the last quarter of the seventeenth century the value of the cruzado had risen to 400 reis.

The African in Colonial Brazil

By 1655 the trade had grown enormously, with over a hundred ships involved. The crown, concluding that more revenue could be obtained through closer control, chartered two agents, the Companhía de Cacheu (1685) and the Companhía de Estanco do Maranhão (1682). They were given monopoly privileges over the transport and sale of slaves to Brazil, the latter company having rights to Maranhão and Grão Pará, while the other held title to the rest of Portuguese America. Owned primarily by metropolitan citizens, the Companhía de Cacheu lasted exactly five years. Reorganized as the Companhía de Cabo Verde e Cacheu de ne-gócios dos prêtos (1690) it also held a monopoly over the slave trade to Spanish America from 1696 to 1701; loss of the contract eventually bankrupted the organization.[14]

Even less fortunate were the entrepreneurs who owned the Com-panhía de Estanco do Maranhão; by terms of its contract, 10,000 *peças* were to be delivered over a twenty-year period. In actuality, the company delivered none, for in response to a petition from settlers in that territory the crown established 100$000 a *peça* as the maximum charge. The contract holders refused to deliver at that price, and in 1684, angry Luso-Brazilians[15] in the town of São Luís (Maranhão) rioted and de-manded that the monopoly be ended; King Pedro II ordered the contract canceled forthwith.[16]

With the demise of these two organizations, Brazil again experienced open trade in slaves, but under the aegis of the energetic Marquis de Pombal (1750-1778) the metropolitan government reasserted itself in forms reminiscent of times past. He sold the rights to deliver slaves in northern Brazil to the Companhia do Grão Pará e Maranhão (1755), and for part of the northeast to the Companhia do Comércio de Pernambuco e Paraíba (1759).[17] Both commercial syndicates were owned by favored

14. Mendonça, *A influência*, 52-57. In 1701 Philip of Anjou succeeded the last Hapsburg king of Spain, and he and his grandfather, Louis XIV, went into the slave trade for themselves.

15. "Luso-Brazilian" in this essay refers to all American- or European-born whites who lived in colonial Brazil.

16. For the complete story, see Arthur César Ferreira Reis, "O Estado do Maranhão catesque do gentía: rebeliões pacificadas," *RIHG, Anais, IV Congresso* (Rio de Ja-neiro, 1950), II, 148-156; Correia Lopes, *A escravatura*, 124-125.

17. The reader may be confused as to the number of *capitanías* involved and the jurisdictions of the companies. Paraíba and Pernambuco were separately ruled units,

LESLIE B. ROUT, JR.

metropolitan interests (the Marquis de Pombal himself being a stock-holder) who intended to supply not only slaves, but also funds toward the economic development of their respective areas. By 1778 they had shipped at least 63,522 slaves to Brazil, but with the dismissal of the Marquis de Pombal (1778) came the loss of their special privileges.[18] After that date, claims Mendonça, the slave trade was characterized by "great confusion" and "contraband."[19] What actually occurred was a tacit reversion to the free-trade policy, an event which signified the crown's grudging recognition that centralized control of the slave trade to Brazil was simply not feasible.

The Illicit Trade: Bahia and the Gulf of Guinea Traffic

From 1580 until 1640, Portugal was under the control of the kings of Spain. This change in dynastic rule proved disastrous for colonial trade, for when Dutch sea-dogs began ravaging Spanish-American ports and treasure fleets, those of Portugal also became fair game. The resourceful Dutch West India Company made a determined bid to acquire both the Brazilian sugar trade and the slave traffic on which the former depended. West India Company forces seized Bahia for ten months in 1624-1625 and held Pernambuco from 1630 to 1654. Meanwhile, on the African coast, they captured São Jorge da Mina (1638) and occupied both Angola and the island of São Tomé from 1641 to 1648.

Recovering their independence from Spain in 1640, the Portuguese initiated a desperate campaign to regain their American and African holdings. They succeeded everywhere except São Jorge da Mina, but this single failure meant that Portugal now lacked a slave station in the Gulf of Guinea. After 1648, however, the Dutch West India Company began

---

the civil governors of which were subject to the authority of the viceroy of Brazil. Maranhão and Grão Pará were separate regions, but they were administered as one *capitanía*, the governor of which (from 1621 to 1774) was not subject to the viceroy, but only to Lisbon.

18. The figures are from Taunay, "Subsídios," 567, and Alfredo Gomes, "Archegas para a história do tráfico africano no Brazil: Aspectos numéricos," *RIHG, Anais, IV Congresso,* V. 63. Some 25,365 slaves were delivered to Maranhão-Grão Pará, and 38,167 to Pernambuco and Paraíba. Even after the monopoly rights were voided, both companies continued trade and investment operations in the *capitanías* cited.

19. Mendonça, *A influência,* 59.

allowing vessels flying the Portuguese flag to trade at four depots it held east of São Jorge.[20] This concession was not without a price tag, for other than gold dust, the Dutch would only accept in exchange for quality *peças* the Bahian rolls of tobacco so highly esteemed by Africans.[21] Even after negotiations between Bahian slavers and a Dahomey princeling culminated in the establishment of a Portuguese concession at Whydah (1725), Dutch patrol ships continued to force Luso-Brazilians to land 10 percent of the tobacco rolls carried at São Jorge, or suffer total confiscation of cargo.

Lisbon had previously banned the payment of this tobacco tax, but as Bahian traders had the product, and the demand for Minas steadily increased, royal officials chose not to enforce this order. After 1725, the crown became increasingly exasperated with Dutch tactics and seriously considered enforcing a decree prohibiting slave trading in the Gulf of Guinea. This step was never taken, however, for Bahians effectively argued that if the trade stopped, the economic life of the *capitania* would be permanently injured and royal tax revenues would suffer accordingly.[22] Furthermore, they guardedly hinted that prohibition of the trade would encourage contraband traffic and indelicately suggested that Lisbon could easily end Dutch extortion by reconquering São Jorge. Reluctantly concluding that the most judicious step was not to force the issue, João V in 1743 authorized twenty-four Bahian ships to trade in the Gulf of Guinea.

Portuguese policy took an abrupt turn under the Marquis de Pombal, who had no intention of allowing the impertinent colonials to determine the parameters of royal commercial policy. Intent upon ruining the defiant Bahians, in 1756 he authorized vessels flying the Portuguese flag to trade on the Guinea Coast, but barred the twenty-four recipients of the 1743 privilege from operating there. The Marquis de Pombal had

20. Specifically, these stations were Jaquín, Apa, Grand Popo, and Whydah, all in contemporary Benin (Dahomey).

21. Verger, *Bahia*, 5. The role of tobacco in the Dahomean slave trade, the African preference for what was third-class Bahian tobacco, and the European scramble to obtain the Bahian product is related in Verger, 5-10. Eight to sixteen rolls of tobacco bought one slave.

22. *Ibid.*, 10-20. Verger relates the long struggle between the crown and the Bahian slave merchants (who organized the Mesa de ben comun dos homens de negócios da Bahia in 1723).

LESLIE B. ROUT, JR.

played an ace in opening this traffic to other traders, but the Bahians still held the tobacco trump. Thus, the clever maneuvering failed to prevent the 1743 monopolists from continuing to trade in the forbidden area.[23]

Slave Trade Statistics

A favorite sport among Portuguese and Brazilian scholars has been to estimate how many heads, or *peças*, were landed in Brazil between 1550 and the end of Portuguese rule in September 1822. These figures are of questionable validity,[24] but they do give some indication of why it is said that almost one-third of the value of Brazil's colonial empire commerce consisted of slave imports.[25]

Authors	Total	Period of Time
Mauricio Goulart	2,250,000	1550-1800
Affonso de E. Taunay	2,500,000	1550-1822
Edmundo Correia Lopes	2,750,000	1550-1800
Luiz Viana Filho	4,300,000	1550-1830
Renato Mendonça	4,830,000	1550-1830
Caio Prado Júnior	5-6,000,000	". . . to 1800"
João Calógeras	8,175,000	1550-1800

Even if Goulart's or de E. Taunay's modest computations are the most accurate, more slaves were probably shipped to Brazil than to any other area of the New World.[26] This suggests that without the mobility provided by the dusky mass of backs, arms, and legs, colonial Brazil would have ground to a halt.

---

23. *Ibid.*, 16-18. Bahian dealers beginning in 1757 moved to circumvent the Marquis de Pombal's ruling by trading at stations in the Bight of Benin.

24. The sources for these figures are: Goulart, *Escravidão*, 272; Affonso de E. Taunay, *Subsídios para a história do tráfico africano no Brasil* (São Paulo, 1941), 305; Correia Lopes, *A escravatura*, 150; Luiz Viana Filho, *O negro na Bahia* (São Paulo, 1946), 100; Mendonça, *A influência*, 72; Caio Prado Júnior, *The Colonial Background of Modern Brazil* (Berkeley, 1967, 1st English ed.), 116; João Calogeras, *Política exterior do Império*, special ed. from *RIHG* (São Paulo, 1927), I, 302.

25. Prado Júnior, *Colonial Background*, 270. The actual estimate by this author is between 30 and 35 percent of the total trade.

26. Philip Curtin, *The Atlantic Slave Trade: A Census* (Madison, 1970), 268.

Slavery In Brazil

Overview

Pedro de Magalhães de Gandavo, who visited Brazil during the sixteenth century, proffered the following advice to future Portuguese immigrants:

> As soon as persons who intend to live in Brazil become inhabitants of the country, however poor they may be, if each one obtains two pairs or one-half dozen slaves . . . he then has the means for sustenance.[27]

Given the millions of blacks subsequently imported into the colony, it would appear that the Luso-Brazilians took Magalhães de Gandavo's counsel to heart. But he never could have envisioned the multiplicity of occupations in which Africans would be used. Not only were they field hands, domestics, peddlers, miners, bodyguards, skilled laborers, and objects of sexual gratification, but also soldiers, overseers, and thieves. In Minas Gerais, blind whites had their slaves beg for them; in both that *capitanía* and Bahia, female properties were rented to brothels or ordered to sell their favors to whoever desired to pay the going price. In some cases whites lived off the proceeds gathered from renting their blacks to entrepreneurs, and occasionally slaves owned other slaves, thereby obtaining money for themselves while laboring for someone else.[28]

The very diversity of labor performed by slaves had a tremendous impact on the kind of tasks free persons regarded as fitting. Like the Spaniard, the Portuguese immigrant felt that he was a *fidalgo*, or "son of somebody." This in itself made manual labor abhorrent, and as the English writer Robert Southey laconically reported of late eighteenth-century Brazil, "never is it seen [that] a white man . . . [will] take an agrarian instrument in his hands."[29] This disdain for physical exertion even extended to modes of personal accommodation. Only slaves and

---

27. Pedro de Magalhães de Gandavo (John B. Stetson, Jr., ed.), *The Histories of Brazil* (New York, 1922), II, 152.

28. For examples of the unusual nature of slaveholding in Brazil, see C. R. Boxer, *The Golden Age of Brazil, 1695-1750* (Berkeley, 1962), 138, 156, 199; Robert E. Conrad, "The Struggle for the Abolition of the Brazilian Slave Trade: 1808-1853," unpub. Ph.D. thesis (Columbia University, 1967), 29-30.

29. Robert Southey, *History of Brazil* (New York, 1970), III, 828.

LESLIE B. ROUT, JR.

free colored walked; persons of any social stature either rode horses or were carried about in sedan chairs or hammocks. In the city of Salvador, horse-drawn carts and carriages did not supplant the sedan chairs as the favored means of locomotion until 1850.[30]

Nevertheless, it would be a distorted picture if the African slave were presented only as a human tool or beast of burden, for the African bondsman was at once both labor and capital. The Brazilian colonial economy was geared to the production of otherwise unobtainable raw materials for Portugal. Colonial initiative in creating iron-making, textile, and gold-manufacturing industries was vetoed by the crown, and since there were virtually no banks, the slave often became the unit of value. Hence, Pascoal de Silva Guimares in eighteenth-century Minas Gerais might have many gold coins, but he was rich because he possessed a retinue of 3,000 slaves.[31] The possession of blacks thus became a hedge against inflation, for they could always be exchanged for some other material object.

Economic considerations were not, however, the only ones which made slavery in Brazil indispensable. Robert Walsh relates that during the 1820s a mechanical crane was brought from England to Rio de Janeiro. Installed on the unloading pier, it allowed two slaves to accomplish the work of twenty. Alas, this step toward modernity was successfully resisted by the port authorities. While many of them owned slaves who worked as stevedores, Walsh's report suggests that the opposition to the crane was engendered by more than fear of economic loss.[32] One could not, after all, cajole, joke with, beat, threaten, or share with a machine. In Brazilian society at least, the ownership of another human being provided certain intangible social and psychological benefits.

While France promulgated the Code Noir (1685) for its possessions, and Charles IV of Spain issued the Código Negro Español (1789) to govern slave conduct in his American domain, all that existed for Brazil was a confused jumble of decrees and recommendations, based on the

---

30. See L. Anselmo da Fonseca, *A escravidão: O clero e o abolicionismo* (Bahia, 1887), 182-184.

31. See Calmon, *História social*, I, 146. This author's succinct statement is that the "unit of value was the Negro," 78. See also Conrad, "The Struggle," 18-20.

32. Robert Walsh, *Notices on Brazil in 1828 and 1829* (London, 1830), II, 362.

Ordenações Filipinas of 1603.[33] The slave provisions therein were probably intended primarily to govern the activities of slaves in Portugal, while the Leis Extravagantes[34] were subsequently added to regulate the conduct of bondsmen in Brazil. Many of these were intended for enforcement in one *capitania* and not another, and no effort was made to clear up any contradiction which may have developed.

The failure of Portugal's crowned heads to create a systematic slave code does not mean, however, that Lisbon chose to ignore the treatment of slaves in Brazil. In 1684, Pedro II ordered the governor of Pernambuco not to permit the excessive punishment of slaves, and also decreed that those mistreated be sold to more compassionate persons. Fourteen years later, this same monarch deplored the barbarity with which slaves were treated in Bahia and ordered the viceroy to look into the matter, but also cautioned him against either antagonizing the slavocracy or exciting the slave population. Given these strictures, one wonders what kind of investigation the king's chief representative was expected to make. The point would seem to be that a plea for human charity was to be made, but disruption of the social order was not contemplated.

Freyre, possibly the leading apologist for Brazilian slavery, points out that the sugar planters of the northeast considered themselves loyal subjects of Portugal, but exercised "absolute power" over their human properties; they would brook significant interference from neither crown nor clergy.[35] An historical example of the power of the landholding aristocracy and the desire of the crown to assure itself of the loyalty of this class can be seen in the developments surrounding the publication of the general *alvará* of 1741.[36] Intended for proclamation throughout Brazil, this decree commanded that all escaped slaves apprehended in a *quilombo*[37] were to be branded on the shoulder blade with the letter *F* (*fujão*). It further stipulated that if the captured slave was known to have committed a serious crime, or had been previously branded, he was to

---

33. I.e., *Laws of Philip III*, who was then king of Spain and Portugal.
34. Literally, "extra laws" added to the Ordenações.
35. Gilberto Freyre, *Brazil: An Interpretation* (New York, 1945), 38.
36. *Alvará*, a royal decree which had the force of law for one year unless, as was most common, there were clauses in it which kept it in effect indefinitely.
37. A *quilombo* was defined as a settlement of five or more escaped slaves; some, like the celebrated *quilombo* of Palmares, might have had thousands of inhabitants.

lose an ear. A total of forty lashes plus additional torture could be dealt the captive, depending on the circumstances, and he was to be either jailed or tied to a whipping post until retrieved by his master.[38]

In executing this statute, the Luso-Brazilians proved themselves much more inclined toward drastic action than the crown. Some colonial officials and security forces simply dispensed with the symbolic act of branding the escapee and hung him on the spot, claiming the bondsman would flee at the first opportunity. Such presumptive action angered slave owners, who insisted that they alone would decide whether their "properties" should live or die. Obligingly, Lisbon modified the 1741 *alvará* to state that only the slave's owner could decide the fate of a runaway.[39]

There can be no doubt that some masters allowed their slaves to cultivate private vegetable patches, and others taught their bondsmen trades and respected the integrity of the slave family. The point is that these allowances were precisely that, for the fundamental law of the slave was the will of his master. Demonstrative of this situation is the fact that over one half-century after independence, the Imperial Court in Rio de Janeiro (1879) ruled that since a slave was not legally a person, he could enter a plea in a court of law only against another slave.[40]

At no time prior to 1822 did the Brazilian clergy as a group question the legitimacy of the African slave trade. That the Roman Catholic church in Portuguese America would have done so was unlikely, since the crowned heads of Portugal exercised the powers of *padroado*[41] over it, and the slave trade was a state-sanctioned industry. Probably the majority agreed with Father Antônio Vieira that cheap labor was absolutely vital, and if the Indian were to be saved, then the African had to suffer. Yet in 1758 Father Manoel Ribeira da Rocha published a tract condemning the transoceanic slave trade as being "against all divine and

---

38. Affonso Cláudio, "As tribus negras importadas," *RIHG, Anais, I Congresso* (Rio de Janeiro, 1915), I, 643-645.

39. *Ibid.*, 645-647.

40. Carneiro, *Antología*, 70.

41. Rights of royal patronage. As a result of a series of agreements signed between 1456 and 1514, the king of Portugal gained the right to name all New World bishops, collect tithes, and regulate all papal correspondence with Portuguese or Brazilian bishops.

human law." In contrast, Bishop José Joaquim da Cunha de Azevedo of Bahia published in 1809 a sophisticated justification of both slavery and the Atlantic trade, and another priest, Junario de Cunha Mattos, became a tiger in defense of these institutions during the early years of political independence.[42] Throughout the colonial era individual clerics and religious orders owned slaves, while agricultural lands owned by the church produced wealth thanks to the sweat of their human properties. On occasion, a priest or bishop might attempt to secure milder treatment or a remission of punishment for a slave in some diocese or parish, but no formal pattern of ecclesiastical intervention on behalf of the African bondsman emerged between 1550 and 1822.

What the church did conceive to be its primary mission was the conversion of the African to Catholic Christianity and the eventual salvation of his soul. The majority of the slaves landed in Brazil were probably baptized sooner or later, but a moot point is the degree of religious instruction received and the spiritual care given. Note that slave unions were supposed to be blessed in the sacrament of matrimony, but the weight of evidence demonstrates that most such matings were "natural and illicit," the owners reserving the right to sell small children and separate married couples.[43] Probably the only assistance consistently supplied by the church to the African slave was in the formation of the religious brotherhoods (irmandades), an institution which will be discussed in the third section of this study.

Provided in many cases with only a smattering of Christian doctrine, millions of blacks simply intermixed Catholic and African religious beliefs. The African deities (orishas) became identified with various Christian saints, and modified in their nature under the influence of fresh waves of slave importations from different sections of sub-Saharan Africa. The emerging mélange of beliefs and practices became known as macumba in Rio de Janeiro and Pernambuco, where Bantu bondsmen seem to have been more numerous. In Bahia and other areas where

42. The source for all these examples is José Honório Rodrigues, Brazil and Africa (Berkeley, 1965), 36. For Ribeira da Rocha's quotation, see Cláudio, "As tribus," 646. For other defenses of slavery, see André João Antônil, Cultura e opulência do Brasil por suas drogas e minas (Rio de Janeiro, 1963, 3rd ed.), 19; Manoel da Nóbrega, Cartas do Brasil (Rio de Janeiro, 1931, 2d ed.), 126.

43. Agostinho Marques Perdigão Malheiro, A escravidão no Brasil (São Paulo, 1944, 2d ed.), I, 56.

LESLIE B. ROUT, JR.

Yoruba influence predominated, the amalgam of rites was called *candomblé*. Students of Afro-Brazilian syncretism have attempted to explain these ceremonial practices and the process of their evolution, but published studies of these matters have produced little in the way of a scholarly consensus.[44]

The Luso-Brazilian reaction to *candomblé* and *macumba* varied considerably. Some rural slave masters allowed the dances and chants which were inevitably a part of the ceremonies, believing that such activities helped make the slave more content with his lot. Others would not allow their slaves to participate, so such services had to be conducted in secret. Particularly in towns, ecclesiastical authorities tried to ensure that the "new Christians" did not relapse into the paganism of their ancestors. Some city councils banned public celebrations (i.e., religious singing, dancing) by all colored persons.[45]

Still another form of religious worship introduced into Brazil (especially in Bahia) by African slaves was that of Islam, the major advocates of which were Hausá. The Luso-Brazilians would not tolerate the propagation or outward manifestation of Muslim principles, but priests called *alúfas* conducted clandestine services for the faithful. In time, however, even the Muslims tended to incorporate other religious practices into the rites, but they maintained a separate identity throughout the colonial period.[46]

Africans were forcibly Christianized, but many passively accepted the new religious beliefs; the degree to which Christian principles were understood, however, was a different matter. It is very easy to visualize the slave at mass, the crucifix in one hand and a *fetiche*[47] in his pocket. He was probably not certain which artifact would provide him with the

---

44. Outstanding studies on assorted aspects of Afro-Brazilian syncretism include Roger Bastide (trans. Peter Green), *African Civilisations in the New World* (New York, 1971); Arthur Ramos, *O negro brasileiro: Ethnographía, religiosa e psychanalyse* (Rio de Janeiro, 1934); José Ribeiro, *Candomblé no Brasil: Fetichísmo religioso afro-americano* (Rio de Janeiro, 1957). A typical discussion of conflicts in findings and interpretations in the study of this phenomenon is found in Carneiro, *Ladinos*, 223-227.

45. Boxer, *Golden Age*, 9; Octavio Ianni, *As metamorfoses do escravo* (Sao Paulo, 1962), 149.

46. On the Muslims imported into Brazil, see Ramos, *Introdução*, I, 423-429.

47. Or fetish, a magical charm which is supposed to protect its possessor from evil spells or bad fortune.

greatest aid and comfort and, given his subordinate social position, there was no reason to take any chances.

Slavery in the Northeast

The history of colonial Brazil's economy is a record of shifts from one export product to another, the most important being sugar cane, which was shipped to Europe from 1546 on. Grown first in what is now São Paulo state, sugar cane came to be cultivated primarily on the northeastern seaboard. The *capitanías* of Pernambuco and Bahia became the chief centers, but Rio de Janeiro, Espírito Santo, Paraíba, and Rio Grande do Norte were also significant producers. Between 1600 and 1700 some 2,925,000 tons of sugar were exported, but during the last quarter of the seventeenth century West Indian sugar began to replace the Brazilian product in European markets. By 1700 prices had fallen as much as 90 percent, and planters in Bahia and Pernambuco began abandoning their landholdings and moving their slaves to the gold fields of western Bahia, Minas Gerais, and Mato Grosso.[48] Prices for Brazilian sugar remained low through the eighteenth century until the slave rebellion in Saint-Domingue suddenly sparked a new demand for this product in European markets.

In discussing the relationship between the African slave and sugar, Antônil, the Jesuit chronicler, relates that "the slaves are the hands and feet of the *Senhores de Engenho.*"[49] We have already seen that as early as 1549 Bahian planters had equated increased sugar production with a ready supply of blacks; during the 1645-1654 war against the Dutch in Pernambuco one of the passwords of the Brazilian rebels was "sugar," to which the countersign was "slaves."[50] Truly the reign of "King Cotton" in

---

48. See Goulart, *Escravidão*, 123. The sugar export figure, given by Goulart as 180,000,000 arrobas, has been converted at 1 arroba = 32½ pounds avoirdupois. On the collapse of the sugar boom, see J. F. Normano, *Brazil: A Study of Economic Types* (New York, 1968, 2d ed.), 21.

49. "Gentlemen of the sugar mill" was the name given to owners of large sugar plantations in northeastern Brazil. The source of the quotation is Antônil, *Cultura*, 91.

50. C. R. Boxer, *Salvador de Sá and the Struggle for Brazil and Angola: 1620-1686* (London, 1952), 388.

LESLIE B. ROUT, JR.

the antebellum U.S. South was no more pervasive than that of "O Rei Açucar" in the Brazilian northeast.

Life on the sugar plantations from about 1550 until national independence has been the subject of conflicting interpretations. For almost three centuries, the accepted theory was that a complex system of social and psychological relationships developed which tended to mitigate the most deleterious aspects of the slavery regimen, resulting in the creation of kinship ties between master and slave. The sexual liaisons that developed between the *senhor de engenho* and his female slaves resulted in the birth of numerous mulatto offspring. Although born slaves like their mothers, these *crias de casa*, or "house children," as they were called, often received their freedom and occasionally financial assistance or patronage from their white fathers. The sexual bond between master and slave and the emotional tie between male parent and his mixed-blood offspring were said to have been bridges which reduced the social distance between white and black.[51]

This seemingly logical interpretation is in reality grossly inadequate. The mass of plantation slaves were not occupants of the *casa grande*, the plantation manor house, but residents of the *senzala*, or slave quarters. Furthermore, the polygamous instincts of the planter should not obscure the fact that since more male slaves were imported than females, if the *senhor de engenho* had many concubines, polyandry and/or homosexuality resulted in the *senzala*. Lastly, the mulattoes of the master's household generally wanted nothing to do with field slaves.[52] Consequently the sexual adventures of the sugar barons and the favoritism shown the *crias de casa* may have created kinship ties between whites, mulattoes, and house servants, but the mass of slaves could hardly have benefited.

The problems of profit, production, and work regimen also suggest that life on a colonial sugar plantation was not exactly the idyll that some authors have pictured it to be. Particularly in Pernambuco, sugar lords estimated that a labor force of 100 slaves was necessary for the effective

---

51. This theory is presented in Gilberto Freyre, *Masters and Slaves* (New York, 1946, 1st English ed.), 181-182; Viana Filho, *O negro*, 123; Donald Pierson, *Negroes in Brazil* (Chicago, 1942), 345-346.

52. Mendonça, *A influência*, 152, stated the problem starkly: "The mulatto hates the white because he is not yet white, and despises the negroes. . . . "

operation of the *engenho*, and if a reasonable profit were to accrue, this labor force must annually produce about 1,138 pounds of sugar. During the 1600-1700 period, the production per hundred slaves reached almost 1,700 pounds yearly, a development which goes a long way toward explaining the tremendous wealth of the seventeenth-century planter class.[53] Whether in Pernambuco, Paraíba, Bahia, or elsewhere in the sugar cane country, certain labor conditions were standard. During the harvest season, work began before dawn and, except for two meals, continued long after dark. After the cane was harvested and processed, there were boxes and crates to be made, rum or cane brandy to be distilled, and new fields to be planted. Controversy exists as to the adequacy of the slave's diet, but most students of the question agree that manioc bread, corn gruel, perhaps a scrap of salted beef, or a few vegetables was all the field hand could expect to get.[54] Naturally there were benign masters who provided their workers with better food, an extra ration of rum, or an additional day off, but others simply ignored such considerations.

An important aspect of the servitude system existing in the northeastern sugar country was the prevailing philosophy of slave utilization. Slave reproduction was quite low, but fresh shiploads could easily be obtained from Angolan or Gulf of Guinea stations and rapidly shipped to Brazil. For these reasons, plantation owners generally held that raising young slaves was a time-consuming and uneconomical proposition. The common practice therefore was to work a slave to the limit of his capabilities, and after he had died, fled, or injured himself severely, buy a fresh replacement.[55] Recent scholarship suggests an allied concern. In the his-

53. The formula is found in Correia Lopes, *A escravatura*, 112, who establishes "one chest of sugar" as containing 35 arrobas (35 x 32½ pounds). The production figure comes from Roberto Simonsen, *História econômica do Brasil: 1500-1820* (Sao Paulo, 1937, 4th ed.), I, 202.

54. On the spartan nature of the slave's diet, see Renato Mendonça, "O negro e a cultura no Brasil," in Congresso Afro-Brasileiro (2nd), *O negro no Brasil* (Rio de Janeiro, 1940), 123-124; Alfredo Brandão, "Os negros na história de Alagoas," in Congresso Afro-Brasileiro (1st), *Estudos Afro-Brasileiros* (Rio de Janeiro, 1935), 81; Manoel Querino, *A raça africana* (Salvador, 1955), 39; María Stella de Novães, *A escravidão e a abolição no Espírito Santo* (Vitória, 1963), 45.

55. Corroboration of this slave replacement policy is found in Carl N. Degler, *Neither Black nor White: Slavery and Race Relations in Brazil and the United States* (New York, 1971), 65-67; Conrad, "The Struggle," 49; Boxer, *Golden Age*, 173. Most succinct is Denslow, "Economic Considerations," 5-6, who quotes a British consul

LESLIE B. ROUT, JR.

tory of the great slave systems established in the Americas, fatalities were apparently higher where sugar cane was the major product.[56] The implication of this hypothesis is clear: in assessing the relative brutality of a slave system, the kind of agricultural labor the slave performed may be much more important than establishing whether or not specific legal and moral safeguards actually protected the slave from arbitrary treatment. Cogent too is the fact that during the eighteenth century an increasing number of sugar lords left their rural properties and took up permanent residence in towns like Salvador or Recife. As a result, the direction of the labor force was in the hands of an overseer, often a mulatto, whose interest in the slaves' welfare was likely to be slight.

More fortunate were the bondsmen living in towns like Salvador, Recife, Rio de Janeiro, or Pôrto Seguro. Here one would find slave porters and stevedores, assorted domestics, prostitutes, and some skilled personnel. There were also numerous males and females employed as day laborers, whose major obligation was to supply their owners with an agreed-upon sum of money.[57] Possessed of some freedom of movement and a choice of jobs unavailable in the rural areas, the urban slave was undoubtedly better off than his plantation counterpart. Furthermore, those involved in the money economy (shoemakers, barbers, etc.) had much better prospects for purchasing their liberty than cane cutters or mill hands.

One may conclude that although the field hands (the largest body of captives) were indeed the "hands and feet of the *Senhor de Engenho*," individually they meant as much to the latter as a pair of boots, a horse, or a yoke of oxen. Witness an incident chronicled by an English visitor to Bahia in the twilight of the colonial epoch:

---

concerning the practices of Pernambuco sugar planters: " . . . it was the interest of the proprietors to obtain the greatest possible work in the least possible time, and at the smallest cost, from the slave; and they [proprietors] carried this principle to the fullest extent. They would not breed slaves; it was cheaper to buy them. If any of these unfortunates became ill, they were left to die. . . . " See also Peter L. Eisenberg, "Abolishing Slavery: The Process on Pernambuco's Sugar Plantations," *Hispanic American Historical Review*, LII (1972), 581-582.

56. See Denslow, "Economic Considerations," 5-7, 10-11.

57. See Carneiro, *Ladinos*, 8-10. These slaves were called *prêtos de aluguel* (literally, "blacks for rent"). The slave was to pay his owner an average of one pataca a day, or six patacas a week (1 pataca = 320 reis; thus, 1$920 a week).

> A poor Negro woman was lying in a dying state by the road. The English gentlemen applied to their Portuguese companions to speak to her and comfort her . . . but they said, ' 'tis only a black, let us ride on'; and they did without further notice.

Two days later, the same black woman, who had been recently "freed" because she could not work, expired.[58]

Slavery in Minas Gerais

About 1695, a major gold strike was made in what is today the state of Minas Gerais. New finds were subsequently made in the contemporary states of Goías (1715, 1730, 1734), Mato Grosso (1718-1719), and western Bahia (1719-1720). Production was carried on almost entirely by manual labor, and after 1770 it declined rapidly; between 1691 and 1820, roughly 926,100 kilograms were reportedly obtained.[59] In addition to gold, the existence of diamonds in Minas Gerais was also reported to Lisbon in 1729. Determined to reserve the lion's share of the proceeds for the House of Braganza, João V made the mining of precious stones in Brazil a royal monopoly, and placed the diamond district of Tijuco under special royal supervision. Between 1740 and 1821, 3,021,331 carats of diamonds were legally mined.[60]

When news of the gold strike reached Portugal, thousands of peasants and ne'er-do-wells departed the homeland and joined Brazilian vagrants, *senhores de engenho*, and frontiersmen in the mining camps and centers of Minas Gerais. Nevertheless, "the work of the mines was the work of Negroes,"[61] and to them went the actual task of digging. Slaves possessed of stamina were especially sought after, and in this regard, captives from the Gulf of Guinea (all called Minas in Minas Gerais, no matter what their port of embarkation) were much preferred to either Bantu or Indians. Between 1728 and 1748, at least 99,000 blacks were shipped

58. Maria Dundas Graham, *Journal of a Voyage to Brazil and Residence there during part of the Years 1821, 1822, and 1823* (New York, 1969, reprint), 144-145.

59. The figure on gold production is from Normano, *Brazil*, 31.

60. Boxer, *Golden Age*, 220, 225. John Mawe, *Travels in the Interior of Brazil* (London, 1821, 2d ed.), 445, claims that £ 2,000,000 worth of gems had been smuggled out of Tijuco by 1819.

61. Carneiro, *Ladinos*, 12.

to Salvador from the Guinea Coast and then overland, or by sea (via Rio de Janeiro) to the gold fields. Other records reveal that in 1734 there were 13,500 slaves at three gold sites in western Bahia, and in 1738 over 100,000 in five counties of Minas Gerais. During the eighteenth century over half a million bondsmen were shipped into the mineral-producing zones of the Brazilian interior.[62]

Naturally, prices were abnormally high. New blacks who sold for 100$000 in Bahia in 1703 and 160$000 in Maranhão during the same year went for as much as 420$000 in Minas Gerais. *Crioulos* (American-born) slaves and craftsmen brought prices of 500 drams of gold (600$000), while attractive *mulatas* often brought bids of 600 drams (720$000) each.[63] Given these exorbitant prices, along with the fact that the slaves served as both an investment and a labor unit, one might assume that the owners treated their slaves with great kindness, or took pains to ensure their good health, but this does not seem to have been the case. The *mulata* mistress, the slave cobbler, or the blacksmith were well taken care of, but otherwise the proprietors were content to maximize their gains, and then buy new properties when the old ones perished.

In any event, digging for gold was a curse for the slave. Those involved in placer mining worked constantly in water, often entirely nude, exposed to the sun, rain, and cold. Those working in underground galleries had to contend with changes in temperature, the release of gases, frequent accidents, and various forms of respiratory ailments contracted as a result of subterranean work. The toll in the lives of bondsmen is said to have reached 7,000 annually,[64] a figure which does not seem extreme in the light of observations made by several authors:

---

62. The Bahian figure is from Boxer, *Golden Age*, 153; the Minas Gerais figures from Correia Lopes, *A escravatura*, 131, who places it at 101,477. Goulart, *A escravidão*, 141, postulates the number to be 101,607 for the same year. The total figure for 1700-1770 is from Carneiro, *Ladinos*, 11; Simonsen, *História econômica*, II, 94, raises the total to 800,000, but he takes into account the entire eighteenth century.

63. The 1703 figures are from Calmon, *História social*, I, 54, 174. The conversion figure (1 dram or oitava = 1$200) is found in Carneiro, *Ladinos*, 16, 21. The totals in milreis are based on that formula.

64. The source of this figure is Wilhelm Von Eschwege (1777-1855), a German mining engineer who was hired early in the nineteenth century to assist in the revitalization of the Minas Gerais mining industry. See Carneiro, *Ladinos*, 22.

In the space of a year, 100 slaves died [in a gold mine in Goias], something which never happened to the plantation landlords. . . . [65]

The high death rate of African males in the gold mines was reflected in the new introduction of slaves which was continually being made. . . . [66]

The mines, insatiable . . . absorbed all the human mass brought in by the traffic. [67]

Paradoxically, in the absence of a large number of white women, female captives of color enjoyed unaccustomed opportunities for social and financial advancement. In Brazil the keeping of Negroid mistresses was a common practice, but in the gold fields this tradition was accentuated because Luso-Brazilians believed that sleeping with a Mina woman brought good luck. Indeed, some priests preached that a Luso-Brazilian committed no sin if he kept slave concubines, and one priest who argued otherwise was run out of a town. [68] A royal *alvará* of 1704 forbade female slaves to wear silk, gold jewelry, or facial make-up, but in Minas Gerais, this decree became still another that was generally honored with non-compliance. [69] The gold rush in eighteenth-century Minas Gerais resulted in the death of thousands of male slaves, but for a while the *mulata* was queen, and a few of these were able to parlay their physical talents into freedom and wealth.

The second greatest source of mineral wealth obtained during the eighteenth century was precious stones. Lisbon first sold the diamond monopoly in 1740, and to prevent the smuggling of precious stones out of the diamond district around Tijuco allowed the purchaser to bring in only 600 registered slaves. A head tax of 230$000 was to be paid on each of these, and all other blacks and mulattoes, slave or free, were banned from the district. In the diamond diggings there was supposed to be one

---

65. Taunay, "Subsídios," 624.

66. Augusto de Lima Júnior, *A Capitanía de Minas Gerais* (Rio de Janeiro, 1943, 2d ed.), 142.

67. Carneiro, *Ladinos*, 13.

68. Boxer, *Golden Age*, 179. See also Nóbrega, *Cartas*, 116, who pointed out that during the sixteenth century some priests preached that it was licit for masters to sleep with their bondswomen since they were slaves.

69. Calmon, *História social*, I, 53. The author also notes that in coastal cities like Rio de Janeiro this stipulation was more comprehensively enforced.

LESLIE B. ROUT, JR.

overseer for every eight slaves, but even though he watched the captives carefully, no really effective means was discovered which completely thwarted theft. One diabolical security measure was to force a slave suspected of having swallowed diamonds to englut large doses of Malaga black pepper, a substance having an awesome purgative effect.[70] Slaves found to have swallowed a gem could expect at the very least a flogging; nevertheless old hands continued to teach new arrivals ways and means of hiding gems and eluding detection. Naturally, the continued intake of either diamonds or purgatives was bound to cause intestinal disorders, a consideration which highlights the desperation and avarice of the slaves.

After 1771 the Portuguese government took over direct control of mining operations in the Tijuco district, and rented 3,500 slaves to work the diggings. These slaves were supplied by local residents and royal administrators, all of whom were usually paid 60 reis daily for the care and feeding of the laborers rented, but the diet fed the work force was said to be "poor and scanty," and "the treatment harsh."[71] The governing officials did, however, attempt a different stance in dealing with the problem of contraband: immediate freedom and an assortment of clothes were offered to any slave finding a stone of 17½ carats. But gems of this size were quite rare, and it was easier for the slave to conceal a small stone, sell it to a smuggler, or even trade it to his master in exchange for emancipation. Of course royal officials knew that some smuggling continued, a fact which did nothing to improve relations between slaves and royal overseers.

Slavery in Northern and Southern Brazil

In the *capitanía* of Grão Pará-Maranhão, Indians constituted the bulk of the servile labor force; thus there were continuing clashes between the Jesuits, who sought to protect the indigenous people, and the Luso-Brazilian settlers, who wanted them as laborers.[72] Both the Jesuits and the

---

70. Carneiro, *Ladinos*, 22.

71. Mawe, *Travels*, 20, 359. For a description of punishments suffered by slaves working the diamond pits and the rewards offered for those who found large stones, see 320-323.

72. Concerning the century-long struggle for control of the Indian population, see Boxer, *Golden Age*, 21. The best example of how protracted the struggle between the Jesuits and Maranhão Luso-Brazilians became is found in Ferreira Reis, "O Estado do Maranhão," II, 128-143.

settlers would have preferred to have had African bondsmen, but sugar cane did not prosper in the region, and neither gold nor precious stones were to be found in the rivers and streams.[73] Under these conditions, Grão Pará-Maranhão whites had little money to buy Africans, and many of those they did obtain were the infirm and rebellious souls who could not be sold elsewhere.[74]

The situation did not begin to change significantly until the Companhía do Grão Pará e Maranhão began making regular slave deliveries in 1755. There had been perhaps 12,000 to 13,000 African slaves landed at Belém (Grão Pará) between 1692 and 1750; by 1782 an additional 30,000 had been disembarked. A few of these saw service as stockmen, cowboys, and domestics, but after 1750 most of them became field hands in the growing coffee and cacao plantations.[75] Nevertheless, prices for skilled and prime *peças* remained unusually high in Grão Pará, in some cases reaching 1:200$000,[76] but, here as elsewhere, slaveholders exhibited an ambivalent attitude toward the health of their properties. In 1792, for example, the idea of vaccinating slaves was rejected because *capitanía* officials in Belém insisted that Negroid skin was too thick to penetrate![77]

Further south in Maranhão, the Companhía do Grão Pará e Maranhão was also responsible for economic development, but in this case the product was cotton. By 1818, exports from São Luís reached $4 million to $5 million annually, and between 1757 and 1823 at least 42,000 Africans arrived in order to cultivate the product which made Dixie famous. This sudden prosperity was not without a price; during the eighteenth century Maranhão became known as the place slaves were most harshly treated.[78] Available information suggests that Sundays were gen-

---

73. Celso Furtado, *Economic Growth of Brazil* (Berkeley, 1963), 73.

74. *Ibid.*, 97-98.

75. On the development of slavery in Grão Pará during the eighteenth century, see Altamirano Nunes Pereira, "Negros escravos na Amazonia," unpub. paper, read at tenth Geographical Congress, Rio de Janeiro, 1943, 25.

76. *Ibid.*, 54. This was an actual price for a twenty-year-old *crioulo* cowhand sold in about 1700.

77. *Ibid.*, 29.

78. On the terrible reputation of Maranhão as a slave center, see Prado Júnior, *Colonial Background*, 125; Henry Koster (C. Harvey Gardiner, ed.), *Travels in Brazil* (Carbondale, 1966), 81-82; Gilberto Freyre, *Mansions and Shanties* (New York, 1962, 1st U.S. ed.), 187; Nunes Pereira, "Amazonia," 57.

LESLIE B. ROUT, JR.

erally days of work, church holidays being the only universal days of rest. Domestics and favored concubines may have been able to extract extra privileges from the master, "but the greater part [were] treated as slaves, that is, with little to eat and much work."[79] By 1817, 66 percent of Maranhão's population consisted of Negroid slaves, a situation which doubtless heightened white fears and contributed immeasurably toward building the territory's reputation as a species of hell on earth.[80]

In the extreme south was the *capitanía* of Rio Grande do Sul, a region long considered too cold for Africans. After 1700 a popular practice among slave owners in Minas Gerais and Rio de Janeiro was to banish rebellious slaves to Rio Grande, and so this territory became known as a land of "vile masters and vile slaves."[81] As in Maranhão, economic growth did not commence until late in the eighteenth century. Cattle raising had steadily gained in importance, with Indian or *mameluco* cowboys tending the expanding herds.[82] According to the 1775 census, there were 20,000 inhabitants (not counting hostile Indians), a fourth of whom were black and mulatto slaves working chiefly as domestics and stockmen. After 1780, however, the meat-packing industry in the towns of Pôrto Alegre and Pelotas began growing rapidly, and in two decades Rio Grande replaced Ceará as the chief provider of salted beef for Brazilian tables. This growth necessitated a rapid escalation in the number of servile workers. By 1814 the *capitanía's* inhabitants numbered perhaps 70,655 souls, of whom 30.1 percent were slaves. Ninety percent of these were committed to permanent service in the *charqueadas*, or meat-packing plants.[83]

Slavery in Rio Grande do Sul was unique in that the mass of the unfree labor force was urban and industrial. The *charqueada* bondsmen

---

79. For a description of slavery in Maranhão and the source for the quoted material, see Francisco de São José, "Paranduba Maranhense," *RIHG*, LIV, 1 (Rio de Janeiro, 1891), 138.

80. For this statistic, see Arthur Ramos, *The Negro in Brazil* (Washington, D.C., 1951, 2d ed.), 21.

81. John Luccock, *Notes on Rio de Janeiro and the Southern Parts of Brazil* (London, 1820), 145.

82. *Mameluco*, a person of white-Indian heritage. In northeastern Brazil, this kind of mixed-blood was often called a *cabra*.

83. See Fernando Henriques Cardoso, *Capitalismo e escravidão no Brasil meridional* (São Paulo, 1962), 69-71; Nestor Ericksen, *O negro no Rio Grande do Sul* (Pôrto Alegre, 1941), 18-19.

worked a minimum of twelve hours a day, beginning about midnight and ending at noon. The critical factor in the system's harshness was that *charqueada* slaves worked all year round, there being no rainy or growing season that would significantly vary the pace of work. The Maranhão practice was reversed—slaves got Sundays off, but not necessarily the church holidays. Perhaps the worst torture of all was that with slave cost high, the emancipation of *charqueada* workers was relatively uncommon.[84]

According to Caio Prado Júnior, the small number of African slaves originally in Maranhão and Rio Grande do Sul, plus the sudden and rapid influx of a predominantly male slave population, prevented the creation of a mulatto contingent such as existed in northeastern Brazil. In both *capitanías*, the Brazilian scholar argues, "the blacks were blacker, the whites whiter," and for this reason a harsher form of slavery developed.[85] More plausible to this writer is that the educated and affluent white elements in Maranhão and Rio Grande do Sul were conscious of the opulence which had characterized the earlier mineral and sugar booms. The increasing demand for meat and cotton signaled the arrival of their opportunity to cash in, much as northeastern landlords and Minas Gerais prospectors had previously done. But if this economic advancement was to be rapidly accomplished, the captive laborers had to toil harder and faster. It is little wonder, then, that African slaves wanted no part of Maranhão or Rio Grande do Sul.

Slave Resistance and Rebellion

Naturally, a great number of blacks rebelled against their masters, and intimidating punishments were necessary to keep the labor force in line. A few defiant souls were actually thrown alive into burning furnaces, and the *novena*, or nine days of whipping, the thumb screw, the iron collar, the stocks, and metal weights were commonly employed methods of enforcing obedience.[86] What some owners discovered, however, was that

---

84. Henriques Cardoso, *Capitalismo*, 146-147; Ericksen, *Rio Grande do Sul*, 23-24. In this region, slaves were occasionally freed if they enlisted in the local militia.
85. Prado Júnior, *Colonial Background*, 125, 324.
86. On slave punishments, see Conrad, "The Struggle," 51, 61-63; Querino, *Raça africana*, 37; and particularly, Arthur Ramos, "Castigos de Escravos," *Revista do arquivo municipal do São Paulo*, IV (1938), 89-104.

LESLIE B. ROUT, JR.

mental cruelty could produce a kind of servility that physical brutality alone might not. One Bahian planter who could not prevent his slaves from committing suicide finally solved the problem by digging up the bodies of several of those who had killed themselves, and hacking off their limbs. Thereupon he informed the assembled captives that if they chose to end their lives, he would also mutilate them, and thus when they were reborn, they would come back minus an arm, hand, or leg.[87]

Although many slaves felt that they could no longer endure these punishments, they were not as aggressive as a mulatto bondsman named André, who in 1791 killed his master. Apprehended by the authorities, André was hanged. His hands and head were then severed from his body and placed on a pole in a public place for eight days.[88]

The general means of resisting oppression became suicide or flight, with the majority opting for the latter course of action. Apprehending these fugitives was a serious problem in colonial Brazil. The chief security agent, the *capitāo-do-mato* (bush captain), was a bounty hunter, who sold his services to a group of slaveholders and received up to 2$000 for each slave recaptured. The *capitāo-do-mato* was generally a free black or mulatto, a factor pregnant with significance; who but a colored person would make the best catcher of another black or mulatto? Furthermore, slave-catching provided a means for putting freed blacks to work and making them a part of the existing social structure. The *capitāes* were known for their relentlessness and cruelty, and certainly were not above deceiving their employers in hopes of maximizing a reward.[89]

A few escaped slaves took up residence in urban areas, where they tried to pass as free persons. Most, however, sought to reach organized settlements of fugitive slaves established in virtually inaccessible places. These independent hamlets and towns were beacons of freedom, and thus their destruction was necessary for the maintenance of the Brazilian slave system. Easily the most famous and largest of these settlements was the celebrated *quilombo* of Palmares, situated in the present state of Ala-

---

87. Viana Filho, *O negro*, 123.
88. Nunes Pereira, "Amazonia," 58.
89. Ramos, *Negro in Brazil*, 35. In Grão Pará, probably because of the hazards of operating in the Amazon jungles, *capitāes-do-mato* received high salaries. See Nunes Pereira, "Amazonia," 59. Those operating in Minas Gerais were paid on a sliding scale, and usually in gold dust. See Boxer, *Golden Age*, 170-171.

goas and established perhaps as early as 1612. Beginning in 1630, Palmares withstood at least twenty major attacks or sieges by the Dutch, the Portuguese, and Brazilians before succumbing in 1695. At the height of its development, Palmares encompassed some ten subdivisions, and 20,000 to 30,000 persons lived within its confines. It would remain the largest independent American settlement of persons of African origin until Haitian sovereignty was recognized in 1804.[90]

There was simply no way for the Luso-Brazilians to prevent the establishment of hundreds of *quilombos* between 1550 and 1822, but when large-scale settlements were reported the Luso-Brazilians shook off their indolence and acted with some energy. Other than Palmares, the largest *quilombos* were established in Minas Gerais, in the mountains and wooded areas near several of the larger towns. An estimated 20,000 ex-captives were said to have inhabited these settlements, and they were considered "a plague scattered about the remote areas and without remedy." Fugitives sallying from these hideouts kidnapped and killed whites and made the roads of the *capitania* unsafe. When Lisbon finally agreed to finance a major campaign against these *quilombos*, Bartolomeu Bueno do Pardo (1757) attacked and destroyed a "quasi-kingdom of fugitive negroes," reportedly returning with 3,900 pairs of ears as proof of the number of inhabitants encountered. Subsequent attacks by Diogo Bueno da Fonseca and Antônio França da Buena temporarily removed the menace to white rule which the *quilombos* had represented in Minas Gerais.[91]

For some slaves, however, the *quilombo* was an unacceptable method of self-determination, in that once the settlement was discovered, Luso-Brazilians could organize at leisure an attack of such overwhelming force that the rebels must eventually be defeated. The solution to the problem was the planned rebellion, in which a sudden attack would result in the death or dispersal of whites. In 1719 and 1724 slaves in Vila Rica de Ouro Prêto, capital of Minas Gerais, plotted a giant insurrection, but these

90. The best source for the history of Palmares is Edison Carneiro, *O Quilombo dos Palmares: 1630-1695* (Rio de Janeiro, 1958, 2d ed.). Another valuable source is Nina Raimundo Rodrigues, *Os africanos no Brasil* (Sao Paulo, 1932, 2d ed.), especially 125-137.

91. On *quilombos* in Minas Gerais, see Diogo de Vasconcellos, *História média de Minas Gerais* (Belo Horizonte, 1918), 164-175. The quoted materials are from Vasconcellos, 165, 167, and Taunay, "Subsídios," 626.

LESLIE B. ROUT, JR.

schemes collapsed because Angolan and Guinea Coast blacks could not agree as to which group would have supreme power after white rule was overthrown.[92] Another conspiracy, formed by slaves in the town of São João del Rei (Minas Gerais) and fugitives from a nearby *quilombo*, called for a surprise attack during church services on Maundy Thursday (April 15), 1756. The execution of both whites and mulattoes was intended, but the plan was discovered, and an undetermined number of conspirators were captured and punished.[93] Several rebellions were also attempted in Maranhão, but the best known was an Afro-Indian revolt which took place in the town of São Tomé in 1773. Information regarded this uprising is scanty, but as one source tersely summed up the fate of the rebels, "they had to be annihilated."[94]

The sugar-growing northeast also was the scene of serious challenges to white authority. The first reported insurrection took place in Bahia in 1607, but a worse crisis developed early in the nineteenth century. In 1807, 1809, 1813, and 1816 Muslim-led slaves made determined efforts to seize political control of the *capitanía*. The 1807 plot was scotched by informers, but both the 1809 and the 1813 uprisings resulted in the death of white planters and overseers, as pitched battles swirled around the city of Salvador. The 1816 affair commenced on seven plantations in the sugar-rich Recôncavo district,[95] and reached "frightening proportions" before Jerônimo Moniz Fruga Barreto succeeded in quelling the slaves. Awarded the title of "Savior of the Recôncavo," Fruga Barreto had hundreds of suspects and prisoners executed, flogged, or deported to penal colonies in Africa.[96] Nevertheless, these repressions and punishments only temporarily succeeded in intimidating the slaves, a fact which the Luso-Brazilians would soon discover, to their dismay.[97]

The evidence of slave resistance to Luso-Brazilian hegemony should

---

92. Boxer, *Golden Age*, 177.
93. See Vasconcellos, *História média*, 170-171; Raimundo Rodrigues, *Os africanos*, 137-138.
94. Raimundo Rodrigues, *Os africanos*, 149.
95. Recôncavo is the name given the land surrounding the Bay of All Saints. It is noted for its rich soil, and some of the richest sugar plantations in Bahia were located here.
96. See Raimundo Rodrigues, *Os africanos*, 77-81. The quotation is from Viana Filho, *O negro*, 140-141.
97. Subsequent Muslim or Nagô-led uprisings took place in 1826, 1830, and 1835.

not be construed as proof that all African captives hated their masters or planned to kill them. Some slaves were simply overawed and submitted meekly, while others chose to drown their discontent in alcohol or the mysticism and frenzy of *macumba* or *candomblé*. The lesson to be drawn from this recital of rebellious acts is that during the colonial period, a significant number of bondsmen (usually African-born) refused to reconcile themselves to white rule. Their continuing flights, conspiracies, and attacks did not effect a breakdown of the slave system, but it meant that political and administrative authorities could not afford to lay down their guard.

Brazilian Slavery on the Eve of Independence

By decree in 1755 and 1758, the Marquis de Pombal officially abolished Indian slavery in Brazil. As in so many other cases, these edicts were often ignored, but they do establish that after the years in question, only Africans were to be considered subject to the rigors of involuntary servitude. We may therefore conclude that in the following estimates[98] the overwhelming majority of those counted as slaves were blacks and mulattoes:

	Free persons	Slaves	Total population	Percent enslaved
José Correia de Serra (1798)	800,000	1,500,000	2,300,000	65.2
F.P. Santa Apolônia (1818)	1,668,000	1,582,000	3,250,000	48.7
Adrien Balbi (1819)	1,917,000	1,980,000	3,897,000	50.8
Antonio Veloso de Oliveira (1819)	3,917,743	1,107,389	4,396,132	25.1
Affonso de E. Taunay (1938)	—	1,400,000	—	—

According to Veloso de Oliveira, the five provinces having the greatest number of slaves in 1819 were: Minas Gerais (168,543), Bahia (147,263), Rio de Janeiro (146,060), Maranhão (133,332), and Pernam-

98. These estimates are from Taunay, "Subsídios," 626–627; Gomes, "Archegas," 48.

LESLIE B. ROUT, JR.

buco (97,633). Those provinces having the greatest percentages of slaves in their total population were: Maranhão, 66.6; Goias, 42.5; Mato Grosso, 38.6; Alagoas, 38.3; São Paulo, 32.6; Amazonas, 31.6; Bahia, 30.8; Rio Grande do Sul, 30.6; Rio de Janeiro, 28.7; Espírito Santo, 27.7.[99]

When on September 7, 1822, Prince Pedro raised his sword and shouted "Liberty or death!" Brazilian dependence upon the institution of African slavery was much more pervasive than it had been in 1550 or 1600. For the black or mulatto slave, however, the end of colonial rule was imperceptible, for society continued to define his role as toter of barges and lifter of bales. Fortunately, there was always plenty of *cachaça* (Brazilian rum).

The Freedman in Colonial Brazil

Manumission

The only significant organizations of colored people which worked to effect the release of slaves were the black and mulatto lay brotherhoods, or *irmandades*, the first of which was founded about 1639. These were religious organizations created to strengthen the spirit of Christianity among persons of African origin, and were divided along racial and even tribal lines. Many *irmandades* assessed their membership an annual sum specifically for the emancipation of members or for the liberation of other deserving bondsmen.[100]

While the work of the *irmandades* stood as the best example of co-operation among Negroid peoples in colonial Brazil, most manumissions were accomplished by self-purchase or through owner benefaction. In the first case, the master and the bondsman agreed upon a price for the freedom of the latter, and when this sum was paid the bondsman was

---

99. These statistics are presented in Gomes, "Archegas," 49; Ramos, *Introdução*, I, 323.

100. For the history of these brotherhoods, see Manoel S. Cardozo, "The Lay Brotherhoods of Colonial Bahia," *Catholic Historical Review*, XXXIII (1947), 12-27; A. J. R. Russell-Wood, "Colonial Brazil," in David W. Cohen and Jack P. Greene (eds.), *Neither Slave nor Free* (Baltimore, 1972), 91, 108, 122. Wood determines that several *irmandades* limited their memberships to Yoruba (Nagô)- and Gegê-speaking blacks. Cardozo, 27, points out that in Bahia no money could be spent on freeing slaves without the permission of the bishop.

awarded a *carta de alforria* (letter of liberation) which acknowledged his emancipation. It is historically disputable whether or not the master had to accept final payment,[101] but in any case the mass of manumissions were unquestionably gratuitous awards. Trusted retainers, slave concubines, and illegitimate mulatto offspring could often expect liberation in a will, or on a church holiday or a birthday, and a few even received a small bequest of land or money.

But Brazilian manumittive customs also had their dark side. Many *cartas de alforria* were given to the sick, the aged, and the crippled, and for these persons release from bondage was a death sentence. An outlandish custom was the provision that if a freedman demonstrated disrespect for his ex-owner, he could be reenslaved.[102] Another common but rarely discussed aspect of manumission was the practice of conditional release. For example, a slave would be freed in his master's will, but with the added provision that the ex-slave continue serving the master's heirs for life, or for a specified number of years. Under these conditions, the bondsman was only semifree, and it was really his descendants who made the final step to emancipation.[103]

Possibly the most tragic aspect of manumission practice was that many of those released had neither skills nor resources, and were bound to be ravaged by the new realities they had to face. For example, except for barbers and midwives, many slaves with skills found that they could not meet the standards of proficiency required for admittance to craft guilds. Socially, the emancipated found themselves in a state of limbo, for many of the white persons encountered did not take cognizance of the colored person's change in status. Only the *irmandades* seem to have provided assistance in helping ex-bondsmen make the psychological and social readjustments necessary.

---

101. Russell-Wood, "Colonial Brazil," 86, argues that if the master refused the money, the slave might appeal his case to the crown, who could rule in his favor. Graham, *Journal of a Voyage*, 197-198, reveals that, whatever the reason, some masters did not set a price on valuable slaves and refused to free them.

102. Russell-Wood, "Colonial Brazil," 92; Conrad, "The Struggle," 43.

103. See Vivaldo V. F. Daglione, "A libertação dos escravos no Brasil através de alguns documentos," *Anais de História*, I, (São Paulo, 1968/69), 131-133.

LESLIE B. ROUT,JR.

The Status of Free Negroes

When the situation of freed persons of color in colonial Brazil is discussed, the question of which persons were freed takes on a special relevance. Most *capitanías* did not, unfortunately, separate blacks and mulattoes in their censuses, so our information is limited, but the tremendous disproportion between the numbers of free blacks and free mulattoes (see table) requires some explanation.[104] It has already been pointed out that white fathers often emancipated their bastard mulatto offspring. Furthermore, the mixed-blood was likely to be Brazilian-born and acquainted with Luso-Brazilian linguistic and cultural predilections. Thus when liberation opportunities presented themselves, it was the mulatto who would most likely be able to exploit them. One scholar has pointed out that among Luso-Brazilians, allowing light-complexioned slaves to perform the same heavy labor as blacks was considered disgraceful,[105] while another has stressed the notion that "a light mulatto . . . even as a slave was more likely to receive acceptance from the white community than a free black man."[106] Further research on this point is necessary, but the possibility is strong that in colonial Brazil the story of the nonenslaved person of color was essentially a mulatto saga.

Admittedly, the mass of emancipated mixed-bloods and blacks possessed neither money nor powerful patrons, so society allotted to them the proletarian tasks which no one else desired. By working hard at these occupations and obeying the laws, the optimum most people of color (except for certain paramours) could expect to achieve in their lifetime was the ownership of a few slaves or a small shop. But these goals could not be gained without a good deal of physical exertion, and in colonial Brazil manual labor was performed only by blacks and slaves. Rather

---

104. The sources are (Rio Grande do Sul and Mato Grosso) Dauril Alden, "The Population of Brazil in the late Eighteenth Century: A Preliminary Study," *Hispanic American Historical Review*, XLIII (1966), 198; (Minas Gerais) Goulart, *Escravidão*, 144; (Goias) Gomes, "Archegas," 65; (Paraíba) Ascendio Carneiro da Cunha, "A revolução de 1817 na Paraíba do Norte," *RIHG, Anais, I Congresso* (Rio de Janeiro, 1915), I, 593; (Curitiba), Ianni, *As metamorfoses*, 90; (Piauhy) José Martins Pereira de Alencastre, "Memória cronológica, histórica e corográphica da Província de Piauhy," *RIHG*, XX, Primeiro Trimestre (Rio de Janeiro, 1857), 79.
105. Perdigão Malheiro, *A escravidão no Brasil*, I, 116.
106. Russell-Wood, "Colonial Brazil," 99.

TABLE 6.1 Demographic Data for Some *Capitanías* in Colonial Brazil

Category	Rio Grande do Sul (1802)	Minas Gerais (1821)	Mato Grosso (1803)	Paraíba (1817)	City of Curitiba (1818)	Piauhy (1826)
Whites	20,248	136,693	5,813	65,000	6,140	21,945
Free mulattoes	1,486	152,921	7,903	28,000	3,036	32,034
Slave mulattoes	1,093	22,788	1,569	—	544	5,920
Total mulattoes	2,579	175,709	9,472	—	3,580	37,954
Percent mulattoes free	57.6	87.1	79.2	—	84.9	84.4
Free blacks	713	53,719	3,356	8,000	251	5,755
Slave blacks	12,011	148,416	8,619	—	1,043	19,193
Total blacks	12,724	202,135	11,975	—	1,294	24,948
Percent blacks free	5.6	26.6	28.0	—	19.4	23.1
Total slaves	13,104	171,204	10,188	17,000	1,587	25,113
Total Negroid population	15,683	377,844	21,447	53,000	4,874	62,902

Source: See n. 104.

LESLIE B. ROUT, JR.

than "disgrace" themselves in this regard, an unusual number of mulattoes preferred to be vagrants, their vanity not allowing them to perform servile work.[107] For other persons of an assortment of shades, banditry, diamond smuggling, or some other form of criminal activity were the preferable alternatives, because they offered the prospect of greater financial remuneration. These attitudes are not completely unreasonable, for in addition to the previously mentioned strictures, colored persons had to pay taxes, and all males were theoretically subject to militia service.

In Brazil, the ticket to clerical, civil, or administrative appointments was proof of "cleanliness of blood" (*limpeza de sangue*), and since all persons of African origin were slaves or descendants of slaves, they were inherently "unclean." A 1671 law banned from clerical and civil appointments Jews, Moors, mulattoes, and all persons who married women of "infected" ancestry. A 1719-1720 series of synodal ordinances by the archbishop of Bahia required that persons applying to enter the priesthood prove themselves free of Jewish or mulatto taint, and all religious orders maintained a rigid ban against the entry of colored Brazilians. Also comprehensive on paper were royal statutes governing the opportunities available to Negroids. When in 1724 the governor of Minas Gerais appointed a mulatto as a judge in Vila Rica de Ouro Preto, the enraged white citizens demanded that Lisbon invalidate this action. João VI sanctioned the appointment, but in 1726 moved to mollify white sentiment by issuing an *alvará* banning the accession to clerical or civil office of any person having a grandparent who had African blood. Twenty-nine years later, in 1755, the Marquis de Pombal issued still another decree commanding that white persons of legitimate birth obtain royal consent before they married a black, mulatto, or Jew.[108]

---

107. *Ibid.*, 107-108.
108. For the events mentioned, see C. R. Boxer, *The Portuguese Seaborne Empire: 1415-1825* (London, 1969), 260; *idem, Race Relations in the Portuguese Colonial Empire: 1415-1825* (Oxford, 1963), 120-121; Lima Junior, *Minas Gerais*, 149-150. On the prejudicial nature of colonial justice, see Russell-Wood, "Colonial Brazil," 89, 92, 95, 99-100; Dauril Alden, *Royal Government in Colonial Brazil* (Berkeley, 1968), 483; Boxer, *Race Relations*, 120-121; Augusto Tavares de Lima, "Sinopse histórica da Capitanía do Rio Grande do Norte," *RIHG, Anais, IV Congresso* (Rio de Janeiro, 1950), II, 165-210.

In addition to these legal bars, court decisions were notoriously color-oriented, but it is the regionally promulgated ordinances which most clearly revealed the obsession of the ruling whites with preventing Negroid social ascension. In 1719, the Count of Assumar, chief official in São Paulo and Minas Gerais, prohibited all blacks and mulattoes from owning either slaves or stores. In 1734, the governor of Rio Grande do Norte implored João V to ban mulattoes from holding any office or entering militia service. Nevertheless, it was Dom Luís de Almeida Lavradio, viceroy of Brazil (1769-1777), who approached the ultimate in upholding the principle of white supremacy. He refused to allow mulatto militia officers to approach him to pay their respects, and on the word of some Indians he relieved of command a *capitão-mor*[109] who was suspected of being a mulatto. Possibly his most outrageous act was his deposition of an Indian chief in 1771 for marrying a black woman. In ordering the red man's removal Almeida Lavradio declared that the marriage was proof of the chief's mental derangement.[110]

Superficially less discriminatory were crown decisions involving racial matters. In 1680 Lisbon ordered the readmission to a Jesuit school in Bahia of several mulattoes whom whites had forced out. Two decades later, over the objection of school administrators, a Brazilian mixed-blood was enrolled at Coimbra University in Portugal, and in 1731 João V overruled the governor of Pernambuco, allowing Antônio Ferreira Castro to practice law even though he was a mulatto. In 1759 the Marquis de Pombal granted to wealthy mulattoes in Minas Gerais and Rio de Janeiro the right to carry swords.[111] In 1802 Prince João set aside the governor of Bahia's order removing colored officers from command positions in colored militia units.[112] Note, however, that all these dispensations were granted either to individuals or to a very small group of privileged per-

---

109. This position, often a pseudo-military rank, denoted that its holder was a commander of a militia regiment or field commander of a *capitania*'s militia force.

110. Boxer, *Seaborne Empire*, 315.

111. By law, no black or mulatto could bear arms without legal permission, under pain of 100 lashes. For the other events mentioned, see C. R. Boxer, "The Color Question in the Portuguese Empire, 1415-1825," *Proceedings of the British Academy*, XLVII (1961), 134-139; Sergio Buarque da Holanda, *Raices del Brasil* (Mexico City, 1955, 1st Spanish ed.), 34.

112. Russell-Wood, "Colonial Brazil," 121-122.

LESLIE B. ROUT, JR.

sons. Moreover, the kings of Portugal were not prepared to risk serious confrontation over racial matters if the Luso-Brazilians displayed violent opposition. In both 1731 and 1733 King João V ordered the integration of Brazilian militia units (at least in Bahia and Minas Gerais) but when it was reported that white soldiers refused to serve with colored troops, the king quietly dropped the issue. This same monarch, nevertheless, ordered a secret inquiry in Minas Gerais to discover whether blacks and mulattoes enjoyed "excessive liberty," and in 1735 and 1743 he ordered all free colored removed from the diamond district around Tijuco under pain of heavy fine and harsh punishment.[113] In essence, the crown might allow itself an occasional display of benignity, but there was always the understanding that the colored masses were really a debauched and inferior people.

Probably the most famous nonwhites to reach positions of status in colonial Brazil were Antônio Vieira, a Jesuit priest and court advisor, João Fernandes Vieira, governor in both Paraíba and Angola, and Henrique Dias, a black soldier who was knighted in 1652. Unquestionably of critical importance was the fact that Fernandes Vieira and Dias were the most heroic figures to emerge from the 1645-1654 "War of Divine Liberation" against the Dutch in Pernambuco. Of significance too is the fact that both Vieiras were European-born; in any case, no other known mulatto became governor in Brazil, and Dias is the only Brazilian black ever to be knighted. The other acknowledged nonwhites to receive civil appointments were a small group of blacks and mulattoes, chiefly in Minas Gerais, who were granted minor posts primarily because no white man would perform the chores which the jobs entailed.[114] But too many royal dispensations would ultimately have undermined the principle of white supremacy, and such a development was unthinkable. Therefore, colored persons hoping to gain civil or religious offices had to apply other stratagems. One such individual, the illegitimate son of Francisca (Xica) da Silva, literally purchased his acceptability, eventually becoming a judge.[115] There was, nevertheless, still another indispensable requisite for those who hoped to "cross the Jordan":

---

113. *Ibid.*, 110; Calmon, *História social*, III, 94-96.
114. Russell-Wood, "Colonial Brazil," 112-113.
115. Francisca (Xica) was the mistress of João Fernandes de Oliveira, who bought

Only persons who were not too dusky of hue, the so-called *brancar-rões* [very fair-complexioned mulattoes] were allowed to rise. . . .
Dark mulattoes and Negroes found the barriers too strong.[116]

Under the conditions delineated, dark mulattoes and blacks were doomed to frustration, their only hope being that someday their descendants might somehow become lighter. Acceptable pigmentation plus wealth and influence were necessary for persons who hoped to obtain the *limpeza de sangue* document, but how dark one could be and still "pass" varied from region to region. In southern Brazil, where whites were proportionately more numerous and *mamelucos* were adjudged white, few mulattoes were allowed to merge with the dominant racial group. Even in cities like Salvador or Rio de Janeiro persons suspected of mixed heritage did not become city council members.[117] It seems that it was one thing to be legally "white" if the position at stake were a relatively minor one, but when the more prestigious offices were to be awarded, persons lacking the necessary pedigree knew better than to compete. Yet, by allowing some mulattoes who most approximated the white phenotype to rise, a potentially dangerous situation was avoided. Insofar as this represented conscious policy, the Portuguese rulers proved themselves sage judges of how to maintain sovereignty in a distant land.

Black versus White versus Brown

A revealing incident reported by both the Englishman Henry Koster and the French artist Jean Rugendas is the following:

In conversing on one occasion with a man of color who was in my service, I asked if a certain *capitão-mor* was not a mulatto man; he answered, 'he was, but he is not now.' I begged him to explain, when he added; 'Can a *capitão-mor* be a mulatto man?'[118]

---

the first diamond monopoly from the crown in 1740. See Calmon, *História social*, I, 53; Boxer, *Golden Age*, 219-220.

116. Prado Júnior, *Colonial Background*, 319. Almost the same language and virtually the same conclusion are found in Boxer, *Race Relations*, 121.

117. Boxer, *Seaborne Empire*, 281.

118. Koster, *Travels*, 175. See also João Maurício Rugendas (trans. Sergio Milliet), *Viagem pitoresca através do Brasil* (São Paulo, 1954), 94-95. The incident is reported in both works in almost exactly the same way.

LESLIE B. ROUT, JR.

This exchange has been cited as proof that unusual opportunities for social ascent existed for mulattoes in colonial Brazil.[119] In fact, these mixed-bloods were generally discriminated against by the Europeans and consistently held up for ridicule and derision. All the mulatto could do in retaliation was to vent his rage and frustration on those darker than himself. Perhaps Koster and Rugendas should have asked themselves instead: did Luso-Brazilians consider the *capitão-mor* in question to be white?

There were, however, a few mulattoes who realized that spurning the black man and accepting white domination was not likely to allow many of them to penetrate the upper echelons of Brazilian society. In 1798 a group of mulatto tailors, engravers, and militiamen in Salvador plotted to overthrow Portuguese rule and ostensibly to create a republic in which there would be equality of opportunity for all races. Nevertheless, as Lucas Dantas, one of the ringleaders, constantly emphasized, the primary goal was the abolition of distinctions between whites and mulattoes, rather than true legal and social equity. Thus, as any cynic could have predicted, "the only black invited to participate not only refused, but betrayed the uprising."[120] Displaying hardly a trace of generosity, Governor Dom Fernando José do Portugal initially detained hundreds, but eventually had four mulattoes executed, six exiled or sentenced to hard labor in Africa, and numerous slaves given 200 lashes.[121]

Conclusion

Colonial Brazil was a place where "perennial rivalry" existed between Bantu and Mina,[122] while Muslim blacks despised their Christian counterparts. The mulatto strove to disassociate himself from the black man, and though conditions necessitated the absorption of some mulattoes,

---

119. Among those noting the incident and suggesting this conclusion (in addition to the works cited in n. 118) is Russell-Wood, "Colonial Brazil," 113. Charles Expilly (trans. Gostão Penalva), *Mulheres e costumes do Brasil* (São Paulo, 1935), 290, takes a different view of the incident, as does Ianni, *As metamorfoses*, 263.

120. On Lucas Dantas, see Carneiro, *Antología*, 114. For the quoted material, see Russell-Wood, "Colonial Brazil," 119.

121. The best history of this event is found in Luiz Viana Filho, "Homens e causas da revolução Baiana de 1798," *RIHG, Anais, III Congresso*, IV, 643-663.

122. Boxer, *Golden Age*, 177, 313.

the whites held the mass of them in ill-concealed contempt. There was also competition between American- and European-born persons of Portuguese origin, but faced with a racial threat to the social order, the whites united. Most of the recorded divisions and antagonisms between the peoples of African origin were not the product of some subtle master plan conceived and subtly effected by the Luso-Brazilians; nonetheless, had the Negroids been able to overcome these differences, it is difficult to visualize how the whites could have remained in power.

Writing in the nineteenth century, Sylvio Romero, Brazilian literator, pointed out that while his countrymen were undeniably a "mixed people," the mulatto himself was "a condition of victory for the white man."[123] During the colonial period, the mulatto in Brazil strove to make himself acceptable to whites. A century and a half later, he is still attempting to do so; it is the haphazard acceptance of these mixed-bloods which gives the country its otherwise unjustified reputation of being some sort of "racial democracy."

---

123. Sylvio Romero, *História da literatura brasileira* (Rio de Janeiro, 1943, 3rd augmented ed.), II, 104, 119.

7

Paul Edwards and James Walvin

Africans in Britain, 1500-1800

First Arrivals: Before 1600

The first record we have of a black African in Britain dates back to Roman times. The Emperor Septimius Severus is recorded in the *Scriptores Historiae Augustae* as having met outside the walls of Carlisle a certain "Ethiopian soldier, famous among buffoons and always a notable jester." The soldier made a jest at the emperor's expense whereupon "Severus in a rage ordered that the man be removed from his sight, troubled as he was by the man's colour."[1] Other evidence for black Roman soldiers in Britain is more tentative, but work on Romano-British cemeteries has produced skull measurements which suggest Negro African burials. Recently, the excavation of an Anglo-Saxon burial at North Elmham in Norfolk has revealed a "skull whose characters leave little doubt that it comes from a negress or a woman with predominantly negro genes in her chromosomes."[2] And there are Irish records of a Viking raid on Spain and North Africa in 862; a number of Negroes were captured and some carried to Dublin, where they were known as "blue men" (Irish, *fir gorma*; Old Norse, *blámenn*).[3] There must have been considerable trading

---

1. David Magie (ed.), *Scriptores Historiae Augustae* (London, 1922), I, 424-427.

2. Privately communicated by Calvin Wells, from a report to be published by Leicester University Press. For articles which hint at African burials at Romano-British and Anglo-Saxon sites see, e.g., Roger Warwick, "The Skeletal Remains," in L. P. Wenham, *The Romano-British Cemetery at Trentholme* (London, 1968), 111-176; M. L. Tildesley, "The Human Remains from Roche Court Down," *Wiltshire Archaeological and Natural History Magazine*, XLV (1930-1932), 583-599.

3. John O'Donovan (ed.), *Annals of Ireland* (Dublin, 1860), 162. The entry is under the title "Three Fragments Copied from Ancient Sources" by Donald MacFirbis,

between Africa and Europe at this time, including Anglo-Saxon England; two typical Anglo-Saxon beads have been found on the East African coast.[4] But it is not until around 1500 that we begin to get more documentary evidence.

In 1506 or 1507 the Scottish poet William Dunbar wrote "Of Ane Blak Moir,"[5] describing a black woman, called Helenor in the Court Accounts, possibly Ellen More, who reached Edinburgh by way of the port of Leith and acted a principal role in "the turnament of the black knicht and the black lady," in which the king of Scotland played the part of the black knight.[6] The winner of the tournament was to be rewarded with a kiss from the black lady, but the loser had to "cum behind and kis hir hippis." Dunbar is far from complimentary about the lady's looks—she is said to be "thick mouthed like an ape" ("tute mowitt lyk an aep")—but it seems that she and another black lady had positions of some respect at court, if we are to judge by the amount spent on clothes for them shown in the Court Accounts.[7] There are also entries for "xij½ elne Birge satin to be tua gownis to the blak ladyis madinnis,"[8] indicating that she had her own personal maid-servants at the expense of the crown, and the accounts for 1513 show, as a New Year gift "to the twa blak ledeis, x Franche crounis."[9] Helenor took part in a spectacle organized by one "Bischope Androw forman quha was ane Igramanciar [i.e., necromancer]" held in the royal banqueting hall, in which a cloud was seen to descend from the roof "and cleikkit up the blak lady in presence of thame all that scho was no moir seine."[10] A number of "Moors," probably

---

and reads: "After that, the Scandinavians went through the country, and ravaged it; and they burned the whole land; and they brought a great host of [the Moors] in captivity with them to Ireland. These are the 'blue men' (*fír gorma*); because the Moors are the same as negroes; Mauretania is the same as negro-land."

4. Privately communicated by Calvin Wells.

5. W. Mackay Mackenzie (ed.), *The Poems of William Dunbar* (London, 1970), 66-67.

6. AE. J.G. Mackey (ed.), *The Historie and Cronicles of Scotland [by] Robert Lindesay of Pitscottie* (Edinburgh, 1899), I, 242-243.

7. James Balfour Paul (ed.), *Accounts of the Lord High Treasurer of Scotland* (Edinburgh, 1902), III, xlix.

8. *Ibid.*, IV, 64.

9. *Ibid.*, 401.

10. Mackay, *Pitscottie*, I, 244.

PAUL EDWARDS AND JAMES WALVIN

North Africans, were also at court, and one of them, Taubronar, devised a dance for "Fasteringis Evin, be the Kingis command."[11]

It was common enough at this time for people to dress up as Africans for dances, and characters with blackened bodies or clothes feature in folk processions and folk drama from medieval times. Play costumes were designed for four Moors to celebrate the baptism of the king's son at Stirling on December 17, 1566, including bonnets of false hair. And Jones quotes a description of the entertainment attended by Henry VIII and the Earl of Essex in 1510, "appareled after Turkey fashion," in which six ladies appeared with "their faces, neckes, armes and handes covered with fyne pleasaunce black . . . so that the same ladies seemed to be nigrost or blacke Mores."[12]

Among the earliest records of black Africans actually being carried to Britain from Africa is John Lok's account of his second voyage to Guinea, which took place in 1554-1555. He acquired "certaine blacke slaves, whereof some were tall and strong men, and could wel agree with our meates and drinkes."[13] From his voyage to Morocco in 1551 Windham brought back "two Moores being noble men, whereof one was of the King's blood."[14] Towerson took two Negroes with him to act as interpreters on his second voyage to Guinea:

> We found a faire Bay where we ran in, and found a smal towne, but the Negros in a long time would not to us, but at the last by the perswasion of our owne Negros, one boat came to us, and with him we sent George our Negro a shore, and after he had talked with them, they came aboord our boates without feare, and I gave their captaine a bason, and two strings of Margarets. . . . This place is called Bulle, and here the Negros were very glad of our Negros, and shewed them all the friendship they could, when they had told them they were the men that were taken away being now againe brought by us.[15]

11. Paul, *Accounts*, II, 477.

12. Eldred Jones, *Othello's Countrymen: The African in English Renaissance Drama* (London, 1965), 28; Paul, *Accounts*, XII, 401.

13. Richard Hakluyt, *The Principal Navigations, Voiages, Traffiques and Discoveries of the English Nation* (Glasgow, 1903-1905), VI, 176.

14. *Ibid.*, 137.

15. *Ibid.*, 217.

The names of two other Africans, Anthonie and Binnie, are given in the same account: they are said to have "bene at London in England, and should be brought home the next voyage."[16]

At this stage the English had not become deeply involved in the flourishing slave trade, but they had already begun to display toward Africans the signs of fear, revulsion, or contempt that were to be closely associated with attempts to justify the barbarities of the trade. A common argument against Negroes was that they were descended from Noah's son Cham, and that God had placed a curse on their race as a punishment for their ancestor's wickedness. In the eighteenth century, abolitionists still took this argument sufficiently seriously to spend time disproving it.[17] It appears that Noah gave orders to his sons to "abstain from carnall copulation with their wives" while in the Ark,

> which good instructions and exhortations notwithstanding his wicked son Cham disobeyed, and being perswaded that the first childe borne after the floud (by right and Law of nature) should inherite and possesse all the dominions of the earth, hee contrary to his fathers commandment while they were yet in the Arke, used company with his wife, and craftily went about thereby to dis-inherite the off-spring of his other two bretheren: for the which wicked and detestable fact, as an example for contempt of Almightie God, and disobedience of parents, God would a sonne be borne whose name was Chus, who not onely it selfe, but all his posteritie after him should bee so blacke and lothsome, that might remaine a spectacle of disobedience to all the worlde. And of this blacke and cursed Chus came all these blacke Moores which are in Africa, for after the water was vanished from off the face of the earth, and that the lande was dry, Sem chose that part of the land to inhabite in, which nowe is called Asia, and Japhet had that which now is called Europa, wherein wee dwell, and Africa remained for Cham and his blacke sonne Chus, and was called Chamesis after the fathers name, being perhaps a cursed, dry, sandy, and unfruitfull ground, fit for such a generation to inhabite in.[18]

---

16. *Ibid.*, 218.

17. Ottobah Cugoano, *Thoughts and Sentiments on the Evil of Slavery* (London, 1787; reprint ed. Paul Edwards, London, 1969); Thomas Clarkson, *On the Slavery and Commerce of the Human Species* (London, 1786).

18. Hakluyt, *Voiages*, VII, 263-264, quoted in James Walvin, *The Black Presence* (London, 1971), 36-37.

In this and related ways blackness came to be widely associated with sin, and often with sexual incontinence. We learn from Lok's second voyage, in a passage added to Lok's account by his editor, Richard Eden, that the Guinea coast was inhabited by "a people of beastly living, without a God, lawe, religion, or common wealth, and so scorched and vexed with the heat of the sunne, that in many places they curse it when it riseth."[19] Jones has recently shown that Negro characters in Elizabethan and Jacobean drama are, with very few exceptions, presented as lecherous, treacherous villains and, indeed, the Devil himself was commonly represented as black in both painting and popular drama. A pale complexion was sought after as a particular mark of beauty and ladies extravagantly praised for their "whiteness" or dispraised for their "blackness."[20] And into this world of whiteness and chastity the black African entered, in person and in print, his color imaging all that was contrary to prevailing English values of beauty and goodness.

In *Othello* Shakespeare shows himself aware of the effect of these current ideas upon an African personality. Quite apart from Iago's sneers behind Othello's back at the "thick-lips" and "the old black ram," there is Brabantio's display of pseudo liberalism. Brabantio is happy to welcome the distinguished black man to his home, but the underlying race prejudice spills out when he learns that Othello has married his daughter. He cannot believe that Desdemona

> Would ever have, t'incur a general mock,
> Run from her guardage to the sooty bosom
> Of such a thing as thou. . . .

Brabantio sees the marriage as "against all rules of nature," giving a lead to Iago who, at a crucial point in the play, suggests that the marriage is sexually perverse:

---

19. Hakluyt, *Voiages*, VI, 167.
20. Jones, *Othello's Countrymen*, 37-119. For the eighteenth-century use of the expression "black devil" see James Albert Ukawsaw Gronniosaw, *A Narrative of the Most remarkable Particulars in the Life of James Albert Ukawsaw Gronniosaw an African Prince* (Dublin, 1790), 16; and reference to Bill Richmond below, 184. See also James Walvin, *Black and White* (London, 1973), 23-24.

Ay, there's the point, as (to be bold with you)
Not to affect many proposed matches
Of her own clime, complexion and degree,
Whereto we see in all things nature tends—
Foh! one may smell in such a will most rank,
Foul disproportion, thoughts unnatural.

Not surprisingly, the man who has been made to feel himself loved in spite of his color—"For she had eyes and chose me"—blames his color, along with his age, when made to feel cheated and ugly, and sees his reputation "now begrimed and black / As mine own face."[21]

But there were other reasons for prejudice against Negroes in England at the end of the sixteenth century, economic ones in particular. A period of dearth coincided with an expanding population which included many immigrants, the most noticeable being the Negroes, though some of the latter found stable employment as servants to the nobility and even at court. Lord Derby employed a black servant as early as 1569 and Elizabeth herself had a black page as well as an African court entertainer. The Lord Mayor's Show employed black entertainers in the early seventeenth century. "The Grocers generally exhibited a King of the Moors, an island of spices, and mounted Blacks who liberally distributed foreign fruit from panniers at their side to the crowding spectators." According to the accounts, they were mounted on "griffins and camels."[22] A census of "straungers" in the London parish of All Hallows for about 1599 lists three women as "negras," Clar, Maria, and Marea, and one "negro," presumably a man though his name is illegible. It is not clear whether they were servants at the houses listed, or boarders.[23] But one community with black members built their own houses in London and got into trouble over the strict building regulations. In 1597 the attorney-general took action against "a certain Negroose and others" for building cottages "contrary to the proclamation," and the houses were destroyed "for their

21. William Shakespeare (Alvin Kernan, ed.), *The Tragedy of Othello* (New York, 1963), I.ii.65-70; I.iii.101; III.iii.228-233; III.iii.189; III.iii.384-385.

22. C. S. L. Davies, "Slavery and the Protector Somerset; the Vagrancy Act of 1547," *Economic History Review*, XIX (1966), 548n; *Calendar of State Papers, Domestic* (1595-1597), April 7, 1597, 381; Charles Knight (ed.), *London* (London, n.d.), VI, 155-156.

23. *Notes and Queries* (April, 1961), 138.

PAUL EDWARDS AND JAMES WALVIN

base condition."[24] But even if some Africans were comparatively well settled in Britain, there were others who were considered a social threat. In
1596 Elizabeth wrote to the lord mayors of the major cities noting that
"there are of late divers blackamores brought into this realm, of which
kinde of people there are already to manie consideryng howe God hath
blessed this land with great increase of people of our nation as anie coun-
trie in the world"; her instructions were that "these kinde of people
should be sent forth from the land."[25] She repeated this later in the year,
saying that "these kind of people may be well spared in this realme, being
so populous,"[26] and licensed a merchant, Caspar van Senden of Lübeck,
to deport Negroes. This license was issued again in 1601:

> Whereof the Queen's majesty, tendering the good and welfare of her
> own natural subjects, greatly distressed in these hard times of
> dearth, is highly discontented to understand the great number of
> Negroes and blackamoors which (as she is informed) are carried into
> this realm since the troubles between her highness and the King of
> Spain; who are fostered and powered here, to the great annoyance
> of her own liege people that which co[vet] the relief which these
> people consume, as also for the most of them are infidels having no
> understanding of Christ or his Gospel: hath given a special com-
> mandment that the said kind of people shall be with all speed
> avoided and discharged out of this her majesty's realms.[27]

So, while there is no firm evidence that the African in Britain at this time
was brutalized to the degree and on the scale of later periods, the economic and legal ground had been prepared for his future degradation and
dehumanization.

The Growth of a Black Community: 1600-1800

Legal Status

In the first half of the seventeenth century, the English involvement with
the slave trade was still haphazard, and there is no evidence of any great

---

24. E. M. Leonard, *The Early History of English Poor Relief* (Cambridge, 1906),
297n.
25. *Acts of the Privy Council*, XXVI (1596-1597), 16.
26. *Ibid.*, 20-21.
27. P. L. Hughes and J. F. Larkin, *Tudor Royal Proclamations* (New Haven,
1969), 3.221.

increase in the numbers of Africans in Britain, though the employment of black servants was growing more common. But numbers began to expand as a consequence of English settlement in the Caribbean and the need for slaves on the sugar plantations, particularly after Jamaica was taken from Spain in 1655. From the middle of the century, slaves were brought to Britain both directly from Africa, and from the West Indies traveling with their masters. In 1651, for instance, the Guinea Company asked one of its factors in West Africa to "buy for us 15 to 20 lusty young Negers of about 15 years of age [and] bring them with you to London."[28] There were free Negroes, but they appear to have been exposed to ill-treatment by their masters,[29] and the newspapers of the time frequently advertised for runaway slaves:

> Run away the first Instant from Sir Phineas Pett at the Navy Office, a Negro about 16 years of age, pretty tall, he speaks English, but slow in Speech, with a livery of dun coloured Cloth, lined with Blue, and so edged in the Seams, the Buttons Pewter, wearing a Cloth Cap, his Coat somewhat too short for him, he is called by the name of Othello.[30]

Such escapes by black slaves invariably involved robbery, since even the clothes they stood in, often elaborate liveries, belonged to their masters.

Another factor to encourage the slave trade in the second half of the seventeenth century was the stability of the Restoration period after the economic disruption of the Civil War. The Company of the Royal Adventurers of Africa was reorganized in 1663, backed by the king and the Duke of York. In 1672 it was replaced by the Royal African Company, which held effective control until the end of the century during a period of simultaneous and associated growth in British imperial and economic ambition, the West Indian sugar industry, and the trade in African slaves. In the process the African slave became a vital economic commodity, and by 1700 an Englishman was able to write of a Negro in his will, "I take [him] to be in the nature of my goods and chattels."[31] But the

---

28. Elizabeth Donnan, *Documents Illustrative of the Slave Trade to America* (Washington, 1930), I, 128.

29. *Calendar of State Papers, Domestic* (1619-1622), "Petition of John Anthony," March 1620, 131.

30. *Notes and Queries* (1917), 146.

31. Will of Thomas Papillon, 1700/1, v. 1015, T. 44, Kent archives.

PAUL EDWARDS AND JAMES WALVIN

economic importance of the Negro resulted in a fundamental confusion in English law. On the one hand the black slave was guaranteed basic human rights in England by the Habeas Corpus Act of 1679;[32] on the other, he was, as we have seen, viewed as a mere chattel and movable property, as defined by the Navigation Acts. So, although in the 1660s the Royal African Adventurers tended to speak of Africans transported to the New World as "Negro-Servants," by 1677 a process of dehumanization was completed when in the opinion of the solicitor-general "negroes ought to be esteemed goods and commodities within the Acts of Trade and Navigation."[33] The stamp of government approval was buttressed by a common law decision that same year: "Negroes being usually bought and sold among Merchants, so Merchandise."[34] From this time on, legal decisions were dogged by these contradictions: thus in 1706 Lord Chief Justice Holt declared that "By the common law no man can have property in another . . . there is no such thing as a slave by the laws of England,"[35] and yet subsequent decisions in the following century by Yorke and Talbot in 1729 and by Lord Hardwicke (formerly Yorke) in 1749 held that a slave remained the property of his master, even though baptized and in England, and so was returnable to slavery in the colonies. "They are like stock on a farm," declared Hardwicke quite unequivocally.[36] By the 1760s, however, the volume of resistance to the slave trade and to the very idea of slavery had begun to swell, and under the leadership of Granville Sharp a significant victory was won in the Mansfield Decision of 1772, though the case was not as decisive as has often been claimed. This case, judged by Lord Chief Justice Mansfield, was between a "slave," James Somerset, and his "master," Charles Stewart. It was claimed at the time, and since, that Mansfield declared the slaves of England free, but in fact his decision gave them only freedom from forcible repatriation to the Americas.[37]

32. W. S. Holdsworth, *A History of English Law* (London, 1926), IX, 112.

33. *Calendar of State Papers, Colonial America and West Indies* (1677-1680), 118, 120.

34. H. T. Catterall, *Judicial Cases Concerning American Slavery and the Negro* (Washington, 1926), I, 9.

35. *Ibid.*, 11-12.

36. *Ibid.*, 9-11.

37. Edward Fiddes, "Lord Mansfield and the Somersett Case," *Law Quarterly Review*, L (1934), 499-511, gives precise legal details. For a more general account, see Walvin, *Black and White*, 117-131.

In the years following the Mansfield Decision the London black population grew into an increasingly active, coherent, and articulate body. Among their leaders was Olaudah Equiano, about whom more will be said below. He had been a slave, but had learned to read, write, and speak English well, as can be seen in his own account of his resale by his master, Captain Henry Pascal, to a Captain James Doran:

> When I came there Captain Doran asked me if I knew him; I answered that I did not; 'Then,' said he, 'you are now my slave.' I told him my master could not sell me to him or to any one else. 'Why,' said he, 'did not your master buy you?' I confessed he did. 'But I have served him,' said I, 'many years, and he has taken all my wages and prize-money, for I only got one sixpence during the war; besides this I have been baptized; and by the laws of the land no man has a right to sell me;' and I added, that I had heard a lawyer and others at different times tell my master so. They both then said that these people who told me so were not my friends; but I replied—it was very extraordinary that other people did not know the law as well as they. Upon this Captain Doran said I talked too much English; and if I did not behave myself well, and be quiet, he had a method on board to make me.[38]

This incident took place in 1762, and shows the confusion of popular opinion on the legal status of slaves: but even more important, it shows that the slaves were beginning to listen, think, and speak for themselves. By 1774, Equiano was active on behalf of other slaves in London and reporting the case of one John Annis to Granville Sharp.[39] And it was he who first reported to Granville Sharp the case of the Zong murders in 1783, when over 130 slaves were deliberately drowned in a West African port to save insurance money.[40] Other London blacks were also reporting to Sharp on the trepanning and carrying aboard ship of their fellows.[41] And there was a group of London blacks in court when Mansfield gave his decision, described in a contemporary newspaper:

38. Olaudah Equiano, *The Interesting Narrative of the Life of Olaudah Equiano* (London, 1789; reprint ed. Paul Edwards, London, 1969), I, 176-177.
39. *Ibid.*, II, 119-123.
40. Prince Hoare, *Memoir of Granville Sharp* (London, 1820), 238.
41. *Ibid.*, 247. Ottobah Cugoano ("John Stewart") reported the trepanning of a Negro servant, Harry Demane, to Sharp on July 28, 1786. Demane later went to Sierra Leone with the freed slaves and himself turned slaver: see Hoare, *Memoir*, 345.

PAUL EDWARDS AND JAMES WALVIN

> [They] bowed with profound respect to the Judges, and shaking each
> other by the hand, congratulated themselves on their recovery of the
> rights of human nature, and their happy lot that permitted them to
> breathe the free air of England.[42]

In spite of this growing activity and self-help, Africans continued to
be treated for some years in England as slaves, and newspapers regularly
advertised the sale of Negroes in London and elsewhere. Mansfield explained that his decision was not to deny masters the right of ownership,
only the right to "forcibly take the slave and carry him abroad."[43] But
even this was too severe a limitation for the slave owners, who devised
plans to circumvent the law and deprive the slaves of what little advantage they had gained. Slaves traveling with their masters to Britain were
compelled to sign indentures, and their status on arrival in Britain converted from bondage to that of indentured worker, rendering them liable
to prosecution under English law if they tried to escape or refused repatriation.[44] In view of the shuffling and ambiguous attitude taken by English
law toward slavery it is not surprising that the feelings revealed by black
spokesmen of the period should show similar ambivalence, shifting between respect and affection on one hand and profound distrust on the
other.

In Scotland, however, a less ambiguous progress of justice was seen.
In July 1757 a slave brought to Scotland from Virginia was baptized and
at once asked a Scottish court for his freedom. His master promptly put
him aboard a vessel bound for Virginia and the slave's death, before any
court hearing could be completed, prevented any resolution of "the respective claims of liberty and servitude by the master and negro."[45] Another case is recorded between 1769 and 1770. The Negro slave of a West
Indian trader resident at Methil was baptized by a local minister, Dr.
Harry Spens, and took the name David Spens. He too claimed his freedom as a result of baptism, and his master, characteristically, made plans
to ship him back to the West Indies. However, Spens was "delighted with

---

42. J. J. Hecht, *Continental and Colonial Servants in Eighteenth-Century England*
(Northampton, Mass., 1954), 48.
43. Quoted in *A Letter to Philo-Africanus* (London, 1788), 39.
44. Catterall, *Judicial Cases*, I, 21.
45. *Ibid.*, 18.

the freedom he had in the bracing village of Methil, and having an inkling of his master's intention, he left him and took up his abode with a farmer in Wemyss parish."[46] Four Scottish advocates and a solicitor took up his case, refusing all fees, though considerable sums were raised locally for his defense. He won his case and returned to work for the farmer who had befriended him, becoming a popular local figure. What is particularly remarkable is that most of the funds raised to help David Spens were collected by the salters, miners, and agricultural laborers of the district. The miners and salters were virtually slaves themselves,[47] and this case illustrates the good relations that the black slaves in Britain and the black population in general often enjoyed with the working people of the country, though there is evidence to the contrary as well. Sir John Fielding remarked how, at times, those attempting to apprehend an escaped slave might find themselves confronted by a mob gathered to assist the escaper.[48] And the large number of black seamen in the Royal Navy seem to have lived on perfectly good terms with their white fellows.

The case which firmly established the freedom of black slaves in Scotland was that of Joseph Knight, who came to Glasgow with his master, John Wedderburn, in 1771, and remained with him for some years. "A love affair then set the man upon the idea of attempting to recover his liberty, which a recent decision of Lord Mansfield in England seemed to make by no means hopeless."[49] Knight ran away from Wedderburn but was arrested and ordered by the justices to return to his master. Knight's appeal to the sheriff of Perthshire was successful, however, and presumably with the Mansfield case in mind the sheriff declared that "the state of slavery is not recognised by the laws of this kingdom."[50] Wedderburn's appeal to the Court of Sessions was turned down by a narrow majority, much of the credit being due to the lord advocate, Henry Dundas, whose speech "generously contributed to the cause of the sooty stranger."[51]

46. A. S. Cunningham, *Rambles in the Parishes of Scoomie and Wemyss* (Leven, 1905), 154-156.

47. A. S. Cunningham, *Mining in Mid and East Lothian* (Edinburgh, 1905), 25-32.

48. John Fielding, *Extracts from Such of the Penal Laws, as Particularly Relate to the Peace and Good Order of This Metropolis* (London, 1699), 144.

49. Robert Chambers, *Domestic Annals of Scotland* (Edinburgh, 1874), 453.

50. Catterall, *Judicial Cases*, I, 18.

51. G. B. Hill (ed.), *Boswell's Life of Johnson*, revised by L. F. Powell (Oxford, 1934), III, 213.

PAUL EDWARDS AND JAMES WALVIN

Though restricted in application to Scotland, this decision was firmer and much more far-reaching than Mansfield's. In the words of Boswell, the case "went upon a much broader ground than the case of Somersett . . . being truly the general question, whether a perpetual obligation of service to one master in any mode should be sanctified by the law of a free country."[52]

Numbers and Distribution

It is impossible to give reliable figures for the number of Africans in Britain at any time during this period though there was ample speculation. The figure usually quoted with most confidence is Lord Mansfield's assertion, in 1772, that there were 15,000 Africans in Britain.[53] But in 1764 the *Gentleman's Magazine* had hazarded a guess of 20,000,[54] a figure increased a year later to 30,000 by the *Morning Chronicle*.[55] On the other hand, Edward Long in his viciously antiblack pamphlet *Candid Reflections* at first proposed a mere 3,000, which he increased to 15,000 in a postscript as soon as he heard Mansfield's estimate.[56]

Clearly there was a large black population, expanding steadily, particularly in London, and causing considerable concern by the 1780s. But until the end of the American War of Independence loosed onto the London streets a stream of black poor, the concern appears to have been rooted in race prejudice rather than any clear economic threat. The prejudice is recorded largely by the servant-employing class, but the servants' "misconduct" and the reports of their "unreliability" are often a consequence of the servants' (or slaves') very understandable desire for a freedom they should never have lost.

Free Africans settled in all parts of Britain, often marrying white wives and apparently living harmoniously in white society, though racial incidents occurred, as might be expected. A black boxer and publican, Bill Richmond, is on record as having given a "milling" to one Frank

---

52. *Ibid.*, 212.
53. William Cobbett, *A Complete Collection of State Trials . . . compiled by T. B. Howell* (London, 1820), XX, 71, 77.
54. *Gentleman's Magazine* (1764), 493.
55. Walvin, *Black and White*, 46.
56. [Edward Long], *Candid Reflections* (London, 1772), 53, 75-76.

Myers, who called him a "black devil etc." for walking out with a white girl.[57] Some such outbursts were understandable in view of the success enjoyed by a number of Africans with the ladies. Dr. Johnson's black servant, Francis Barber (who married a white woman), was said by the doctor to have "carried the Empire of Cupid farther than most men," and was on one occasion pursued from Lincolnshire to London by a local lady haymaker.[58]

Edward Long, known as "the planters' friend," was not pleased by such goings-on. "The lower order of women," he declared, "are remarkably fond of the blacks, for reasons too brutal to mention," not that this prevented him from mentioning some of them.[59] However, such scandals as the conduct of the Duchess of Queensberry's protégé Soubise,[60] or the emotional crisis caused by the birth of a black child to a white couple in Midgham, Berkshire,[61] have to be set against a number of stable marriages between black and white. Olaudah Equiano announced his marriage to a Cambridgeshire girl of respectable family, Susan Cullen, with Boswellian earthiness in a letter to some Nottingham friends:

> I now mean as it seem Pleasing to my Good God, to leave London in about 8 or 10 Days more, and take me a Wife (one Miss Cullen) of Soham in Cambridge shire and when I have given her about 8 or 10 Days Comfort, I mean Directly to go to Scotland and sell my 5th Editions.[62]

They had two daughters, one of whom, Anne Maria, died at the age of four and is commemorated in a tablet at St. Andrew's Parish Church, Chesterton, near Cambridge.[63] Another African writer of the period, Gronniosaw, tells how he fell in love at first sight with a white girl, Betty,

57. [Pierce Egan], *Boxiana; or Sketches of Ancient and Modern Pugilism by One of the Fancy* (London, 1812), 440-449.

58. G. B. Hill, *Johnsonian Miscellany* (Oxford, 1897), I, 291; Hester L. Piozzi, *Anecdotes of the late Samuel Johnson* (London, 1786), 210.

59. Long, *Candid Reflections*, 48.

60. See below, 193.

61. Midgham Parish Register, 1769, Berkshire Record Office.

62. Equiano, *Narrative*, editor's introduction, xiv-xv.

63. *Ibid.*, vi-vii. The inscription adjoins the main entrance and has been identified by D. H. Simpson, librarian of the Royal Commonwealth Society.

PAUL EDWARDS AND JAMES WALVIN

and married her.[64] A free Negro, Charles Morett, raised a mixed family in an English village, North Ashton,[65] and another mixed marriage on record is of an African to the landlady of a York tavern.[66] There was racist abuse for some mixed marriages, but a black man's choice of partner must have been severely limited in Britain at this time since there appear to have been many more black men than black women.[67] The degree of prejudice seems to have been less than in America. One American traveler records with surprise his encounter with

> A well dressed white girl, who was of a ruddy complexion, and even handsome, walking arm in arm, and conversing very sociably, with a negro man, who was as well dressed as she, and so black that his skin had a kind of ebony lustre.[68]

The "little race of mulattoes" noted in 1710 by Philip Thicknesse[69] is further evidence of the inevitable racial mingling taking place during these years.

There is abundant evidence for the ill-treatment of free Negroes, for example in the writings of Equiano, Sancho, and Cugoano, but this appears to have come principally from the middle class. In Equiano's autobiography we read again and again of his good relationships with British seamen; he suffered bad experiences too, but mostly from West Indian and American planters and their ships' captains. Hecht, discussing prejudice against Africans revealed in the letters and pamphlets of the period, concludes:

> Unlike the numerous attacks directed against continental domestics, these fulminations represented no widespread body of hostile opinion. At most they reflected the sentiments of a relatively small number of scattered individuals. The public at large does not seem to have felt that negro domestics constituted a menace.[70]

---

64. Gronniosaw, *Narrative*, 32.
65. *Notes and Queries* (December, 1878), 453.
66. Walvin, *Black and White*, 52.
67. Hecht, *Servants*, 42-47, 89n.
68. *Ibid.*, 47.
69. Quoted in Cedric Dover, *Hell in the Sunshine* (London, 1943), 159.
70. Hecht, *Servants*, 46.

In 1783, however, opinion appears to have hardened against Negroes, notably in London, when the postwar dislocation of the British defeat in America led among other things to the influx of Negroes from America. Black soldiers who had been promised their freedom in return for joining the British army, black seamen discharged from the navy, black servants with returning dispossessed masters, and others who had lost their employment in America poured into Britain, particularly London. Again, it is impossible to estimate the numbers involved, though it did produce an unrealistic nervousness about the problems posed by black immigration. One consequence was the encouragement given to immigrants to settle in Sierra Leone, but the number which ultimately went was small and the black population appears to have been absorbed into Britain without any need for mass deportations.

As early as the sixteenth century there were Africans settled as far from London as Barnstable and Plymouth in Devonshire,[71] and in Edinburgh were the "twa blak ledeis" already mentioned. A full exploration of the evidence for African settlement in Britain would be too massive an undertaking for so short an essay as this, but, in brief, it points to a range of settlements covering the whole country by the early eighteenth century. London predominates, particularly the black ghettos of Mile End, Paddington, and the riverside parishes, but many immigrants entered through west-coast ports, notably Liverpool and Bristol. Some became permanent residents, but not all: in 1789 an estimated number of fifty boys and twenty-eight girls from Sierra Leone were being educated in London, Liverpool, Bristol, and Lancaster. In Liverpool, John Hanson established himself as a joiner, an unusual occupation for an African since few in Britain were trained as skilled artisans, though in 1728 a young slave was offered for sale in Bristol "fit to be Instructed in any Handycraft trade." In northern Britain, besides the Africans resident in Scotland, there are several recorded in Cumberland (one of them a prisoner in a Cumberland jail), and on the other side of the country we find the African previously mentioned who was married to the landlady of a York tavern.[72] In the same county a slave called Beswick was the only

---

71. Walvin, *Black and White*, 8, 14n.
72. *Ibid.*, 51-58.

PAUL EDWARDS AND JAMES WALVIN

regular member of his parish church not to be baptized. He was described as "a Youth of no Learning and but of slender capacity," and though two local ministers prepared him for baptism, there seems to have been some reluctance in Yorkshire to baptize black people without the consent of the archbishop.[73] In Lincolnshire the slave of the Jenkinson family of Claxby-by-Normanby was killed by his master in a fit of drunken rage late in the seventeenth century, and in Nottinghamshire twelve black slaves and their families are on record around 1680.[74] Further south, Africans, both slaves and freemen, are recorded in Bedfordshire, Berkshire, Kent, Essex, Shropshire, and Sussex,[75] as well as the Isle of Wight.[76]

In addition to those settled in particular places, there were a number of itinerant Africans. Equiano, for instance, made several journeys outside Britain to the continent of Europe, the Arctic, and Central America, and also traveled within Britain, selling copies of his book in Ireland and Scotland as well as northern England and the Midlands.[77] Ignatius Sancho traveled as a servant of the Duchess of Montagu to Dalkeith in Scotland and wrote in 1770 of trips to the Highlands.[78] Another African writer, the impoverished Gronniosaw, described his wanderings in search of employment: after service with the army in the Caribbean, he traveled from Portsmouth to London, then to Colchester and Norwich, and at the close of his book he was living in Kidderminster.[79] Traveling theaters and fairs also had their black actors and performers.[80]

Occupations

Most Africans in Britain during this period were employed as personal servants, but within this profession the social range was considerable. There is ample evidence of the good treatment of African servants in Britain, and their lot was generally more happy than that of their fellows in

---

73. *Ibid.*, 65.
74. *Ibid.*, 11.
75. *Ibid.*, 11, 50, 53, 58, 65.
76. Equiano, *Narrative*, I, 152-153.
77. *Ibid.*, Appendix B.
78. *The Letters of the Late Ignatius Sancho an African* (London, 1782; 5th ed., London, 1803; reprint ed. Paul Edwards, London, 1968), 20-22.
79. Gronniosaw, *Narrative*.
80. Walvin, *Black and White*, 81-82.

the New World, particularly the plantation slaves. All the same, until 1772 the threat of being returned to American or West Indian slavery hung over most African servants in Britain, as was the case with Equiano and David Spens, already noted. Sancho's biographer Jekyll tells how Sancho's first owners, three tyrannical ladies, "even threatened on angry occasions to return Ignatius Sancho to his African slavery." On this, he left them and took service with the Montagu family, who treated him with the greatest kindness. When in 1773 "repeated attacks of the gout, and a constitutional corpulence, rendered him incapable of further attendance on the Duke's family,"[81] he was helped by the family to set up a chandler's shop in Westminster, where he lived, a respected middle-class London citizen, until his death in 1780. In a number of similar examples of good treatment a convincing picture of the life of servants in such homes emerges, though the condescension of a "good" master could for obvious reasons be a sore irritant, as in the case of Equiano discussed below. Hecht quotes a letter sent by the Duchess of Devonshire to her mother as illustrating the "tenderness and attachment" felt towards black servants:

> George Hanger has sent me a black boy, eleven years old and very honest, but the Duke don't like me having a black, and yet I cannot bear the poor wretch being ill-used; if you like him instead of Michel I will send him; he will be a cheap servant and you will make a Christian of him and a good boy; if you don't like him they say Lady Rockingham wants one.[82]

Hecht comments that "when a brief relationship could inspire so much solicitude, it is scarcely surprising that a longer one often produced deep devotion." But this seems to us a superficial view: the "tenderness" is no more than surface feeling here; the emphasis seems to be on the boy's cheapness, his reliability, and his function as commodity, veiled only by the sentimental tone of the letter.

For the more fortunate Africans—or the less unfortunate—there were opportunities for education, although, as we have seen in the case

---

81. Sancho, *Letters*, Jekyll's memoir, ii-iii, v.
82. Hecht, *Servants*, 41.

PAUL EDWARDS AND JAMES WALVIN

of Equiano's knowing "too much English," this could prove a disadvantage to the slave owner. Equiano had the good fortune to meet up with people who were willing to teach him or send him to school. Even when he was serving aboard the *Namur* provision was made for schooling.[83] Sancho was provided with books by the Duke of Montagu even before he entered service with him.[84] Both Sancho and Equiano achieved a competence in English well above the average, but Gronniosaw's autobiography had to be "taken from his own mouth and committed to paper by the elegant pen of a young lady of the town of Leominster," and although he speaks several times of reading printed books, he also tells us that he was unable to read his wife's handwritten letters.[85] Ottobah Cugoano's *Thoughts and Sentiments* appears to show a high degree of competence in English, but a manuscript letter written five years later is packed with errors of grammar and spelling; it seems impossible for him to have written his book without considerable assistance.[86] There is other evidence indicating a wide range of fluency in English among black servants,[87] but in general they would be expected to achieve a fair level of articulateness if only in order to cope with their household duties.

Other Africans came to Britain as students. African chiefs began to send their sons to Europe for an education; John Corrente, Braffo of Annamaboe, sent one of his sons to France and another, named Cupid, to Britain. However, the ship's captain, who was supposed to carry Cupid to London, sailed for Barbados and sold the boy, claiming that Corrente owed him money. An agent was sent to trace Cupid and, along with another black boy, he was at last brought to London and treated, amongst other entertainments, to a performance of Mrs. Aphra Behn's *Oroonoko* in Thomas Southerne's dramatized version at the Covent Garden Theatre, "with which they were so affected, that the tears flow'd plentifully from their eyes; the case of *Oroonoko*'s being made a slave by the treachery of a captain being so very similar to their own."[88]

---

83. Equiano, *Narrative*, I, 151-152.
84. Sancho, *Letters*, Jekyll's memoir, ii.
85. Gronniosaw, *Narrative*, i, 38.
86. Cugoano, *Thoughts and Sentiments*, editor's introduction, x-xi, xxi-xxiii.
87. Walvin, *Black and White*, 63.
88. Douglas Grant, *The Fortunate Slave* (London, 1968), 145-147.

In the 1790s, Chief Naimbana of Sierra Leone sent one son to France, another was placed under a Mandingo teacher, and the eldest, John Frederick, resolved to make his way to England for his education. Hoare tells us that "he learned, in the space of a year and a half, to read very fluently, and to write a letter in English without much difficulty."[89] Hoare adds a a striking anecdote in a footnote to this account of John Frederick, illustrating "the extreme sensibility which he felt, when any circumstance arose which touched the honour of his country." When someone made a remark on the inferiority of Africans, John Frederick, despite being reminded of his Christian duty, was moved to reply in "violent and vindictive language":

'If a man should rob me of my money, I can forgive him; if a man should shoot at me, or try to stab me, I can forgive him; if a man should sell me and all my family to a slave-ship, so that we should pass all the rest of our days in slavery in the West Indies, I can forgive him;—but' (added he, rising from his seat with much emotion,) 'if a man takes away the character of the people of my country, I never can forgive him'.[90]

He develops this theme with great vigor and at some length. It is a sad postscript to the tale that he died within a few hours of landing on his return to Freetown.

Another Sierra Leonean, Anthony Domingo, also the son of a local chief, came to England for his education and wrote in June 1797 from Freetown to Granville Sharp expressing his gratitude and "hearty thanks to the Directors of the Sierra Leone Company, for giving me education and bringing me to the knowledge of God. . . . When I left England I felt a violent struggle in my mind between inclination and duty. I could have wished to have spent my advanced years in that place where I first obtained your acquaintance. But I hope I shall be one of the numbers that shall teach my countrymen."[91] Probably the best known African student in Britain during this century was Job ben Solomon, one of the few Afri-

---

89. Hoare, *Memoir of Sharp*, 369.
90. *Ibid.*, 368-369n.
91. *Ibid.*, 365-366.

PAUL EDWARDS AND JAMES WALVIN

cans taken in slavery ever to return to his native home. He was freed from slavery by James Oglethorpe, the founder of the colony in Georgia and a leading abolitionist, into whose hands had come a letter from Job to his father written in Arabic. On his arrival in England in 1733, Job was lionized in London, elected to the Gentlemen's Society at Spalding (whose members included Alexander Pope and Sir Isaac Newton) and presented at court. Later, Job worked as an interpreter for the Royal African Company.[92] Yet another African student in England, Philip Quaque, became the chaplain at Cape Coast Castle in Ghana. Quaque was sent to England with two other boys in 1754 but he was the only survivor. He married an Englishwoman, Catherine Blunt, who went to Cape Coast with him. His interpreter, John Aqua (Quaque did not keep up his knowledge of African languages), was educated in England in the 1750s. The children of Quaque's second marriage, which was to an African, were also sent away to England "in order to secure their tender minds from receiving the bad impressions of the country, the vile customs and practices and above all, the losing of their mother's vile jargon."[93]

There were Africans in a number of other kinds of employment. Some, like Gronniosaw, joined the army, others the British navy or merchant service. We have already referred to an African tavern-host in York, a joiner in Liverpool, and David Spens, who became an agricultural laborer.[94] A small number entered some of the professions. Shortly after the end of the eighteenth century a mulatto applied for a teaching post at Bisley, and his referee observed that "where so dark a complexion is not objected to, he would make a very valuable schoolmaster."[95] A free Negro worked as a clerk in the Admiralty in the late seventeenth century,[96] and Equiano was appointed to a civil post of importance as Commissary for Stores for the 1786 expedition of the London black poor to Sierra Leone.[97] John Marrant, a black Nova Scotian, was ordained a minister of the Countess of Huntingdon's Connexion, an independent

92. Grant, *Fortunate Slave*, gives a full account of Job's life.
93. Margaret Priestley, "Philip Quaque of Cape Coast," in Philip Curtin (ed.), *Africa Remembered* (Madison, 1967), 99-139.
94. See above, 182, 186, 187.
95. Letter of Richard Raikes, July 5, 1815, Gloucester County Record Office.
96. Joel A. Rogers, *Nature Knows No Color-Line* (New York, 1952), 165.
97. Equiano, *Narrative*, II, 231-246; editor's introduction, I, xxx-xlv.

church which had seceded from the Church of England; he died in Islington in 1781.[98]

Many Africans in Britain became musicians, some professionally, others simply for pleasure. Equiano writes several times of his enthusiasm for the French horn,[99] and Sancho not only played, but published music.[100] In 1764 "no less than 57 [Africans], men and women, supped, drank, and entertained themselves with dancing and music, consisting of violins, French horns and other instruments, at a public-house in Fleet Street. No whites were allowed to be present, for all the performers were black."[101] There are many examples of black musicians in army regiments.[102] And at a different level, George Bridgewater, born in Poland in 1789 of an African father and a Polish or German mother, became a virtuoso violinist and a friend of Beethoven; he was a guest of the Prince of Wales after having played before King George III at Windsor.[103]

Of the more eccentric occupations of Africans at this time perhaps the weirdest was that of George Alexander Grattox, "the Spotted Negro Boy," and Harlequin, "the White Negro woman," both of whom were displayed at traveling shows.[104] Equally unusual was the profession of Macomo, the most famous lion-tamer of his age,[105] whose son kept up the tradition and ran a circus in the nineteenth century. Harriet, an African from Guinea, was a highly successful London prostitute,[106] and Soubise, a protégé of the Duchess of Queensberry, said to be "as general a lover as Don Juan," was almost equally successful as a gigolo. The Duchess had taken great pains educating him in the other qualities of an English gentleman, for he was a skilled rider, musician, and conversationalist, but eventually, as the result of a scandal, he was packed off to

98. Christopher Fyfe, *A History of Sierra Leone* (Oxford, 1962), 31-32.

99. Equiano, *Narrative*, II, 84, 119.

100. Sancho, *Letters*, editor's introduction, viii.

101. Hecht, *Servants*, 49.

102. Walvin, *Black and White*, 70-71.

103. J. A. Rogers, *Great Men of Colour* (New York, 1972), II, 92-97.

104. *Notes and Queries* (1900), 506; (1910), 56; Papers on Harlequin, Q/SBb, 372/60-62, Essex Record Office.

105. Rogers, *Nature Knows No Color-Line*, 165.

106. *Nocturnal Revels* (London, 1779), 98-105.

PAUL EDWARDS AND JAMES WALVIN

India, where he died after falling from a horse.[107] Several of Sancho's letters are addressed to him or refer to his escapades.[108]

Two of the most attractive African figures of the period are the boxers Bill Richmond and Molyneaux. Richmond, born in New York in 1763, was taken up by the Duke of Northumberland, with whom he went to London in 1777. He had a successful career as a boxer, became a skilled cabinet-maker, and retired to keep the Horse and Dolphin at Richmond. He was also said to be an excellent cricketer.[109] An even more famous boxer of the period was Molyneaux, who also came from America but established his reputation in England. His two most memorable fights were with the heavyweight champion Tom Crib; the first was exceptionally bloody and fought for over forty rounds before a violent and prejudiced audience.[110] Molyneaux was said to be "remarkably civil and unassuming in his demeanour"; a ballad composed on the first fight with Crib ends,

A bumper to brave Crib, boys, to the black a bumper too,
Tho' beat, he prov'd a man my boys, what more could a man do![111]

Spokesmen for the Black Community

Although there is no reason to think that the numerous black servants were treated any worse than their white fellows, or suffered from any more prejudice than continental servants of the period, it is clear that some prejudice existed at all levels, particularly later in the eighteenth century. Consequently, the black population of Britain developed a firm sense of community. The articulate element looked after the interests of their fellow blacks, as when Equiano and Cugoano reported cases of ill-treatment to Granville Sharp, and joined with ten other Africans in writing a letter of thanks for his aid.[112]

---

107. Henry Angelo, *Reminiscences* (London, 1828), I, 446-452; *Nocturnal Revels*, 210-232.
108. Sancho, *Letters*, 5, 171-174, 184-185, 249-250, 287.
109. [Egan], *Boxiana*, 440-449.
110. *Ibid.*, 360-371, 401-414.
111. *Ibid.*, 480-481. A traveler on the A1 through Rutlandshire will find several fine early nineteenth-century prints of the first Crib-Molyneaux fight at the Ram Jam Inn, near where the fight took place.
112. Hoare, *Memoir of Sharp*, 374-375.

Equiano similarly took his appointment as Commissary for Stores for the 1786 expedition to Sierra Leone as an opportunity to create solidarity among his fellow Africans, against both white corruption and white authority. At one point he persuaded the Africans not to attend the services of the chaplain, "Fraser the Parson," "for no other reason whatever"—to use Fraser's words—"than that I am *white*."[113] That there was considerable color-feeling is indicated by the persistence with which the promoters of the expedition insisted upon the improvement of relations. In June 1787 Granville Sharp was able to write to his brother that "all the jealousies and animosities between the Whites and Blacks has subsided, and that they had been very orderly since Mr. Vasa [Equiano] and two or three other discontented persons had been left behind at Plymouth."[114] In the discussion of these problems in the press, even the white supporters of the expedition seem at times distinctly racist, as when one correspondent accuses Equiano of "advancing falsehoods as deeply black as his jetty face" and concludes with remarks on *"black* reports" and how "the *dark* transactions of a *Black* will be brought to *light.*"[115] Captain Thomas Thompson reported to the Navy Board that Equiano had been "turbulent and discontented, taking every means to actuate the minds of the Blacks to discord," but complained too that the leader of the expedition, Irwin, had taken no steps "which might indicate that he had the welfare of the people the least at heart."[116] The Navy Board came down on Equiano's side, and what emerges fairly clearly is that Equiano, in promoting the interests of his fellow blacks, found himself up against a rigid white authority on the expedition whose view of the blacks' rights was both paternalistic and limited.[117]

The Sierra Leone settlers were in fact to continue to experience such problems. There was some confusion in the 1790s, when the land grants promised by John Clarkson to the "Nova Scotian" settlers failed to mate-

113. *Public Advertiser*, July 2, 1787, reprinted in editor's introduction to Equiano, *Narrative*, xli.

114. Hoare, *Memoir of Sharp*, 313.

115. *Public Advertiser*, April 14, 1787, reprinted in editor's introduction to Equiano, *Narrative*, xlii.

116. T.i/643, 681, Public Record Office.

117. An account of Equiano's dispute is to be found in the editor's introduction to Equiano, *Narrative*, xxx-xlv.

PAUL EDWARDS AND JAMES WALVIN

rialize. The settlers sent two representatives to England at their own expense to claim these rights, but the representatives, Cato Perkins and Isaac Anderson, had no success. Correspondence with Clarkson and arguments with the Sierra Leone Company continued for some years. Eventually the settlers made a declaration of independence, but the affair subsided only after two of them had been hanged.[118]

In London, a spirit of black cooperation exhibited itself in a number of ways. A visitor wrote that "London abounds with an incredible number of these black men who have clubs to support those out of place."[119] We have quoted a news item about a dance held in 1764 at which "no whites were allowed to be present, for all the performers were black."[120] A few years later, in 1772, another such occasion is described which indicates that African dancing had assimilated local English conventions:

> Near 200 Blacks, with their ladies gathered in that year at a public house in Westminster, to celebrate the triumph which their brother Somerset had obtained over Mr Stuart his master. Lord Mansfield's health was echoed round the room, and the evening was concluded with a ball. The tickets for admittance to this Black assembly were 5s each.[121]

There was mutual aid at other levels of black society. When in 1773 two blacks were committed to Bridewell for begging, they were "visited by upwards of 300 of their countrymen" and the black community "contributed largely to their support during their confinement."[122]

Although there is ample evidence of continuing friendly relations between black and white, the special situation of the black poor and the former slaves in Britain created tensions and ambiguities toward white men which often appear to have been intensified by kindness as much as by cruelty. The African in Britain understood his position in relation to

---

118. Add. Ms. 41263, British Museum. This contains a large number of manuscript letters from settlers to John Clarkson. A full account is to be found in Fyfe, *History of Sierra Leone*, 38-87.

119. Philip Thicknesse, quoted in Dover, *Hell in the Sunshine*, 159.

120. Hecht, *Servants*, 49.

121. *Ibid.*

122. *Ibid.*, 48.

his declared enemies, but the problem, as it appears in the written work of the two principal black public spokesmen against slavery, Sancho and Equiano, was often to define his relation with those who claimed to be, and were felt to be, friends.

Although there is good reason to think that, at least by the latter part of the eighteenth century, a considerable number of Africans had received sufficient education to read and write, their cause was largely defended in print by white abolitionists. Hoare, quoting a letter to Granville Sharp from twelve London Africans (including Equiano and Cugoano), saw it as "the composition of some person better acquainted with the construction of the English language than the poor negro slaves can be supposed to have been."[123] Gronniosaw's autobiography, as we have noted, was admittedly ghosted by "the elegant pen of a young lady of the town of Leominster."[124] And Cugoano, on the evidence of a holograph letter dated 1791, clearly could not have written *Thoughts and Sentiments*, published four years earlier, without a very great deal of help. But Sancho undoubtedly, and Equiano with little doubt,[125] were able to articulate the black experience of eighteenth century life in Britain.

Their lives present a contrast, as do their published works. Sancho's letters are predominantly those of a man thoroughly assimilated to the middle-class English life of his day, though we should not be deceived by his often flippant and casual manner into thinking him unconcerned about the sufferings of his fellow Africans in Britain and the Americas. He was a devotee of literature and music, and a friend of David Garrick and Laurence Sterne. The family he served, the Brudenell family, which included the Dukes of Montagu and Buccleuch, treated him with respect and affection, and he ended his life as a prosperous shopkeeper (despite regular complaints about his lack of money). He had reached London at the age of two or three, and though we know little about his early life, it could not have involved him in sufferings on the scale endured by most American and West Indian slaves. When Equiano was being carried into slavery at the age of eleven, Sancho was already, at about twenty-five,

123. Hoare, *Memoir of Sharp*, 374n.
124. Gronniosaw, *Narrative*, i.
125. For a discussion of the authenticity of the *Narrative* of Equiano, see the editor's introduction, x-xviii.

PAUL EDWARDS AND JAMES WALVIN

an established servant in a generous home with no distinct memories of Africa or the slave trade.

Equiano, on the other hand, had seen it all. After a childhood and boyhood in a West African society, he suffered slavery in both Africa and the Americas, the horrors of the Middle Passage, warfare at sea, and shipwreck, followed by middle-class English life, polar exploration, and a period among the Central American Indians as assistant to an English doctor. Compare this with the progress of Sancho from an unhappy youth as a servant to three unpleasant maiden ladies, to a good post in his late 'teens, youthful excesses with women and cards, marriage to a nice, quiet West Indian girl, good prospects, an addiction to port, consequent gout, an expanding waistline, and a small respectable business to which to retire in one of the better parts of central London.[126] It is not surprising, then, that their approach to the matter of the slave trade and the plight of the London blacks should be different. At the same time, each reveals the inner tensions of the black man in a white-dominated world.

Taking Sancho first, we can see his assimilated "Englishness" in letter after letter. "When I look back," he laments, "on the glorious time of a George II and a Pitt's administration, my heart sinks at the bitter contrast."[127] He writes of "our English oak" and glories in the victory of "five ships of our line. . . . We fought like Englishmen, unsupported by the rest," he declares.[128] He delights in a royal birth: "The Queen, God bless her! safe;—another Princess"[129] and revels in a defeat of "Washintub's army" in America.[130] But all this is deceptive. At other times "our" England becomes "yours":

> I am sorry to observe that the practice of your country (which as a resident I love—and for its freedom, and for the many blessings I enjoy in it, shall ever have my warmest wishes—prayers—and blessings); I say, it is with great reluctance that I must observe your country's conduct has been uniformly wicked in the East—West Indies—

126. Sancho, *Letters*, Jekyll's memoir.
127. Sancho, *Letters*, 274.
128. *Ibid.* 9, 213.
129. *Ibid.*, 117.
130. *Ibid.*

and even on the coast of Guinea.—The grand object of England navigators—indeed of all Christian navigators—is money—money—
money—for which I do not pretend to blame them. Commerce was
meant by the goodness of the Deity to diffuse the various goods of
the earth into every part. . . .[131]

And so he proceeds to praise Commerce "with Religion for its companion." The signs of a characteristic tension are here, between the assimilated values of an admired white society, and a recognition of the barbarities on which so much that was admirable was based. The same tension
is recognizable in a letter which records extravagantly Sancho's feelings
on reading a white abolitionist tract:

Indeed I felt a double or mixt sensation—for while my heart was
torn for the sufferings—which, for aught I know—some of my nearest kin might have undergone—my bosom, at the same time, glowed
with gratitude—and praise towards the humane—the Christian—
the friendly and learned Author of that most valuable book.[132]

But the letter ends with his comments on those gentlemen who, although
writing of their admiration of the black poet Phyllis Wheatley, permitted
her to remain a slave. This letter raises the problem with which Equiano,
too, was to wrestle: if slavery is evil, how, irrespective of individual acts
of kindness by those directly or indirectly involved with the slave trade,
can one accept the idea of a *good* slave owner? Equiano's "good" master,
Mr. King, was a Quaker. What kind of Christianity is it that is used to
encourage the slave to be submissive, yet does not totally and irrevocably
reject slavery? Are these acts of kindness, even on the part of white abolitionists, truly charitable or mere condescensions—assertions of black
inferiority in the guise of Christian charity?

Sancho deals with the problem of his own ambivalent feelings sometimes by adopting a comic mode of submission—"I am utterly unquali-
fied through infirmities—as well as complexion. —Figure to yourself, my
dear Sir, a man with a convexity of belly exceeding Falstaff—and a black

---

131. *Ibid.*, 149.
132. *Ibid.*, 125-127.

PAUL EDWARDS AND JAMES WALVIN

face into the bargain,"[133]—but some of the self-mockery can have a sharp edge to it. Even in friendly letters we find greetings to the friend "and to all who have charity enough to admit dark faces into the fellowship of Christians,"[134] and in another letter this bitter note:

> I thank you for your kindness to my poor black brethren—I flatter myself you will find them not ungrateful—they act commonly from their feelings:—and I have observed a dog will love those who use him kindly.[135]

To a fellow African—Soubise—he is candid enough:

> Look round upon the miserable fate of almost all of our unfortunate colour—superadded to ignorance,—see slavery, and the contempt of those very wretches who roll in affluence from our labours. Superadded to this woeful catalogue—hear the ill-bred and heartracking abuse of the foolish vulgar.[136]

Sancho's letters express what must have been a common experience of the black population in Britain: the need to adopt poses of supplication and respect despite an inner rage. But Sancho's considerable social position would place him under much less pressure than most of his poorer and less articulate fellows, and his most famous letter, written to Sterne in response to his *Sermons* and to *Tristram Shandy*, speaks with a voice closer to the sentimental fashion of the time than that of immediate feeling.[137] The plea on behalf of the slaves is eloquent; but when Sancho asks Sterne to "think in me you behold the uplifted hands of thousands of my brother Moors . . . figure to yourself their attitudes;—hear their supplicating cries," we are more aware of Sancho's gestures than those of his brothers. The terms are those of the liberal cliché and hardly different from the white abolitionist rhetoric of the day. And in an earlier reference to Sterne as "an epicurean in acts of charity," enjoying his generous

---

133. *Ibid.*, 238.
134. *Ibid.*, 143.
135. *Ibid.*, 30.
136. *Ibid.*, 31-32.
137. *Ibid.*, 71-72.

impulses as "a feast to a benevolent heart" when a single slave is freed and befriended, we find a self-indulgent and sentimental liberalism more concerned with its own virtuous acts than those cruelties it claims to alleviate. The letter was popular in its day and it is not hard to see why: it invites a virtuous glow and a kindly tear without actually confronting the reader with the bare brutalities of slave ownership and the trade. For this, the reader must turn to Equiano.

Equiano was, as we have said, more directly and more deeply involved in the abolitionist movement and black self-help. His autobiography went into eight British editions and one American in his own lifetime, and several more after his death, and was translated into Dutch and German. Its audience would thus have been a large one: the first edition of 1789 had a subscription list of 350 and Equiano, in a letter of February 1792, mentions having sold 1,900 copies in Ireland during the previous eight and a half months. He was an active propagandist against the slave trade, traveling widely in England, Ireland, and Scotland selling copies of his book and speaking publicly on abolition.[138]

Contemporary commentators on Equiano's *Narrative* appear to have been particularly struck by its descriptive immediacy. "The simplicity that runs through his Narrative is singularly beautiful, and that beauty is heightened by the idea that it is *true*," wrote one.[139] A reviewer observed that "the Narrative appears to have been written with much truth and simplicity" and another, "The Narrative wears an honest face."[140] Equiano's account of life in "Eboe" and aboard the slave ship (the first three chapters of the first volume) must indeed have had a persuasive impact on its readers, and the narrative as a whole provides examples in abundance of precisely observed incidents in the common life of a slave.

But the *Narrative* goes beyond a full and in general well-authenticated record of events. It also makes significant revelations about the workings of Equiano's mind, particularly on questions of authority and paternalism, similar to those found in Sancho's letters but intensified by Equiano's more immediate experience. His relations with his masters and

---

138. Equiano, *Narrative*, Appendix D.
139. *Ibid.*, Appendix B, xiv-xv.
140. *Ibid.*, xv-xvii.

PAUL EDWARDS AND JAMES WALVIN

captains are of particular interest. He praises Robert King, his last owner, for his benevolence, but at the same time makes clear King's reluctance to give him his freedom, and King's insistence on being paid by Equiano the same sum for which he was bought. There is a sharp sting in the tail of some of his comments on King's "benevolence":

> I have often seen slaves, particularly those who were meagre, in dif-
> ferent islands, put into scales and weighed, and then sold from three
> pence to six pence or nine pence a pound. My master, however,
> whose humanity was shocked at this mode, used to sell such by the
> lump.[141]

It is only through Captain Thomas Farmer's intercession that King is persuaded to release Equiano, and consequently it is now Farmer who becomes ambiguously "benevolent." Equiano wants to head straight back with his freedom to England, but Farmer wants him aboard his trading ship to work between America and the West Indies, where, as Equiano knows only too well, even the free black man remains frighten-ingly vulnerable. "Here gratitude bowed me down," he writes, "and none but the generous can judge my feelings, struggling between inclination and duty."[142] So now Farmer begins to play the role of benevolent tyrant, later to repent his tyranny and to die, leaving Equiano in charge of the ship.

> I now obtained a new appelation and was called Captain. This
> elated me not a little, and it was quite flattering to my vanity to be
> thus styled by as high a title as any man in this place possessed.
> When the death of the captain became known, he was much regret-
> ted by all who knew him; for he was a man universally respected. At
> the same time, the sable captain lost no fame; for the success I had
> met with increased the affection of my friends in no small meas-
> ure.[143]

---

141. *Ibid.*, I, 220.
142. *Ibid.*, II, 20. An almost identical expression is used by Anthony Domingo (see above, 191) in a letter in Hoare, *Memoir of Sharp*, 376; "When I left England I felt a violent struggle in my mind between inclination and duty."
143. *Ibid.*, II, 35.

Incidents of this kind are repeated with variations throughout the *Narrative*.[144]

Further ambiguities emerge in his attitude to Christianity. Equiano was a Calvinist and at times comes close to the view that his enslavement was a special dispensation of Providence for his salvation. Yet this Christian society which has revealed to him the truth of the Lord is also practicing the greatest barbarities contrary to its own creed. Like Sancho he often uses the word "Christian" ironically, and contrasts such conduct with that of the virtuous unbeliever. His visits to the eastern Mediterranean had a great impact on him. He feels close to the Muslims he meets in Smyrna and tells the brutal Captain Hughes, "I had been twice among the Turks, yet I had never seen such usage with them, and much less could I have expected anything of this kind amongst Christians."[145] In his time of religious doubt he declares himself "again determined to go to Turkey and . . . never more to return to England."[146] Indeed, "finding those who in general termed themselves Christians not so honest or so good in their morals as the Turks, I really thought the Turks were in a safer way of salvation than my neighbours."[147]

The *Narrative* displays a considerable talent for revealing the perplexities in the mind of an eighteenth-century slave and freedman, and the ways in which these were sometimes reconciled. The society which snatched him away to slavery also persuades him to respect it:

> I now not only felt myself quite easy with these new countrymen, but relished their society and manners. I no longer looked on them as spirits, but as men superior to us; and therefore I had the stronger desire to resemble them; to imbibe their spirit and imitate their manners; I therefore embraced every opportunity of improvement; and every new thing that I observed I treasured up in my memory.[148]

It is inadequate to claim that Equiano is writing here to please his white friends; he has plenty to say which reveals them at their worst.

---

144. Paul Edwards, "Equiano and His Captains," in Anna Rutherford (ed.), *Common Wealth* (Aarhus, 1972), 18-25.
145. Equiano, *Narrative*, II, 195, 201.
146. *Ibid.*, 124.
147. *Ibid.*, 118-119.
148. *Ibid.*, I, 131-132.

PAUL EDWARDS AND JAMES WALVIN

Like Sancho, Equiano appears to experience contrary impulses toward the white world. The importance of these two writers goes further than their immediate effect on contemporary feelings about the slave trade and abolition; they also give us an insight into the tensions which must have been present in the thoughts and feelings of many thousands of inarticulate black men and women in eighteenth-century Britain.

8

James W. St. G. Walker

The Establishment of a
Free Black Community
in Nova Scotia, 1783-1840

The serious study of black Nova Scotian history is still in its infancy despite the major contributions of some recent scholarship. Until Winks and Clairmont wrote their surveys there existed only a few specific articles and books covering small parts of the early black experience in Nova Scotia. Two articles dealing with the black loyalist leaders Thomas Peters and David George appeared in *Sierra Leone Studies.* They contained general background information on the black situation in eighteenth-century Annapolis and Shelburne, but the authors, Fyfe and Kirk-Greene, were drawn to the black loyalist period primarily by their interest in the later historical development of the Nova Scotian emigrants in Sierra Leone. This motive also served Walls, whose insightful description of the formative influences of black loyalist religion in Nova Scotia was intended to explain the characteristics of the nineteenth-century churches in Sierra Leone.[1]

In their own right the founders of the black community have attracted little attention. The black Baptist church, as an outstanding example, has been the subject of only two general accounts, by Mackerow in 1895 and Oliver in 1953. Though both present much factual information, there is little analysis of the implications and repercussions of a sep-

Grateful acknowledgement is made to the Canada Council, through the generous support of which the research for this article was financed.

1. Christopher Fyfe, "Thomas Peters: History and Legend," *Sierra Leone Studies,* 9 (1953), 4-13; Anthony Kirk-Greene, "David George: The Nova Scotian Experience," *Sierra Leone Studies,* 14 (1960), 93-120; Andrew F. Walls, "The Nova Scotia Settlers and Their Religion," *Sierra Leone Bulletin of Religion,* I (1959), 19-31.

arate religious development. Most valuable of the earlier studies is Fergusson's *Documentary Study of the Establishment of the Negroes in Nova Scotia.* Unfortunately Fergusson has interpreted "establishment" almost exclusively in physical terms. Within its chronological boundaries his selection of documents admirably illustrates the numbers and geographical location of the black settlers, their hardships, and the relief policies of the provincial government, but contains scant information on the establishment of a separate black society. Rawlyk's brief account of the "Guysborough Negroes" does consider the role of the church and of education in the economic and cultural development of the Guysborough black community, though its value is limited by its brevity and its geographical concentration.[2]

The black community of Nova Scotia, though rich in a history of two hundred years' duration, had therefore been left relatively poor in historiography until the appearance of several articles by Winks, culminating in his impressive work, *The Blacks in Canada.* Winks has been supplemented by Clairmont and Magill's *Nova Scotian Blacks: An Historical and Structural Overview.* Yet the student of black history does not find in Winks or Clairmont either a description or an explanation of a distinctive black historical development that has preserved the heritage of the past and continues to motivate black initiatives today. Winks concludes that black history is "a depressing story," told in terms of disadvantage, racism, and opportunities lost through the blacks' failure to produce a united structure akin to the American civil rights movement of the 1960s. For Winks the significance of separate black institutions has been in their contribution to segregation, rather than in the protection they afforded to an evolving black identity that has always been necessary to withstand the pressures of white racism. From a different perspective, black history is no less than a heroic story: values have been retained that have long questioned the materialistic orientation of white

2. P. E. Mackerow, *A Brief History of the Coloured Baptists of Nova Scotia* (Halifax, 1895); Pearleen Oliver, *A Brief History of the Colored Baptists of Nova Scotia, 1782-1953* (Halifax, 1953); C. B. Fergusson, *A Documentary Study of the Establishment of the Negroes in Nova Scotia between the War of 1812 and the Winning of Responsible Government* (Halifax, 1948); George A. Rawlyk, "The Guysborough Negroes: A Study in Isolation," *Dalhousie Review,* XLVIII (1968), 24-36.

society, and a black community structure, though localized, has prevented the complete degradation and demoralization of its members. Clairmont and Magill have brought sociological analysis to bear on the black situation, but the burden of their study is directed toward an explanation of the contemporary "marginal" condition of the black population. For them an examination of the past has been important for the discovery of the roots of present economic disadvantage, and they have therefore tended to avoid more positive strains in the black historical development or to interpret them only as factors in a continuing story of deprivation. Thus the evolution of a unique black culture and the strength the black people have derived from their community life is overlooked in the Clairmont and Magill overview.[3]

Both the Winks and the Clairmont publications contain enough information, source directions, and interpretations to make a fundamental contribution to an understanding of black history in Nova Scotia, and in fact they do so to a degree that compensates for the omissions noted here. However, there remains room for a different approach, for different questions to be asked of the historical records, which could examine black concerns, motives, and initiatives and suggest their influence upon the course of black history. Of course the following article cannot claim to rework in a few pages a field that others have spent many hundreds of pages in doing, but it is meant to introduce the dominant forces in early black Nova Scotian history, within an overview of the formative years of black community consciousness and institutions, and to indicate the degree to which this community has been formed by, and has influenced, the events of the black past.

In November 1775 Lord Dunmore, the governor of Virginia, unwittingly committed the British forces to the cause of the American slave in the ensuing colonial rebellion. To enforce his declaration of martial law

---

3. Robin W. Winks, "Negroes in the Maritimes: An Introductory Survey," *Dalhousie Review*, XLVIII (1968), 453-471; *idem*, "The Canadian Negro: A Historical Assessment," *Journal of Negro History*, LIII (1968), 283-300, and LIV (1969), 1-18; *idem*, "Negro School Segregation in Ontario and Nova Scotia," *Canadian Historical Review*, L (1969), 164-191; *idem*, *The Blacks in Canada: A History* (New Haven, 1971); Donald H. Clairmont and Dennis W. Magill, *Nova Scotian Blacks: An Historical and Structural Overview* (Halifax, 1970).

JAMES W. ST. G. WALKER

Dunmore offered freedom to any rebel-owned bondsman who would participate in "speedily reducing this Colony to a proper sense of their duty, to his Majesty's crown and dignity."[4] Although the British Empire was still determined to maintain the institution of slavery, and of course slaves owned by loyalists were not eligible to accept Dunmore's offer, yet the belief was born in slave society that a British victory would mean emancipation.[5] This belief was reinforced by Sir Henry Clinton's Philipsburg Proclamation of July 1779 in which he promised "to every Negro who shall desert the Rebel Standard, full security to follow within these Lines, any Occupation which he shall think proper."[6] Clinton also indicated that after the war the black troops would receive the same allowances of land and provisions as "the Rest of the Disbanded Soldiers of His Majesty's Army."[7]

Thousands of slaves were drawn to the British by the prospect of freedom, and their number was swelled by "free Persons of Colour" who joined the British out of some motive other than a simple desire to leave a condition of servitude. Testimony given by black loyalists after the war revealed that the overriding motive of the escaping slaves, and one that was shared by the free blacks who became loyalists, was to achieve security in their freedom. In the confusion of war it was frequently easy to desert a master, and many thousands of escapees headed for Indian territory or established free "maroon" communities in the wilderness. But the ideal of the black loyalist went beyond freedom: it was to become a small proprietor, self-sufficient upon land of his own and secured by British justice in his rights as a subject of the crown.[8]

The British, on the other hand, had no program for the blacks attracted to their ranks beyond their immediate value in putting down the "unnatural rebellion" of the colonists. Britain's manpower needs were

---

4. Peter Force (ed.), *American Archives: A Documentary History of the American Colonies* (Washington, 1837-1853), 4th ser., III, 1385.

5. Benjamin Quarles, *The Negro in the American Revolution* (Chapel Hill, 1961), 19-32; Herbert Aptheker, *The Negro in the American Revolution* (New York, 1940), 16-18.

6. New York Public Library (NYPL), Carleton Transcripts, doc. 2094.

7. Public Archives of Nova Scotia (PANS), vol. 359, doc. 65.

8. E.g., PANS vol. 423, *passim*; PANS, Shelburne Records, Special Sessions, August 5, 1786; British Museum (BM) Add. Ms. 41262B, Clarkson Papers, II, 8-9.

pressing, and, besides the mass of black recruits anticipated as a result of the proclamations, it was expected that the southern economy would break down as the workers deserted it and that slave owners would be forced to leave the war in order to protect their families from vengeful slaves.[9] In success the British command could afford to go without any explicit policy regarding the treatment and status of the black loyalists, but in defeat and retreat decisions had to be made. Arguing that "an attention to Justice, and good faith, must plead strongly in behalf of the Negroes," British officers evacuated some 10,000 black loyalists from Boston, Savannah, and Charleston as those cities fell to the American rebels.[10] After the signing of the provisional peace, and the evacuation of New York, a further 3,000 blacks were removed from the new American republic. Informed that "their past services will engage the grateful attention of Government," the blacks were carried to the West Indies, East Florida, and London, and about 3,500 were sent to Halifax in the loyalist province of Nova Scotia.[11]

With the free blacks who accompanied the main loyalist body to Nova Scotia in 1783 and 1784 went more than 1,200 slaves, owned by white loyalists and therefore unable to claim the protection of a magnanimous majesty.[12] Though it offered a haven to fleeing American slaves, Nova Scotia was itself no stranger to slavery. Slaves participated in the building of Halifax in 1749, and by the 1770s there were several hundred living in various parts of the province.[13] In a society conditioned to

9. Colonial Office (CO) 5/175: Dunmore to Germain, February 5, 1782; G. W. Williams, *History of the Negro Race in America from 1619 to 1880* (New York, 1882), I, 325; Quarles, *American Revolution*, 21, 112; Aptheker, *American Revolution*, 6.

10. Public Record Office (PRO) 30/11/2: Clarke to Cornwallis, July 10, 1780; PANS, Executive Council Minutes, 1777, 343; PRO 30/55/46: docs. 5268 (2) and (3); Quarles, *American Revolution*, 163-167; Aptheker, *American Revolution*, 19.

11. Public Archives of Canada (PAC), MG 23 A2, vol. 9, bundle 344; NYPL, Carleton Transcripts, doc. 10427, orders dated April 15 and May 22, 1783; PANS vol. 423; PANS vol. 369, doc. 198.

12. T. Watson Smith, "The Slave in Canada," *Collections of the Nova Scotia Historical Society*, X (1899), 23, 32.

13. *Ibid.*, 9; Thomas Akins, "History of Halifax City," *Collections of the Nova Scotia Historical Society*, VIII (1895), 246; PANS vol. 443, Poll Tax and Census Returns, 1767-1794; W. R. Riddell, "Slavery in Canada," *Journal of Negro History*, V (1920), 362.

JAMES W. ST. G. WALKER

thinking of blacks as slaves, the claims of the free black loyalists for equality were not always to be taken seriously. Constituting over 10 percent of the total loyalist influx, the free blacks were regarded more as the slaves whose race they shared than as the loyalists whose status they had earned. In the confusion surrounding the settlement of over 30,000 refugees, it was easy to overlook an insignificant group of former slaves.

According to imperial policy, all loyalists were to be placed upon free land in Nova Scotia, the amount depending on the rank and former holdings of the recipient. Ordinary soldiers and refugees were eligible to receive one hundred acres plus fifty acres for each family member. Priority was given to "such as have suffered most" in the American war, that is, those who had lost the most in property or position.[14] Many whites of low station had to wait two or three years for their land, as Governor John Parr and his beleaguered officials strove to settle the officers and gentlemen, but at the lowest end of this system of priorities came the freed slaves who had lost no large estates or high positions. By the late 1780s less than one-third of the black families had been placed on lands. Even this fortunate minority had waited several years beyond the settlement of the whites; the farms they received, never more than fifty acres, averaged about one-quarter the size of those granted to their closest white neighbors; and they were usually located in the most isolated and least fertile regions of the province.[15]

The procedure established for administering loyalist grants called for disbanded troops from the same regiment, or civilian refugees from the same home district, to be settled together on one tract of land in Nova Scotia.[16] Out of this procedure grew three separate black communities and several smaller concentrations of black settlers on the fringes of white settlements. The largest was at Birchtown, near Shelburne, where over 1,500 free blacks were located by 1784. Of the 649 male heads of

14. PANS vol. 349, doc. 33; PANS vol. 369, doc. 6; PANS vol. 32, doc. 78; PANS vol. 33, doc. 3; CO 217/56: North to Parr, August 7, 1783.

15. PANS, Land Papers; PANS vol. 371, List of Grantees of Land; PANS vol. 394A, Abstracts of Surveys; PANS vol. 459, Docket of Land Grants.

16. Margaret Ells, *Settling the Loyalists in Nova Scotia* (Ottawa, 1933), 105; PANS vol. 346, Proclamations, March 1 and June 22, 1784; PANS vol. 369, doc. 6.

family, 184 received thirty-four acres each in 1788.[17] At Brindley Town, on the outskirts of Digby, one-acre town lots were laid out for the seventy-six black families settled there.[18] The third all-black settlement, Little Tracadie in Lower Sydney County (later Guysborough County), had seventy-four families each placed on a farm of forty acres in 1787.[19] Most important of the semi-integrated concentrations was Preston, on the eastern side of the harbor near Halifax, where fifty-one black families gained fifty-acre farms as part of several larger loyalist grants.[20] The newly created province of New Brunswick laid out 121 lots in three tracts for the blacks, but the land was so remote that only five farms were occupied and the other 100 or more families remained around the city of St. John.[21] About 400 blacks remained in Halifax, and scattered families squatted on vacant lands or sought employment in a dozen other Nova Scotian settlements.[22] The physical circumstances, at least, were therefore present for the development of separate black communities in Birchtown, Brindley Town, Little Tracadie, Preston, St. John, and Halifax.

The intention of the British government had been that no loyalist should be required to become a wage-laborer in order to survive. Provisions were promised to loyalists, partly as a reward for their loyalty and

17. PAC, MG 9 B9-14, I, "Muster Book of Free Blacks of Birch Town," 1784; PANS, Shelburne Records, "A List of those Mustered at Shelburne in the Summer of 1784"; PANS, Land Papers, Raven, Joseph, and 182 others (sic), Shelburne, December 8, 1787; PANS vol. 213, Council Minutes, February 28, 1788.

18. PANS vol. 376, "Return of Negroes and their families mustered in Annapolis County between May 28 and June 30, 1784"; CO 217/63; Bulkeley to Dundas, March 19, 1792, enclosing Millidge to Parr, March 1785; PANS, Nova Scotia Land Grants, Leonard, Joseph, and others, Digby Township, 1785.

19. PANS, Land Papers, Brownspriggs, Thomas, and 73 others, Tracadie, September 28, 1787; PANS, Box of Guysborough County Land Grants, folder 1, doc. 17.

20. PANS, Land Papers, Chamberlain, Theophilus, and 163 others, Preston Township, September 3, 1784, and Young, Thomas, and 34 others, Preston, December 5, 1787; PANS vol. 370, Names of Original Grantees, February 1784, December 1784, March 1786, February 1787.

21. Public Archives of New Brunswick (PANB), Raymond Collection, "Return of the Total Number of Men, Women and children of the Disbanded Loyalists Mustered on the River St. John," September 25, 1784; PANB, Colonial Correspondence, III, Carleton to Dundas, December 13, 1791; CO 217/63: "The Humble Memorial and Petition of Thomas Peters, a Free Negro."

22. Akins, "History of Halifax," 103; Nova Scotia Archives Report (1934), Appendix B, 27-61; Society for the Propagation of the Gospel in Foreign Parts (SPG) Journal, XXV, 60-62, 71, 157, 308-309, 340, 358.

JAMES W. ST. G. WALKER

a compensation for their losses, but primarily to sustain them during their first few years in Nova Scotia until their new farms should become productive and enable them to support themselves.[23] The same confusion that surrounded land distribution, however, affected the granting of provisions. Poor whites were served last, blacks usually not at all. When black loyalists did receive provisions they were often required to earn them by laboring on public works, the supplies never lasted more than a few months, and the quality was inferior to that given the whites.[24] With neither land nor provisions, or at best an inadequate supply, the mass of free blacks was forced to seek some other means of support. Large numbers became tenant farmers, working the lands of white loyalist grantees under a share-cropping agreement. For others only indentured servitude provided a way to avoid starvation.[25] But in the larger centers, such as Shelburne, Halifax, St. John, and Annapolis, a general shortage of labor created a demand for a pool of day workers. Those blacks settled on the outskirts of such towns were able to hire their skills or their labor by the day, and though at wage rates of eightpence to one shilling per day they were receiving only about one-quarter the prevailing rate for whites, at least they were able to sustain themselves or, if they had received lands, to supplement the produce of their inadequate farms.[26] With most people in the province pioneering their own farms or businesses, the blacks constituted the bulk of the free labor reserve that cleared the lands, laid the

23. PANS vol. 366, doc. 33.

24. PANS, Family Papers, Clarkson's Mission to America, 188; CO 217/63: Bulkeley to Dundas, March 19, 1792, enclosing "Enquiry into the Complaint of Thomas Peters, a Black Man"; David George, "An Account of the Life of Mr. David George," *Baptist Annual Register*, I (1790-1793), 478; PANS, Halifax County Quarter Sessions, 1766-1801, June 7, 1791; James S. MacDonald, "Memoir of Governor John Parr," *Collections of the Nova Scotia Historical Society*, XIV (1910), 54.

25. BM, Clarkson Papers, II, 8-15; PANS, Clarkson's Mission, 66-67.

26. Akins, "History of Halifax," 85; T. C. Haliburton, *An Historical and Statistical Account of Nova Scotia* (Halifax, 1829), II, 280; SPG, Dr. Bray's Associates, Unbound Papers, box 7, Canadian Papers, 1784-1836, Rowland to Associates, November 17, 1813; Boston King, "Memoirs of the Life of Boston King, A Black Preacher," *Arminian Magazine*, XXI (1798), 210; CO 217/63: "List of the Blacks of Birch Town who gave in their Names for Sierra Leone," November 1791; C. B. Fergusson (ed.), *Diary of Simeon Perkins, 1790-1796* (Toronto, 1961), III, 194, 197-201, 344; PANS, Shelburne Records, General Sessions, September 2, 1784; CO 217/64: Proprietors of Lands to Dundas, May 16, 1793.

roads, and erected the public buildings of loyalist Nova Scotia.[27] Under such circumstances the black loyalists provided a valuable addition to the provincial economy.

Land, independence, and equality were denied the majority of black loyalists. So too was security. Tenant farmers could be moved arbitrarily to a virgin part of their landlord's estate, just after having cleared one area for planting.[28] Five-year indentures were forged to become thirty-nine-year terms, and indentured children were sold out of the province, in America or the West Indies, as outright slaves.[29] Some were reclaimed as slaves, through the courts, by loyalists who disputed the blacks' claims to have escaped from rebel masters, and others were simply kidnapped and sold back into slavery.[30] When economic depression and food shortage struck "Nova Scarcity" in 1789, jobs disappeared and many more blacks had to opt for indentured servitude or face the prospect of starvation.[31]

Either as war veterans or as loyalists, the free blacks had a right to expect treatment as full citizens. On the one hand they were required to perform the duties of citizenship, on the other their rights fell far short of equality. Those with lands were obliged to pay taxes and serve in the militia, yet they were denied the vote and trial by jury.[32] In addition they

27. PANS, Clarkson's Mission, 73; CO 271/68: Howe to Quarrell, August 9, 1797; CO 217/63: Skinner to Dundas, n.d. (received April 1792); PANS vol. 48, docs. 81, 87.

28. E.g., PANS, Bishop Charles Inglis, Journal, no. 2, book 5, 8.

29. BM, Clarkson Papers, II, 15, 19; PANS, Clarkson's Mission, 197-201; PANS, Shelburne Records, General Sessions, November 1, 2, 3, 1791.

30. BM, Clarkson Papers, II, 8, 22; PANS, Unpassed Bills, 1789, "A Bill Intituled an Act for the Regulation and Relief of the free Negroes within the Province of Nova Scotia"; PANS, Shelburne Records, Special Sessions, August 25, 1785, August 5, 1786, General Sessions, April 12, 1786, April 5, July 8, 11, 19, 1791.

31. PANS vol. 346, doc. 115; PANS vol. 213, Council Minutes, July 9, 1789; MacDonald, "John Parr," 51, 75; Akins, "History of Halifax," 95; PANS vol. 302, doc. 11; King, "Memoirs," 209-210; PANS, Clarkson's Mission, 294-295; BM Add. Ms. 41262A, Clarkson Papers, I, Clarkson to Hartshorne, December 13, 1791; SPG, Dr. Bray's Associates Minute Books, III, Millidge to Associates, October 13, 1788; George, "Life," 499; PAC, MG 9 B9-14, III, "From the Overseers of the Poor to the Magistrates of Shelburne," February 3, 1789.

32. FO 4/1: Peters to Grenville, n.d. (received December 26, 1790); BM, Clarkson Papers, II, 15, 21; PANS vol. 444½, Poll Tax Returns, 1791-1796; SPG, Bray Minutes, IV, Stanser to Associates, November 18, 1811 and October 8, 1812; PANB, Colonial Correspondence, III, Carleton to Dundas, December 13, 1791.

often suffered restrictions in their private lives. The Shelburne magistrates issued orders "forbidding Negro Dances and Negro Frolicks in this Town." Contravention of the order meant being "ordered out of their home for keeping a disorderly house."[33] In Shelburne and Lower Sydney Counties blacks were whipped, mutilated, and even hanged for crimes that, when committed by whites, were often punished by the same magistrates with monetary fines.[34] During the eighteenth century no man or woman of low station could avoid the constant threat of physical suffering, yet it appears evident that for black Nova Scotians, as a group, the threat was greater and more frequently realized than for any others. In many ways their life as freemen was not altogether different from the life of slavery they had left behind. As sharecroppers, indentured servants, or subsistence day-laborers they were still completely dependent upon white people and subject to the whims and prejudices of their employers. The law denied them equal privileges and services yet expected as much of them as any other resident, and when they strayed they were corrected with greater severity. There was no incentive for provincial officials to help or even allow the blacks to become self-sufficient, for to do so would be to deprive the province of a major pool of available labor.

While the economic climate in Nova Scotia created a peculiar position for the black loyalists, setting them apart from white society as a dependent and exploited class, the social environment of the 1780s set the conditions for their development as a distinct and separate community. Dominant among these social influences was a fundamentalist religious revival then sweeping the province. As slaves in the American colonies the blacks had been discouraged, and sometimes prevented, from embracing the religion of their owners. Most of them, therefore, though probably aware of Christian teachings, had never belonged to a formal congregation.[35] It is possible that this very prohibition, by associating

---

33. PANS, Shelburne Records, Special Sessions, May 12, 19, 1785, General Sessions, July 3, 1799.

34. E.g., PANS, Quarter Sessions, Guysborough County, 1785-1800, October 10, 1787, August 12, 1789, February 8, March 31, August 11, 13, November 3, 1791; PANS, Shelburne Records, Special Sessions, February 24, June 7, 9, 1785, General Sessions, April 12, November 3, 1792; PANS, White Collection, VI, doc. 553.

35. See John Wesley, *The Works of John Wesley* (London, 1872), II, 337, 355; idem, *The Journal of the Rev. John Wesley* (London, 1909), I, 350-353; SPG, Bray Minutes, III, July 11, 1785; George, "Life," 478.

Christianity with the status of freeman, made them anxious to exercise their new liberty by seeking baptism. They may also have been moved by the promise of equality of all men before a welcoming God. For whatever reason, it was the case that religious gatherings of any description—and the revival ensured that there were many—attracted free blacks in the hundreds.[36]

As the largest and best organized colonial church, the Anglicans initially garnered the most converts. From Halifax, Preston, Digby, and Shelburne, and even from remote Tracadie, Anglican clergymen reported that blacks were flocking to the font for baptism and full church membership.[37] A Methodist crusade resulted in the conversion of over 200 blacks, of a total Methodist membership of only 800 across the province.[38] This was still, however, an age of slavery and of belief in the separation of the races. A special gallery was fitted in St. Paul's Church, Halifax, in 1784, to which blacks were confined "during divine worship." When even that space was needed for white worshipers the blacks were excluded altogether; as an alternative they gathered in private homes and the rector commissioned "several capable Negroes to read the Instructions to the Negroes and other pious Books to as many of them as assemble for that purpose."[39] Thus, though nominally members of the Church of England, the blacks living in Halifax were in fact segregated into their own congregations.

In the separate all-black settlements no such complications arose. Neighboring Anglican priests, after establishing black congregations, would visit them once or twice a year, leaving black lay readers in charge in the meantime. In Brindley Town the black Anglicans selected Joseph

36. George, "Life," 478; King, "Memoirs," 157-158.

37. *SPG Report* (1784), 36; (1785), 40, 43; (1787), 15; SPG Journal, XXIII, 379, 425, XXIV, 264, 314, 372, XXV, 149; PANS, Shelburne Records, Baptisms, 1783-1869; W. O. Raymond, "The Founding of the Church of England in Shelburne," *Collections of the New Brunswick Historical Society*, III (1907), 284; PANS, Memoirs of Bishop Inglis, no. 1, 53-56, 115-118, 124.

38. John Wesley, *The Letters of the Rev. John Wesley* (London, 1931), VII, 218-219; G. G. Findlay and W. W. Holdsworth, *The History of the Wesleyan Methodist Missionary Society* (London, 1921), I, 290, 293, 297; Isaiah W. Wilson, *A Geography and History of the County of Digby, Nova Scotia* (Halifax, 1900), 90.

39. SPG Journal, XXIV, 24; SPG, Bray Minutes, III, Weeks to Associates, November 27, 1786; SPG, C/Can/NS 1, 1722-1790, Breynton to SPG, November 15, 1784.

JAMES W. ST. G. WALKER

Leonard as their religious leader. When Bishop Charles Inglis visited them in 1791 he was shocked to find that Leonard was not merely leading services of worship but was actually baptizing children and new converts and administering the communion sacrament to some sixty families.[40] Isaac Limerick performed a similar service for his fellow black Anglicans at Birchtown, as did Thomas Brownspriggs at Little Tracadie and Adam and Catherine Abernathy at Preston. Initially converted and organized by whites, the blacks were in each case subsequently left on their own, with only occasional supervision, to create what were in effect separate black churches under their own leadership.[41]

The Methodist evangelists followed a similar pattern after their mass rallies and conversions. Moses Wilkinson, a blind and lame former slave, took charge of the Birchtown meetinghouse. Boston King at first assisted Wilkinson, then went on a mission circuit, and finally was placed as pastor over the Preston black Methodists. Another of Wilkinson's black assistants, John Ball, also went on the circuit, preaching in Methodist halls but to all-black gatherings meeting at a separate hour from the whites' regular service.[42] In their isolation the black Methodists, like the Anglicans, were free to interpret Christian doctrines according to their own needs and inclinations, and to develop distinctive styles of worship that became, in time, scarcely recognizable to their formal denominations.

Two other Christian sects gained large black followings, the Huntingdonians and the Baptists. John Marrant, a black loyalist discharged from the Royal Navy in England after the war, received a call from his brother at Birchtown to help satisfy the religious needs of the people there. Marrant sought ordination in the Countess of Huntingdon's Connexion, an evangelical group that had broken with orthodox Anglicanism, and in 1785 he arrived in Nova Scotia with a black assistant, Wil-

---

40. PANS, Bishop Charles Inglis, Journal, no. 2, book 5, 15.

41. SPG, Bray Associates, Canadian Papers, Viets to Associates, April 18, 1789; SPG Journal, XXV, 163, 229, 318; *SPG Report* (1791), 32; (1792), 42; CO 217/64: Panton to Sydney, March 17, 1786; Raymond, "Church of England," 289; PANS, Memoirs of Bishop Inglis, no. 1, 115-118; SPG, Bray Minutes, III, September 1, 1791.

42. PANS, Clarkson's Mission, 262; King, "Memoirs," 157-161, 213; D. C. Harvey (ed.), *Diary of Simeon Perkins, 1780-1789* (Toronto, 1958), II, lvi, 365, 371, and III, 130.

liam Furmage, to begin his crusade.[43] The Baptist faith was introduced by David George, formerly associated with the Silver Bluff Black Baptist Church in South Carolina, who had taken refuge with the British at Savannah and was eventually evacuated to Halifax.[44] George established his headquarters in Shelburne and Marrant his in Birchtown, but both stumped the province with their message of sin and salvation and left a string of black Huntingdonian and Baptist chapels in their wake, completely unconnected with any white agency.[45]

Whether Anglican, Methodist, Huntingdonian, or Baptist, the black chapels had in common their segregated blackness and their independence from white supervision. Forced to grow separately, they retained the fervor and intense personal involvement that had characterized the crusade for their conversion. The Holy Spirit had to be felt to be believed, and God regularly appeared to visit their meetings of worship. Liturgically the various sects were distinct, each preferring a different form of service, but doctrinally their differences were minimal. In a sense they were arrested at the point of emotional excitement that persuaded them to be not as other men were. As they looked out to their white coreligionists, they saw that God did not give the white worshipers the same attention he gave the blacks. In the white churches there were no visions, convulsions, or voices, no visible proof that God had made a personal call. There developed in the black churches a sense of distinction, a confidence that they were a chosen people who must be kept apart from and uncontaminated by the evidently lapsed Christians of the white churches. Allowed to develop by the neglect of the white ministry, the black churches took on a deliberate posture of separation. Segregation

43. John Marrant, *A Narrative of the Lord's wonderful Dealings with John Marrant, a Black* (London, 1788); *The Harbinger* (May, 1852), 154; (May, 1856), 78; Christopher Fyfe, "The Countess of Huntingdon's Connexion in Nineteenth Century Sierra Leone," *Sierra Leone Bulletin of Religion*, IV (1962), 53-54.

44. George, "Life," 475-476; Walter H. Brooks, "The Evolution of the Negro Baptist Church," *Journal of Negro History*, VII (1922), 15-16; *idem*, "The Priority of the Silver Bluff Church and its Promoters," *ibid.*, 172-184.

45. Harvey (ed.), *Diary of Simeon Perkins*, II, lvi, 365; Akins, "History of Halifax," 102; PANS, Memoirs of Bishop Inglis, no. 1, 87-93; *The Harbinger* (January, 1857), 2; George, "Life," 478-481.

JAMES W. ST. G. WALKER

was regarded as necessary and good, for it was their role to preserve the truth of the moment of salvation.[46]

The black pastors inevitably became the natural leaders of their local communities, for they represented the first all-black institution in most of their congregations' lives. In several cases the preachers were in fact chosen by the congregations, and in others the preacher had at least to be accepted by the congregation before becoming its pastor. God gave the license to preach, but the people gave the church and the consent to preach in it. Petitions for land or provisions, and complaints of injustices, were usually organized by the preachers and submitted by them on behalf of the congregation.[47] The chapels, therefore, took on an importance beyond a simple location for religious services. The first community identity felt by the black Nova Scotian was his membership in a Christian chapel.

Another institution that was also introduced into the black settlements in the 1780s, the school, helped further to create a separate black identity and, incidentally, to confirm several preachers in their leadership position. The Associates of the late Dr. Bray, a London-based Anglican charity devoted to black education, was forced by the revolution to give up its work among American slaves, and in 1785 transferred its attention to the free blacks still within the empire in Nova Scotia. The Associates' donations built schools and paid for black teachers in Brindley Town, Halifax, Preston, and Birchtown. Joseph Leonard, Isaac Limerick, Catherine Abernathy, and William Furmage, all of them preachers, were selected to act as teachers in their communities. Colonel Stephen Blucke, a mulatto officer of the Black Pioneers, received the appointment to teach at Birchtown, and was the only schoolmaster not associated with chapel leadership.[48] The Society for the Propagation of the Gospel, an

46. Walls, "Nova Scotia Settlers," 24; PANS, Clarkson's Mission, 208, 250, 262; Maritime Baptist Archives (MBA), Personal Letters of Henry Alline, Joseph Dimock, Harris Harding, Edward Manning, and others, dated from 1778 to 1793, Harding to Lavina D'Wolf, August 20, 1791.

47. E.g., the roles of Joseph Leonard and Thomas Brownspriggs in procuring land. See also PANS, Clarkson's Mission, 71-73, 79, 250; BM Add. Ms. 41263, Clarkson Papers, III, 174.

48. H. P. Thompson, *Thomas Bray* (London, 1954); SPG, Bray Minutes, III, July 1, 1784, February 3, July 11, 1785, February 5, March 26, 1787, July 3, 1788; SPG, Bray Associates, Canadian Papers, Breynton to Associates, November 15, 1784, Barton to Breynton, January 25, 1785; *An Account of the Designs of the Associates of the late Dr. Bray, with an Abstract of their Proceedings* (London, 1787), 31-32.

Anglican mission, established the fifth school at Little Tracadie where the local preacher, Thomas Brownspriggs, was installed as its teacher.[49]

From 1785 to 1791 several hundred black children received an elementary education through the aid of the Church of England, and another hundred adults attended Sunday or evening classes in Halifax and Brindley Town.[50] Just as the white missionaries paid only infrequent visits to the black churches, so the schools were left in considerable peace by the inspectors who authorized the payment of salaries and supplied books but rarely interfered in the running of the schools.[51] Each of the five major black communities in Nova Scotia had its own school which, with the chapel, encouraged the development of a parallel society, black, Christian, and to some extent educated, different from their white neighbors but different too from the slave culture they had left behind.

In their own institutions, sheltered from the interference of white society, the black loyalists perpetuated cultural characteristics carried from slavery and added new attitudes and characteristics to meet the needs of their daily lives. All-night meetings, usually devoted to prayer and praise (the "Negro Frolicks" banned by insomniac whites in Shelburne), became common. Formal marital ties were treated more casually than by white society, and women assumed an independence unusual for the times.[52] In the slave situation, formal marriage had not always been possible or, even when it was, the opportunity to live together was never assured and there was no role for a male provider. Yet the black loyalist family, though loosely defined, was powerfully constructed. Family membership was extended to include bastards, orphans, widows, and neighbors, without distinction by blood.[53] It grew to include the whole chapel community, and even spanned chapel boundaries to envelop all the black brethren in one geographical location. The Baptists, Anglicans, and Methodists of Preston claimed in 1791 that they had lived as neigh-

---

49. PANS, Memoirs of Bishop Inglis, no. 1, 53-56, 115-118, 125, 162-168; *SPG Report* (1790), 44.

50. SPG, Bray Minutes, III, July 7, November 3, 1791.

51. *Ibid.*, September 3, 1787, April 3, 1788, September 3, 1789, February 4, 1790.

52. *Ibid.*, July 3, 1788; PANS, Shelburne Records, Baptisms, 1783-1869. A typical entry: "31 December 1785—Katherine, Daughter of John Moody, by Ann Johnson, Black."

53. CO 217/68: Howe to Quarrell, August 9, 1797; PANS, Clarkson's Mission, 92-93; BM, Clarkson Papers, II, 11.

bors for so long that they could not contemplate separation; in Shelburne County blacks with property actually sold it to pay the debts of their neighbors; the Methodists and Huntingdonians of Birchtown met in a joint meeting to discuss the future of their settlement.[54] After less than a decade in Nova Scotia, each black settlement had become conscious of its own identity and of its distinction from white society. In all but economic terms the black loyalists were isolated from the rest of Nova Scotia.

Despite the solace they evidently received from their own institutions and communities, the ideals that drew them to the British during the revolution did not pass from the black loyalists' minds. They continued to seek land, equality, and security as independent British subjects.[55] In 1790, after several attempts to gain satisfaction from local officials had failed, the blacks of the Annapolis and St. John regions deputed Thomas Peters to proceed to London, there to present their grievances directly to the British cabinet. Peters, a sergeant in the Black Pioneers during the American war, bore a petition which stated that "some Part of the said Black People are earnestly desirous of obtaining their due Allotment of Land and remaining in America but others are ready and willing to go wherever the Wisdom of Government may think proper to provide for them as free Subjects of the British Empire."[56] In London Peters met Granville Sharp, Henry Thornton, and William Wilberforce, members of the Bray Associates and promoters of the new colony of Sierra Leone in West Africa. These influential men helped Peters present his petition to Secretary of State Henry Dundas, and they also offered to accept as many black loyalists as might choose to emigrate to their colony. The Sierra Leone Company was in need of a free black Christian population for their colonization venture; the free black Christians of Nova Scotia were in need of a Promised Land wherein they could realize their destiny as a chosen people. When Peters returned to Nova Scotia in 1791 he was

54. PANS, Clarkson's Mission, 79-90, 175-176, 245, 293-294.

55. *Ibid.*, 138.

56. FO 4/1: Peters to Grenville, two letters, n.d. (received December 24 and 26, 1790); CO 217/63: "The Humble Memorial and Petition of Thomas Peters a Free Negro on behalf of himself and others the Black Pioneers and loyal Black Refugees," 1790.

accompanied by John Clarkson, brother of the famous abolitionist, bearing an offer of free land and full equality in an independent British African colony.[57]

After receiving Thomas Peters's petition, Secretary Dundas wrote to Governors Parr and Thomas Carleton advising them that the government intended to correct the blacks' situation in Nova Scotia and New Brunswick. "If what the Petitioner represents be true," Dundas commented, "they certainly have strong grounds for complaint." He ordered an immediate enquiry into Peters's charges, and offered three alternatives "to make them some attonment for the injury they have suffered": they could be placed on good lands in Nova Scotia, they could enlist in the army, at regular pay rates, for service in the West Indies, or they could accept the Sierra Leone Company's offer.[58] The third alternative, as far as the blacks were concerned, was the most attractive. During October and November 1791 Clarkson visited Halifax, Preston, Shelburne, and Birchtown, while Peters carried the news to the St. John and Annapolis regions, including Brindley Town. Between them they recruited 1,196 black loyalists for the voyage to Africa.[59]

Interestingly, the 1,196 emigrants represented the more advantaged group from among the black loyalists. Indentured servants and debtors, including many sharecroppers who had borrowed seed from their white landlords, were not allowed to leave, and the Sierra Leone Company would not accept unattached women or anyone unable to present a certificate bearing witness to his "honesty, sobriety and industry."[60] Since landowners and skilled craftsmen were the most independent and able to support themselves, they were the least susceptible to the shackles of debt and indenture and therefore constituted the largest proportion of those

57. Fyfe, "Thomas Peters"; PANS, Clarkson's Mission, 1-15; BM, Clarkson Papers, I, Orders of the Directors of the Sierra Leone Company to John Clarkson, August 12, 1791; BM, Clarkson Papers, III, Clarkson to Wilberforce, n.d.; *Report of the Directors of the Sierra Leone Company* (1794), 2.

58. CO 217/63: Dundas to Parr, August 6, 1791. Misspelling is in the original.

59. PANS, Clarkson's Mission, 32-45, 55-56, 71-73, 79-90, 106-109, 205-206; George, "Life," 482.

60. BM, Clarkson Papers, III, 158; *Report of the Directors of the Sierra Leone Company* (1794), 4-6; PANS, Clarkson's Mission, 79, 92-94, 101, 139, 147, 163, 204, 230, 237-238, 240-247, 292, 317.

JAMES W. ST. G. WALKER

who were free to consider the African opportunity. They were also in a better position to resist the opposition thrown up by interested parties desirous of scuttling the emigration. The provincial establishment, both private and official, rallied its forces to obstruct the black exodus: white Nova Scotians were not anxious to lose at a stroke the bulk of their cheap labor reserve, nor did they wish to have Peters's complaints confirmed by a successful emigration.[61]

That opposition was determined, "making use of every artful device," Clarkson reported, to keep the blacks in their state of dependence in Nova Scotia.[62] A public campaign disparaged the Sierra Leone scheme, warning that the blacks were to be reenslaved in Africa. False indentures and debts were produced, or court proceedings instituted, to delay the black loyalists until after the Sierra Leone fleet had departed. Peters was physically attacked, and both Clarkson and David George, an early recruit, were threatened with violence. The official recruitment agents appointed by Parr and Carleton discouraged prospective emigrants or simply declined to announce or explain the Sierra Leone Company's proposals. The entire northern section of the province, including Little Tracadie, remained in ignorance of the emigration; since Clarkson and Peters limited their activities to the Halifax-Shelburne-Annapolis triangle, the north was left in the hands of a government agent, who did not fulfill his duties.[63]

The 1,196 who actually quitted Nova Scotia were not a discontented minority of the black population, but the majority of those who had an effective choice whether to leave or stay. And they were not merely seeking an opportunity for individual economic improvement. Clarkson was offering more than free land, he was offering them a homeland. Slavery was absolutely forbidden in the new colony, taxes were light, and settlers were promised control of their own affairs, religious liberty, and the full

61. PANS, Clarkson's Mission, 29-31, 44-47, 72-73, 207; PANB, Colonial Correspondence, III, Carleton to Dundas, December 13, 1791; SPG, C/Can/NS 1, Houseal to Morice, November 21, 1791.

62. PANS, Clarkson's Mission, 109.

63. *Ibid.*, 36, 53, 73-78, 105, 116-117, 120-123, 171-172, 193, 204-206, 231, 240-243, 435; BM, Clarkson Papers, I, Peters to Hartshorne, October 10, 1791; PANB, Colonial Correspondence, III, Carleton to Dundas, March 2, 1792; BM, Clarkson Papers, II, 15; George, "Life," 482; CO 267/9: Peters to Dundas, n.d. (received July 6, 1792).

rights and protection of British subjects.[64] In the event, these promises remained unfulfilled, but in 1791 the black loyalists had faith that Clarkson spoke with the authority of the company's board of directors.[65]

The decision to participate in the emigration, characteristically, was most often a collective one. Unwilling to break up the society, everyone free to leave would do so if the majority in that particular chapel or community so decided. All but one of the teachers and preachers from the settlements visited by Clarkson and Peters accepted the opportunity to build a new society in Africa, and they were joined by those members of their congregations who were not restricted by law, debt, or indenture. From Shelburne County, after a mass meeting in Birchtown's Methodist chapel, went David George, Moses Wilkinson, John Ball, Cato Perkins, and William Ash. George's converts in New Brunswick were also persuaded to leave, by his example, after consulting among themselves. Joseph Leonard's Anglicans and the Brindley Town Methodists left as intact as conditions would permit, as did the Halifax County churches led by Boston King, Hector Peters, and Adam and Catherine Abernathy.[66]

The exodus, which took place in January 1792, had the economic effect that had been feared by the province's employers and proprietors. Trade was depressed by the removal of so many black consumers, and the province was deprived of "useful labourers." The new governor, John Wentworth, and several other dignitaries recorded their conviction that Nova Scotia had been seriously damaged by the departure of the major pool of available casual labor.[67] One might therefore have expected an improvement in the wages and working conditions of the remaining black laborers, for their assets were in short supply. That this did not happen may partly be explained by the fact that the free blacks' impor-

64. BM, Clarkson Papers, III, 158; *Report of the Directors of the Sierra Leone Company* (1794), 4-6; BM, Clarkson Papers, II, 8-9.

65. On the later history of the black loyalists see James Walker, *The Black Loyalists in Nova Scotia and Sierra Leone*, forthcoming.

66. PANS, Clarkson's Mission, 125, 179, 193, 205, 217-218, 237-238, 293; CO 217/63: "List of the Blacks of Birch Town," November 1791; George, "Life," 482; SPG, Bray Minutes, III, December 1, 1791, July 5, 1792, February 7, 1793, IV, April 1, 1809; BM, Clarkson Papers, III, 169; Wilson, *County of Digby*, 90-91.

67. PANS vol. 48, docs. 81, 87; CO 217/63: Skinner to Dundas, n.d. (received April 1792); CO 217/64: Proprietors of Lands to Dundas, May 16, 1793; PANS, White Collection, VI, doc. 560; PANS, Bishop Charles Inglis, Letters, no. 3, 58.

tance to the Nova Scotian economy had always been as a labor reserve: they were available to work when required, but had never become an integral or permanent component in a continuing process of production. Clarkson had recruited his emigrants from among that free labor reserve, and particularly from the skilled group within it. Left behind were the slaves, indentured servants, and sharecroppers, by definition excluded from the free labor pool, and the weak, the aged, the indebted, and the unskilled.[68] Such people were neither free to choose their employment nor capable of bargaining an equitable share in Nova Scotia's economy. The increased demand and higher wages for labor did not devolve benefits upon the black remnant as an immediate consequence of Clarkson's mission.

Nor did the provincial government take steps to improve conditions in the depleted black settlements. In accordance with the secretary of state's order, Parr had instituted the "Enquiry into the Complaint of Thomas Peters, a Black Man," which met at Annapolis in November 1791. The commissioners appointed by the governor were not directed to enquire into the whole pattern of black loyalist land grants, however, but merely to examine and explain the situation in Annapolis-Digby where Peters claimed to have been refused land and provisions. Evidence at the enquiry revealed that after an unsuccessful petition for land at Brindley Town Peters had left for New Brunswick, where he hoped that a new government would be more generous. The commissioners were therefore able to conclude that Peters was left landless only because he "hastily quitted" Nova Scotia before lands could be distributed. Disregarding the landless state of blacks throughout the province, including those who had remained at Brindley Town but had received confirmed grants only to one-acre town lots, the enquiry found Peters personally to blame for his failure to gain his promised land.[69]

Thus, as far as the province was concerned, ended the Peters affair. The commissioners found that it was unnecessary to amend the process of granting lands to black loyalists or to consider making any "attonment," as Dundas had requested. If any blacks had decided to remain in

---

68. PANS vol. 48, doc. 81; CO 217/68: Howe to Quarrell, August 9, 1797.

69. CO 217/63: Bulkeley to Dundas, March 19, 1792, enclosing "Enquiry into the Complaint of Thomas Peters, a Black Man."

Nova Scotia in the hope of having their promises fulfilled, the enquiry report, completed in February 1792, effectively quashed that possibility. Petitions from black loyalists in both Nova Scotia and New Brunswick continued to flow into Halifax and Fredericton, indicating that many of them remained landless until well into the nineteenth century.[70] In fact the situation actually deteriorated for the blacks at Little Tracadie, where 2,720 acres of the 3,000-acre tract granted to Thomas Brownspriggs and seventy-three others in 1787 was reallocated in 1799 to thirty-six "Acadians and Negroes."[71]

Clearly the controversies and promises attendant upon the 1792 removal did not result in the creation of a Promised Land for the black loyalists still in Nova Scotia; rather, the exodus was detrimental to their economic interests. Preston was almost immediately deserted. Once the landowners had left for Sierra Leone, another fifty families who had lived with them were forced to seek employment and residence in Halifax. Birchtown and Brindley Town were also reported to be suffering from the loss of many employed or landed families.[72] Wentworth acknowledged that throughout the province "this emigration proves exceedingly distressful to those that remain, many of whom are . . . unable to provide for themselves, having been heretofore assisted and supported by their black friends and brethren."[73] Without the aid of their relatively more prosperous neighbors, and with neither land of their own nor economic opportunity to enable self-support, black families were increasingly forced to adopt the alternative of placing their children, usually around age eleven or twelve, into indentured servitude or apprenticeship.[74]

Even more significant than the economic repercussions of the exodus was the social dislocation it caused. The black remnant of Nova Scotia was a decapitated community, having lost most of its teachers, preach-

70. E.g., PANS vol. 224, doc. 103; PANS, Land Papers, Memorial of Samuel Ball, September 9, 1809, of Abraham Clements, November 7, 1822, of Peter Johnson, December 7, 1825; PANB, Land Petitions, York County, no. 530, September 10, 1795, no. 732, June 27, 1808, Kings County, no. 744, February 18, 1796.

71. PANS, Box of Guysborough County Land Grants, folder 1, docs. 29, 30.

72. SPG, Bray Minutes, III, February 7, 1793; CO 217/68: Wentworth to Portland, October 29, 1796.

73. PANS vol. 48, doc. 81.

74. SPG, Bray Minutes, III, May 3, 1802, IV, January 13, 1810, March 7, 1811.

JAMES W. ST. G. WALKER

ers, and other leaders to Sierra Leone. The core of the black clergy from each settlement had gone, and though religious faith remained, the separate black churches collapsed after 1792. The school at Preston was closed, since there were no black children there after 1792, and the Birchtown school ceased operation in 1795 when only fourteen pupils were enrolled.[75] After the departure of Joseph Leonard from Brindley Town the school there continued sporadically under white teachers, but it no longer provided a social focus as it had before 1792.[76] White teachers continued the Halifax school as well, after Isaac Limerick left for Africa, but the instruction the children received was specifically intended to prepare them for jobs as servants.[77] No more than in Brindley Town did the post-exodus school serve as a force to develop an independent and self-supporting black community. New schools founded by the Bray Associates in Fredericton and Shelburne were similarly served by white teachers,[78] who could not combine the roles of educational, religious, and community leaders.

Finally, the exodus had resulted in the physical shattering of the black settlements. Brindley Town was reduced by three-quarters, Birchtown by half, and Preston was completely depopulated.[79] This, combined with the disruption of the church and school, meant that there were no longer in existence large and isolated concentrations of black people served by institutions under their own effective control. Instead there was a widely scattered black population, located on white-owned farms as sharecroppers or in white homes and businesses as servants. This trend was accentuated by the economic decline of the outlying settlements and the education received in the remaining schools, which encouraged the younger blacks to relocate in the city of Halifax as servants

75. *Ibid.*, III, April 11, 1793, February 4, March 3, 1796.

76. *Ibid.*, February 7, 1793, May 12, 1800, November 2, 1801, September 29, 1802, April 1, October 1, 1803, April 1, October 1, 1805, September 2, 1806, April 19, 1807, April 1, 1808; *Bray Abstract* (1793), 35, (1794), 28-29.

77. SPG, Bray Minutes, III, February 7, 1793, July 3, 1794, July 2, 1795, December 5, 1796, June 12, 1797, February 5, 1798, April 25, October 23, 1800, October 27, 1801, May 21, 1802, December 5, 1803, October 23, 1807, October 24, 1808, May 19, July 6, 1809, IV, January 10, 1811.

78. *Ibid.*, III, July 3, August 7, 1797, July 2, November 12, 1798, January 5, 1801, November 1, 1802, July 6, 1807, IV, November 13, 1813.

79. See above, n. 66.

and apprentices. Brindley Town, Birchtown, and Shelburne's North Division were gradually depleted in favor of Halifax, where the nature of their employment and the pattern of their residence in white homes prevented the revival of a separate cultural development.[80] Only Little Tracadie, in its remoteness, was left intact by the exodus. In 1792 Thomas Brownspriggs abandoned his post as teacher and church leader, but he was replaced after a short interval by Dempsey Jordan, who conducted classes and led the religious life of the community.[81]

Economically, at least, the free blacks' position began to show a decided improvement by the second decade of the nineteenth century. As indenture terms were fulfilled, and as apprentices qualified in trades, the young men once again constituted an available labor reserve in a province that was short of manpower. During the War of 1812 wages for blacks in Halifax ranged from five shillings to seven shillings and sixpence per day, and so great was the demand that any able man could find constant employment. Once more the lament was heard that there were not enough free blacks in Halifax to perform all the available work.[82] The blacks won approval, too, for their loyalty and readiness to defend the empire. A black company attached to the first battalion of the Halifax militia attracted 120 volunteers, and they were described as "fine young men, equal in every respect to the White Militia, both in Discipline and Appearance." When the new governor, Sir John Coape Sherbrooke, reviewed the troops in 1812 he expressed his satisfaction with the black company's "neat and soldierlike Appearance. Of their loyalty and steady attachment to the Parent State there can be no doubt."[83]

At no time in the history of black Nova Scotia were conditions more favorable for the achievement of racial equality than in 1812. Though blacks were still a disadvantaged class, slavery and its repugnant racial distinctions had effectively been abolished, residential segregation was breaking down, and economic and social advance were visible. Ironi-

---

80. SPG, Bray Minutes, III, April 3, 1807, IV, October 24, 1808, November 13, 1813.
81. PANS, Bishop Charles Inglis, Letters, no. 3, Inglis to Morice, June 25, November 25, 1792.
82. PANS vol. 111, Sherbrooke to Cochrane, October 5, 1814; SPG, Bray Minutes, IV, February 5, 1812.
83. SPG, Bray Minutes, IV, November 18, 1811, October 8, 1812.

cally, just as the blacks' fortunes were turning upward, Nova Scotia was swamped with the very thing provincial employers claimed they wanted: a sudden influx of free black labor. In September and October 1813 several British ships landed in Halifax, bound from the United States, bearing runaway slaves who had sought the protection of the British forces then fighting their masters. Sherbrooke welcomed them, for he felt that they would afford "a large accession of useful Labour."[84] But attitudes would change as more and more black refugees entered the province.

As had happened during the Revolutionary War, American-owned slaves had faith that the British were enemies of slavery, and hundreds fled to the Union Jack in hope of gaining freedom. Vice-Admiral Sir Alexander Cochrane, caught by surprise, sought a statement on imperial policy from Lord Bathurst. Assured that His Majesty's government welcomed the refugees and would provide them with "the necessaries," Cochrane issued a proclamation in April 1814 inviting any American residents to avail themselves of the opportunity to become British subjects. Those who did so, the proclamation promised, would be "sent as Free Settlers to the British Possessions in North America or the West Indies, where they will meet with all due Encouragment."[85] The Cochrane proclamation, as had Clinton's thirty-five years earlier, brought a flood of runaway slaves to the British: over 3,500 of them responded, about 2,000 of whom were carried to Nova Scotia to join the few hundred who had arrived in 1813.

Some organization was required for the refugees' reception in Halifax, and so Sherbrooke opened the poorhouse to them. When that quickly proved inadequate a special depot was established on Melville Island, where the refugees' illnesses were treated and they were supported pending their removal to other parts of the province.[86] Preston, with a history of black occupation, was selected as the first new black settlement, and in 1815 refugees began moving onto the Preston lands originally cleared by the black loyalists in the 1780s. They were granted provisions, clothing,

---

84. PANS vol. 420, docs. 1-8; PANS vol. 111, Sherbrooke to Bathurst, October 18, 1813; PANS vol. 305, doc. 2.

85. PANS vol. 111, Cochrane to Sherbrooke, October 5, 1814, enclosing the Proclamation dated April 2, 1814.

86. *Ibid.*, Sherbrooke to Cochrane, October 5, 1814; PANS vol. 112, Dalhousie to Bathurst, December 2, 1816.

and farm implements, and placed on farms measuring eight to ten acres each.[87] Refugees were also settled in other parts of the province, principally at Hammond's Plains northwest of Halifax city, under similar conditions. By 1820 there were 958 blacks at Preston, 469 at Hammond's Plains, 76 at Refugee Hill near Halifax, and twenty families "on the Windsor and Colchester Roads." Over a hundred located within the Halifax city limits.[88]

The men at Preston were organized into work parties to clear the land and to build one house each day, and while construction was progressing the families shared the houses already built. To supplement their government rations they undertook to cut cordwood for neighboring white farmers.[89] However, the tiny farms, of no more than ten acres of marginal land, were not sufficient to support the refugees at Preston, Hammond's Plains, or elsewhere. An epidemic of mice and a heavy frost destroyed potato crops in 1815 and 1816, and though the more fortunate families shared their harvest with the destitute, provincial relief continued to be necessary to keep them from starvation.[90] A postwar depression and the arrival of white immigrant labor reversed the favorable employment situation that had existed before 1814. Once their wooded areas had been stripped there was little other means of support for the refugee settlers; when employment was available, only whites were hired for it. Many were forced to beg or steal for a living in Halifax, or to engage in prostitution.[91] Unable to sell their land to finance a move, for their farms were given on licenses of occupation, not freehold grants,[92] the black refugees were tied to uneconomical holdings with scant prospect for additional income.

Thus from the outset the refugee settlements were doomed to poverty and economic marginality. Frequently their condition was appalling. A visitor to Hammond's Plains in January 1827 found that potatoes,

---

87. PANS vol. 419, docs. 39-42, 46, 70, 71, 101, 102.
88. PANS vol. 422, docs. 19, 28, 110-113.
89. PANS vol. 419, docs. 46, 88.
90. PANS vol. 112, Dalhousie to Bathurst, December 2, 29, 1816; PANS vol. 422, doc. 28.
91. PANS vol. 112, Dalhousie to Bathurst, December 2, 1816; PANS vol. 420, doc. 132; PANS vol. 422, doc. 49.
92. PANS vol. 419, docs. 29, 30, 36, 119.

JAMES W. ST. G. WALKER

of a poor quality, served as the only food for the settlement, most people had few clothes or bedding, and one woman and two children were discovered "in absolute nakedness." An epidemic of scarlet fever was raging, for which there was no medicine.[93] Private philanthropists and the provincial assembly sent emergency relief of medicine, blankets, and food, but without preventive measures the same situation arose again in succeeding years. Poor potato harvests in 1832 and 1836 brought the people to an "abject State of poverty and wratchedness"; living at the line of absolute subsistence, they were vulnerable to the slightest variations in weather and growing conditions.[94] Preston shared the same fate. Sworn statements from their white neighbors testified that the black settlers worked hard and had improved their meager landholdings, but the poor potato crops of 1832 and 1836, upon which they relied, brought them to the point of starvation.[95]

Such was in fact the case in black settlements throughout the province. Even in the Guysborough area, the loyalist-descended blacks were able to subsist "only by the charity of their white neighbours" in 1836-1837. The remoteness of the district prevented their marketing any surplus crops in favorable seasons, and there was little employment available there for laborers.[96] The provincial Assembly was forced to vote special relief distributions almost annually just to keep the scattered black population, loyalist and refugee, from death by starvation and exposure.[97]

One result of the almost universal black poverty, especially as it was concentrated to such an extent within Halifax County, was a burst of antiblack sentiment among the white officials and population of Nova

---

93. PANS vol. 422, docs. 35-37.

94. *Ibid.*, docs. 42, 44.

95. *Ibid.*, docs, 43, 49; PANS, Box, Negroes, Negro Refugees, 1815-1857, "Return of the Distribution of Relief of Poor Coloured People at Preston," 1833.

96. PANS vol. 313, doc. 116; PANS vol. 422, doc. 43.

97. E.g., *Journal and Proceedings of the House of Assembly* (Nova Scotia) (1847): Relief voted to the blacks at Hammond's Plains, Beech Hill, Sackville, and Preston in Halifax County, £300, to the blacks in Hants County, £25, in Guysborough, £50, in Tracadie, £25, in Shelburne, £25, in Queens County, £25, in Annapolis, £25, in Digby, £25, March 23, 1847. PANS, Box, Negroes, is largely made up of receipts, bills, and accounts for relief funds or materials sent to poor blacks from the 1820s to the 1850s.

Scotia. Discriminatory restrictions had of course been introduced since the very arrival of the black loyalists in 1783, but such acts had as their apparent object the keeping of the black man "in his place." As the white resistance to the Sierra Leone emigration would indicate, an exploitable black community was deemed useful to the province. The arrival of the refugees, however, coincided with economic depression and a surplus of white immigrant labor; there was no longer any valid role for the black man in the general provincial economic structure. After 1815, therefore, white feeling went beyond the earlier restrictions to the point where the black was denied any "place" at all. In a reversal of the 1812 argument, the Assembly claimed that there were already too many "Africans" in Nova Scotia, and "the introduction of more, must tend to the discouragement of white labourers and Servants."[98] Black poverty, too evident to be denied, was blamed on the fact that the refugees (and presumably the native-born children of loyalist immigrants) were "Slaves by habit and education." With the "dread of the lash" removed, they were "quite incapable of Industry."[99]

Another consequence of the economic distress and attendant prejudice was a gradual inward movement of the black population; vulnerable outlying farms and smaller centers were deserted, particularly in favor of Halifax and Guysborough Counties, as the blacks sought employment, mutual support, and freedom from racial discrimination.[100] In cities such as Halifax, Guysborough, and Manchester, and in new all-black settlements such as Guysborough Road (later Lincolnville), the descendants of loyalist and refugee blacks merged, creating a new black population that eventually lost its awareness of the particular origin of its ancestors.[101] The loyalist tradition, therefore, was lost, but in its place the new black population created a new community awareness: existing under similar conditions to those which had pertained after 1783, the blacks of Nova Scotia underwent a similar social development.

---

98. PANS vol. 305, doc. 3.
99. PANS vol. 112, Dalhousie to Bathurst, December 29, 1816.
100. PANS vol. 422, docs. 43, 47; Rawlyk, "Guysborough Negroes," 31.
101. Numerous conversations with black Nova Scotians between 1968 and 1971, and with black students from every part of Nova Scotia attending the Transition Year Programme at Dalhousie University, 1970-1971, failed to discover anyone able to identify positively the immigrant group from which he descended. Most knew of the

JAMES W. ST. G. WALKER

Geographically the black communities were once again distinct from white society, being located on the fringes of white towns or in all-black neighborhoods. The physical possibility for a revival of community life was therefore present as it had not been since the shattering of 1792. Schools, where they existed, were separate from white schools, and by the mid-1830s the school in Halifax was supplying graduates who could act as teachers in the other black districts. Halifax, Preston, Hammond's Plains, Birchtown, Port Latour, Little Tracadie, Brindley Town, and Liverpool all received provincial and private aid for education, chiefly from the Bray Associates, and most were served by black teachers.[102]

In some areas, therefore, an institutional foundation for a new cultural development was being laid during the 1820s and 1830s. The trend was greatly strengthened by the appearance of successors to the mantle of David George. Many of the black refugees were "rigid Baptists" on their arrival in Nova Scotia, due to the success that the church had enjoyed in converting American slaves.[103] Two white evangelists, John Burton and David Nutter, organized chapels in the black settlements and made new converts; in 1821 even the loyalist Anglicans of Little Tracadie fell to the Baptist persuaders. But it was Richard Preston, a black American who followed after the refugees, who did most to ensure the almost universal adherence of the black Nova Scotians, refugee and loyalist, to the Baptist faith. After his ordination in London in 1831, Preston re-

---

refugees' arrival and their interlude at Melville Island, and simply assumed that their ancestors must have been part of that group. Even at Birchtown, once the largest free black settlement in North America, memory of the loyalist roots has apparently been lost. Robin Winks suggested in 1970 that Annapolis County is an exception to this general trend. He met several blacks there who retained a memory of and a pride in their loyalist origins. I have been unable to corroborate this with personal interviews, but it is true that Annapolis County received few refugee immigrants after 1814 and therefore the merger described here may not have taken place to the extent that it did elsewhere.

102. SPG, Bray Associates, Canadian Papers, Inglis to Associates, March 21, July 20, 1818, July 21, 1820, Dec. 16, 1830; PANS vol. 289, doc. 63; PANS vol. 293, doc. 104; PANS vol. 422, doc. 22; PANS, Petitions, Education, 1816-1830, Petition of John Pleasant and 17 others, February 1825, of the Residents of Hammond's Plains, Feb. 12, 1828; PANS, School Papers, Shelburne County, 1811-1846, Annual Reports of the Commissioners for Schools, Abstracts of the Returns of Schools, Petition of John Fells and others, Coloured Persons at Port Latour, n.d.; Assembly Journal (1841), March 9, April 7, 1841.

103. SPG, Bray Associates, Canadian Papers, Inglis to Associates, March 21, 1818.

turned to Nova Scotia, became pastor of the church at Preston, and embarked on a crusade that led eventually to the establishment of the African Baptist Association in 1854.[104] Almost every black settlement had its own chapel and local preacher, and within the community a common religious outlook gave strength to a feeling of belonging together. Like the earlier loyalist churches, the new chapels of the 1820s and 1830s insisted on a direct experience with a personal God, on visions, dreams, and proof that the Holy Spirit had touched the individual believer.[105] Such doctrines set them apart, just as much as did their physical separation, from the white society surrounding them.

Though the blacks of Nova Scotia were economically dependent on the white community for employment, charity, and government relief, they were not involved in the life of the province or in provincial affairs.[106] Local loyalties predominated as the blacks looked inward to their own communities for their religious, social, and educational existence. A deep attachment to the community had developed by the 1830s, to the extent that people were prepared to forego individual advantage for the sake of keeping the community intact. Two incidents from that decade illustrate the strength of the blacks' commitment to their local identity. The island of Trinidad, suffering a labor shortage after the abolition of the slave trade, made several attempts to recruit black immigrants from Nova Scotia. In 1820 a total of ninety-five, all from Hammond's Plains, accepted Trinidad's offer of free lands and promise of high wages, but all efforts to recruit more ended in failure. In a vain attempt to imitate John Clarkson, a British army lieutenant, Richard Inglis, toured the black districts extolling the virtues of Trinidad, and Governor Sir James Kempt added his personal persuasions "to induce them to remove." The offer was rejected without so much as an expression of thanks.[107] Trinidad tried again and again, passing special laws to encourage black immigration, sending envoys to Nova Scotia, promising free houses on half-acre

---

104. Mackerow, *Coloured Baptists*, 15-31; Oliver, *Colored Baptists*, 22-30.

105. E.g., SPG Journal, XXXVIII, Report of the Rev. William Nisbett, December 31, 1826.

106. For a detailed account of black "marginality" see Clairmont and Magill, *Nova Scotian Blacks*, especially part II, 96-142.

107. PANS vol. 422, docs. 19, 29, 30; PANS vol. 113, Kempt to Harrison, Jan. 20, 1822, to Bathurst, Oct. 16, 1823.

JAMES W. ST. G. WALKER

plots and wages of four to five shillings a day plus provisions, and even offering assistance in the establishment of churches and schools. But by 1839, despite the crop failures and economic hardships of the preceding few years, the blacks of Nova Scotia had roundly and finally dismissed the possibility of a second exodus. "They seem to have some attachment to the soil they have cultivated, poor and barren as it is," one agent reported, and another noted perceptively that several community leaders refused to go and the others, "poor and miserable though they be, are unwilling to remove without them."[108]

The blacks were, as the title of a modern black-produced play put it, *Here to Stay*. Roots were struck deep after a quarter-century in Nova Scotia, and it would take more than physical hardship to induce them to move. A second incident, also culminating in 1839, bore a similar message. The blacks' persistent refusal to emigrate, and their apparent inability to prosper on ten acres of marginal soil, prompted attempts to secure new, larger, and more fertile farms for them in other parts of the province. Governor Sir Colin Campbell urged Whitehall to finance a black relocation, but Lord Glenelg, reflecting the current view that the blacks' problems derived from a lack of ambition, replied that "If the want and privations from which they have so long suffered have not furnished sufficient inducement to active and industrious habits, I should fear that the mere occupation of rich land would fail of that effect." Besides, crown land was no longer being made available free to settlers, and the British government hesitated to set a precedent that could cause problems for the future administration of colonial lands.[109] However, the continued need for relief funds convinced the government that a few hundred pounds spent in relocation could save thousands in special assistance, and so in 1839, "considering the peculiar circumstances under which those people were originally sent to Nova Scotia," an exception was made and Nova Scotia was authorized to place the blacks on "any unoccupied Crown Lands in the Province."[110]

---

108. PANS, Box, Negroes, Gray to James, May 11, 1836; Lowe to James, June 7, 1836; PANS vol. 422, docs. 43, 51-53.
109. PANS vol. 115, Campbell to Glenelg, August 25, 1837; PANS vol. 422, doc. 50.
110. PANS vol. 77, Glenelg to Campbell, January 8, 1839.

Had such a policy been advanced in 1815 and in 1783, there can be little doubt that the blacks would have accepted, established comfortable farms, and become part, eventually, of the districts in which they settled. But by the late 1830s it was too late. White prejudice had become entrenched, and the surveyor-general feared that black neighbors would not be well received by white farmers.[111] The blacks must have been aware of this, and had no desire to expose themselves individually to racial attack on holdings scattered around the province. In their all-black settlements they at least had the support and protection afforded by their numbers. Removal would also have meant 'he destruction of the black community, the disappearance of the church, the severing of ties welded in shared poverty and mutual assistance for an entire generation. Unless they could remove in a body, they informed the government, so that their entire communal life could be transplanted to the new location, they preferred to stay where they were.[112] Since removal as a body was not possible the plan was dropped; the black community survived at the expense of the people's economic future.

The conditions, prejudices, and insecurities that drove their brethren to Sierra Leone drove the Nova Scotian blacks into their own isolated society during the nineteenth century. The separate churches and schools and residential neighborhoods, at first forced upon the blacks by a hostile or indifferent white society, had gained a positive meaning by about 1840. In an atmosphere of physical and institutional segregation, black communities developed that were economically stagnant and politically sterile, but were viable and valid cultural entities. As yet there was no institutional unity among the various black settlements spread from Tracadie to Shelburne; physical isolation and the importance of the local community prevented even the African Baptist Association from including all the black Baptists. But a cultural unity was becoming visible. All the blacks shared a heritage of American slavery and of disadvantage in Nova Scotia, and had common continuing experience with racial prejudice, neglect, and poverty. In their peripheral society they produced their own leadership, developed their own religious style, and nourished a

---

111. *Assembly Journal* (1838), Appendix 32, Morris to George, August 1, 1837.
112. PANS vol. 115, Campbell to Glenelg, August 25, 1837.

JAMES W. ST. G. WALKER

belief that in separation they could best realize the salvation of their souls and the integrity of their group identity. For the black Nova Scotians the Promised Land became a realm of the spirit, a place where they could be themselves and find their own destiny even though engulfed by a society that denied them all other means of self-expression.

The blacks in Nova Scotia have remained a peripheral society, economically marginal and socially distinct. As a group they have encountered discrimination in employment, housing, and education, and as a result share the lowest standard of living in a province that is itself marginal to the rest of Canada.[113] Most efforts to improve their situation have been directed towards their own communities, at the expense of any unified thrust that could have confronted white society in an attempt to win recognition as an equal and accepted part of a multiracial Nova Scotian mosaic. That this should be the case is a product of their early historical experience and of continuing racial barriers to their economic and social advancement within the larger community. Only recently has there been a concerted program to carry the struggle into the white community, and particularly into the political arena, and this program's inspiration can be traced more to the black American example than to their own historical development in Nova Scotia. The victory of the black community hitherto has been in its endurance, the more impressive for the conditions it has faced. Without that endurance there could be no contemporary basis for unity, and no community consciousness that could be mobilized to seek equality. Aside from the inherent value in the preservation of a valid cultural tradition in Canada, the black Nova Scotians' communal response to the racism of the past has made possible a united attack on the racism of the present.

---

113. E.g., see Dalhousie Institute of Public Affairs, *The Condition of the Negroes of Halifax City* (Halifax, 1962); *idem, Poverty in Nova Scotia* (Halifax, 1969); K. S. Wood, *Profile of Poverty in Nova Scotia* (Halifax, 1965); Jules Oliver, "Report on the Problem of Unemployment for the Negro" (Halifax, 1968), unpub. report; Nova Scotia Human Rights Commission, *Visible Minorities in Nova Scotia* (Halifax, 1973); Donald Clairmont *et al., A Socio-Economic Study and Recommendations: Sunnyville, Lincolnville and Upper Big Tracadie, Guysborough County, Nova Scotia* (Halifax, 1965); Clairmont and Magill, *Nova Scotian Blacks; idem, Africville Relocation Report* (Halifax, 1972).

9
Brian Weinstein

The French West Indies:
Dualism from 1848
To the Present

Central to the post-slavery history of Martinique and Guadeloupe, islands in the Lesser Antilles, and Guyane, on the South American littoral between Brazil and Surinam, is the struggle between two competing models of community. The proponents for each have sought to replace the pluralist society typical of the Caribbean area with different social and cultural systems. To achieve their purposes they have tried to find structures upon which to build movements for change. They have not been able to avoid dealing with the heritage of the plantation system, which still influences the leadership styles and social structures and which frustrates basic change.

Other societies in the Caribbean have similar problems, but the tension is greater here because Martinique, Guadeloupe, and Guyane are not independent. Instead of following the path of English colonies to political independence after World War II, the French possessions in the Caribbean, 90 to 95 percent of the population of which are of at least partial African descent, became *départements* of France in 1946, along with the island of Réunion in the Indian Ocean. Despite earlier colonial status, their inhabitants had been citizens since 1848. Now their juridical status is almost identical with that of other French *départements*, and together they send twelve representatives to the French legislature.

For their advice and assistance I am grateful to Martin Kilson, Robert Rotberg, Marie Perinbam, Daniel Racine, Jean Benoist; to M. Pouliquen and Marie-Antoinette Ménier of the Archives Nationales, Section Outre-Mer; to Hugues Petit-jean Roget; and to Jean-Claude Courbain. For a small grant I am also thankful to the political science department of Howard University.

BRIAN WEINSTEIN

Policy makers in Paris are attempting to assimilate further their 675,000 people culturally and socially into the French nation. At the same time, counter elites, whose most articulate representatives often live in Paris, have asserted a different identity as yet poorly defined. For some, it is a collective sense of *Antillanité* which includes the three small areas[1] in a new entity or nation; for others, it is a separate Guadeloupan, Martiniquan, or Guyanese identity, either within the French state or independent of it. These national solutions are rejected by a small but significant group often labeled "Trotskyites," "socialists," or simply "gauchistes." Their goal is a socialist state in the Caribbean after a violent worker-peasant revolution; despite their refusal to articulate demands in terms of nationhood, they will, like all other socialists, be forced to accept some form of national community if they ever come to power.

The masses generally do not perceive that they fully belong to any of these potential communities of the nation-builders or to the classes of the revolutionaries. Unconsciously, they do belong to large unorganized communities. Linguistically, for example, they are part of the Creole-speaking area including Haiti; racially, they belong to Afro-America, which includes Brazil and the United States; geographically, they are part of the entire Caribbean from Cuba to the South American coast. Consciously, however, they are part of small highly particularistic groups based on neighborhood, kinship, livelihood, and fine color gradations. Even these allegiances are tenuous. Extreme individualism, distrust of voluntary organizations, weak family structures, lack of universalistic ideology—which are the direct result of slavery and centuries of political and economic manipulation by distant authority for the benefit of France and some of the white settlers—accordingly have prevented the growth of the larger insular or French-oriented communities or even class solidarities desired by competing elites.

---

1. Martinique consists of one island of 1,100 square kilometers; Guadeloupe is composed of eight islands, principally Grande-Terre, "Guadeloupe" or Basse-Terre, and Marie-Galante, with a combined area of 1,780 square kilometers. Guyane, on the mainland, composed of a narrow inhabited strip on the ocean and a large hinterland called Inini, has an area of about 9,000 square kilometers. The population of Martinique is about 300,000, that of Guadeloupe more than 330,000, and that of Guyane barely 45,000.

One problem for all elites is thus how to bring the passive, conservative masses out of the narrow structures of the past to a new level of solidarity and community which will make life better for them. The second problem for the future is to determine who will provide leadership for the Antillean[2] peoples who remember the betrayals of the past and the allurements of French governmental aid, and are suspicious, as well, about any political change. Dual patterns of community structure and leadership present elites and masses with an inescapable dilemma and a permanent conflict.

Community Structures

Heritage of the Plantation System

The plantations or *habitations* of these former colonies created racial classes and were the key to a permanently dependent economy. In spite of their humble origins, often as indentured laborers and soldiers of fortune, many whites became rich while the blacks were kept down as slaves. The poor whites allied themselves with the rich. All groups lived in and around the cane *habitations*, the products of which—sugar and, later, rum—had to be sent to France. In the eighteenth and early nineteenth centuries the *habitation* was an autonomous unit within the colony: the white owner lived surrounded by his black slaves who cultivated and cut the cane and transformed it on the spot into sugar and rum. A little land set aside for food crops supplied some of the needs of the population. Social life revolved around this unit: "The principal social groups were created within it, others on its periphery in symbiosis with it. Finally, there were those created in reaction to it, but no element in the complex tableau of this society appeared independent of it."[3]

French policy stifled local leadership and insured the colonies' political and economic isolation from the rest of the Caribbean, South America, and the United States by manipulating local production, restricting

---

2. By "Antilles" I generally mean Martinique, Guadeloupe, and Guyane, although the Guyanese do not use that term to refer to their country.

3. Jean Benoist, "Types de plantation et groupes sociaux à la Martinique," *Cahiers des Amériques Latines*, 2 (1968) 139.

trade to French ships, and maintaining exclusively bilateral forms of communication—a typical "colonial pact." To minimize, for example, the strength of the Roman Catholic Church as a source of organization and leadership, the government would not permit Rome to create bishoprics in the Caribbean until 1850.[4] Economically, one of the best ways to prevent the growth of commercial ties in the Caribbean was to control the source of capital. The French Antilles therefore had no banks until after 1848 and were dependent on money men in the French port cities, such as Bordeaux, to which they sent their sugar. Planters could obtain loans on future crops to pay for new machinery or construction only from metropolitan France. The results were limited ties within the Caribbean, lack of local leadership, and a continuing bilateral communication with Paris or Bordeaux.

In spite of the absence of intensive communication with each other, similar changes took place in each colony. The first important social change altered the racial bipolarity of the Antilles and Guyane: inevitably, children were born of white owners and black slave women. In 1664 in Martinique there were 1,081 whites, 2,416 blacks, and 18 mixed. By 1767 the mixed or brown-skinned group increased to 2,141.[5] In Guyane in 1695 there were 398 whites, 1,047 black slaves, 143 Indians, and 4 freedmen who were probably brown. By 1789 there were 1,307 whites, 10,748 slaves, 806 Indians, and 494 freedmen.[6] During the earliest period of French settlement, 1635 to 1680, these *métis* or mulattoes were automatically freed on birth and became French citizens. Gradually, however, whites perceived this intermediate group as a danger to their position and privileges, and they insisted on restrictions to its freedom. Consequently, the famous Code Noir of 1685 established a subtle distinction between whites who supposedly had "natural liberty" and free

4. Camille Fabre, "De la Restauration aux temps modernes: La Guadeloupe au XIXe siècle," *Bulletin de la Société d'Histoire de la Guadeloupe*, 15-16 (1971), 113. See also J. Rennard, *Histoire religieuse des Antilles françaises des origines à 1914 d'après des documents inédits* (Paris, 1954).

5. Edith Kovats-Beaudoux, "Une minorité dominante: Les blancs créoles de la Martinique," unpub. thesis, troisième cycle (Université de Paris, 1969), Appendix, n.p.

6. Alexandre Moreau de Jonnès, "Essai sur la statistique de Cayenne," unpub. ms. (1816) in Archives Nationales de France, Section Outre-Mer (ANSOM), Guyane carton G 9 (dossier 1), 29.

mulattoes who had "acquired liberty." This distinction opened wide the gates to discrimination and set the context for the struggles of this new social group.[7]

Brown men and women contributed to the social and cultural change of the Antilles, but in fact they never played the revolutionary political and economic role that whites feared. Lack of numbers could not have been a reason, for on the eve of the French Revolution Martinique had about 10.7 percent white, 84 percent slave, and 5.3 percent freemen "of color" out of a total population of about 100,000. By 1848 the freemen numbered 35,000, or more than 29 percent of the total population.[8] Similarly, Guadeloupe's brown population in the same period grew from 3,125 to 31,405, or to about 24 percent of the total population.[9] They were a symbol of nonwhite social and economic mobility and were called "colored" even though many were doubtless black as time went on. This interesting association of the color brown with an intermediate, middle-class, or bourgeois status extends into social and economic relations today—a rich black man may be called a "Big Mulatto," for example.[10]

As the nonwhite population grew, the whites declined in both absolute and relative terms. The sugar economy did not encourage white immigration, and many of them died in Martinique in 1902 during the eruption of Mount Pélé volcano. The result is that the present white population numbers about 3,200 in Guadeloupe, 2,340 in Martinique, and about 1,500 in Guyane, or less than 1 percent of the total populations.

The whites were increasingly conscious of their numerical weakness, and they perceived the mulattoes as the greatest threat to their economic and social power. The brown-skinned people embodied all the threats to

---

7. Yvan Debbasch, *Couleur et liberté: Le jeu du critère ethnique dans un ordre juridique esclavagiste* (Paris, 1967), I, 7-23. Also, see Henri Bangou, "Groupements humains et institutions à la Guadeloupe," *Bulletin de la Société d'Histoire de la Guadeloupe,* 22 (1974), 3-63.

8. Auguste Armet, "Esquisse d'une sociologie politique de la Martinique: De l'assimilation au sentiment national," unpub. thesis, troisième cycle (Université de Paris, 1970), 179.

9. Guy Lasserre, *La Guadeloupe: Etude géographique* (Bordeaux, 1961), 302-303.

10. Michel Leiris, *Contacts de civilisations en Martinique et en Guadeloupe* (Paris, 1955), 165.

BRIAN WEINSTEIN

the status quo that the whites could think of, two of the most important being a weakening of the sugar cane economy due to the declining number of slaves, and an increase in potential leaders who, because they had more education, might have the skills to drive out the whites and declare the Antilles independent as had the black and brown creoles in Haiti. The loss of that colony in 1804 after a violent revolutionary struggle haunted the whites of the remaining French possessions, for many had worked there and knew what revolution meant. Haiti had been considered France's best colony in the new world—"the most beautiful colony in the universe"—and it was said that no less than 30,000 whites died in the "catastrophe."

As a result, the whites vainly attempted to limit the increase of the free mulatto population, and, failing that, took all possible measures to prevent solidarity between it and the enslaved blacks. The governor of Guadeloupe wrote in 1828: "it is necessary, in order to strengthen the action of the government over an agitated population . . . to divide the masses as much as possible and thereby to break resistance."[11] Segregation, discrimination, and a racist ideology helped to divide the nonwhites and undermine developing leadership skills.

According to the developing racial ideology of the Antilles, the whites were landholders—rich, powerful, French-speaking, and monogamous. Blacks were pictured as potentially dangerous if aroused by others or by hot drink; they were usually weak, Creole-speaking, and without family ties. The brown people were seen as innately immoral and sinful because they had been born "illicitly." One governor of Guadeloupe wrote to the ministry that the brown population had grown because of "unrestrained passion."[12] Altogether, they were pictured by whites as untrustworthy, ambitious, venal, and the projection or embodiment of an assortment of other vices which obsessed whites. Many blacks adopted white sterotypes about the men of color and about themselves, too.

To create further antagonism among nonwhites and to encourage

---

11. ANSOM, Guadeloupe 259 (1556), Report from Governor, September 20, 1828.
12. *Ibid.*

fine color distinctions many suggestions were put forward. For example, the governor of Guadeloupe wanted persons of color who had been *born* free to be given the titles Monsieur, Madame, or Mademoiselle. Those who *acquired* their freedom should not have the right to such titles of respect, he thought. Whites created countless names for color distinctions and then treated people accordingly. *Capre* was a person born of a black mother and a mulatto father, for example, and *chabin* had blond or red hair with a whitish skin.[13] Obsessive study of genealogies facilitated the classification of everyone, including whites, according to the almost limitless combinations in racial ancestry. Distinctions were also made according to the way in which a man or woman had been freed. He might have purchased his freedom but the colonial administration may have delayed recognizing it, and this fact created a new category.

After the decision to free the slaves in 1848, Paris instructed each governor to find out which slaves had been introduced after 1817 "in violation of the laws prohibiting the slave trade" and which ones had come "legally." The implication was that the government would not feel obliged to indemnify owners of slaves brought after 1817. The result was that those for whom no indemnity had been paid might eventually feel and be considered less free than those for whom the government had paid.[14]

The inevitable result of these artificial distinctions was a "subracism" which prevented, in a self-sustaining way, solidarity among nonwhites: "Each subgroup wants to be and feels itself to be different from those who the racist ideology indicates are located at lower levels. . . ."[15] Thus divided among themselves, the freemen of color were restricted by laws passed to limit their social mobility. Even though they had been increasingly mobile in the late seventeenth and early eighteenth centuries, they could not attain high levels of education or well-paid positions

---

13. Lasserre, *La Guadeloupe*, 324.
14. ANSOM, Guyane 90, Conseil Privé, 1847-1848, *Procès-Verbaux*, Discussion of October 21, 1848, about ministry dispatch of May 7, 1848.
15. Debbasch, *Couleur et Liberté*, 309. Also, see Léo Elisabeth, "The French Antilles" in David W. Cohen and Jack P. Greene (eds.), *Neither Slave nor Free: The Freedmen of African Descent in the Slave Societies of the New World* (Baltimore, 1972), 153, 166.

in the civil service and professions until the 1830s. A series of decrees had smothered their ambitions in the Antilles. For example, a decree in 1764 forbade the free colored to practice medicine or pharmacy. In 1765 they were barred from employment in the courts.[16] On the other hand, they were allowed to become artisans and to enter the colonial economy by producing indigo and other dyes for export, coffee, some cotton, and sugar cane. In Guyane in 1828 at least 937 freemen, women, and children out of 1,559 lived on *habitations* they owned themselves. Another 85 ran *habitations* belonging to others.[17] The average size of the holdings, however, was generally less than that of the whites or the government, which owned the spice-producing "La Gabrielle" plantation.

In Guadeloupe in 1835 freemen owned 12 sugar plantations, 91 cotton plantations, 249 food-producing farms, and 294 coffee plantations. They also owned 9,916 slaves. An official who counted these enterprises said that the freemen as a class were "becoming like the class of whites [and are] . . . much quieter in Guadeloupe than anywhere else. No doubt the reason is that they would have much more to lose if there were disturbances, and they know it."[18] In Martinique in 1844 the free colored owned 12,343 out of a total of 76,117 slaves but a proportionately small share of the sugar, and they too were regarded with approval by officials. The government wanted to insure that no bourgeoisie—white, brown, or black—would challenge the political status quo. On this point, the white policy makers and the white planters, sensitive to their status, did not agree.

Despite increasing economic similarities, divisions ran deep. The society created by color divisions and an outwardly-oriented economy was not unified and had no viable locally-oriented island-wide structures other than those created and controlled by the whites. The most solid subgroup was, in fact, that of the white settlers who, terrified of losing their economic and social predominance, stuck together in the face of

---

16. *Ibid.*, 162.
17. ANSOM, Guyane G 9 (6), "Renseignements de statistique sur la Guyane Française au 31 decembre 1828," 150-151.
18. ANSOM, Guadeloupe 259 (1556), "Relevé des habitations rurales des terres et des esclaves de ville, de bourg, et de campagne appartenant d'après les dénombrements de 1835 à la classe dite autrefois de couleur."

intense internal divisions. They stuck together best in Martinique, where the thunder of the French Revolution was muffled because of British occupation from 1793 to 1804. White settlers collaborated enthusiastically with the enemy, as they would again from 1809 to 1814, and thus insured that French decisions freeing the slaves would not be promulgated. Therefore, the continuity of the power of the Martinique whites, the famous *békés* who live on the Route de Didier in Fort-de-France, has been unbroken. In contrast, in Guadeloupe the rich whites fled during the revolution or were killed. Those who remained or returned, the so-called *blancs pays*, never had the cohesion of the *békés*. The whites of Guyane were the most divided.

Against all the odds, some blacks and browns built small isolated associations, too. In 1793, for example, a slave dancing club was noted. Others were formed on the basis of African ethnic identity or the ship in which the slaves and been transported. An Igbo (Ibo) group existed. In 1830 officials counted seventeen such clubs in Fort-Royal (Fort-de-France). Each organization had officers, a flag, a motto, dues, and a regular meeting place.[19]

In Guyane some slaves had escaped to the nearly impenetrable hinterland called Inini from Dutch Surinam and from Guyane itself. These *marrons* constituted new ethnic groups. Since 1760 the Boni and Djuka had been recognized by treaty as free. They built closed, isolated communities on the basis of their memories of Africa and the exigencies of their environment, but racist ideology pictured them as "savages" and other blacks regarded their way of life as retrograde and unattractive.[20]

Other escaped slaves formed more temporary associations about which little is known. On July 1, 1828, the governor of Guyane reported 163 *marrons* at large. Another 333 escaped during the year; 140 returned voluntarily, 102 were arrested, and 3 were killed, he said. At the end of

---

19. Yvan Debbasch, "Les associations serviles à la Martinique au XIXe siècle: Contribution à l'histoire de l'esclavage colonial" in *Etudes d'Histoire de Droit Privé Offertes à Pierre Petot* (Paris, 1959), 6.

20. Jean Hurault, *Africains de Guyane* (La Haye, 1970). Also, Silvia W. De Groot, *From Isolation Towards Integration: The Surinam Maroons and Their Descendants, Official Documents Concerning the Djuka Tribe (1845-1863)* (The Hague, 1963).

BRIAN WEINSTEIN

the year 251 freemen still hid from the administration.[21] The size and topography of Guyane and Guadeloupe permitted the establishment of isolated communities. A large group also fled to British-controlled Dominica, between Guadeloupe and Martinique, after slavery had been abolished in the British Empire in 1833.[22]

A different type of community was founded by a Roman Catholic sister, Mère Anne-Marie Javouhey, who led freemen at the town of Mana, west of Cayenne, the capital of Guyane, during the 1820s and 1830s. The entire population of Mana remained in a closed autonomous society until 1847, when whites and others began taking land in the area.[23] Two more groups had no consequence for the rest of the country. One was the American Indians, who survived in the Guyanese hinterland; they continued to live much as they had before the arrival of the Europeans. The other was a penal colony formed by the French government in the vain hope of solving its problem of lack of labor; the colony received about 70,000 prisoners, mainly white, from 1852 to 1946.[24]

Lack of labor after the abolition of slavery in 1848 led plantation owners to agitate for the recruitment of a new group of workers. The government thus approved the transportation of East Indians and Africans from 1852 to 1887. These supposedly free workers signed five-year contracts, but in fact they had been "purchased" in more or less the same fashion as slaves; they lived in unhealthy houses, were given strange, inadequate food, and died in great numbers. In this period Guadeloupe received 45,000 Indians and 5,800 Africans while Martinique received 29,400 Indians and 10,500 Africans.[25] Guyane received 7,333 workers, of

---

21. ANSOM, Guyane G 9 (6), "Renseignements," 132-133.

22. See Raphael Bogat, "Dominique: Terre de refuge," *Bulletin de la Société d'Histoire de la Guadeloupe*, 11-12 (1969), 149-154.

23. M-J. Jolivet, "Une approche sociologique de la Guyane française: Crise et niveau d'unité de la 'Société Créole,' " Office de Recherches Scientifiques et Techniques Outre-Mer (ORSTOM), *Cahiers: Séries Sciences Humaines*, VIII (1971), 284-286.

24. Pierre Dupont-Gonin, *La Guyane française* (Genève, 1970), 54.

25. Lasserre, *La Guadeloupe*, 303, 309; Jean Benoist, "Population Structure in the Caribbean Area" in F. Salzano (ed.), *Ongoing Evolution of Latin American Populations* (Springfield, 1971), 221-249; Eugene Revert, *La Martinique: Etude géographique* (Paris, 1949), 241.

whom 1,370 came from Africa, 4,924 from India, 492 from China, and 547 from Indochina.[26]

Of these various groups the East Indians have been best able to maintain cohesiveness, mainly because of their religion and culture, which separates them from the rest of the society. As of 1960, 15,000 lived in the south and east of the "Guadeloupe" (Basse-Terre) island of Guadeloupe. Other East Indians live in the eastern half of Grande-Terre island of Guadeloupe. All have always been regarded as being at the very bottom of Antillean social structure. They are still called "coolies."[27]

Africans were able to maintain some cohesion for years on the basis of their ethnic identity, most often Kongo, or on the basis of the ship which brought them to the islands. After dispersal to the various *habitations* in Martinique, for example, many Africans succeeded in reestablishing the ties forged aboard ship by locating one another on market days. Marriages often took place within these ex-ship communities. The Africans were also reputed to have brought their religions with them and to have come with superior talents in occult matters, so that they were feared by others. It now seems that these later arrivals have melded into the general black population, although their names can be found in some families.[28]

This extreme pluralism and outward economic orientation of Martinique, Guadeloupe, and Guyane were mitigated by two factors. In the first place, whites as well as blacks were cut off from their original societies, and the browns were the product of the West Indies. Even when the whites had been living in France, most belonged to the periphery of French society; they had been poor, from the underdeveloped northwestern part of the country, and had never seen Paris. They adapted to plantation society just as the blacks did. Living on the isolated *habitations* over 7,000 kilometers from their homeland they formed ties with their slaves and with the freemen of color. Everyone spoke Creole, a language which developed in the Caribbean from French, Portuguese, English,

---

26. E. Abonnenc, *Aspects démographiques de la Guyane française* (Cayenne, 1951), 19.

27. Lasserre, *La Guadeloupe*, 318, data from 1960.

28. Hugues Petitjean Roget is preparing a dissertation about these "Congoes."

African, and Indian tongues. Although nominal Catholics, many whites and nonwhites shared beliefs in the magic of the *quimboiseur*, who, like the *obeah* of the English Caribbean, supposedly helped solve medical and psychological problems. In spite of the fears and mutual antagonism, whites frequently served as godfathers for children of freemen, and they often left property to their mulatto children.[29] These were some of the symbiotic ties which helped keep these fragmented and semiautonomous groups together.[30]

Secondly, it is important to note that the men of color who owned land began to produce food for sale locally in addition to the industrial crops for export. In 1835 they were devoting 728 carrés of land (a carré equaled 122.5 square feet) for the production of food compared with 993 for coffee, 263 for sugar cane, and 216 for cotton in Guadeloupe.[31] They were becoming artisans and small businessmen. In 1828, for example, only 12 freemen were small businessmen compared with 28 whites, but 26 were furniture makers compared with only 12 whites; 3 were shoemakers compared with 2 whites; 62 were dressmakers compared with 2 whites; 10 were tailors compared with 1 white. In addition, 12 colored men were masons for only 1 white, 40 colored carpenters built the wooden houses, and there were 51 free hunters and 33 launderers. In the town of Cayenne there were 157 militia men of color compared with 117 whites.[32] Thus, whites were increasingly dependent on nonwhites for specialized services outside agriculture. The seeds of a more autonomous community were planted in the *habitation* society of the French possessions, but as later events showed, the harvest was too small.

Antillean-Guyanese Community Development

Growth of consensus and solidarity is obviously hindered in a society where the majority of the population is enslaved. Thus, the dispatch sent to the colonies on February 28, 1848 saying that the French government

29. For many years, however, mulattoes and blacks could not inherit property from whites, a measure taken to prevent the rise of a nonwhite landowning group.

30. See S. F. Nadel, "Social Symbiosis and Tribal Organization," *Man*, XXXVIII (1938), 85-90. Also, M. G. Smith, *Stratification in Grenada* (Berkeley, 1965), 255.

31. ANSOM, Guadeloupe 259 (1556), "Relevé des habitations rurales."

32. ANSOM, Guyane G 9 (6), "Renseignements," 150-151, 152-153.

intended to free the slaves soon was an important step in the building of either an Antillean-Guyanese community or an enlarged French community.

Although blacks greeted the news published March 26 in Martinique[33] with an outburst of joy, a vague sense of insecurity about the nature of freedom and citizenship has lingered to the present like the acrid odor of smoke long after a fire. Slaves knew from their elders that freedom had been declared once before. In 1794 the revolution had proclaimed all men and women on French territory to be free. The decree was never promulgated in Martinique because of British occupation, but freedom came to the other French possessions. A few years later hopes were smashed everywhere, except in Haiti, by Napoleon's cruel order of May 20, 1802, reestablishing slavery and the slave trade.

Even in 1848 the 67,000 slaves of Martinique and the 88,000 in Guadeloupe wondered when the decree would be written and promulgated. Governor Marie Jean François Layrle of Guadeloupe declared on April 4, 1848: "Liberty is coming!" He asked for patience, explaining that the slave owners had requested that their slaves be freed—a bald lie—but that it would take some time to work out the details and draw up the decree. Therefore, he said with unrivaled callousness, "You are still slaves." Ominously he reminded the blacks of the previous declaration of freedom in 1794 and wickedly blamed them for the reestablishment of bondage:

> During the time of your fathers a Republic existed in France. It proclaimed liberty without indemnity for the owners, without organizing labor. It thought that the slaves would understand that they had to work and avoid creating disorder. But, they deserted their work and became increasingly unhappy. They forced the government to put you back into slavery. That is the reason you are still slaves.

He advised the blacks to continue as before, particularly to follow the advice of the priests not to leave their work in the cane fields, and to get married "in order to obtain the rewards of the next life."[34]

---

33. Henry Lémery, *Martinique: Terre française* (Paris, 1962), 99.

34. ANSOM, Guadeloupe 7 (72), Proclamation of Governor Layrle to the slaves, April 4, 1848.

BRIAN WEINSTEIN

Heedless to these words, slaves left the *habitations* in droves, and disorder grew in Martinique, where some whites were killed during demonstrations. The governors of Martinique and Guadeloupe moved quickly; even before they received orders from Paris, they declared all slaves free. Martiniquans received their governor's declaration on May 22, and Guadeloupans on May 27. Guyane remained quiet in its isolation, apparently without news of events in the two islands. Incredibly, at the June 16 session of the Guyane governor's council, the Conseil Privé, only sixteen individuals were officially freed. (Either their owners had made the request or the slaves had purchased their own freedom.) It was not until August 10 that slavery was officially abolished in Guyane.[35] Here too the governor seems to have acted on his own. A dispatch from Paris dated May 7 concerning the abolition did not arrive in Cayenne until August 22, almost two weeks after the local declaration. Such problems of communication were a reason why colonial administrators had much more power in all empires than laws and regulations gave them.

In the case of the Antilles, one possible reason for the delay in communication was the ability of white landowners to put pressure on high government officials in Paris, either directly or through their allies in Bordeaux. They knew that France depended on the landowners to keep the islands loyal and to keep the sugar flowing. By extravagant claims that the colonial economy was collapsing, disorder was reigning, or massacres were filling the streets with rivers of blood, the whites hoped to stop efforts to free the slaves or at least to provoke the government to send the troops which would then use their guns to intimidate and harass the blacks. Tendentious articles fed to leading newspapers, embarrassing questions put to a minister by members of parliament friendly to settler interests, or anguished letters served the same purpose. As one owner wrote in June 1848:

> The ruin of this colony is consummated. A false philanthropy has made a holocaust of it. We beg you, Monsieur le Ministre, to understand the position of the unfortunate Colons and to take all neces-

---

35. ANSOM, Guyane 90, Conseil Privé, 1847-1848, *Procès-Verbaux*, Session of June, July, and August 1848.

sary measures to preserve their existence and the debris of their property. This means the dispatch of sufficient forces and the granting of enough power to the governor to prevent any weakness in the face of the uprising.[36]

Relief came from Napoleon III, whose coup d'état in 1851 relegated the liberal Second Republic to the history books. The new emperor did not reinstitute slavery, but decrees of 1852 and 1853 introduced forced labor, thus saving sugar *habitations* from loss of workers. Other decisions also weakened the significance of freedom and citizenship. In 1852, for example, universal suffrage and parliamentary representation were abolished in the Antilles; in 1853 a decree brought an end to the free primary public schools, which had only recently been established in 1848. In 1854 an important decision, called a Senatus-consulte, declared that the Antilles and Guyane would be governed mainly by ministerial decree rather than by laws. Guyane was lumped together with Senegal and New Caledonia; thus demoted, Guyanese possessed even fewer rights than Martiniquans and Guadeloupans.

The curtain came down on the Second Empire after the Franco-Prussian war of 1870, and the French proclaimed their Third Republic, one of the most important acts in the continuing drama of France. The 1854 Senatus-consulte remained in force, and the Antilles continued to be governed by a large corps of colonial administrators and the colonial ministry in spite of the fact that their inhabitants were citizens who once again elected representatives to Parliament. During the transition to the Third Republic rumors abounded that blacks and browns would once again lose their rights. In order to insure that this could never happen again and to obtain more rights, the elected Conseil Général of Martinique, most of the members of which were landowning mulattoes, requested, in vain, that the island become a *département* of France. That change would have to wait another three-quarters of a century.

These Martiniquans had good reason to be concerned about their status in the Third Republic. France was beginning a second overseas empire, racing against the British and the Belgians to plant the tricolor on river banks and desert dunes in Africa and Asia, and was not granting

---

36. ANSOM, Martinique 56 (464), Letter to Ministry, June 25, 1848.

BRIAN WEINSTEIN

citizenship to the peoples there. Calls were heard for the integration of Caribbean colonies into this new empire, with all it meant in terms of status, but the Antilleans kept their rights until World War II.

Under the Pétainiste regime from 1940 to 1943 the citizenship of Antilleans and Guyanese was diluted once again. The Conseils Généraux were suspended, and the nonwhites' freedoms curtailed; racist laws were applied, and the white planters allied themselves with a quasi-fascist administration. Blacks and browns supported the Free French movement of General Charles de Gaulle, and many fought in his ranks believing his promises for reform after the war.

At the end of the world conflict Aimé Césaire, the then communist deputy from Martinique, and a great poet and writer, spoke for the complete integration of Martinique, Guadeloupe, and Guyane (as well as Réunion) into the French Republic. Parliament passed a law to that effect in 1946. The islands and Guyane thus became overseas *départements,* and the governors were replaced by the same prefects who headed these administrative divisions in metropolitan France. French minimum wage laws and social security provisions were applied gradually, but subtle distinctions remained, leaving some doubt in Antillean minds about the quality of their citizenship. For example, the overseas *départements* have their own ministry, located in the endless corridors of the former Ministry of Colonies on rue Oudinot. Some Antilleans perceive this special treatment as symbolic of a difference in status between themselves and whites.

Despite the ambiguity of freedom and citizenship from 1848 to the present, the game of politics has been open to increasing numbers of players. In 1837 municipal councils had been organized. In 1854 elected Conseils Généraux were created to discuss the budgets of the colonies, although most blacks were not permitted to vote for another twenty years. Until the Third Republic whites controlled both councils. From the 1870s brown and black men took their seats while whites, who withdrew from most active direct political involvement, tried to influence decision-making through their economic power. The masses were disgusted by the all too frequent successful manipulation of votes by the rich, an unfortunate reputation for venality in the administration, and the fairly open tendency of governors to interfere in the electoral process to insure the election of candidates favorable to this or that party in metropolitan France. A high rate of abstentions during elections thus became as traditional as rum punch.

More important than politics was the great increase in educational opportunities. Unlike the white planters whose status depended on land and color, not literacy, the mulattoes and then the blacks rushed to the schools, such as they were. The church controlled almost all schools in the Antilles and Guyane until 1886, when the government decided gradually to laicize them. Partly because of the church's association with the monarchy, white settlers, and slavery, few black and brown men and women sought careers within its hierarchy, but they all profited from its educational establishments.

The government opened lycées first in Martinique, then in Guadeloupe, and lastly in Guyane. A small number of scholarships to French institutions of higher learning opened a tiny door to the professions, and a law school was set up in Fort-de-France in 1882.

More important than politics was a change in the pattern of land ownership and usage. A simultaneous process of both land deconcentration and land concentration contributed on the one hand to a sense of local community and reinforced on the other hand a new colonial pact.

Surprising as it may seem, Guadeloupe and Martinique always had a considerable amount of uncultivated land. In 1790, for example, only 43 percent of the total land area of Guadeloupe was cultivated.[37] The hilly and dry areas were, of course, unsuitable to cane, but after the end of slavery many blacks moved to these *mornes* or hills where they cultivated food crops by very archaic methods. On the seacoast they set up fishing communities similar to those of the poor whites. The cultivated land available for blacks also increased after 1848 because some sugar estates went bankrupt.

As a result, interesting agricultural communities formed. More or less self-sufficient families cultivated the soil, but they did not isolate themselves from others. A web of interrelations grew through the collective practices reminiscent of the development of the American West. For example, families living around Guisanbourg, east of Cayenne, partici-

---

37. Lasserre, *La Guadeloupe*, 378.

BRIAN WEINSTEIN

pated in the religious and social activities of the town; they went to church there and bought their cloth in its market or shops. Townsmen purchased food from the farmers, and families helped each other clear land and harvest food crops. A type of cooperative movement called *mahury* grew: according to Jolivet, it "united the farmers about 40 times a year," and "these small family units were thus closely bound by an institution of collective and mutual aid, veritable expression of a feeling of belonging to a single community and the principal arena of social interaction."[38]

Concurrently with these social changes the production of plantation crops for export declined. Guyanese sugar exports, for instance, declined from a value of 882,000 francs in 1847 to 570,000 francs in 1848.[39] Similarly, the tonnage of Guadeloupan sugar shipped declined from 38,000 to 20,000 from 1847 to 1848 and even further to 13,000 in 1850.

Distribution of publicly owned lands by the Conseil Général of Guadeloupe in 1875 increased the alternatives to sugar, and in the period "between 1898 and 1922 around a thousand parcels of land from one to two hectares in size were given out."[40] In the 1880s more *habitation* land got into the welcoming hands of smallholders because some planters went bankrupt when they could not compete with sugar beet producers in metropolitan France. In 1884 cane sugar sold for 64 francs per kilogram; in 1885 the price dropped to 46, then to 30 in 1893 and 27 in 1894.[41] Even more middle-level planters went out of business after 1946 when they could not pay the new minimum wages which came with departmentalization.[42] Small holdings consequently grew, and by the mid-twentieth century Guadeloupe had 16,000 small landholders each with one hectare or less.[43]

---

38. Jolivet, "Une approche sociologique," 280.

39. ANSOM, Guyane G 9 (8), "Résumés annuels du commerce colonial 1846-1868," note 14.

40. Henri Bangou, "Le problème paysan à la Guadeloupe après 1848," *Bulletin de la Société d'Histoire de la Guadeloupe*, 13-14 (1970), 119.

41. *Ibid.*, 116. Unfortunately, the author does not make clear whether this is the price paid the producers or the retail price in France.

42. Don R. Hoy, "Changing Agricultural Land Use on Guadeloupe, French West Indies" in Michael M. Horowitz (ed.), *Peoples and Cultures of the Caribbean* (Garden City, 1971), 275.

43. Lasserre, *La Guadeloupe*, 433.

The significance of this change is that these small farmers produced food for local consumption. By 1871 a total of 3,368 hectares was devoted to food-growing in Guyane compared with 2,456 for *rocou*, a red dye plant which was exported, and 391 for cane. The net value of the food produced was estimated at 268,876 francs compared with 86,499 francs for *rocou* and 79,132 for cane.[44] This increasing self-sufficiency presented a threat to the colonial economy, and the plantation owners knew it: "They believed that 'this invasion' of food crops menaced the colonial future: not the future of Guadeloupe but the 'colonial future,' that is to say, the future of a system which brought advantages to the colonizing country and the colons."[45] (Their concern was, at the time, unfounded, for although the peasants took the crumbs of land, a few aggressive *habitations* took the slices. This was part of the counterforce of French community development, which will be discussed below.)

Until the end of the nineteenth century and the beginning of the twentieth, therefore, the elements of a new economic base in a society of free men and women appeared. These embryonic communities had a much more positive social foundation for consensus than the old *habitations*, even though criteria of color, wealth, and level of education differentiated their populations.[46] In the words of Benoist, noted observer of French West Indian society, "Despite their often precarious character . . . [these communities] represent one of the alternatives for Antillean society."[47]

French Community Development

The French alternative presented itself forcefully for three reasons. In the first place, French society in the metropole is highly centralized and organized; this does not mean that the model is automatically adopted, but

---

44. ANSOM, Guyane G 9 (9), "Statistique générale de la Colonie au 1 Janvier 1871."

45. Michel de la Fournière, "Le problème de la main d'oeuvre à la Guadeloupe de 1848 à 1870," unpub. Diplôme d'Etudes Supérieures, n.d., in library of ANSOM, 124.

45. Michael M. Horowitz, *Morne-Paysan: Peasant Village in Martinique* (New York, 1967), 22.

47. Jean Benoist, "L'étude anthropologique des Antilles" in Jean Benoist (ed.), *L'archipel inachevé: Culture et sociétés aux Antilles françaises* (Montréal, 1972), 33.

BRIAN WEINSTEIN

it is already fairly well defined—much better defined than in an Antillean community whose only model until recently has been Haiti, where despotism and a deteriorating economy have been widely publicized. Secondly, beginning with the Third Republic the islands and Guyane have been more closely integrated with France than previously, and, thirdly, new structures in the colonial economy tied the West Indies more closely to the colonial pact than ever before.

Schools of the Third Republic, for example, effectively taught those West Indians who could attend classes to be good Frenchmen. Academic programs modeled on those of the metropole were supervised by educational officers from Bordeaux. Suggestions of one governor for the transformation of an academic program into a trade school inspired an uproar from the colonial middle class and middle-class aspirants; these attempts to adapt schools to what colonial officials considered "local needs" were perceived as threats to citizenship and mobility by insecure browns and blacks who wanted an educational system exactly like the one in France. In 1864 the governor of Guyane received a questionnaire from Paris which asked, among other things: "Does the educational system exercise some influence in the French point of view?" His response showed no ambiguity: "There are only French students here; nothing is forgotten in order to keep the students in the spirit and love of their nationality."[48] Illiteracy has now reportedly declined sharply to less than 10 percent.

The most important contribution of these schools has been the transmission of French culture and history, which means French language, literature, and symbols. Creole, the language of all native residents, could not be used in schools because until recently almost everyone disdained it, and because French tradition allowed no room for vernacular language education in France or in the empire. Command of French was considered the first prerequisite for social mobility. The author of a recent sociolinguistic study of Creole found that mulattoes in particular insist on speaking French, and on being spoken to in French outside the circle of family and intimate friends, as a "sign of recognition of their status."[49]

---

48. *ANSOM*, Guyane 140, R 3 (1), Governor's report.
49. Gilles Lefebvre, "Les diglossies françaises dans la Caraïbe," *Français et Créole dans la Caraïbe* (Fort-de-France, 1971), 29.

Without French language and education no one could hope for a position in the civil service, an attractive source of jobs for West Indians because of the security of income and a pension. Many West Indians joined the colonial service; in Africa, where the government often sent them, they could expect an increase in their salaries, paid vacations to go home, and many other perquisites. In 1910 about 10 percent of all colonial officers came from Guadeloupe, Martinique, and Guyane.[50] They sent their children to French schools in the African colonies or to similar institutions in metropolitan France, and many of them became civil servants and professionals.

More job opportunities opened after 1946, and important transfers of funds from Paris started in order to develop the Antilles. By 1966 in Martinique, for example, 130,000 children of 42,000 families received money from the government, and two-thirds of the total population received some form of social security.[51] The Sixth French Development Plan is providing 830 million francs for Guadeloupe and 770 million for Martinique.[52]

The economic underpinnings for these social programs consisted in the efforts of some old family *habitations* and banks—the latter new to the scene—to consolidate land and to transform themselves into industrial establishments. As a result, although Guadeloupe had its 16,000 small landowners, it also had by the mid-1950s "three powerful companies controlling 60% of the sugar production of the country."[53] The same process took place in Martinique, until 5 percent of the landowners owned 75 percent of the cultivated land.[54]

Moreover, in Guadeloupe the new investors never set foot on the island. By 1960 only about 14 percent of the capital was controlled and owned locally. Martiniquans held 23 percent of the capital invested in Guadeloupe, and metropolitan Frenchmen and metropolitan corporations obtained 62 percent of it. In Martinique, in contrast, the local

50. Brian Weinstein, *Eboué* (New York, 1972), 22.

51. Henri Leridon, Elisabeth Zucker, and Maïté Cazenave, *Fécondité et famille en Martinique: Faits, attitudes et opinions* (Paris, 1970), 165.

52. *Le Figaro,* October 17, 1972.

53. Lasserre, *La Guadeloupe,* 421.

54. P. Albussac and B. Martin Laprade, "Les Antilles françaises," *Tendances* (Juin 1971), 354-359.

whites owned 66.4 percent of the capital and local blacks and browns had 22.6 percent of it. Metropolitans owned only 11 percent of the capital invested there. Guyane had very few investments of any kind except for French governmental installations.

In Guadeloupe, metropolitan banks, which opened offices after 1848, gradually became large landholders. The Crédit Foncier Colonial, established in 1863, lent money to the planters. When they defaulted on the loans because of cyclone destruction, lack of labor, or lower income due to intense competition, Crédit Foncier seized the property and received an indemnity from the colony's treasury to boot. The bank then consolidated its holdings and set up large central factories called *usines* or *centrales*. Later, it transformed itself into the Compagnie Française des Sucreries, one of the largest landholders on the island.[55]

The internal structure of the *usine* differed from that of the old *habitation*. One sugar mill with modern equipment and a great capacity served several formerly independent *habitations*. Owners kept their anonymity, and workers lost some of their identity too. They became factory workers: "Instead of the house of the planter built in the center of the property which constituted an economic unit, there were some factories from which fanned out roads to various agricultural areas."[56]

The new *usine* discouraged the growth of a sense of community and prevented economic autonomy. Most important, the small neighborhood or area provided the only arena for social contacts and organization. *Usine* life is best described by Joseph Zobel in his famous novel, *La Rue Cases-Nègres*. Josy, the principal character of the story, grows up in a section of *usine* property where his family works. Until he goes to secondary school in Fort-de-France his community is "composed of about three dozen wooden shacks covered with sheet metal and lined up in regular intervals on the side of a hill." The manager, probably a brown-skinned man, has his house on the top of the hill; his wife has the only

55. Alain Buffon, "Note sur l'organisation bancaire aux Antilles dans la seconde moitié du XIXe siècle," *Colloque d'Histoire Antillaise*, II (Point-à-Pitre, 1969), 82-101.

56. Louis Joubert, "Les conséquences géographiques de l'émancipation des noirs aux Antilles (1846)," *Les Cahiers d'Outre-Mer* (Avril-Juin 1948), 114-115.

shop. Below the hill the cane fields extend for miles about, and way in the distance Josy can see the smoke from the sugar mill.[57] He seldom sees a white and feels a vague antagonism toward blacks who work in white houses in Fort-de-France, as well, of course, as toward the group of brown or black managers and businessmen. Thus, the old divisions of plantation society remained, but the ties that had nonetheless managed to develop weakened.

A totally different phenomenon dramatically transformed the economy of Guyane. In 1855 gold was discovered, and the successive rushes which followed took young men away from their agricultural communities to the rivers deep in the Inini hinterland. Immigrants from Martinique and Guadeloupe arrived to try their luck, too. In 1870 Guyane exported gold worth 891,286 francs, compared with 152,448 for *rocou* and 132,157 for sugar. It also still produced food worth 806,628 francs. Workers scrambled from the farms to the gold hunt. In just one year, from 1869 to 1870, the number of Guyanese in gold increased from 62 to 228, a significant change in a small population.[58] In addition, the prison administration offered secure jobs, and a Guyanese, Herménégilde Tell, became director of the system in 1919. This movement to gold and the administration, and thus away from agriculture, has meant a permanent dependence on outside sources for food. One source reports that Guyane imports about 27 percent of its food, but the figure is doubtless higher because only 0.1 percent of its land surface is cultivated.[59] In addition, the middle classes and civil servants are even more dependent on imports of protein foods, such as beef, than the rest of the population.

Both gold production and sugar exports have declined in the French West Indies. Bananas and pineapples were introduced in the early 1920s. In 1922 Guadeloupe exported 35 tons of bananas to France; forty years later white, brown, and black entrepreneurs exported over 100,000

---

57. Joseph Zobel, *La Rue Cases-Nègres* (Paris, 1950), 23.
58. ANSOM, Guyane G9 (9), "Statistique Générale de la Colonie au 1 janvier 1871."
59. Dupont-Gonin, *La Guyane française*, 125, 103. The 17,000 hectares used for food cultivation in Martinique in 1890 declined to 4,000 in 1961. Martinique and Guadeloupe must import 25 percent of their food (Armet, "Esquisse d'une sociologie politique," 197). Elites depend on imports for about 80 percent of their food, according to a personal communication from Daniel Racine.

BRIAN WEINSTEIN

tons.[60] These bananas provided more of an opportunity for nonwhites than sugar, partly because they could be grown efficiently in hilly areas where large machinery, which only big companies could afford, was useless. Banana producers, like cane producers, had to use the ships of the French Compagnie Générale Transatlantique—the "Transat"—and they have often complained about its high rates.

Since World War II the business and commercial sector has become increasingly important. The whites have been moving from the land into commerce, often in alliance with mulattoes, who have had considerable experience in this sector of the economy, or a few blacks. Their interests are mainly in export-import. Such businesses have attracted a few young people fleeing from agriculture into the cities.

This flow of young people to urban areas from agricultural and fishing villages—a worldwide phenomenon—has been encouraged by the improvement in communications since 1946. Roads permit the sale of agricultural products in Fort-de-France, Basse-Terre, and Pointe-à-Pitre directly, thus weakening small village and regional markets.[61] As a result, many young men and women have sought civil service jobs in the towns and in the rapidly expanding tourist industry.

By 1968 agriculture, fishing, and related economic areas in Martinique produced only 17.8 percent of the total value of goods and services compared with 18.4 percent in business and a remarkable 63.8 percent in the civil service and tourism, the mainstays of the tertiary sector. Out of 28,000 permanently-held jobs, 8 percent were in agriculture, 22 percent in business, and 70 percent in the civil service, tourism, and related areas.[62] (The fact that agricultural jobs are seasonal is one reason for the low figure in agriculture, but the data are significant nonetheless of the trend to the tertiary sector in the Antilles.) The civil servants and the tourist industries are responsible for a tremendous increase in imports, particularly of luxury items, to the Antilles. Before 1946 Guadeloupe and

---

60. Lasserre, La Guadeloupe, 679, 680. See Jean-Claude Maillard, "Eléments pour une histoire de l'industrie bananière en Guadeloupe," Bulletin de la Société d'Histoire de la Guadeloupe, 8 (1967), 43-59; 9-10 (1968), 85-106; 11-12 (1969), 121-143.

61. Jean-Claude de l'Orme, "Les transformations économiques et sociales d'un marché martiniquais" in Benoist (ed.), L'archipel inachevé, 321-334.

62. Albussac and Laprade, "Les Antilles françaises," 360-24.

Martinique (but not Guyane) generally had a favorable balance of trade, or at least deficits were generally kept within limits. By 1962, however, Martinique's imports totaled 275 million francs compared with only 171 million francs in exports.[63]

Landless Antilleans who cannot get jobs in business, tourism, or the civil service are unemployed, or they leave. Each year the Office of Migration for the Overseas Departments (BUMIDOM) helps 2,400 individuals from Martinique and 2,400 from Guadeloupe to move to metropolitan France, where most must be trained. At various times efforts have been made to encourage a movement toward underpopulated Guyane, but lack of development and amenities there has thwarted these efforts, and the 6,380 native-born Guadeloupans living in metropolitan France in 1954 increased to 30,000 in 1968.[64] Current estimates of the total West Indian population in metropolitan France place it over 100,000.

France's contemporary interest in the West Indies may create a few more jobs there. A satellite launching station was built at Kourou in Guyane, but it is an isolated enclave contributing little to the economy. Also, efforts to protect the French language and encourage its use in the Americas have an important role for the Antilles. The recent establishment of a university in Guadeloupe could serve as a center—a "cultural relay station"—for the transmission of French culture to Haiti, Louisiana, Quebec, and other areas. In the words of a former minister for overseas départements, Martinique, Guadeloupe, and Guyane have a "national mission" to extend French cultural influence.[65]

The results of these various trends are the growth of a rootless, landless proletarian class and a reorientation of the society to reflect the fact that the Antilles and Guyane are becoming part of the tertiary sector of the French state, a more exotic Côte d'Azur with beautiful beaches, a base for experiments, a labor reservoir, and a conference center.

---

63. J-M. Albertini, "La fausse croissance," *Economie et Civilisation* (September, 1965), 20.

64. Jean-Pierre Guengant, *Problèmes démographiques guadeloupéens* (Basse-Terre, 1970), 22.

65. Xavier Deniau, "Les Départements d'Outre-Mer et la Francophonie," extraits des *Comptes Rendus des Séances de l'Académie des Sciences d'Outre-Mer* (Paris, 1972), 1-2.

BRIAN WEINSTEIN

At the apex of the society is thus a newly enlarged group of high-ranking civil servants. These mainly white metropolitan-born men and women live in segregated neighborhoods around Basse-Terre, Fort-de-France, and Cayenne. They receive 40 percent increases in their normal salaries for "hardship pay" and enjoy many perquisites. In 1964 the average salary of a functionary was 1,838 francs each month, compared with 343 francs for the average agricultural worker.[66] Martinique has at least 7,000 civil servants, or one for every 44 people, compared with one for every 43 people in metropolitan France, which is a high concentration of functionaries. Guyane in the 1960s had about 5,100 government employees out of a total active population of about 17,000.[67] These civil servants collect about 50 percent of the total salaries disbursed in Martinique, Guadeloupe, and Guyane each year.[68] Taxes paid by metropolitan Frenchmen provide for the salaries.

White landholder-businessmen hover about the summit, too; then come the middle-ranking businessmen and professionals—white and, increasingly, brown and black—and then the lower-ranking civil servants, many of whom are Antillean-born. At the bottom are still the poor black agricultural workers, hotel employees, domestics, and the unemployed. The landholders, civil servants, and businessmen are the best organized in their chambers of commerce, professional associations, and Masonic lodges. Small landholders have been organized, but the workers have not done so successfully. With the possible exception of Guadeloupe with its port area and dockers at Pointe-à-Pitre, the workers have only a weak sense of economic class. Many observers, Marxists and non-Marxists, have been surprised to note that the general pattern of relationships between locally born whites and locally born blacks does not seem to have changed very much since the days of the *habitation*, particularly in Martinique. In the words of Gresle, blacks and whites are "fixed within their archaic roles."[69]

---

66. Armet, "Esquisse d'une sociologie politique," 195.
67. Dupont-Gonin, *La Guyane française*, 104.
68. Armet, "Esquisse d'une sociologie politique," 29, citing *Le Monde* of November 20, 1968.
69. Francois Gresle, "Ambiguité des modèles et spécificité de la société martiniquaise," *Revue Française de Sociologie*, XII (1971), 530.

The peasant communities of Guyane, Guadeloupe, and Martinique had failed to develop to a level of cohesion sufficient to resist the social effects of the gold rush and the rise of the *usine,* and they have not made much progress since. Dramatic social change, therefore, could now depend on conscious decision-making by leaders.

Patterns of Leadership

Heritage of the Plantation System

The leaders of colonized or enslaved peoples are usually anonymous in the history books. Consequently, little is known about black and brown Antillean and Guyanese leaders of the seventeenth and eighteenth centuries.[70] What was their status or background? What groups followed them? What were their goals? It is not even certain that there were always clearly defined leadership roles in the demonstrations and revolts that took place.

Joubert has written that skilled workers who ran and took care of *habitation* machinery provided a pool of leaders prior to 1848. House servants also may have been leaders.[71] Without a careful inventory of *habitations* it is difficult to know the size of such groups. However, in Guyane in 1828 a census found that 11,228 slaves were ordinary field workers, compared with 2,235 "workers, servants, peddlers, fishermen, washerwomen." In addition, seventy slaves worked on ships belonging to the colony.[72]

Did representatives of this group lead the reported slave revolts of 1790, 1791, and 1792 and the demonstrations of 1848 in Martinique which forced the governor to declare all slaves free? Joubert asserts, without much proof, that skilled workers "attempted to become leaders of poorly organized groups recruited among the former plantation slaves and sought to win political power against the whites."[73]

---

70. Gabriel Debien has published several bibliographies. The free colored also had archives but less is known about them.
71. Joubert, "Les consequénces géographiques," 109.
72. ANSOM, Guyane G 9 (6), "Renseignements."
73. Joubert, "Les consequénces géographiques," 109.

BRIAN WEINSTEIN

Surviving documents prove, however, that skilled workers, artisans, and small landholders were among the most important leaders of
an uprising against large *habitation* owners in 1870 in southern Martinique. In February of that year a black farmer and landowner, Léopold
Lubin, was beaten by a group of whites who judged that he had not
shown them "the proper respect." Lubin got his revenge by beating one
of his attackers later. The all-white court before which Lubin then appeared sentenced him to prison for five years. His friends, furious at the
partiality of the court, paid for an appeal.[74]

Meanwhile, in Europe the French were losing a war to the Prussians,
and rumors about the future flew everywhere. The most important rumor was that slavery would be reestablished, and, reportedly, a few
whites flew royalist fleur-de-lis flags in happy expectation of it. In September at Rivière-Pilote in southern Martinique blacks and browns began to attack whites and their property. A state of siege was proclaimed
in fifteen towns; the *habitation* of one of Lubin's white judges was attacked, and the crowd killed the owner. Some blacks who defended the
properties of their white employers were also killed, and fifty *habitations*
suffered damage. The panicking whites predicted that the island would
follow Haiti's example, and demanded vigorous action to prevent a
bloodbath.[75]

Government troops made mass arrests of black and brown native-
born Martiniquans. They also held several African immigrants and possibly a couple of men from English colonies. Most of these men and
women were cultivators and artisans, according to the Antillean historian Adelaïde: thirty-one farmers (including three Africans), seven carpenters, three sailors, two dressmakers, one baker, one former teacher,
one blacksmith, and one barrel maker. The number also included six
owners of *habitations* who were probably mulattoes.[76]

---

74. Roget believes Lubin was a mulatto, but the documents imply that he was
black.

75. For a partisan view see Armand Nicolas, "L'insurrection du sud à la Martinique (Septembre 1870)," *Action* (Fort-de-France), 19 (December 1970), supplément.

76. Jacques Adelaïde, "Lutte de race ou lutte de classe à la Martinique dans la seconde moitié de XIXe siècle: Essai de problématique," *Colloque d'Histoire Antillaise*,
II (Point-a-Pitre, 1969), 18-19.

At their trial the African-born prisoners claimed that they had been forced to follow the black and brown creoles by threats of physical harm. The court must have believed them because it seems to have acquitted them when it rendered its verdict on April 15, 1871. The condemned were mainly locally born; one was Louis Telgard, who records show was black, a butcher by profession, and in his late thirties.[77] It is likely that most of the others were black, too.

The *métis'* struggle against discrimination was waged both in Paris, where they had early found a more secure freedom and a greater hope of educational opportunity, and in the islands. The whites were happy that the mulattoes did not always return from the metropole, because they realized that years spent in France would give the mulattoes more self-confidence, skills, contacts among liberal Frenchmen, and leadership ambitions. A governor of Guadeloupe admitted that if they were to return home they would "see themselves hurt by prejudice which does not exist in the metropole. They [would] become angry about such a state of affairs and mobilize their forces to improve their position."[78]

The governor was correct, although he did not perceive that a growing middle class of generally brown-skinned professionals wanted to enjoy their full civil rights within existing political and economic structures. They had limited goals which did not always include the interests of other nonwhite groups.[79]

For example, in 1829 the freemen of color sent two petitions to Parliament. In Pointe-à-Pitre 130 freemen signed a petition on October 25, 1829, and in Martinique 334 individuals signed a similar document December 14, 1829; the two groups probably worked together.[80]

---

77. *Ibid.*, 41; "Documents relatifs à l'insurrection du sud de la Martinique (1870)," part of minutes of Conseil de Guerre set up for the trial, copy in Laboratoire d'Anthropologie Sociale, Collège de France.

78. ANSOM, Guadeloupe 259 (1556), Report of Governor to Direction des Colonies, September 20, 1828.

79. See the case of Marc Cyrus, a colored militia man, in ANSOM, Martinique 51 (428), Report of Governor to Direction des Colonies, October 1, 1829, no. 25.

80. "Pétition des Hommes de Couleur de la Guadeloupe" (Paris, March 1830), printed in Chambre des Députés, *Extrait du Procès-Verbal de la séance du 4 septembre 1830*, in ANSOM, Guadeloupe 107 (750). Also, "Pétition des Hommes de Couleur de la Martinique" (Paris, March 1830), in ANSOM, Guadeloupe 107 (750).

BRIAN WEINSTEIN

Both groups appealed to the sense of justice of metropolitans against the constant threat to their rights by the whites of the Antilles: "We are asking for equality with individuals of the white class before the law." Decrees from faraway ministries could not provide the necessary guarantees, they said, because they could be manipulated by governors under pressure from the local whites.[81] The Martiniquans in particular asked for protection of their property, a reflection of the fact that freemen of color had significant holdings which whites sometimes threatened. The free colored complained specifically that every time they went to court to sue their white debtors, judges who were sympathetic to the whites made them prove that they were freemen. They also asked for the titles of Monsieur, Madame, and Mademoiselle.[82] Both groups insisted on their unfailing loyalty to France.

In addition, the Martiniquans showed concern for the enslaved; they asked for a strict application of laws against the slave trade, which was still continuing in clandestine fashion, and they requested that the process of manumission be streamlined. The Guadeloupans showed a willingness to unite with the slaves if it served their own narrower purpose as landowners and professionals: "It is not by pushing the free population of color toward the slave population that the property and security of the whites, who do not constitute even a tenth of the population in our country, will be preserved."[83] The threat to use the slaves, the logic of the petition, and the strength of metropolitan allies helped win more rights for the freemen of color of Martinique, Guadeloupe, and Guyane in 1830, but the slaves do not appear to have benefited.

The type of leadership offered by these freemen of color was more articulate than that of the artisans and smallholders—at least they left written statements—but all the leaders shared certain similarities. In the first place, goals were relatively limited to a narrow grievance or to upward mobility despite white fears of Armageddon; second, complaints were about local whites, not metropoli'an policy; third, there was no appeal to universal standards of morality or to an ideology for general and basic economic or political change; fourth, no one attacked the colo-

---

81. Guadeloupe petition, 6.
82. Martinique petition, 10.
83. Guadeloupe petition, 5.

nial pact; fifth, leaders often seemed to become leaders because the whites blamed them for some trouble. Lastly, leadership lacked continuity: A man appeared as a leader and then disappeared after a brief sporadic action. No individuals seem to have filled such roles over a long period of time, or at least long enough to build something more than an ad hoc organization. Antillean-oriented leadership and French-oriented leadership have attempted to change these patterns.

Antillean-Guyanese-Oriented Leadership

The most articulate Antillean-oriented leadership has been educated in France. Instead of belonging to the artisan or small landholding group like their fathers and grandfathers, they have been physicians, lawyers, and high-ranking civil servants with diplomas from leading French universities and institutes. In recent times, civil servants have provided a large number of leaders.

Locally trained men and women participating exclusively in local politics like the Conseil Général or elected town councils are less important. Election to these offices has not procured an adequate base for island-wide leadership because power is too limited, the spoils of victory and patronage too modest, and ability is dissipated in endless quarrels about petty matters. More power belongs to representatives elected to Parliament, but their leadership potential is limited because of the power of the local prefect and the Ministry for Overseas Departments, which dispenses vast sums. Députés and sénateurs from the Antilles have a reputation for taking care of the "relatives" and friends who cluster about them in huge extended families once they win an election—and little else. Naturally, there are some notable exceptions to this harsh judgment.

The first elected officials were mulattoes, who quickly took over most positions of local leadership from the whites. The people voted for a few whites for Conseil Général or for municipal councils to show that they wanted an integrated system. For example, in 1875 in Fort-de-France, Martinique, the blacks and browns who were registered to vote outnumbered the whites 4,726 to 224, but they nonetheless chose to elect 11 whites to the municipal council of 27 members.[84] Most often these whites

---

84. Lémery, *Martinique*, 118.

BRIAN WEINSTEIN

refused to take office because they objected to the principle of universal suffrage which permitted nonwhites to vote for them.

Metropolitan whites, on the other hand, found representing the Antilles and Guyane too good to resist. By keeping a governor friendly and by doing favors for mayors and other local notables, who were the only voters for the Senate seat, a man could assure his reelection without difficulty. Some rarely visited the areas they supposedly represented. Henry Bérenger, a white metropolitan, represented Guadeloupe in the Senate from 1912 to World War II, and Guyane had a white senator, Vignon, until the 1970s. Few metropolitans represented Martinique because of a larger elite; Henri Lémery, a very fair colored Martiniquan lawyer, represented his island in Parliament from 1914 to World War II.

In the 1880s the black elites of Martinique and Guadeloupe began to organize against the whites and the browns. One group in Martinique explicitly excluded mulattoes, claiming with some justification that mulattoes had never pursued the interests of blacks when they had power.[85] In Guadeloupe Hégésippe Légitimus, a black man, founded a newspaper, Le Peuple, in 1888, to defend the interests of blacks, as opposed to the interests of whites and mulattoes. He wrote that blacks should become socialists and run for public office. He himself was subsequently elected to the Chambre des Députés in 1898, where he served until 1902 and again from 1906 to 1914. Once there he allied himself with the metropolitan Jules Guesde and the radical wing of the French socialist party. Achille René-Boisneuf, another great figure in Guadeloupan political history, called for the unity of mulattoes and blacks and was also elected to the French Parliament.[86] Thus, although color differences have been keenly felt between black and brown, they do not appear to have hardened permanently around opposing parties or ideologies.

The socialists, the radicals, and later the communists and Gaullists attracted followers, but local sections of metropolitan parties often had their own quite particularistic programs and broke with the central Paris

---

85. Ibid., 121.
86. Lenis Blanche, Contribution à l'histoire de la presse à la Guadeloupe (Basse-Terre, 1935), 44-45, 47. For an excellent discussion of early colonial representation see Jacques Binoche, "Les élus d'outre-mer au Parlement de 1871 à 1914," Revue Française d'Histoire d'Outre-Mer, LVIII (1971), 82-115.

headquarters. Leaders have found the ideologies of these parties to be unsatisfactory in recent years, and they have searched for ideas to support separation from France and possibly some level of unity within the Antilles.

Aimé Césaire is the most interesting of these leaders. Poet, teacher, mayor of Fort-de-France, deputy to the French Assemblée Nationale, and member of the communist party, he spoke in favor of the integration of the Antilles with France in 1946. Within the next ten years his attitude changed, however; in 1956 he broke with the communists, claiming that, among other things, they had the same colonialist mentality toward blacks as did the other whites. The same year he wrote that Martinique and the other French possessions had a national identity.[87] He has never explained what he meant, but more recently he wrote that the identity comes from the "confluence of two traditions—French and African. To deny the reality of an Antillean personality is to deny the nature of things." In recognition of this identity he would like to see the island granted "internal autonomy" just short of independence, but with "an elected assembly, an executive, and institutionalized cooperation with France which would be represented by a high commissioner."[88]

Césaire, along with Léon Damas of Guyane and Léopold Sédar Senghor of Senegal, had already articulated an ideology of *négritude* in the interwar period, and this, presumably, would be part of Antillean identity. But *négritude* only provided Antillean intellectuals, already completely assimilated by French culture, a satisfying pride in a non-white identity from which they would otherwise feel alienated. It is unlikely that uneducated rural and urban masses could be mobilized by such ideas. Césaire's party, the Parti Progressiste Martiniquais, founded in 1958, has been unable to mobilize these groups either.[89]

Like Césaire, other Antilleans' consciousness of their color, and of the Caribbean culture they had left behind, grew in metropolitan France

---

87. Aimé Césaire, Introduction to Daniel Guérin, *Les Antilles décolonisées* (Paris, 1956), 14-15.

88. Interview in *Le Figaro*, October 17, 1972. Also, Jack Corzani, "Guadeloupe et Martinique: La difficile voie de la Négritude et de l'Antillanité," *Présence Africaine*, 4 (1970), 16-42; Wilson Lima, "Recherche de l'Antillanité," *ibid.*, 43-62.

89. Auguste Armet, "Césaire et le Parti Progressiste Martiniquais: Le nationalisme progressiste," *Nouvelle Optique*, I (1971), 57-84.

where they studied and worked. Whites often discriminated against them, lumping them together with Africans, to whom Antilleans felt very superior. Nonetheless, they remained in the metropole, where they felt freer to discuss their ideas, or they went to Africa as French civil servants. In only a very few cases—Frantz Fanon is a notable example—did they actively oppose French colonialism in the name of a universalistic ideology.

On the contrary, these civil servants, physicians, lawyers, and teachers oppose the status quo most often for the reason that competing white elites bar the door to power and economic benefits. The competitor is no longer the Antillean-born white planter who has been content with his land or new business. The threat is, rather, the white metropolitan civil servant who occupies the best positions in France and in the French West Indies, to which some Antilleans say they want to go now. Bertène Juminer portrays this struggle for jobs in his novel *Les bâtards* (Paris, 1967), in which a Guyanese physician wants to return home after spending many years in the metropole. He finds, however, that the administration will not give him an attractive post and that he must struggle against metropolitan civil servants to survive.

The French administration quickly recognized the danger in this situation. Thus, in 1960 prefects in the overseas *départements* received the authority to remove civil servants quickly and without need for much explanation. The government also prefers not to appoint Antilleans to posts in the Antilles, despite increasing requests for such assignments on the part of blacks and browns discouraged by discrimination in France. It was only after a much publicized hunger strike that Fanon's brother was named to a post in the Antilles as he wished.

Civil servants in 1960 organized a new political group in alliance with students, physicians, lawyers, and others. They called themselves the Committee for the Study of Problems of the Antilles and Guyane and issued a manifesto in Paris, where most were living. They said that they wanted political change, and objected to the large transfers of money to the Antilles in the form of social security payments, which they saw as "humiliating."[90] This is, of course, another example of the gulf between elites and masses: elites with secure employment can afford to denounce

---

90. Comité d'Etude des Problèmes des Antilles et de la Guyane, *Manifeste et annexes* (Paris, 1960), 7. For a recent history of efforts to change the status of Guadeloupe see Laurent Farrugia, *Autonomie pour la Guadeloupe* (Paris, 1967).

payments to large families and the unemployed as humiliating, whereas the masses are more concerned about getting enough to eat. Shrill slogans demanding a cessation of payments in the name of dignity will neither build a more autonomous economic structure nor create a greater sense of Antillean identity.

In a more constructive vein, Antillean intellectuals have begun to rewrite Antillean and Guyanese history from the point of view of black and brown inhabitants. They have also begun to provide a basis for national identity by seeking to reevaluate the *habitation* chapter of the Antillean past, and are teaching children more about it. In the process they have found new models for leadership.

Among the models discovered are Louis Delgrès and Ignace, heroic figures who fought the decision to restore slavery in Guadeloupe in 1801. According to one writer, Delgrès, a mulatto, was born at Saint Pierre, Martinique, about 1722. He joined the French army and fought the British. He then served further in France and was promoted to lieutenant, head of a battalion, and finally aide-de-camp to Admiral Jean-Baptiste Raimond Lacrosse. Lacrosse had gone to Guadeloupe first to carry out the orders of the revolution to free the slaves; he returned in 1801 to reestablish slavery, and Delgrès accompanied him.

In the general disorder that naturally greeted the news he brought, Lacrosse, as well as Delgrès, was seized by a group of blacks who refused to return to their previous condition of servitude. Eventually the Guadeloupans permitted Lacrosse to leave for a nearby island. Delgrès joined forces with the insurgents, who welcomed his military and organizational skills; he went to Basse-Terre and took charge of the military forces there.

The French thus faced the loss of both Haiti and Guadeloupe while Martinique had already been seized by the British. They sent a military expedition to Haiti under Leclerc and another to Guadeloupe under the direction of Admiral Antoine Richepance. Richepance arrived at Pointe-à-Pitre in May 1802. After landing, his soldiers reportedly brutalized the local population for daring to revolt, and then they moved toward Basse-Terre, where Delgrès prepared his defense. The battle began May 10. Delgrès fought off the French until May 28, when he and the 300 men still by his side committed suicide rather than surrender.[91]

---

91. Germain Saint-Ruf, *L'Epopée Delgrès* (Paris, 1965), 103-133.

BRIAN WEINSTEIN

Delgrès's colleague, Ignace, has been portrayed in a more attractive way. Young leaders who belonged to what recently was one of the most active separatist organizations, GONG (Groupe d'Organisation Nationale de la Guadeloupe), created in 1963, have said that Ignace was the better model of a revolutionary leader: "Everything would have perhaps changed if Ignace, Delgrès' lieutenant, had been in command from the beginning."[92] By this they meant that a poor black man should have been in charge rather than a brown-skinned man of higher status, for Ignace, like most Guadeloupans, was black rather than brown. In addition, he was born in Guadeloupe, he became an artisan, a carpenter, and he had escaped from slavery to lead a band of *marrons* or escaped slaves. Contemporary interpretations claim that this black man wanted complete independence for Guadeloupe, unlike Delgrès, whose views are pictured as being somewhat ambiguous despite his heroic struggle. Delgrès was almost another Toussaint L'Ouverture; Ignace might have been Jean-Jacques Dessalines. Like Delgrès, Ignace was killed fighting the French on May 25.[93]

Although this carpenter is held up as a model leader, those who seek to shepherd the Antillean masses do not claim that leaders will necessarily emerge from the lowest stratum in society. To do so would be to weaken their own claims, because for the most part they are of bourgeois origins. On the other hand, these professionals and civil servants hope that school teachers who are very close to the masses will help them mobilize peasants and workers. The sociologist Gresle considers primary school teachers to be a "socially dynamic group," who are a force for change because their roots are in the common people and they desire mobility: 65.5 percent of male teachers and 60.5 percent of female teachers surveyed in Martinique were children of urban and agricultural workers, for example.[94]

GONG members agreed with this interpretation and added other

---

92. Cited by Monique Vernhes and Jean Bloch, *Pour la Guadeloupe indépendante* (Paris, 1970), 32; also, interviews by author.
93. Saint-Ruf, *L'Epopée Delgrès*, 93–132.
94. François Gresle, "Les enseignants et l'école: Une analyse socio-démographique des instituteurs et des professeurs de la Martinique," *Les Cahiers du Centre d'Etudes Regionales Antilles-Guyane* (1969) 19, 150, 34.

middle- and low-ranking functionaries and members of the liberal professions to the leadership category. Successful recruitment of these lower-
middle-class and middle-class Antilleans depends on drawing them

> away from the influence of colonialists and their pressures (such as
> high salaries, social mobility, vacations and trips to France, Legions
> of Honor, etc.), by reminding them persistently of their class origins
> and by awakening in them a feeling of solidarity with their suffering
> brothers, a love for their oppressed and downtrodden country, and
> [a sense of] the great national role that awaits them.[95]

A problem is, however, that teachers are looking out for their own
advancement in a society that promises many benefits to the ambitious
but obedient civil servant. Increasingly, secondary school teachers come
from richer families, and future generations of primary school teachers
will be children of civil servants rather than of farmers.[96] Another problem for Antillean leadership is exactly what they can promise the masses.
Dignity is important, and so is identity, but the masses have seen nothing
to convince them that Antillean-oriented elites such as teachers will offer
improvement to their lives. Therefore, the least assimilated Antilleans
and Guyanese, the poorest of the poor, probably still look to the French-
oriented leaders for an improvement in their condition.

French-Oriented Leadership

Most potential Antillean and Guyanese leaders have been siphoned off
into the French community, because education and employment opportunities opened the way to a better life, particularly in the metropole.
One famous example of the French choice was Magloire Pélage who, in
the dramatic days of 1802, opposed Delgrès's and Ignace's fight for freedom. A mulatto, he was born a slave in Martinique in about 1766, ac-

95. GONG charter, cited by Vernhes and Bloch, *Pour la Guadeloupe indépendante*, 50. For testimony of GONG members and others at the 1968 trial in Paris see *Le
procès des Guadeloupéens: Dix-huit patriotes devant la Cour de Sûreté de l'Etat Français* (Paris?, 1969). Also, Félix Rodes, *Liberté pour la Guadeloupe: 169 jours de prison*
(Paris, 1972).
96. Gresle, "Les enseignants," 36-41.

BRIAN WEINSTEIN

cording to Saint-Ruf. After working with white Martiniquan planters and joining the French army, he was freed. His commanding officer assigned him to Guadeloupe as an aide-de-camp like Delgrès. After the departure of Admiral Lacrosse, Pélage was left in charge of the troops at Pointe-à-Pitre. In the confusion about where Guadeloupe was going, and in the absence of any other clear authority, the people of Pointe-à-Pitre recognized Pélage as head of a type of provisional government at the end of 1801.

In messages to Admirals Lacrosse and Richepance, Pélage claimed unflagging loyalty to France, and he welcomed the French expedition after it landed in Pointe-à-Pitre in May 1802. He chose to ignore the brutality of the troops and brushed off French accusations of treason. Ignace pleaded with him to join his forces and those of Delgrès, but he decided to lead French soldiers against the Antillean leaders. After the victory of the French, Pélage was nonetheless imprisoned for a short time because of questions about his loyalty. The army eventually released him and welcomed him back into its ranks, where he fought energetically for France in Europe.[97]

Another example is Cyril Charles Auguste Bissette, a man of color and a landholder, who in Paris in 1823 helped draw up a highly provocative pamphlet considered anti-French at the time. The mulatto authors of *De la situation des gens de couleur libres aux Antilles françaises*[98] vigorously attacked the whites of Guadeloupe and Martinique, calling them "the privileged caste" despite their unsavory origins as "pirates, drunks, and outcasts."[99]

Colonial authorities refused to recognize the difference between Antilleans who wanted freedom to participate in the French system and Antilleans who wanted their freedom from the French system. These elegant, educated, landholding and slaveholding men of color wanted only to be better Frenchmen, but the courts sentenced them to prison and exile. Bissette was included, but he lived to forgive and forget. After the general abolition of 1848 and the rise of the black and brown population

97. Saint-Ruf, *L'Epopée Delgrès*, 65-76, 134.
98. No author indicated. It was printed in Paris in 1823 by J. MacCarthy.
99. *Ibid.*, 7. See also ANSOM, Martinique 51 (417), Conseil Spécial du Gouvernement, 5ème décision, January 25, 1824.

in politics he ran for a seat in Parliament from Martinique and allied himself with white planters who opposed further democratization. He thus supported the colonial-oriented economy and remained loyal to France.

The list of distinguished men and women who expressed their desire to be fully accepted as French, like Bissette, is very long, and West Indians have seen their countrymen achieve the highest posts in French politics, professions, sports, music, and the arts. Gaston Monnerville, born in Guyane of a Martiniquan family, was elected president of the French Senate after World War II; René Maran, poet and writer, won literary prizes; Félix Eboué, colonial administrator and governor, brought reform to Guadeloupe, and played a heroic role in World War II as General de Gaulle's governor-general of French Equatorial Africa. In 1949 the government buried him in the Panthéon, resting place of heroes of the French nation.

Unlike Eboué, who served as acting governor of Martinique and governor of Guadeloupe, French-oriented Antilleans seldom seem to be in a position to work directly for the improvement of the Antilles' economic and social condition. Prefects and other high-ranking civil servants in the three overseas *départements* are almost always white metropolitans; they make the most important decisions affecting the French West Indians in collaboration with metropolitan officials in the tiny, sad offices of the rue Oudinot. Moreover, these elites do not invest their money in the Antilles and they depend on the French government for the money for necessary improvements.

These Antilleans are the furthest away from the masses, but they are still models. They are not leaders so much as they are models for escape from a confrontation between different ideas of community, and for flight from countries where ambition and talent are thwarted by the barriers of the past and the limits to material development. They show that one solution to the problem of the West Indies is an atomization of the population so that successful individuals can assimilate themselves to France. Escape from the need to choose between two communities is possible through the exercise of extreme individualism, but these elites have succeeded in suppressing the dualism of their situation only by internalizing the conflict and tension which it arouses.

Conflict

The conflict and tension born of the opposition between two ideas for community have always had a potential for both creation and destruction. The search for a closer political and economic relationship between France and the Antilles or a new basis for an autonomous economy has challenged the heritage of the *habitation* system, and each model for community competes with the other. An important literature expresses the desire for a new identity, but no one has defined it. Antilleans committed to active politics have experimented with universalistic ideologies and new organizations to unite fragmented societies, but the French West Indies have still produced no C. L. R. James, Fidel Castro, Norman Manley, or Eric Williams, who brought new choices to their own countries.

Thus, social stagnation and destruction, rather than creative community formation, have been the dominant themes in Antillean history since 1848. It is difficult to believe that more Africans were brought to Guadeloupe, Martinique, and Guyane than to all of North America—707,600 compared to 427,000, according to Curtin.[100] Over the centuries the West Indian population declined in both absolute and relative terms and for years could only be maintained by constant imports of new laborers. Although today a high birthrate insures the physical survival of Antilleans, the failures of the economy, as well as the blockage in the intellectual development of free Antilleans by an educational system designed for others, mean a waste of human potential.

Riots and other acts of violence in reaction to this situation have encouraged greater doses of material assistance, but neither the emotional outbursts nor the new funds have provided long-term relief for the ferment. The local whites were the first to use violence to strike out against the anomalous position of the islands. In 1717 the *habitation* owners of Martinique, following the example of their brethren in Guadeloupe, challenged the colonial pact. Like other settlers in the new world they demanded the right to trade freely with nearby foreign countries. They threatened colonial officials and demonstrated throughout the

---

100. Philip D. Curtin, *The Atlantic Slave Trade: A Census* (Madison, 1969), 80, 84, 91.

island,[101] but once they realized the weakness of their position compared with the blacks and browns led by men like Delgrès and Ignace, they grasped at the French community alternative.

The local whites, whose interests were still not the same as those of the white-controlled administration, tried to manipulate its representatives and structures to suit their social and economic interests. No longer able to use violence or the threat of violence to maintain their status, the whites attempted to control the administration's use of it. Thus, whites distorted the language and action used by blacks and browns in defense of their civil rights. Respectful refusals to obey unfair orders were called "rebellions"; the search of newly freed men for lands and decent jobs was labeled dangerous "vagabondage"; a request in elegant French for further integration within the French community was "proof" that the bloody "revolution" was at hand.

Too quickly convinced of the need for action, Paris sent the troops; it consented to almost unlimited action by the governors to protect order, or it learned too late about the initiatives taken. Thus, in 1900 when Martiniquan workers, attempting to organize a trade union, demonstrated peaceably in the town of François, white troops fired on them, killing ten and wounding twelve. (They were shot in the back as they fled.)[102]

Seemingly small sparks set off riots regularly, a sign of the deep frustrations in Antillean-Guyanese society. In 1850 and 1851 the government was obliged to declare a state of siege in Martinique; 1908 was another tense year; in 1910 a violent strike shook Guadeloupe; in 1928 several people died after the mysterious death of a popular white candidate for Parliament in Guyane; and in 1959 riots occurred after an accident between a Martiniquan motorcyclist and a metropolitan automobile driver. The 1967 riots in Guadeloupe took place after a white set his dog upon a black shoe cobbler. And the 1974 riots and deaths in Martinique were partly due to a crushing inflation and a rate of unemployment soaring beyond 25 percent of the active population.[103]

---

101. See Jacques Petitjean Roget, *La Gaoulé: La revolte de la Martinique en 1717* (Fort-de-France, 1966), 31-111, 251-414.

102. ANSOM, Martinique 59 (503, 490).

103. Nöel-Jean Bergerous, "Le calme est revenu, mais les difficultés demeurent," *Le Monde*, February 24, 1974, 9.

BRIAN WEINSTEIN

Increasing distrust of the distant metropole and its local representatives, the white civil servants, is replacing antagonism toward local
whites. *Békés* of Martinique, *blancs créoles* of Guyane, and the *blancs
pays* of Guadeloupe are less a target of the anger of the masses than
formerly, and with some exceptions black and brown spokesmen say
they accept them as part of the island communities they envisage. The
fact that these whites speak Creole and that several of their children have
worked closely in recent years with blacks and browns seeking to build a
new community has contributed to their assimilation. In addition, in
Guadeloupe and Guyane local whites do not have the power of the *békés*
of Martinique. It is the government and metropolitan interests which
have taken over the factories and land, the Kourou satellite station in
Guyane, and, of course, the civil service. The Martiniquan whites of the
Route de Didier are still who they are, but they have been transforming
their investments from land into business and are reportedly placing their
profits in Latin America and elsewhere. With the greater mobility that
these capital transformations give them, they have less need to try to
manipulate the government, despite their continuing fears for the future.

Because of their larger populations, greater material development,
and increasing communication with nearby elites on independent islands,
Guadeloupan and Martiniquan leaders would be able to change the
political status of their islands more easily than Guyanese elites. The
French warn, however, that for them it is all or nothing: Antillean
demands for more autonomy would lead directly to independence
without metropolitan material assistance afterwards. Unity of the three
areas is not a plausible solution for the moment because elites are divided
and the economies competing. Although Guadeloupans, Martiniquans,
and Guyanese are learning a little more about their own history and may
be prouder now of the Creole language, they also know that many
leaders of the past were serving their own narrow economic or color
interests and are still suspicious of the ambitious. The artisan leaders who
were closer to the interests of the masses have been replaced by professionals and civil servants who have much more personal security than
the rest of the population and who represent a distant government, no
matter what they claim.

In the meanwhile almost all school-age children are in primary
school learning the French language and culture as their own, although
the failure rates are high. It is also true that metropolitan France continues to try to absorb thousands of migrants each year, but these men

and women discover that the old solution of individual assimilation is no longer as effective as it used to be. Unlike the elites which preceded them to the metropole in the nineteenth and early twentieth centuries, they get jobs closer to the bottom of the ladder than to the top of it. And they discover that in spite of their French culture, white metropolitans may treat them in offensive ways showing them that they are not full citizens. Rates of unemployment are increasing in the metropole, although they will not be so high as in the West Indies.

Thus, neither model of national community and neither group of leaders have been able to provide the "central tradition through which [West Indians] could mediate their relationships to each other."[104] Another type of leader with a promise of a new level of community based on class could perhaps capture the imagination of the skeptical masses of Guadeloupe, Martinique, and Guyane, and it is likely that many are following more closely than ever the experimentation in nearby Caribbean islands, particularly in Cuba and in Jamaica, which is now undertaking "Democratic Jamaican Socialism."

The socialist slogan might mobilize the masses, but its goals would ultimately be national. The national community is today the highest level of community—the supreme loyalty group. Only the nation can provide peoples with a meaningful order. Within this context the best remaining solution may be the cultivation of Antillean-Guyanese history, language, and culture to raise the unconscious identities of the masses to the level of consciousness, thus transforming Guadeloupans, Martiniquans, and Guyanese into one or three clearly identified ethnic groups within the larger French nation or within a larger future Caribbean nation.

One barrier to this solution is that the French nation, already threatened by the assertions of ethnic identity among the Catalans, Bretons, and Corsicans, may consider any such recognition as a threat to its national unity rather than as a solution to continuing diversity. Another barrier is that the prospects for a Caribbean nation are still very dim. However, the failure to experiment with new community alternatives may drive the peoples of Martinique, Guadeloupe, and Guyane to extreme individualism or back to the narrow family and neighborhood groups of the past. Thus divided and isolated, they would become the damned of the African diaspora.

---

104. Sidney W. Mintz, "The Caribbean Region," *Daedalus*, CIII (1974), 48.

10 George Eaton Simpson

Religions of the Caribbean

Nearly all the studies of religions in the Caribbean have been separate accounts of major denominations, esoteric groups, syncretistic cults, or Pentecostal churches. Most of these reports have lacked the historical or the comparative dimension, or both. The present paper is an attempt to provide some historical perspective on religious developments in the region, and to indicate some of the relationships that have existed there among the many religions of the past and the present.

In the Latin colonies of the Caribbean, Roman Catholic missionaries baptized and served large numbers of African slaves. In these countries, Protestant ministers had little success until relatively recent years.

In the British possessions, the Church of England was the religion of white settlers and officials in the seventeenth and eighteenth centuries; it was not a missionary church for the slaves.[1] The arduous work of the nonconformist missionaries resulted in the conversion of only a small minority of the slaves in the non-Catholic countries. In Jamaica, the Native Baptists were without serious competition for forty years (1780-1820) as George Gibb, Moses Baker, and other subordinates in George Lisle's "leader system" founded their own groups, and as these classes split into new cult groups. During this period a reinterpretation of Christianity spread throughout the island, and by 1830 the Native

---

An earlier version of this chapter was presented to the Conference on Popular Religious Movements sponsored by Oberlin College in 1973.

1. J. B. Ellis, *The Diocese of Jamaica: A Short Account of Its Growth and Organization* (London, 1913), 41.

Baptists had become "another religion competing with the Christianity of the European missionaries."[2]

Because they were not exposed to Christian doctrine, or were only partially instructed, or were not welcomed as participants, many persons of African descent in the West Indies never became members of the churches established by whites. Instead, they have participated regularly or occasionally in syncretistic cults or independent religions.

Part I: Christian Religions in the Caribbean
through the Nineteenth Century

The Catholic Church

In 1667, Jean-Baptiste du Tertre, a Catholic priest who came to the Antilles in 1640, asserted: "There is scarcely a Negro in all the French Antilles that is not a Christian, scarcely one that they [the missionaries] have not regenerated in the waters of Baptism." Du Tertre claimed that more than 15,000 slaves had already been baptized in the French islands; he claimed also that these slaves went to mass, confession, and Holy Communion. In 1685, the Code Noir prescribed that all the slaves in the French islands were to be baptized and given instruction in the Catholic religion.[3] Catholicism came later to the English possessions in the West Indies. In Jamaica, the largest of the British islands, the first Catholic priest arrived in 1792, and in 1829 the congregation in Kingston consisted of "Spaniards, French, Dutch, some Italians, and a few Irishmen, scarcely twelve in number."[4]

It has often been claimed that slavery was harsher in the English and Dutch colonies than in the Latin possessions. Probably the differences have been exaggerated, but at least during the early years of slavery the

---

2. Philip D. Curtin, *Two Jamaicas: The Role of Ideas in a Tropical Colony, 1830-1865* (Cambridge, Mass., 1955), 34.

3. Jean-Baptiste du Tertre, *Histoire Générale des Antilles Habitées par .les François* (1667). Quoted in C. Jesse, "Du Tertre and Labat on 17th Century Slave Life in the French Antilles," *Caribbean Quarterly*, VII (1961), 153-155.

4. Francis X. Delany, *A History of the Catholic Church in Jamaica, B. W. I., 1494 to 1929* (New York, 1930), 43.

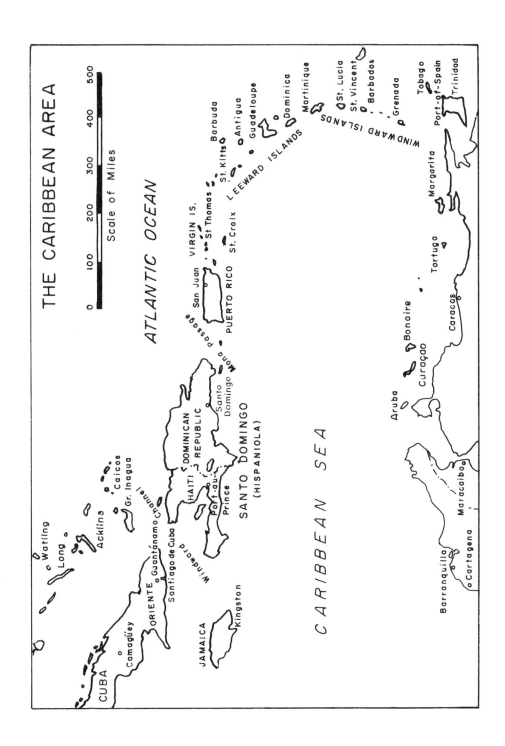

Spanish, Portuguese, and French governments supported the attempts of the Catholic church to ameliorate the system. Among other things, the state-supported church was influential in the formation of more humane laws in Latin America. Conformance fell short of the standards set in law, but concern for the religious and social well-being of the slaves was stronger in the Latin colonies. Protestant churches in the West Indies did not receive the same kind of support from their governments, and the laws enacted by slave owners in the British colonies were not influenced to any extent by religious principles.[5]

The Anglican Church

The Anglican bishops of London in the eighteenth century cared little or nothing about the persons of African descent in the West Indies; their concern in many cases was to oblige a friend or to find a home for some "family encumbrance."[6] Not only was there a lack of interest in the slaves on the part of most of the clergy; the churches in Jamaica were understaffed and many of the rectors were incompetent or dissolute. An eighteenth-century writer described the majority of the Anglican clergy as being "of a character so vile that I do not care to mention it; for, except for a few, they are generally the most finished of all debauchees."[7]

Most of the slave owners in the British West Indies opposed the preaching of the Christian gospel to the slaves because of their fear that conversion would make them difficult to manage and give them ideas of revolt and freedom. The argument that Christian doctrine would produce more obedient and docile slaves made little impression on most of the plantation owners.[8] Anglican teaching was considered less dangerous than the instruction given by the dissenting missionaries, but planters believed that any teaching would make labor less efficient and reduce

5. Frank Tannenbaum, *Slave and Citizen* (New York, 1947), 52-104; Robert W. Smith, "Slavery and Christianity in the West Indies," *Church History*, XIX (1950), 186.

6. Ellis, *Diocese of Jamaica*, 40-41.

7. *Ibid.*, 42-43.

8. Tannenbaum, *Slave and Citizen*, 82.

profits. In short, missionaries were regarded in the British Caribbean as renegades who threatened the solidarity of white society.[9]

In 1823, the British government attempted to inject some vitality into the Anglican church in the West Indies by creating two new bishoprics and providing a special grant for work with the slave populations. Also, Anglican societies, including the Church Missionary Society and the British and Foreign Bible Society, were becoming interested in the West Indian slaves, and it was at this time that the Society for the Conversion and Religious Instruction of the Negro Slaves in the British West Indies was formed.[10] Between 1824 and 1832, thirteen Anglican churches were built and nine were under construction in Jamaica, with funds provided by the Assembly and the vestries. It was claimed that instruction in religion was being given to slaves on 280 estates in the diocese.[11]

Disestablishment of the Church of England was accomplished in most of the British colonies between 1868 and 1870, but in Barbados the legislature refused to take this action and the Anglican church continued to be the established church of the island. In Trinidad the Church of England and the Catholic church both received grants from the government; in British Guiana the Church of England, the Presbyterians, and the Dutch Reformed church had all received grants and these arrangements were continued.[12]

The Moravians

New efforts at Christianizing the slaves in the West Indies were started in the second third of the eighteenth century. Three groups undertook this work: the United Brethren, or Moravians, from Germany; the Methodists from England; and the Baptists from America. The first Moravian missionaries in the Caribbean arrived in St. Thomas on December 13, 1732. The official language of the island was Danish, but the Negroes spoke Creole and the Brethren spoke "in a jargon of Dutch and German."

9. Smith, "Slavery and Christianity," 181-182, 184.
10. Ibid., 178-179.
11. Ellis, Diocese of Jamaica, 69.
12. Alan Burns, History of the West Indies (London, 1969, 2d ed.), 667.

A church historian exclaims that "they made it clear that Christ died for blacks as well as whites [and] the poor slaves clapped their hands for joy." One of the first missionaries remarked that the slaves "felt the truth rather than understood it."[13]

Although Count Nikolaus von Zinzendorf, the founder of the Moravian missions, defended slavery, telling converts at a mass meeting in St. Thomas in 1739 that "conversion will make you free, not from the control of your masters, but simply from your wicked habits and thoughts, and all that makes you dissatisfied with your lot," the Brethren at first met considerable opposition from the planters. However, the zeal of the missionaries, aided by friendly assistance from the Danish government and some of the planters, resulted in the rapid growth of the mission after 1740.[14] Beginning in the 1760s, the Moravians successfully used a system of "native helpers." The outstanding helper, a stonemason who had purchased his own freedom, preached in Creole, Dutch, English, and Danish.

In the British West Indies most of the planters despised the first Moravian missionaries, but a few planters in each island favored Christianizing the slaves. The Brethren built their first stations on the estates of sympathetic planters. Some of these churchmen were given tracts of land, became plantation operators themselves and preached mainly to their own slaves.[15] Although the Brethren arrived in Jamaica in 1754 and were the first to attempt seriously to Christianize the slaves there, they had baptized fewer than 1,000 Negroes by 1800. In the British West Indies as a whole, the Methodists and the Baptists had gained many more converts.[16] In the tense period in Jamaica just before emancipation, the Moravians, who had always stressed law and order, were charged with being seditious. The reply of the Brethren was so convincing that they were then praised for their loyalty.[17]

---

13. J. E. Hutton, *A History of Moravian Missions* (London, 1922), 22, 28, 29, 33-34.

14. *Ibid.*, 44-45, 49; Jens P. M. Larsen, *Virgin Islands Story* (Philadelphia, 1950), 66-69.

15. Hutton, *A History*, 50-51.

16. Smith, "Slavery and Christianity," 173.

17. Hutton, *A History*, 214-215.

GEORGE EATON SIMPSON

The Lutherans

After the Danish government acquired the Virgin Islands from the West Indian Company in 1754, sentiment favoring the opening of a Lutheran mission among the slaves of the colony developed rapidly. On February 3, 1755, a royal ordinance issued by King Frederick V provided that God's Word should be preached to the slaves, they should be instructed in the Christian religion, and their children should be baptized like other people's children. Within a few years, ten Lutheran missionaries were dispatched to the colony.[18] In 1785, the Lutheran mission in the Virgin Islands was small only in comparison to the Moravian work. In 1788, the Lutherans instituted a system of helpers similar to that of the Moravians to assist in mission work.[19] At the beginning of the nineteenth century, there were two Lutheran congregations in each Virgin Islands parish— both with the same minister, the same church building, and the same government supervision. The Danish Lutheran "missionary pastor" conducted services and ceremonies in both congregations—in Danish in one, in Creole in the other.

The Methodists

Methodist missionaries began their work in the West Indies in Antigua in 1770. The Rev. Thomas Coke visited the British West Indies in the 1780s and was one of the founders of the Methodist Missionary Society in 1789. The first missionaries who asked permission to visit the slaves were met with reluctance and hostility by the planters. Some planters, however, were converted to Methodism. After hearing John Wesley preach during a visit to England, Nathaniel Gilbert, a lawyer, planter, slave owner, and speaker of the House of Assembly in Antigua, joined the Methodist Society and opened his house to Methodist worship by whites and Negroes alike.[20]

Both the Methodists and the Baptists used a system of slave leaders

---

18. Larsen, *Virgin Islands Story*, 61, 75.
19. *Ibid.*, 94-95, 99, 138.
20. G. G. Findlay and W. W. Holdsworth, *The History of the Wesleyan Methodist Missionary Society* (London, 1921), II, 29-30.

to supervise their followers. Because it was difficult for missionaries to gain permission to enter the estates, they relied on black assistants to visit the sick, hold prayer meetings in the evenings, and oversee the conduct of the members over whom they had charge. Usually the missionary could talk to his charges quarterly, when their membership cards were renewed.[21]

Slave uprisings in the 1790s produced new expressions of anger against the dissenting missionaries, and the local legislatures in the West Indies enacted repressive acts. For example, the Assembly of St. Vincent prohibited the holding of religious services by unlicensed, itinerant preachers—an act disallowed by the home government. In 1796 the Methodist church in Nevis was set afire. In Dominica, a Methodist missionary was ordered to report for militia service on Sunday and later was ordered to leave the island.[22]

The persecution of dissenters through legislative acts in Jamaica in 1802 and 1807 was revived in 1826 when the Code of Slave Laws was revised. New provisions prohibited the holding of religious services "by sectarian Ministers or other teachers" before sunrise or after sunset. Since Presbyterians, Roman Catholics, and Jews were exempted from this rule, it applied only to Methodists, Baptists, and Moravians. Despite religious harassment preceding the Act of Emancipation (1824-1833), Methodist church membership grew to almost 13,000.[23]

Slave uprisings in Cornwall (Jamaica) in 1831 led to the proclamation of martial law throughout the island, and on January 26, 1832, an association called the Colonial Church Union was formed in the rectory of St. Ann's Bay. The objects of this organization were said to be the defense by constitutional means of the interests of the colony, exposure of the falsehoods of the Anti-slavery Society, and the support of the established church, but its real purpose was to attempt to drive out the free church missionaries.[24] In the wave of vandalism that followed the founding of this organization, a number of Baptist and Wesleyan chapels were

21. Smith, "Slavery and Christianity," 174.
22. Findlay and Holdsworth, *The History*, II, 25-26; Lowell J. Ragatz, *The Fall of the Planter Class in the British Caribbean* (New York, 1928), 284.
23. Findlay and Holdsworth, *The History*, II, 89, 92.
24. Frederick Pilkington, *Daybreak in Jamaica* (London, 1950), 67.

destroyed, and several ministers were imprisoned and mistreated. Even clergy of the Anglican church who had been friendly with the slaves were suspected and abused.[25]

In 1833, 23,000 of the 32,000 Methodist church members in the West Indian districts were slaves. No other church had so large a slave membership. Within a few months of emancipation, the missionary committee of the Wesleyan Methodist Missionary Society sent reinforcements to the West Indies. The staff of 54 in 1833 became 85 by 1840, and by 1844 the church membership had reached 54,552.[26]

Within a decade after emancipation, a period of decline set in for West Indian Methodism. The Jamaica district lost 1,000 members during 1845, and the Antigua district half that number. The enthusiasm accompanying emancipation had been expended and disappointment followed the previous excitement and high hopes. A major reason for the disillusionment of the former slaves was the continuing gulf between white and black after 1833. With some exceptions, the propertied and official classes continued to regard the Negro as "fit only for subjection." The Methodist church became increasingly the church of the black and colored people. Whites were not excluded; they withdrew. The estrangement had begun during the struggle for emancipation, and when, after 1833, the Church of England increased the number of clergy for West Indian parishes, many middle- and upper-class white families moved in that direction. The Methodist enterprise in the West Indies revived somewhat after 1866. The excesses of the great revival of 1861-1862 had passed, and the reports of missionaries became more hopeful.[27]

The Baptists

George Liele (Lisle), a manumitted slave who came to Jamaica in 1783 with his fugitive former master, was one of the first Baptist missionaries in the West Indies. Lisle had preached in Virginia, and he soon organized a church in Kingston. By 1791 his church had 450 members—all Negroes

---

25. Ernest A. Payne, *Freedom in Jamaica: Some Chapters in the Story of the Baptist Missionary Society* (London, 1933), 30-31.

26. Findlay and Holdsworth, *The History*, II, 321, 326-327, 341.

27. *Ibid.*, II, 355-358, 391.

and most of them slaves. Thirty years after Lisle's arrival in Jamaica, the Baptist Missionary Society began to send out missionaries from England. Although they worked in a hostile atmosphere, the Baptist missionaries acquired a growing following among the slaves. By 1831 they had built twenty-four churches, acquired 10,000 members, and claimed another 17,000 "inquirers."[28]

After emancipation in 1834, Baptist congregations in Jamaica quickly grew; by 1837, sixteen Baptist missionaries and schoolmasters served 16,000 church members and an equal number of "inquirers." In the confusion and disillusionment that followed the failure and termination of the apprenticeship system four years after emancipation, some of the missionaries tried to assist in reconstructing economic and social life. William Knibb, a leader among the Baptist ministers, and his associates established free townships and villages where Negroes could have their own small holdings.[29]

The Baptist church in Jamaica continued to grow in the late 1830s and early 1840s and, in response to repeated requests, two dozen new missionaries were sent from England within four years. In 1842, the Jamaica Baptist Association asked that the work of their church be made self-supporting. The enthusiasm for self-support led to the launching of several new projects: the establishment of a training college for a native ministry, the beginning of a mission to western Africa, and the starting of a program in other West Indian islands (Haiti, Cuba, the Bahamas, and Panama).[30]

The Presbyterians

The Scottish Missionary Society, a nondenominational body, sent three pioneers to Jamaica in 1800, and like other missionaries already in the field, they met with much opposition. In 1819, the established Church of Scotland initiated its work in Kingston, and in 1823 the Scottish Missionary Society began the program that was carried on later by the United

---

28. Payne, *Freedom in Jamaica*, 19-20, 26.
29. *Ibid.*, 61-62.
30. *Ibid.*, 65, 68-70, 80-81.

GEORGE EATON SIMPSON

Presbyterian church. The missionaries from Scotland were active in teaching the people in the rural districts of Jamaica. In 1846, the Presbyterian workers in Jamaica sent a band of missionaries to Calabar (Nigeria).[31]

The United Presbyterian church was formed in 1847, and by the end of 1865 the Presbyterian mission in Jamaica included twenty-six congregations with memberships of 5,124 and 467 candidates. Members of this denomination had been active for twenty-five years in education, and at the end of 1865 were operating twenty-nine day schools with 2,326 students enrolled. In 1869 the mission board in Scotland decided that efforts should be made to train a native ministry and that European missionaries should be withdrawn from the field.[32]

During the apprenticeship period (1836), a Presbyterian missionary was sent from Scotland to Port of Spain, Trinidad, and within a few years additional appointments were made to Arouca and San Fernando. In 1911, the Presbyterian program in Trinidad became self-sustaining.[33]

Conclusion

Within the framework of the system of slavery, colonial society in the Caribbean, and a diversity of religious formulations, the black slaves and free men and women attempted for centuries to work out their salvation. In the British Caribbean, the established churches were closed to the slaves for a century and a half.[34] Despite the prodigious labors of the nonconformist missionaries, only a small fraction of the slaves in the non-Catholic colonies were converted to Christianity. After emancipation, the Protestant denominations increased their missionary staffs throughout the West Indies in their drive for converts. Large numbers of persons of African descent were added to the rolls of the Methodist, Baptist, Presbyterian, and other Protestant churches in the non-Catholic countries, and rapid population increases in the twentieth century have

31. George McNeill, *The Story of Our Missions in the West Indies* (Edinburgh, 1911), 21, 32, 34-36.

32. *Ibid.*, 37, 40-41, 44, 46.

33. *Ibid.*, 85-88.

34. Alfred Caldecott, *The Church in the West Indies* (New York, 1898), 63.

swelled their memberships. Little attention was paid by Protestants to the black and colored populations in the Catholic countries so long as they were slaves, but after 1834 serious efforts were made to proselytize them. Protestant ministers, however, met with little success in these countries, and 100 years later, Catholics constituted approximately two-thirds of the population in such places as Grenada, Carriacou, and the Grenadines.[35]

Part II: Caribbean Cults

The syncretistic cults of the Caribbean have evolved because persons of African ancestry in the diaspora were cut off from contact with Africa and could not preserve intact their traditional religions, or because lower-class persons of African origin have been excluded from, or have not felt comfortable in, the denominations or class churches.[36] Although Caribbean religious cults have similar social and psychological functions, they vary greatly in form and content.

Cultural Content

From the viewpoint of cultural content, black religious cults of the Caribbean may be classified under five categories: (1) remodeled African religions, (2) ancestral cults, (3) revivalist cults, (4) spiritualist cults, and (5) religio-political cults. These labels are somewhat unsatisfactory because the ancestral cults and the revivalist cults include some African cultural elements; the "remodeled African" religions are, however, the most African of the Caribbean cults.

Remodeled African Cults. These cults are found in countries which are predominantly Catholic. This cult type includes Haitian *vodun*, the

---

35. Raymund Devas, *Conception Island: Or the Troubled Story of the Catholic Church in Grenada, B. W. I.* (London, 1932), 255.

36. The popular religious movements under consideration here are those which have developed among lower-class populations of African descent in the Caribbean. We have not included the cults that have been formed by persons of American Indian or East Indian descent.

GEORGE EATON SIMPSON

candomblé of certain parts of Brazil, Cuban *santeria*, and the *shango* cult of Trinidad, Recife (Brazil), Grenada, and Venezuela. In all of these cults old African gods are worshiped and frequently an African deity is equated with a Catholic saint. In Africa each deity has specialized priests, societies, and cult centers, but in the New World a syncretistic cult honors a number of hyphenated African-Catholic deities, and in addition some Catholic saints who do not have African counterparts and some supernatural figures who appear to be of local origin. Multiple "soul" concepts, common in West African religious belief, have been reinterpreted in the Caribbean, and in many of the New World syncretistic cults ritual objects which play a prominent part in West African religions are used— thunder stones, double-bladed wooden axes, swords, ceremonial brooms, and water jars. Moreover, there is a general similarity in a major ceremony of a *vodun, candomblé, santeria,* or *shango* cult and a traditional annual ceremony in West Africa: drum rhythms and songs designed to summon and to honor each god, possession-trances for a minority of the participants, dancing, propitiatory verses, animal sacrifices, and feasting.[37]

Aspects of Caribbean cult life that are closely related to religious behavior include divination, conjuring, and folk medicine, often strikingly similar to West African procedures. There is, however, one important difference between some remodeled African religions in the Caribbean and the traditional religions in Africa from which they are derived. In the *shango* pantheons of Trinidad and Grenada, Orunmila, the Yoruba deity of divination, is absent. This is not the case in the *santeria* cult in Cuba, a religion also derived from Yoruba traditions. Perhaps fear of the gods served by the *babalawo* (diviners) caused relatively few priest-

---

37. Melville J. Herskovits, "African Gods and Catholic Saints in New World Negro Belief," *American Anthropologist,* XXXIX (1937), 635-643; William R. Bascom, *Shango in the New World* (Austin, 1972), 5-20; Harold Courlander, *The Drum and the Hoe: Life and Lore of the Haitian People* (Berkeley, 1960); Roger Bastide, *Les Religions Africaines au Brésil* (Paris, 1960), 82-92, 365-382; George E. Simpson, "Afro-American Religions and Religious Behavior," *Caribbean Studies,* XII (1972), 7-12; Angelina Pollak-Eltz, "The Shango Cult in Grenada, Westindies," *Proceedings, VIIIth International Congress of Anthropological and Ethnological Sciences* (1968), III, 59; Isaac Barreal, "Tendencias Sincreticas de los Cultos Populares en Cuba," *Etnologia y Folklore,* I (1966), 17-24.

diviners who knew the Ifa system to be sold into slavery. Since full knowledge of the Ifa geomantic system of divination requires years of study, it would have been difficult for those who were sent to the Caribbean to have trained competent assistants under conditions of slavery. The lack of the fixed mode of Ifa divination has driven devotees of *shango* to find their own substitutes for determining the causes of events in order to learn which ritual actions must be taken. In the Caribbean, these substitutes include "looking" or "seeing" with crystal balls, cards, or leaves, as well as reliance on dreams, visions, and prophecy. Ifa techniques gave indirect access to a knowledge of the causes and sequence of events, but New World techniques through visions and messages to possessed individuals are direct and immediate. As Smith points out, this factor "allows progressive individualization of cult practice and organization, and hence increasing variability of belief and rite over time in Shango worship as practiced by West Indians."[38]

Ancestral Cults. The rituals associated with cults that we call ancestral—the Big Drum Dance (Nation Dance) of Grenada and of Carriacou, the *kele* cult of St. Lucia, and *cumina* in Jamaica—are less African than those to which we have just referred. The *kele* ceremony in St. Lucia resembles the *shango* ritual in Trinidad, but the belief system associated with it seems to be much simpler. The ceremony is given to ask the African ancestors of present devotees for protection in all matters of importance—good crops, good health, and good fortune. The paraphernalia essential for this rite consists mainly of Amerindian polished stone axes (thunder stones), drums, and agricultural implements (cutlasses, axes, hoes, and forks). The stone axes, called *chango* (*shango*), symbolize the African ancestors, but present-day devotees have no knowledge that Shango is the deity of thunder and lightning in traditional West African belief. Preliminary preparations for the *kele* ceremony are similar to those for a Trinidadian *shango* ritual. At the beginning of the ceremony, the leader asks the ancestors to intercede with God in behalf of the person or family sponsoring the occasion. Drumming, singing, dancing, and possession of some participants by the spirits of the African ancestors

---

38. M. G. Smith, *Dark Puritan* (Kingston, 1963), 139.

continue during the rite and toward the end a ram is sacrificed to the ancestors.[39]

On the island of Carriacou, the Big Drum Dance is celebrated as a
sign of respect for the ancestors, and as a means of avoiding their dis-
favor. This festival is held in cases of ill health or misfortune, at a Stone
Feast (the raising of a tombstone to a deceased member of the family), at
the start of any critical undertaking, and before the marriage of a son or
a daughter. The "parents' plate," a table containing food for the guests, is
set in the best room of the house. During the dance the ancestors are
called by beating a hoe with a spoon to a Cromanti song, libations are
made by members of the family, and the participants kneel and ask the
ancestors to pardon them, saying "If I deserve it punish me, if I don't
deserve it, pardon me."[40]

According to Smith, the Big Drum Dance was the representative
African cult of the Grenadian folk at the beginning of the twentieth century. In 1849, more than 1,000 post-emancipation immigrants arrived in
Grenada from Ijesha, Nigeria; eventually, they and their descendants
began to move away from the closed communities where they had settled
after completing their indentures. As they scattered around the island,
their cult (shango) spread, attracted many followers, and became marked
by "syncretisms of form and content, numerous traits being taken over
from the Nation Dance as well as from Catholicism until Shango is now
the representative form of African ritual among the Grenadians."[41]

In Jamaican cumina the three ranks of spirits are the sky gods, earthbound gods, and ancestral zombies. Among the thirty-nine sky gods
listed by Moore, only one has the name of a West African deity (Shango).
Of the sixty-two earthbound gods in Morant Bay cumina, at least seven
have Biblical names: David, Ezekiel, Moses, Cain, Shadrach, Meshach,
and Abednego. The twenty-one ancestral zombies are the spirits of men
and women (Jimmy Snate, Margaret Miller, Archie Pierce, Obi Beck-
ford, Sophie Bartly, James Grasset, Grace Bailey, and others) who, in

39. George E. Simpson, "The Kele (Chango) Cult in St. Lucia," *Caribbean
Studies*, XIII (1973), 110-116.
40. Andrew C. Pearse, *The Big Drum Dance of Carriacou*, Ethnic Folkways
Library Album (No. P. 1011, 1956), 1-2.
41. M. G. Smith, *The Plural Society in the British West Indies* (Berkeley, 1965),
33-34.

their lifetimes, were dancing *zombies* (persons who have experienced possession by a god and who dance to the spirits of this cult group), drummers, and *obeah* men. *Cumina* dancing is known to the residents of Morant Bay as "African dance." All *zombies* are invoked through the use of drums and songs. *Cumina* is not as African as the cults in our first category, but in the framework of the sky gods, earthbound gods, and ancestral *zombies, cumina* belief resembles West African and Congo religions. The names and duties of the *cumina* gods are different, but their behavior and the theological rationale show little evidence of Christian Western European influence.[42] Because of the emphasis placed on the Jamaican forebears of present-day devotees, we consider *cumina* as an ancestral cult in our classification.

Revivalist Cults. Under this heading we include Revival Zion (Revivalist, Pocomania, Convince) in Jamaica, the Shouters (Spiritual Baptists) of Trinidad, the Shakers of St. Vincent, and the Grenadian revivalists. These are fundamentalist groups which stem from the Afro-Christian cults of the late eighteenth century. In Jamaica, interest in separatist churches as well as in the regular missions was greatly stimulated by an emotional religious revival which swept the island in 1861-1862, but the enthusiasm and the excitement dwindled within a short time.[43] Present-day revivalist cults in Jamaica are descended from the Native Baptists and the Afro-Christian cults of one to two hundred years ago. They are revivalistic in the sense of religious awakening rather than of attempts to restore the customs and values of an ancient culture.[44]

Unlike the devotees of African religions in Haiti, Brazil, Cuba, Trinidad, and Grenada, members of Revival Zion and of Convince groups in

---

42. Joseph G. Moore, "Religion of Jamaican Negroes, A Study of Afro-Jamaican Acculturation," unpub. Ph. D. thesis (Northwestern University, 1953). See also J. G. Moore and G. E. Simpson, "A Comparative Study of Acculturation in Morant Bay and West Kingston, Jamaica," *Zaire,* 9-10 (1957), 979-1019; *ibid.,* 1 (1958), 65-87. (These articles are reprinted in G. E. Simpson, *Religious Cults of the Caribbean: Trinidad, Jamaica, and Haiti* [Rio Piedras, 1970], 157-200; see especially 161-163, 174-175, 178-179.)

43. Curtin, *Two Jamaicas,* 171.

44. Anthony F. C. Wallace, "Revitalization Movements," *American Anthropologist,* LVIII (1956), 267, 276.

GEORGE EATON SIMPSON

Jamaica do not worship old African gods. These cults are polytheistic in orientation, but the important spirits are Old Testament prophets, New Testament saints, angels and archangels, Satan, Rutibel, and beings from the de Laurence books on the occult and magic (published in Chicago), especially from *The Sixth and Seventh Books of Moses*. Drumming, handclapping, singing (both collective and antiphonal), praying by the leader and individual prayers by the members speaking simultaneously, Bible-reading, personal testimonials, counterclockwise "spiritual" dancing around the front part of the church, preaching in brief intermittent installments, spirit possessions, and, in some cases, public healing constitute the main features of "divine worship." Special revivalist ceremonies include baptismal rites, the numerous death rites, the dedication of a new church, the installation of a new officer, healing rites, and divinatory and conjuring rituals. A reinterpretation of the West African concept of multiple "souls" is found in the belief that each person has a *duppy* (shadow) in addition to a soul. Other reinterpretations of African traditions are seen in the ritual uses of stones, blood, and leaves. The words and melodies of most of the revivalist songs are derived from Methodist and Baptist hymns, but the use of drums and rattles, handclapping, and dancing are African retentions.[45]

The Shouters in Trinidad place greater emphasis on handclapping, shouting or "rejoicing," dancing, and trances than on formal worship.[46] Herskovits thought that the Spiritual Baptists constitute "a point of transition between African religion, represented in Trinidad by the Shango cult, and undiluted European forms of worship, as found in the Church of England, among the Moravians, and, to a lesser extent, the Seventh Day Adventists and the Baptists."[47] The origins and history of the Shouters have not been studied in detail, but apparently this syncretistic religion evolved in Trinidad during the nineteenth century. A substantial

---

45. George E. Simpson, "Jamaican Revivalist Cults," *Social and Economic Studies*, V (1956), 342-358, 360-371. On the Convince cult, see Donald Hogg, "The Convince Cult in Jamaica," *Yale University Publications in Anthropology*, 58 (1960), 3-24.

46. George E. Simpson, "Baptismal, 'Mourning,' and 'Building' Ceremonies of the Shouters in Trinidad," *Journal of American Folklore*, LXXIX (1966), 537.

47. Melville J. and Frances S. Herskovits, *Trinidad Village* (New York, 1947), 305.

number of natives from the Windward Islands, especially St. Vincent, Grenada, and Barbados, migrated to Trinidad about 1880, and it is possible that the Spiritual Baptist configuration was introduced from St. Vincent.[48] As Bourguignon points out, however, while the Trinidadian Shouters have had contact with *shango* cults and some borrowing between these groups has occurred, "no spirit cults exist on St. Vincent and no such influences have been exerted on the Shakers."[49] Shakerism in St. Vincent seems to have been derived from Methodism. In the pre-Methodist period, the Anglican church did not welcome the slaves, but Catholic missionaries did work among slave groups. According to Bourguignon, "many Shakers receive their first religious training in the Catholic Church, and certain minor Catholic influences are to be seen in their practices: the references to saints, the use of chromolithographs representing various saints, and the use of a bell during the ritual being perhaps the most noteworthy."[50]

The founder of one noteworthy Grenadian revivalist cult, Norman Paul, combined segments of diverse traditions: the Big Drum Dance, Puritanism, *shango*, Shakerism, and African and European witchcraft.[51] Other revivalist groups in Grenada have been of the Shaker type.

Spiritualist Cults. Since its introduction into Brazil in 1863, spiritualism has gone through three phases: the spiritualism of intellectuals, spiritualism of the white lower class, and spiritualism of the lower class of blacks.[52] In the latter phase, the *candomblé* in Rio de Janeiro was transformed in the early 1900s into the *macumba*. A syncretism between African and American Indian cults, Catholicism, and spiritualism, it is characterized by violent possessions, advice given by spirits, animal

48. *Ibid.*, 25-26.
49. Erika Bourguignon, "Ritual Dissociation and Possession Belief in Caribbean Negro Religion," in Norman E. Whitten, Jr., and John F. Szwed (eds.), *Afro-American Anthropology* (New York, 1970), 91. Bourguignon states that "there is some evidence to suggest that African-derived religions did exist during the eighteenth century in areas where they are no longer to be found today" (*ibid.*, 94). She mentions that this point applies also to Martinique and Guadeloupe (*ibid.*, 101).
50. *Ibid.*, 94-95.
51. Smith, *Dark Puritan*, 8.
52. Bastide, *Les Religions*, 435-442.

sacrifices, use of incense, drumming, and the chalking of designs on the ground (similar to making "verver" in Haitian *vodun*).[53] In Rio de Janeiro, "the spiritualism of Umbanda" developed from the *macumba*.[54] In the *umbanda* cult in urban industrial centers in southern Brazil, mediums make spirits available to anyone for consultations concerning illness, professional success or failure, the passing of examinations, and other personal problems.[55] Ritual elements are derived from African religions, American Indian cults, Christianity, and spiritualism; the membership is ethnically diverse; and the cult appeals to both middle- and lower middle-class persons. Participants engage in trance states and are not merely clients of practitioners. *Umbanda* is not a revitalization movement; its concern is in helping individuals to solve their personal problems. Bastide claims that the spiritualism of *umbanda* is the only form of religious adaptation which can exist in the urbanized and indus- trialized community. In 1970, however, Bascom found that the worship of *shango* flourished in Havana, Port-au-Prince, and Port of Spain; in Brazil it centered in the state capitals—Belém, São Luiz, Recife, Salva- dor, Rio de Janeiro, São Paulo, and Pôrto Alegre. As a result of the dis- persal of Cuban refugees, the worship of Shango, the thunder god, is now important in Miami and New York City, and the *santeria* cult has expanded to Newark, Savannah, Detroit, Chicago, Gary (Indiana), Caracas, and San Juan.[56]

In Puerto Rico, spiritualism is "the one institution to which the people turn for help in their hours of need."[57] Typically, a spiritualist group in Puerto Rico revolves around a head medium and contacts between this person and a patient take place mainly in a private consulta- tion or in a session involving some fifteen or twenty participants. A group meeting is organized around four social roles: those of the head

53. *Ibid.*, 411-414.
54. Roger Bastide, *African Civilisations in the New World* (New York, 1972), 86.
55. Erika Bourguignon, "Trance Dance," *Dance Perspectives*, XXXV (1968), 40.
56. Bascom, *Shango*, 19-20.
57. L. H. Rogler and A. B. Hollingshead, *Trapped: Families and Schizophrenia*, (New York, 1965), 260.

medium, the auxiliary medium(s), and participants with and without "faculties" (alleged degree of influence over spirits).[58]

A Religio-Political Cult: Garveyism and the Ras Tafari Movement in Jamaica. During the period 1914 to 1940, Garveyism was regarded as a religion by many Negroes in the United States, the West Indies, and elsewhere, a religion led by "the black Moses." Writing in the *Negro World,* the Rev. R. R. Porter asserted that a true Garveyite "is true to himself, others and his religion—through the right understanding of One God, One Aim, One Destiny [The Universal Negro Improvement Association motto] he shall enjoy life and live abundantly in the Kingdom of Heaven on earth, and know that Africa shall once more become the land of the Good, Strong, and Wise."[59]

According to Garveyite theology, blacks are the chosen people of God, and Marcus Garvey's followers often likened themselves to the Jews, especially the Zionists. Rabbi J. Arnold Ford, the UNIA's musical director, was a black Jew from Barbados who had adopted Judaism before he joined the association.[60] Most of his Beth B'nai congregation came to the Garvey movement with him, and he had hoped that Judaism would become the official religion of the UNIA.[61]

Garvey had been brought up as a Roman Catholic. To further the religious side of his movement, he persuaded the Rev. George Alexander McGuire, an Antiguan Episcopal clergyman in Boston, to accept the post of chaplain general of the UNIA. Ordained a bishop in a service conducted by an archbishop of the Greek Orthodox church, McGuire became the head of the new African Orthodox church.[62]

---

58. L. H. Rogler and A. B. Hollingshead, "The Puerto Rican Spiritualist as a Psychiatrist," *American Journal of Sociology,* LXVII (1961), 19-20.

59. Theodore G. Vincent, *Black Power and the Garvey Movement* (Berkeley, 1971), 134.

60. In the 1950s there was at least one congregation of black Jews in Jamaica (the writer attended one of the Saturday afternoon services in 1953). The founding date of this group is not known, and I do not know whether groups of black Jews have existed in the Caribbean other than in Barbados and Jamaica.

61. Vincent, *Black Power,* 134-135.

62. The approximate number of African Orthodox churches in the United States presently is 25-30, and the approximate number of members 6,000 (Charles V. Hamilton, *The Black Preacher in America* [New York, 1972], 75).

GEORGE EATON SIMPSON

Mrs. Garvey asserts that her husband taught all peoples of African descent "to visualize Christ—the Redeemer of all Mankind, as a man of color," and she asks: "Who can best portray 'the man of sorrow, and acquainted with grief,' but the down-trodden Negro in modern times?" According to her, the wandering Jew portrayed this figure many years ago when "he was the persecuted, the spurned, the wanderer on the face of the earth, seeking a return to his homeland. Today . . . the New Negro's Icon is of dusky hue."[63] Garvey was not, however, the first advocate of a black God; many religious cults and sects among American Negroes had rejected the worship of a white god before Garvey came to New York.[64]

During the 1924 convention of the UNIA, Bishop McGuire asked Negroes to set a time for burning pictures of the white Madonna and the white Christ that they might own and to start Negro painters supplying "a black Madonna and a black Christ for the training of our children." At the same time, McGuire declared that henceforth the Negro's devil would be white.[65] For various reasons, including economic considerations, three-fourths or more of the regular Negro preachers opposed the new black religion,[66] and the majority of Garveyites never joined the African Orthodox church.

An offshoot of the UNIA, the Ras Tafari movement in Jamaica, began to take shape about 1930. Rastafarians considered Marcus Garvey as the forerunner of their movement. His slogans—"Africa for the Africans, At Home and Abroad" and "One God! One Aim! One Destiny!"—are proclaimed frequently at Ras Tafari meetings. The basic Rastafarian doctrines are: first, black men, reincarnations of the ancient Israelites, were exiled to the West Indies because of their transgressions; second, the wicked white man is inferior to the black man; third, the Jamaican situation is a hopeless Hell; fourth, Ethiopia is Heaven; fifth, Haile Selassie is the Living God; sixth, the invincible Emperor of Abyssinia will soon arrange for expatriated persons of African descent to

---

63. Amy J. Garvey, *Black Power in America* (Kingston, 1968), 38.
64. E. David Cronon, *Black Moses, The Story of Marcus Garvey and the Universal Negro Improvement Association* (Madison, 1955), 177.
65. *Ibid.*, 179, 180.
66. *Ibid.*, 182.

return to the homeland; and seventh, in the near future black men will get revenge by compelling white men to serve them.[67]

The Ras Tafari movement might be called a religio-political cult. Despite the hostility of the Rastafarians toward clergymen and their congregations, passages of the Bible are read or quoted at meetings and interpreted in ways that give support to Rastafarian doctrines, and many of the cult's songs are adaptations of Methodist or Baptist hymns.[68]

In the early 1950s, participation in Ras Tafari meetings was an escapist-adjustive type of activity, and that is true of some of the groups today. These occasions have provided lower-class and disaffected Jamaicans with opportunities to denounce the enemies of the people: "the white man" and the Jamaican "traitors": politicians, businessmen, clergymen, and the police.[69] By 1960, the Ras Tafari movement had become a more complex phenomenon. Some groups are committed to a political and military struggle, others are still escapist. Psychologically, the latter groups resemble the revivalist cults of Jamaica.[70] The former groups believe that deliverance from poverty and humiliation must come in Jamaica and not from Haile Selassie in Ethiopia. These members have shifted from earlier Rastafarian doctrine, and they share with the secular "rude-boys" the belief that the social system must be changed, by violence if necessary.

The religious doctrines of Rastafarianism constitute one of its most persistent features. Central in the belief system of this cult is the divinity of Haile Selassie. Selassie stands "as a symbol of black glory and ancient African lineage dating back to Solomon and the Queen of Sheba." Nettleford points out that it is the Rastafarians who have deified Selassie, and adds:

---

67. George E. Simpson, "Political Cultism in West Kingston," *Social and Economic Studies,* IV (1955), 133-149. The effects of Selassie's downfall in 1974 and death in 1975 on the beliefs of Rastafarians are not yet clear, but early reactions included denials that reports in white newspapers were true, and the assertion that Selassie chose humiliation in order to redeem his people.

68. George E. Simpson, "Social Stratification in the Caribbean," *Phylon,* XXIII (1962), 43.

69. George E. Simpson, "The Ras Tafari Movement in Jamaica in Its Millennial Aspect," *Comparative Studies in Society and History,* Supplement II (1962), 160-165.

70. Rex M. Nettleford, *Mirror Mirror: Identity, Race and Protest in Jamaica* (Kingston, 1970), 43.

GEORGE EATON SIMPSON

> The implication for the Jamaican society will continue to turn on
> whether Rastafarianism can be accepted as a legitimate form of reli-
> gious worship. It is somewhat tolerated now but . . . there are those
> who view as blasphemous the belief in the divinity of Haile Selassie.[71]

Just as others have declared the man Jesus to be the son of God, so the
Rastafarians have declared the divinity of Haile Selassie. They assert that
the histories of other religions prove that eventually they will gain legitimacy for their creed. As other cultists have done, they reinterpret the
Old Testament in claiming that they are true present-day prophets, the
"re-incarnated Moseses, Joshuas, Isaiahs, and Jeremiahs." They believe
that they are "destined to free the scattered Ethiopians who are black
men."[72] It seems likely, however, that it will be a long time before
Jamaican society will accept, if it ever does, Rastafarianism on its own
religious terms.

Although this paper is concerned primarily with Caribbean cults,
some reference to Garvey's influence on Father Divine's movement and
on the Black Muslims in the United States may be of interest. On the relationship between the UNIA and Father Divine's movement, Vincent comments:

> Though the Divine Peace Mission's only tie to the UNIA was
> through its large ex-Garveyite membership, the movement's life-
> style was not unlike that of the UNIA. Whites were present, but the
> Peace Mission was run by blacks under a black God. Grass-roots
> followers in both movements found spiritual escape from estab-
> lished Christianity, and sought to build separate economic institu-
> tions, and overcome white racism primarily by developing indepen-
> dent power bases within black society. Many Garveyites were no
> doubt reluctant to join a movement which officially rejected the con-
> cept of race, and many more rejected the spiritual aspects of the
> Peace Mission, but a sizeable contingent of Garveyites saw in Di-
> vine's movement the opportunity to continue building a world of
> their own.[73]

---

71. *Ibid.*, 108-109.
72. *Ibid.*, 109.
73. Vincent, *Black Power*, 226-227.

Many Garveyites joined the Moorish American Science Temple of Noble Drew Ali in the 1920s. Later, in recruiting for the Black Muslims, Elijah Muhammad declared: "I have always had a very high opinion of both the late Noble Drew Ali and Marcus Garvey and admired their courage in helping our people (the so-called Negroes) and appreciated their work. Both of these men were fine Muslims. The followers of Noble Drew Ali and Marcus Garvey should now follow me and cooperate with us in our work because we are only trying to finish up what those before us started."[74] Mrs. Garvey asserts that all of the "freedom movements" in America in the 1960s "were initiated by the work and teachings of Marcus Garvey," and she adds that the "entire Black Muslim philosophy . . . is feeding upon the seeds that were planted by Marcus Garvey."[75]

The Socioeconomic Context

Most of the cults in the Caribbean have arisen among peoples who were economically disadvantaged, socially subordinated, and politically powerless: slaves, peasants, or lower-class workers. Their religious behavior has been part of their attempt to identify with forces in the universe greater than themselves, to express themselves, to escape—at least temporarily and imaginatively—from rejection, discrimination, and exploitation, and, in some cases, to change their life situations. These cults must be seen, therefore, in the light of the economic-social-political contexts of the Caribbean. We cite two instances of these matrices.

In the post-slavery period, Haiti has been among the least developed countries economically in the West Indies. The national average per capita gross national product in the 1960s was about $67, the country ranking "at the bottom of the Latin American and near the bottom of most global scales."[76] Public service declined early in the history of the republic, evidence of neglect is seen everywhere, life expectancy is low, agricultural production has declined, the system of education is inappro-

---

74. *Ibid.*, 222-223.
75. Garvey, *Black Power*, 7.
76. Robert I. Rotberg, *Haiti: The Politics of Squalor* (Boston, 1971), 9.

priate, the peasants are cut off from modern developments in the capital and even in the coastal towns, and child-rearing patterns seem to occasion complicated tensions.[77] Christian doctrine has not been offered in connection with education, health programs, better rewards for labor, rising expectations, and alternative activities to *vodun* that meet the emotional needs of ordinary Haitians. In the absence of such alternatives, *vodun* has provided the peasant with meaningful explanations and relationships. As Courlander points out, if there is failure in Haitian life, it is not a failure of *vodun*, which offers something essential, but a failure of the society at large to provide any other satisfactory choices.[78]

In Jamaica, lower-class individuals have continually struggled since emancipation against exploitation. Higher wages, civil and political rights, and other gains have come slowly and against bitter opposition. Uprisings have occurred now and then, but much of the hostility on the part of those who have sought social and economic advancement has been repressed. For more than a century, Afro-Christian cults—Native Baptists, Revivalist, *cumina*, and Convince—have provided outlets for the expression of repressed resentment.[79]

Personality Factors in Cultism

Unfortunately, details concerning the effects of the socialization process on the personality tendencies of Caribbean cult leaders are not available.[80] Among lower-class people, the extended family system tends to reduce the chances of rejection within the kinship group. However, some disadvantaged individuals, smarting under the exploitation inherent in relatively rigid color-class systems, have rebelled against existing structures.

---

77. *Ibid.*, 9-24.

78. Harold Courlander, "Vodoun in Haitian Culture," in Harold Courlander and Rémy Bastien, *Religion and Politics in Haiti* (Washington, 1966), 22. See also Rotberg, below, 344-346.

79. Curtin, *Two Jamaicas*, 32-34, 168; Simpson, "Jamaican Revivalist Cults," 411-415; Hogg, "The Convince Cult," 21; Moore and Simpson, "A Comparative Study," 82-83.

80. A discussion of personality development in general in Jamaica is given in Madeline Kerr, *Personality and Conflict in Jamaica* (Liverpool, 1952), 34-73, 165-174; for Haiti by Rotberg, *Haiti*, 19-24.

Leaders or active members of the cults may have become participants in part because of a serious physical or mental illness. Such individuals believe that temporary blindness, crippling, emotional disturbance, or a debilitating illness has been relieved or cured through appeals
to supernatural agents related to a cult. Some cultists experience dis-
sociational states such as trance and visions, but, as a class, cult leaders
are not seriously disturbed persons. Those who believe that they become
possessed by the gods or the ancestors, and whom others believe are thus ,
possessed, cannot be sweepingly categorized as "abnormal." Dissociation
is a normal phenomenon in some cases and it may be experimentally
induced.[81] In Recife, Brazil, the psychiatrist, Ribeiro, found severe
maladjustments in some persons who became possessed, but he says that
"their social and religious behavior was by no means appraised as
abnormal by their relatives, employers, work partners, priests, and cult
fellows."[82]

The Emergence and Continuation of Caribbean Cults

No single variable can explain the existence of a Caribbean cult. The
remodeled African cults, the ancestral cults, and the forerunners of the
revivalist cults arose in part because persons of African descent were cut
off from Africa and could not perpetuate in entirety their traditional
religious beliefs and rituals. In the diaspora, cultural elements from the
diverse religious traditions of Africa, Europe, and the United States were

---

81. Gardner Murphy, *Personality: A Biosocial Approach to Origins and Structure* (New York, 1947), 16.

82. René Ribeiro, "An Experimental Approach to the Study of Spirit Possession"
(Recife, 1960), unpub. ms., 17. After observing behavior in *candomblé* cult groups in
Bahia, Brazil, an American psychiatrist, Stainbrook, wrote that a possessed individual must be "in sufficient control of autistic and regressive behavior and of reality-
testing to be acceptable within the relatively rigid ritualistic group action"; he added
that "no frankly schizophrenic person would be able to pass the probationary
scrutiny." Stainbrook did find that some schizophrenic lower-class patients acted out,
on an individual basis, possessions by African gods. In these psychotic cases, the
major psychological goal appeared to be similar to "the brief and transitory intro-
jection and identification" achieved by participants in *candomblé* rituals (Edward
Stainbrook, "Some Characteristics of the Psychopathology of Schizophrenic Behavior
in Bahian Society," *American Journal of Psychiatry*, CIX [1952], 330-335).

GEORGE EATON SIMPSON

combined in new religions. A second factor of importance is the oppression on the basis of race or class, or both, that has characterized the Caribbean region during and after the period of slavery. The development of the spiritualistic and the religio-political cults, as well as the other three cult-types, is a functional adaptation to the economic-social-political situation in the diaspora. A third basic variable contributing to the emergence of cults in the Caribbean is found in the personality tendencies of cult leaders. Without their dreams and visions, drive, and organizing ability, the cults would not have appeared.[83]

The presence of these three interacting variables at a certain time and place does not necessarily result in the appearance of a religious cult, nor does the emergence and continuation of such a cult mean that alternative modes of adjustment, including orthodox Christian religions, labor organizations, political parties, and mutual aid societies, may not be available. Among the additional factors that have contributed to the development of religious cults of the Caribbean and the differences found among them are the following: the physical isolation of cult members, continuing contact with Africa, continuity of leadership, the presence of rival cults, and group cohesion.

Physical isolation, especially in the early days of a cult, furthers its development. In the Caribbean and in those parts of South America where the ratio of persons of African descent in the total population was highest during the period of slavery, and where those persons were most severely isolated from Europeans, the likelihood that African religious traditions would persist in easily recognized form was greatest.[84] Physical isolation continued in many places after slavery was ended. In the case of the African immigrants who came to Grenada in 1849 and their descendants, the original settlements were closed communities at Concorde, La Mode, and Munich.[85] In 1870, the Rada, Yoruba, Ibo, Congo, and Mandingo peoples in Port of Spain, Trinidad, lived in

---

83. See J. Milton Yinger, *The Scientific Study of Religion* (New York, 1970), 387-392, on "A Field Interpretation of the Relationship of Protestantism to Capitalism" for a discussion of social change in relation to social structure, culture, and character.
84. Melville J. Herskovits, *The Myth of the Negro Past* (New York, 1941), 121.
85. Smith, *Plural Society*, 33-34.

separate communities, and the Rada cult was an integral part of the life of those who traced their ancestry to Dahomey.[86] In Jamaica, the Convince cult seems to have developed among the Maroons who fled to inaccessible regions of the island in the 1830s, or among the neighbors of these fugitives, who were only slightly less isolated. Likewise, the *cumina* cult may be derived from the religion of the Blue Mountain Maroons.[87]

Where physical isolation was less extreme, social isolation existed in varying degrees. The slaves had greater freedom to conduct their own religious services without white supervision than they had in work or in African-style political activity. African types of singing and dancing were tolerated in slave quarters when they did not interfere with work or were performed on holidays; at times, white onlookers enjoyed them as much as the participating slaves.[88] Sometimes the "amusements" of the slaves provided channels for the enactment of segments of West African religious rituals and for the planning of revolts.

In Brazil, Trinidad, and Grenada, continuing contacts with Africa furthered the retention of Africanisms. The Herskovitses noted in Bahia, Brazil, that such contacts were continuous until the outbreak of World War II: "To the Afro-Bahians, Africa is no vague, mythical land. . . . It is a living reality, whence many of the objects they use in their rituals are imported, where people they know have visited and where other acquaintances live, where their fathers or grandfathers came from."[89] Slavery was abolished in the West Indies in 1834, and the abolition of the apprenticeship system followed in 1838, but African immigrants continued to settle in Trinidad until at least 1855.[90] As we have already noted, more than 1,000 Africans came to Grenada from Ijesha in Yorubaland in 1849.[91]

Caribbean cults vary greatly in continuity of leadership. Where units of a cult are closely tied to extended families, as is the case in rural

---

86. Andrew T. Carr, "A Rada Community in Trinidad," *Caribbean Quarterly*, III (1953), 35-41.

87. Hogg, "The Convince Cult," 16-17.

88. Herskovits, *Myth*, 137-138.

89. Melville and Frances Herskovits, "The Negroes of Brazil," *Yale Review*, XXXII (1942), 256.

90. Carr, "A Rada Community," 38.

91. Smith, *Plural Society*, 33-34.

GEORGE EATON SIMPSON

Haiti, the groups are permanent. In Haiti, ritual mechanisms exist for insuring the continuation of the *vodun* cult. When a *houngan* (*vodun* priest) dies, it is necessary to arrange for his "degradation." Catholic chants and prayers are interspersed with African-style chants and dances as the officiating *houngan* supplicates both the Catholic saints and old African deities. Eventually, the principal *loa* (deity) that the dead man had served is withdrawn from his head. This ceremony is followed by the rite of "transmission" or "transference" to discover the successor to the dead leader.[92] In Trinidad, a *shango* leader may arrange before his death for his spouse or for the second-in-command to succeed him. The person who takes over must be a follower of the same "power" as his predecessor. If a leader has appointed no one to succeed him, an *amombah* conducts a rite of drumming, singing, and praying during which the spirit of the dead leader is dismissed. Whoever gets a message from the "power" of the dead leader then takes up the work. If no one takes over, the ritual objects are given away and the cult center disappears.[93] To take the other extreme in stability, the revivalist cults in Jamaica (Revival Zion, Pocomania, and Convince), the Shouters or Spiritual Baptists in Trinidad, and the Shakers of Grenada and St. Vincent are highly unstable. All of these groups are intensely competitive, and the survival of a given "church" depends mainly upon the personality and ingenuity of the leader. Shifting memberships and secessions are common, and a leader who loses all or most of his following simply tries to recruit another.[94]

Smith argues that the displacement of the Big Drum Dance in Grenada shows the importance of group cohesion in the persistence of a culture complex. Although *shango* was a late arrival, it had a priesthood and a formal organization.[95] In Jamaica, the struggle of the rebellious Maroons to maintain their independence promoted solidarity among them. Rejecting Christianity, they utilized African spirits to assist in that struggle, and the present-day *cumina* cult seems to have some connection

92. George E. Simpson, "Four Vodun Ceremonies," *Journal of American Folklore*, LIX (1946), 154-167.
93. George E. Simpson, *The Shango Cult in Trinidad* (Rio Piedras, 1965), 93-94.
94. Simpson, "Jamaican Revivalist Cults," 404-405.
95. Smith, *Dark Puritan*, 34.

with the Maroon religion which developed in the nineteenth century.[96] Undoubtedly, group cohesion has been influential as well in the continuation of *vodun* in Haiti, *shango* in Trinidad and in Recife, Brazil, *santeria* in Cuba, and the *candomblé* in Bahia, Brazil.

Where two or more Caribbean cult-types—remodeled African religions, ancestral cults, revivalist cults, spiritualist cults, and religiopolitical cults—exist in one area, cultural borrowing and social interaction occur, and some persons rely on more than one cult-group. In Trinidad, many shangoists attend Shouters ceremonies during the intervals between the annual ceremonies of the numerous *shango* groups. Moreover, *shango* priests and priestesses go to a Shouters leader to be baptized and to be guided in advanced spiritual experiences known as "mourning" and "building." Or, to take another example, despite the hostility of Rastafarians toward revivalists in West Kingston, Jamaica, participants in the former cult are acquainted with and have been influenced by revivalist rituals.

The cults referred to here range from forty to two hundred years in age. Specific cult-groups have been revised, replaced, or transformed, but none of the five cult-types has disappeared from the region. Among the revised cults are the remodeled African religions: *vodun, candomblé, santeria*, and *shango*. In Rio de Janeiro, many centers of the *candomblé* have been replaced by the *macumba* or by *umbanda*; and in Jamaica, Trinidad, Grenada, St. Vincent, and St. Lucia one revivalist cult has replaced another. The Big Drum Dance in Grenada has been supplanted to a considerable extent by the *shango* cult; the other ancestral cults— *cumina*, Convince, and *kele*—are declining in popularity. Garveyism has been transformed into Rastafarianism in Jamaica, and in the United States into the Black Muslim and black power movements.[97]

What the Cults Have Accomplished

What rewards do the cults offer to devotees? Some of the faithful experience "religious thrills" through speaking in unknown tongues and by

---

96. Hogg, "The Convince Cult," 20.
97. In a later study the writer plans to expand the treatment of the topics covered in this chapter and to present a fuller assessment of black religions of the Caribbean and elsewhere in the New World at the present time.

becoming possessed by an African deity, an ancestor, or the Holy Spirit. The cults contribute to a sense of belonging and of identity with fellow believers. The esoteric rites, and the mysterious magic sometimes associated with them, may permit the expression of behaviors which are ordinarily unacceptable. Cult offices and important roles in cult ceremonies provide opportunities for exercising leadership and gaining recognition from confreres. The most sophisticated members of a cult derive intellectual satisfaction from discussing and elaborating the many points of the belief system. They share with the rank and file devotees the satisfactions that come from joint participation in the familiar routines of the rituals.[98] Frequently, mutual aid in time of crisis is an important feature of cult life. Cult participation may involve costs as well as rewards: economic exploitation of cultists by a leader, physical injuries, or a heightening of emotional disturbances. From the standpoint of those who are concerned with social change, preoccupation with cult rituals reduces the time, thought, energy, and resources that can be devoted to political activity. Given the life situations of the lower class in the Caribbean, the gains derived from cult participation seem to most believers to outweigh the costs.

Haitian *vodun* exemplifies, perhaps in extreme form, what a Caribbean syncretistic cult has and has not done. It has changed little in a half-century, and it makes heavy demands on its believers. At the same time, it offers a sense of community, social diversion, and protection against unseen dangers, and it enhances solidarity in the extended family. But *vodun* has stagnated; it does not have the capability of formulating new policies for the benefit of the rural people. Courlander comments that, to his knowledge, "no houngan has ever sponsored the building of a school, promoted a program of community development, sought to introduce new crops, or innovated an agricultural technique. . . . The type of change needed today is beyond the comprehension of Vodoun and contrary to its interests."[99]

---

98. This point is developed in James W. Fernandez, "Symbolic Consensus in a Fang Syncretist Cult," *American Anthropologist*, LXVII (1965), 902-909. On the value of two analytic perspectives—cultural and social—see also Talcott Parsons, *The Social System* (New York, 1961), 6; Clifford Gertz, "Ritual and Social Change: A Javanese Example," *American Anthropologist*, LIX (1957), 32-54.

99. Courlander, "Vodoun in Haitian Culture," 24-25, 48.

An assessment of the accomplishments of the Rastafarians, the cult at the other end of the Caribbean religious spectrum, is more difficult. They are neither an anachronism nor the wave of the future in Jamaica. There is no Rastafarian political party, and no member of the group has been elected to political office. Some of the Rastafarian beliefs and their fight for the recognition of black Jamaicans may be seen in the black power movement. The question which has not yet been answered is whether black nationalism in Jamaica is a form of strategy, the substance of recent protests, or a mixture of the two. If it is political strategy, this movement has much in common with the agitation of 1938 against foreign exploitation of the country's resources and control of its economic and intellectual life. As substance—that is, as a forced and sudden black control of the country—it would reverse Jamaica's commitment of the early 1940s to evolutionary development.[100]

Conclusion

In time, the religions of the whites in the Caribbean—Roman Catholic or one form or another of Protestantism—became the religions of millions of descendants of slaves, but only in the last two or three decades has the majority of the ministers in the largest denominations come from the West Indies. Meanwhile, tens of thousands of persons of African descent in the region have become involved to a greater or lesser degree in the beliefs and rituals of a wide variety of syncretistic cults. For more than a century these groups have met needs of the most disadvantaged sections of West Indian populations that have not been met by the conventional churches, the Pentecostal churches, or secular organizations.

---

100. Nettleford, *Mirror Mirror*, 125, 218-219.

11

Raymond T. Smith

Religion in the Formation of West Indian Society: Guyana and Jamaica

> The debauched and profligate lives which so large a proportion of the white inhabitants of Jamaica lead is owing to many causes. It has already been observed that all those in the planting line . . . seldom or never attend any religious institution; nor do they read pious books themselves nor enjoin their children to do so. . . . If religion and religious instruction were more in repute than they are in this island; if its inhabitants, instead of sneering at, and turning all that regards them into ridicule, were even to pay the homage of exterior respect, there is no doubt that this would in time contribute to effect a reformation in the morals and manners of the people.[1]

Prior to about 1820 the white inhabitants of the West Indies, on the evidence of contemporaries and in the accounts of many historians, appear to have been completely irreligious. It is said repeatedly that the few churches were in poor condition, the clergy corrupt and the free population lax in their morals to the point of depravity. The African slaves, allegedly sunk in superstition, were regarded as being incapable of appreciating the truths of a "higher" religion.

By 1840 a mighty effort at conversion was well under way; Christianity had become the chosen instrument for the stabilization and reintegration of West Indian society. The Africans, almost without exception, appeared to have embraced Christianity in some form or other.

This view of the complete absence of religion in slave society, followed by the sudden conversion of a waiting slave population from

---

1. [J. Stewart], *An Account of Jamaica and its Inhabitants* (Kingston, 1809), 147.

heathenism to Christianity, is an exaggeration, created during the period of the abolition movement—roughly from 1795 to 1830. More recent research, concentrated upon the survival of African culture in the New World, has shifted the focus but left intact certain assumptions about the slaves and their interests. Some writers have depicted Africans as possessing a religious sense which, if not actually innate, derived from the central concern of all African cultures and which survived all the vicissitudes of the diaspora.[2] According to some accounts this basic religiosity was "reinterpreted" during the conversion movement, while others have viewed the sudden enthusiasm for Christianity at the time of abolition of slavery as a short-lived affair, quickly followed by revitalization movements which established, or reestablished, a West Indian folk culture quite different from the basically European traditions of the elite.[3] In either case a purely religious interest is seen to be the central concern of African, black, or West Indian folk culture.

These interpretations are inadequate. West Indian colonies have always been an extension of European Christian society, with an established church of sorts. African slaves began to be incorporated into a local society from the moment of their arrival in the New World. Even though that mode of incorporation was specific to the plantation as a form of organization, Christianity was never entirely absent.[4] No matter how irreligious planters and their white employees might appear to be, they came from a society in which religion had been the vehicle for the expression of social and political doctrine for at least 300 years. There was a lively awareness of the potentially unsettling effects of teaching slaves the doctrine of brotherly love and the equality of human souls. One response to this danger was to deny the slaves any access to

---

2. Herskovits is the best-known exponent of this view. See Melville J. Herskovits, *The New World Negro* (Bloomington, 1966). Also George E. Simpson, *Religious Cults of the Caribbean: Trinidad, Jamaica and Haiti* (Rio Piedras, 1970).

3. Michael G. Smith, *A Framework for Caribbean Studies* (Kingston, 1955); Philip Curtin, *Two Jamaicas: The Role of Ideas in a Tropical Colony 1830-1865* (Cambridge, Mass., 1955); Orlando Patterson, *The Sociology of Slavery* (Rutherford, 1969).

4. Raymond T. Smith, "Social Stratification, Cultural Pluralism and Integration in West Indian Societies," in Sybil Lewis and Thomas G. Mathews (eds.), *Caribbean Integration, Papers on Social, Political, and Economic Integration* (Rio Piedras, 1967).

Christian teaching, but this does not appear to have been stressed as deliberate policy until near the end of the eighteenth century, and the effort then was to keep them away from the *wrong kind* of Christian teaching. During the eighteenth century there were few clergy anyway, and certainly too few to engage in the proselytization of an overworked slave population made up in considerable part of people brought directly from Africa and still learning the rudiments of West Indian language and customs. On the other hand, there are few indications that Africans or free people of color were specifically excluded from church services. The more usual response to the potential danger of Christian doctrine was to stress the complete separation between earthly fate and heavenly reward, and to emphasize those aspects of Christianity which pointed to the virtues of submission and obedience. This is well exemplified by the statement of Count Nikolaus von Zinzendorf, the Moravian leader responsible for the early missions to the West Indian slaves, on the occasion of his visit to St. Thomas in 1739. Addressing the Moravian converts in that island he said: "God punished the first negroes by making them slaves, and your conversion will make you free, not from the control of your masters, but simply from your wicked habits and thoughts, and all that makes you dissatisfied with your lot."[5]

Cultural transmission rarely proceeds according to conscious intent. The social doctrines of nonconformist Christianity, which had been forged in the political atmosphere of Europe, lay waiting for the ripening of the contradictions within the system of plantation slavery and mercantile capitalism which supported it. The manner in which the slaves embraced Christianity in an outpouring of fervor had less to do with pure religiosity, innate or otherwise, than it had to do with social and earthly expectations in specific historical circumstances. In order to understand the remarkable success of the evangelical movement in the West Indies and the subsequent development of religion among West Indians of African descent, it is not enough to speak of "folk" and "elite" cultures, nor to trace the provenience of elements of ritual and belief to their Old World

---

5. Cited in Elsa V. Goveia, *Slave Society in the British Leeward Islands at the End of the Eighteenth Century* (New Haven, 1965), 272, n.6. See also Simpson, above, 285.

sources; one must examine the social, political, and economic contexts in which the varying symbolic structures of religion operated and into which they diffused their meaning.

My argument is that while Christianity functioned briefly as a vehicle for the radical expectations of those in the West Indies who most desired change—the slaves—the missionary effort never transcended its origins in the ideal and material interests of the English bourgeoisie. In the West Indies Christianity soon became the major ideological support of colonialism, and the churches were carried by the incipient middle and lower middle classes of post-emancipation society. The lower classes turned increasingly to magical, enthusiastic, and socially despised forms of religious participation, which, whether they contained African, European, or East Indian liturgical and doctrinal elements, were firmly rooted in the social experience of their practitioners.

In examining religion in the West Indies one should not treat various forms of religious belief and practice as if they were completely separate entities derived from "African," "Indian," or "European" cultural traditions, or even as syncretisms of these elements. The array of belief and practice found in any one territory has to be seen as a whole, with internal variations being related to the various dimensions of social differentiation—local, class, and racial. Only in this way can one discover the common elements in such differing forms of religiosity as Jamaican lower-class cults and some forms of Guyanese Hinduism, and only in this way is one led to seek the structural core to which apparently disparate forms of religious symbolism are anchored.

West Indian religion is West Indian, in all its complex diversity, and not African, Indian, European, or anything else. Christianity came to symbolize the stable integration of the society around the core elements of the colonial social order, while the persistence and growth of radically different or even opposed religious forms have equally symbolized differentiation and conflict.

This paper deals particularly with the establishment of free African villages in Guyana after 1838.[6] In order to render the events of that pe-

---

6. Prior to emancipation a distinction was made between African and creole, or locally born, slaves. During the latter part of the nineteenth century this distinction

RAYMOND T. SMITH

riod explicable I briefly describe the growth of Guyanese society up to that time. Finally, to demonstrate the relation between social class and the varying modes of religious expression, I make some comparison with Jamaica, where the fate of the rural population and the development of Christianity after emancipation were rather different.

Religion under Slavery

Christian churches, and the organization of local government according to parishes, were among the first artifacts of European civilization imported into the West Indian colonies. Barbados was the first fully developed English settlement in the region; its Assembly, representing the rights and interests of the free settlers, and its vestry system of local government, quickly became the model for other territories. Jamaica was captured from the Spanish in 1655 by William Penn and Robert Venables, two of Cromwell's men. One of the first acts of the king after the Restoration was to establish there the same social and political arrangements as existed in Barbados.

Just as the Roman Catholic church was an integral part of the governance of the Spanish, Portuguese, and French territories in the New World, so the established church of England and the Dutch church were an integral and important part of the social life of the West Indies.

The coastal area of Guyana was not opened up for settlement before the middle of the eighteenth century.[7] Although some plantation cultivation had been undertaken along the banks of the major rivers, it was the drainage and irrigation of the Demerara coastal plain that led to large-scale and profitable planting of cotton, coffee, and sugar. A majority of the plantations along the coast were owned and operated by British planters who brought their skill and their capital (mainly in the form of slaves) from the West Indian islands. There is no evidence that these British planters were any more or less religiously inclined than the generality of

---

disappeared, and all black people came to be termed either Africans (in contrast to Indians, Chinese, etc.) or Negroes. I shall generally use the term African to apply to Guyanese black people.

7. See Raymond T. Smith, *British Guiana* (London, 1962), chs. 2, 3, for a fuller account.

British in the West Indies, but as early as 1753 they petitioned the Dutch director-general to be allowed to build a church and provide themselves with an English minister.

> The inhabitants of Demerara, who were here in large numbers last week, have placed two matters before me with a request that I should submit them to the Court of Justice at its next meeting.
>
> Firstly, that they are compelled to live like heathens, without divine worship, in that Colony, which was very hard for them and that they begged, since by far the greater number consisted of English or of those understanding the English language, that the precentor of Saba who was shortly expected there might be permitted to perform divine service on Sundays in the house of the Commander by reading a sermon, singing psalms, etc. This most laudable request I immediately granted, not doubting that YY.HH. will give the same Your Honors' approbation. On one occasion they asked me whether YY.HH. might consent to the appointment of an English preacher, to which I replied that I would write about it but that I had no doubt YY.HH. would certainly consent thereto.[8]

By the end of the eighteenth century things had not changed very much; there was one Dutch and one English clergyman and they conducted separate Sunday services in the same room under the courthouse. In a letter dated December 20, 1796, Pinckard said that "No church or temple is to be found in the settlements; nor have the inhabitants even appropriated any house, or other building, for the performance of divine service."[9] There is no indication that any plantation had a chapel,[10] although some planters held daily prayers and included their domestic servants in the household rituals.

Despite these negative indications, the lives of the slaves were pro-

---

8. C. A. Harris and J. A. J. de Villiers, *Storm Van 's Gravesande, The Rise of British Guiana Compiled from his Despatches* (London, 1911), I, 292-293.

9. George Pinckard, *Notes on the West Indies Including Observations Relative to the Creoles and Slaves of the Western Colonies and the Indians of South America* (London, 1816), II, 131.

10. Some Jamaican planters certainly built private chapels and even maintained their own clergymen. See Michael Craton and James Walvin, *A Jamaican Plantation* (London, 1970), 169.

gressively structured according to the requirements of plantation economics and the Christian calendar. Sunday was set aside as a day of rest on which the slaves were free to attend weekly markets, there to sell produce from their provision grounds. Christmas and Easter had become major festivals in all the West Indian territories. On the day after Christmas in 1796, Pinckard wrote in a letter to a friend in England:

> On the subject of Christmas I should tell you that it is not less a period of festivity here, than in England. The planters make parties, and the merry feasting of the season goes round, unchilled with its frosty coldness. It is likewise a holyday to the slaves, who usually receive some indulgence of food, and some present of clothing to augment the happiness of the festival. . . . in the evening their loved African dance crowned the holyday. Parties of them go from the different plantations to spend the mirthful hours with their more particular friends or acquaintances of the neighbouring estates, and it is a happy meeting of relatives, lovers, and fellow-passengers who made the voyage together from their native land. The whole country exhibits one moving scene of dancing gaiety.[11]

There was, doubtless, some carry-over of Arican elements in these festive activities, as there was in funeral and marriage ceremonies performed by the slaves, but the major outlines of Christian ceremonial gradually permeated the whole society. Bolingbroke describes a funeral in Stabroek (the central portion of what is now the capital, Georgetown), around 1805, which could well apply today:

> . . . the respect and attention paid at funerals of free people, and even of negroes, is very considerable. Not only all their relatives, but strangers feel it an incumbent duty to go. If a coloured free person dies in Stabroek, the remains are followed to the grave by everyone in town. I have seen upwards of two hundred people of colour followers. They are either in white muslin dresses, or deep black mourning, according to whether the deceased is female, or male. . . . The coffin, which though merely covered with black cloth and lined with linen, costs twenty-five pounds sterling, is conveyed in a hearse, attended by twelve bearers, then the clergyman, mourners and followers.[12]

---

11. Pinckard, *Notes on the West Indies*, II, 140-141.
12. Henry Bolingbroke, *A Voyage to the Demerary, Containing a Statistical Ac-*

The situation among field slaves on the plantations must have been very different, of course, and there is evidence that funeral rituals were provided for and organized on the basis of tribal affiliation.[13] We know relatively little of the religious beliefs of the slaves, but even if the structure of African religious doctrine had not become disorganized, that doctrine must have been difficult to relate to the new situation of plantation life. Witchcraft, sorcery, and divination, however, not only persisted and played an important part in the daily life of the plantation, but *was* appropriate to the new conditions, inasmuch as such belief and practice dealt with interpersonal problems of conflict and suffering which were very real. There is abundant evidence of the important part which drumming and dancing played in the lives of the slave population, but we can only speculate as to the shifts in the meaning with which these liturgical elements of African religious performance were invested. The slave displayed relatively little interest in Christianity (which was after all even less related to his social condition than African beliefs) until it came to symbolize an improvement in the condition of his daily life, or until he could see in it an expression of his own situation and a message of hope for the future.

Mass Conversion and the Abolition of Slavery

It is against this background that one must view the remarkable success of the movement to convert the laboring population of the West Indies to Christianity. Without going into the complex question of how the evangelical movement developed in Britain, one can say that despite the sporadic appearance of missionary activity in the West Indies, it was not until after the abolition of the slave trade in 1807 that a real *movement* began to build, and this was closely linked to the development of evangelism in England itself.

According to one account the first missionary to land in Guyana was a Wesleyan from Dominica who arrived on September 30, 1805. On October 2 the governor politely suggested that he leave on the first avail-

count of the Settlements there, and of Those on the Essequebo and Berbice, and Other Contiguous Rivers of Guyana (London, 1809), 44.
13. Raymond T. Smith, The Negro Family in British Guiana (London, 1956), 9-10.

RAYMOND T. SMITH

able boat, which he did on October 8.[14] However, by this time the idea of slave conversion was rapidly becoming British government policy and the opposition of planters and administrators was unable to stop it.

The first Anglican church was opened in Georgetown in 1810, intending to cater to people of all conditions. This was part of an expanded effort on the part of the Church of England to develop missionary activity in overseas territories—an effort aimed in part at forestalling the effects of radical nonconformist activity. Eventually the Episcopalian and Presbyterian churches were to take on the major work of conversion and education, simply because they were supported out of public funds, but it was the Congregationalists of the London Missionary Society who pioneered in the conversion of slaves and who bore the brunt of the opposition from the planters.

The first missionary to establish an active station in Guyana was sent by the London Missionary Society at the specific invitation of Hermanus Post, owner of Plantation Le Resouvenir, situated about eight miles from the capital along the Demerara Coast. The Rev. John Wray and his wife arrived early in 1808 and immediately started work on the instruction and conversion of the slaves in that vicinity.

Between the arrival of Wray in 1808 and the first step toward total emancipation which was taken in 1834, Guyana, like the rest of the West Indies, went through a period of internal readjustment in which Christianization came to be accepted as the principal means of rendering slaves tractable. This view did not prevail without opposition, but all the ideas about slavery in circulation during this period were quite old; only the situation was different. Many planters refused to believe that a plantation system could ever be operated by free labor; others, prodded by the British government, came to put their faith in the market system aided by the religious training in Christian obedience and moral virtue. In either case the view was that insofar as people of African descent had any social attitudes whatever they would be produced by European manipulation. If they were not terrorized into obedience they must be indoctrinated with a spirit of humility. Mismanagement of that indoctrination could

14. Edwin Angel Wallbridge, *The Demerara Martyr: Memoirs of the Rev. John Smith, Missionary to Demerara* (London, 1848; reprint, New York, 1969), 16.

produce rebellion. The contemporary view of religion was remarkable for its functionalism; differences of opinion merely revolved around the question of what functions it would fulfill. The autonomous political action of the slaves was discounted completely.

Christian doctrine proved to be a rich source of symbols which could be marshaled by different groups in the coming struggle over what were essentially political issues. The variety of meanings which could be attached to those symbols is well illustrated by the case of the Rev. John Smith, whose trial and conviction on charges of aiding a slave rebellion led him to be styled "The Demerara Martyr."[15]

Smith arrived in Guyana in 1817, sent by the London Missionary Society to take over the chapel and mission station at Le Resouvenir which had been without a resident minister since Wray had gone to Berbice in 1813. For six years Smith worked to increase the number of converts in his district, becoming increasingly incensed by the restrictions placed upon him by hostile planters, and becoming increasingly involved with the lives and concerns of those among whom he worked. In 1823 disturbances broke out among the slaves all along the east coast of Demerara but the rebellion was soon crushed with considerable loss of life among the slaves. Some were killed in confrontation with the militia, some executed summarily by detachments of militia, some tried by courts-martial and sentenced to execution or flogging. Not more than one or two whites were killed, and those in large confused confrontations. No whites were killed with deliberation, though many were confined in the stocks which existed on every estate. Most remarkable of all, no property was destroyed.

The proximate cause of the rebellion was the rumor which began to circulate in July regarding dispatches received by the governor from Britain ordering a series of measures in amelioration of the condition of the slaves. They were intended to pave the way for the ultimate ending of

---

15. Apart from Wallbridge cited above, the most useful source is *The London Missionary Society's Report of the Proceedings Against the Late Rev. J. Smith, of Demerara, Minister of the Gospel, Who Was Tried Under Martial Law, and Condemned to Death, On a Charge of Aiding and Assisting in a Rebellion of the Negro Slaves: etc.* (London, 1824). See also David Chamberlain, *Smith of Demerara* (London, 1924); Thomas Rain, *The Life and Labours of John Wray, Pioneer Missionary in British Guiana* (London, 1892).

RAYMOND T. SMITH

slavery. The governor and the Court of Policy discussed these measures but made no public announcement either of their contents or of the action they proposed to take. News of the dispatches soon spread among the slaves, especially along the east coast of Demerara where communications with Georgetown were frequent and the slaves politically aware. Whatever the immediate occasion for the rebellion, it is clear that the slaves nursed deep-seated grievances rooted in the conditions of their life and work in the sugar plantations. Since the abolition of the slave trade the number of workers had been steadily declining while at the same time the slaves developed rising expectations of improved conditions. The planters were of two minds as to the best way to control their labor force. One moment they were inclined toward more liberal treatment and the extension of religious instruction in the hope that it would result in greater obedience; at other times they fell back upon physical punishment as the only method of restraint. It was precisely this contradictory behavior that bred increased dissatisfaction, along with such continuing aggravations as the separation of families through slave sales.

Smith argued at his trial that neither he nor the members of his church had been in any way involved in the plotting of the rebellion, but it seems clear from the evidence presented at the trial that the church at Le Resouvenir was one nodal point in the dissatisfaction and in the resolve to take action. On the other hand the slaves were not at all sure that Smith would support them when it came to the test. They certainly allowed him to go unmolested, but the evidence is that he tried to dissuade them from any illegal action and that many of them expected him to side with the whites if it came to a showdown.

What, then, was the part played by Christianity and the missionaries in outbreaks of this kind? At Smith's trial the prosecution built its case around the contention that he had deliberately stirred up the slaves by thinly veiled attacks upon the planters and the slave system in the form of sermons based on texts from the Old Testament. The planters and the government were anxious to arrive at a simple explanation of the rebellion, and they seized upon the activities of this representative of the English antislavery movement and were determined to make an example of him. The case was certainly exaggerated. The missionaries, including Smith, were sincerely interested in teaching submission to the law, and their identification with the slaves stopped far short of fomenting rebellion or of drastically reordering secular society. They shared many of the racial prejudices of the other whites, differing only in their opinion that Africans were capable of ultimate redemption provided they conformed absolutely to the rules of the church.

The volatile and unpredictable element in the whole situation was the slave himself. Rather than being a passive element manipulated by the missionaries, the slave used the missionaries and Christianity to further his own ends. Despite the earnest instructions of the London Missionary Society to avoid interference in the relations between masters and slaves, it is clear that the main attraction of Christianity was the promise of an improved social order. To become a Christian in 1820 meant an open association with the local representative of the abolition movement and participation in activities which promised social as well as spiritual uplift. This, rather than any intrinsic interest in religion, seems to have been the key reason for the striking success of missionary activity.

Smith was found guilty by court-martial and sentenced to death, but was recommended for clemency. He was held in Georgetown until he died early in 1824 of the consumption from which he had been suffering before his trial. After the rebellion had been crushed, with considerable loss of life among the slaves from militia action and executions, the planters were determined to put an end to the activities of the missionaries. However, it is significant that they did not try to stop religious instruction. At a public meeting held at the Royal Hotel in Georgetown in February 1824, a few weeks after Smith's death, it was resolved to petition the Court of Policy to expel all missionaries from the colony. But it was also resolved to recommend that financial aid should be given to the Dutch, English, Scottish, and Roman Catholic churches in order to create "by means of pure and genuine religious instruction, an effective moral power for the government and control of the labouring population."[16] The next fifteen years saw a greatly expanded effort at Christianization; in 1826 a complex system of parishes was created and clergymen of the four churches mentioned were placed on the public establishment. The

---

16. James Rodway, *History of British Guiana, From the Year 1782 to the Present Time* (Georgetown, 1893), II, 256.

RAYMOND T. SMITH

mission chapels were taken over for a while by the established churches, though they were eventually allowed to resume their work.

The stage was now set for the transition to a new social order, and the part that Christianity was to play had been decided. In 1833 the vestrymen of St. Paul parish (which now included Le Resouvenir) wrote in their annual report that they needed more money for the repair and expansion of the parish church. In arguing for this they set out very clearly what they believed to be the role of the churches.

> At a period of time so interesting as the present, when a change is about to take place in our community the most momentous that we have ever witnessed, and in its probable effects the most uncertain, it is of the utmost importance that religion and moral instruction should be placed fully within the reach of that class of the population, whom this sudden transition from bondage to apprenticeship, and thence progressively to complete freedom, will chiefly affect. Christianity is eminently a religion of order, and a due subordination to lawful authority is a duty which stands high among the requisite qualifications of its followers; and its doctrines strenuously inculcated will be our greatest safeguard against any mischief that might probably occur in the important crisis, which is so near at hand. Every facility therefore, which can be afforded to the negroes, of obtaining a full and intimate acquaintance with these doctrines, will be an additional bulwark to the peace, well-being and happiness of the country. . . . they think it of considerable moment that the religious and moral education of the peasantry should be, as much as possible, in the hands of—and the field of instruction preoccupied by—authorised and accredited ministers of the Gospel, who act in subordination to Known Regulations, and are answerable to the Head of their Church for the conscientious discharge of the sacred trust reposed in them; rather than be left open to irresponsible persons, who, however well-meaning and pious, are not always endowed with a zeal duly tempered by discretion, and have no acknowledged religious superior in this part of the world.[17]

17. "Report to His Excellency, Major-General Sir James Carmichael Smyth, Baronet, C. B., Lieutenant Governor, and the Honorable Court of Policy from the Vestry of St. Paul, 21st. October 1833," from a collection of copies of documents obtained by the author in the 1950s from the Public Buildings, Georgetown, before the archives had been transferred to their present location. Many of these documents had been worked through by previous students of Guyanese history and left unfiled.

Religion in the Free Villages

The slaves were given limited freedom in 1834 when they became "apprentices," and slavery was finally abolished on August 1, 1838. Between 1838 and 1850 the ex-slave population of Guyana demonstrated its feelings about plantation labor by a mass exodus into free villages, none of which had existed prior to this time. By 1850 there were less than 20,000 Africans resident on sugar plantations, while the population of the villages had reached 44,456 persons.[18] Many of these villages were simply portions of the front lands of sugar estates which were laid out into plots and offered for sale by the owner, who hoped thereby to retain a pool of laborers who would wish to work on the plantation for wages.

The earliest and most significant development was not the growth of these "proprietary" villages confined to the front lands of estates,[19] but the cooperative purchase of whole plantations by groups of ex-slaves who intended to go into business on their own account. Significantly, the first village to be set up in this manner was on the east coast of Demerara in the area which had been most affected by the 1823 rebellion. In November, 1839, eighty-three laborers purchased an abandoned cotton plantation of 500 acres for a total sum of $10,000, of which $6,000 was paid in cash. This was the first of twenty-five such purchases over the next ten years, all of which were part of a movement of revolutionary expectations which had been a long time developing, and which ran its course very quickly before settling down into the state of quiescent disillusionment which persisted for the next 120 years.

The communal villages were bought collectively, with title being vested in the representatives of the shareholders. The intention was to run them as cooperative plantations. None continued in this manner for more than a few years, and eventually all were divided into individual shares, most of which were subsequently subdivided for sale or lease. The principal reason for the failure of the cooperatives was a lack of capital to maintain the drainage and irrigation works and roads, combined with poor markets for profitable cash crops. Export crops were difficult

---

18. Allan Young, *The Approaches to Local Self-Government in British Guiana* (London, 1958), 23.

19. *Ibid.*, 11-13, distinguishes between "proprietary" and "communal" villages.

RAYMOND T. SMITH

to manage in a depressed market, particularly when the villagers were dependent upon the established planters for the grinding of sugar cane and upon the white merchants for shipping facilities. Many of them cultivated food crops, such as plantains, for sale to people living in the towns and on plantations, but this market was soon saturated. Other crops such as arrowroot were tried, which had a limited success, but the fact was that the ex-slaves were buying up plantations that had been abandoned for the very good reason that they were no longer profitable in the changed circumstances of the 1840s.

Since the clergy were well established among the slaves by the time emancipation came, it is easy to see them as the chief architects of the free village movement. In Jamaica the free villages are often referred to as being "church based."[20] It is certainly true that by 1838 clergymen, teachers, and catechists were present in large numbers, and a body of special "stipendiary magistrates" had also been appointed to supervise the transition to a free society. The Church of England had eighteen clergymen, twenty-eight schoolmasters, ten clerks and catechists, and an unspecified number of schoolmistresses; the Church of Scotland had seven clergymen; the Roman Catholics raised Guyana to the level of a bishopric and had five priests plus several catechists and schoolteachers; the London Missionary Society and the Wesleyan Missionary Society operated schools and/or churches in about twenty-seven communities; six schools were operated by the Mico Charity and one by the De Saffon Trust for the legitimate orphans of white parents; and, finally, there were a number of private schools in both Georgetown and the rural areas.[21]

This enormous expansion in the number of churches and schools affected virtually every person in Guyana. The total population at the census of 1841 was only 98,133. Compensation had been paid for 69,579 slaves and another 13,245 slaves were either under six years of age or noneffective owing to old age or chronic sickness. It can be appreciated

20. See Hugh Paget, "The Free Village System in Jamaica," *Jamaica Historical Review*, I (1945), 31-48.

21. These figures are compiled from Richard Schomburgk, *A Description of British Guiana* (London, 1840); Robert Duff, *British Guiana: Being Notes on a Few of Its Natural Productions, Industrial Occupations, and Social Institutions* (Glasgow, 1866); *British Guiana Blue Book 1841* (London), section on Educational Returns.

therefore that this upsurge in the activity of clergy and teachers must have had a dramatic impact upon a population concentrated in settlements along the coast. Christianity and church membership had come to symbolize progress and, in the West Indian vernacular, "upliftment," and it created avenues of social mobility for the ex-slaves—avenues which tied them in directly with the highest status levels of the total society.

It is remarkable that the progress of Christianization in Guyana was never attended by the development of new forms of liturgy, nor, so far as we know, was it marked by enthusiastic forms of worship. On the contrary, it appears to have been highly controlled, hierarchical and authoritarian in structure, and was closely linked to the development of formal education, which symbolized admission to civilized society. (This conclusion is not vitiated by the knowledge that many of the clergy arriving in Guyana during this period quickly succumbed to tropical fevers or to the evils of strong drink and/or venereal disease.[22]) Church services, music, speech, and subsidiary associational activities were kept very close to British patterns, and clergymen from Britain were preferred by the congregations. Institutionalized Christianity of this kind created a rural elite whose position was based in the schools and the churches, and whose lifestyle was modeled on that of the respectable missionaries and clergy from Britain. The more successful children of this elite gradually moved into the civil service and the professions, thus creating links with the national middle class—which was essentially urban-based.

Despite these later developments it does not seem likely that the establishment of the free villages was inspired and directed solely by the clergymen or the leading members of their churches. The leaders among the slaves had long been either the "drivers," the headmen, or elected

---

22. Duff, writing in the 1860s, calculated that of the fifty-seven Presbyterian ministers who arrived in Guyana between 1818 and 1866 "the average life of 41 ministers has been three years and three months; of 6, 22 years;—and 11 are now in the service, only four of whom have been five years in the colony" (Duff, *British Guiana*, 360). Elsewhere he says: "No fewer than nineteen of the clergy of the different religious bodies in the colony have to my knowledge been compelled by the authorities in those churches to resign on a few months' leave of absence. . . . The crimes of which they were all guilty were drunkenness, concubinage, or adultery" (*Ibid.*, 351).

RAYMOND T. SMITH

"kings" who were responsible for arranging funerals and other matters. It seems likely that the leaders of the free village movement came from this group, though no doubt some men of this kind achieved important positions in the church hierarchy as well.

The upsurge of interest in Christianity which characterized the period of transition to freedom was neither uniform in its distribution nor total in its effect. Not all ex-slaves were baptized nor did all of those who were baptized become church members, though over the next few decades nominal adherence to Christianity became accepted to the extent that few children remained unbaptized. Elements of belief and practice which appear to be African, such as witchcraft, drumming, and dancing, persisted into the later nineteenth century and still exist today. The reason for their preservation in relatively unmodified form is, paradoxically, that Christianity remained both strong and orthodox, so that instead of syncretism one got the parallel existence of two types of belief and practice.

Evidence on the exact nature and extent of African forms of religious belief is scarce and difficult to evaluate, but it is clear that few, if any, blacks denied the validity of Christianity and openly claimed to be the adherents of a rival religion. There may have been some tendencies in that direction in the early stages, just as there were some tendencies toward the development of syncretic forms within the churches, but they were nipped in the bud. All apparently African belief and practice tended to be classed together as *obeah* and characterized as superstition or devil worship. In a dispatch to the secretary of state for the colonies dated November 26, 1840, the governor of British Guiana wrote:

> Obeah practices, mixed up with portions of scripture, and repetitions of prayer, have come to my notice within the last few months; they seem to pay so well, that no opening should be allowed to the knavish negro, to assume the sacerdotal power.[23]

He goes on to cite a case in which a stipendiary magistrate had recently punished an *obeah* man who was headman on an estate and a class leader

---

23. Henry Light to John Russell, Guiana Despatches no. 157/1840, Guyana archives.

"of one of the sects." The legal suppression of all forms of non-Christian ritual and the relegation of African beliefs to the category of superstition was extremely important.

In the same year that he forwarded this dispatch to London, Henry Light recommended to the inhabitants of the new African villages that they should draw up, and subscribe to, agreements for the management of the plantation lands.[24] Such agreements were usually constructed with the assistance of the stipendiary magistrates and signed by all the shareholders. In 1952 I found a copy of one of these agreements, dating back to at least 1866, for a village which had been established in 1840.[25] The agreement contained two clauses dealing specifically with the prohibition of non-Christian practices.

> 9th And be it known to all shareholders that no ungodly dance shall be held in the village Mingy Mamma. Mingy drumming, persons found in such act to be carried before Magistrate of the district.
>
> 10th Should any person be found practising Obeah or receiving money under false pretence to be dealt with according to law.[26]

During the slavery period little attention had been paid to African dancing and drumming. It was very common and has been mentioned by many writers.[27] The fact that drumming and dancing should be specifically mentioned in these village agreements is some index to their continuing importance.

In the 1860s Robert Duff, a Presbyterian clergyman, claimed to see a revival of *obeah*. He attributed it to the tolerance shown to the "performance of the heathen rites practised in open day by the coolies and the Chinese, at their annual festivals."[28] The Africans needed no encouragement from the indentured immigrants, and the fact is that the early 1860s saw

---

24. Young, *Approaches to Self-Government*, 35.

25. The text of the agreement is reproduced in full in Smith, *Negro Family*, 16-18.

26. *Ibid.*, 17.

27. The materials are much richer for Jamaica than for Guyana, as can be seen from Edward Brathwaite, *The Development of Creole Society in Jamaica 1770-1820* (Oxford, 1971), ch. 15. See also Patterson, *Slavery*.

28. Duff, *British Guiana*, 320.

RAYMOND T. SMITH

an upsurge of enthusiastic forms of religion spreading throughout North America, Britain, and the West Indies.[29] The effect in Guyana was relatively unorganized and unnoticed, which is probably due to the tight control which the established churches had imposed and the lesser proportion of dissenting clergy—lesser than in Jamaica, for example. Nonetheless, Duff notes that

> The negro villages, and even the suburbs of our county towns, which, for many years after emancipation, were free from such superstitious and licentious practices, are now once a week the scenes of disorder, immorality, and vice—the natural accompaniments of every Obeah exhibition. Thousands of the peasantry may be seen, from the rural districts for miles around, congregating in the places dedicated to midnight revelry, now no longer secretly and by stealth, but openly and in defiance of the law and the police authorities. Collisions between the latter and the deluded votaries of Obeahism and Watermammaism frequently take place, and though a few of the ringleaders may be secured and brought before the magistrate, from want of evidence they can only be convicted of riot and assault, not of practising Obeahism.[30]

These dances have persisted into the present. I witnessed several in the early 1950s which accord quite closely with the following description provided by Duff.

> The ceremonies vary in form, but they always consist of a dance, sometimes called cabango, comfoe, or catamarrha. During this dance, the performer throws himself into every possible variety of attitude; tumbles, jumps, and foams at the mouth, while the assembled multitude follow him in singing some nonsensical words, understood neither by him nor them.

> When all have, by the physical effects of such gymnastics on their nerves, reached a sufficient degree of frenzy, the special worshippers are beaten with a bush rope, or piece of root, often until the blood flows, to punish them for their neglect of the water mamma worship or some offence that they have given to her.

---

29. See Curtin, *Two Jamaicas*, 170-172.
30. Duff, *British Guiana*, 320.

> When this has been sufficiently done to appease the anger of the water mamma, a calabash of water, after certain mumblings, is thrown on them while kneeling, and the performer then informs his dupes that the water mamma's favour has been secured, and that he will meet her alone in the bush and obtain what is wanted; generally, the name of the person who has been the cause of someone's sickness, of some disease among stock, or some death in a family.[31]

It will be noted that there is virtually no blending of Christian elements into these ritual performances; the central elements are drumming, dancing, and spirit possession.

There appears to have been little change in the main outlines of this cult activity in over a hundred years. In the spring of 1952 I was living in a village on the West Coast of Berbice, the first section of which had been founded as a communal village in 1840. Most of the villagers were at least nominal adherents of either the Anglican or the Congregational churches. As I have described elsewhere, there was a powerful undercurrent of belief in magic, spirit intervention in everyday life, and witchcraft.[32] A frequent complaint was that of being "troubled" by spirits, and for these problems it was customary to call in a specialist—a man who was generally classed as an *obeah* man but who was just as frequently termed a "scientist," a "doctor," or a "professor" by the villagers themselves. One of these specialists had diagnosed the case of a particular young woman as indicating that she had special spiritual gifts which could perhaps be harnessed and demonstrated by holding a *cumfa* dance under the guidance of appropriate experts. The girl's family sought out a team of drummers and dancers from Georgetown and invited them to the village for a prolonged stay. A dance square, or *ganda*, was set up and for several days and nights the drummers and dancers held sporadic sessions in which they sought to bring out the propensity of the girl for spirit possession. The procedure was to try to create an atmosphere in the *ganda* which would induce spirits to come and possess the girl and lead her down to the sea where she would encounter a "fair maid" or water mamma, who would give her a token in the form of valuable objects (gold

---

31. *Ibid.*, 139.
32. See Smith, *Negro Family*, chs. 7, 8.

RAYMOND T. SMITH

jewelry in this case) and impart to her special occult powers and esoteric knowledge. Eggs, water, and white rum were used to "wash the *ganda*" and to attract spirits, and care was taken to keep clear a path to the burial ground on one side and the sea on the other. It was believed that a special indication of the girl's power would be if she were able to "dance on her head,"[33] which would show that she had caught "Wind." These dances are sometimes known as "Wind" dances; the word seems to be a corruption of "Winti."[34]

There is no need to go into the further details of what actually happened on this occasion; the point is that here we had a flourishing cult, the elements of which were apparently of African origin with no Christian elements at all. I might say that the whole performance was treated with somewhat less than reverence and respect by most of the villagers, and the consensus among the young men was that the only thing peculiar about the young female initiate was that "she want man." In discussing religion we are apt to forget that whatever the capacity of religious symbols to formulate conceptions of ultimate meaning and make those conceptions immediate, and no matter how prominent the pious part of the population may seem, there is always a sizable group of people who take their religion with a grain of salt, regarding ritual performance more as insurance than as a certain path to salvation. Certainly the West Indian folk have a sharp sense of humor and an ability to puncture the pretensions of those who feign Christian charity while practicing worldly selfishness, just as they can mock their own credulity in lining the pockets of charlatans, be they *obeah* men or less shady characters.

Contrast with Jamaica

Jamaica is the home of a multitude of syncretistic religious movements of a type almost completely absent from Guyana. They began as long ago

---

33. See Simpson, *Religious Cults*, 176, for a description of the dancing style involved.

34. The word Winti is commonly used among the Bush Negroes of Surinam for a possessing deity. The term Mingy in the village agreement cited above is also probably a corruption of Winti, though this would require careful linguistic analysis in order to be certain.

as the late eighteenth century, when Baptist churches were established among some slave populations as the result of the activities of black preachers from the United States. Curtin presents a view of this Native Baptist tradition which elevates it to the position of an Afro-Christian sect, largely beyond the control of the European Baptist missionaries who came in large numbers later on. The argument is that these early Baptist congregations were led by men who had the religious authority of *obeah* men, or Myal men,[35] and who were also often plantation officials such as headmen or skilled tradesmen.[36] Curtin's thesis of the two Jamaicas—one African and one European—sometimes inclines him to treat syncretism as an uneasy conjunction liable to fall apart into its constituent elements, but he is correct in his argument that the black leaders in these early Christian congregations were the prototype of the independent cult leader. They were also the prototype of the respectable church official, and it would be more correct to say that religious leadership became differentiated into two contrasted types: the religious virtuoso who became the leader or the "shepherd" of an independent group, and the official (member, lay preacher, vestryman, deacon, or clergyman) of one of the respectable churches. Once the European missionaries established control, the Native Baptist tradition of Afro-Christian syncretism tended to be squeezed out of the church, but it did not disappear.

In twentieth-century Jamaica we find an extremely wide range of expressions of religiosity. The "respectable" churches are well established, as they are in Guyana, supplemented in recent years by a host of evangelical denominations coming mainly from North America. Seventh-day Adventists, Jehovah's Witnesses, the Church of the Open Bible, Church of God, the United Brethren, and a host of others now compete for followers, as indeed they do in Guyana. Apart from these churches there are the Rastafarians with their well-developed doctrine preaching the necessity for blacks to be repatriated to Africa and a complex theology which places Haile Selassie as a divine incarnation in the direct line

---

35. Myalism is generally distinguished from *obeah* on the grounds that it is a collective cult organized around dance and spirit possession ritual. See Patterson, *Slavery*, 185-192.

36. Curtin, *Two Jamaicas*, 31-35.

RAYMOND T. SMITH

of succession from David, Solomon, and the Queen of Sheba.[37] Rastafarianism is organized not into a church but into relatively independent groups loosely tied into a number of competing associations. Its doctrines are highly political but there have been few attempts to shape it into a movement for political action in Jamaica.[38]

A very large but unknown number of cults are grouped under the designations of "revival Zion" and "Pocomania."[39] The range of variation in the doctrines and rituals of these groups may be considerable but they are all quite clearly syncretistic, employing such liturgical elements as drumming and dancing and spirit possession, but using Christian or Old Testament theology.

Finally there is a large but less overt body of belief and practice ranging from the *cumina* dance cult of St. Thomas[40] to the curing cults of "balm yards" and the practice of *obeah*. The *cumina* cult is the most apparently African in its derivation and most clearly comparable to Guyana's *cumfa* dance cult.

Why did Jamaica develop such a wide range of syncretic forms of religious belief and practice while Guyana had virtually none? In order to answer this question fully one would require an extended comparative study of the history of the two colonies over the years since emancipation. All I can do here is to suggest the main factors such a study would have to examine.

There is first the difference in the geographical configuration of the two countries. Jamaica is extremely mountainous, and the scattered settlement patterns made it difficult—even impossible—for the orthodox churches to maintain control over their members and to prevent the development of deviant movements. However, one should not exaggerate the effects of geographical isolation; as Simpson points out, the majority of Jamaicans profess some attachment to one or another of the orthodox

---

37. See Simpson, above, 301; *idem, Religious Cults*, 208-228; Leonard E. Barrett, *The Rastafarians, A Study in Messianic Cultism in Jamaica* (Rio Piedras, 1968).

38. Rex M. Nettleford, *Identity, Race and Protest in Jamaica* (New York, 1972), 39-111.

39. Martha Beckwith, *Black Roadways: A Study of Jamaican Folk Life* (Chapel Hill, 1929), 157-182; Simpson, *Religious Cults*, 157-207.

40. Joseph G. Moore, "Religion of Jamaican Negroes, A Study of Afro-Jamaican Acculturation," unpub. Ph.D. thesis (Northwestern University, 1953).

churches and are apt to be quite promiscuous in their attachment to a range of different religious bodies.[41] A more important reason for the Jamaican religious developments is the greater complexity of Jamaica's rural social structure.

Jamaica has always had a much wider range of agricultural enterprises than Guyana, and a greater diversity in the size and profitability of agricultural holdings. Even before emancipation some medium-sized farms had been owned by free people of color who produced food crops for export as well as for local consumption. These exports increased after emancipation, and were usually handled by a class of produce merchants, mainly colored (racially mixed) or Jewish, who shipped direct to Britain or to the Gulf ports of North America. This trade was outside the control of the large Kingston merchants, and it expanded overall during the nineteenth century, particularly after the start of the banana trade in the 1870s. At the same time that this small-to-medium farm activity was growing, the structure of the plantation sector was changing. After the passage of the Encumbered Estates Act in 1854 it became easy to allow estates which had been abandoned, because of their excessive indebtedness, to change hands. The act did not really begin to take effect in Jamaica until the late 1850s and early 1860s, but once the special court, which had been established in England, began to operate, it had the effect of permitting London mercantile houses to purchase estates cheaply and to put them back into operation. Between the beginning of the operation of this court and 1893 no less than 148 sugar estates were sold in Jamaica, and in many cases one buyer would purchase a considerable number of estates and consolidate them.[42] Such consolidation was rapidly becoming a necessity for the efficient operation of a modern sugar plantation, and it usually resulted in a shift in ownership from individuals to companies.

Jamaica imported relatively few indentured immigrants after emancipation, and the sugar estates continued to rely upon black labor to meet

---

41. Simpson, *Religious Cults,* 161.

42. See R. W. Beachey, *The British West Indies Sugar Industry in the Late Nineteenth Century* (Oxford, 1957). Donald K. Robotham, "Class Structure and Community Structure in Jamaica," unpub. M.A. thesis (University of Chicago, 1969), draws attention to the eviction of squatters which resulted from repossession of abandoned estates, and which produced widespread distress and even violent protest.

most of their needs. However, few blacks remained as resident laborers. The vast majority established themselves as small holders, whether upon their own freeholds, on rented lands, or as squatters on the marginal or abandoned lands of plantations. Whereas the economic condition of the small- and medium-sized farmers engaged in the cultivation of cash crops generally tended to improve over the years, the plight of the people who depended upon wage labor to supplement the subsistence farming carried on around their houses became worse. Apart from the efforts of the sugar estates to keep down wages and to deny workers access to profitable holdings on good land, the sugar industry itself was always subject to fluctuations of fortune which had their harshest effect upon labor.

Curtin identifies the early 1860s as the turning point in the development of relations between "African" and "European" Jamaica.[43] The great religious revival of 1860 to 1862 started among the Moravian congregations and was generally encouraged by clergymen of all denominations. However, as it progressed it became increasingly evident that more and more enthusiastic elements were being introduced into revival meetings, and that many of them at least appeared to be derived from such "African" cults as Myalism. As Curtin says, "there was no getting around it: the Great Revival had turned African."[44] This somewhat dramatic way of putting it tends to obscure the complexity of the situation, but Curtin's discussion shows that it was not a simple matter of Jamaica dividing into two segments. The independent cults such as Revival Zion and Pocomania developed and flourished among the marginal peasants, who left the more orthodox churches to the substantial small- and medium-sized farmer elements. By this time the latter were also frequently employers of labor and often no more kindly disposed toward paid laborers than the sugar planters. Migration to the cities from these two segments of the rural population followed different paths over the next hundred years. The more prosperous farmers educated their children to the limit possible with the facilities available, and when they moved to the city it was generally into dignified employment of some kind: in teaching, the lower ranks of the civil service, police, nursing, or shop-

---

43. Curtin, *Two Jamaicas*, 172.
44. *Ibid.*, 171.

keeping. The drift into town of the more impoverished people deposited them in the slum areas of West Kingston, which eventually became the most concentrated home of religious cults.[45]

Although Guyana experienced some differentiation in the free black population, particularly between the villagers and those who remained resident on the sugar plantations (many of them immigrants from Barbados), there was no class division comparable to that between marginal peasants and middle-sized farmers in Jamaica. Furthermore, the growing East Indian population in Guyana almost equaled that of the blacks by 1891, and their alien "heathen" religions came to symbolize low status in the society as a whole. There is a sense in which Hinduism and Islam were the counterpart of Jamaican cult movements in symbolizing marginal social status within the developing colonial society. The parallel is limited, of course, since Hinduism, once purified of its "low" features derived from non-Brahmanical sources, and Islam were eventually brought up to the level of "respectable" Christianity as a vehicle for status affirmation.[46] Perhaps the parallel will become less limited, for there are clear signs in Jamaica that the rituals and doctrines developed in the syncretistic cults are being used by a new generation of young people in their quest for a new identity and a new political expression in postcolonial society.[47]

Conclusion

In this chapter I have attempted to analyze some aspects of the part played by religion in the creation of post-emancipation colonial society in the West Indies by showing the relation between varying forms of religious organization and expression, and the status contexts in which they developed. Most interpretations of religion in the West Indies concentrate heavily on the origins of particular items of ritual or belief, a procedure which inevitably diverts attention from the creative use to which

---

45. George E. Simpson, "Political Cultism in West Kingston, Jamaica," *Social and Economic Studies*, IV (1955), 133-149.

46. See Chandra Jayawardena, "Religious Belief and Social Change: Aspects of the Development of Hinduism in British Guiana," *Comparative Studies in Society and History*, VIII (1966), 211-240.

47. Nettleford, *Identity, Race and Protest*, 127.

RAYMOND T. SMITH

these items are put in the ongoing processes of social life. Fascinated though we may be by the evidence of continuity of African belief and practice in such cults as *cumina* or *cumfa*, we should not be distracted from the impact which Christian individualism has had upon the people of African descent. On the other hand, in recognizing that impact we should not imagine this to be a passive population gratefully accepting the view of religion as the guarantor of obedience and social order which was current in the 1840s, and is still evident today among those who see Christianity as the "bulwark against communism." West Indians have used and interpreted Christian tradition in as many ways as have Europeans, and for much the same reasons. One can detect at least three major trends in West Indian religious development, quite apart from the role which Christianity played in symbolizing the transition from slave status to free citizen in the first half of the nineteenth century.

For want of better terms, we may label these three trends hierarchical paternalism, ethical and sectarian individualism, and participatory enthusiasm.

The paradigm of the first trend was, of course, the Church of England, but all the denominations shared some of the same characteristics. They were all dominated by clergy sent from Britain or trained there, and the church members felt themselves to be connected through the church to the very center of metropolitan society. Like the education they sponsored, these respectable churches were, and still are to a very considerable extent, "English." They self-consciously served the ends so clearly stated by the members of the vestry of the parish of St. Paul in Guyana in 1833. Even the nonconformist churches which had grown out of a European tradition of individualism and dissent became establishment-oriented and hierarchical after the major battle of emancipation was past. The most active core of these churches consisted of the descendants of the old "free coloured" (the nucleus of the post-emancipation middle class), and those members of the laboring population oriented to upward mobility—mainly African, but also containing some Indian, Chinese, and Portuguese. The social mobility of these elements was largely sponsored mobility, arising from the growth of the civil service, teaching, and the churches themselves. Those who were successful in agriculture or business emulated the bureaucratic middle class and tried to ensure that their children entered it.[48] Beneath this core element was a large body of nominal adherents who attended church occasionally, sent their children when they could afford to clothe them suitably, and used the services of the minister for baptism, weddings, and funerals. The most significant thing about these churches is their hierarchical structure and the controlled, orderly, and eminently respectable quality of their proceedings. Surrounded by a halo of service organizations and attended by the highest in the land, they seem to bring the church member into touch with God only through a careful adherence to correct social form.

In stressing the hierarchical and paternalistic quality of these churches, one should not overlook the individualistic trend: the core members are not drawn from a hereditary gentry class, but are in many cases individualistic strivers imbued with some elements of the social ethic of European Protestantism. The self-reliance which such an orientation would normally produce, of course, tended to be overlaid by the effects of a racial ideology which created self-doubt as well as resentment. But still, some elements of individualism did find expression in the use made of the respectable churches by the upwardly mobile. Extreme dedication to improvement of the self, frequently through adoption of an ascetic lifestyle and the application of rational principles to work, could exist in the middle reaches of church organization, particularly in the rural areas. This is not the only area of religious life and organization, of course, in which individualistic striving appears. Numerous Christian denominations or sects less firmly tied to the existing colonial establishment have provided favorable opportunities and a congenial atmosphere for the religious and social life of those emerging from the lower class. Many of these smaller denominations came from the United States rather than from Britain, and some of them, like the Seventh-day Adventists and the Jehovah's Witnesses, were not so small, either. The same kind of cultural orientation which is characteristic of the really active members of these churches can be found among some Hindus and Muslims in Guyana and Trinidad.[49]

---

48. See Nancy Foner, *Status and Power in Rural Jamaica: A Study of Educational and Political Change* (New York, 1973).

49. See Jayawardena, "Religious Belief and Social Change."

RAYMOND T. SMITH

Finally, what I have called participatory enthusiasm has its roots in the lower class and finds expression in a very wide range of religious settings. Apart from the apparently African cults mentioned in the body of this chapter, and the syncretistic sects such as Pocomania and Revival Zion, there are numerous sects, such as the Pentecostals, the various forms of the Church of God, the Salvation Army, the Church of Christ, Pilgrim Holiness, and many others which are lesser known. Virtually all such sects place some restrictions upon the worldly activities of members, be it abstinence from alcohol, dancing, or the use of make-up, and virtually all involve such practices as congregational participation—in the form of testifying, glossolalia, hand-clapping or other musical expression, and sometimes spirit possession. While there is certainly differentiation within these sects, with gradations of organizational and spiritual authority, there is a pervasive feeling of egalitarianism and a marked preoccupation on the part of the members with questions of doctrine, biblical interpretation, and so on.[50]

I do not wish to suggest any simple spectrum of religious belief, practice, and orientation which corresponds directly to position in the hierarchy of social status or the structure of occupations; there are too many discrepancies and anomalies, and sufficient flexibility so that different cultural orientations can appear within each type of religious organization. However, it is clear that there are broad variations in world view which have some connection with social structural factors and which correspond in a general way to the trends in religious development set out above. It is more effective to begin with a framework of this kind than to start from supposedly pure types of European, African, or Indian religion. Elements from all these sources may enter into religious expression at any level; speaking in tongues, the use of percussion instruments, and the direct experience of spiritual power occur in all three continents and could have come to the West Indies from any or all of these sources. What is of interest is the manner in which these elements are used in social practice and what they mean to the practitioners.

Symbols derived from the African tradition have been pushed into a

---

50. See Malcolm J. C. Calley, *God's People: West Indian Pentecostal Sects in England* (London, 1965), 72-95.

subordinate position and identified with witchcraft, idolatry, and devil worship; traces of legal proscription linger on in the form of *obeah* laws. Rastafarianism is the only example in the English-speaking West Indies of an attempt to fashion an aggressive social ethic based on a well-developed religious doctrine and incorporating African symbols in a clear way. It does not have the spread and vitality of Haitian *vodun*, and it seems unlikely that its popularity among a small group of university students and intellectuals will have sufficient dynamic to carry it to the level of a national religion. In Guyana and Trinidad, East Indians have built Hinduism and Islam into respectable churches (not free, however, from internal processes of fission) in which members of all classes may participate. Surprisingly enough, even Islam has remained an "Indian" religion though some small groups of Black Muslims have come into being in recent years. There is no intrinsic reason why West Indians cannot develop more self-consciously African modes of religious expression, and every likelihood that they will.

Whether religion will be the vehicle for the expression of a new ethic of social transformation is another question. In the early nineteenth century Christianity was the only means available to the slaves for seeking a society-wide system of social justice—and certainly the only one acceptable to those with power—and we know just how ambiguous that justice was in practice. While it would be wrong to ignore the fact that religion is more than social ideology, and that Africans in the West Indies derived more from Christianity than an avenue to social justice, we cannot fail to see the Christianization was a deliberate piece of social engineering. It surely stands as a case study in that art, for although the predictions of chaos and disorder to follow emancipation were exaggerated, there can be little doubt that Christianity helped to ease the transition— and to put off the day of reckoning.

12

Robert I. Rotberg

Vodun and the Politics of Haiti

"Haiti," says one authority writing about the years of Duvalier, "came under the control of a high priest of the voodoo cult who retains the loyalty of the superstitious masses through fear."[1] Is this true? And, if true, what does it mean and how did it come about?

It is widely affirmed that *vodun* (voodoo) has played a significant role in Haitian political development. At a commonsense level, since *vodun* has for long been the religion of the great mass of Haitians, a political importance for *vodun* is often posited a priori. The presumption of power and the ability and willingness to wield that power also exists on behalf of *vodun*. But the essence of *vodun* is not easily expressed within institutional frameworks, and measuring the impact of *vodun* upon Haitian politics has always been an abstruse and doubtful enterprise. Most of the scholarship which has been expended on *vodun* has concentrated, for obvious reasons, upon the explanation of the state of possession, *vodun*'s least obviously explicable manifestation, and upon taxonomic appreciations of its theism. The sociology of *vodun* has been comparatively neglected despite the presumed bases on which it exerts parochial social control. Similarly, few of those who have studied *vodun* have concerned themselves with the political component of social control, or with

An earlier version of this chapter was read at Stanford University in 1971. I am grateful to G. Wesley Johnson and the Rockefeller Foundation for providing the opportunity and the encouragement.

1. Thomas G. Mathews, "The Caribbean: The National Period," in Roberto Esquenazi-Mayo and Michael C. Meyer (eds.), *Latin American Scholarship Since World War II* (Lincoln, 1971), 139.

the larger, national influence exerted by what, despite a nominal adherence to Roman Catholicism, has always been the national religion. This chapter provides a longitudinal framework for the examination of prevalent if unstated assumptions about the conjunction of *vodun* and politics in Haiti.

Any simplified working definition of *vodun* will occasion controversy. In large, *vodun* is "an integrated system of concepts concerning human activities, the relationship between the natural world and the supernatural, and the ties between the living and the dead." It encapsulates a cause and effect system which explains otherwise inexplicable and unpredictable events. It sets out guidelines for social behavior and demands that its gods respond. Like all true religions, it ties the known to the unknown and establishes theological order in place of chaos. No event is a unique occurrence.[2]

God, the Creator, rules the universe, but from a distance. He shares this task with Christ, the Holy Ghost, and many saints. Man, endowed with a soul which comes from God, is judged by God, and his soul returns to God at the end of its sojourn on earth. The intermediaries between men and God during the earthly period are the deities or their representatives, called *loa*. The *loa* have varying characteristics and number in the hundreds; many are African in origin and inspiration, others are indigenous to Haiti or the Caribbean, and some are specifically Christian.[3] (*Vodun* has its Afro-American analogues in Cuba, Brazil, and Trinidad.) *Loa* lurk in the background, regularly providing advice, courage, and consolation, sometimes behaving benevolently, sometimes not, and always acting in unexpected ways.

Vodun proposes that man has a material body animated by a spirit which, being nonmaterial, does not share the death of the body. It is this spirit or soul which may achieve by stages the status of a *loa* and come to represent a quality of divinity or some critical natural or moral principle. When, as an archetypal representative of some principle, it has the power temporarily to displace the soul of a living person and become the ani-

---

2. Harold Courlander, "Vodoun in Haitian Culture," in Harold Courlander and Rémy Bastien, *Religion and Politics in Haiti* (Washington, 1966), 12.
3. For a list of *loa*, see George E. Simpson, "The Belief System of Haitian Vodun," *American Anthropologist*, XLVII (1945), 40-43.

mating force of his physical body, the soul becomes possessed. Possession is a manifestation of rapport between the deities and their representatives and men.

Vodun is "neither the practice of black magic nor the unorganized pathological hysteria it is so often represented to be. The gods are known to their worshippers, and the duties owed them are equally well understood. The reward for the performance of these duties is good health, good harvests, and the goodwill of fellow-men."[4] But if a Haitian neglects his gods or fails to serve his *loa*, he forfeits the goodwill of his fellow men and submits himself, and his soul, to the vagaries of ill fortune. Conformity to group goals and punishment for social deviance is implicit, as is its oblique enforcement and the use of nonspecific sanctions.

Vodun is an all-encompassing belief system which depends only marginally upon the existence of specific places of worshi. "It is an integrated system of concepts concerning human behavior, the relationship of mankind to those who have lived before, and to the natural and supernatural forces of the universe."[5] The living are related to the dead and to those not yet born. Unpredictable events—and traditional societies constantly live with a lack of predictability—are explained. Chaos is converted into order. In this sense, as in some others, *vodun* is a profoundly conservative force. It, and the patterns of life which radiate from its core, substitute in Haitian rural existence for the kinds of formal or governmental institutions which are and have always been lacking in Haiti. Nothing else in Haitian life so fully integrates nature and human experience, provides the psychological and social cushions which make rural poverty bearable, and gives color and mystery to years otherwise drab and bleak. *Vodun* also provides a central reference point above and outside of the local or national instruments of government. For a long time, and still to some extent now, *vodun* was the major if not the only focus around which rural Haitians could begin to organize.

Yet *vodun* is the most decentralized of religions. There is no national organization, no hierarchy, and even no statewide agreement about the identity of the *loa* or the form of propitiatory rites. Profoundly, genu-

---

4. Melville J. Herskovits, *Life in a Haitian Valley* (New York, 1937), 153. See also Maya Deren, *Divine Horsemen: The Voodoo Gods of Haiti* (New York, 1970).
5. Harold Courlander, *The Drum and the Hoe* (Berkeley, 1960), 9.

inely congregational, the *vodun* religion is in fact a thousand or more parochial variations on a single theme. The center of each node of worship is a *hounfour*, a wood and thatch temple, and each *hounfour* is presided over by a *houngan*, or priest. Within the *hounfour* there is a recognition of differences in priestly authority, but there are no formal or institutional links between *hounfours*, few ties between the *houngans* of different *hounfours*, and very little interchange, association, or conflict between the various *hounfours*.

Vodun is a belief system which "pushes out from below." Rather than being imposed from above, like most religions, it is "bred and nurtured in the family, in the towns, and in the fields. It is common law, with deep roots in an unbroken and continuous past." It is democratic, ordinary worshipers having direct access, without going through the *houngans*, to the deities or their ancestors. The *houngans* only interpret and serve; they cannot control *loa*. But they articulate beliefs, teach, "give form to abstraction," become "the intellectualizing agency of a tremendous emotional force," and manipulate the substance and the mysteries of life.[6] They are central and dynamic in a community with few other resources, and their power, although it may come by indirection, is nevertheless real. Depending upon the priest and the situation, the *houngan* can predominate, always providing that his power evolves out of the traditional belief system and that its exercise wears the clothes of legitimacy.

A local cult center flourishes if it has the support and trust of the surrounding community. It fades away if and when the *houngan* fails to impress the community with his strength. Worshipers recognize the difference between a *houngan* who has *connaissance* and one who cannot fully appreciate the character of the deities, tradition in its full regalia, and the political variables of local and regional settings.

Vodun is inescapably Haitian. It reflects the idiom of rural reality, reinforces it, and expresses much of the contents of any personality inventory that might be considered especially indigenous. Or, turning this analysis around, it is equally plausible to suppose that *vodun*, drawing upon notions of the cosmos which were brought by the slaves from West

---

6. *Ibid.*

ROBERT I. ROTBERG

Africa, may have helped profoundly to shape Haitian attitudes toward life and work. Whatever the case, *vodun* is an accessory to and a support of the kinds of rural mental attitudes which have inhibited modernization and made the imposing and maintaining of dictatorship easier. Rural Haitians are generally said to be more suspicious, jealous, and full of intrigue than their counterparts in other traditional societies.[7] These casts of mind may have been derived from the necessary mental accommodation to slavery: "The first Haitians were rootless, lacking any bonds common to them all except revolution. They were originally of many tribes [speaking many] languages of Africa, and naturally lacked the cement of a shared culture, religion, or language, or, as time went on, even—as peasants and freed men—the group socialization which might have been [engendered] by a modern colonial experience." Instead, separated from their forefathers and denied an opportunity to acquaint themselves in normal ways with the benefits of cooperation, they remained both submissive to authority and able, deviously if necessary, to cope under stress.[8]

Throughout the history of Haiti, from independence in 1804 to the death of François Duvalier in 1971, these habitually sensitive responses of rural Haitians have been reinforced by socioeconomic deprivation and acute isolation. Although the country includes only 10,700 square miles, 21 percent of the land mass lies below 700 feet and 35 percent is over 1,600 feet. Its northern and southern arms jut out wildly toward Cuba and Jamaica, making Haiti's narrow, flat waist the only area with easy access to Port-au-Prince, the capital. Geographical impediments accentuate the separation of peasants from one another, and from their government, by valleys, mountains, and rushing rivers. Then too, Haiti has never had any roads. In 1969, outside of the main towns, there were about 50 miles of paved, properly repaired highways, 200 miles of badly surfaced main roads, and another 2,000 miles of the most execrable roads in the world. (Tiny Barbados in 1964 had about 1,300 miles of paved highway.) Nor are there or have there been many functioning telephones, radio receivers, widely circulating newspapers, or homes with electricity

---

7. Rémy Bastien, "Haitian Rural Family Organization," *Social and Economic Studies*, X (1961), 483-484; Francis Huxley, *The Invisibles* (London, 1966), 26.
   8. Robert I. Rotberg, *Haiti: The Politics of Squalor* (Boston, 1971), 18.

or waterborne sanitation. On all of these indices of economic strength, Haiti ranks lowest in the Western Hemisphere.

Haitian poverty is nevertheless difficult to describe statistically. In the 1960s, the national average per capita gross national product equaled $67. Rural Haitians were probably even more impoverished than their urban counterparts, and no wealthier on the average than the citizens of Botswana ($55), Malawi ($52), or Ethiopia ($52). No other country in the Western Hemisphere even approximated Haiti on this scale. Bolivia, the second poorest country, had a per capita gross national product of $164; Jamaica and Martinique had $440. Elsewhere, India at $90 and Tanzania and Chad at about $70 exceeded the Haitian figure.[9] The Haitian recurrent national budget has in recent years totaled about $25-30 million, roughly the same size as the annual budgets of Brandeis University and Lexington, Massachusetts (pop. 31,000).

Nearly 90 percent—an abnormally high proportion—of all Haitians live outside of the towns. Since only about 23 percent of Haiti's tangled land mass is arable, Haiti for many years, perhaps a century or more, has been the most densely populated rural region in the Western Hemisphere. Its eroded, wasted lands carry upwards of 2,000 persons per square mile. In these crowded conditions, where the average nuclear family controls no more than an acre of land (Haiti has no latifundia), malnutrition and its related diseases have accompanied high levels of morbidity and excessive infant mortality: 7-15 percent of all Haitian children die during the first eight weeks of life from umbilical tetanus—which can be easily prevented—alone. Numbers of physicians and nurses per thousands of population are again the lowest in the Western Hemisphere, and life expectancy averages about thirty-three years. Given soils which are far less fertile than they were in the eighteenth century, when Haiti was the wealthiest colony in the world, declining productivity in subsistence agriculture, an underfed, crowded, and chronically ill population with few resources and almost no opportunities for cash employment (Haiti lacks large-scale extractive or plantation industries), it is hardly surprising that Haitians turned (and continue to turn) their backs on the Roman Catholic church and gave themselves fervently to a system of cognitive order-

---

9. For more details, and references, see *ibid.*, 9-10.

ROBERT I. ROTBERG

ing capable of rationalizing the harshness of everyday life. What is more, Haitians have always been staggeringly illiterate. Schooling, theoretically accessible to all Haitians, in practice has been limited since the days of the revolution to members of the urban elite and the families of relatively advanced peasants.[10] Even in 1970 more than 90 percent of all Haitians could not read and write, a figure similar to that usually given for believers in *vodun*.

The religion of *vodun* is a significant component of Haiti's political culture. From 1513, when Africans began to replace Carib Indians in the pearl-fishing economy of Hispaniola (the island of which Saint-Domingue, later Haiti, formed the western third) until the early eighteenth century, there were but few plantations, and modest numbers of slaves. Before the end of the Seven Years' War in 1763, the cotton, sugar, coffee, and indigo plantations of the French colony of Saint-Domingue were expanded only gradually. Then, with the loss to France of Canada, the development of more favorable markets, and the attendant expansion of plantation acreage, there was rapid growth. By 1775, the white and mulatto population had multiplied threefold to 15,000, and the number of slaves had increased by a factor of five—to 250,000. (During the 1720s, Saint-Domingue imported about 4,000 slaves yearly. In the 1750s, about 5,000 slaves entered the colony. Twenty years later, the number of landed slaves had doubled.) Working fertile and well-irrigated soils, the slaves and their talented, well-capitalized overlords had begun to create an impressive and efficient economic machine. By the end of the American Revolution, it produced two-thirds of French-grown tropical produce, as much sugar as all of the British islands in the Caribbean, and large amounts of coffee, cotton, and indigo. Culturally and physically, Haiti had become a colonial jewel.

Black slaves polished the orb. On the eve of the French Revolution, the population of Saint-Domingue included 30,000 whites, 27,500 free

---

10. In the Caribbean, 98 percent of the inhabitants of Barbados, 85 percent in Costa Rica, 82 percent in Jamaica, and 77 percent in Cuba are literate. Zambia, an African country with a population about the same size as Haiti's, counts 50 percent of its people as literate. The Yemen, Ethiopia, and Moçambique are among the very few countries which have lower rates of literacy than Haiti.

mulattoes and blacks, and 465,000 slaves.[11] The majority of the slaves were very recent arrivals, a surprisingly small proportion of their number having been born or socialized on the island. From 1786 to the outbreak of revolution, between 27,000 and 40,000 slaves had been imported annually from innumerable scattered villages and regions in western Africa. Although it is widely assumed that most of the slaves who landed in Haiti before the revolution were from Dahomey and the coasts of what is now Nigeria (thus linking modern *vodun* naturally with the religion of their African origins), the sources upon which most writers have relied provide little substantial evidence on which to base conclusions about the provenance of Haitian slaves. Records of the individual ships and their loads have not survived, but there are lists of plantation populations, and contemporary discussions of the composition of the slave majority of the colony at various periods. Nothing indicates that the slave markets of Saint-Domingue were ever dependent upon supplies from Dahomey, the putative home of *vodun*. Rather, late eighteenth-century Haitian slaves stemmed from at least thirty-eight different areas of Africa, and from more than 100 different tribes and ethnic divisions.[12] They came from the widely separated savanna and forest of what have since been called Senegal, Mali, Guinée, Ghana, Zaire, Angola, and Moçambique. Without a common language or religion, sharing no common social principles or technologies, and united only by virtue of residence, color, and station, they constituted a pool of uprooted exiles ripe for the twined appeals of *vodun* and revolution.

During the 1780s, the planters of Saint-Domingue were opening up virgin lands in the interior. Thanks to the American Revolution and new patterns of trade, there was a heightened demand for sugar and other tropical crops from the most efficient producer in the Western Hemi-

---

11. Support for these figures and other data may be found in Rotberg, *Haiti*, 33, *et passim*.

12. The most comprehensive collation of the origins of Haitian slaves is James G. Leyburn, "The Making of a Black Nation," in George Peter Murdock (ed.), *Studies in the Science of Society* (New Haven, 1937), 381-386. See also Gabriel Debien, "Les Origines des Esclaves aux Antilles," *Bulletin de l'Institut Fondamental d'Afrique Noire*, *XXIX* (B) (1967), 536-558; *idem*, *Plantations et Esclaves à Saint-Domingue* (Dakar, 1962). There is a discussion of the other sources in Rotberg, *Haiti*, 34-35n. Cf. Higgins, above, 118-127. In 1975 Dahomey was renamed Benin.

ROBERT I. ROTBERG

sphere. Hence the unprecedented increase in the numbers and frequency of slave importations into the colony, and the consequent massing on the newest plantations of large numbers of newly landed, inexperienced, intractable, impoverished, resentful, and not yet broken Africans who still carried memories of a freedom forcibly surrendered. There was little danger, too, of conditions on the plantations making them cherish their American surroundings. Work in the sugar and indigo fields was hard and their treatment inhumane, slaves being ill-housed, ill-fed, ill-cared for, and continually abused. They were mistreated physically and mentally, mutilated for trivial offenses or in order to satisfy the sadistic pleasures of their masters, shackled, masked with metal, occasionally tortured or punished with boiling cane sugar. The lot of most slaves was vile, and beyond the comprehension of most modern readers.[13] When spiritual and political liberation were once seen to be available, the slaves of Haiti, particularly those who had so recently entered the society, proved supremely receptive to the message of conspiracy. They were readily mobilized. Subjectively, they had little to lose.

Whether or not *vodun* developed in Haiti before the middle of the eighteenth century, and whatever its specific African origins (evidence for the Zaïrese is as impressive as that for the Dahomean line of descent), *vodun* does not appear to have been used as an overt instrument of political mobilization until about that time. An anonymous French essay on slavery alluded to secret nocturnal meetings of slaves where, presumably, their state of helotry was discussed, methods of gaining their freedom were explored, and—conceivably primarily—their memories of Africa were compounded into a transmittable assemblage of cultural, religious, and magical information. By this time slaves spoke Creole, which has a vocabulary of contemporary regional French (or Norman) with some African-derived words, an African syntax, and a grammar derived from French and one or more Bantu languages. African attitudes

---

13. There is a good description of life on a sugar plantation in Justin Girod-Chantrans, *Voyage d'un Suisse dans différentes colonies d'Amérique* (Neuchatel, 1785), 136-138. See also Pierre de Vaissière, *Les origines de la colonisation et la formation de la société française à Saint-Domingue* (Paris, 1906), 186-188; François Alexandre Baron de Wimpffen (trans. J. Wright), *A Voyage to Saint Domingo* (London, 1817), 216-218.

regarding time, circumstance, sorcery, and the worship of gods were probably more fully shared than concepts about any specific attributes of a deity. Presumably, too, *vodun* evolved without any central inspiration. Separate, roughly contemporaneous growth constitutes a more plausible model for *vodun* than does diffusion from a single source.

By 1750, in at least one area, Africans had begun to participate in a dance called "the water mother" of which the slaves were said to make a great mystery. "All that is known . . . is that it excites very much their imagination." They become so ecstatic that they lose consciousness, claiming that God has spoken to them. "But as they do not worship the same God they hate each other and spy on each other reciprocally."[14] The "water mother" notion has affinities with the later use of water as a carrier of magical properties in African and American Indian religious resistance movements and rebellions, but the theme is common enough to indigenous revitalization and anticolonial assertions throughout the subjected world, and across time; it would be misleading to link this fragmentary report either to Africa or to the religion which *vodun* became.

Makandal, a slave born in Africa who gathered a following in the late 1750s in the Limbé district, may have been a *houngan*. He is said to have had apocalyptic visions, and to have represented himself as the emissary of a powerful divinity. Mobilizing hundreds of slaves, he and his followers began pillaging plantations, stealing cattle, and poisoning whites and collaborationist blacks. But whether or not Makandal spread his message from *hounfour* to *hounfour*, and whether or not religious expressionism rather than some larger revolutionary impulse was his motive, he may have helped to politicize *vodun* and assist in its spread throughout the fertile northern plain of Saint-Domingue. In 1758, however, Makandal's plot was discovered and he was burned by the French in Cap Haitien.[15]

---

14. Quoted in Simpson, "Haitian Vodun," 35-36.
15. Thomas Madiou, *Histoire d'Haiti* (Port-au-Prince, 1847), I, 23, says that in Africa Makandal had become a Muslim. Whether or not Makandal's rampage ever reached fruition or not is unclear. Simpson, "Haitian Vodun," 36, implies that it did. Médéric-Louis-Elie Moreau de Saint-Méry, *Description Topographique, Physique, Civile, Politique et Historique de la Partie Française de l'isle Saint-Domingue* (Paris, 1958; orig. ed. 1797), II, 630; Madiou, *Histoire*, 23; Cyril L. R. James, *Black Jacobins* (New York, 1963), 21, indicate that the rebellion was aborted before its culmination.

ROBERT I. ROTBERG

Among Makandal's successors as leaders of rebellious slaves were many who may have first emerged as *houngans* or who made use of the apparatus of *vodun* to mobilize and motivate their legions of followers. Distinctions between the two were rarely sharp, however, and should not be exaggerated retrospectively. Even if *vodun* primarily provided a means of sublimating the frustrations of enforced servility, its rituals and shared spiritual secrets created cohesion among an often subordinated and oppressed populace. "The fact cannot be denied that Vodoun was the cement which bound the members of the conspiracy and that it served as a catalyst when the time for action came."[16]

The time for large-scale, decisive action came in 1791. Two years before, the Haitian ruling classes enjoyed unquestioned wealth and could confidently look forward to the perpetuation of a priviliged and highly rewarding system of economic and social exploitation. Saint-Domingue was an oasis of prosperity, the very success of which made the possibility of radical change as unthinkable to those who were profiting from the system as it must have made psychological sense to the oppressed. But the surge of events in the mother country suddenly engulfed the distant planters of the colony. Louis XVI summoned the Etats-Généraux, the Bastille fell, and the abolitionists in the Assemblée bitterly attacked the bourgeois colonial apologists. In early 1790, the Assemblée established a universal franchise for all taxpayers, including mulattoes. But overseas the colonists refused to accept equality regardless of color and acted vigorously to nullify the application of the French declaration to Saint-Domingue. This was, in effect, a counterrevolution which, like so many initiatives in the colonies, might have achieved a mute acquiescence from the ranks of the mulattoes and the blacks. But among the many Haitians who appreciated the importance of widening the door of opportunity which the Assemblée had opened were Vincent Ogé and Jean-Baptiste Chavannes, two young mulattoes. Ogé had personally witnessed the events of Paris and listened with dismay to the news of their rejection by the whites of Saint-Domingue. Encouraged by abolitionists in England and the United States, he purchased weapons, sailed home, and, with

---

16. Rémy Bastien, "Vodoun and Politics in Haiti," in Courlander and Bastien, *Religion and Politics*, 42.

Chavannes, demanded the promulgation of the French instructions. Re-buffed, he tried to march on Cap Haitien (then called Cap Français, the colony's capital) leading a small detachment of armed mulattoes. Over-whelmed, Ogé, Chavannes, and many of their co-conspirators were tor-tured, broken alive on the wheel, and beheaded.

Ogé had been unwilling to recruit or arouse the slaves, and they, lacking a sense of common destiny or an awareness of their potential strength, were in turn slow to make the revolution their own. They may have heard of the slave uprisings in Guadeloupe and Martinique, but Haitians at first responded only in an uncoordinated manner to word of *liberté, fraternité*, and *égalité*. A few garrisons mutinied, but only after French troops arrived in 1791 with news that all men, irrespective of color, were free and equal, did the slaves on scattered plantations murder their overseers, set the cane fields alight, and begin roaming the country-side. As often as before, however, repression triumphed, and rebellious slaves literally lost their heads in increasing numbers. A concerted organ-izational framework was lacking which, given the racial antagonisms of the day, could most easily be supplied by a social catalyst capable of evading the suspicions of an anxious ruling class. Whether or not *vodun* had been used for these purposes before, and despite the nuclear nature of each *hounfour*, it was well adapted—as were the rain-shrine cult cen-ters in nineteenth-century Rhodesia—to the conspiratorial and mobiliza-tional needs of a revolution.

Boukman, the headman of a plantation in the northern plain, pro-vided the necessary inspiration. Although he was born in Jamaica, his qualities of leadership had attracted the attention of whites and, as it transpired, blacks as well. He is said to have been of impressive physical stature, and to have had a gift of oratory. He may also have been able to read and write. Most significantly, he had become a well-respected *houn-gan*. By mid-1791, he had managed to gain the cooperation of other *vodun* priests and to have begun to weld their congregations into a sup-ple and responsive whole. Slaves gathered throughout the north to sing, dance, and express themselves in a frenzy of religiosity. Presumably, they schemed as they worshiped, and the *loa* provided many with a con-temporary inspiration, or the courage to act. Certainly the mystery with which the *vodun* rituals were invested helped to embolden the wills of

ROBERT I. ROTBERG

disparate, desperate individuals. Those who partook of the substance of ritual, and swore the oaths that could so easily have been grafted upon the eclectic ceremonies of *vodun*, were promised invulnerability. Ritualization and oathing persuaded *vodun* adepts that their spirits would be rendered invulnerable to the superior fire power of the French colons. Oaths sworn religiously were also difficult to disregard in the heat of battle. There must have been many scenes like the eve-of-battle ceremony in August 1791, when an older female slave, presumably possessed, danced wildly, sang robustly, and finally plunged a huge cutlass into the throat of a black hog so that the excited celebrants could drink its blood and swear to follow the dictates of Boukman.[17]

The percentage of worshipers among the subsequent revolutionaries, like the quality of their religious commitment, is unknown. But the informal network of *vodun* forged by Boukman held together long enough for about 40,000 slaves throughout northern Saint-Domingue to rise against their masters. Seeking revenge as well as freedom, they raped, tortured, and killed whites, pillaged plantations, set the hated sugar cane alight, destroyed the aqueducts, and put in motion a tortuous chain of events which not so much directly, but inadvertently, led eventually to the independence of Haiti in 1804. Yet *vodun*, particularly after Boukman was captured and decapitated, also came to play a less and less central role in the process of fiery civil war. There were some emergent leaders, like Jean François, in the north, the self-styled Grand Admiral of France, and Biassou, who called himself Viceroy of the Conquered Territories, who wore elaborate uniforms, surrounded themselves with men of magic and the bones of the dead, and exuded an aura of *vodun* religiosity. They were fond of symbolism and preceded each attack by a lengthy and extraordinary session devoted to dancing and, presumably, the rites of possession. Biassou voiced the instructions of God and promised his followers that those who fought bravely against the French and had the misfortune to die would have their souls transported home to Africa. In the south, there was Romaine Rivière, who claimed descent from the Virgin Mary and plundered Léogane in her name after an elaborate high mass. In the west, Hyacinthe Ducoudray, a young slave, gath-

---

17. Cf. Jean Price-Mars, *Ainsi Parla l'Oncle* (Port-au-Prince, 1928), 145.

ered thousands of followers, promised those who fell a return to Africa, and attacked Croix-des-Bouquets and Port-au-Prince. Halaou, also in the west, received the words of God through a white rooster which was carried, flapping, under his arm. He and a host of priests used long ox-tails to turn gunpowder to dust and deny the force of onrushing bullets.

These were valiant men for whom *vodum* provided a refuge, a rationalization, and a source of virtue capable of being transmitted to slaves determined to overthrow better-equipped and more experienced counter-revolutionaries. But as the slave insurrection gained stature and a collective rabble was transformed into a disciplined army, so *vodun* receded in importance. Toussaint L'Ouverture, the household slave who had become commander-in-chief of the freed armies by about 1794, refused to countenance *vodun*. In his eyes it perpetuated the kinds of ignorance and superstition which he, as a self-conscious modernizer, was bound to find anathema. Acculturated to French values and disdainful of the African heritage, he distrusted *vodun* and held in contempt the many *houngans* who led so many religiously excited men against the enemy. Toussaint, a leader who had risen rapidly and brutally from the ranks, knew the capacity of *vodun* to sway the masses. He feared its secrecy and its potential challenge to the state. "Quite often while fighting the British invader or the French, he had to divert some of his forces to destroy bands of dissidents led by Vodoun priests."[18] Even during those brief honeymoon years between the rise of Toussaint and Napoleon's attempted reconquest, *vodun* was attacked, *hounfours* destroyed, and worshipers punished. Toussaint, after all, was a centralizer, and *vodun* was the most decentralized and individualistic of religions. For Toussaint, Roman Catholicism was an ally, and both he and Jean-Jacques Dessalines, his angry successor and the first emperor of Haiti, tried to impose the foreign religion and its French priesthood on the seething mass which had supposedly freed itself from the oversight of all whites and foreigners. Toussaint prohibited dancing or nightly meetings. Dessalines ordered all followers of *vodun* shot on sight. (Yet he alone of the early leaders is now revered as a *loa*.) Presumably, they feared the spread of sedition, the

18. Bastien, "Vodoun and Politics," 49.

ROBERT I. ROTBERG

fomenting of new revolts, and *vodun*'s potential for focusing existing antagonisms against the state.

Bastien believes that the death of Henri Christophe in 1820 signified the triumph of *vodun*. Since Toussaint, Dessalines, and Christophe (although there is much ambiguity about the policies of the latter) had failed to eradicate *vodun* and impose Roman Catholicism in its stead (lacking a concordat with the Vatican, the priests in Haiti were few, irregular, and uninterested in the backwoods), their deaths were a signal for the resurgence of ritual and the proliferation of *houngans* and *hounfours*. From 1820, "no head of state had the same opportunity, resources, personality, or energy to launch a movement of national proportions to stamp out this apparent obstacle to the Europeanization of Haiti. Rather, the balance of power changed and rulers began to compromise with Vodoun instead of repressing it."[19]

Or did they care? Jean-Pierre Boyer (1820-1844) and many of his successors as president of Haiti were little interested in modernization. Like Alexandre Pétion, who ran southern Haiti during Christophe's reign in the north, Boyer and others were laissez-faire rulers. They avoided trouble whenever possible, and, so long as *vodun* presented no obvious challenge, were content to regard the religious pursuits of the masses with a certain equanimity. (The exception was President Jean-Baptiste Riché, a sixty-year-old illiterate black general who hated *vodun*. During his brief rule, from 1845 to 1847, he often followed the beat of distant drums to their source, personally pummeling worshipers with his heavy walking stick). Then too, from the time of Christophe almost to the era of Duvalier, Haitian governments ignored the countryside and scorned the preoccupations of their uneducated subjects.

It is often said that *vodun* kept Haiti backward. Probably the reverse is true: *vodun* flourished because the rulers of Haiti denied their multitudinous citizenry a chance to transform a socially and economically stagnant rural life. Poverty engulfed the Haitian subsistence farmer. His plots of land grew smaller and more fragmented as a result of generations of partible inheritance. As density increased, isolation from the main towns intensified and, we may assume, the importance of *vodun*

---

19. *Ibid.*, 50.

(particularly with the widespread absence of any effective Roman Catholic or Protestant missionary endeavors) to villagers grew naturally, even functionally.

But despite its unquestioned preeminence throughout the nineteenth century, *vodun* never again sought the political power that such a widespread system of worship and belief could—in another setting—have rightfully demanded and expected. The fiercely independent nature of its constituent parts inhibited any quest for power on a national level, and, given the minimal extent to which early Haitian governments administered their villages, *houngans* could exercise locally relevant power without reference to the established political hierarchy. Had national integration ever been imposed on Haiti, *vodun* might have emerged as a force to be reckoned with nationally. Instead, occasional charismatic presidents themselves tried to use *vodun* as a source of political support. Championing the otherwise reviled superstitions of the illiterate, they thereby broadened the base of political support. The effect was twofold; in the eyes of the urban elite, linking himself to the mysterious and poorly understood rites of the people gave a president a reservoir of power peculiarly Haitian. Then too, although most Haitians played almost no part in the routine political process, they were capable of being mobilized periodically in support of an insurrection or coup d'état. Presidential support of *vodun* could neutralize this threat.

Before Duvalier, only one Haitian despot made *vodun* politically his own. In 1847, when Riché died, the republic's Senate turned for a leader to Faustin Soulouque, an illiterate sixty-two-year-old black who headed the presidential guard. According to the older accounts of his reign, Soulouque was at first uninterested in politics and had no expectations of being summoned to high office.[20] But his qualities and, presumably, his ambitions were more advanced than these simple reports would indicate. He had a high reputation as a military commander under Boyer and Riché, and his last position would have afforded him a superb opportunity of appreciating the convoluted intrigues of Haitian political life. He was also a vain man whose modesty had never compelled him to refuse a

---

20. Dantès Bellegarde, *Histoire du Peuple Haitien (1492-1952)* (Port-au-Prince, 1953), 153.

ROBERT .I. ROTBERG

promotion. Yet it is still true that his robust character and innate shrewd-ness may have been underestimated by the "coterie which, having gov-erned pretty much the country through his predecessors, expected to find in him the easy tool or lay figure with which to work."[21] Like Duvalier so much later, an antipathy toward being manipulated impelled him to seek other sources of support. For political survival, it was essential that he gain independence from the predominantly mulatto ruling elite to whom he owed his new office. He purged the army and promoted men person-ally loyal. He reshuffled the cabinet, bringing in darker-skinned men who would be responsive to him alone. He established a secret police, and, as a forerunner of Duvalier's *tonton macoutes*, recruited the *zing-lins*, an informal paramilitary group which terrorized Port-au-Prince and participated in presidentially-ordered massacres in other sections of the country. Simultaneously, Soulouque openly promoted that which his predecessors had feared and scorned. MacLeod hints that Soulouque's wife may have urged him to tolerate *vodun*.[22]

But whatever his initial reasons, as the self-proclaimed protector of indigenous religion, Soulouque (who became the Emperor Faustin I in 1849) involved the city in the countryside for almost the first time, in turn developed a new and potent source of rural intelligence, and, con-ceivably consciously, created the kind of mass-based political founda-tions which were new to Haiti. A man from the people, the new emperor did more than most Haitian presidents to try to become a man of the peo-ple. Soulouque was also a nationalist at a time when the French were harassing Haiti and the Vatican and the United States were continuing to ignore it. *Vodun*, after all, was the national religion. Leyburn waxes grandiloquent: "As Soulouque had broken with the tradition of presi-dents who wished Haiti to be recognized as one of the community of civ-ilized Western nations, so he allowed the traditional respect for Catholi-cism to die. As an emperor he was a transplanted African chief; as a believer he was a follower of Vodun. The rites were practiced and the sacrifices made openly now. Men in high places dared to reveal their

---

21. Samuel Hazard, *Santo Domingo Past and Present* (New York, 1873), 427.
22. Murdo J. MacLeod, "The Soulouque Regime in Haiti, 1847-1859: A Reevalua-tion," *Caribbean Studies*, X (1970), 44.

belief in native tenets. For twelve years Vodun flourished with official approval."[23] A *houngan* on her way to prison told a foreign bystander not to fear for her life: "If I were to beat the sacred drum and march through the city, not one from the Emperor downwards but would humbly follow me."[24]

Leyburn, and MacLeod perhaps following him, assert that Soulouque legitimized *vodun*, his recognition welding the folk beliefs of Africa for the first time into a form comprehensible as a religion rather than a society dedicated to "vulgar claptrap" and secret, sensual dancing. But this is a misleading interpretation: *vodun*, the collective name for the worship of thousands of separate *hounfours* and the ministrations and leadership of thousands of jealous *hougans*, existed to be used or not used. Supple, passive, fragmented, it could provide rural assistants and foci of backwoods authority for a charismatic autocrat, but it could never be taken over as a closed system or incorporated institutionally. The ties between *houngan* and autocrat were, perforce, also direct. When the strong man departed, as Soulouque did as a result of a coup d'état in 1859, the lines of communication were sundered and new ones had to be created, from individual to individual.

Vodun did not again become a force on the national scene until the end of the American occupation. This is not to say that *vodun* failed to flourish. Everywhere fires burned on Saturday evening, rude rum was sipped by tired dancers, and women (and sometimes men) were ridden by their *loa*. There is some evidence that Sylvain Salnave, a dark northerner who was president from 1867 to 1869, consulted *houngans* and took part in a number of oathing ceremonies in order to buttress his slipping grip on Haiti's highest office. Antoine Simon, a peasant who was president from 1908 to 1911 and who had the misfortune to embroil himself and his countrymen with unscrupulous foreign concessionaries, may have permitted the rites of *vodun* to be performed within the national palace. His daughter was said to have been a *houngan* and to have participated in the sacrifice of humans. But although both heads of state may have consulted and looked to the mystery of *vodun* for support, there is

---

23. James G. Leyburn, *The Haitian People* (New Haven, 1966), 126.
24. Spenser St. John, *Hayti or the Black Republic* (London, 1889), 190.

ROBERT I. ROTBERG

no evidence that they managed to bring *vodun* back into the larger political arena. They, and the other twenty men who ruled Haiti from 1859 to 1915, may have refused to persecute the religion of the people, and may even have been staunch believers, but in other and more important respects their involvement was limited.

During this period *vodun* made no claims on politics. It resisted the periodic heavy-handed attempts of the Roman Catholic and Protestant churches to prohibit manifestations of *vodun* worship, and suffered silently (if at all) when a British diplomat with long experience in Haiti publicly linked *vodun* with the practice of human sacrifice and cannibalism. When the first edition of Sir Spenser St. John's *Hayti* appeared in 1884, it was heavily criticized in Port-au-Prince for exposing the seamier sides of Haiti's life to the obloquy of the antagonistic world. Sir Spenser's two chapters on *vodun* contained "attested" reports of lurid occult practices and hearsay evidence of human sacrifices connected with *vodun*.[25] (For it he claimed no political role.) These connections were all denied locally, and it is now clear that Sir Spenser—like so many other nineteenth-century observers—had an incomplete understanding of *vodun*. But no one denied that the religion existed, was healthy, and was thoroughly Haitian.

There was little political stability in Haiti from 1859 to 1915, and little in the way of economic development. Traditional society was untouched by the fingers of modernization. During most of this period, rural Haiti was in no respect governed. Almost the same can be asserted for the urban centers. But the practitioners of *vodun* do not seem to have tried to fill the resultant political vacuum. Content as before and since to operate parochially, they shunned the kinds of power which would have brought them into conflict with other institutions. A shadowy but nevertheless real existence sufficed. Even during the hated American occupation, and especially the anti-American *caco* war of 1918-1919, *vodun* played an essentially passive part. Many of the 40,000 *caco* troops who took the field against the U.S. Marines exuded a sense of invincibility because they had obtained *vodun* potions. Indeed, they at first proved far tougher than the Haitian gendarmerie, even daring to attack Port-au-

---

25. *Ibid.*, 187-257.

Prince. Marine reinforcements and air support were needed before the rebellion could be crushed. But no *houngans* led the *cacos*. There were no *vodun*-inspired revitalization movements. Individual priests manufactured protective amulets and tried to swing the gods in favor of their people. But, as a religion, *vodun* never opposed the occupation. Again passive, it preserved what little it had, and provided—especially when the authorities, prodded by the church, banned drumming and dancing in an attempt to stamp out "backwardness"—a refuge for the faith of a troubled people.

The Marine administration failed to change Haiti fundamentally. Its initiatives were politically and socially sterile. Nothing in the character of the occupation, except possibly its ultimate willingness to dissolve itself, and its emphasis upon probity and efficiency, altered the basic preconceptions of Haitian life. As tutors, the Americans reinforced a set of unfortunate and retrogressive stereotypes. They reemphasized the stigma of color and favored mulattoes over black members of the elite, thus reviving class antagonisms. But most of all, by unambiguously stressing the worthlessness of men of color and black religious pursuits, they unwittingly helped bring about an intellectual renaissance among Haitians which ultimately was to make *vodun* respectable and revered as the authentic religion of the people.[26] Increased educational opportunities, a general broadening of horizons, a renewed appreciation of Africa, and the spread of notions of *négritude* from Guadeloupe, Martinique, and Paris, all stimulated this renaissance. Its proponents sought authenticity and, whatever their color, began to realize that in the masses, and in the religion of the majority of Haitians, lay their salvation. Jean Price-Mars, a physician and civil servant, gave lectures in 1920 and 1923 which were published in 1928 as *Ainsi Parla l'Oncle: Essais d'Ethnographie*. A pioneering examination of the life of the rural population of the republic, it proved surprisingly influential. Price-Mars urged his countrymen to cease denying their African heritage.

Shortly before the publication of these essays Jacques B. Roumain, a wealthy young mulatto, joined six or seven other educated Haitians in founding a journal which would foster the rediscovery of *vodun* and the

---

26. Rotberg, *Haiti*, 144-145.

other contributions of Africa to Haiti. Roumain also wrote a number of novels, the first of which appeared in 1930, celebrating the folkways of Haiti's citizens. Within a few years there were many blacks and mulattoes busily collecting information about Haitian customs and their presumed origins, and using prose and poetry to glorify their discoveries. A contemporary has called their efforts "emotional ethnography, at times frankly mystical, written in a rococo style and showing little or no capacity to grasp the overall problem" of Haiti, but for most elite Haitians the case had to be overstated if it were to be made at all.[27]

Among the many young professionals influenced by this case were those, of whom François Duvalier was one, who popularized their ideas in a weekly review called *Les Griots* and a journal of the same name. They concerned themselves with *vodun*, and Duvalier wrote for them all when he praised its authenticity. In addition to contributing to the achievement of national independence, *vodun* was "the supreme factor of the unity of Haiti." It "came to crystallize, in the dynamism of its cultural manifestations, the past of the African on native soil, his martyrdom in the colonial hell, and the heroism of the knights in realizing the miracle of 1804. And as this religion is a constant creation, it sublimates, in its perpetuation through generations, the tragedy of . . . the Haitian masses." Moreover, the rural masses with their *vodun*, which epitomized the psychology of a forgotten continent, constituted the authentic population of the state. They embodied "humanism," a concept which encapsulated and affirmed the dignity of man, took account of his original grandeur, implied the possibility of man's perfection, and found its fullest flowering in individualism.[28]

Duvalier may have romanticized *vodun*, but he never underestimated its grip on the minds of most Haitians or ignored its very real political potential. He was not ignorant of his country's history, and may have made a particular study of Soulouque. Most of all, he had a knowledge of the occult which he deployed and displayed to impress *houngans*

---

27. Rémy Bastien, "The Role of the Intellectual in Haitian Plural Society," *Annals of the New York Academy of Sciences*, LXXXIII (1960), 846.

28. François Duvalier, "L'évolution stadiale du vodou" (1944), in *Oeuvres essentielles* (Port-au-Prince, 1968), I, 173; *idem*, "Pour un humanisme totalitaire" (1939), *ibid.*, 118.

and overawe his peers and the great mass of Haitians. Dressing somberly, with a gray homburg on his head, round spectacles, and a sickly smile, and speaking deliberately, he imparted an aura which reminded many of Baron Samedi, the master of cemeteries and lord of *zombies*. During his years as a rural physician, a member of a yaws eradication team, and as a traveling cabinet minister under President Dumarsais Estimé, he—unlike most Haitian politicians—became acquainted with the needs and beliefs of common Haitians. From his reading and his experience he would have understood the political uses to which the social power of the *houngans* could be put.

If there had ever been free elections in Haiti, the *houngans* would have been accustomed to deliver the parish vote. But in circumstances where governments refrained from governing, and most *houngans* managed to retain their independence and their power—providing they had *connaissance*—the *houngans* had not had or wanted to flex their political muscles. They successfully fought against the Catholic-sponsored massive anti-*vodun* purge of the early 1940s, and were henceforth treated as an ineradicable, quasi-respectable, uncontrollable, rural religious factor. Under the presidency of General Paul Magloire during the middle 1950s, *vodun* was promoted as a useful tourist attraction.

But Duvalier had loftier purposes in mind. A compromise president who gained power as a supposedly moderate, well-intentioned, middle-class intellectual with friends in the army and an understanding of the needs of the rural masses, Duvalier knew the fragility of his position. Magloire, like so many previous Haitian presidents, had been toppled from the pinnacle of power when one or more interest groups perceived that the spoils of office were being shared unfairly. It was essential to Duvalier's grand personal design[29] that he remain in power, and, emerging for the first time as a consummate political tactician, he knew that staying in power meant subordinating to his will all potential institutional or informal foci of opposition. The army was purged once, then a second time and a third time yet again. The bicameral legislature was converted into a single chamber, and the rights and duties of the deputies

---

29. See the chapter entitled "The Personalization of Power" in Rotberg, *Haiti*, 197-258.

were limited forcibly. The judiciary was easily cowed. Foreigners were insulted. The Catholic church and then the Anglican church were attacked, priests, bishops, and archbishops deported, a papal excommunication defied, and the hierarchy made subservient to the divine demands of Duvalier. Student strikes were crushed. The *tonton macoutes* were created as a direct military arm of the master. They could carry out specific assassinations or a program of random terror—the more effective for being capricious. The *macoutes* could extort, hassle, and kill. And there was never any redress. Equally important, Duvalier gained the kind of control over *vodun* which no one before had ever managed. He gave cooperative *houngans* special privileges, small incomes, and made some *chefs de section* (district commissioners) or local *macoute* leaders. He became the first chief *houngan* of Haiti—his mysterious manner, deviousness of mind, and ability to evoke the superstitions of his countrymen, along with his sheer power, gaining him legitimacy. Obstinate *houngans* were eliminated. The *houngans* supplied him with intelligence and loyalty, and the unsophisticated—and even some of the supposed sophisticates—credited him with malevolent powers of second sight. Without tampering with the parochial rituals of *vodun* or altering religious practices, from it he absorbed power and gained significant personal stature.

Whether or not Duvalier believed in *vodun*, he used it. He made himself the master of age-old ceremonies. The demonic energy of a thousand *loa* was his. Did he bathe himself in blood? Did he spend the nights brooding naked in the basement of the palace? Did he stare stonily at his cabinet ministers and thereby glean their innermost thoughts and read their future intentions? The facts are less important than the knowledge that the people (and cabinet ministers) believed that he did these things and thus had power over the occult and over them.

Within months of his accession, Duvalier was successfully exploiting the credibility of Haitians for political purposes. For example, in 1959 Clément Jumelle, who had opposed Duvalier in 1957 and spent twenty-one months in hiding in peasant huts and holes in the ground, staggered, gravely ill with uremia, into the Cuban Embassy and died. *Vodun* demands the proper interment of the dead so that the spirits will not wander or be put to illegitimate use. Jumelle's family tried to give him a decent burial, but as the coffin started out toward its last resting place, *macoutes* forcibly hijacked the hearse, sped north to St. Marc, and disposed of poor Jumelle.[30] Why would Duvalier interfere? Believers in *vodun* immediately knew that the great president planned to transform Jumelle into a *zombi* and use him and his essential organs in order magically to strengthen the dictatorship. Equally bizarre is the explanation for the power that Clément Barbot, Duvalier's first secret police chief, exerted over the dictator until he was outlawed, hunted, and killed in 1963. Barbot had taken the precaution to disinter the skull of Duvalier's father from its resting place in the main Port-au-Prince cemetery. With it he made an *ouanga*, or fetish and—until his death—could thus exert some magical control over his ruler.

Duvalier became the head of a sociopolitical institution of immediate relevance to the bulk of his people. No other Haitian institution could have claimed such a hold, and Duvalier was able to subvert it to his ends providing those ends did not interfere with, and even strengthened, the autonomy of the individual *hounfours*. Each used the other, but as Duvalier possessed an overarching design and the *houngans* had limited, easily satisfied goals, the degree of compatibility was circumscribed. *Vodun* was the original instrument of social control in the Haitian countryside. Under Duvalier, this sociological abstraction was given a pragmatic dimension without which invasions, internal opposition, revolutionary movements, and widespread disaffection might all have proved real threats to the stability of the dictatorship. The sanctity of *vodun* gave Duvalier the kind of legitimacy which he could never have achieved on his own, as a traditional Haitian despot. By embracing *vodun*, Duvalier entered the heart of rural Haiti. There the terror of the towns was unnecessary; the mystery of *vodun* incorporated terror and Duvalier was the chief *houngan*. He was theirs and they his—at least for all of the political purposes which mattered.

Vodun is resilient. Without Duvalier, as without Soulouque, its links to the state will fade away. Its small, secure, parochial base of power will remain until that distant day when modernization—if it ever comes to innermost Haiti—erodes the very foundations of a protective security-giving cognitive universe.

---

30. This incident provided the basis for the interrupted funeral in Graham Greene, *The Comedians* (Harmondsworth, 1967), 119-126. The fullest account of the actual incident is in the *Haiti Herald*, April 19, 1959.

13 Adele Simmons

Class or Communalism?
A Study of the Politics of
Creoles in Mauritius

Curtin has developed a profile of the Atlantic slave trade;[1] no such record presently exists for the Indian Ocean trade. We cannot document how many people were taken from African ports to the variety of Indian Ocean ports; however, we can begin to piece together a history of the African slaves once they landed. This chapter will consider some aspects of the political development of the African or "creole" community on the island of Mauritius.[2]

While members of the creole community participated as individuals in Mauritian politics in the nineteenth century, creoles did not become active as a community in politics until the twentieth century. Precisely because the creole community is the most heterogeneous of the five ethnic and/or religious communities of the island, it has been the most politically divided. Occasionally the creole community has united to support creole causes; generally, however, the community has divided along class lines. In either situation, the creole community, which since 1900 has constituted approximately 25 to 30 percent of the Mauritian population, has not been able to have a decisive influence at the polls. However, individual creole leaders have become major political figures on the island and have had an influence that has extended beyond the bounds of their own community.

---

1. Philip Curtin, *The Atlantic Slave Trade* (Madison, 1969).
2. The term creole, which in some French colonies referred to a Frenchman born in the colonies, in Mauritius originally referred to the lower classes of the colored population. Today it is used more freely to refer to all those who are mulatto or black. I shall follow this usage.

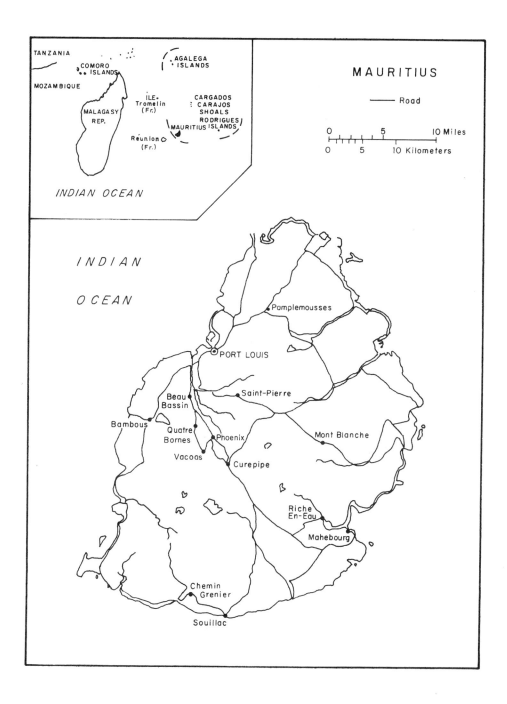

ADELE SIMMONS

Mauritius: The Plural Society

Over 800,000 people, representing four ethnic and five religious communities, are crowded into the 720 square miles of the island of Mauritius. Once uninhabited, Mauritius is now one of the most densely populated countries of the world, with 1,100 people per square mile. Since the eighteenth century, sugar has been the main source of income for the island. Today 46 percent of the island's area, representing 90 percent of the arable land, is planted with sugar; sugar constitutes 90 percent of Mauritius' exports, and nearly half of the labor force works in the sugar industry.

Dutch efforts to settle Mauritius in the sixteenth century failed. The first successful settlements were French. The present creole community in Mauritius, then, is descended from the several thousand slaves imported by the French to build houses, clear and cultivate the plateau, and man the privateering ships. During the Napoleonic Wars, Mauritius was captured by the British and transferred to the British crown; when the British abolished slavery in their colonies in the 1830s approximately 76,000 Mauritian slaves were freed.

Between 1834 and 1900, 420,000 indentured laborers were imported from India to replace the slaves. In their wake came traders from Muslim regions in India as well as from China. As the table below shows, the largest population group in Mauritius today is Indo-Mauritian. Three-quarters of the Indo-Mauritians, and just over half the total population of the island, are Hindu; 23 percent of the Indo-Mauritians are Muslim, and 2 percent are Christian. However, the term Indian usually refers to those Indo-Mauritians who are not Muslim. Three percent of the total population is Chinese.

Hindu	437,365
General population (of European descent and mixed African descent)	230,465
Muslim	137,760
Chinese	24,990
Total:	830,580

Source: Mauritian Government, 1970 Census, Port Louis, 1971.

The census takers, aware of the difficulties of drawing a line between creoles and Franco-Mauritians, lump these two Catholic groups together into the "general population." But only 2 percent of the general population is Franco-Mauritian; the rest, nearly 28 percent of the population of the island, is creole.

As in many plural societies, the population is divided by class as well as community.[3] Until recently, class divisions coincided with communal divisions. Until the mid-1950s the Franco-Mauritians were the dominant community both politically and economically. The creoles were next in line and the Indians were at the bottom. The Chinese and the Muslims—the shopkeepers, traders, and importers of the island—were generally outside of the class system of the island and only became active in politics as communities in the 1950s. In the last twenty-five years, the Indian population had acquired both wealth and political power, so that class lines no longer coincide with ethnicity.

As important as divisions between communities are the stratifications within each community, yet until recently Mauritians had little understanding of the class and social differences within each community.

The Creoles

The creole community is the most diverse and, as a result, the most factionalized community in Mauritius today. While creoles can be found in nearly every job on the economic ladder,[4] the stratification resulting from differences in color, education, and wealth impedes mobility within the community.[5] The creole fishermen and dockers at the bottom of the social and economic hierarchy generally have a darker skin than the creole urban middle class who are clerks and civil servants.

---

3. I have followed the Mauritian practice of using the words "community" and "communal" to describe ethnic, religious, and/or cultural groups that usually act as a political unit. For a further discussion of the theory of pluralism see J. S. Furnivall, *Colonial Policy and Practice* (New York, 1956); Clifford Geertz (ed.), *Old Societies and New States* (New York, 1963); M. G. Smith, *The Plural Society in the British West Indies* (Berkeley, 1965); Leo Kuper and M. G. Smith, *Pluralism in Africa* (Berkeley, 1969).

4. The only occupation creoles consistently avoid is that of cane cutter. In a homicide case it was argued that the accused creole could not have been guilty because the murder weapon was a *pioche*, a scythe for cutting cane. The defendant argued that a creole would not be likely to use such a weapon.

5. Smith, *Plural Society*, 308.

ADELE SIMMONS

The divisions on the basis of color within the creole community have a historical origin. Those in the light-skinned elite are descended from slaves who were freed before the emancipation in 1835. Most of the darker creoles are descended from slaves who were freed by law in 1835.

The French imported their slaves from the east coast of Africa and from Madagascar. They treated them harshly, and the British administrators failed to bring about any improvement in the treatment of slaves.[6] While Parliament abolished the slave trade in 1807 and the law was extended to Mauritius in 1813, the slave trade continued, sanctioned by the British administrators on Mauritius who were anxious to avoid antagonizing the Franco-Mauritian community. A minor and ill-fated revolt in the 1820s is the only recorded organized protest on the part of the slaves.

On January 17, 1835, Governor Sir William Nicolay freed the slaves,[7] who then constituted nearly three-fourths of the total population.[8] The freed slaves were required to work as apprentices for six years, but this period was reduced to four, and in 1839 the slaves left the plantations to seek an independent life. Their descendants claim that they would have stayed on the plantations had they been offered adequate wages.[9] For whatever reasons, the slaves scattered so quickly and so completely that by 1872 "they had disappeared from agricultural labour, from the precincts of the plantations, from any contact with the whites."[10] Some began new settlements on the plateau; others went to the coast to become fishermen; others stayed near the plantations to become skilled craftsmen; and still others went to Port Louis to work as dockers. By

---

6. James Stephen, permanent law officer in the Colonial Office, was distressed that one governor, Sir Lowry Cole, failed to prohibit the use of chains, fetters, and collars for punishment. Stephen reluctantly concluded that Cole and his council were unfit "to legislate at all on any subject connected with the condition of the slave population" (Vincent Harlow and Frederick Madden, *British Colonial Developments 1774-1883* [Oxford, 1953], 577-578).

7. The planters received a little more than £ 2 million in compensation out of a total of £ 20 million distributed throughout the colonies.

8. In 1835 there were 24,695 free men and 76,774 slaves (P. J. Barnwell and Auguste Toussaint, *A Short History of Mauritius* [London, 1949], 159).

9. Raymond Smith suggests that the slaves would have stayed on the plantations in British Guiana if the planters had been willing to pay them (Raymond Smith, *British Guiana* [London, 1962], 43).

10. *Report of the Royal Commissioners Appointed to Enquire into Treatment of Immigrants in Mauritius*, C 115 (London, 1875), 20.

1900 many had managed to obtain an education and perhaps a job as a teacher or a civil servant, forming the core of the growing creole middle class. But in 1835, the newly freed slaves were at the bottom of the social and economic hierarchy. They were politically inarticulate and seldom a focus for the concern of colonial administrators or sugar planters. For these groups, Indian immigration was the primary issue. Between 1835 and 1910, official correspondence, Royal Commissions, and local newspapers discussed conditions for immigration, the status of Indian immigrants, and the problems on sugar estates. The creoles and their problems were rarely mentioned.

Wedged between the slaves and the Franco-Mauritians in the hierarchy were the light-skinned "free coloreds," the creole elite. Members of the creole elite rarely mixed socially with the Franco-Mauritians; but they sat in the Colonial Assembly which was established during the French Revolution, and were equal before the law until 1803. At this time Governor Charles Decaen issued laws designed to separate free coloreds from whites.[11] The British legally abolished the color bar in 1829, and the Royal College, then the only secondary school in Mauritius, admitted its first creole students shortly afterwards. In 1830, five years before the emancipation of the slaves, there were 18,019 "free coloreds" in Mauritius and only 8,135 whites.[12]

This large colored community grew from liaisons between French settlers and their slaves. The French father freed his child, but did not accept him into his family. The child, for his part, sought to become a part of the European community.[13] The creoles began to adopt the customs and the habits of the Franco-Mauritian community from which they were excluded; their goals became a white skin, wealth, and a classical education. Slavery had left them without language or traditions so, like the creoles in other countries, they acquired the customs of the most

---

11. Burton Benedict, *Indians in a Plural Society* (London, 1961), 14.
12. Barnwell and Toussaint, *Mauritius*, 225.
13. For a discussion of a similar phenomenon in the West Indies, see Douglas Hall, "Slaves and Slavery in the British West Indies," *Social and Economic Studies*, XI (1962), 305-318.

ADELE SIMMONS

prestigious and influential community.[14] While the Jamaican creole looked at the world through British eyes, the Mauritian creole adopted the Franco-Mauritian politics on the Franco-Mauritians' terms, seeking a constituency within the Franco-Mauritian community. Many were highly educated and occupied important positions in society and government, becoming Franco-Mauritians in all but color.[15]

Most prominent creoles at the end of the nineteenth century were political conservatives. Distinguished lawyers, journalists, and literary figures, they rested their claim to participate in government on their European culture. This elite, in Mauritius as well as in the West Indies, was rarely more sympathetic than the Europeans to the plight of the creole lower classes or the Indian indentured laborers. Jealous of their position, they were careful to avoid associating with or even admitting knowledge of the creole lower classes. They were often rewarded with honors, decorations, and knighthoods from the British crown. The first Mauritian K.C.M.G. was a creole.

The role of the creole elite in the Reform Movement of 1881-1886 exemplifies the attitudes and position of this group in the nineteenth century. In 1881, the creole elite joined with the Franco-Mauritians to oppose efforts of the British administration to try to enforce an old French regulation limiting ownership of land on the sides of streams. Three of the most prominent leaders of the movement were creole: Laurent Louis Raoul, then president of the Chamber of Notaries, Sir Virgile Naz, who was both an articulate lawyer and a wealthy landowner, and Sir William Newton, who had been legal advisor to the Chamber of Agri-

---

14. Smith, *Plural Society*, 5. Similarly, in the West Indies the goal of the creole elite was to become a part of the dominant European oligarchy. The creoles of the West Indies and Sierra Leone copied their British rulers. According to Martin Kilson, "this acculturation, in turn, minimized the apprehension of the colonial oligarchy over granting political concessions to articulate African interests." In Mauritius, where the creoles identified with the Franco-Mauritians, the British were less enthusiastic about incorporating them into the political system (Lloyd Braithwaite, "Social Stratification and Cultural Pluralism in the Caribbean," *Annals of the New York Academy of Sciences*, LXXXIII [1960], 816-831; Martin Kilson, *Political Change in a West African State* [Cambridge, Mass., 1966], 101).

15. For a discussion of the same phenomenon in British Guiana see Smith, *British Guiana*, 42; E. F. L. Wood, *Visit to the West Indies and British Guiana*, Cmd. 1679 (London, 1923), 6.

culture. Two of the three had been nominated by the governor to serve on the Council of Government. Two of the three had given evidence on behalf of the planters before the 1872 commission investigating the conditions of the Indian laborers.

The members of the Reform Movement believed that the nominated members of the Council of Government were not in a position adequately to represent their interests. For this reason, they sought constitutional change that would allow them to elect their own representatives to the Council of Government. After considerable hesitation, the secretary of state agreed to permit Mauritians to elect ten representatives to the council, one short of an unofficial majority. The secretary of state, however, designated a wider franchise than the more conservative members of the Reform Movement, including the creoles, wanted. In this case, the creole leadership was not seeking social change or additional rights and privileges for the entire creole community. Rather the creole elite, who were the only creoles to have a political voice in the nineteenth century, sought to protect the interests of the Mauritian elite—creole and Franco-Mauritian. Their primary concern was that the colonial government, through laws governing the use of land and the rights of laborers, would undermine the economic and social position of the sugar planters.

Descendants of these creole leaders remained closely tied to the Franco-Mauritian community, but in the twentieth century a number of younger creoles, who were not part of the traditional elite, became active in politics and worked to gain greater participation of the creole community as a whole in politics. The social and economic divisions within the community have been so sharp that, except during a brief period between 1907 and 1911, the creoles failed to act as a political unit until 1963, when the threat of Indian domination, which was seen as the inevitable result of independence, forced creoles to overcome their divisions and work for the Parti Mauricien, the party that opposed independence.

If the various creole interest groups since the 1880s have had any single goal, it was to assure creole participation in the political system and by so doing to prevent one of the other communities—the Franco-Mauritians or the Indians—from dominating the politics of the island. The importance of retaining a position of political power was underlined during the process of decolonization in the 1950s and early 1960s. During these years crucial decisions about the composition of the legislature, electoral procedures, and the franchise were made. In addition, the economic problems of the island, particularly unemployment, became acute. Yet at this time the basis for creole political power became increasingly tenuous. The creole community, constituting 28 percent of the population, could not have the voting power of the Indians, who composed the majority of the Mauritian population. Nor did the creoles have the economic power of the Franco-Mauritians, or even the Muslims. They were neither traders nor landowners. Rather than creoles, it was the Indians, descendants of the indentured laborers, who acquired land from the 1890s on and became the island's second largest landholding community. The creoles for the most part were salaried employees, and usually civil servants. Since the government is the island's largest single employer, access to jobs in the government, often through patronage, was important to the creoles.

The political power of the creoles was consistently greater than their numbers or status might suggest. The creole population was generally concentrated in Port Louis and the towns. Thus the creoles regularly controlled the influential Municipal Council of Port Louis, and when town councils were introduced in Rose Hill—Beau Bassin, Curepipe, and Vacoas—the creoles were fairly certain of controlling these councils. With municipal and town council control went a number of patronage jobs, important decisions about taxes, and a chance to make a name in politics. In addition, the creole community produced a number of political leaders whose charismatic qualities helped to extend the influence of the creole leadership beyond the community. And finally, creoles had a reputation for being the community that drank the most, and the most easily provoked to violence. In a place as small as Mauritius, the threat of violence is a strong political weapon.

Although creoles might have agreed about the goals of the community, they disagreed about how to achieve those goals. Some leaders advocated alliance with the Indian laborers; others opted for alliance with the economically powerful Franco-Mauritians. Mistrust among the creole leaders was significant. It is easy to understand why Guy Rozemont, the leader of the dockers and the cane cutters in the 1940s, did not have the same political program as Raoul Rivet, intellectual, bon vivant, and literary figure. But it is harder to understand why Dr. Maurice Curé and Dr.

Edgar Millien, who both promoted programs to benefit the workers in the 1940s, could not coordinate their efforts, or why Harold Walter and Gaeten Duval, both of whom were trained as lawyers and professed interest in the problems of workers, joined different parties and paid agents to spy on each other. In so small a political community, the differences between factions that are tolerated within one political party in larger countries become sharper and often require resolution.

The restricted size of Mauritius affects the nature of politics in the island. Until the advent of television, political happenings were the chief form of entertainment. Mauritians would travel for hours from one end of the island to another to participate in a large political rally, not necessarily out of burning desire to support one candidate or another but because the political rallies were among the few events on the island. Market day was enhanced in any village by the presence of political figures. By 1874, there were some eight daily newspapers on the island, and political issues filled most of their columns.

The description of the three twentieth-century political movements that follows illustrates the political dynamics within the creole community and between the creoles and other communities.

Retrocession and the Creole Elite

Between World War I and 1936, creole politics was the province of the creole elite. During this period, the creole professionals learned through experience that there were not enough registered creole voters to force political reform in Mauritius and that the creole community would have to rely on political alliances with other communities to protect its interests. The failure of the Retrocession Movement in 1919 underscored the limitations of the creole elite as a political force in the island. In 1919, the creole professionals organized a political movement without the support of the creole lower classes or other communities. While they expected Franco-Mauritian support they failed to recognize that the primary goals of the Franco-Mauritian community—a high price for sugar and political power—precluded such support.

Inspired by President Wilson's principle of self-determination, a group of young creoles, mostly professionals, became convinced that

ADELE SIMMONS

Mauritius should again become a French colony.[16] French was still the dominant language on the island and French customs and the French way of life were very much in evidence. Most of the creole community was Catholic.

But there was more than emotional sympathy for France behind the move for retrocession. The retrocessionists felt that Britain had ignored Mauritius during the war, and they illogically assumed that France would not have done so. During the war creole Mauritians had been to South Africa and been shocked by the low status accorded to the African population. Segregation contrasted with assimilation in neighboring French Réunion. There, universal suffrage ensured that the colored community had political power.[17] Creoles from Réunion served as deputies in the French Assembly. After a century of British rule, Mauritian creoles had learned that although equal before the law they were not in fact equal in any other respect to the Franco-Mauritian elite or the British administrators. As the governor, Sir Hesketh Bell, pointed out, in Mauritius creoles were "British *subjects*. In Réunion they would be French citizens."[18]

The creoles were also anxious about the Indians. They saw an increasing number of Indians becoming small planters and professionals, and realized that the Indian majority could one day dominate the politics and economics of the island. The people who would suffer, as Governor Charles Bruce had said in 1900, would be the colored community, which would be pushed out of jobs.[19] If Mauritius became French, it would unite with Madagascar and Réunion. Such a federation would turn the Indian majority into a minority and offered the only hope of obtaining political power for the creoles in Mauritius.

The retrocession leaders were mostly young colored professionals

16. Retrocession to France was not a new idea. Ever since the British abolished the slave trade and finally slavery itself in Mauritius, some Franco-Mauritians had talked of returning the island to France. Sir Arthur Hamilton Gordon suggested exchanging Mauritius for French trading posts in India in the 1870s.

17. Colonial Office 167/833: Sir Hesketh Bell, Governor, to Viscount Milner, Secretary of State, July 20, 1920.

18. C.O. 822/11, no. 148, 4: Bell to Thomas, February 28, 1924; see also C.O. 167/826: J. Middleton, Acting Governor, to Milner, April 19, 1921.

19. C.O. 882/6, no. 78, 8: Governor Charles Bruce to Joseph Chamberlain, June 25, 1900.

who had had experience outside Mauritius. Among the early promoters was Edouard Laurent, a Réunionais who in 1914 published *L'Ile Maurice entre la France et l'Angleterre*.[20] Another early retrocessionist was Dr. Edgar Laurent. When he left Mauritius, Laurent was, according to Governor Bell, a member of the Indian community with the family name of Rambojan. After obtaining a medical degree from Montpelier University, he returned to Mauritius with the creole name of Laurent and from then on identified himself with the creole community.[21] Although a Protestant, Laurent was deeply immersed in French culture and firmly believed that Mauritians, especially colored Mauritians, would have a better life under French rule.

The Retrocession Movement was just gathering momentum when Curé, who was later to found the Mauritius Labour Party, returned from his medical studies in London. During the war, when he was in England, he had offered his services to the British army but had been turned away because of his color. By 1918, he had established a name for himself in Mauritius as a doctor and was looking for an entrée into the political life of the island. Another young creole, who, like Curé, began a long and prominent political career in the retrocession movement, was Raoul Rivet. Using the anagram Tevir, Rivet wrote editorials for *Le Mauricien*, one of the island's four daily newspapers, to support retrocession.[22]

Two months after their program became public, it was clear to the retrocessionists that they would have to rely on creole support exclusively. The Franco-Mauritians would not support them. First, India and Britain were their best markets for sugar; the prices that Britain was offering for sugar were high and going up. Secondly, the Franco-Mauritians feared that the French might grant universal suffrage to Mauritius and thus the Franco-Mauritian elite would lose the control over the island's affairs which it had been exercising for so many years. The gover-

---

20. Edouard Laurent, *L'Ile Maurice entre la France et l'Angleterre* (Paris, 1914).

21. C.O. 882/11, no. 148: Bell to Thomas, February 28, 1924. Although Mauritians frequently changed communities by changing names, this fact in the case of Laurent is disputed. Bell is confident of it, but Laurent's descendants dispute it, claiming that Laurent's father was called Jean Rodolphe Laurent.

22. The others were *Croix et Patrie*, *Le Vrai Progrès Colonial*, and *Le Journal de Maurice*.

nor felt that Franco-Mauritians would have supported retrocession "if a transfer to the French flag did not connote the Republic system of Government, universal suffrage, and the consequent preponderance of coloured influence in the colony."[23]

In spite of attempts of the retrocessionists to woo the Indian community, most Indians condemned retrocession as a plot to prevent Mauritius from being annexed to India and thus to prevent Indians from taking part in the Council of Government. They feared that under French rule the Franco-Mauritians and the colored elite would assume greater control of the island's affairs at the expense of the Indians.[24]

The Colonial Office understandably took a dim view of the retrocessionists. In July 1919, John Middleton, the officer administering the government, assured the members of the council that "Mauritius will remain a cherished part of the Empire." In 1920, Governor Bell, whose fluent French made him popular with the Franco-Mauritians, repeated that Mauritius was, and would remain, British and that he "trusted, therefore, that a movement for the impractical object and which would bring nothing but discord and dissension among the people [would] be abandoned."[25] According to Bell, the retrocessionists were "malcontent and mischievous individuals."[26] Bell considered deporting Curé, but instead decided to ensure a strong British presence in the island at election time. As the day for the poll approached, a British cruiser, H.M.S. *Comus*, appeared in the Port Louis harbor and her crew paraded through the streets. In spite of the apparent strength of the retrocessionist newspapers, the vote was decisive. Not one retrocessionist candidate was elected.

Looking back several years later, the staunchest retrocessionists considered the whole campaign a farce. Creole intellectuals and professionals struggling to be free from the domination of the Franco-Mauritian planters dreamed that France could bring *liberté, fraternité, égalité* to Mauritius. But it was just a dream. Like most political organizations in Mauritius, particularly until 1936, the Retrocession Movement was formed by a group of friends who had not carefully thought out the im-

23. C.O. 882/11, no. 148, 4: Bell to Thomas, February 28, 1924.
24. *Croix et Patrie*, January 8 and 9, 1921.
25. *Debates*, Mauritius Council of Government, July 27, 1920, 69.
26. C.O. 167/833: Bell to Milner, November 22, 1920.

plications of their program. Retrocession had a romantic appeal, and provided a means for the growing creole intellectual class to express their cultural and emotional loyalty to France, as well as an opportunity for them to suggest to the colonial government that they would in the future demand a greater part in the island's politics.

Retrocession as a policy had the active support of the intellectuals only. The creole dockers and artisans did not have the franchise, and their links with French intellectual circles were far more tenuous than those of the creole elite. If the creole elite had chosen a political issue of greater importance to the creole lower classes, they still would not have won at the polls. But they might have laid a basis for communal loyalty. The failure of the Retrocession Movement made it clear to the creole leadership that they did not have a sufficient political base to determine an important national issue. The 1921 national election emphasized their dependence upon forming alliances with other groups. With the exception of Duval in 1963, creole political leaders since 1921 have talked openly about their need for non-creole support. However, they have disagreed with each other about the source of support. The elite remained tied to the Franco-Mauritians. While they resented the exclusive nature of the Franco-Mauritian community, culturally and economically, they had far more in common with the Franco-Mauritians than with the Indians. A second group of creole political leaders turned to the disenfranchised and poorly paid, seeking support among the creole lower classes and the Indian community. Efforts to reach beyond the creole community for a constituency, then, often led to a division within the community on the basis of class.

The Labour Party: A Class Alliance

Between 1936 and 1952, the Labour Party was an alliance of creoles and Indians working to improve the political, social, and economic conditions of laborers in Mauritius. Although creoles dominated the party leadership, Indians were on the Executive Committee. The party membership, which fluctuated in the 1930s and 1940s between several hundred and 20,000, included both Indian cane cutters and creole laborers. In the 1930s when the party was formed, Mauritian laborers were among the lowest paid in the British colonies; at the same time they were more

ADELE SIMMONS

heavily taxed than any other economic class on the island.[27] Petitions to the governor, the crown, and the International Labour Organization failed to produce action. Peaceful protest meetings were no more successful. Excluded from the political process, ignored by the planters, and provided with only token assistance from the Poor Law Office, the laborers eventually understood that only violence would bring their plight to the attention of the colonial authorities.

The leader of the Labour Party was Curé, who became aware of the conditions on the estates through his medical practice, and who was still seeking an entrée into Mauritian politics. He was assisted by another creole, Emmanuel Anquetil, who had spent twenty-five years in England during which he assisted in the organization of the local branch of the National Union of Shipwrights. Embittered by his experiences abroad, where he felt he was often "victimized because of the colour of [his] skin," Anquetil determined to use his experience to help Mauritian labourers.[28]

With Anquetil and Pandit Sahadeo, an Indian and a follower of Gandhi, Curé toured Mauritius and spoke to small groups of laborers about the need for constitutional reform, trade union legislation, better housing and medical facilities, minimum wage and maximum hours, old age pensions, and regulations ensuring a fair price for the sugar that small Indian planters grew and sold to the large estates with mills. These were the concerns of a class, not of a community. However, the governor, Sir Wilfrid Jackson, failed to see this distinction and continued to perceive politics in Mauritius as a communal affair. Because the Labour Party leadership was creole, the governor did not expect the party to gain Indian support. Rather he felt that Curé "must not be regarded as representing the sentiment of any large section of the population,"[29] and believed that the creole community, which was "the more educated and more politically minded class as compared with the Indian section," would oppose a wide extension of the franchise.[30] He correctly stated the

---

27. *Financial Situation of Mauritius: Report of a Commission Appointed by the Secretary of State for the Colonies*, Cmd. 4034 (London, 1932), 208.

28. *Le Mauricien*, November 30, 1937.

29. C.O. 167/890, file 57004: Sir Wilfrid Jackson to Thomas, March 16, 1936.

30. C.O. 167/897, file 57227: Jackson to Ormsby-Gore, May 27, 1937.

views of the creole elite with whom he had regular contact. But he did not understand how divided this elite was from the creole labourers. Perhaps because the situation in Mauritius resembled that in so many other colonies in the 1930s, officials in the Colonial Office understood the dynamics of the Mauritian situation better than the governor. One of these officials noted in 1937:

> My own instinct is that if we are to avoid storms, we ought to set our political course a few points to the left. The situation of the working classes is deplorable. The white planters are excessively ancien regime.[31]

But it was too late. In August 1937, eighteen months after the Mauritius Labour Party had been formed, small planters and laborers joined together to strike against the estates. Cane fields burned in all sections of the island, and riots on three estates, one of which was owned by an Indian, resulted in six deaths. For the first time since 1911, political activity resulted in loss of life.

The violence of the 1937 riots led to a commission of inquiry chaired by the procureur général, C. A. Hooper. In its report, the commission absolved Curé of responsibility for the strikes and found most of the complaints of the laborers and small planters justified.[32] Following the publication of the Hooper report, the government began to implement the recommendations for political, economic, and social reform. The governor appointed two representatives of the small planters to the Legislative Council, but refused to appoint a laborer.[33] Committees of representatives of the estates and small planters were formed to regulate the payment for canes to small planters, and the Poor Law Office and Office of the Protector of Immigrants were replaced by a Labour Department which included six labor inspectors, four of whom were Indian. The 1938 Labour Ordinance outlined minimum standards of health and diet for

---

31. C.O. 167/894, file 51227: Minute by Dawe, August 30, 1937.
32. C. A. Hooper, *Report of the Commission of Enquiry into Unrest in Sugar Estates in Mauritius* (Port Louis, 1938), 194-200.
33. C.O. 167/897, file 57172: Sir Bede Clifford to Ormsby-Gore, November 9, 1937.

workers and required that the workers be paid in cash.[34] An Industrial Association Ordinance legalizing a limited form of trade unionism was passed in 1938. In spite of the new legislation, there was little real change. The legislation was not enforced, and the governor, rather than working with the leaders of the Labour Party, sought to break the power of the Labour Party. He succeeded, at least temporarily.

As the Labour Party leadership became increasingly discouraged, and as its membership fragmented to join a more local organization, usually some kind of trade union, Curé, once the leader of all workers in Mauritius, began to articulate his fears that the basis for political divisions in Mauritius would become communal.

Speaking at the annual meeting of the party in 1940, he prophetically warned his much-reduced following:

> The workers, Creole or Indians, are all basically the same colour, with the same interests united under the same banner. Today, the leader of the Labour Party is a Creole; tomorrow he will be an Indian. That is right, but the workers are to be aware of the Indian intellectuals who one day will try to found a party ostensibly for the labourers, but in reality for themselves.[35]

Curé's tone was bitter, for he resented those educated Indians who failed to support the Labour Party during its early years and who had not identified with the Indian laborers on the estates even though their parents and grandparents had been among these laborers. Curé felt that he, a creole, had been largely responsible for the awakening of the Indian laborers. But he knew that the alliance of creole and Indian laborers in the Labour Party would break down as soon as established Indian politicians began to appeal to Indian laborers on communal terms. Once that happened, creole laborers would have to find allies in order to maintain their position in Mauritian politics. In the 1930s and 1940s creole leadership had been essential to the Labour Party in Mauritius, but later the role of the creole community in the Labour Party would become peripheral.

---

34. Labour Ordinance of 1938: *Hansard's Parliamentary Debates* (Commons), 5th ser., 338 (July 29, 1938), cols. 3504-3505.
35. *Le Mauricien*, May 3, 1940.

Creole Communalism and Decolonization

For twenty years, between 1947 and 1967, the recurring issue in Mauritius was constitutional change, and, more specifically, the nature of representation, the extent of the franchise, the size and boundaries of constituencies, and the electoral process. At first the creole community was divided. The creole elite argued that the franchise should be limited and that representation of minority communities should be guaranteed. The creole laborers and their leaders asked for a wide franchise and no special provision for representation. By 1963 the divisions had been overcome, and the creole community united in an effort to block independence and Hindu domination of Mauritian politics.

From the time constitutional change appeared imminent in 1945, the creole elite spoke of the need for constitutional safeguards. As Edgar Laurent told the Consultative Committee established to advise the governor on constitutional change:

> As a responsible leader of the coloured community in the island, I cannot allow myself to be led by the bright idea that we are all Mauritians, that we should not be divided . . . I can now only come to one conclusion and it is that if no safeguard is provided in the new constitution for some communities, and [sic] one of them in particular, and I have in mind the coloured community, will not have the representation to which it is entitled.[36]

But neither Laurent nor most of the leaders of the creole community advocated outright communal representation by which members of that community would elect their own representatives. According to Governor Sir Bede Clifford, "the Creoles resented any attempt to define the line of demarcation between them and the Europeans, which was not always easy to discern."[37] The Colonial Office, influenced in part by experience in other colonies such as Ceylon, did not want to institutionalize communalism and therefore resisted pressure from some creoles and most Muslims for reserved seats.

---

36. Chief Secretary's Office: Minutes of the First Consultative Committee, memorandum by Edgar Laurent, April 1945.
37. Sir Bede Clifford to author, December 1965.

ADELE SIMMONS

The second issue which caused greatest controversy in the constitutional talks was the franchise. The Franco-Mauritians and the creole elite agreed that universal suffrage, the demand of the Labour Party, would cause "dissension and would aggravate class and racial antagonisms." Aroused in part by India's impending independence, they argued that "given the Indian nationalistic tendencies which have become apparent, universal suffrage might open the door to external interference in the affairs of the Colony."[38]

In its final form, the 1948 constitution supported the Labour Party in that it extended the franchise to men and women over twenty-one who could write simple sentences in any language. Thus the constitution ensured that neither Franco-Mauritians nor representatives of the creole elite would have success at the polls in any numbers. At the same time, the constitution provided that twelve out of the thirty-four members of the council would be nominated by the governor to ensure adequate representation of all communities. In 1948 and 1953 the governor used this power to nominate Franco-Mauritians and members of the creole elite. By 1954, however, it was clear that the system of nominated members could not last. The elected members, who were mostly Indians and creole supporters of the Labour Party, were bitterly angered when, following two consecutive elections, the results of the poll were virtually overturned by the governor's nominations. Constitutional change was inevitable. It was clear that a new constitution would transfer power and responsibility from the Colonial Government to Mauritians, but the question remained which Mauritians. The nature of the constitution would, in part, determine the answer to that question.

Between 1954 and 1958 the shift began from political alliances based on class interests to those based on community. The educated Indian elite, of which Curé had warned a decade earlier, became the elected representatives of the Labour Party. While the Labour Party retained a creole president, the president had little power, in part because he did not have the qualities of personal leadership to attract a creole constituency.

---

38. Chief Secretary's Office: Minutes of the Second Consultative Committee, 1946, memorandum to Sir Donald Mackenzie-Kennedy from A. Gelle, R. Hein, A. Raffray, R. Rivet, E. Laurent, J. Koenig, and A. Nairac.

Once the center of the Labour Party, the creole workers moved to the fringe, uncertain about their political future. They did not feel comfortable in the Labour Party, but they were not attracted by the Parti Mauricien, which had formed recently to represent the interests of the Franco-Mauritians and the creole elite.

The 1959 constitution gave little encouragement to creoles of either party. The secretary of state, Alan Lennox-Boyd, believed that the constitution should encourage the existence of a second party which could have a "reasonable opportunity for election," and should assure that the party in power "did not achieve such a preponderant position that it could disregard minorities."[39] Between the time when Lennox-Boyd set forth his goals and 1959 when the constitution was promulgated, the Labour Party was able to persuade the secretary of state to revise aspects of the constitution in its favor. Universal suffrage was granted. A provision outlining a system of proportional representation and a single transferable vote designed to give greater weight to minorities was abandoned. The governor's power of nomination was limited.

In the 1959 elections, held under the new constitution, the Labour Party won 41 percent of the popular vote and 57 percent of the seats (twenty-three out of forty). In addition, the Muslims, allied with the Labour Party, won five seats. The creoles, who then constituted 25 percent of the population, won 25 percent of the seats, but they were not elected to represent creoles per se. The creole members of the Labour Party were better known for their willingness to work with Indian leaders than for their ability to protect creole interests effectively. Creoles elected by the Parti Mauricien were tied to the Franco-Mauritian sugar interests. As self-government approached, creoles in both parties became increasingly worried about the future of the creole population in the island, but they had no organization, no platform, and no leadership. By 1963, however, the situation had changed, largely in response to the energy and dynamism of Duval, then a young barrister recently returned from England.

Duval was elected to the Legislative Assembly in a by-election in 1960. A lively and charismatic speaker, Duval chose Curepipe, where

39. *Constitutional Development in Mauritius*, Sessional Paper No. 3 of 1956 (Port Louis, 1956), 47, 48.

ADELE SIMMONS

creoles comprise most of the population, as his constituency. There he talked openly of the dangers of Hindu domination and the need for the general population to work together to protect its interests. The Parti Mauricien, pleased with Duval's ability to attract voters, did not look beyond his immediate success to the dangers of provoking communal conflict.

In the 1963 election, Duval campaigned throughout the countryside for the Parti Mauricien, giving young creoles a feeling that they could effectively participate in politics. He talked for hours with them, exchanging ideas and creating an image of a prosperous Mauritius with creoles playing a leading role. Duval's leadership enabled lower-class creoles to overcome their fears of being associated with the party of the sugar interests. Creoles and Franco-Mauritians, both Catholic communities, united to block independence and to keep the Indians from controlling the political life of the island. Concerned with gaining support from traditional Parti Mauricien members, Duval was unable to see the need for non-creole support. In 1963 he was content with the fact that the Parti Mauricien had increased its representation from three to eight, with his new title, "King of the Creoles," and with the handsome salary provided by the sugar estates.

The growth of communal politics succeeded in forcing the creole community to overcome internal differences that had a long and deep history. But the response to creole communalism was an intensification of Hindu communalism. If the creoles were to vote for the Parti Mauricien to keep the Hindus out of power, then the Hindus were compelled to vote against the creole party. Communal feelings aroused during an election are not easily dampened. Because the Labour Party leadership included a number of creoles, it was difficult for the Labour Party to respond directly to Duval's communalism. Instead, Hindu communalism was expressed through a new party, the All Mauritius Hindu Congress.

Organized by a group of young and radical Hindus in 1965, Congress demanded that 52 percent of the government jobs be allocated to Hindus, since Hindus comprised 52 percent of the population of Mauritius. Holding secret meetings in the countryside, Congress aroused intense feelings of communalism at the village level. Duval's response to Congress was militant. He began to use militaristic terms in his speeches, calling for national mobilization to block Congress.[40] The criminal fringe of both parties increased their activities, and on May 10, 1965, the creoles and Hindus took up arms against each other in the south of the island. The rioting lasted two days; only two people were killed; but Mauritius was in a state of shock. In a place as small as Mauritius, the consequences of widespread communal violence are clear to everyone. The fear of such violence and the knowledge that there is no place to which people can escape serve to bring coalitions together to call for calm.

Predictably, each community blamed the other for the violence. But if violence itself could be seen as a benefit to any side, it had to be to the benefit of the Parti Mauricien and hence the creoles. Communal violence was proof that Mauritius did not have the political stability to survive independence. Furthermore, as Duval argued at the Constitutional Conference in 1965, a Hindu-dominated government, no matter how noble its intentions, would be subject to pressure from extremist Hindu groups.[41] Mauritius, Duval argued, was not ready for independence.

The Parti Mauricien realized that its campaign against independence required a positive program. The Parti Mauricien's goal was "association" with Great Britain, a status comparable to that of Puerto Rico to the United States, the Cook Islands to New Zealand, and the Overseas Territories to France. The primary benefits of "association" would be economic. According to the Parti Mauricien,

> the basic ailment of Mauritius is economic, though its symptoms have largely been racial and political. The remedy is, therefore, a constitution which will primarily ensure jobs locally and elsewhere, and a long term market for the whole of our sugar production at a remunerative price.[42]

The Parti Mauricien argued that if Mauritius were "associated" with the United Kingdom, Mauritians wishing to work in or emigrate to Eng-

40. Confidential Police Report on the Disturbances at Trois Boutique, Port Louis, Mauritius.

41. Mauritius Constitutional Conference Papers, 1965, Memorandum of the Parti Mauricien Social Democrat.

42. *Ibid.*

land would be given a special status, that Mauritius would automatically benefit from Britain's eventual common market membership, and that there would be an outside power to guarantee that the constitutional safeguards for minorities were upheld. At a time when independent nations were coming under one party or military rule, "association" would be more likely to assist in preserving a multiparty system.

At the conclusion of two weeks of discussion at the 1965 Constitutional Conference the secretary of state rejected the Parti Mauricien's appeal for a referendum on the issue of independence alone and agreed to the Labour Party's proposal for a general election. The older Parti Mauricien leaders felt betrayed, and returned to Mauritius depressed, discouraged, and convinced that the interests of minority communities were of little concern to the British government. Duval, however, was resilient and determined to win the general election.

Winning a general election required a new tactic. Duval, the creole communalist, saw that he needed the support of other communities. Believing that the merits of his case against independence were compelling and that there were Indians who were disenchanted with the Labour Party, he gave the Parti Mauricien a new slogan: "Hindoo, mon frère." He would no longer tolerate communalism, and reprimanded members of his party who advocated or participated in communal activities.[43]

Duval remained optimistic during the two-year period between the Constitutional Conference and the 1967 elections, but the long delay between the time when he enthusiastically sought Hindu support and the time when Mauritians went to the polls was costly. Other strong leaders to share the burden of the campaign did not emerge within the party. Duval's own personality was no longer a novelty. And in spite of the highly organized campaign, the creoles lost the 1967 independence election. The Independence Party, an alliance of the Labour Party, Congress, and the Muslim Committee of Action, won thirty-nine seats; the Parti Mauricien won twenty-three. The results reflected marked gains for the Parti Mauricien, which claimed one-third of the seats of the assembly as compared to one-fifth of the seats prior to the election. Yet one-third of the seats was not enough to block independence, nor was it enough to effect legislation in the independent state.

---

43. *The Times*, December 7, 1965.

Conclusion

Mauritius celebrated its independence in 1968. While the position of the creole community on the island has changed little with independence, the creoles have come to accept their position. They understand that the Mauritian government will not be dominated by creoles. But creoles also understand that the leaders of the present government, like the British colonial administrators and the Franco-Mauritian sugar planters before them, realize that the creoles cannot be ignored. Their influence on the political, social, and economic life of the island remains disproportionate to their numbers. Although the creoles are only 28 percent of the population, they live mainly in the urban areas where political disturbance can have the greatest impact. The island's dockers are still creoles, and a dock strike as late as 1972 reminded every Mauritian of their power. If there is a distinctive Mauritian culture, it is creole; creole language and creole songs are regularly publicized to promote tourism. Finally, creole political leaders have a style and a flair that will continue to make them popular with Mauritians of all communities.

There have been times when the creoles exerted great influence on the political and economic life of the island by allying themselves with the Indian or Franco-Mauritian community. Similarly, there have been times when the creole leaders thought they could have the greatest influence by forming a creole-based communal party. However, the creole politicians can no longer expect to lead the Indian cane cutters. Nor can a strictly communal creole party be effective. To ensure the well-being of the creole community in Mauritius in the 1970s, the creoles have only one option—to participate in the Indian-dominated government.

Those creoles who predicted that independence would bring disaster for the creole community have been proven wrong. Sir Seewosagur Ramgoolam's government has sought and welcomed creole help. The position of the creoles has been helped considerably because the Mauritian economy has grown rapidly since independence. The price of sugar has increased by over 100 percent; sugar production itself has reached a record of 700,000 tons. Mauritius is now a free industrial port, and products from diamonds to wigs pass through its harbor and factories. Unemployment has dropped from the 40 to 50 percent levels reached in the 1960s. Economic prosperity has alleviated communal tensions of the late 1960s. But the communal divisions have not disappeared. Social, cultural, and

ADELE SIMMONS

economic divisions—the basis for communal politics—remain, although they may be less rigid then they were fifty years ago. The Mauritian middle class—which has traditionally been creole—is now growing to include Indians, but class divisions between and within communities are also sharp. A sudden drop in the price of sugar could heighten all these tensions, and force the creoles to choose once again between action as a community or dividing their allegiance on a class basis. At present, however, the symbiotic nature of Mauritius' economy provides some assurance to the creoles that they will continue to be an important part of Mauritian society.

14 I.K. Sundiata

Creolization on Fernando Po: The Nature of Society

The early nineteenth century saw the creation of several West African communities composed of Africans recaptured from the slave trade or of American freedmen—people who may in the broadest sense be classed as "creoles."[1] It has been suggested that study of the acculturation of such groups may throw light on general patterns of African Westernization.[2] No doubt it is in the cultural sphere that much of the true significance of creole communities emerges. The material aspects of the creole lifestyle have often been described;[3] still not fully analyzed are the conditions which gave rise to such a style, for it exhibits traits which are common to Westernized blacks in widely varying contexts.

From the Gambia and Sierra Leone to the Bight of Biafra, the influence of nineteenth-century creole groups was evident. Among these groups were the Fernandinos of Fernando Po (an island of approximately 800 square miles lying off the Cameroonian coast). The island provides a

---

1. "Creole" is used in this chapter only in its West African sense. It usually refers to the descendants of Africans, who, enslaved for the Atlantic slave trade, were recaptured and freed in Sierra Leone. However, the term has been given broader application and applied to repatriates from the Americas. As P. C. Lloyd has noted: "One of the most clearly distinguished elites is the creole type of Sierra Leone, of Liberia, and of nineteenth- and early twentieth-century Lagos. The term creole is applied only in Sierra Leone, but the other elites mentioned have the same characteristics, deriving from their alien origin." P. C. Lloyd, *Africa in Social Change* (Baltimore, 1969), 128.

2. Kenneth Little, "The Significance of the West African Creole for Africanist and Afro-American Studies," *African Affairs*, XLIX (1950), 309.

3. See Arthur Porter, *Creoledom* (London, 1966); John Peterson, *Province of Freedom: A History of Sierra Leone 1787-1870* (London, 1969).

I. K. SUNDIATA

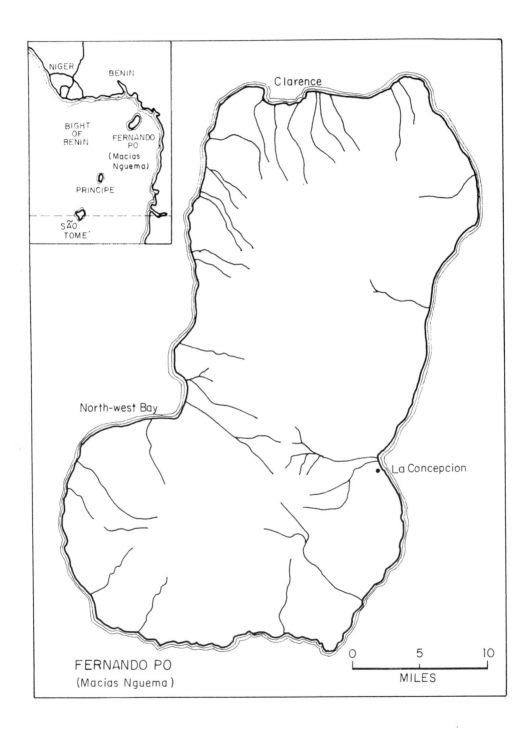

FERNANDO PO
(Macias Nguema)

well-documented case of the creation of a creole community, one which shows many similarities in socioeconomic development to the mainland creole settlements. Its divergences, especially in the economic sphere, question certain assumptions long held about Westernized elites in West Africa.

The creole community on Fernando Po had its origin in British efforts to make the Bight of Biafra the focus of their antislaving activities. Between 1827 and 1834 over a thousand recaptives from slave ships were landed at a settlement (Clarence, later to become Santa Isabel) on Fernando Po's northern coast. In 1834 the official British presence was withdrawn following protests from Spain, the nominal owner of the island. From that time until 1858, the creole settlement was left almost entirely on its own resources; from 1858 to the opening decades of the present century it was usually subject to a miniscule Spanish colonial establishment. In its early days Clarence was composed of a congeries of African groups: Sierra Leoneans, Cape Coasters (Fanti), liberated Africans (mostly from Gabon and the Congo), Cameroonian and Calabar; migrant laborers, refugees from Principe and São Tomé (mostly "Congos"), and Kru laborers from Liberia. Power was wielded by the most Europeanized elements—whites, Sierra Leoneans, and Cape Coasters. Gradually, as the nineteenth century progressed, the disparate groups coalesced into a new ethnicity—the "Fernandinos." Descendants of liberated Africans intermarried with Sierra Leonean and Cape Coast immigrants and the socioeconomic barriers between them yielded. Yet the community remained small, never rising to much more than 1,500 persons. The least Westernized groups—the Kru laborers and the indigenous Bubis—led largely separate existences, their chief contact with the Westernizing elite coming through the elite's exploitation of their labor and produce.

Culture and Black Enterprise

In discussing the culture of creole communities it is first necessary to separate cause from effect as one confronts past stereotypes. Critics assumed that the Western education received by recaptured or repatriated blacks inhibited industry and self-reliance. Culture was attributed the power to mold the socioeconomic aspect of communities: creole culture was seen as exerting significant influence over economic preoccupations. Creole

I. K. SUNDIATA

lifestyle and aspirations seemingly militated against an interest in the soil, and Europeans frequently criticized the effete disdain of agriculture.[4] It is correct to note that "clearly no attempt at large-scale farming in either country [Sierra Leone or Liberia] achieved sustained success in the nineteenth century."[5] Yet the backward state of creole agriculture should not be attributed solely to the mercantile predilections of educated (or "overeducated") blacks. Dearth of labor, laterite soils, and competition in international markets all contributed to the retardation of nonsubsistence agriculture. Where opportunity presented itself, a creole community could respond to agriculture with alacrity. Fernando Po, largely neglected by whites in the nineteenth century, is striking as a place in which an alien and Westernized group was able to assert its agricultural preeminence in the last quarter of the century.

After mid-century, cocoa was introduced to Fernando Po, producing a shift away from palm oil trading as the economic mainstay of the community.[6] On the island the crop produced a dramatic movement to agriculture. In the 1890s a Catholic missionary complained: "The island of Fernando Po above all, has been captured by the English blacks of Sierra Leone . . . and thus, the major part of the island is in the hands of the English blacks, and they have herded the Bubis, the natives of the island, into the interior of the island, the worst part of all, where the means of subsistence are hardly found and those foreign English blacks, have, for the most part, the better coastal soil."[7] Sierra Leonean immi-

---

4. Some blacks, like the Americo-Liberian Edward Blyden, also complained: "Nothing should be allowed to interfere between us and the soil. In bestowing so much attention upon commerce, we have mistaken true policy." Edward W. Blyden, "Liberia as She Is," in Henry S. Wilson (ed.), *Origins of West African Nationalism* (New York, 1969), 83.

5. John D. Hargreaves, "African Colonization in the Nineteenth Century: Liberia and Sierra Leone," *Boston University Papers in African History* (Boston, 1964), I, 66.

6. The new crop had been taken from Brazil to São Tomé in 1822 and thirty-two years later introduced to Fernando Po. In the 1860s a Spanish colonial functionary made a trip to the Portuguese island, where, with the aid of the Spanish vice-consul, he succeeded in obtaining 400 cocoa pods. From Fernando Po cocoa cultivation was spread by migrant workers to the Gold Coast, Nigeria, Liberia, and other parts of West Africa. Manuel de Teran, *Síntesis geográfica de Fernando Póo* (Madrid, 1962), 84; R. J. Harrison Church, *Africa and the Islands* (New York, 1964), 278.

7. Cristóbal Fernandez, *Misiones y misioneros en la Guinea española* (Madrid, 1962), 109.

grants and descendants of Fernando Po recaptives invested capital accumulated from palm oil trading in cocoa. A good example was William Allen Vivour, a Sierra Leonean oil trader who by 1871 had earned enough to purchase a schooner.[8] In 1874 Vivour was still engaged in the oil trade, but within a decade he had become an important planter on the western side of the island. By 1886 he was Fernando Po's largest landowner. By the beginning of this century Vivour was dead, but his widow, Amelia Barleycorn Vivour, owned the largest cocoa plantation on the island—400 hectares.[9]

Vivour's eminence was succeeded by that of several other black planters—Joseph Dougan, Samuel Kinson, J. W. Knox, and, most notably, Maximilian (Maximiliano) C. Jones. By the end of the 1880s a few planters had begun to trade directly with Manchester trading houses, among them Vivour. Planters prospered; in 1895 the island's Protestant mission reported: "We have, at the moment . . . 58 members distant at their farms and otherwise. . . . Indeed, were it not for the Church, many of our people assert that they would rather live on their farms altogether . . . ."[10] Two years later a traveler wrote of the "Portos" (Fernandinos) having farms all around the island, "collecting palm oil from the Bubis, and making themselves little cocoa plantations and bringing these products into Clarence every now and then to the white trader's factory. Then, after spending some time and most of their money in the giddy whirl of that capital, they return to their homes and recover."[11]

Cocoa was king on Fernando Po; competing crops were abandoned as the race to participate in the cocoa boom continued. Coffee failed to compete and the trade based on the oil palm became of secondary importance. Cocoa, 474 kg of which had been produced in 1889, was being produced at the rate of 1,440,398 kg per annum in 1899. However, as in other creole areas, black agriculturalists faced significant obstacles. In

8. John Holt, *The Diary of John Holt* (Liverpool, 1948), 178.
9. José A. Moreno-Moreno, *Reseña histórica de la presencia de España en al Golfo de Guinea* (Madrid, 1952), 118n.
10. Nathaniel Boocock and W. N. Barleycorn, Yearly Report, Santa Isabel, 1895, Primitive Methodist Mission, Fernando Po, box 5, Methodist Missionary Society archives, London.
11. Mary Kingsley, *Travels in West Africa* (London, 1897), 71.

I. K. SUNDIATA

spite of the increase in production, the exploitation of cocoa was halting. By the end of the nineteenth century only 6,500 hectares had been granted to farmers. Narrow paths to the uplands made more land available but the total amount in cultivation remained low. In 1912, 12,000 hectares were in agricultural use, or only 3.5 percent of the land area.[12] The next year, a member of a German party noted: "The island has never produced more than six million pounds in the year, whereas in the year 1909 the island of St. Thomas [São Tomé] exported over sixty million pounds. Coffee is scarcely to be reckoned as an export, and the same may be said of palm oil. . . . "[13]

Labor shortages were a great burden to the black cocoa farmer. It was evident that with the indigenous population, the Bubis, declining and hostile, the traditional support of the island's economy, migrant labor, was vitally needed. Because of persistent rumors of labor abuse, labor migration from British West Africa (e.g., the Mende of Sierra Leone) was embargoed in 1900. Thereafter, labor from the Kru coast of Liberia assumed the utmost importance. Liberian labor was siphoned off to the plantations of Fernando Po in large and increasing numbers and, in 1901, there were already 933 Liberians on the island.[14]

Fernando Po had suffered great neglect in the nineteenth century. Such neglect had benefited black trading intermediaries and agriculturists. It also deprived the island of the infrastructure needed for continued and expanding exploitation. Labor was in short supply and transport facilities were rudimentary. The Spanish colonial regime, with meager economic resources, had hardly taken an interest in linking the capital with other centers of settlement. The agriculturists of the second largest center of population, for instance, had to send their produce to Clarence by sea because there was no road spanning the thirty miles between the two. Above all, the colony lacked capital and organization. Many planters were, in the words of a Spanish official, constantly "enveloped in the coils of usury . . . [there] existing a nucleus of small farmers representing

12. Luis Ramos Izquierdo, *Descripción geográfica y gobierno, administración y colonición de las colonias españoles del Golfo de Guinea* (Madrid, 1912), 343.
13. J. Mildraed, "Fernando Po," in Adolf Friedrich, Duke of Mecklenburg, *From the Congo to the Niger and the Nile* (London, 1913), 259.
14. De Teran, *Síntesis*, 65.

a large part of the cocoa plantations producing a fair amount of the . . . crop imported into the Peninsula, and [who] neither command [enough] capital nor have sufficient power to protect themselves from major debt, in as much as the security that they were able to offer was not considered enough to obtain the same advantages as those enjoyed by the big agriculturists, some of whom, in spite of having proper funds and being able to withstand the consequences of a loan, were ruined."[15]

By the second decade of the twentieth century, a winnowing process had begun and insolvent blacks were its first victim. In 1913 the British consul pointed out "that the prosperity of three British firms and several planters who are British Protected Subjects is at stake and that they cannot continue to thrive without an increased supply of labour."[16] This was true of the island generally. A visitor of 1913 noted the fate that had overtaken the property of the greatest of the nineteenth-century planters, William Vivour. "Since his death," it was said, "this large property has been somewhat neglected, and in the face of the present dearth of labourers it would be difficult for even the most energetic owners to keep it up."[17]

The financial predicament of the black planters led them to overwork laborers and to detain workers beyond their contracts. The colonial regime's efforts to ameliorate the situation worked to the detriment of most of the blacks. A labor bureau (the *curaduria*) was established and laws were passed to deny labor to debt-ridden farmers. The inability of most of the planters to rid themselves of debt, coupled with increasing competition from Europeans, proved disastrous. In addition, for all agriculturists, the supply of Liberian labor remained precarious. In 1926, after altercations between Liberian and Spanish officials, it was abruptly cut off, creating panic among the planters. The following year, the Liberian secretary of state officially terminated a 1914 labor agreement. The rupture caused consternation in Spanish Guinea, and two representatives of the island's agriculturists, one black and one white (Edward Barleycorn and Emanuel Gonezrosa), were sent to Monrovia to arrange for the

---

15. Jabez Bell to Wiles, Jan. 16, 1905, PMM, box 5, MMS archives, London.
16. Great Britain. Foreign office 367/353: Lewis E. Bernays to F.O., Oct. 30, 1913.
17. Mildraed, "Fernando Po," 252.

continuation of the labor traffic. As a result of their negotiations, private labor agreements were made with several Liberian politicians. These agreements, last desperate attempts to solve the labor crisis, resulted in a League of Nations investigation in 1929-1930. Liberia was charged with promoting a modern "slave trade" and further labor shipments prohibited. Unfortunately for Fernando Po, the embargo came at a time when the island was already beginning to feel the effects of the worldwide economic depression.

By the second decade of the twentieth century, Fernando Po had ceased to be the exclusive agricultural preserve of a miniscule creole elite. The exiguous European presence of the previous era had been replaced with a mounting number of Portuguese and Spanish agriculturists and entrepreneurs. By 1930 it was obvious that a shift had taken place; 18,000 hectares had been conceded to Africans, and some 21,000 hectares had gone to Europeans,[18] a situation which remained legally frozen until 1948.[19]

The worldwide depression made even more apparent the trough into which the community had fallen. In 1930 the Fernandinos were appealed to in the pages of *La Guinea española*, the voice of the Roman Catholic mission. The community was urged to reflect on its decline and reminded that "your parents made a fortune, that all have recognized. . . . Through the substitution of vagrancy for constant work, vain consumption for seriousness, and the life of the bar and saloon for the intimacy of family life, has come the socioeconomic disaster that we deplore."[20] Unfortunately, the socioeconomic eclipse of the black elite could not be reversed by the exercise of individual or group probity. New conditions had been brought on by the fumbling yet inexorably tightening grip of European imperialism and the subservice of a colonial monoculture to a system of unstable international commerce.

The economic decline of the Fernandinos was only a peculiar manifestation of a general economic constriction which overtook West African creoledom in the latter half of the nineteenth century. Such constric-

18. Juan Bravo Carbonell, "Posibilidades económicas de la Guinea española," *Boletín de la Sociedad Geográfica Nacional*, LXXIII (1933), 525.

19. De Teran, *Síntesis*, 87.

20. Ruiaz, "Año Negro," *La Guinea española* (21 diciembre, 1930), 386.

tion cannot be seen as simply the result of increased entrance into the professions or the advent of scientific racism, nor was it the simple result of the lack of black business acumen. Both were concomitants of the rise of European economic domination following increased European interest in West Africa.[21] As long as white interest remained relatively small, the Westernized or semi-Westernized African had found economic scope in which to operate. Sometimes black merchants were able to become entrepreneurs trading directly with Europe; however, such a period of ascendancy ended with the coming of full-blown European imperialism. In the economic struggle, the creole commercial class was squeezed into an increasingly marginal position, their commercial function often being abandoned for a clerical role in colonial bureaucracies. If the creole community remained active, it was as the agent of and under the dominance of European capital.

The economic ascendancy of the creole varied in time depending on the area of the West African coast.[22] In Liberia the period came in the decades following the republic's independence in 1847.

But the commercial boom did not continue into the latter part of the century. A number of factors combined to end it. The introduction of European-owned steamships, which provided regular and relatively low-cost transport, drove Liberian sailing craft off the sea. The establishment of shipping lines permitted small European traders to operate, in addition to the large companies owning private vessels: these small traders competed with Liberians and the European-owned shipping lines gave preference to their own nationals. And finally, competition developed among the producing countries:

21. See Porter, *Creoledom*, 114: "The rise of a professional class corresponded with the decline of commerce among the Creoles. This decline was in part caused by the lack of adequate personnel with the zeal and drive of the entrepreneur which had characterized the merchant-owners. Those sons who returned to their fathers' business, came back largely because they had failed to qualify for one or another of the professions. It was not too surprising, therefore, that in the hands of these sons, business declined. Another factor contributing to the decline, and in some ways a resultant of the decline, was the increasing participation of the Lebanese and Syrian traders in the retail trade of the country."

22. It is interesting to note that in the Gambia, creoles had supplanted another nonindigenous group, the Afro-Portuguese traders. See Florence Mahoney, "Government and Opinion in the Gambia, 1816-1901," unpub. Ph.D. thesis (University of London. 1963). 19.

I. K. SUNDIATA

between 1885 and 1900, with rapidly increasing coffee exports from
Brazil, Liberia's coffee exports were halved. The introduction of beet
sugar cultivation in Europe had an even worse effect on Liberia's
cane sugar industry. . . . By 1904, Monrovia had no less than twenty
trading houses whose head office was in Hamburg, and Liberians
whose fathers had controlled the republic's business were working as
agents or employees of foreign firms.[23]

The same constriction of economic activity can be seen elsewhere; in
Lagos "in the third quarter of the nineteenth century, trade was buoyant,
there was little competition, and the market was small and demanded
neither a complex business structure, nor large reserves of liquid capital."
However,

by about the turn of the century, African merchants were faced with
a number of new and complex problems. In the first place, the export trade was less profitable than it had been because of a fall in the
prices of palm oil and kernels. It was possible for merchants to com-
pensate for this fall by handling an increased volume of produce, but
this implied a larger organization and greater overhead costs. Secondly, the last years of the nineteenth century saw an increase in
competition as a result of the rise of a number of new expatriate import and export firms. Thirdly, the expansion of the market (largely
as a result of the construction of railways) made new demands on
skill in business. These demands were met more quickly by the European firms than by the African merchants, because the expatriate
concerns had greater capital resources and lost no time in adopting
new forms of business organization, such as the limited liability
company.[24]

On Fernando Po a parallel process took place. In the decade following 1827 the small community began trading as middlemen in palm oil
(just as in Freetown the recaptives turned to commerce, first as petty
traders and then as owners of capital). On Fernando Po the wealth
amassed in trade was invested in land; the 1890s were the halcyon days
of incipient creole monoculture. Land was available, the terms of conces-

---

23. Merran Fraenkel, *Tribe and Class in Monrovia* (London, 1964), 17-18.
24. A. G. Hopkins, "Richard Beale Blaize, 1845-1904: Merchant Prince of West
Africa," *Tarikh*, I (1966), 70-79.

sion were not difficult, production was small, and the black planters were able to recruit an almost adequate supply of Kru and Mende labor. The Spanish and Portuguese presence was small, and European administration lacked continuity and direction.

However, the situation changed for reasons analogous to those on the coast. The establishment of a steamship line to Barcelona by the Compañía Transatlántica in 1887 not only facilitated the export of the colony's produce, but also stimulated the interest of Catalan business houses. The 1897 decree which made the concession of additional land conditional upon having lands already conceded in cultivation became especially burdensome after 1900 when the British embargo made the labor shortage acute. Labor was expensive; without it many blacks could not retain what they already possessed. The attempt to maximize the output of an inadequate labor force resulted in labor abuses which only furthered the limitations placed on labor importation. The control of labor distribution by the *curadoría* favored the allotment of workers to Spanish nationals. The black planters were dependent upon the *curadoría*, which was, in turn, dependent upon foreign companies empowered to contract labor. The mortgaging of farms and crops to obtain capital with which to maintain production created greater dependence on European firms at a time when these were entering the field with greater capital and organization.

It has been said that "in 1910 a new stage [was] initiated, politically and administratively characterized by the duration and continuity of the governing function."[25] A somewhat increased European presence and tighter regulation of colonial affairs coincided with the greater economic dominance of large European companies (e.g., Compañía Colonial de Africa). Between 1910 and 1925 the production of cocoa increased by 143 percent, but the increment was due to new economic forces and not to the expansion of production by the old elite.[26] The cessation of Liberian labor migration in 1929, coupled with the economic depression, gave the *coup de grâce* to an already depressed class of black proprietors.

The second and third decades of the twentieth century witnessed the

---

25. De Teran, *Síntesis*, 87.
26. *Ibid.*

I. K. SUNDIATA

same closing of economic horizons seen in other places; no doubt the economic constriction of the community would have come earlier if Spain had been able fully to exploit the island. This decline cannot be seen as the working of racism per se; indeed, the withering away of the economic power of the Fernandinos occurred while the community was undergoing acculturation which moved it closer to the colonial regime.[27] In the 1920s the creation of *emancipado* (*evolué*) status reflected the assimilationist tendency of colonial policy. Thus it is difficult to see the economic decline as the result of a consciously applied ideology. Neither can it be explained as the outcome of a growing anticommercial ethic. The exodus of the Fernandinos from the land was not induced by a desire to enter the professions and abandon commerce. In 1903 it was noted: "Black Doctors who have at no small expense and with no small labour qualified themselves for the profession may be found engaged in cocoa planting in preference."[28] Economic change, in other words, preceded occupational shift, and not vice versa.

In 1848 Fernando Po was described by an outsider as a place "where a lazy population of liberated Africans from Sierra Leone neglected the advantages of one of the richest soils in the world."[29] Yet, as later experience showed, the Fernandinos had no bias against or lack of ability in agriculture per se. The failure of creole agriculture (and West African black capitalism in general) arose out of competition and the nature of the market for tropical produce, and not out of an innate prejudice on the part of educated blacks. Prejudice existed, however, against praedial labor rather than agriculture—an important distinction. It was no doubt natural for communities possessing technological skills not found among their neighbors to believe that the latter should perform the menial tasks of society. Greater leisure is usually a concomitant of higher status; the

27. The decline of the Fernandino cocoa planters proceeded for many of the same reasons that Brazilian coffee planters declined in the late nineteenth century, the chief difference in the Brazilian situation being the existence of openly recognized slavery. Stanley J. Stein, *Vassouras, A Brazilian Coffee County 1850-1890: The Roles of Planter and Slave in a Changing Plantation Society* (New York, 1970), 213.

28. Johnson Report, G.3 A3/0, 1904, no. 110, Church Missionary Society archives, London.

29. William Allen and Thomas Thomson, *A Narrative of the Expedition sent by Her Majesty's Government to the River Niger . . .* (London, 1848), I, 226.

Westernized African was no doubt acting out the role considered most in keeping with his status. It could also be argued that escape from forced labor prejudices the individual against labor in general. One historian noted of the black settlers of Liberia that "it was as though, being come to Africa to escape the strictures of slavery, many of the colonists did not want to engage in the manual labor with which they had been so closely associated."[30] The attitude towards labor can, no doubt, generalize to include the laborer. And racial similarity does not necessarily ease the impact of settlement: "In fact, the colour of their skins [in the Liberian case] made it more important for them to stress the social distance between themselves and the local Africans. The fact that they were not obviously physically different accentuated the fear—shared by other colonial communities—of being submerged in what was to them a barbarous and heathen society."[31] On Fernando Po these factors were clearly operative: for most of its history reports of excessive abuse of labor were common. Flogging was both instrumental and symbolic. Masters used corporal punishment to encourage the performance of tasks and to punish their nonperformance. Beyond this, physical punishment was viewed as inherent in the master-servant relationship: "It did good, people could not manage servants without it."[32] The ability to command labor was, like the ability to command wealth, a symbol of high status.

Lifestyle: Between Image and Reality

The creole lifestyle has been extensively commented upon: "Their houses were styled after those of the white traders and missionaries. . . . Furnishings, furthermore, closely followed European patterns, with upholstered settees and chandeliers in vogue. European dress was usual, with wing collars and crinolines the essential accompaniment of high status."[33] In terms of lifestyle, later Fernando Po was part of a larger West African

---

30. George W. Brown, *The Economic History of Liberia* (Washington, D.C., 1941), 117.
31. Fraenkel, *Tribe and Class*, 13.
32. John Clarke, Journal, I (1st ser.), 380, quoting John Scott, Baptist Missionary Society archives, London.
33. Lloyd, *Africa*, 128.

I. K. SUNDIATA

ecumene. Culturally, Clarence (now Santa Isabel) lay on the borders of Freetown; a visitor described the Fernandinos as "very much like the Sierra Leoneans of Free Town, but preferable," concluding that they had "some of the same 'Black gennellum Sar' style about them, but not developed to the same ridiculous extent as in our institutions."[34] Ties of consanguinity bound the settlements; many of the Clarence people were immigrants and many returned to Sierra Leone to select a spouse.

Yet similarities between communities have their origin not so much in contact as in similar conditions of life. Not all the components of the stereotypical creole lifestyle were present in all West African creole communities, nor did all members of such communities participate in the lifestyle to the same extent. However, its salient characteristics are widely evident: conspicuous consumption and the strict maintenance of social distance vis-à-vis subordinate groups. It has been observed that, in general, "in order to distinguish themselves from the indigenous peoples, the creoles tended to identify themselves closely with the European communities and their values."[35]

The formation of creole attitudes is in part molded by the outlook of their European mentors. On Fernando Po, for instance, the creoles were consciously subjected to a program of planned acculturation. The premises upon which the Clarence settlement was founded were heavily loaded with a paternalism which viewed the African as "redeemable" and African culture as worthless. Fernando Po was envisioned as an important step in the "improvement" of Africa; the base would block the slave trade, turning back upon its sources liberated Africans bearing the accouterments of "civilization." The British planned to introduce a regimen which would "civilize" the recaptive, inculcate the value of work and render him a productive member of an embryonic polity. As blacks were not, in the opinion of the British superintendent, deficient in reason, the creation of correct models and agencies of socialization would achieve the desired ends:

The liberated African when first taken from a Slave Ship requires to be subjected to a peculiar mode of management in order to render

34. Kingsley, *Travels*, 71.
35. Lloyd, *Africa*, 128.

him a useful member of the Community—In his own Country his state even at the best is a species of Slavery, as he is robbed by his Chief of whatever Property he may acquire that is more than sufficient for his own support; deprived thus of every stimulus to industry, he is consequently the laziest of Human Beings, and until he can be taught some of the wants of civilized life, and convinced that by his own exertions he can obtain the means of satisfying them it is both cruel and impolitic to abandon him to his own guidance. . . . It is therefore some time after he comes amongst us before he can believe his bondage is ended, and still longer before he feels any security of our keeping faith with him respecting the indoucements [sic] held out to make him work—after finding for a short time that he is punctually paid for his labour and seeing amongst his fellows many articles for Necessity and Luxury which he desires and which this Pay will enable him to obtain, he begins to see the advantages of industry and becomes voluntarily industrious.[36]

Clarence seemed to justify British faith in African cultural malleability. No doubt deracination was significant in this; uprooted "western-educated Africans had . . . reason to see a wide gap between their own technology and that of the Europeans."[37] Not only was Western technology superior, but aspects of Western culture might enter the breach created by removal from traditional society. Yet the early image of uprooted and "civilized" blacks as the vanguard of Africa's "redemption" proved illusory. European society became the cultural referent, creating a type of racial inversion in which being less African and more European was positively valued. The creole's acculturation included disparagement of African society and often produced an alienation which inhibited him from acting as a channel of cultural interchange. It has been observed that "creoles tended to adopt many European stereotypes of the 'depraved native'—such sentiment effectively impeding the adoption of the culture and values of the indigenes—and did little to advocate or advance education in the interior, for such could only result in an increasing threat to their monopoly of prestige status in the capital."[38] Contrary to European

36. C.O. 82/3: A Description of the Harbour and Defenses of the Settlement of Clarence upon the Island of Fernando Po, October 25-30, 1830.
37. Philip Curtin, "African Reactions in Perspective," in Philip Curtin (ed.), *Africa and the West: Intellectual Responses to European Culture* (Madison, 1972), 243-244.
38. Lloyd, *Africa*, 129.

expectations, the tendency was for uprooted and Westernized groups to constitute endogamous and inward-looking elites.

The acculturation of creole groups seldom reached the point at which European culture completely effaced its African predecessor. The process was one of synthesis and in many instances African culture predominated. Yet devotion to aspects of a European culture could be tenacious, as was amply demonstrated on Fernando Po. Throughout the nineteenth century English culture played a dominant role in molding the Fernandino lifestyle, even in the face of a competing model. Only gradually was the culture of the metropole taken on; with great difficulty an Anglophone and Protestant community became Hispanophone and Roman Catholic.

The technological and material gap between Africa and Europe no doubt encouraged identification with European culture. Yet the peculiar manifestations of this identification are open to varying interpretations. The lifestyle of the creoles has been seen as the result of "transfrontal culture learning," in which the European cultural paradigm is derived from the narrow segment of European society represented by missionaries and colonial officials.[39] No doubt the creole lifestyle was greatly influenced by the ideas and concepts of the European missionaries, yet the emphasis on conspicuous consumption should not be seen as a direct implantation of the nineteenth-century ethos of the European middle classes. Indeed, on Fernando Po, European visitors were usually critical of the extravagance of creole society. Some, as in Sierra Leone and elsewhere on the Coast, thought them parodies of Europeans. In 1862 an English trader wrote: "The beaux and belles of the place dress themselves in their finest and most brilliant feathers and strut and mince up and down like our own fashionables."[40] Forty-two years later, another Englishman condescendingly appraised the community:

A wedding among this aristocracy is well worth beholding. The bride's dress and other accessories are generally ordered from Eu-

---

39. K. E. DeGraft-Johnson, "The Evolution of Elites in Ghana," in P. C. Lloyd (ed.), *The New Elites of Tropical Africa*, 109, citing Gail P. Kelly, "The Ghanaian Intelligentsia," unpub. Ph.D. thesis (University of Chicago, 1959), 87.
    40. Holt, *Diary*, 26.

rope, and on the happy morning, or sometimes afternoon, the bride proceeds to church, leaning on her father's arm, or that of some gentleman friend of the family. Six or fewer little girls waddle behind holding up the train, with their feet squeezed into boots too small for them. Then follow all the black society of the town. The gentlemen wear evening dress, or a frock coat. Some of the fashions are rather antiquated, especially the silk hats, which are much in evidence. In some cases a lady friend goes before the bride waving a Spanish flag. After the religious ceremony is over the bride is paraded through the town in a hammock chair borne by four laborers. Her husband walks by the side, and the fife and drum band also forms part of the procession. The lady friends sing, throw rice and flowers at the bride, and yell out their wishes for her happiness. After the parade they all go and have a good repast, and the desire seems to be to eat and drink as much as possible.[41]

Criticism of the extravagant quality of the black community was also voiced by an officer of the Primitive Methodist Missionary Society. A leading Fernandino, James McFoy, answered that "Mr. P. [Pickering] said he never saw a grand marriage as he has seen in Fernandopo I doubt it" and also replied to other cultural criticisms:

Mr. P. did . . . tell the people in England that we are very imitative the people of our Church I believe the people in England and in other countries make clothes and send them out for us to wear if they did not want us to put them on they ought not to sent them out for sale this shows that Mr. P. never was please when he sees us dress he would be please to see us with leaves tied around us or a slip of cloth say about 4 inches wide it will rejoicis more so he will be able to give a fine speeches about us then the meeting will have a big laugh at us and yet in all Mr. P. says he loves us.[42]

The creole lifestyle was not that of a frugal and emerging bourgeoisie. On Fernando Po a Spanish official noted that it led the Fernandinos into debt and that "hitherto there has been a great difficulty in getting the

---

41. T. J. Nunan, "Fernando Po," *Journal of the Manchester Geographical Society,* XX (1904), 32.

42. James McFoy to the General Missionary Secretary, February 6, 1895, PMM, Fernando Po, box 5, Boocock file, MMS archives, London.

I. K. SUNDIATA

judge to compel the completion of . . . agreements, and money which should have been paid to the merchants has been squandered by these debtors in trips to Sierra Leone and Europe and the buying of luxuries such as horses, bicycles, musical boxes, etc., to such an extent has this taken place that merchants are now in many cases not willing to advance money for development and the Island suffers in consequence."[43] The impetus toward conspicuous consumption travels by a devious route and involves more than "symbolic justification."[44] Conspicuous consumption can better be seen as arising from the ambiguities inherent in being a creole. Having internalized many of the values of nineteenth-century Europe, many creoles also accepted the theory of African inferiority, in the process accepting their own.

Dress has long been recognized as an index of status in most cultures; the creole's dress affirmed his adherence to European culture, to which he attached a high value. If the creole were trapped inside his skin, which marked him as inferior, clothing allowed him to transcend it; clothing was a second skin compensatory for the defects of the first.[45]

Dress, therefore, has an externally symbolic function. It also has a more internal function which might be called "aesthetic justification." Having internalized the values of prevailing European society, the creole views Africans not only as inferior, but as less aesthetically pleasing. There is a disjunction between the community and its "somatic norm image," that is, "the complex of physical characteristics which are accepted by a group as its norm and ideal."[46] At the extreme, an African

---

43. Suggestions re Fernando Po Constitution, notes and comments on Reorganization of Fernando Po and with its Powers (1904), 10.16, John Holt Papers, Liverpool.

44. See Bernard Barber, *Social Stratification* (New York, 1957), 404: "Where there is a lag, large or small, [between status and lifestyle] there may take place a progress that we may call 'symbolic justification.' This is a process in which the socially mobile individual or family acquires, consciously or unconsciously, the various symbolic accompaniments of their social class position."

45. This occurs not only in West Africa, but in the Americas as well. Thus, "at the present time on the island of Trinidad in the British West Indies, wearing a coat and tie is an indispensable symbol for a middle-class colored man; otherwise, he is not marked off from lower-class people. These symbols of social class position are jealously guarded" (*Ibid.*, 147, citing Lloyd Braithwaite, "Social Stratification in Trinidad," *Social and Economic Studies*, II [1953], 203).

46. Harry Hoetink, *Caribbean Race Relations: A Study of Two Variants* (New York, 1971), 120. Hoetink deals specifically with "segmented" societies. A segmented

could say that the African, including the creole, "is ugly, because his woolly pate is not so becoming as the flaxen hair of the Anglo-Saxon, because the flat nose of the Negro is more like the nasal organ of the ape than is the aquiline nose of the Aryan races, because blubber lips are not as pretty as thin ones, because a black complexion is displeasing compared with a fair or olive one."[47]

The contradiction dealt with in the phrase "black, but comely" is partially resolved by clothing. It is not only that European clothing is worn, but that it is costly clothing. The inherent aesthetic defect is surmounted by emphasis on cleanliness, cost, and opulence of attire; the body will be black, but the covering is beautiful. As was said in another context: "There is a beauty, a transformation, as it were, a regeneration, that takes place in the physical make-up of a young man or young woman who gets into the habit of living on the high side of life rather than on the lower side."[48]

It has been suggested that from a study of creoles "may . . . be gathered enough evidence to reconstruct phases of the New World scene which are still blurred through inadequate documentation or lack of empirical data."[49] Indeed, it may be possible to speak of "creole society" in a broader context if we consider "creolization" that facet of the more general process of Westernization which occurs with the juxtaposition of a

---

society is defined as "one in which two or more groups occur which had originally, apart from their cultural differences, clearly different somatic norm images, of which that of the dominant segment has, in the process of intersegmentary acculturation, been adopted and accepted by the lower segments" (*Ibid.*, 137).

47. Joseph Renner Maxwell, *The Negro Question, or Hints for the Physical Improvement of the Negro Race, with Special Reference to West Africa* (London, 1892), 10, cited by Leo Spitzer, *The Creoles of Sierra Leone* (Madison, 1974), 134-135. Maxwell, a Sierra Leonean of Yoruba ancestry, obtained his B.C.L. degree at Oxford in 1880 and in the same year was converted to Roman Catholicism, which he felt to be a universalistic and color-blind faith. Eventually he became chief magistrate of the Gambia. Maxwell looked forward to the physical elimination of the "ugly" black race through miscegenation; should this not occur, "the progress of civilization, the struggle for existence, will not admit of the solution of questions of abstract right; if the white man wants room the black, being the weaker and uglier, will have to make room for him."

48. Booker T. Washington, *Black-Belt Diamonds: Gems from the Speeches, Addresses and Talks to Students of Booker T. Washington* (New York, n.d.), 86, quoted by E. Franklin Frazier, *Black Bourgeoisie* (London, 1962), 70.

49. Kenneth Little, "Significance of the West African Creole," 309.

I. K. SUNDIATA

deracinated black population and a dominant European cultural paradigm.[50]

In such a society, the upwardly mobile black will exhibit many facets of the world view and lifestyle identified as "creole" in the West African context. Thus, stretching right across the Atlantic from the West African littoral to the islands of the Caribbean and up to the North American mainland, we find creole culture. The hypostatization of such a process as "creolization" does not rule out significant differences in the sociocultural content of the many creole societies. For example, the Aku (Yoruba) who returned to Yorubaland from Sierra Leone in many cases collaborated with and sought integration in indigenous African life.[51] However, this instance only helps to emphasize the importance of deracination in the creation of the creole world view and lifestyle; the severance of the community from traditional African political and cultural patterns creates a situation in which a new paradigm can be most readily accepted.

Creolization is an outcome of European attitudes imbibed in the process of Westernization and is an attempt to deal with the problems posed by the adoption of a paradigm which must involve a certain degree of self-rejection. The contradictions thus imposed create similar conflicts and reactions in widely varying circumstances. Until recently in the United States, for instance, "in attempting to escape identification with the black masses, [the black bourgeoisie] have developed a self-hatred that reveals itself in their depreciation of the physical and social characteristics of Negroes. Likewise, their feelings of inferiority and insecurity are revealed in their pathological struggle for status within the isolated Negro world and craving for recognition in the white world."[52]

---

50. The possibility for comparison was mentioned by Frazier in 1957 (although he detected a purely American origin for Afro-American culture): "Our study may have a broader significance than the group which we have studied. It may have some relevance for the study of the emergence of a middle class in colonial societies, especially in African societies at present undergoing rapid changes." He added: "The characteristics of this class in the various societies will have to be studied in each case in relation to its history and the economic and social forces which are responsible for its development" (Frazier, *Black Bourgeoisie*, 192).

51. See Jean Herskovits Kopytoff, *A Preface to Modern Nigeria: The "Sierra Leoneans" in Yoruba, 1830-1890* (Madison, 1965).

52. Frazier, *Black Bourgeoisie*, 176.

The *embourgeoisement* of deracinated blacks in West Africa and the Americas is no doubt similar to the process in Europe or elsewhere. However, creolization has its own character. In a society in which racial hierarchies are recognized, symbolic justification of status is never complete; the symbols of status are contradicted by ethnic identification. Creolization, taking place in a racially or culturally heterogeneous community, contains inherent contradictions which become more manifest as the process unfolds: "the Negroes' inferiority complex is particularly intensified among the most educated, who must struggle with it unceasingly."[53]

Creolization on Fernando Po bears interesting comparison with part of the Caribbean and Latin America. The island almost reproduces a color-caste system in a monochromatic setting. In the past occasional confusion of culture and phenotype resulted in reference to the elite by foreigners as "half-bred mulattos."[54] Usually, however, distinctions were drawn on an ascriptive basis. In the late 1940s a Spanish writer noted that members of the elite had "climbed to a high social level because of their education, work and wealth, being in a way an aristocracy of color, to which in polite Spanish we refer as 'Fernandinos' in order to distinguish them from the rest of the blacks, with whom they don't want to confuse themselves, and to which they have a right by virtue of a high degree of civilization."[55]

For certain purposes, the elite ceases to be socially defined as "black." In this there is some parallel with Brazilian situations in which a "shift in color typing does not reflect changed sensory perceptions of the persons engaging in it, but is, rather, a recognition of social merit reflected in the more courteous designation."[56] On Fernando Po, an acculturated black

---

53. Frantz Fanon (trans. Charles Lam Markmann), *Black Skin, White Masks* (New York, 1967), 25-26, citing Diedrich Westermann, *The African To-day* (London, 1934), 331.

54. F.O. 367/286: Admiralty to Foreign Office, Sept. 24, 1912, enclosure 1; Report by Lt. Strong on the Exportation of Native Labour from Liberia to Fernando Po, August 5, 1912.

55. Abelardo de Unzueta, *Geografía histórica de la isla de Fernando Póo* (Madrid, 1947), 298.

56. John Saunders, "Class, Color and Prejudice: A Brazilian Counterpoint," in Ernest O. Campbell (ed.), *Racial Tensions and National Identity* (Nashville, 1972), 162.

group occupying an intermediate socioeconomic position (at least in the twentieth century) became nonblack—politely they had ceased being *negros*. This suggests that, in a largely nonwhite society dominated by a white norm image, status differentiation tends to take on racial coloration. This may take place even where somatic differences among the population are negligible. Color conflict can be seen as an epiphenomenon of economic competition between groups. As has been noted in Guyana, "the groups involved are not only trying to gain as much as they can from the economic system, but one is trying to monopolize those traits in Western culture that make for high station. . . . "[57] In the Caribbean the "sometimes muffled, sometimes open struggle which brings Negroes and mulattos to grips is, in a certain measure, a class struggle."[58] The conflict is the result of a colonial heritage of income and prestige maldistribution. In this situation, the liquidation of the mixed middle class, in and of itself, will not automatically obviate invidious status distinctions and the maintenance of a sense of color. It is possible that those black individuals or groups having the means to approximate the elite life style will claim to constitute an ersatz class of "racial" intermediacy. The solution lies in the destruction of both paradigm and bourgeoisie.

In the present century the fate of the Fernandinos has been similar to that of many other creole groups. Having opposed the imposition of Spanish authority in the nineteenth century, the Fernandinos proved to be the ultimate defenders of that authority in the twentieth. Fearful of the surrounding African mass, the Fernandinos could do little else but uphold the metropolitan connection. On Fernando Po "Bubis and Fernandinos taken together . . . still constitute a minority [43 percent in the 1950s] in the midst of a mass of temporary Nigerian labourers."[59] A more

---

57. Elliott P. Skinner, "Group Dynamics and Social Stratification in British Guiana," in Vera Rubin *et al.* (eds.), *Social and Cultural Pluralism in the Caribbean, Annals of the New York Academy of Sciences,* LXXXIII, 905.

58. Daniel Guérin, "Racial Prejudice and the Failure of the Middle Classes in the West Indies," in Richard Frucht (ed.), *Black Society in the New World* (New York, 1971), 188.

59. René Pélissier, "Spanish Guinea: An Introduction," *Race,* VI (1964), 120. Equatorial Guinea had an estimated total population of 290,000 in 1970. In 1960 Santa Isabel had a population of 37, 237; it is probably not very much more at present. The Fernandinos, concentrated in the capital, have, in essence, been politically swamped

permanent threat presented itself in the guise of the population of Spanish Guinea, a colony comprising not only Fernando Po but also the mainland territory of Rio Muni. The mainland Fang are, unfortunately for the insular elite, in the majority. In the late 1960s, as talk of autonomy and independence accelerated, the Fernandinos' Unión Fernandina found itself opposing the creation of a unified and independent state. Since the creation of the Republic of Equatorial Guinea in 1968, the Fernandino community has undergone a second winnowing. The black elite has witnessed the exodus of its former European patrons and is viewed suspiciously by the new government. The traditional masses have emerged and are attempting to escape the consequences of creolization. Old forms are consciously disparaged; the new government has noted that formerly "education was cast in European models and did not correspond to the necessities of African countries."[60] The cry of the government has become "¡ Cultura sí, pero africanizada!"

Creolization diminishes as the racist content of European thought changes and as movements for political change arise in the black community. Rejection of white political authority often involves a conscious rejection of European models. Yet even here contradictions exist; although rejection may seek to end the problem of deracination and return to pre-European roots, it cannot do so. The result is not nativism or even syncretism, but appropriation of Western thought in an attack on Western society (e.g., the formerly missionized using Judeo-Christian ethics as a gauge of the present "decadence" of the West). Although the creole elites of West Africa have faded in importance and although the lifestyles of black elites in the Americas have undergone considerable change, creolization has left its mark. The cultural dilemma posed by the impingement of the West on Africa has yet to be resolved. The problem of black-white relations lies not only in the field of economic exploitation and competition, but also in the tension engendered by the creation of black men encapsulated in white minds.

(Dan Golenpaul [ed.], *The New Information Please Almanac, Atlas and Yearbook* [New York, 1971], 212).

60. Ponciano Mbomio Nvó, "Relaciones entre la educación y el desarrollo económico," *Organo informativo del Ministerio de Educación de Guinea Ecuatorial*, 7 (Marzo 1970), n.p.

15 Marion D. de B. Kilson

Afro-American Social Structure, 1790-1970

There's a wheel in a wheel,
The big wheel runs by faith,
And the little wheel runs by the grace of God,
There's a wheel in a wheel.
Afro-American Spiritual

Within the pluralistic social system of the United States, Afro-Americans have occupied a subordinate position initially as slaves and later as citizens. Consequently, at any given time the external parameters of the Afro-American experience have been drawn by the dominant white stratum and defined by the dynamic interaction between subordinate and superordinate strata. After 1830, for example, white fears of slave insurrection led to the imposition of severe restrictions upon free black communities. From the last decade of the nineteenth century until 1965, most Afro-Americans living in the South were legally disenfranchised. More subtle limitations upon Afro-American participation in American life are reflected in the career contingency and family income differentials as well as unemployment ratios for black and white Americans today.[1] Although

I wish to express my appreciation to the Simmons College Fund for Research for a grant supporting the research for this paper.

1. Kenneth M. Stampp, *The Peculiar Institution, Slavery in the Ante-Bellum South* (New York, 1956), 215; J. Merton England, "The Free Negro in Ante-bellum Tennessee," *The Journal of Southern History*, IX (1943), 41. W. E. B. DuBois and Augustus Granville Dill, *The Common School and the Negro* (Atlanta, 1911), 115-116. Peter M. Blau and Otis Dudley Duncan, *The American Occupational Structure* (New York, 1967), 209. See tables 15.1, 15.2, 15.3.

the subordinate status of Afro-Americans within American society and its sociological implications cannot be denied or neglected, I am primarily concerned with the internal development of the Afro-American social system rather than with its relation to the wider society.

Several national demographic changes during the period between 1790 and 1970 indicate the contours of important changes in Afro-American society. While the black population increased decennially from 757,208 in 1790 to 22,580,289 in 1970, the proportion of Afro-Americans in the United States population consistently diminished from 19.3 percent in 1790 to 9.7 percent in 1930 and 1940, rising slightly in subsequent decades to 11.1 percent in 1970. Of greater sociological import are three related trends: urbanization, occupational redistribution, and regional redistribution. During the past century the Afro-American population has changed from a predominantly rural (86.6 percent rural in 1870) to a predominantly urban (74 percent urban in 1970) population. Associated with this ecological transformation has been a significant change in the Afro-American occupational profile during the twentieth century. Between 1910 and 1970, significant decreases occurred in the proportion of farmers (from 25.3 to 0.7 percent) and unskilled workers (63.3 to 30.9 percent) including farm laborers (30.8 to 3.1 percent) among Afro-American men, with a corresponding increase in semiskilled (4.7 to 26.0 percent,) skilled (3.6 to 13.2 percent), clerical (1.0 to 7.2 percent), and professional (1.1 to 5.2 percent) occupational categories.[2] During this period the occupational profile of Afro-American women changed even more strikingly. The proportion of unskilled workers, mainly farm laborers and domestic workers, declined from 88.4 percent in 1910 to 39.9 percent in 1970, while the percentage of clerks increased from 0.3 to 18.4 percent, professionals from 1.4 to 10.3 percent, and semiskilled workers from 5.4 to 14.6 percent. As these data imply and, as Price's detailed analysis of changing Afro-American occupational patterns demonstrates, "the occupational status of the Non-white female has improved more rapidly than that of the Non-white male."[3] A final demographic trend of importance has been the regional redistribution of black Americans. Throughout the

2. See tables 15.4, 15.5, 15.6.
3. Daniel O. Price, *Changing Characteristics of the Negro Population* (Washington, D.C., 1969), 183.

MARION D. de B. KILSON

nineteenth century more than 90 percent of the Afro-American population lived in the South. Although in 1970 a majority (53 percent) continued to live in the South, the regional distribution of Afro-Americans changed significantly during the twentieth century, especially in the post-World War II era. The proportion of Afro-Americans living in southern states has diminished consistently from 89 percent in 1910 through 78.7 percent in 1930 and 68 percent in 1950 to 53 percent in 1970; correspondingly, the proportion of blacks living in the North has risen from 10.5 percent in 1910 to 39 percent in 1970 and in the West has grown from 0.5 percent in 1910 to 8.0 percent in 1970.[4] These three fundamental trends are related, for the occupational redistribution of blacks results primarily from the decreasing number of farmers and farm laborers left in rural areas as blacks moved cityward, and the regional redistribution of blacks is essentially an aspect of the urbanization of Afro-Americans.

During the past century the most important demographic trend has been the urbanization of black Americans. For every decade from 1870 to 1970 both the black urban population in the South and its decennial increase have exceeded the number and decennial increase of Southern-born blacks living in other parts of the country.[5] In 1924, Work observed that "the so-called migration to the North is a part of the movement of Negroes to cities, both North and South."[6] Work's observation is as appropriate for blacks in 1970 as at the time of its initial formulation.

Between 1790 and 1970 the fundamental social process involving Afro-Americans has been the transformation of a rural slave population into one of urban citizens. In ideal terms, this transformation has meant a change in status, from slave to citizen, initially achieved through the Emancipation Proclamation in 1863 and the Fifteenth Amendment in 1870 and reaffirmed through the Voting Rights Act of 1965; a change in community, from rural to urban or from the racially heterogeneous and culturally isolated plantation to the racially homogeneous and culturally heterogeneous ghetto; a change in economic activity, from participation in an agricultural economy in which unskilled labor plays an essential

---

4. See table 15.7.
5. See table 15.8.
6. Munroe N. Work, "Taking Stock of the Race Problem . . . 1923," *Opportunity* (Feb., 1924), 41-46.

role to involvement in an industrial economy in which unskilled work is peripheral; a change in social stratification, from minimal to maximal social differentiation; and a change in institutional development, from minimal to maximal elaboration. Such an ideal representation of aspects of the basic social process involving black Americans for the past two hundred years necessarily glosses over major differences in the social experience of significant segments of the population.

Both ecological and temporal variables are relevant in attempting to understand the varied complexity of Afro-American society over two hundred years. Certain blacks have always lived in cities, especially in the North, while a fair number continue to live in rural southern districts. For analytical purposes, the temporal continuum is divided into three periods: 1790-1860, the slavery period; 1865-1914, the after-freedom period; 1915-1970, the out-migration period. By looking at both the general structural contours of Afro-American society and the nature of urban and rural communities within each of these periods, I hope to indicate both the essential attributes of Afro-American society at different periods in time and the overall pattern of development of the black social system.

Afro-American Society, 1790-1860

Throughout the antebellum period, the Afro-American population was divided into two socially and numerically unequal strata: freemen and slaves. Freemen, who occupied an intermediary position between slaves and whites, represented a small but growing proportion of the Afro-American population (8 percent in 1790; 11 percent in 1860). Both strata mushroomed in size during the seventy-year period: slaves increased from 697,624 in 1790 to 3,953,760 in 1860, and freemen expanded from 59,557 to 488,070. Moreover, members of both strata were concentrated in the South. While the slave population was overwhemingly southern (94.3 percent in 1790; 97.1 percent in 1860) and a small majority of freemen also lived in the South (54.6 percent in 1790 and 52.9 percent in 1860), a significant proportion of freemen lived in the North (46.2 percent in 1790; 45.4 percent in 1860). Although most slaves and freemen in the South lived in rural communities, some slaves lived in southern cities and freemen constituted the "most urbanized group in Dixie"; northern

MARION D. de B. KILSON

freemen, however, were predominantly city-dwellers.[7] For understanding social developments in the Afro-American community after freedom, the experiences of the plantation slave and the urban black, both free and slave, are particularly relevant.

Social Structure of Freemen

The Afro-American freeman occupied an intermediary status between slave and white in antebellum America. His superiority over the slave was reflected in various legal rights that the latter did not possess, such as the rights to own and dispose of property, to use his earnings, to contract legal marriages, and to develop religious and economic institutions. Although the relations between slave and freeman are relatively uninvestigated, social mobility between strata was possible through manumission, intermarriage occurred, and slave ownership by freemen existed to a limited extent.[8] While freemen enjoyed such important rights that were denied to slaves, they did not enjoy others that remained the exclusive prerogatives of white citizens. Especially after 1830, limitations were placed on the manumission, movement, franchise, education, occupation, and cultural participation of northern and southern freemen. Apart from such statutory restrictions, the intermediary status of freemen is reflected in the fact that they appear to have suffered more from competition with white workers than slaves. According to DuBois and Dill, slave and white artisans often worked together without friction in the South; in northern cities, however, white immigrants not only replaced free blacks in occupations such as stevedore and waiter, but rioted against freemen

---

7. Bureau of the Census, *Negro Population, 1790-1915* (Washington, D.C., 1918), table 2, 55. John Hope Franklin, *The Free Negro in North Carolina* (Chapel Hill, 1943), 19; Richard C. Wade, *Slavery in the Cities: The South 1820-1860* (New York, 1964), 247; Carter G. Woodson, *Free Negro Heads of Families in the United States in 1830* (Washington, D.C., 1925), xx.

8. Woodson, *Free*, xxxi, lvi-lvii; Wade, *Cities*, 249. John Hope Franklin, "James Boon, Free Negro Artisan," *Journal of Negro History*, XXX (1945), 150-180; John H. Russell, *The Free Negro in Virginia, 1619-1865* (New York, 1969), 131, 89-107. In 1790, 165 free black slaveholders; in 1830, 3,777; in 1860, 6,000 (Edward Byron Reuter, *The American Race Problem* [New York, 1927], 266; Irving J. Sloan, *Blacks in America, 1492-1970* [Dobbs Ferry, 1971], 11).

in Cincinnati, Philadelphia, New York, and Washington during the 1830s and 1840s.[9] Thus, the freeman legally occupied an intermediary status between slave and citizen; although social mobility between the two strata of Afro-Americans was possible, freemen could not achieve membership in the superordinate white caste. Freemen, therefore, constituted a jurally intermediate class between slave and citizen and were simultaneously members of a socially inferior color caste.

Within the free black population various social distinctions existed. Occupational differentiations appear to have been primary and were associated with a number of social and cultural criteria such as moral code, color, and possibly a socially salient discrimination between free-born and ex-slave. Among southern rural freemen the major occupational distinctions were between a small group of farmers, a large group of tenant farmers, and a sizable group of landless laborers; correspondingly, urban freemen were differentiated into a small group (10-20 percent) of artisans and businessmen largely in personal service occupations such as waiter and barber, and a large group of unskilled laborers. In both North and South, whites differentiated freemen into a class of respectable "men of color" and an economically insecure and disreputable class of "free niggers," the latter representing perhaps 20 percent of the free black population. These two classes differed not only occupationally but in family patterns and institutional participation. Frazier argues that the family organization of skilled artisans was as stable as its white counterpart, whereas the family structure of the impoverished class was characterized by greater disorganization than that of the slave family. Hershberg has shown that in antebellum Philadelphia, the proportion of two-parent households varied with economic fluctuations, falling from

9. See William Jay, "Condition of the Free People of Color," in *The Free People of Color* (New York, 1969), 374-395; Eugene D. Genovese, "The Slave States of North America," in David W. Cohen and Jack P. Greene (eds.), *Neither Slave Nor Free* (Baltimore, 1972), 259; Ira Berlin, "From Slavery to Freedom: The Emergence of the Free Negro Caste, 1775-1812," in *ibid.*, 16-17; St. Clair Drake and Horace Cayton, *Black Metropolis* (Chicago, 1961), I, 41. W. E. B. DuBois and A. G. Dill, *The Negro American Artisan* (Atlanta, 1912), 30; Theodore Hershberg, "Free Blacks in Antebellum Philadelphia," *Journal of Social History*, V (1972), 183-209; Robert A. Warner, *New Haven Negroes* (New York, 1969), 22; Carter G. Woodson, *The Education of the Negro Prior to 1861* (New York, 1968), 284.

MARION D. de B. KILSON

70 percent in 1833 to 63 percent in 1848 among the poorest 20 percent of Philadelphia freemen.[10]

Woodson has maintained that southern freemen were more economically secure than northern freemen, who faced greater economic competition from Irish immigrants, but that institutional life was more developed in the North than the South. Among the freemen's institutions none was more central to their community than the church, which served both as a center of community activity and as a seedbed for other institutions, including schools, mutual aid societies, and fraternal orders. Although considerable independent religious and educational institution-building occurred within northern and southern communities of freemen in the late eighteenth and early nineteenth centuries, such activity was sharply curtailed in the South during the last thirty years of the antebellum period.[11] In the North, however, separate institutions proliferated throughout the antebellum years.

Emerging from the dual forces of black initiative and white hostility, the independent church movement had two aspects. The initial one entailed the establishment of separate congregations of existing denominations, as exemplified by the founding of the first black Baptist church in Silver Bluffs, South Carolina, in 1773 and various other Baptist congregations; the second involved the creation of independent denominations as initiated by Richard Allen's break with Methodism in Philadelphia in 1794. By the close of the antebellum period, northern cities with sizable Afro-American populations had several black churches of different denominations. The black churches of Philadelphia increased from six in

---

10. Russell, *Virginia*, 159, 149; E. Horace Fitchett, "The Origin and Growth of the Free Negro Population of Charleston, South Carolina," *Journal of Negro History*, XXVI (1941), 421-437; Marina Wikramanayake, *The World in Shadow* (Columbia, 1973), 71-92. Laura Foner, "The Free People of Color in Louisiana and St. Dominique," *Journal of Social History*, IV (1970), 415-416; Jeffrey R. Brackett, *The Negro in Maryland* (Baltimore, 1889), 206; Franklin, *Free*, 131-150; England, "Tennessee," 52; Carter G. Woodson, "The Negroes of Cincinnati Prior to the Civil War," *Journal of Negro History*, I (1916), 10; Dorothy Provine, "The Economic Position of the Free Blacks in the District of Columbia, 1800-1860," *Journal of Negro History*, LVII (1973), 61-72; Warner, *New Haven*, 28; E. Franklin Frazier, *The Negro in the United States* (New York, 1949), 311.

11. Woodson, *Free*, xxxvi-xxxviii. See Russell, *Virginia*, 145; Woodson, *Education*, 95-131; DuBois and Dill, *School*, 16; E. Franklin Frazier, *The Negro Family in Chicago* (Chicago, 1932), 16.

1813 to twenty in 1867, and those of New Haven expanded from one Congregational church in 1824 to six in 1860, of which three were Methodist and one Baptist. Toward the end of the antebellum years in New Haven and probably other northern cities, social differentiation within the black population was reflected in church membership: the black elites attended one church and members of other strata were associated with other churches.[12]

Growing out of and paralleling the development of separate churches were separate educational institutions. During the late eighteenth and early nineteenth centuries, Afro-American communities founded Sabbath schools and to a lesser extent private "common" schools. Such endeavors were restricted in the South after 1830 to such an extent that in 1840 there were only fifteen black Sabbath schools. During this period northern black communities did not experience such limitations on their educational institutions. Moreover, in several northern cities and states the policy of public, albeit segregated, schools was implemented. By 1828, there were public schools for blacks in Boston, New Haven, Salem, and Portland; the policy of segregated public education was introduced in Pennsylvania in 1818, Rhode Island in 1828, New York in 1841, New Jersey in 1844, and Ohio in 1849.[13]

Free blacks also established and participated in several other kinds of institutions at both local and national levels. Mutual aid societies were founded initially through churches; in 1848 Philadelphia had 106 societies with 8,000 members. Fraternal lodges originated with the organization of the Masons in Boston in 1784; in 1860 Masonic lodges existed in eighteen states and Canada. At the national level, blacks participated actively in anticolonization and abolitionist movements.[14]

12. Eugene D. Genovese, *Roll Jordan Roll* (New York, 1974), 364-365. Carter G. Woodson, *The History of the Negro Church* (Washington, D.C., 1921), 76-78. W. E. B. DuBois, *The Philadelphia Negro, A Social Study* (New York, 1967), 199-200; Warner, *New Haven*, 308-331.

13. Woodson, *Education*, 184, 308-331.

14. DuBois, *Philadelphia*, 222. John Daniels, *In Freedom's Birthplace* (New York, 1969), 21; Edward Nelson Palmer, "Negro Secret Societies," *Social Forces*, XXIII (1944), 208. William H. Pease and Jane H. Pease, "The Negro Convention Movement," in Nathan I. Huggins *et al.* (eds.), *Key Issues in the Afro-American Experience* (New York, 1971), 191-205; Larry Gara, "The Professional Fugitive in the Abolition Movement," *Wisconsin Magazine of History*, XLVIII (1965), 196-204.

MARION D. de B. KILSON

The institutional life of the small number of urban freemen foreshadowed the institutional experience of large numbers of Afro-Americans after freedom. After the Civil War the church became the central institution in rural and urban black communities, though after 1900 the church became less influential in urban centers. Institutional development among Afro-Americans in the past 100 years has involved the increasing differentiation and elaboration of institutions around activities and services initially performed within the black church.

Social Structure of Slaves

During the antebellum period most slaves lived on farms and plantations in the South, while a dwindling number resided in southern cities. Southern slaves were engaged in three major economic sectors: personal service, agriculture, and industry. The slaves working in agriculture and industry included foremen, skilled laborers, and unskilled workers.[15] Urban slaves were engaged primarily in personal service and secondarily in industry, both as factory workers and as individual artisans, whereas rural slaves were employed primarily in agriculture and to a lesser extent in personal service and mechanical trades. Although slave society was inextricably linked to white society, possibilities for the development of an independent community life "from sundown to sunup" were greatest for urban slaves and nondomestic workers on large plantations and least for plantation house servants and slaves living on isolated farms.

Rural Slavery

Southern plantations were devoted to the raising of a commercial monocrop and to being as economically self-sufficient as possible. In 1850, 75 percent of the more than 101,000 plantations raised cotton, 15 percent grew tobacco, and the remaining 10 percent produced hemp, sugar, and rice; a corresponding proportion of slaves were engaged in cultivating and harvesting these crops: 73 percent cotton, 14 percent tobacco, 6 percent sugar, 5 percent rice and 2 percent hemp. Stampp has cogently argued that the extent of occupational differentiation on plantations varied

---

15. Genovese, *Roll*, 365-398; Wade, *Cities*, 4. Robert Starobin, "Disciplining Industrial Slaves in the Old South," *Journal of Negro History*, LIII (1968), 125.

with the size of the unit: on small plantations of ten to thirty slaves, occupational differentiation was limited to field hands, a slave foreman, a couple of artisans, and a domestic worker, whereas on larger units, in addition to these jobs, distinctions would be made between plow and hoe gangs among field hands, and between driver and white overseer among administrators.[16]

The relationship between occupational differentiation on the plantation and social stratification within the slave community is not clear cut. While field hands occupied the lowest status, social ranking at the elite level is more difficult to ascertain. House slaves appear to have enjoyed high prestige because of their association with the master's family and their greater acculturation to its mores, but effective leadership in the slave community probably was exercised by drivers and plantation artisans who often served as preachers, the most influential personalities among slaves.[17]

With respect to social institutions within the slave community, Rawick has argued persuasively that the slave community was more important than the nuclear family, for "while the family could be—and was—regularly broken up, the individual slave could be taken to another plantation hundreds of miles away and become part of another community where he knows how to behave and where he would be accepted."[18] "The slave community acted like a generalized extended kinship system in which all adults looked after all children."[19] Nevertheless, as Rawick also points out, the bio-social slave family was of greater importance than is often realized, for ex-slaves in the 1920s and 1930s often had considerable knowledge of kin ties and recounted searching for relatives after freedom. As among the freemen, the slave family or household had two predominant forms: the matricentric family consisting of a woman and her children, and the nuclear family composed of man, wife, and children.[20] Given the structure of the plantation, however, the inde-

---

16. Charles H. Wesley, *Negro Labor in the United States, 1850-1925* (New York, 1927), 2-3. Stampp, *Peculiar*, 30-42.

17. See Genovese, *Roll*, 384; E. Franklin Frazier, "The Negro Slave Family," *Journal of Negro History*, XV (1930), 208-214.

18. George P. Rawick, *From Sundown to Sunup* (Westport, 1972), 9.

19. *Ibid.*, 93.

20. *Ibid.*, 90. Frazier, *Negro*, 309; W. E. B. DuBois, *The Negro American Family* (Atlanta, 1909), 48.

pendent household unit was less functionally autonomous than after freedom. The slave household was neither a unit of production nor—except to a limited extent—one of consumption and socialization; it functioned as an affective and residential unit.

Undoubtedly the most important and enduring institution within the plantation slave community was the "invisible" religious institution.[21] Although slaves participated in the religious observances of their masters and worshiped in white churches throughout the antebellum years, they also met with and without their masters' approval in their own meetings "under the arbors" where elements of African and Christian worship fused, creating a vital synthesis that contributed distinctively to the independent black church, especially after freedom.

The plantation slave community, both in its own right and as part of a wider system of reciprocal relations based upon paternalistic assumptions involving blacks and whites,[22] established a tradition that has been salient throughout the Afro-American experience. Writing of an Alabama cotton plantation county in 1934, Johnson observed that

> the Negro population [of the county] . . . has its own social heritage which . . . has had little chance for modification from without or within. Patterns of life, social codes, as well as social attitudes were set in the economy of slavery. . . . Macon County has a Negro population with a tradition much older than that of a Negro population in any city of either the North or the South.[23]

Urban Slavery

During the antebellum period, the slave population of southern cities was characterized by decline and instability. These attributes related partly to the nature of slavery insofar as masters might move or sell their slaves at will, as they did more often in cities than in rural areas, and partly to the nature of slavery in the city, in that social control was more difficult to maintain in cities, particularly after 1830, than in rural areas.[24]

---

21. See E. Franklin Frazier, *The Negro Church in America* (New York, 1971).
22. Stampp, *Peculiar*, 326-327; Genovese, *Roll*, 2-18.
23. Charles S. Johnson, *Shadow of the Plantation* (Chicago, 1966), 16.
24. Wade, *Cities*, 19, 244.

In the cities, slaves were engaged predominantly in personal service, but also in industry as individual artisans and as factory workers. By 1860, 200,000 industrial slaves were engaged in extractive and manufacturing industries. In the later antebellum period urban industrial slaves, who included slave managers as well as skilled and unskilled workers, were increasingly owned by corporations rather than individuals. In 1840, two mills in Charleston each owned more than seventy slaves, while in 1860, fifty-four Richmond corporations each owned at least ten slaves and the Virginia Central railroad owned 274 slaves. Not only was the corporate ownership of slaves distinctive to urban industrial slavery, but individual urban artisans' control of their labor and time was greater than in rural areas and urban artisans tended to be more skilled than their "jack-of-all-trades" plantation counterparts.[25] During the later antebellum period urban artisans were increasingly hired out by the day or by the year, often on their own time, which enabled them to earn money for themselves as well as their masters and thereby at times their freedom. Such independent slaves often "lived out" in their own dwellings away from their masters' surveillance. The autonomy of such slave artisans made the *de facto* status differences between them and urban freemen much less than appeared *de jure*, especially as the period of increasing autonomy for urban slaves coincided with that of increasing restriction and repression for urban freemen.

Given the correspondence in occupational differentiation between urban and rural slaves, albeit in different economic sectors, a similar stratification pattern may be presumed, entailing particular prestige for house servants and effective leadership for industrial slave managers and skilled workers, including independent artisans, and lesser prestige for unskilled industrial workers. Further, comparable domestic patterns existed. Although independent institutional development among urban slaves was formally restricted by the slave code, slaves met informally with one another and with freemen "throughout the city—in homes, grog shops, grocery stores, and in the churches."[26]

---

25. *Ibid.*, 30, 23; Starobin, "Industrial," 111. W. E. B. DuBois, *The Negro Artisan* (Atlanta, 1902), 20.
26. Wade, *Cities*, 146.

Clearly the social universe of the urban slave was vastly different from that of the plantation slave: its horizons were wider, its restrictions less, its social contacts more diversified with greater opportunity for multiple role playing and for developing personal initiative and self-reliance. Not surprisingly, slaves who had enjoyed the freedom, diversity, and responsibility of urban life rarely wished to live in rural society.[27] Like antebellum freemen, urban slaves, especially those belonging to the industrial elite, had acquired standards of behavior and experiences that would be useful in adapting to social conditions after freedom.

Afro-American Society after Freedom, 1865-1914

Although the Emancipation Proclamation issued in the midst of civil war and the aftermath of the war created an initial period of social chaos, southern society soon reintegrated around the fact of "freedmen," and important institutional developments in Afro-American society characterized the decades after freedom. For many freedmen, the essential attribute of being free was freedom of movement; many quickly exercised this new prerogative: in some instances, leaving their slave homes permanently, and, in as many others, returning to them after some travel. Before freedom, the movement of slaves had entailed two basic patterns: the flight of a few intrepid slaves northward from servitude, primarily through the Ohio Valley, and the involuntary movement of a large number of slaves from Virginia, Maryland, and South Carolina through the domestic slave trade into the lower South and Southwest, facilitating the expansion of cotton culture. After freedom, Afro-Americans began to move in a variety of directions, as they have continued to do until the present. During the 1860s some freedmen sought refuge in southern cities; others voluntarily followed the expanding cotton culture southwestward into Mississippi and Texas, thereby perpetuating the pattern of the slave trade. During Reconstruction some northern blacks moved south, where they perceived greater opportunity for social mobility; in 1879 freedmen from Louisiana, Mississippi, Alabama, and Georgia joined in an "exodus" to Kansas. Beginning in the 1880s blacks began to seek

27. *Ibid.*, 246; DuBois, *Artisan*, 21.

greater economic opportunities in southern industrial centers such as Birmingham and in the Appalachian mines, as well as to move from the border states of Maryland, Virginia, Kentucky, Tennessee, and North Carolina to northern cities in Pennsylvania, New Jersey, and New York. Three distinctive patterns of Afro-American movement, therefore, emerged in the period after freedom: the first, a movement between rural areas from the upper South to the Southwest, was largely completed by 1910; the second, a movement from rural areas to urban areas within the South, and the third, a movement between southern cities and others in the North and West, still persist.[28]

Following the initial social upheaval created by war and emancipation, Afro-Americans embarked upon a period of institutional foundation and participation. For rural freedmen the twenty years following the Civil War appear to have been especially important for the "upward economic mobility" of landless farm workers into farm owners; even as late as 1910 the number of black farm owners in the South continued to increase significantly, rising from 120,738 in 1890 to 218,972 in 1910. Moreover, under the cultivation of free black labor, southern cotton production between 1878 and 1882 exceeded that of its Civil War heyday of 1857-1861. The growth of Negro entrepreneurship, estimated at 4,000 enterprises in 1866, as well as the concomitant growth of southern urbanization, is reflected in the development of banking, first through the federally supported Freedman's Saving and Trust Company and subsequently through the foundation of private banks, beginning in the late 1880s in such southern cities as Washington, Richmond, Chattanooga, and Birmingham, and in the establishment of the National Negro Business League in 1900. In the religious sphere even more impressive institutional growth occurred, primarily in the South; the number of black churches increased from 700 with 600,000 members in 1866 to 36,770 with 3,685,097 members in 1906. In the educational sector, the policy of integrated public schools was adopted in the North after freedom, while

---

28. Carter G. Woodson, *A Century of Negro Migration* (New York, 1969), 27-36, 91-124, 146; Frederic Bancroft, *Slave-Trading in the Old South* (Baltimore, 1931), 19, 269, 275; Stampp, *Peculiar,* 237-239; Joseph A. Hill, "The Recent Northward Migration of the Negro," *Opportunity* (April, 1924), 100-101; Wesley, *Labor,* 213; Dean Dutcher, *The Negro in Modern Industrial Society* (Lancaster, 1930), 20-21.

MARION D. de B. KILSON

the foundations for public segregated education in the South were laid through the Freedman's Bureau that operated 975 schools with 90,778 pupils in 1866 and 2,677 schools with 149,581 pupils in 1870. In this period variously sponsored institutions of higher education for blacks were also established. In addition to three antebellum colleges, the Freedman's Bureau founded thirteen colleges, religious denominations established fourteen colleges—five of which were those of black churches—and state educational systems under the Land Grant Acts of 1862 and 1890 founded four colleges for blacks. The period after freedom was also the heyday of the fraternal beneficial societies; starting in 1869, these organizations reached their zenith between 1890 and 1910. Although most of the fraternal societies were limited to one community and many were short-lived, in 1902 there were twenty national Afro-American secret societies.[29] In part, the burgeoning of institutions created by or for blacks after freedom reflected the lack of opportunity for such development in the antebellum years.

Moreover, in the after-freedom period, ominous trends emerged in the relationship of the wider society to Afro-Americans, promising severe limitations on the future quality and development of the Afro-American experience. The most important of these trends occurred in the economic and political spheres. As the economy of the South moved toward industrialization, the role of the Afro-American was defined as unskilled. Thus, whereas in the antebellum agrarian economy of the Old South, most skilled workers had been Afro-American slaves and freemen, in the industrial economy of the New South, skilled workers were to be white and unskilled were to be black, in accordance with the model for industrial labor previously established in the North. Concomitantly, in the political sphere, with the failure of Reconstruction, southern states (beginning with Mississippi in 1890) effectively disenfranchised Afro-American residents, with disastrous consequences not only for their civil

---

29. Allison Davis et al., Deep South (Chicago, 1941), 299; Wesley, Labor, 227, 193. Munroe N. Work, Negro Year Book, 1931-32 (Tuskegee, 1931), 137-138, 118; Frazier, Negro, 387. Woodson, Church, 286-287. Policy of integrated education established in Rhode Island in 1866, in Pennsylvania and New Jersey in 1881, in New York in 1900 (DuBois and Dill, School, 20). W. E. B. DuBois, The College-Bred Negro (Atlanta, 1900), 12-13; Palmer, "Secret," 207-212.

rights but for their acquisition of publicly funded services.[30] Disenfranchisement led to the curtailment of funds for black schools to such an extent that in 1930 Horace Mann Bond is quoted as saying that relative to whites less money was "spent for the public education of Negroes today than was spent in 1880."[31] Thus, from an overall perspective, for Afro-Americans the formative years after freedom were characterized by institutional development and initial socioeconomic advance, and by increasing limitations upon further social advancement for freedmen within industrial American society, as became increasingly evident in the subsequent period.

Rural Social Structure

After freedom the largest rural community for blacks became the county, with its county seat, sparse clusters of villages, and isolated farms and plantations. At any given time, reciprocal ties of service and obligation formed a network of relations uniting town and countryside, white and black into one ecosystem. The black landless population of the county moved frequently from tenant farm to tenant farm within the county but rarely outside it. The town with its stores and public buildings drew the country folk on market day for economic and convivial exchanges. In time the small towns became way-stations in the urbanization of black folk. By the turn of the century, a clear migration pattern had emerged in the upper South whereby rural families moved from the farm into the village and then to the rural town; from the rural town some young men and women as individuals or couples without children moved on to the nearest southern cities, from which some progressed to northern urban centers.[32] After 1910 this migratory pattern had developed in the lower

30. Charles S. Johnson, "Negro Workers in Skilled Crafts and Construction," *Opportunity* (Oct., 1933), 296-297. DuBois and Dill, *Artisan*, 28; Kathleen Bruce, "Slave Labor in the Virginia Iron Industry," *William and Mary Quarterly*, VII (1927), 1-20; Kathleen Bruce, *Virginia Iron Manufacturing in the Slave Era* (New York, 1931). See John G. Van Deusen, *The Black Man in White America* (Washington, D.C., 1938), 57.

31. Ira DeA. Reid, *In A Minor Key* (Washington, D.C., 1940), 36.

32. See Johnson, *Shadow*, 25. W. E. B. DuBois, "The Negroes of Farmville, Virginia," *Bulletin of the Department of Labor*, XIV (Jan., 1898), 9; DuBois, *Philadelphia*, 76; George E. Haynes, "Negro Migration, Its Effects on Family and Community in the North," *Opportunity* (Oct., 1924), 30.

MARION D. de B. KILSON

South as well. Thus, the rural town became a "clearing house" for black folk turning from the country toward the city.

Within the rural countryside after freedom, relatively little occupational differentiation existed: blacks were farmers or more often farm laborers. Consequently, throughout the period, cultural criteria based on nonoccupational standards were salient for social stratification, including the differentiation between descendants of freemen and those of freedmen; between mulatto and black, and increasingly between "thrifty" and "improvident," with highest status associated with thrifty mulatto descendants of freemen. Perhaps one of the most significant developments of the period was the emphasis upon the nuclear family composed of husband, wife, and children as a unit of agricultural production as well as of consumption and socialization. Matricentric families existed as they had in slavery, but during the period after freedom, families of nuclear and other forms assumed more autonomous functions than during the antebellum years. Frazier characterized the after-freedom period as one in which "the progressive stabilization of Negro family life" occurred.[33]

Although social stratification in the countryside was based on nonoccupational criteria, within rural towns a new form of stratification, based in part on occupational and educational criteria, began to emerge. Thus, by the turn of the century DuBois remarked upon a threefold status system in rural communities throughout the South. In the highest category were more affluent farmers as well as artisans and professionals; the intermediate category, which was by far the largest numerically, was comprised of laborers and domestic workers, as well as less affluent farmers and artisans; the lowest category consisted of the "slum" element of underemployed and unemployed unskilled workers.[34] Associated with these occupational differentiations were variations in family structure and educational achievement. In 1898, DuBois assessed "the growing differentiation of classes among Negroes, even in small communities" as the "most natural and encouraging result of thirty years' development."[35]

---

33. Frazier, *Negro*, 273-274. Frazier, *Chicago*, 49.
34. See DuBois, *Philadelphia*, 192-195; DuBois, "Farmville," 36.
35. DuBois, "Farmville," 38.

In almost all of the rural southern communities studied by DuBois and his associates at the turn of the century, the church occupied a central position, serving spiritual, social, and political needs and functions. DuBois, for example, observes of the church in rural Georgia: "here he [the Afro-American] learns the price of cotton or the date of the next circus."[36] Most communities of any size had several churches, representing primarily Baptist and Methodist denominations. The church was also the center for other organizations, including minimally an Odd Fellows or Masonic lodge for men and a "benevolent society" for women, while in larger, more prosperous rural towns several lodges and as many as ten sickness and burial societies might be organized through the church. Schools were variously associated with churches—some were run by rural churches and many "public" schools were housed in churches. In 1910, 61 percent of the schools in Alabama, 63 percent of those in Georgia, almost 100 percent of those in Louisiana, and 39 percent of those in South Carolina were housed in nonschool buildings. In many areas the school term for black children was half the length of that for white children; in more isolated villages and plantation communities, the term ran for three or four months of the year, and in rural towns for six months.[37] The community without a church or a benevolent society was hardly a community, for even with such institutions DuBois asserted that "a sketch of the social life of Negroes in the rural districts of the South is almost like an essay on the snakes in Ireland."[38]

Urban Social Structure

During the years after freedom the social process began that has been transforming Afro-American society for the past 100 years—namely, the

---

36. W. E. B. DuBois, *The Negro Church* (Atlanta, 1903), 57.

37. See J. Bradford Laws, "The Negroes of Cinclare Central Factory and Calumet Plantation, Louisiana," *Bulletin of the Department of Labor*, XXXVIII (Jan., 1902), 117, 104; William Taylor Thom, "The Negroes of Sandy Spring, Md.," *Bulletin of the Department of Labor*, XXXII (Jan., 1901), 100; William Taylor Thom, "The Negroes of Litwalton, Virginia," *Bulletin of the Department of Labor*, XXXVII (Nov., 1901), 1167; DuBois, "Farmville," 35-36, 13; DuBois, *Philadelphia*, 403-417. Carter G. Woodson, *The Rural Negro* (Washington, D.C., 1930), 184, 204-205.

38. DuBois, *Family*, 130.

MARION D. de B. KILSON

urbanization of the rural freedman. At the opening of the twentieth century. DuBois observed that the city attracted extremes within the black
rural population, both "idle floaters" and "thrifty aspiring" blacks. Initially, Afro-Americans were drawn to the city through a desire for
greater economic and social opportunity. As time went on, the process
developed its own momentum and became a causative factor in its own
right, in such a way that the blacks' own perception of the process of
transformation from an agrarian way of life to an urban lifestyle within
industrial and commercial centers became a predominant factor in generating further urbanization. Although the urbanization of Afro-Americans has always been primarily a southern phenomenon, in the period
after freedom it was virtually limited to the South until the turn of the
century. Nevertheless, some blacks did leave southern cities for northern
and ultimately western urban centers throughout the period. During
these after-freedom decades, most northern-bound blacks went to northeastern cities and secondarily to north-central urban centers. Relatively
speaking, the urbanization of blacks in the North was less than in the
South; nevertheless, by the end of the nineteenth century the influx of
freedmen had made a significant impact on the established black communities in northern cities. By 1900, the northern-born blacks of free parentage represented approximately one-third of the population of northern
cities, while the southern-born of slave parentage constituted two-thirds.
Relations between northern-born and southern-born residents were often
strained, for their social values, experiences, and goals differed.[39]

Probably the most significant consequence of Afro-American urbanization was the development of cohesive, racially homogeneous black
communities within the cities. The process of ghettoization had developed to such an extent by 1900 that DuBois observed of the black urban
community: "Here, then, is a world of itself, closed in from the outer
world and almost unknown to it, with churches, clubs, hotels, saloons,
and charities; with its own social distinctions, amusements, and ambi-

39. W. E. B. DuBois, "The Negro Land Holder of Georgia," *Bulletin of the Department of Labor*, XXXV (July, 1901), 676. See DuBois and Dill, *Artisan*, 127-218. For a
decennial analysis of regional net migration between 1870 and 1960, see Reynolds Farley, "The Urbanization of Negroes in the United States," *Journal of Social History*, II
(1968), 251. W. E. B. DuBois, *The Black North in 1901* (New York, 1969), 190. See
Warner, *New Haven*, 169; DuBois, *Philadelphia*, 25-26.

tions."[40] A few years later, he noted some of the positive socioeconomic consequences of ghettoization: "today in every city of the United States with a considerable Negro population, the colored group is serving itself with religious ministration, medical care, legal advice, and education of children: to a growing degree with food, houses, books, and newspapers."[41]

Throughout the after-freedom period urban blacks were engaged primarily in unskilled jobs as domestic servants and laborers, as they had been before freedom. In Raleigh, North Carolina, the proportion of blacks in domestic and personal service categories rose from 57 percent in 1876 to 69 percent in 1888; in Boston in 1880 and Philadelphia in 1898, unskilled laborers and domestic workers represented 87 percent and 80 percent, respectively, of the black workers, while in Chicago domestics constituted 64 percent of the black workers in 1900. Some urban blacks owned small businesses such as catering and barbering establishments that served white clientele; while the few professionals were usually teachers and clergymen serving the black community. A few blacks were involved in the industrial sector, primarily as unskilled workers.[42] Not until the subsequent out-migration period did the occupational profile of Afro-Americans begin to alter in response to new needs within the wider society.

At the turn of the century DuBois found greater social differentiation in northern than southern cities. In part this differentiation arose from the distinction between free and freed and its sociological ramifications. Analysts of the period stratify the black population into three or four groups based primarily on occupational and cultural criteria. Thus, Spear distinguishes three strata in Chicago during the years 1870 to 1890: refined, respectable, and riffraff. DuBois, Daniels, and Warner isolate

---

40. DuBois, *North*, 18.

41. W. E. B. DuBois, *Economic Cooperation Among Negro Americans* (Atlanta, 1907), 179-180.

42. Frenise A. Logan, "The Economic Status of the Town Negro in Post-Reconstruction North Carolina," *North Carolina Historical Review*, XXXV (1958), 449-458; Elizabeth H. Pleck, "The Two-Parent Household, Black Family Structure in Late Nineteenth Century Boston," *Journal of Social History*, VI (1972), 10; DuBois, *Philadelphia*, 100; Allan H. Spear, *Black Chicago, The Making of a Negro Ghetto, 1890-1920* (Chicago, 1967), 301-303; Charles S. Johnson, "Negroes at Work in Baltimore, Maryland," *Opportunity* (June, 1923), 12; DuBois, *North*, 22.

four groups in their respective cities: an upper class or aristocracy; a middle class including waiters and artisans; a common class comprising unskilled and personal service workers as well as laborers; and finally a "criminal" or "incapable" class.[43]

Associated with such status differences were variations in family structure. At the turn of the century in Philadelphia, DuBois noted a "pleasant family life" among the upper class in sharp contrast to that of the lowest class, which was characterized by multiple short-term liaisons in which women often supported men. Pleck found that two-parent households were greater among literate than among illiterate black Bostonians, while Blassingame has noted comparable correlations for black families in New Orleans after freedom.[44]

With respect to communal institutions, there were also status differentiations in church attendance and participation in voluntary associations. Many upper-class blacks in northern cities were oriented toward an integrated social life, as symbolized by their membership in predominantly white churches. Members of this class resented the relatively large influx of rural-born southerners which threatened their integrationist orientation, as the enlarged black community, both voluntarily and in response to white pressure, developed a segregated communal lifestyle.[45] Within the black ghetto of this period, DuBois wrote, "the church is a centre of social life and intercourse, acts as newspaper and intelligence bureau, is the centre of amusements."[46] Although membership in the urban church was less than in rural areas, there were many churches in urban centers at the turn of the century: fifty-four in Atlanta, fifty-five in Philadelphia, and thirty to forty in New York City. These churches attempted to meet the new needs of urban folk in various ways, including serving as employment agencies and sponsoring night schools.[47] The

43. DuBois, *North*, 28. Spear, *Chicago*, 6. Daniels, *Boston*, 174.
44. DuBois, *Philadelphia*, 5. Pleck, "Boston," 18. John W. Blassingame, *Black New Orleans, 1860-1880* (Chicago, 1973), 79-106.
45. See Daniels, *Boston*, 227. DuBois, *North*, 41.
46. DuBois, *Philadelphia*, 201.
47. Church membership: 50 percent in Atlanta, 1900 (DuBois, *Philadelphia*, 68-69); 50 percent migrants in Chicago (Spear, *Chicago*, 93). DuBois, *Philadelphia*, 199-207; DuBois, *North*, 16-17.

urban church, therefore, began to adapt to the secular socioeconomic needs of its new members after freedom.

Afro-American Society, 1915-1970

As the time of World War I approached, the character of Afro-American urbanization altered significantly. Although the basic pattern of internal southern movement continued to be maintained, for the first time thousands moved northward in response to the promise of job opportunities in northern industry, and for the first time substantial numbers came from the Deep South. In addition to past causes of urbanization, two particular complementary factors facilitated this movement out of the South; on the one hand, northern industry actively recruited black workers as European immigration ceased, and, on the other, the southern cotton economy collapsed due to the ravages of the boll weevil. In retrospect, the social magnitude of the period of the "great migration" lay not in its numerical aspect—for in the 1940s and 1950s many more blacks moved northward, virtually unheralded—but in its import for the cities into which Afro-Americans moved. For the first time these northern centers had to cope with large numbers of blacks, many of whom had had limited urban experience in the South. During the 1910-1920 decade, the black population increased from 2.0 to 4.1 percent in Chicago, from 1.2 to 4.1 percent in Detroit, and from 1.5 to 4.3 percent in Cleveland. From the perspective of the receiving cities of the North, it was indeed a great migration; it was also a great migration for black society as a whole, for the World War I years set the pattern for the black experience in modern industrial cities, North and South, where 74 percent of the Afro-American population resided in 1970.[48]

Blacks moving out of the South have followed three principal routes. One route follows the Atlantic seaboard from Georgia, the Carolinas,

---

48. See Hill, "Recent," 102; Louise Venable Kennedy, *The Negro Peasant Turns Cityward* (New York, 1930), 27-30; Spear, *Chicago*, 138-140. It is important to note that during World War I, white out-migration from the South was twice that of black (V. D. Johnston, "The Migration and the Census of 1920," *Opportunity* [Aug., 1923], 236). Benjamin Elijah Mays and Joseph William Nicholson, *The Negro's Church* (New York, 1933), 94; Van Deusen, *Black*, 32-33. Blanche J. Paget, "The Plight of the Pennsylvania Negro," *Opportunity* (Sept., 1936), 309.

MARION D. de B. KILSON

and Virginia northward to Philadelphia, New York, and Boston; the second moves north from Alabama, Mississippi, and Louisiana to Chicago, Detroit, and Cleveland; the third stretches west from Louisiana and Texas to California. Within the North, at this time as earlier, considerable intercity mobility developed as migrants sought better opportunities elsewhere. Particularly interesting in this regard are the circuitous routes whereby migrants arrived at peripheral northern cities such as Buffalo, N.Y. In 1927, ten migrants' routes to Buffalo were charted; they included one from Memphis through Muncy, Pennsylvania, to Buffalo; another from Texarkana, Texas, through St. Louis and Chicago to Buffalo; another from Winston-Salem, North Carolina, through Columbus, Ohio, to Buffalo, and also one from Aiken, South Carolina, through Pittsburgh to Buffalo. Carpenter, who studied Buffalo blacks in 1918, characterized the migrant who completed such an arduous route and settled permanently in Buffalo as an exceptionally purposeful family man.[49]

Although migrants to Buffalo may well have been especially enterprising, throughout the period migrants were better educated and often held better jobs than those who stayed behind. Migrants to northern cities aspired to better conditions of life in both social and economic senses. Although it is generally assumed that these expectations were satisfied during the "great migration," this was not unequivocally true in cities such as Pittsburgh. In 1918 the southern migrants to Pittsburgh had held more skilled jobs (11 percent South; 4 percent Pittsburgh) and fewer unskilled jobs (54 percent South; 95 percent Pittsburgh) in the South; more had worked less than ten hours per day in the South (27 percent South; 16 percent Pittsburgh), though more had worked over twelve hours a day (14 percent South; 4 percent Pittsburgh) and more had received high wages and also low wages in the South ($3.60 per day or over: 15 percent South; 5 percent Pittsburgh; less than $2.00: 56 percent South; 5 percent Pittsburgh). On balance, new residents in northern cities probably found housing conditions more congested than in the

49. See Charles S. Johnson, "Present Trends in the Employment of Negro Labor," *Opportunity* (May, 1929), 146-148; Karl E. Taeuber and Alma P. Taeuber, "The Changing Character of Negro Migration," *American Journal of Sociology*, LXX (1965), 432. On Boston, Buffalo, and Poughkeepsie in 1880-1890, see Pleck, "Boston," 8-9. Niles Carpenter, *Nationality, Color and Economic Opportunity in the City of Buffalo* (Buffalo, 1927), 159.

South, but had better food and clothing. Nevertheless, while the black worker may have improved his overall standard of living by moving North, he continued to be deprived relative to white workers.[50]

Rural Social Structure

Despite the continued loss of more capable young members of the community, the social structure of rural communities did not begin to alter radically until after World War II. At that time plantation agriculture was becoming mechanized and changing over from cotton to other forms of produce such as cattle, resulting in a further reduction of economic opportunity for Afro-American unskilled workers. Only in the late 1960s, with the reenfranchisement of blacks, did the power structure of southern rural communities begin to alter from white domination and black subordination toward one of black and white coeval participation. For most of the out-migration period, however, the legacy of the early after-freedom period was a viable reality.[51]

The largest communal unit continued to be the county, comprised of ecologically linked town, plantation, and farm. But whereas the early years after freedom had been ones of economic growth, the early out-migration years were ones of economic decline. Throughout the period the number of black farm owners decreased, from 218,972 in 1910 to 127,000 in 1959. In the Cotton Belt of the 1930s, owners constituted 10 to 13 percent of the black farmers of a county.[52] Johnson eloquently summarized aspects of the social and psychological issues confronting black owners within an Alabama county in the 1930s.

---

50. See Arthur F. Raper, *Preface to Peasantry* (New York, 1968), 193; C. Horace Hamilton, "The Negro Leaves the South," *Demography*, I (1964), 287; Taeuber and Taeuber, "Changing Character," 435. Abraham Epstein, *The Negro Migrant in Pittsburgh* (New York, 1969), 27, 21-23. Kennedy, *Peasant*, 99-100.

51. Morton Rubin, *Plantation County* (New Haven, 1963), *passim*.

52. Between 1910 and 1959 both black and white southern farmers decreased sharply; white farm owners declined from 3,707,501 in 1910, through 3,691,898 in 1920 and 1,390,000 in 1935, to 1,142,000 in 1959; white farm tenants numbered 1,676,558 in 1910, 1,740,363 in 1920, 1,202,000 in 1935, and 288,000 in 1959, while black farm owners fell from 218,972 in 1910, through 218,612 in 1920 and 186,000 in 1935, to 127,000 in 1959 and black farm tenants from 678,118 in 1910 through 714,441 in 1920 and 629,000 in 1935, to 138,000 in 1959 (Woodson, *Rural*, 26-28; Editors of

MARION D. de B. KILSON

> The present Negro population of these old plantation areas can best
> be understood . . . in the light of this plantation tradition, with its
> almost complete dependence upon the immediate landowner for
> guidance and control. . . . Such families as escape from the prevail-
> ing economy of dependence into the new responsibilities which go
> with independence find economic complications and shades of social
> conflict . . . sometimes prompting them to migration, but as often
> leading to resignation and relapse from the ownership status to ten-
> antry.[53]

Nevertheless, the importance of such farm owners to their communities
is clearly conveyed in the overlapping leadership roles played by owners
in the communal institutions of Greene and Macon counties, Georgia,
during the same period. Of the landowners, 80 percent were church
members and a third were church officials; over 50 percent were lodge
members and more than 20 percent were lodge officials; just under 40
percent were school trustees; and two-thirds of the lodge officers were
also church officers. The leadership role of landowners within the community undoubtedly relates both to the enterprise and initiative required
of owners and to their permanent residence within the community, for
tenant farmers were highly mobile within counties. In fact, Frazier attributes the lack of institutional stability within rural Afro-American communities to the mobility of tenant farmers.[54]

Within the context of a numerically diminishing and increasingly
impoverished community, the occupational opportunities, stratification
patterns, and types of communal institutions remained essentially as they
had been earlier. Since occupational and economic differentiations were
relatively slight, educational achievement and moral standards represented the principal criteria for differentiating one stratum from another.
In "Cottonville" and its county in Mississippi in the mid-1930s, Powdermaker differentiated a small upper class (5 percent) of professionals and
businessmen of at least high school education whose families were char-

Ebony, The Negro Handbook [Chicago, 1966], 335). For specific counties, see Johnson, *Shadow,* 10; Davis, *Deep,* 322; Raper, *Preface,* 21. Cf. Hortense Powdermaker,
After Freedom (New York, 1969), 81, 95.

53. Johnson, *Shadow,* 3.

54. Raper, *Preface,* 383. Frazier, *Negro,* 213.

acterized by "patriarchal" structure and stability, a large middle class (87 percent) of agricultural workers, manual laborers, domestic workers, and clergymen, and thirdly a small lower class (7-8 percent) of occasionally employed persons whose own families were extremely unstable but for whom the ideal family form was that of the upper class. In the late 1940s in Wilcox County, Alabama, Rubin also differentiated a three-class stratification system on the basis of similar criteria: an upper class, whose members had at least a high school education and whose family structure was comparable to that of the white middle class, consisting of teachers and plantation owners; a middle class, whose members had achieved an elementary school education and whose adults ultimately settled down to a long-term marital relationship, comprised of domestic workers, artisans, and regularly employed workers; and a lower-class category, whose members had very little education and whose matricentric households were involved with a succession of adult males, consisted of occasional workers and indebted tenants. Analyzing the Piedmont town of Kent at the same period, Lewis considered that class differentiation was incipient rather than manifest and that the important social differentiation in Kent was between respectable and nonrespectable lifestyles, as symbolized by the church and the tavern, respectively.[55] From an overall perspective, however, it is noteworthy that the differentiations of the after-freedom period, based less on occupational criteria than on codes of conduct, have persisted in rural areas into the present.

In addition to the previously noted association between family form and social status, several other attributes of these rural families are noteworthy. Not only is there considerable variation in form, ranging from the male-headed nuclear family of the upper class through a variety of extended family patterns to the female-headed household of lower-middle-class and lower-class families, but there is fluidity in family membership as adopted children and relatives of the household head move in and out for shorter or longer periods of time. Moreover, the internal authority structure of the family depends upon the economic role of the

55. Powdermaker, *After*, 60-71; Rubin, *Plantation*, 124-126; Hylan Lewis, *Blackways of Kent* (New Haven, 1964), 3, 223-236. Cf. Lee Rainwater, "The Crucible of Identity," *Daedalus*, XCV (1965), 172-216.

MARION D. de B. KILSON

adults in such a way that family authority and economic responsibility are positively correlated. This association helps to explain the "patriarchal" nature of upper-class families in Cottonville and among tenant managers in "Old County," Mississippi, as well as the predominant role of the mother with more stable earning power than the father among middle-class and lower-class families, and also the increasing stability of families with more certain incomes in the sawmills of "Plantation County" in the late 1940s.[56] In rural areas, therefore, the form and internal authority structure of families are determined by economic, primarily income, factors.

Just as relatively little occupational change occurred in the rural South during the period of out-migration, so communal institutional patterns changed little. By 1930, 76 percent of all churches were rural and predominantly (67.7 percent) Methodist and Baptist. Most members of the community were church members: in 1928, 74.3 percent in Greene County, Georgia; in the late 1940s, 80 percent of the inhabitants of the little Piedmont town of Kent—many of whom were still affiliated with their natal rural churches rather than ones in Kent.[57] As in after-freedom days, "the church is the one outstanding institution of the community over which the Negroes themselves exercise control, and because it stands so alone in administering to their own conception of their needs, its functions are varied."[58] Undoubtedly with the increased political role of blacks in the rural South, the communal functions of the church will become increasingly limited.

In arguing for essential structural continuity during the past century, it would be erroneous to suggest that significant changes have not occurred that will affect and are affecting the nature of rural communities. Some indications of the magnitude of these changes are suggested by looking at some social trends in southern counties studied at an earlier period. Around the turn of the century, DuBois, Thom, and Laws studied several rural communities, including in their reports brief descriptions of the surrounding counties; in the 1930s and 1940s Johnson, Raper,

56. See Lewis, *Kent*, 88-104; Johnson, *Shadow*, 33-44, 29. Davis, *Deep*, 409-412. Powdermaker, *After*, 145-149, 197-210; Rubin, *Plantation*, 103-104.

57. Mays and Nicholson, *Church*, 230-231. Raper, *Preface*, 365; Lewis, *Kent*, 129-130.

58. Johnson, *Shadow*, 150.

and Rubin made case studies of plantation counties. By looking at available statistical socioeconomic data on these counties over the past ninety years some notion of the extent of rural change can be achieved. Since 1910 a striking decline in the proportion of blacks has taken place in all the counties except Macon County, Alabama, immortalized by Johnson in *Shadow of the Plantation* (see n. 23). While the proportion of blacks in these counties ranged from 29 to 79 percent in 1880 and from 4 to 81 percent in 1970, the mean proportion of county blacks has declined from 59 percent in 1880 to 38 percent in 1970. In all the counties the proportion of illiterates has been reduced radically, from as high as 61 percent and no lower than 26 percent in 1910 to no more than 10 percent and as low as 1 percent in 1970. Not surprisingly, the school-going population has risen significantly during these decades; county children attending school ranged from 28 to 69 percent in the 6-14 year age group in 1910 and from 85 to 100 percent in the 7-13 age category in 1970. Moreover, the proportion of 16-17-year-olds attending school has risen from a range of 22 to 51 percent in 1930 to a range of 71 to 92 percent in 1970. Perhaps most striking of all is the 1970 occupational profile for counties which at the time of their initial study were comprised primarily of agricultural workers and other unskilled laborers. In 1970, the proportion of county farmers and farm workers ranged from 17 to 0.1 percent, other blue collar occupations ranged from 87 to 59 percent, while white collar occupations varied between 37 and 8 percent for men. Finally, a summary of salient socioeconomic attributes of the population of these counties shows that the vast majority (from 82 to 96 percent) were born in the state in which they live; the median number of years in school is low (ranging from 5.4 years to 12.1, with a mean of 6.5 years), and the proportion of high school graduates is also low (ranging from 9 to 53 percent and averaging 19 percent) in these counties, as are median yearly incomes (ranging from $2,394 to $6,745 and averaging $3,751) and unemployment rates (ranging from 1.8 to 16.2 percent and averaging 5.4 percent).[59] Thus, although the popula-

---

59. Census, *1790-1915*, table 2, 776; table 3, 798-839; table 3, 827. Charles E. Hall, *Negroes in the United States, 1920-32* (Washington, D.C., 1935), Appendix. Bureau of the Census, *1970 Census of the Population, General Social and Economic Characteristics*, vols. for Alabama, Georgia, Louisiana, Maryland, Virginia (Washington, D.C., 1972), tables 119, 120, 125, 126, 127.

MARION D. de B. KILSON

tion of these counties has improved in educational achievement and its occupational structure has changed, those who remain in the rural counties are for the most part impoverished folk.

Urban Social Structure

The period of out-migration opened with an influx of southern blacks into northern cities, creating considerable dislocation for established white—and black—residents, as symbolized by race riots after World War I in large cities such as Chicago, Omaha, St. Louis, Springfield, and Tulsa, and in small cities like Chester and Coatesville in Pennsylvania. Moreover, the newly arrived Afro-Americans intensified the pattern of residential segregation. The pattern of ghettoization originated in northern industrial centers and later developed in southern industrial centers, ultimately spreading to older southern cities which previously had had integrated housing patterns as a consequence of the residential proximity of master and slave in the antebellum period. By 1960, urban centers, North and South, had a firmly entrenched ghetto pattern in which certain sections of the city were occupied by 94 to 98 percent black residents.[60]

For blacks in northern cities, the great migration had a number of important consequences: creation of a market for black business, congested housing conditions facilitating higher rates of illness and crime, and disruption of established social patterns leading to fundamental institutional changes.[61]

O'Kane suggests that southern blacks moving to the city first in the South and subsequently in the North migrated from agricultural poverty to industrial poverty. For some this was certainly true. A comparison, however, of the 1920 occupational distribution of blacks in the United States and blacks in selected cities indicates that, in general, urban living

---

60. Clara A. Hardin, *The Negroes of Philadelphia* (Bryn Mawr, 1945), 3; Jesse O. Thomas, "American Cities—Tulsa," *Opportunity* (Feb., 1929), 54. See Frazier, *Family*, 237; Rudolf Heberle, "Social Consequences of the Industrialization of Southern Cities," *Social Forces*, XXVIII (1948), 29-37. See Kenneth B. Clark, *Dark Ghetto* (New York, 1965), 25.

61. See Drake and Cayton, *Metropolis*, 434; Van Deusen, *Black*, 42-43; Clark, *Ghetto*, 86-90; Frazier, *Church*, 47-64.

was associated with occupational differentiation and occupational upward mobility.[62] A reflection of the significance of the more differentiated occupational profile during the out-migration years is the changing criteria for social stratification which Frazier eloquently summarized with reference to border cities in 1940.

> As the social structure has evolved, such social distinctions as free ancestry, white ancestry and color, and even family background and general culture have tended to become less important than distinctions based upon occupation, education, and income.[63]

In the late 1940s, Frazier suggested, as DuBois had forty years before, that occupational differentiation was greatest in northern cities and least in southern metropolitan centers. Drake and Cayton's analysis of social stratification in Chicago in the mid-1940s conveys aspects of the new complexity; they discuss three classes based on occupational and income criteria: a small upper class (5 percent), a sizable middle class (30 percent), and a large lower class (65 percent). Each of these classes is further subdivided into a "respectable" and a "shady" category reflecting the manner in which livelihoods were earned within the category, and finally the "respectable" category is further subdivided into church-oriented and non-church-oriented subcategories.[64] Returning briefly to the analysis of black Chicago in 1961, Drake and Cayton noted that "the norms and values and the styles of living described . . . have changed but little. . . . Changes have been in the direction of a more intensive elaboration of Bronzeville's separate sub-culture, not toward its disappearance."[65]

In the city during the out-migration period, as before, differences in social status were associated with differences in family patterns. At all status levels, however, the ideal family form was the nuclear family of the urban middle and upper classes. Recent studies suggest that the crucial factor with respect to marital stability is income. Farley's finding is

---

62. James M. O'Kane, "Ethnic Mobility and the Lower-Income Negro, A Sociohistorical Perspective," *Social Problems*, XVI (1969), 303. See tables 15.6 and 15.9.
63. E. Franklin Frazier, *Negro Youth at the Crossways* (New York, 1967), 21.
64. Frazier, *Family*, 285. Drake and Cayton, *Metropolis*, 522.
65. Drake and Cayton, *Metropolis*, xi, xiii.

MARION D. de B. KILSON

consistent with Hershberg's analysis of the decline in husband-wife households during an antebellum decade of economic decline in Philadelphia; with Moynihan's correlation of family disorganization with cyclical swings of unemployment since World War II; with Raper's finding in the 1930s that when rural families moved to southern cities, many husbands (25 percent) deserted their families because of lack of funds; and with Rubin's observation that after men began to have reliable work in Plantation County sawmills, the stability of their marriages increased. The problems of earning a living in the city are reflected in the higher desertion rates in urban centers throughout the out-migration period and in the income differentials for black and white citizens in the post-World War II era.[66] Among the consequences of family disorganization are an increase in welfare families, leading to the generation of a new culture of dependency within an urban rather than a rural context.[67]

Through the urbanization process of the out-migration period, the black church was transformed and lost its unique status within the community. Frazier analyzed three major religious responses to urbanization following the "great migration": a secularization of established denominations, whose congregations were differentiated along class lines; an attempt to recreate rural churches in intimate storefront churches; and an innovative response to urban life through cult movements. In 1930, Mays and Nicholson's survey of urban churches showed that in southern cities, 61.5 percent of the churches were Baptist and more blacks belonged to congregations than whites, and in northern cities Baptist churches were 45.3 percent of the urban churches, Holiness 23.7 percent, Spiritualist and African Methodist Episcopal 7.5 percent. The survey further determined that storefront churches were more numerous in the North (57 percent of all churches) than in the South (18 percent), with storefronts constituting 45 percent of the churches in Detroit, 72 percent

---

66. See Warner, *New Haven,* 221. Reynolds Farley, "Trends in Marital Status Among Negroes," in Charles V. Willie (ed.), *The Family Life of Black People* (Columbus, 1970), 173; J. Richard Udry, "Marital Instability by Race, Sex, Education and Occupation, Using 1960 Census Data," *American Journal of Sociology,* LXXII (1966), 203-209; Department of Labor, *The Negro Family, The Case for National Action* (Washington, D.C., 1965), 21; Raper, *Preface,* 196-199. See tables, 15.3, 15.10, and 15.11.
67. 17.2 percent urban black families in 1970.

in Chicago, and 54 percent in Baltimore. Although the church was initially the most important institution assisting newcomers to northern cities to adapt to urban life, other institutions began to take over various community services previously performed by churches. Such institutions included recreational organizations such as YMCAs and city park services, welfare organizations, libraries, and other cultural institutions.[68]

Conclusion

In reviewing the social structure of Afro-Americans from 1790 to 1970, the basic social transformation has been the shift from rural to urban living. In a real sense, the antebellum period saw the intensification of the rural basis of black society with the expansion of the southern plantation economy, while the period since freedom has involved the urbanization of Afro-Americans concomitant with the growth of an industrial economy.[69] Both the agrarian slave and urban freeman of the antebellum period contributed significantly to the traditions of Afro-American society in the years after freedom.

In retrospect, the freeman's experience, especially in northern cities, created a model for the black experience in modern industrial urban America. The society of the urban freeman was more occupationally diversified than any other sector of black society during the same period. Nevertheless, most northern freemen were restricted to unskilled jobs and faced fierce competition from white workers. Freemen were limited by whites with respect to where they could live, and from these small black communities developed in later years the urban ghetto—"a world within a world." Out of the enterprise of urban freemen developed the tradition of separate institutional development, first through the church and later through a variety of secular associations serving many of the social functions of the freeman's church.

---

68. Mays and Nicholson, *Church*, 209-219. See R. Maurice Moss, "American Cities-Grand Rapids," *Opportunity* (Jan., 1929), 14; Eugene Kinckle Jones, "Negro Migration in New York State," *Opportunity* (Jan., 1926), 10; Ira DeA. Reid, *Social Conditions of the Negro in the Hill District of Pittsburgh* (Pittsburgh, 1930), 99; Ira DeA. Reid, *The Negro Community of Baltimore* (Baltimore, 1935), 37.

69. See tables 15.5 and 15.8. Cf. Farley, "Urbanization," 241-258.

MARION D. de B. KILSON

This tradition of enterprise and initiative under adverse circumstances established by black freemen before "Jubilee" helps to account for certain developments since freedom. Such achievements include the notable reduction in illiteracy among blacks from 70 percent in 1880 to 3.6 percent in 1970, associated with a rise in school attendance from 44.7 percent of black youth in 1910 to 74.8 percent in 1970. These educational developments help to account for the occupational upward mobility of Afro-Americans, who, relative to white Americans, nonetheless remain disadvantaged with respect to education, occupation, and income.[70] The tradition of institutional innovation established by freemen is also apparent not only in the proliferation of black churches from 700 in 1866 to 50,293 in 1966, but through the growth of communal institutions at both local and national levels.[71] Thus, black freemen in the antebellum North, both in their relations with white society and in their independent com-

70. See tables 15.1, 15.2, and 15.3. Between 1880 and 1970, the percentage of illiterates among whites and blacks over ten years old declined; illiteracy among whites fell from 9.4 percent in 1880, through 7.7 percent in 1890, 6.2 percent in 1900, 5.0 percent in 1910, 4.1 percent in 1920, 3.4 percent in 1930, 1.6 percent in 1960, to 0.7 percent in 1970, while illiteracy among blacks declined from 70.0 percent in 1880, through 57.1 percent in 1890, 44.5 percent in 1900, 30.4 percent in 1910, 22.9 percent in 1920, 16.3 percent in 1930, 7.5 percent in 1960, to 3.6 percent in 1970 (Work, *Year Book*, 208; Hall, *Negroes*, table 7, 233; Bureau of the Census, *Statistical Abstracts of the United States, 1971* [Washington, D.C., 1971], table 170). During the period 1910-1970, school attendance for whites and blacks increased as follows: black school attendance rose from 44.7 percent in 1910 through 53.5 percent in 1920, to 60 percent in 1930 for 5-20-year-olds, and from 53.1 percent in 1940, through 59.6 percent in 1950 and 69.2 percent in 1960, to 74.8 percent in 1970 for 5-24-year-olds; during these decades white school attendance for the same age categories increased from 64.5 percent in 1910, through 65.7 percent in 1920, 71.5 percent in 1930, 58.5 percent in 1940, 62.5 percent in 1950, 71.8 percent in 1960, to 78.2 percent in 1970 (Hall, *Negroes*, tables 4, 5, 209-210; Bureau of the Census, *General Population Characteristics, United States Summary* [Washington, D.C., 1960], table 166; Bureau of the Census, *1940 Census of Population, General Population Characteristics, United States Summary* [Washington, D.C., 1940], table 11; Bureau of the Census, *Abstracts 1971*, table 160).

71. Black religious institutions have increased from 700 churches with 600,000 members in 1866, to 36,770 churches with 3,685,097 members in 1906, to 42,000 churches with 5,200,000 in 1930, to 50,293 churches with 11,119,000 members in 1966 (Work, *Year Book*, 118; Woodson, *Church*, 286-287; *Ebony, Handbook*, 308). Black national organizations included 15 educational groups in 1930 and 11 in 1970, 19 professional associations in 1930 and 23 in 1970, 60 secret societies in 1930 and 10 in 1970, 7 community service groups in 1930 and 9 in 1970 (Work, *Year Book*, 521-523; Sloan, *Blacks*, 107-110).

munal endeavors, established the pattern for blacks in urban America that persists today.

The agrarian slave also contributed significantly to the subsequent Afro-American experience. Through the slave system, blacks acquired an occupation as unskilled agrarian laborers that engaged a majority of Afro-Americans until the out-migration period and that still engages a small proportion of rural blacks. As important as the means of livelihood acquired during slavery was the establishment of a dependent relationship with white individuals and white society. The tradition of dependence enforced by slavery and perpetuated by the persistence of plantation agriculture within the rural South has contributed in the contemporary impoverished urban context to the development of a culture of dependence upon public institutions.

The ecological transformation of black society within the context of an industrializing American society has led to increasing social differentiation within black America, with domestic and communal institutional forms associated with status distinctions. Nevertheless, despite empirical variations in family forms, members of all strata have aspired to achieve nuclear families throughout the period under review. This aspiration vividly symbolizes the extent to which Afro-Americans quickly became acculturated to the values and ideals of their post-diaspora homeland. Moreover, as a consequence of civil rights achievements since World War II, caste is becoming secondary to class in determining the life chances of Afro-Americans. Thus, the extent of social differentiation within black America associated with more diversified patterns of relationship with the larger society suggests that increasingly class, rather than caste, will explain black participation in the American social system.

MARION D. de B. KILSON

TABLE 15.1   Black and White Occupational Distribution and Education, 1959 and 1970 (percentages)

	White			Black		
	Total years of high school			Total years of high school		
		-4	4+		-4	4+
1959						
Male						
White collar	39.7	20.3	58.3	12.6	5.3	38.8
Blue collar	45.5	58.9	32.3	59.3	65.4	37.3
Service	5.6	7.2	4.0	14.3	12.6	20.2
Farm	9.2	13.7	4.9	13.9	16.7	3.7
Female						
White collar	61.1	31.5	80.3	17.6	5.8	44.5
Blue collar	17.2	31.4	8.0	14.7	15.7	12.4
Service	18.5	31.6	10.0	64.3	73.8	42.6
Farm	3.2	5.5	1.6	3.4	4.7	0.5
1970						
Male						
White collar	44.3	18.5	58.0	23.2	8.8	42.1
Blue collar	45.0	64.8	34.6	61.1	71.6	47.3
Service	5.6	7.5	4.6	11.1	12.6	9.2
Farm	5.0	9.1	2.9	4.6	7.0	1.4
Female						
White collar	64.7	30.3	77.9	35.1	10.3	56.8
Blue collar	16.3	35.6	9.0	18.4	21.5	15.8
Service	17.5	31.0	12.3	45.8	67.0	27.3
Farm	1.5	3.2	0.8	0.7	1.2	0.2

Source: Bureau of the Census, *Statistical Abstracts of the United States, 1971* (Washington, D.C., 1971), table 168.

TABLE 15.2   Black and White Employment, 1910-1970, and Unemployment
Ratios, 1950-1970

	Gainfully Employed (10 years and over, percentages)			
	Black	White Native	White Foreign-born	White Total
Male				
1910	87.4	77.9	90.0	
1920	81.1	75.1	89.3	
1930	80.2	73.4	88.4	
1940	82.2			85.1
1950	92.2			95.1
1960	91.2			96.4
1970	92.7			96.0
Female				
1910	54.7	19.2	21.7	
1920	38.9	19.3	18.4	
1930	38.9	20.5	18.8	
1940	85.5			86.7
1950	92.1			95.4
1960	91.5			94.6
1970	90.7			94.6
	Black-White Unemployment Ratios, 1950-1970			
1950	1.8			
1955	2.2			
1960	2.1			
1965	2.0			
1970	1.8			

Sources: Charles E. Hall, Negroes in the United States, 1920-1932 (Washington, D.C., 1935), table 1, 288; Bureau of the Census, Census of the Population, 1960: Characteristics of the Population, United States Summary (Washington, D.C., 1964), table 88; Bureau of the Census, Statistical Abstracts of the
United States, 1971 (Washington, D.C., 1971), table 335; Bureau of the Census,
The Social and Economic Status of Negroes in the United States, 1969 (Washington, D.C., 1969), 29; Bureau of the Census, 1970 Census of Population,
General Social and Economic Statistics, United States Summary (Washington,
D.C., 1972), table 90.

TABLE 15.3 Black and White Family Income, 1960-1970 (percentages)

Families	-$2,999	$3,000-4,999	$5,000-6,999	$7,000-9,999	$10,000-14,999	$15,000-24,999	$25,000-	Median
Total families								
1970: U.S.	10.3	10.0	11.8	20.6	26.6	16.0	4.6	$9,590
Black	23.6	17.6	16.1	18.8	16.1	6.9	1.0	6,067
1960: U.S.	21.4	20.5	23.0	20.1	10.5	3.3	1.3	5,660
Black	47.9	24.9	14.3	8.7	3.4	0.7	0.1	3,161
Urban families								
1970: U.S.	8.7	8.9	10.9	20.0	28.0	18.0	5.3	10,196
Black	20.7	16.5	16.1	19.9	17.9	7.8	1.1	6,581
1960: U.S.	16.4	19.0	24.2	22.6	12.3	3.9	1.5	6,166
Black	39.6	27.7	17.1	10.5	4.2	0.8	0.2	3,711
Rural farm families								
1970: U.S.	17.7	14.8	15.3	19.6	19.2	9.9	3.3	7,296
Black	44.3	22.4	13.6	11.2	6.1	1.9	0.4	3,445
1960: U.S.	47.1	23.1	14.1	9.0	4.6	1.6	0.6	3,228
Black	83.8	9.9	3.7	1.7	0.7	0.2	0.1	1,263
Rural non-farm families								
1970: U.S.	13.9	12.2	14.2	22.7	23.8	10.7	2.6	8,248
Black	27.2	22.9	15.9	13.6	7.6	2.3	0.4	4,035
1960: U.S.	28.9	24.2	22.3	15.5	6.5	1.8	0.7	4,750
Black	70.1	18.5	6.8	3.3	1.1	0.2	0.1	1,917

Source: Bureau of the Census, *1970 Census of Population, General Social and Economic Characteristics, United States Summary* (Washington, D.C., 1972), table 83.

TABLE 15.4   Black Population, 1790-1970

Year	Number of blacks	% United States population
1790	757,208	19.3
1800	1,002,037	18.9
1810	1,377,808	19.0
1820	1,771,656	18.4
1830	2,328,642	18.1
1840	2,873,648	16.8
1850	3,638,808	15.7
1860	4,441,830	14.1
1870	4,880,009	12.7
1880	6,580,793	13.1
1890	7,488,676	11.9
1900	8,833,994	11.6
1910	9,827,763	10.7
1920	10,463,131	9.9
1930	11,891,143	9.7
1940	12,865,914	9.7
1950	15,044,937	9.9
1960	18,871,831	10.5
1970	22,580,289	11.1

Sources: Bureau of the Census, *Negro Population, 1790-1915* (Washington, D.C., 1918), table 2, 25; Charles E. Hall, *Negroes in the United States, 1920-1932* (Washington, D.C., 1935), table 1, 1; Bureau of the Census, *1970 Census of Population, General Population Characteristics, United States Summary* (Washington, D.C., 1970), table 48, 1-262.

MARION D. de B. KILSON

TABLE 15.5   Black and White Population in Urban Areas, 1870-1970 (percentages)

Region and place	1870	1880	1890	1900	1910	1920	1930	1940	1950	1960	1970
United States											
White	27.5	30.3	38.4	43.0	48.7	53.4	57.6	57.4	64.3	68.5	67.8
Black	13.4	14.3	19.8	22.7	27.4	34.0	43.7	48.6	62.4	73.2	74.0
New England											
White	44.2	50.6	62.5	69.0	74.0	75.7	76.9	76.1	78.7	79.1	
Black	54.0	62.7	71.5	78.3	82.6	86.7	89.0	90.1	94.0	95.6	
North Central											
White	20.5	23.8	32.7	38.2	44.7	51.6	56.9	57.3	62.6	66.8	
Black	37.2	42.5	55.8	64.4	72.6	83.4	87.8	88.8	93.8	95.7	
West											
White	25.3	30.7	37.9	41.2	49.2	53.0	59.6	58.8	69.7	77.6	
Black	44.6	50.8	54.0	67.4	78.6	74.0	82.5	83.1	90.3	92.7	
South											
White	13.3	13.1	16.9	18.5	23.2	29.6	33.4	36.8	48.9	58.6	
Black	10.3	10.6	15.3	17.2	21.2	25.3	31.7	36.5	47.7	58.5	

Sources: Daniel O. Price, *Changing Characteristics of the Negro Population* (Washington, D.C., 1969), table I-3, 11; Bureau of the Census, *Statistical Abstracts of the United States, 1971* (Washington, D.C., 1971), table 14.

TABLE 15.6 Black Occupational Distribution, 1910-1970 (percentages)

Occupation	1910	1920	1930	1940	1950	1960	1970
Male							
Professionals	1.1	1.2	1.5	1.8	2.1	3.9	5.2
Proprietors, managers, administrators	26.3	27.2	23.0	22.5	15.2	6.7	3.4
Farmers	25.3	26.2	21.8	21.2	13.3	4.4	0.7
Wholesale-retail	0.6	0.6	0.7	1.3	1.9	2.3	2.7
Clerks	1.0	1.5	1.7	1.2	3.1	5.0	7.2
Sales	-	-	-	0.8	1.1	1.5	1.8
Skilled workers	3.6	4.6	4.8	4.5	7.7	10.2	13.2
Semiskilled workers	4.7	7.0	9.0	12.5	21.9	23.5	26.0
In manufacturing	1.7	2.8	2.9	-	-	14.3	17.2
Unskilled workers	63.3	58.5	60.0	57.1	48.3	40.9	30.9
Farm laborers	30.8	20.5	18.9	19.9	10.3	7.1	3.1
Factory and building	13.4	17.4	17.8	21.3	23.7	19.4	13.6
Servant	6.9	7.1	9.4	15.9	14.3	14.4	14.2
Female							
Professionals	1.4	2.4	3.3	4.3	5.6	7.5	10.3
Proprietors, managers, etc.	4.3	5.6	4.7	3.7	2.9	1.9	1.4
Farmers	4.0	5.1	4.2	3.0	1.6	0.7	0.1
Clerks	0.3	1.0	1.1	0.9	4.0	8.5	18.4
Sales	-	-	-	0.5	1.3	1.7	2.2
Skilled workers	0.1	0.1	0.1	0.2	0.6	0.7	1.3
Semiskilled workers	5.4	9.0	10.1	6.2	14.6	12.8	14.6
Unskilled workers	88.4	82.0	80.7	83.6	69.2	58.9	39.9
Farm laborers	48.2	33.8	22.8	12.9	7.5	2.9	0.8
Servant	39.4	45.5	56.3	69.9	60.2	55.0	37.8

Sources: Alba M. Edwards, *A Socio-economic Grouping of the Gainful Workers of the United States, 1930* (Washington, D.C., 1938), table 4, 13; Bureau of the Census, *1960 Census of Population, General Population Characteristics, United States Summary* (Washington, D.C. 1960), table 88; Bureau of the Census, *1970 Census of the Population, General Population Characteristics, United States Summary* (Washington, D.C., 1970), table 81; Bureau of the Census, *1950 Census of Population, General Population Characteristics, United States Summary* (Washington, D.C., 1950), table 123; Daniel O. Price, *Changing Characteristics of the Negro Population* (Washington, D.C., 1969), table IV-3, 116.

MARION D. DEB. KILSON

TABLE 15.7 Regional Distribution of Black Population, 1790-1970 (percentages)

Year	The South	The North	The West
1790	91.1	8.9	-
1800	91.6	8.4	-
1810	92.1	7.9	-
1820	92.7	7.3	-
1830	92.8	7.2	-
1840	91.9	8.1	-
1850	92.1	7.8	-
1860	92.2	7.7	0.1
1870	90.6	9.3	0.1
1880	90.5	9.3	0.2
1890	90.3	9.4	0.4
1900	89.7	10.0	0.3
1910	89.0	10.5	0.5
1920	85.2	14.1	0.8
1930	78.7	20.3	1.0
1940	77.0	11.6	1.3
1950	68.0	28.2	3.8
1960	59.9	34.3	5.8
1970	53.0	39.0	8.0

Sources: Bureau of the Census, *Negro Population, 1790-1915* (Washington, D.C., 1918), table 3, 33; Charles E. Hall, *Negroes in the United States, 1920-1932* (Washington, D.C., 1935), table 3, 5; Bureau of the Census, *Statistical Abstracts of the United States, 1971* (Washington, D.C., 1971), table 19; Daniel O. Price, *Changing Characteristics of the Negro Population* (Washington, D.C., 1969), Table I-1, 9; Bureau of the Census, *1940 Census of the Population, General Population Characteristics, United States Summary* (Washington, D.C., 1940), table 25.

TABLE 15.8   Black Population in Urban South and Southern-born Outside the
South and Decennial Increase, 1870-1970

A. Black Population Year	Born in South and living outside South	Living in urban South
1970	3,324,879	8,050,000
1960	3,256,596	6,617,000
1950	2,594,125	4,819,000
1940	1,668,811	3,204,000
1930	1,460,633	2,966,000
1920	780,794	2,251,000
1910	440,534	1,854,000
1900	349,651	1,365,000
1890	241,855	1,033,000
1880	198,029	630,000
1870	149,000	454,000

B. Decennial Increase Years	Born in South and living outside South	Living in urban South
1960-70	68,283	1,433,000
1950-60	662,471	1,798,000
1940-50	925,314	1,264,000
1930-40	208,178	650,000
1920-30	679,839	715,000
1910-20	340,260	397,000
1900-10	90,883	489,000
1890-00	107,796	717,000
1880-90	43,826	403,000
1870-80	48,929	176,000

Sources: Daniel O. Price, Changing Characteristics of the Negro Population
(Washington, D.C., 1969), Appendix B, 245; T. J. Woofter, Jr., Races and Ethnic
Groups in American Life (New York, 1933), tables 35, 36; C. Horace Hamilton,
"The Negro Leaves the South," Demography, I (1964), table 4a, 281; Bureau of
the Census, Negro Population, 1790-1915 (Washington, D.C., 1918), table 14,
68; Bureau of the Census, 1970 United States Census of Population, State of Birth
(Washington, D.C., 1972), table 5, 3; Bureau of the Census, 1970 Census of
Population, General Social and Economic Statistics, United States Summary
(Washington, D.C., 1972), tables 131, 142; Bureau of the Census, Historical
Statistics of the United States, Colonial Times to 1957 (Washington, D.C., 1960),
table C 15-24.

MARION D. de B. KILSON

TABLE 15.9 Black Occupational Distribution in Selected Cities, 1920
(percentages)

City	Proprie-tors, officials, etc.	Clerks	Skilled workers	Semi-skilled	Laborers	Servants	Profes-sionals
Southern							
Atlanta							
Men	2.0	4.3	12.3	17.8	46.4	15.3	1.6
Women	1.3	2.6	-	16.9	1.8	74.8	2.3
Baltimore							
Men	2.5	2.5	3.9	16.4	58.0	14.7	1.7
Women	1.1	0.9	0.2	15.4	1.4	79.0	2.0
Birmingham							
Men	1.3	1.9	11.6	25.7	50.8	6.6	1.8
Women	1.5	1.6	0.2	18.0	2.1	73.0	3.6
New Orleans							
Men	1.2	3.0	10.4	17.5	57.1	9.0	1.2
Women	1.1	1.5	-	50.7	2.8	41.9	1.9
Northern							
Chicago							
Men	2.2	6.1	8.3	13.4	41.4	24.8	2.6
Women	2.6	8.7	0.6	32.1	4.2	48.3	3.4
Detroit							
Men	1.4	2.4	15.8	15.5	51.2	11.6	1.7
Women	4.9	4.1	0.5	28.3	4.0	55.2	2.8
New York							
Men	1.5	8.3	7.9	14.5	28.5	35.0	2.8
Women	1.0	2.7	0.3	30.0	0.7	63.1	2.3
Philadelphia							
Men	2.4	3.8	8.0	15.4	51.1	16.0	1.7
Women	1.6	1.7	0.1	18.7	1.0	75.0	1.9
Western							
Los Angeles							
Men	3.1	4.4	10.1	13.2	30.5	33.7	3.5
Women	2.5	3.6	0.3	17.1	0.7	72.6	3.1

Source: Dean Dutcher, *The Negro in Modern Industrial Society* (Lancaster, 1930), 96-97.

TABLE 15.10 Distribution of Ever-Married Blacks, 1910–1960 (percentages)

Region	Black women				Black men			
	Married Spouse present	*Spouse absent*	*Widowed*	*Divorced*	*Married Spouse present*	*Spouse absent*	*Widowed*	*Divorced*
North and West								
1910	62	8	27	3	......	......	......	......
1940	58	15	25	2	72	18	8	2
1960	63	16	15	6	75	15	5	5
Urban South								
1910	54	8	36	2	......	......	......	......
1940	54	13	—32—		......	......	......	......
1960	60	17	18	5	77	14	6	3
Rural South								
1910	74	4	21	1	......	......	......	......
1940	73	7	—20—		......	......	......	......
1960	72	12	14	2	81	12	5	2

Source: Reynolds Farley, "Trends in Marital Status Among Negroes," in Charles V. Willie (ed.), *The Family Life of Black People* (Columbus, 1970), 177.

MARION D. de B. KILSON

TABLE 15.11 Black and White Family Heads, 1950-1970 (percentages)

Heads	Families		
	1950	1960	1970
White			
Husband/wife	88.0	88.7	88.7
Other male	3.5	2.6	2.3
Female	8.5	8.7	9.1
Black			
Husband/wife	77.7	73.6	69.7
Other male	4.7	4.0	3.5
Female	17.6	22.4	26.7

Sources: Bureau of the Census, *The Social and Economic Status of Negroes in the United States, 1969* (Washington, D.C., 1969), 70; Bureau of the Census, *Statistical Abstracts of the United States, 1971* (Washington, D.C., 1971), table 46.

16 Martin L. Kilson

The Political Status of American Negroes in the Twentieth Century

Background and Context

Following the abolition of American Negro slavery, the federal government's policy of Reconstruction gave the former slaves a brief encounter with modern political participation. This experience included the right to vote and the right to hold political office at all levels of government in the South, including congressional office. By the 1880s, however, the anti-Reconstruction groups in both the South and the federal government had prepared the way for the effective disenfranchisement of the Negro. A combination of constitutional and extraconstitutional methods (including coercion and violence) were used to reduce the majority of American Negroes, who resided overwhelmingly in the South, to effective political subservience.[1] From the 1890s onward, modern political rights were available to blacks on an appreciable scale only through migration out of the South to the cities of the North, Midwest, and West.

Migration out of the South became an established feature of American Negro life in the years 1910-1915 onward. Yet in the succeeding half-century more than half of the Negro population remained in the South. For example, only 10 percent had left the South by 1910, 23 percent by

---

1. See Paul Lewison, *Race, Class and Party: A History of Negro Suffrage and White Politics in the South* (New York, 1932). See also C. Vann Woodward, *The Strange Career of Jim Crow* (New York, 1966). The success of disenfranchisement of southern Negroes is seen in the fact that by 1940. a half-century later, only 250,000 Negroes were registered voters—5 percent of Negro adults in the South.

MARTIN L. KILSON

1930, 32 percent by 1950, and 40 percent by 1960. Migration out of the South was, however, crucial to the acquisition of modern political status by blacks: for the white supremacist barriers to Negro participation persisted until the middle of the twentieth century. What, then, was the experience of that minority of blacks who left the white supremacist South for the cities of the North, Midwest, and West in the first several decades of the 1900s?

For one thing, residence outside the South gave blacks their first intensive experience with urbanization. The significance of urbanization to the political development of Negroes cannot be overemphasized: it afforded them that quality of social organization and institutional spe-- cialization without which effective political influence is impossible. As DuBois, the first systematic observer of the urban Negro, recognized in his study of the Philadelphia Negro at the turn of the twentieth century, there is a strong correlation between the sociological differentiation available to Negroes in cities and their political attributes.[2] Urbanization within the South—limited for blacks in any case—did not permit that quality of sociological development that was conducive to realizing political influence and change.

Yet Negro urbanization outside the South was not free of obstacles to effective social and political development. Negro city dwelling outside the South was also stifled by that cluster of norms and behavior characterized by the term white racism. No other major American immigrant community—Irish, Jews, Italians, etc.—faced a comparable range of restrictions upon its urban adaptation. Warner, the sociologist of mainstream America, discovered this in Yankee City: "The caste barrier or color line, *rigid and unrelenting*, has cut off this small group [blacks—.48 percent of Yankee City's population] from the general life of the community."[3] Such isolation of blacks "from the general life of the community" is central to understanding the dynamics of blacks' political status in cities outside the South in the first half of the twentieth century.

Whatever the general life of a modern community consists of, surely

2. W. E. B. DuBois, *The Philadelphia Negro* (Philadelphia, 1899), 233-234, *et passim*.

3. W. Lloyd Warner and Paul S. Lunt, *The Social Life of a Modern Community* (New Haven, 1941), 217. My italics.

politics is a salient feature, for politics is the process through which a significant share of modern services and benefits is allocated among competing sectors of society. Social restrictions imposed upon Negroes in cities outside the South necessarily jeopardize their political capacity. They become victims of the caprice of white-controlled city governments and organizations. Such victimization was frequent from 1900 into the 1940s for the typical lower-class and working-class urban Negro outside the South. Myrdal identified one notable area of such victimization—by the police—in his survey of the Negro's status in the middle 1940s: "In most Northern communities," he observed, "Negroes are more likely than whites to be arrested under any suspicious circumstances. They are more likely to be accorded discourteous or brutal treatment at the hands of the police than are whites. The rate of killing of Negroes by the police is high in many Northern cities."[4]

City Machines and Afro-Americans 1900-1960

From World War I onward, the party and bureaucratic structures in cities outside the South functioned to preclude an effective political role for Negroes. Not that the black city dwellers were totally ignored by white-controlled city politics; their numbers alone argued against indifference, as shown in table 16.1. Rather, white city machines—with the notable exception of Chicago's—simply dealt half-heartedly with the problem of the political inclusion of Negroes on terms comparable to that of white ethnic groups. In order to ensure a truncated political status for blacks, the typical city machines "gerrymandered ghetto neighborhoods so that [whites] would not have to share their power with Negroes."[5] Such practices distorted Negro political development outside the South for a half-century.

Above all, the half-hearted stance toward blacks by white-controlled city machines during the first several decades of the 1900s deprived Negroes of a primary mode of political influence that had been available to white ethnic groups—namely, the politicization of ethnicity. This means

---

4. Gunnar Myrdal, *An American Dilemma* (New York, 1944), 527 *et passim*.
5. Herbert J. Gans, "The Ghetto Rebellions and Urban Class Conflict," in Robert Connery (ed.), *Urban Riots* (New York, 1969), 52-53.

MARTIN L. KILSON

TABLE 16.1   Number and Percentage of Negroes in Selected Northern Cities,
1910-1940

City	Number of Negroes				Percent Negroes in population			
	1910	1920	1930	1940	1910	1920	1930	1940
New York	91,709	152,467	327,706	458,444	1.9	2.7	4.7	6.1
Chicago	44,103	109,458	233,903	277,731	2.0	4.1	6.9	8.2
Philadelphia	84,459	134,229	219,599	250,880	5.5	7.4	11.3	13.0
Detroit	5,741	40,838	120,066	149,119	1.2	4.1	7.7	9.2
St. Louis	43,960	69,854	93,580	108,765	6.4	9.0	11.4	13.3
Cleveland	8,448	34,451	71,899	84,504	1.5	4.3	8.0	9.6
Pittsburgh	25,623	37,725	54,983	62,216	4.8	6.4	8.2	9.9
Cincinnati	19,639	30,079	47,818	55,593	5.4	7.5	10.6	12.2
Indianapolis	21,816	34,678	43,967	51,142	9.3	11.0	12.1	13.2
Los Angeles	7,599	15,579	38,894	63,774	2.4	2.7	3.1	4.2
Newark	9,475	16,977	38,880	45,760	2.7	4.1	8.8	10.6
Gary	383	5,299	17,922	20,394	2.3	9.6	17.8	18.3
Dayton	4,842	9,025	17,077	20,273	4.2	5.9	8.5	9.6
Youngstown	1,936	6,662	14,552	14,615	2.4	5.0	8.6	8.7

Source: U.S. Census Reports.

simply the use of ethnic patterns and solidary features as the primary basis for interest-group and political formations. It means building upon these to integrate a given ethnic community into the wider politics of the city and the nation. To the extent that a given ethnic group was successful in so organizing itself in this era, it could claim an effective share of city-based rewards and, through congressional and presidential politics, of federal government benefits.[6] On the other hand, to fall outside or to be only partially integrated into this process was necessarily to be without an effective basis for acquiring political power and influence.

As the urban Negro was only partially connected to this politicization of ethnicity through city machines, his political development has

6. For a general study of this process, see Harold Zink, *City Bosses in the United States: A Study of Twenty Municipal Bosses* (Durham, 1930). For a class study of one city, see Theodore Lowi, *At the Pleasure of the Mayor: Patronage and Power in New York City, 1898-1958* (Glencoe, 1964).

borne the mark of such isolation throughout the twentieth century. For one thing, the Negro lower classes were deprived of the participatory incentives associated with an ethnic group's inclusion into city politics. Thus in 1930 only 36 percent of the voting-age Negro population in New York City (Harlem) were registered voters, compared to 44 percent of voting-age whites residing in Manhattan. Actual voting rates were also low for the black urban masses in this era. When combined with low political skill and knowledge, these situations produced a uniquely high sense of powerlessness and estrangement from institutionalized processes. This state of affairs persisted, in fact, into the post-World War II era and was reversed only through Negro political militancy and riotous upheaval, national in scope—a mode of political inclusion into American society experienced by no other major ethnic community.

Second, the city machines' relative neglect of the black ghetto in the first several decades of the twentieth century deprived the Negro elites (the small black middle and upper classes) of the opportunity and incentives to fashion effective ghetto-wide political organization. Whereas the city machines aided in both latent and manifest ways—as Merton would say[7]—the elites among the Irish, Italians, Jews, Poles, and other ethnic groups to establish effective political organization of their communities, the black bourgeoisie was not induced to exert its skills and institutions (e.g., clubs and civic associations, and interest groups like the National Bar Association) to politicize the Negro lower strata into the service of city machines. And in those few instances where city machines did facilitate the political organization of the black ghetto, white politicians exercised local control, denying it to black leadership. For example, in Philadelphia the Negro population increased from 5.5 percent in 1910 to 11.3 percent in 1930, but the first Negro ward leader was not appointed until 1932. Thirty years later Negroes were nearly 30 percent of the population and 26 percent of the registered voters, but still claimed only 10 percent of the ward leaders in the city of Philadelphia, and the progress was exceedingly slow (see table 16.2).

Only in Chicago did the typical pattern of a truncated political inclusion of Negroes into city politics not prevail. A brief discussion of

7. Robert Merton, *Social Theory and Social Structure* (Glencoe, 1956), ch. 5.

MARTIN L. KILSON

TABLE 16.2   Negro Ward Leaders in Philadelphia

Year	Number Negro ward leaders			Total no. ward leaders	% ward leaders who are Negroes	% registered voters who are Negroes
	R	D	Total			
1928	0	0	0	102	0	9.3
1932	1	0	1	102	.98	10.7
1936	1	1	2	102	1.96	12.7
1940	0	0	0	102	0	12.3
1944	1	1	2	104	1.92	13.1
1948	2	1	3	104	2.88	15.3
1952	4	2	6	104	3.84	16.2
1956	5	2	7	104	6.74	18.7
1960	6	4	10	118	8.48	21.5
1964	6	6	12	120	10.0	26.2
1965	11	10	21	132	15.9	—

Source: John H. Strange, *The Negro in Philadelphia Politics, 1963-1965*, unpub. Ph.D. thesis (Princeton University, 1966), 121.

the Chicago case will place in sharper relief the usual relationship Negroes had with city politics.

Owing to several unique circumstances—especially the small-ward organization of Chicago and the keenly contested elections between Republicans and Democrats in the years 1910-1940—the white city machine embraced the black ghetto on terms comparable to white ethnic ghettos.[8] William Hale ("Big Bill") Thompson—unique as a reasonably color-blind white machine boss in this era—initiated the politicization of the Negro elites during his successful campaign for mayor in 1915. His margin of victory in the Republican primary—some 3,000 votes over his nearest opponent—was provided by the Negro Second Ward; Thompson received 91 percent of the votes or 8,633 compared to 1,870 for his opponent. Thompson's bid for a second term in 1923 was also ensured by the votes of the Negro wards. In return, Thompson initiated the full-fledged inclusion of black Chicago into the Republican city machine. Through

8. The following discussion is based upon Harold Gosnell, *Negro Politicians: The Rise of Negro Politics in Chicago* (Chicago, 1935).

Edward Wright, a lawyer, and Oscar DePriest, a businessman, a Negro-controlled ward organization in support of Thompson was effected. Patronage appointments and political office sealed Thompson's bond with the new Negro machine politicians. For example, Edward Wright was appointed in 1919 to a $100-a-day post as lawyer to the State Traction Commission and later (1923) a Republican governor appointed him to the Illinois Commerce Commission, a $7,000-a-year patronage post. DePriest, for his part, became the first Negro member of the Chicago city council in 1915, and in 1928 he won the Republican primary election for Congress and also the general election, becoming the first Negro in this century to achieve this office—an achievement that guaranteed subsequent election of Negro congressmen from Chicago in the 1930s (Arthur Mitchell), 1940s until 1970 (William Dawson) and 1970s (Ralph Metcalfe and Mrs. Cardiss Collins).

The benefits resulting from the full-fledged inclusion of Negro elites and, through them, the black ghetto, into Chicago's machine politics were enormous and variegated. First, the level and range of political participation of lower-strata Chicago Negroes in the era between the two world wars was without peer among city-dwelling black communities. In 1920, for example, some 72 percent of the voting-age Negro population were registered to vote (blacks were then 4 percent of the population) compared to 66 percent registration for the whites; in 1930 some 77 percent of voting-age Negroes were registered, compared to 68 percent of whites. In the 1930 Republican primary election, Negroes were reported to constitute 11 percent of the voters—60,000 out of 526,000 Republican voters—though they were 6 percent of the population. Most significantly, Chicago Negroes realized a share of jobs controlled by the city machine far in excess of their proportion of the city population, as shown in tables 16.3 and 16.4. Although constituting only 6 percent of the population in 1930, Chicago blacks held 25 percent of some 11,888 postal service jobs; in 1932, blacks held 6.4 percent of some 29,702 city civil service jobs. These benefits were not inconsiderable: 22.3 percent of clerk jobs in the postal service were black in 1934, 17.4 percent of carrier jobs, 62.6 percent of skilled laborers, 4.7 percent of special-delivery messengers, and 80 percent of menial jobs.[9] Data in table 16.5 on Chicago's

---

9. *Ibid.*, 309.

MARTIN L. KILSON

police are equally notable, for Negroes claimed nearly 2 percent of these posts in 1920 and 2.2 percent in 1930, including the first black commissioned police officers in any city. Though these advances for Chicago Negroes were not sustained in the 1950s—the era of enormous growth of Negroes in Chicago and thus of sharpening racial competition—they nonetheless underscore the significance for an urban ethnic group of full-fledged inclusion into city politics.[10]

It must be emphasized, however, that the typical Negro urban community in the years between the two World Wars never even approximated the degree of political inclusion experienced by Chicago blacks. This typical pattern of exclusion from city politics was, moreover, especially disadvantageous for lower-class Negroes—that majority stratum of Afro-Americans without even the primary attributes necessary for attracting attention from white politicians. On the other hand, middle-class Negroes did not suffer as many consequences of powerlessness as did the lower classes in the years between the two world wars. Their higher level of education and greater affluence allowed middle-class Negroes in the interwar years to forge alternative modes of political inclusion apart from city political machines. The most prominent of these alternative routes to politicization were clientage politics and the civil rights movement.

Clientage and Civil Rights Politics 1900-1960

In the first several decades of the twentieth century, clientage and civil rights politics involved Negroes in two ways. The first was through associations of Negro professionals. These associations are best characterized as economic interest groups, the most prominent of which in the interwar era were the National (Negro) Bar Association and the National (Negro) Medical Association. These Negro interest groups protected and advanced the needs and concerns of their members—lawyers and doctors— though they also functioned as civic associations, serving needs of other Negroes as well. In this latter role, these Negro interest groups often organized financial and political support for the civil rights organizations

---

10. For the Chicago situation in the 1950s, see James Q. Wilson, *Negro Politics* (Glencoe, 1960).

TABLE 16.3 Persons in Chicago Working in Postal Service, by Color, Sex, and Occupation, 1930

Occupation	Total workers			Negro workers			Per-centage Negro of Total
	Total	Men	Wom-en	Total	Men	Wom-en	
Compositors, linotypers, and typesetters	11	10	1	3	3	—	27.3
Machinists	12	12	—	1	1	—	8.3
Mechanics (not otherwise specified)	51	51	—	7	7	—	13.7
Chauffeurs and truck and tractor drivers	101	101	—	42	42	—	41.6
Foremen and overseers	133	133	—	6	6	—	4.5
Inspectors	27	27	—	1	1	—	3.7
Laborers	531	530	1	369	368	1	69.5
Managers and officials	167	167	—	2	2	—	1.2
Guards, watchmen, and doorkeepers	46	45	1	2	1	1	4.3
Charwomen and cleaners	13	3	10	9	1	8	69.2
Elevator tenders	14	13	1	12	11	1	85.7
Janitors	40	29	11	35	25	10	87.5
Porters	24	24	—	23	23	—	95.8
Clerks	6,512	6,246	266	1,825	1,764	61	28.0
Messenger, errand, and office boys	81	81	—	10	10	—	12.3
Stenographers and typists	47	14	33	2	—	2	4.3
Mail carriers	3,948	3,946	2	631	631	—	16.0
Other occupations	61	58	3	28	28	—	46.0
Pursuits in postal service in Chicago in 1930 in which there were no Negroes*	69	62	7	—	—	—	0.0
Total	11,888	11,552	336	3,008	2,924	84	25.2

*Carpenters (3); electricians (5); engineers (stationary) (6); oilers of machinery (1); painters, glaziers, and varnishers (building) (1); apprentices, other transportation and communication (2); advertising agents (1); policemen (1); draftsmen (1); agents (not elsewhere classified) (6); accountants and auditors (7); bookkeepers and cashiers (24); shipping clerks (1); weighers (3); housekeepers and stewards; office-appliance operators (7).

Source: Harold Gosnell, Negro Politicians (Chicago, 1935), 304.

MARTIN L. KILSON

TABLE 16.4   Negroes in the Classified Service of the City of Chicago, 1932

Service	Total Number on Payroll March, 1932	Negro Employees, 1932			
		Clerical, Profes- sional; Commis- sioned	Janitors, Laborers, and Esti- mated Tempo- raries	Total	Per Cent of Total
Comptroller's Office	143	3	—	3	2.1
City Collector	158	2	—	2	1.3
Police	6,551	143	32	175	2.7
Fire	2,713	22	—	22	0.8
Gas and Electricity, Department of	872	4	1	5	0.6
Public Service	51	—	1	1	2.0
Building, Department of	112	1	—	1	0.9
Weights and Measures, Depart- ment of	31	—	2	2	6.5
Health, Department of	891	70	50	120	13.5
Board of Local Improvements	429	9	—	9	2.1
Public Works,					
Commissioner's Office	13	1	—	1	7.7
City Hall, Bureau of	180	1	26	27	15.0
Bridges, Division of	409	1	—	1	0.2
Streets, Bureau of	4,435	6	500	506	11.4
Sewers, Bureau of	67	—	11	11	16.4
Parks, Recreation, Aviation, Bureau of	328	23	—	23	7.0
Water Works, Engineer	172	1	—	1	0.6
Pumping Stations	1,512	6	6	12	0.8
Construction & Water Pipe Ext.	1,172	4	185	189	16.1
Bureau of Water	462	29	—	29	6.3
Board of Education, Business Department	5,291	69	637	706	13.4
Library Board	949	42	17	59	6.2
Municipal Tuberculosis Sani- tarium	903	3	—	3	0.3
Offices in which no Negroes were found	1,858	—	—	—	0.0
Total	29,702	440	1,468	1,908	6.4

Source: Harold Gosnell, Negro Politicians (Chicago, 1935), 239.

TABLE 16.5   Number and Percentage of Negro Policemen in Chicago by Ranks, 1900-1930

Year	Patrolmen			Sergeants			Lieutenants			Total		
	Total	Negro		Total	Negro		Total	Negro		Total	Negro	
		Num-ber	Per Cent		Num-ber	Per Cent		Num-ber	Per Cent		Num-ber	Per Cent
1900	2,505	20	0.8	257	1	0.4	63	0	0.0	2,825	21	0.7
1910	3,785	45	1.2	370	3	0.8	71	0	0.0	4,226	48	1.1
1920	3,683	79	2.1	864	9	1.0	84	1	1.2	4,631	89	1.9
1930	5,443	129	2.4	570	6	1.3	150	2	1.3	6,163	137	2.2

Source: Harold Gosnell, Negro Politicians (Chicago, 1935), 253.

like the National Association for the Advancement of Colored People. This often entailed an overlapping of leadership and membership among the interest groups and civil rights bodies.

The political experience of Negro interest groups and their leaders is vividly revealed in the career of George E. Cannon, a Negro physician in Jersey City, New Jersey, in the first twenty-five years of this century.[11] Dr. Cannon's political leadership was both realized and sustained through a network of patron-client linkages with influential and power-ful whites, usually Republicans, who were willing to effect a variety of economic and political benefits either for individual middle-class Negroes or for a group of middle-class Negroes, like doctors or lawyers, clergy-men or businessmen. This clientage political process was a common form of politicization of the small black bourgeoisie during the late nineteenth through the early twentieth century. Though it was usually confining for the Negro political leader involved in this clientage process and not as productive of benefits as full-fledged inclusion into party machine poli-tics at city, county, or state levels, it was nonetheless serviceable to both individual blacks and groups. Nor did clientage politics preclude access to party machines, for the resourceful black clientage politician could convert the advantages gained through the clientage process into a more

---

11. The following discussion is based upon Dennis Clark Dickerson, "George E. Cannon: Black Churchman, Physician, and Republican Politician," Journal of Pres-byterian History, LI (1973), 411-432.

institutionalized political role. Cannon was perhaps the most successful Negro clientage politician in this respect in the first several decades of this century. He penetrated Republican party ranks—aided by powerful white patrons—at the city, county (Hudson), state, and national levels. As a delegate to the Republican National Convention in 1924, Dr. Cannon had the honor of seconding the nomination of Calvin Coolidge.

The focus of Cannon's political role as clientage politician was, however, concerned with the needs of middle-class Negroes. For example, from 1920 to 1923 Cannon was chairman of the executive board of the National (Negro) Medical Association, directing its efforts to persuade the federal government to extend medical appointments for Negroes and to ensure Negro control of the federal government's medical facilities for veterans in Tuskegee, Alabama, home of the famous Tuskegee Institute, founded by Booker T. Washington. In addition to this, Cannon was an officer of the Negro Home Benefit Association of New Jersey, president of the Committee of One Hundred of Hudson County (a Negro improvement association), exalted ruler of the Negro Progressive Elks Lodge, and a leading figure in the Negro Welfare League of New Jersey. His biographer sums up Cannon's leadership career quite aptly: "Although George Cannon used his influence in behalf of black Americans, his power did not emanate from them. His acceptability to whites accounts for his sway in politics, education, and religion. . . . His acceptability to whites as a spokesman for blacks guaranteed his influence and prestige among Negroes. . . ."[12]

The civil rights leadership and organizations, though similar to clientage politicians in some respects, differed in their political mode insofar as the Negro community (especially the middle class) was more directly involved in their legitimation. Thus what general-purpose political organizations like the National Association for the Advancement of Colored People and the National Urban League did in behalf of the surmounting of racism derived more explictly from Negro ideas, aims, aspirations, and relationships. Though alliances or coalitions with white individuals and groups constituted an important aspect of the politics of these general-purpose political organizations, this was always secondary

12. *Ibid.*, 431.

to the Negro basis of support and membership. Founded in 1912 with about 300 members, the NAACP had over eighty branches and some 82,000 members—mainly Negro—by 1920. Its leaders were typically militant in matters of racial discrimination and oppression, markedly different from the typical clientage politician in this regard. Yet the pattern of benefits produced by the civil rights organizations was essentially middle-class in character; these organizations lacked that kind of political authority, realized through elected political office within party politics, that enabled Negro machine politicians in Chicago in the 1920s through the 1940s to aid lower-class Negroes with jobs.

It was precisely this kind of limitation of both clientage and civil rights politics that came into sharp conflict with the massive social and economic needs of newly urbanized Negroes in the post-World War II era (see table 16.6). Despite the growth of the NAACP's membership to several millions by the 1960s, its organization outside party politics and competition for elected office restricted the NAACP's ability to serve the new political needs of lower-strata urban Negroes. Both a new political thrust and leadership were required to ensure the eventual inclusion of the urban black ghetto into the dominant mode of political power in American society—party politics and elected office.

Politics of Black Ethnicity in the 1960s

The distinguishing feature of political development among American Negroes in the 1960s through the 1970s was the successful political exploitation of a new and powerful sense of black ethnic consciousness. This politicization of black ethnicity had eluded both the clientage and civil rights leadership in the years between the two world wars because of the typical Negro's lack of a positive self-image, as well as the general exclusion of Negroes from effective political participation.

From the late 1950s onward, however, these conditions no longer obtained. By the early 1960s there were numerous political organizations (including cultural agencies) whose style of activity involved the explicit cultivation and manipulation of pro-black and anti-white attitudes. Organizations like the Congress of Racial Equality (CORE), the Southern Christian Leadership Conference (SCLC), the Student Nonviolent Coordinating Committee, and the Black Muslims recognized that large

MARTIN L. KILSON

TABLE 16.6   Percentage of Negroes in Each of the Thirty Largest Cities

City	1950	1960	1970
New York, N.Y.	10	14	21
Chicago, Ill.	14	23	32
Los Angeles, Calif.	9	14	17
Philadelphia, Pa.	18	26	33
Detroit, Mich.	16	29	43
Baltimore, Md.	21	35	46
Houston, Texas	24	23	25
Cleveland, Ohio	16	29	38
Washington, D.C.	35	54	71
St. Louis, Mo.	18	29	40
Milwaukee, Wis.	3	8	14
San Francisco, Calif.	6	10	13
Boston, Mass.	5	9	16
Dallas, Texas	13	19	24
New Orleans, La.	32	37	45
Pittsburgh, Pa.	12	17	20
San Antonio, Tex.	7	7	8
San Diego, Calif.	5	6	7
Seattle, Wash.	3	5	7
Buffalo, N.Y.	6	13	20
Cincinnati, Ohio	16	22	27
Memphis, Tenn.	37	37	38
Denver, Colo.	4	6	9
Atlanta, Ga.	37	38	51
Minneapolis, Minn.	1	2	4
Indianapolis, Ind.	15	21	23
Kansas City, Mo.	12	18	22
Columbus, Ohio	12	16	18
Phoenix, Ariz.	5	5	5
Newark, N.J.	17	34	54

Source: *U.S. Census Reports.*

numbers of Negroes—especially the lower classes, but the middle-class blacks as well—displayed a deep-seated readiness for aggressive behavior toward white society, its values, ideas, and institutions. The success of this so-called black nationalist or militant movement in the 1960s was revealed in the wide spectrum of Negro leaders involved in it. Moderate leaders like the Reverend Martin Luther King and militant leaders like

Malcolm X (a minister in the Black Muslims) realized the utility of black ethnic assertiveness for stimulating new types of political participation among Negroes. It was also recognized that longstanding social cleavages among Negroes were significantly attenuated through anti-white political appeals; it was now possible for both lower-class and middle-class Negroes to submerge their differences (or at least some of them) and coalesce around a new perception of their collective needs in relation to white America. In short, a politics of black ethnic solidarity was now feasible.[13]

The social class factor in the politics of black solidarity in the 1960s was not, however, a simple affair. For one thing, the anti-white riots which raged in the urban Negro ghettos in the years 1964-1971 involved (see the table 16.7) much greater participation by lower-class than by middle-class blacks.[14] This resulted, in turn, in numerous lower-class blacks seeking ghetto leadership roles, becoming veritable poverty politicians. These individuals recognized correctly that the widespread riots reflected a power vacuum within the Negro community, and if they could seize control of the symbolic and ideological forces which motivated black rioters they could translate this into political advantage. Moreover, the Democratic federal administrations of Presidents John F. Kennedy and Lyndon B. Johnson (1961-1968) established the so-called War on Poverty (through the Office of Economic Opportunity) which provided for local participation of the urban poor in the administration of this public policy, and frequently the poverty politicians achieved control of the local participatory agencies created under the War on Poverty.[15]

---

13. This issue is treated in Martin Kilson, "Blacks and Neo-Ethnicity in American Political Life," in Nathan Glazer and Daniel P. Moynihan (eds.), *Ethnicity: Theory and Experience* (Cambridge, Mass., 1975), 236-266. See also Martin Kilson, *Political Dilemma of Black Mayors: A Study of Carl Stokes' Mayoralty in Cleveland* (Washington, D.C., 1976).

14. See National Advisory Commission on Civil Disorders, *Report* (Washington, D.C., 1968), 173-176.

15. The War on Poverty, officially executed by the Office of Economic Opportunity under the Economic Opportunity Act of 1964, allocated over $5 billion to urban communities between 1964 and 1970. The so-called community action committees that were used to facilitate "maximum feasible participation," to quote the 1964 Act, gave the lower-class militant leaders an instrument for a formal leadership bid in the urban black ghetto. See, e.g., Dale R. Marshall, *The Politics of Participation in Poverty: A Case Study of . . . Greater Los Angeles* (Berkeley, 1971).

MARTIN L. KILSON

TABLE 16.7   Education of Rioters, 1967

Education	% Detroit rioters N = 43	% Newark rioters N = 106
Less than 1-6 grades	2.3	0.0
Grade school	4.7	1.9
Some high school	53.5	63.2
Completed high school	23.3	29.2
Some college	14.0	5.7
Graduated from college	0.0	0.0
Graduate study	2.2	0.0
	100.0	100.0

Note: Those called "rioters" were persons arrested in course of the Detroit and Newark riots.

Source: National Advisory Commission on Civil Disorders, Report (Washington, D.C. 1968), 174.

This leadership bid by those I call poverty politicians did not, however, succeed—owing to the fact that these leaders of lower-class backgrounds (men who were school dropouts and often with criminal records) lacked the habits, values, and skills required for a durable political role. They were, in other words, incapable of institutionalizing the new politics of black solidarity.[16] Their main contribution was, therefore, rather different: they stamped the politics of black solidarity with a lower-class, populist motif. Thus the concerns and situations of the Negro lower classes realized primacy over those of the Negro middle classes, symbolically if not substantively. This change in the social-class focus of Negro politics was readily accepted by the new generation of elected black politicians who emerged by the thousands in the 1960s. The new black politicians employ a political style—a mode of political appeal —which celebrates the lower-class origins of the majority of Negroes and gives primacy to issues affecting the lower classes, thereby reversing the historical tendency of Negro clientage and civil rights politicians to emphasize the concerns of middle-class Negroes.

16. This is elaborated in Martin Kilson, "The New Black Intellectuals," Dissent (July-August 1969), 304-310.

The new Negro politician class, comprising some 4,000 elected officials in 1975, compared to about 100 in 1960, is made up of men and
women with middle-class status and attributes. But the overwhelming
majority of these new black politicians are first-generation middle class:
their fathers were stable semiskilled and skilled workers, often home-
owners, and typically aspiring middle-class status for their offspring.
Their recent origins in the Negro lower stratum—albeit the coping upper
sector thereof—has been effectively manipulated by this new Negro politician class to deepen their legitimacy among the Negro masses. They are
thus ensured a much firmer status as leaders of blacks than their predecessors in the civil rights organizations. The new politician class is exemplified at its best by politicians like Richard Hatcher, son of a steel-
worker, who is a lawyer and the first Negro mayor of Gary, Indiana;
Shirley Chisholm, daughter of a house painter, who is a teacher and the
first Negro woman elected to Congress, representing a new district in the
Bedford-Stuyvesant section of New York City; Carl Stokes, son of a
seamstress, who is a lawyer and the first Negro mayor of Cleveland; and
Kenneth Gibson, son of a factory worker, who is a civil engineer and the
first Negro mayor of Newark, New Jersey.

Conclusion: Institutionalizing a New Black Political Status

The current political status of the American Negro is distinguished from
that of the era between the two world wars by the existence of a sizable
class of Negro elected politicians. In the years 1900-1960, elected Negro
politicians were uncommon; other forms of political leadership—clientage politicians and civil rights leaders—dominated Negro politics, with
only a handful of Negroes obtaining political leadership through city
machine politics. Today there are, as noted, some 4,500 Negro elected
officials, nearly 70 percent of whom are outside the South. They are
found in forty-one of the fifty states; they include 17 congressmen, nearly
200 state legislators, over 50 mayors, nearly 1,000 city officials, and over
500 school-board officials.[17] They constitute nationally almost 1 percent
of all elected American officials. And, of course, both within and outside

---

17. Joint Center for Political Studies, *National Roster of Black Elected Officials*
(Washington, D.C., 1975).

MARTIN L. KILSON

the South the increase in Negro political participation is the primary basis for the rise of the new politician class. As shown in table 16.8, within the South the crucial element underlying greater Negro political participation has been the growth in the number of Negro voters, owing to the federal government's enactment of the Voting Act of 1965. Outside the South the crucial factor in the rise of the new Negro politician class has been the rapid growth of the Negro population in big and medium-size cities, as shown in table 6, for the years 1950-1970. By 1974 there were fifty-nine congressional districts with 30 percent or more Negro population. These factors of voting and population increases have combined to alter the political status of Negroes. Data on selected cities in table 16.9 reveal the new status Negroes hold in American political life.

Several trends will likely be associated with the institutionalizing of the Negro's new political status. First, the Negro elites can be expected to become more politically aware, in contrast to the widespread consciousness of social status that prevailed among them in the era 1900-1960.[18] The voluntary associations (e.g., Elks, Knights of Pythias, Greek-letter fraternities) and interest groups controlled by the Negro elites now display an unprecedented aggressive political consciousness.[19] This development is partly a logical outgrowth of the extraordinary expansion of the Negro elites since World War II. By 1970 nearly 30 percent of American Negroes possessed middle-class status, compared to less than 5 percent in 1930. The maintenance and expansion of this new status for blacks depends necessarily upon greater political participation and thus greater political influence.

There is, however, a limit to the growth of Negro political influence solely within the Negro community. It is, therefore, likely that more Negro politicians will seek office in electoral districts where the Negro population is less than 15 percent. Edward Brooke, Republican senator from Massachusetts, pioneered this trend when he stood successfully for attorney general of Massachusetts in the late 1950s and later for senator,

---

18. For the obsession with social status as a class-identifying orientation among Negro elites, see E. Franklin Frazier, *The Black Bourgeoisie* (Glencoe, 1957).

19. No study of this important behavioral change among the black middle classes since the 1950s has yet been made. But some good reporting on it is found in the excellent black-owned monthly, *Black Enterprise* (New York).

TABLE 16.8   Black Voter Registration in the South, 1940-1968

Year	Estimated number of registrants	Percentage of voting-age population
1940	250,000	5
1947	595,000	12
1952	1,008,614	20
1956	1,238,038	25
1960	1,414,052	28
1964	1,907,279	38
1968	3,112,000	62

Source: Joe Feagin and Harlan Hahn, "The Second Reconstruction: Black Political Strength in the South," Social Science Quarterly, LI (1970), 47.

TABLE 16.9   Political Attributes of Negro Population in Selected Cities

City	Total pop. (1970)	% Negro	Negro % VAP* (1970)	Negro % city council seats (1972)	Negro % police forces (1970)
Baltimore	905,759	46.4	43.7	26.3	13
Detroit	1,511,482	43.7	39.4	33.3	12
Cincinnati	452,524	27.6	24.4	37.5	4.9
Cleveland	750,903	38.3	36.6	36.6	7.7
Buffalo	462,768	20.4	17.8	20	2
New York	7,867,760	21.2	19	5.4	7.5
Newark, N.J.	382,417	54.2	48.6	33.3	15
Camden	102,551	39.1	34	28.6	—
Jersey City	260,545	21	17.4	11.1	5.4
Kansas City, Mo.	507,087	22.1	18.8	33.3	7.5
St. Louis	622,236	40.9	35.9	20.6	14
Philadelphia	1,948,609	33.6	31.1	17.6	18.6
Pittsburgh	520,117	20.2	18.4	22.2	6.4
Oakland	361,561	34.5	29.4	12.5	7
Chicago	3,366,957	32.7	28.2	28	16.5
Wilmington	80,386	43.6	36.7	41.7	11.5

*VAP denotes voting age population.

Source: U.S. Census Reports, 1970, 1972.

MARTIN L. KILSON

becoming the first Negro in this century to hold an elected executive state office and a Senate seat.

What might be called the "Brooke phenomenon" is now in full force among a unique section of the new black politician class. Wilson Riles demonstrated it in California in 1970 when, in a state where blacks are barely 10 percent of the population, he defeated a conservative (a so-called law-and-order) candidate, Max Rafferty, for the office of superintendent of public instruction—perhaps the second most important executive office in California. The Brooke phenomenon was displayed again in California when Thomas Bradley, a lawyer and former police officer, stood successfully in 1973 for mayor of Los Angeles (black population about 12 percent). And in 1974 a Negro state legislator in California, Mervyn Dymally, ran successfully for the office of lieutenant governor, Wilson Riles ran successfully for a second term as superintendent of public instruction, and in Colorado another Negro legislator, George Brown, successfully ran for lieutenant governor, joining Dymally as the first Negroes elected lieutenant governors in the twentieth century.

The essential feature of the Brooke phenomenon is that the Negro candidates involved cannot count on a massive share of the black voters to ensure victory. Success lies instead with white and other nonblack voters (Orientals, Mexican-Americans, etc.), who constitute about 90 percent of the electorate concerned. This is not an easy situation to negotiate because the issue of racial polarization remains salient for a sizable proportion of the white community. Nonetheless, an increasing number of Negro politicians has the personality traits and political capacity necessary for reducing the racial issue as a factor affecting white voters' perceptions of Negro candidates.[20] It is, in fact, not unreasonable to expect a rapid increase in the number of Negro candidates who emerge through

20. Changing attitudes of middle-class whites on major political problems in American society facilitate this new relationship between middle-class whites and Negro politicians. For example, a Louis Harris survey reported to the National Conference of State Legislative Leaders, September 26, 1973, revealed such attitude changes as the following: 67 percent of the population with incomes $15,000 and upward favor consumer advocate Ralph Nader (only 37 percent with incomes $5,000 and below did); only 17 percent of the $15,000 group favored banning radical or revolutionary newspapers (55 percent of the $5,000 group did); and only 21 percent of the $15,000 group believed Negroes are asking for more than they are ready for (59 percent of the $5,000 group did).

the Brooke phenomenon. The implications for the nature of the benefits Negroes derive from the political process are enormous. For unless more whites become more directly connected with the new Negro politician class in this way, the still massive socioeconomic needs of about 60 percent of American Negroes cannot be guaranteed the claim upon federal government resources that they require.

A final trend in the politics of American Negroes is that an increasing number of the new Negro politicians will begin to master the process of alliance and coalition-building that surrounds the creation of public policy at the federal level. Until the past decade, only a small section of Negro political leadership had experienced the coalition process at the federal level. This included several congressmen like William Dawson and Adam Clayton Powell, Jr., and several Negro lobbyists for civil rights organizations.[21] The coalition experience typical of Negro political leadership before the 1960s was basically one-dimensional, involving alliances between civil rights groups and white organizations who shared a common ideological orientation.

The new Negro politician class at all governmental levels, but especially at the federal one, must now enter a more complex process of alliances and coalitions. The process requires one to forsake the natural desire for ideological consistency in political interactions, replacing it with a strictly pragmatic approach. Such a coalition dynamic is both perplexing and traumatic, as reflected in the first two years of the operation of the Black Congressional Caucus—a legislative organization of the new Negro congressmen. Seeking ideological consistency in coalitions, the caucus used a strictly racial criterion for defining the range and mode of legislative behavior for black congressmen. But it soon was apparent that the legislative process in Congress cannot be effectively influenced through such a restricted definition of what Negro congressmen represent.

---

21. No major study of the political experiences of the four Negro congressmen in the era 1930-1970 (Oscar DePriest, Arthur Mitchell, William Dawson, Adam Clayton Powell) has been made; it is much needed. So is a study of the several black political lobbyists in Washington in this period—especially Clarence Mitchell (lobbyist for the NAACP) and Louis Martin (a free-lance lobbyist for Negro interest groups). For a list of Negro congressmen since 1869, see Appendix.

MARTIN L. KILSON

APPENDIX (continued)

Year	Name	Party	State
1888-1890	Henry P. Cheatham	R	North Carolina
	Thomas E. Miller	R	South Carolina
	John M. Langston	R	Virginia
1890-1892	Henry P. Cheatham	R	North Carolina
1892-1894	George W. Murray	R	South Carolina
1894-1896	George W. Murray	R	South Carolina
1896-1898	George H. White	R	North Carolina
1898-1900	George H. White	R	North Carolina
1928-1930	Oscar DePriest	R	Illinois
1930-1932	Oscar DePriest	R	Illinois
1932-1934	Oscar DePriest	R	Illinois
1934-1936	Arthur W. Mitchell	D	Illinois
1936-1938	Arthur W. Mitchell	D	Illinois
1938-1940	Arthur W. Mitchell	D	Illinois
1940-1942	Arthur W. Mitchell	D	Illinois
1942-1944	William L. Dawson	D	Illinois
1944-1946	William L. Dawson	D	Illinois
	Adam Clayton Powell, Jr.	D	New York
1946-1948	William L. Dawson	D	Illinois
	Adam Clayton Powell, Jr.	D	New York
1948-1950	William L. Dawson	D	Illinois
	Adam Clayton Powell, Jr.	D	New York
1950-1952	William L. Dawson	D	Illinois
	Adam Clayton Powell, Jr.	D	New York
1952-1954	William L. Dawson	D	Illinois
	Adam Clayton Powell, Jr.	D	New York
1954-1956	William L. Dawson	D	Illinois
	Charles C. Diggs, Jr.	D	Michigan
	Adam Clayton Powell, Jr.	D	New York
1956-1958	Willaim L. Dawson	D	Illinois
	Charles C. Diggs, Jr.	D	Michigan
	Adam Clayton Powell, Jr.	D	New York
	*Robert N. C. Nix	D	Pennsylvania
1958-1960	William L. Dawson	D	Illinois
	Charles C. Diggs, Jr.	D	Michigan
	Adam Clayton Powell, Jr.	D	New York
	Robert N. C. Nix	D	Pennsylvania

(continued)

*Nix was elected in a special election held in May 1958.

APPENDIX (continued)

Year	Name	Party	State
1960-1962	William L. Dawson	D	Illinois
	Charles C. Diggs, Jr.	D	Michigan
	Adam Clayton Powell, Jr.	D	New York
	Robert N. C. Nix	D	Pennsylvania
1962-1964	Augustus F. Hawkins	D	California
	William L. Dawson	D	Illinois
	Charles C. Diggs, Jr.	D	Michigan
	Adam Clayton Powell, Jr.	D	New York
	Robert N. C. Nix	D	Pennsylvania
1964-1966	Augustus F. Hawkins	D	California
	William L. Dawson	D	Illinois
	John Conyers, Jr.	D	Michigan
	Charles C. Diggs, Jr.	D	Michigan
	Adam Clayton Powell, Jr.	D	New York
	Robert N. C. Nix	D	Pennsylvania
1966-1968	Augustus F. Hawkins	D	California
	William L. Dawson	D	Illinois
	John Conyers, Jr.	D	Michigan
	Charles C. Diggs, Jr.	D	Michigan
	Adam Clayton Powell, Jr.	D	New York
	Robert N. C. Nix	D	Pennsylvania
1968-1970	Augustus F. Hawkins	D	California
	William L. Dawson	D	Illinois
	John Conyers, Jr.	D	Michigan
	Charles C. Diggs, Jr.	D	Michigan
	William L. Clay	D	Missouri
	Shirley Chisholm	D	New York
	Adam Clayton Powell, Jr.	D	New York
	Louis Stokes	D	Ohio
	Robert N. C. Nix	D	Pennsylvania
1970-1972	Ronald V. Dellums	D	California
	Augustus F. Hawkins	D	California
	Walter E. Fauntroy	D	District of Columbia
	George W. Collins	D	Illinois
	Ralph H. Metcalfe	D	Illinois
	Parren J. Mitchell	D	Maryland
	John Conyers, Jr.	D	Michigan
	Charles C. Diggs, Jr.	D	Michigan

(continued)

APPENDIX (continued)

Year	Name	Party	State
	William L. Clay	D	Missouri
	Shirley Chisholm	D	New York
	Charles B. Rangel	D	New York
	Louis Stokes	D	Ohio
	Robert N. C. Nix	D	Pennsylvania
1972–1974	Yvonne Burke	D	California
	Shirley Chisholm	D	New York
	William L. Clay	D	Missouri
	**Cardiss Collins	D	Illinois
	John Conyers, Jr.	D	Michigan
	Ronald V. Dellums	D	California
	Charles C. Diggs, Jr.	D	Michigan
	Walter E. Fauntroy	D	District of Columbia
	Augustus F. Hawkins	D	California
	Barbara Jordan	D	Texas
	Ralph H. Metcalfe	D	Illinois
	Parren J. Mitchell	D	Maryland
	Robert N. C. Nix	D	Pennsylvania
	Charles B. Rangel	D	New York
	Louis Stokes	D	Ohio
	Andrew Young	D	Georgia
1974–1976	Yvonne Burke	D	California
	Shirley Chisholm	D	New York
	William L. Clay	D	Missouri
	Cardiss Collins	D	Illinois
	John Conyers, Jr.	D	Michigan
	Ronald V. Dellums	D	California
	Charles C. Diggs, Jr.	D	Michigan
	Walter E. Fauntroy	D	District of Columbia
	Augustus F. Hawkins	D	California
	Barbara Jordan	D	Texas
	Ralph H. Metcalfe	D	Illinois
	Parren J. Mitchell	D	Maryland
	Robert N. C. Nix	D	Pennsylvania
	Charles B. Rangel	D	New York
	Louis Stokes	D	Ohio
	Andrew Young	D	Georgia
	Harold Ford	D	Tennessee

**Cardiss Collins won a special election in 1973 to fill the seat of her late husband, George Collins.

Authors

MARTIN L. KILSON is professor of government at Harvard University. He is the author of *Political Dilemma of Black Mayors* (Washington, D. C., 1975), *Political Change in a West African State* (Cambridge, 1966), and co-editor of *Key Issues in the Afro-American Experience* (New York, 1971).

ROBERT I. ROTBERG is professor of history and political science, Massachusetts Institute of Technology, and a research associate of the Center for International Affairs, Harvard University, and the African Studies Program, Boston University. He is the author or editor of a dozen books, including *Joseph Thomson and the Exploration of Africa* (London, 1971), *Haiti: The Politics of Squalor* (Boston, 1971), *Protest and Power in Black Africa* (New York, 1970), *Africa and its Explorers* (Cambridge, Mass., 1970), *A Political History of Tropical Africa* (New York, 1965), *The Rise of Nationalism in Central Africa* (Cambridge, Mass., 1965), *The Family in History* (New York, 1973), and *East Africa and the Orient* (New York, 1975). He edits *The Journal of Interdisciplinary History*.

PAUL EDWARDS is reader in English literature, University of Edinburgh. His major interests are Icelandic history and literature, and West Indian, African, and nineteenth century English literature, on which he has written numerous articles. He is the editor of *West African Narrative* (London, 1963), Ignatius Sancho's *Letters* (London, 1968), Ottobah Cugoano's *Thoughts and Sentiments etc.* (London, 1969), Equiano's *Life* (London, 1969), and other works, as well as several volumes of transla-

485

tions from and studies in medieval Icelandic. He taught in Ghana and Sierra Leone from 1954 to 1963.

CHRISTOPHER FYFE is reader in African history, University of Edinburgh. He is the author of *A History of Sierra Leone* (London, 1962), *Sierra Leone Inheritance* (London, 1964), and *Africanus Horton: West African Scientist and Patriot* (New York, 1972).

WILLIAM ROBERT HIGGINS is an independent television producer and visiting fellow in Atlantic history at the Johns Hopkins University. He is the author of several articles on the slave trade and Revolutionary finance and *The Slave Trade of Colonial South Carolina*, forthcoming.

MARION D. DE B. KILSON is Director of Research, The Radcliffe Institute. She is the author of *Kpele Lala: Ga Religious Sons and Symbols* (Cambridge, Mass., 1971), and *African Urban Kinsmen* (New York, 1974).

BERNARD LEWIS is Cleveland E. Dodge Professor of Near Eastern studies, Princeton University, and long-term member of the School of Social Science, Institute for Advanced Study, Princeton. He is the author of *The Arabs in History* (London, 1950; most recent ed. 1975), *Race and Color in Islam* (New York, 1971), *Islam in History* (LaSalle, Ill., 1973), *Islam, From the Prophet Muhammad to the Capture of Constantinople* (New York, 1974), 2v; and *History—Remembered, Recovered, Invented* (Princeton, 1975).

JOSEPH C. MILLER is associate professor of history at the University of Virginia. His current interest is slavery and the slave trade, on which he has published a number of articles. He is the author of *Kings and Kinsmen: Early Mbundu States in Angola* (Oxford, 1975).

LESLIE BRENNAN ROUT, JR. is associate professor of history, Michigan State University. He is the author of *Politics of the Chaco Peace Conference: 1935-39* (Austin, 1970), *Which Way Out?: A Study of the Guyana-Venezuela Boundary Conflict* (East Lansing, Mich., 1971), and

The African Experience in Spanish America (Cambridge, 1976). He is a jazz saxophonist and has played with the Woody Herman orchestra, among others.

GEORGE SHEPPERSON is William Robertson Professor of Commonwealth and American history at the University of Edinburgh. A pioneer in the study of the African diaspora, he is sometimes credited with originating this expression. He is the author of *Independent African* (Edinburgh, 1958), *David Livingstone and the Rovuma* (Edinburgh, 1964), and numerous articles and short studies on African, Afro-American, American, and Scottish history. He has taught in British, American, Canadian, and African universities.

ADELE SIMMONS is Dean of Student Affairs and lecturer in the department of history, Princeton University. She co-authored, with Ann Freedman, Margaret Dunkle, and Francine Blau, *Exploitation from 9-5; Twentieth Century Fund Task Force Report on Working Women* (Boston, 1975). She is currently completing a manuscript on the political history of Mauritius.

GEORGE EATON SIMPSON, emeritus professor of sociology and anthropology at Oberlin College, has done extensive field work in the Caribbean and Nigeria. He is the author of *Melville J. Herskovits* (New York, 1973); *Racial and Cultural Minorities* (with J. M. Yinger), which won the Anisfield-Wolf Award in Race Relations in 1958 (New York, 1972, 4th ed.); and *Religious Cults of the Caribbean* (Puerto Rico, 1970). He received the Wellcome Medal from the Royal Anthropological Institute of Great Britain and Ireland in 1957.

RAYMOND T. SMITH has been professor of anthropology at the University of Chicago since 1966, having taught at the Universities of the West Indies and Ghana. Born in England, he has carried out field research in Guyana, Jamaica, Ghana, and the United States. He is the author of *The Negro Family in British Guiana* (London, 1956), *British Guiana* (London, 1962), and *Class Differences in American Kinship and Family Structure*, with D. M. Schneider (Englewood Cliffs, 1972).

FRANK MARTIN SNOWDEN, JR. is professor and chairman, Department of Classics, Howard University. Besides numerous articles in classical and educational journals, he wrote *Blacks in Antiquity: Ethiopians in the Greco-Roman Experience* (Cambridge, Mass., 1970), for which he received the Charles J. Goodwin Award of Merit in 1973 from the American Philological Association. He also wrote "Témoignages iconographiques sur les populations noires dans l'Antiquité gréco-romaine," in Jean Vercoutter, Jean Leclant, Frank M. Snowden, Jr., and Jehan Desanges, *L'Iconographie des Noirs dans l'Art Occidental,* forthcoming.

IBRAHIM K. SUNDIATA is assistant professor of history at Northwestern University. He has written articles on Liberia and Fernando Po, and is particularly interested in the rise and development of West African elites. He is currently at work on a book on the Liberian Scandal of 1929.

JAMES W. St. G. WALKER is assistant professor of history, University of Waterloo, where he teaches Black North American and African history. He is the author of *The Black Loyalists: The Search for a Promised Land in Nova Scotia and Sierra Leone, 1783-1870* (London, 1975). He was a co-founder of the Transition Year Programme, an educational project for Black and Native Canadian youths at Dalhousie University, Nova Scotia.

JAMES WALVIN is Senior Lecturer in History, University of York. He wrote *Black and White: The Negro and English Society, 1555-1945* (London, 1973), *The Black Presence* (London, 1971), and was co-author of *Britain and Black Slaves: A Thematic Documentary* (London, 1976).

BRIAN WEINSTEIN is professor of political science at Howard University and was a Fellow at the Woodrow Wilson International Center for Scholars in 1975-76. He is the author of *Gabon: Nation-Building on the Ogooué* (Cambridge, 1967), *Eboué* (New York, 1972), and co-author of *Introduction to African Politics: A Continental Approach* (New York, 1974).

Index